THE ESSENTIAL HISTORY OF
TOTTENHAM HOTSPUR

FOREWORD BY STEVE PERRYMAN

BOB GOODWIN

First published in 2001
by HEADLINE BOOK PUBLISHING
for WHSmith, Greenbridge Road, Swindon SN3 3LD

1 3 5 7 9 10 8 6 4 2

ISBN 0 7553 1019 5

Design by designsection, Frome, Somerset
All photographs supplied by EMPICS, except the following:
pages 10, 15, 34, 35, 48 and 52 Bob Goodwin Archive
The author would like to thank everyone at Designsection including Adrian Besley, Julian Flanders, Sandra Morgan, Rhiannon Sully and Kathie Wilson

Printed and bound in Great Britain by Clays Ltd, St Ives PLC, Bungay, Suffolk

HEADLINE BOOK PUBLISHING
A division of Hodder Headline
338 Euston Road
London NW1 3BH

www.headline.co.uk
www.hodderheadline.com

Contents

Foreword
By Steve Perryman

It's a great honour to write about the team that was a part of my footballing life for 19 years as a player, and later, briefly, as assistant manager. I played over 900 games for Spurs and it is a great disappointment to me that I was unable to get to Bill Nicholson's testimonial at White Hart Lane, because he had a huge influence on me, both on and off the field.

I still remember vividly how, all those years ago, the club's chief scout at the time, Charlie Faulkner, came round to my house having seen me play for Ealing Schoolboys. I lived in west London then and north London seemed like the other side of the world, but the name Tottenham Hotspur, with its traditions and great players, like Danny Blanchflower and Dave Mackay, sent a tingle down my spine.

They invited me to train once or twice a week, much to the displeasure of my school. I felt at home there from the start, even though I could have joined most clubs in England. In fact, my brother wanted me to join West Ham, which had a reputation as a teaching club. But I felt immediately welcomed at Tottenham.

It was Bill Nicholson who signed me. He was coming towards the end of his management career, but he told me I would be treated as well as anyone else at the club even though I was only 15 when I joined. He was honest and straightforward, if a little blunt. The first week I was there, I remember being told that Spurs played the game quickly, easily and accurately, making the ball do the work. I still use those words today with the team I am currently coaching in Japan, because it's the right way to play.

So many things have been said about Bill Nicholson, but still his influence cannot be underestimated. His partnership with Eddie Bailey is legendary. They had a style and a purpose about them. You could not but respond to Bill Nic's way of management. I loved talking to him then, and I still do today. I call him once every couple of months because he had a huge effect on my career. His love for Tottenham Hotspur was undying. Bill Nic never wanted you to wear a red tie or drive a red car, it had to be blue or white. The club was in his blood and when he spent the club's money, he spent it as if it was his own. He was totally dedicated, you could drive past his office and his light would still be on at eight or nine o'clock at night. Of course, I also played under Terry Neill, Keith Burkinshaw and Peter Shreeves, and they all had an influence on my career.

While on the field I was always in awe of Dave Mackay. I only played about six months with him but even when we trained indoors, you could feel the power of his voice through the walls. He used to come into training and literally stick out his chest. He was full of pride and ambition. Pat Jennings was always known as Mr Quiet, but he could still make himself heard in front of 50,000 people if he wanted to get his message across. I also had the honour of playing with Ossie Ardiles, Glenn Hoddle, Jimmy Greaves and Alan Gilzean, all of them great players in their own right.

I made my debut in September 1969, when we lost 1-0 at home to Sunderland with a Mike England own goal. If I had realised what that game meant to my career, I'd probably have frozen and been unable to play. Bill Nic warned me two days before that I might be playing, but I only knew for certain on the day of the game. It was a big step for Tottenham as well as myself. They had been seen as a spending club and all of a sudden they were blooding this 17-year-old youngster.

In terms of the fans, much has been written about how fickle the crowd is at Spurs. To be honest, I found them hard but fair. I felt they gave me power. At times they were a harsh audience to play in front of, but if they knew you were trying, they responded brilliantly.

As captain of the club, my proudest moment was picking up the FA Cup in 1981. When I first joined the club I never thought that I would be leading the team up the steps at Wembley, in front of a worldwide audience, after one of the best goals ever seen at the national stadium. Of course, I'm talking about Ricky Villa's fantastic effort.

Even when we were relegated a few years earlier, the supporters turned up in their thousands on the last day of the season to back the club, even though we, as players, felt embarrassed that we were going down. All they chanted was that we would be back and the power of that support made it happen the following year.

You need to feel right about a place and I knew I couldn't expect, in 19 years, to play under the same kind of manager all the time. So I never minded taking on fresh ideas. Even now, sometimes when I go over to my mother's house and dig out some of the old tracksuit tops I wore, it just makes the hair stand up on the back of my neck.

Not that there weren't bad times. As assistant manager of the club under Ossie, I only lasted 18 months. When I left it was a changed place and, of course, I wish I could have gone in different circumstances because I never got a chance to say goodbye to the fans and I regret that to this day.

Nevertheless, I like to think I am part of a special family. I am no longer connected to the club on a day-to-day basis, but I'm delighted with every win and sad about every defeat. Glenn Hoddle has his heart in the club and will want to get them playing stylish football again. Tottenham lost their way for 10 years, but if he is given long enough, Glenn will put it right.

I hope you all enjoy this book.

Chapter One: 1882-96
From Schoolboys to Professionals

There is an old saying about great oak trees growing from little acorns. Nowhere is that more true than in the world of football. All the top football clubs of today, with their grand stadiums, multi-million pound turnovers and superstars, have their roots in far humbler beginnings. Arsenal and West Ham United were works teams of the Woolwich Arsenal munitions factory and Thames Ironworks shipbuilding company respectively. Everton were the Sunday school team of St Domingo's Church; Aston Villa, the cricket team of the Villa Cross Wesleyan Chapel. Even the mighty Manchester United began life as a team for the workers of the London and Yorkshire Railway Company's Newton Heath depot.

Tottenham Hotspur's origins were equally humble, indeed perhaps even more so, for they did not have the advantages of a business or church organisation to call upon for support and help. The club was formed in 1882 when a group of schoolboys who had played cricket under the name of Hotspur Cricket Club decided to turn their attentions to the increasingly popular winter game of association football. The cricket club had been formed two years earlier by pupils of St John's Middle Class School and a few of their friends who attended the Tottenham Grammar School.

Taking the name of Hotspur Football Club was obvious, but how the cricket club first came to adopt the Hotspur title is not so clear. The story that has come to be accepted is that some of the founder members, including brothers Hamilton and Lindsay Casey, were studying early 15th century English history and were fascinated by the heroic tales of Sir Henry Percy. Son of the Earl of Northumberland and a supporter of the deposed and murdered King Richard II, the teenage Sir Henry was one of the leaders of rebel forces fiercely opposed to Henry IV. He earned the nickname 'Harry Hotspur' for his battlefield valour, before meeting his end at the Battle of Shrewsbury in 1403. The name was most appropriate, for the Percy family had at one time owned large tracts of Tottenham and even now the connection remains, with Northumberland Park still one of the major roads in the area.

The record of the cricket club is unknown, only one or two matches being reported, but that is hardly surprising for a club made up of boys of only ten or 11 years of age. Likewise the early records of the football club are practically non-existent, although six pages of what appear to be the original club record book have survived. These show that five shillings (25p) was transferred from the cricket club and a subscription of sixpence (2.5p) was paid by the old cricket club members, the Casey brothers, John and Tom Anderson, Edward Beaven, John Thompson, Fred Dexter, Bobby Buckle, Stuart Leaman, P. Thompson and E. Wall. D. Davies, C. Iverson and John Fisher were called upon to pay one-shilling (5p) subscriptions, as they had not been members of the cricket club. Lindsay Casey was appointed honorary treasurer, John Thompson honorary secretary, Bobby Buckle captain and Hamilton Casey vice-captain. As subscriptions were first paid on 5 September 1882, that is taken to be the foundation date of the football club.

The initial funds were soon expended, purchasing such items as goal and flag posts, flags, tape, white paint and, at a cost of six shillings and six pence (32.5p), a ball. Subsequent members in that first season included Tom Bumberry, R. Howlett and Billy Tyrell, and at the end of the season, the club funds were augmented by the sale of the cricket club assets.

The Tottenham of the 1880s bore little resemblance to the Tottenham of today. Right on the boundary of London, it was rapidly being swallowed up by the ever-spreading metropolis, but still retained plenty of open spaces for the increasing population to utilise. One of those spaces remains to this day. Tottenham Marshes already provided a base for the Park, Radicals and Star clubs, but there was plenty of room and the Hotspur boys had little difficulty identifying a large enough unused patch to provide their first 'home ground'. The club record book shows that the first match played by the Hotspur Football Club was a 0-2 defeat at the hands of Radicals on 30 September 1882. Sadly no further details for that first season were recorded and the only other result known was a 1-8 defeat against an Edmonton schools side, Latymer.

While the marshes provided the ideal venue for a fledgling football club, they were not without their problems. Finding and marking out a pitch was all very well, but there were other, older and bigger lads who wanted to utilise the facilities and they had little compunction in taking over the Spurs' pitch, often by force. Others had no desire to play football, but obtained their enjoyment by abusing a bunch of boys who had the temerity to form their own little club.

The young Spurs battled on through their first season, but soon realised that if their club was to flourish it could not do so without help. They approached John Ripsher, warden of the Tottenham YMCA and a pillar of the Parish Church of All Hallows. He was well known for his work with the local youngsters, had helped out the boys when they played cricket and quickly agreed to support their football club, even buying some of the cricket equipment to provide much needed funds. The club's original meetings had been held in some houses under construction in Willoughby Road or under a gas lamp in Tottenham High Road, but Ripsher quickly secured the use of a basement kitchen in the YMCA. With help from Jim Randall, a county court clerk and former Radicals player, he organised a meeting for the end of August 1883 to properly establish the club.

A Scarlet Shield

The 21 boys who attended voted in Ripsher as president and treasurer, a committee of Tom Bumberry, W.G. Herbert, Fred Dexter and Billy Tyrell, Randall as club captain and Billy Harston vice-captain. Navy blue was adopted as the club colour with all players requested to have a scarlet shield embossed with the letter 'H' on the left side of their shirt. All matches would be played at the Park Lane end of Tottenham Marshes. The first match of the club's second season saw the Spurs beat Brownlow Rovers 9-0. It is the first game for which a full 11 has been recorded, albeit one recalled several years later by Billy Harston. He gave the line-up as: – S. Leaman; W. Tyrell and F. Dexter; H.D. Casey and F. Lovis; W. Lomas, F. Cottrell, Dr Alec Watson, J.T. Fisher, W. Harston and R. Buckle, but makes no reference to Jack Jull who was specifically mentioned in the report sent to the *Tottenham and Edmonton Weekly Herald*. It is noticeable there were six forwards listed, but football was still developing and it was some time before the 2-3-5 formation that lasted for so many years was settled upon.

Due to the absence of official records it is difficult to establish the details of many of the club's very early games. The *Herald* provides the principal source of information, but it did not employ a football reporter, relying upon clubs sending in match reports. Games were not always mentioned and even when they were, it was often in the barest detail. Conflicting reports were not popular with the editor and there were often threats that no report would be published unless opposing teams could agree on what had happened. What is clear is that Spurs were performing well. In their second season they won 15 of their 20 known games, attracted boys from other local teams and even fielded a second 11.

Jack Jull, the first Spurs player ever to win representative honours.

A fixture list was published for the first time in 1884-85, a season that continued in similar vein to the previous one with 18 victories, five draws and only five defeats. It was also a notable season for it saw the club change its name. For several years there had been another club called London Hotspur. Such was the growing success of the Tottenham outfit that post to the two clubs was being confused. To alleviate the problem Spurs added 'Tottenham' to their title. They also cancelled their final game of the season to watch Blackburn Rovers and Queens Park in the FA Cup Final at Kennington Oval. In recognition of Rovers' success Spurs changed their colours to the blue and white halves of the Lancashire club.

It is difficult to imagine what the standard of opposition was like as few, if any, of their early opponents have survived. Certainly there were occasions when one or other team was unable to field a full 11, games did not always last 90 minutes and goals were sometimes disputed. Spurs, though, were successful and were also beginning to build a reputation for entertaining football. Spectators did not just consist of non-playing members or families; local sports fans were beginning to make their way to the marshes specifically to watch Spurs play and a loyal following was growing.

The perfect example of this came in October 1885. For the first time Spurs entered a cup competition; the London Association Cup. In the first round they were drawn at home to St Albans, a London house team. Fully 400 spectators attended to witness a 5-2 victory for Spurs. It was the start of what has since become a glorious cup tradition, although Spurs were quickly put in their place in the next round when they were thrashed 0-8 by the Casuals at Wandsworth. Still, there was no disgrace in what remained little more than a boy's side losing to one of the biggest names in football's early history and it certainly had little effect on Spurs' growing popularity. Over 100 supporters regularly turned up as Spurs won 24 of their games for the season, netting 111 goals.

A growing maturity on the pitch was not always matched off it. Spurs had been kicked out of the YMCA after less than a year as the association tired of their boyish antics. The basement was often used for practice sessions and trouble first began when an association member went to investigate the rumpus disturbing a committee meeting. Just as he entered the kitchen area, the light was switched off and the unannounced visitor found himself on the receiving end of a well-struck volley. It might not have been too bad had the ball not emerged from a chimney barely seconds earlier, a fact that only became apparent when the committee man returned to his meeting covered in soot. Playing cards and eating mulberries from the garden also did little to endear the Spurs to their hosts and John Ripsher was soon called upon the find them new accommodation. He persuaded the vicar of Tottenham, Rev. Wilson, to let them use premises at 1 Dorset Villa, Northumberland Park, that had just opened as a new branch of the Young Men's Church of England Society. The only condition imposed by the vicar was that the boys should attend church every Wednesday evening. This was no problem for two years until the vicar discovered some of the Spurs boys playing cards during service. They were out on the street again and once more turned to John Ripsher for help. Ripsher had never let the boys down, often providing footballs when funds ran low, helping organise transport for away games and defending them for their little misdemeanours. He found them rooms at the Red House in Tottenham High Road, a building that forms part of White Hart Lane to this day and now houses the club's press office. They were to remain the club's headquarters for six years.

League football was still a thing of the future, but cup competitions were proving popular and in 1886-87 Spurs entered both the London Association and East End Cups. In the first competition they lost in the first round to Upton Park, but in the latter tasted competitive success for the first time.

After defeating Phoenix, Park and St Lukes they found themselves meeting London Caledonians in the semi-final at Millwall Rovers' ground in North Greenwich. When the two teams turned up on 19 March, the pitch was in such a terrible state they agreed it was not fit for an important cup match, so played out a friendly match with Spurs losing 0-2. The semi-final was rearranged for the following week at Tottenham, but the Scottish exiles failed to turn up and Spurs claimed the game. The claim was rejected and when the clubs met again in mid-April, it was the Scots who won by the only goal. Cup success spread Spurs' name and brought with it requests for them to meet teams from outside the immediate Tottenham vicinity. This in turn increased demands on finances and to help augment funds the club held its first concert, raising over £15.

From the Marshes to Northumberland Park

The increasing number of supporters Spurs were attracting to the marshes, sometimes as many as 4,000, was a welcome tribute to the club's success, but not so welcome were the problems that accompanied them. The pitch was roped off, but the marshes were still a public area and the thought of an afternoon's free entertainment attracted the more unruly members of society. Anxious to see their favourites win, they were keen to assist, often resorting to the throwing of mud and rotten vegetables if it might gain Spurs an advantage. Verbal abuse was common, frequently coarse and offensive, and resulted in many complaints from opponents. There was nothing Spurs could do though, unless they could control the crowds, and they could only do that if they had a private ground.

The conduct of some spectators made life very uncomfortable for Spurs and even threatened the club's very existence. Opponents were not keen on visiting if they were going to be subjected to all sorts of abuse and even the Spurs players were unhappy at their enjoyment of their favourite pastime being ruined. A private ground where spectators could be charged for admission (and ejected if they misbehaved) was the only solution. Many club members were in favour of such a move, but there were also many concerned at the likely cost. Would people be prepared to pay or would they just switch to another of the local teams they could still watch for free? It was a difficult problem, but fortunately Spurs had men of foresight in Bobby Buckle, Jack Jull, Ham Casey and secretary Frank Hatton. They persuaded the doubters, began the search for a suitable ground and soon found one just off Northumberland Park. Part of it was already home to Foxes FC, but there was an area used by a tennis club in the summer that would make a perfect pitch for Spurs. A £10 per season rent was quickly agreed with the landlord, dressing room accommodation secured at the Northumberland Arms and the ground made ready for the start of the 1888-89 season.

The decision to secure their own enclosure marked a big step forward in Spurs' history and again proved a successful one. Results were not so good – the first team won 11 and drew five of their 24 games, the reserves won 11 and drew four of their 19 – but Spurs were playing at a higher level now. No longer schoolboys meeting other schoolboys, they were young men moving into adult football circles. The real success was that people were prepared to pay to watch them play. Crowds were nowhere near as large as on the marshes, but with an admission charge of 3d (1.25p) costs were being covered and at the end of the season the club accounts showed a profit of £6. The big game of the season came in October when the first round of the London Senior Cup saw Old Etonians visit Northumberland Park. Although not the power they once were, the former public schoolboys had reached the FA Cup final five years earlier and justified a doubling of the normal entry price. Spurs did remarkably well to hold them to a 2-3 scoreline at half-time, but the age, strength and experience of a team who were still one of the biggest names in Southern football eventually told, and in the second half they ran in five goals without reply.

The wisdom of moving to Northumberland Park was well illustrated by the growing number of people keen to be associated with the club. The area's MP, Joseph Howard, was appointed patron and several local businessmen, conscious that a successful club would draw trade to the area, joined the list of vice-presidents, although John Ripsher continued to hold the senior position. It also helped Spurs attract a better standard of opposition to Tottenham, which in turn meant better players wanted to play for the club – an essential factor if the paying public were to be enticed along. Spurs were rapidly moving from a local club for local boys to Tottenham's sporting flagship.

Steady Progress

For the three seasons from 1889-90 through to 1891-92, Spurs continued to make steady if not spectacular progress. They were not yet in the top level of London football, not serious competitors to the likes of Woolwich Arsenal and Millwall Athletic, but they were developing as serious rivals to Crouch End and City Ramblers as the top team in north London. They were getting reasonable results, attracting good crowds and playing attractive football. Off the pitch they had an excellent ground and a far-sighted and ambitious committee, but there was something missing and it was not difficult to see what that was. Friendly matches were all well and good, but it was the cup games that drew the biggest crowds. Regular competitive football was needed.

The Football League had been formed in 1888, continuing the drive to dominance of clubs from the North and Midlands. Top level football had once been the preserve of the Old Boys clubs but since the legalisation of professionalism in 1885, the balance of power had rapidly shifted. The Football League's success was obvious and as early as March 1890 efforts had been made to form a 'Southern league', but at a meeting called by the London FA the proposal had been rejected by 47 votes to 46. Woolwich Arsenal may not have been the first southern club to realise that unless a challenge was mounted to the Football League the gap would become unbridgeable, but they did try to do something about it. When they decided to adopt professionalism in 1891, they quickly incurred the wrath of the London FA, were expelled and banned from all cup competitions under its jurisdiction. They responded by organising a meeting of London's leading clubs and in February 1892 26 clubs voted to form a league for 'London and Southern clubs'. Twelve clubs, which did not include Spurs, were elected to membership, but the plan quickly fizzled out when several pulled out, fearing the response of the London and home county FAs would see them ostracised.

Despite the rebuff, Spurs remained convinced of the benefits league football would bring and when John Oliver, president of Westminster Criterion, sponsored the formation of the 'Southern Alliance' for 1892-93, Spurs were quick to join. Erith, Old St Stephens, Polytechnic, Slough, Upton Park and Windsor and Eton may not have been as big or popular as Chatham, Luton Town, Millwall Athletic, Reading, Swindon Town or Woolwich Arsenal, but at least Spurs would be meeting them with something more than pride at stake. As it turned out, the Southern Alliance was not a success. Not all their opponents were as well organised as Spurs and certainly not as strong. Spurs finished third to Old St Stephens, but enthusiasm for the competition waned when it became clear not all the clubs would fulfil their fixtures.

While the London and home county FAs were stuck in their amateur time-warp, the Football Association itself could see that southern football was getting left in the wake of those more forward-looking clubs from the North and Midlands. By 1893 Football League clubs were dominating the FA Cup, so much so that for the first time in its history, the final had been held outside the capital. If football in the south was not going to lose all its popular appeal, something had to be done to rekindle interest. The Football Association's answer was to introduce the FA Amateur Cup. It would be open to all amateur outfits, but as the south remained the amateur stronghold it was hoped it would prove popular there.

'Payne's Boots'

In the inaugural competition, a first round home victory saw Vampires defeated 3-1 in November 1893, but Spurs went no

Stanley Briggs joined Spurs from local rivals Tottenham FC and soon became skipper of the side.

further in the competition, despite being drawn to meet Clapham Rovers in round two. The reason has come to be known as the 'Payne's Boots Affair', one of the most momentous events in the club's history – not that anyone would have realised this at the time.

In the first round of the London Senior Cup, Spurs had been drawn to meet Old St Marks with the match set for 21 October. Always keen to secure new talent, they invited Ernie Payne, unable to get a game with Fulham, to play for them. He accepted, but was bereft of kit when he arrived at Tottenham, having found it had 'disappeared' on his way to Northumberland Park. Spurs provided shirt, shorts and socks, but no suitable boots could be found, so they gave Payne ten shillings (50p) to buy a pair on the understanding the boots would belong to the club.

Fulham accused Spurs of poaching and professionalism as soon as they heard what had happened and within ten days Spurs were before the council of the London Football Association to answer Fulham's charges. The allegation of poaching was thrown out, but Spurs were found guilty of misconduct by offering 'an unfair inducement'. The penalty was harsh: Northumberland Park was closed for two weeks, with Spurs suspended for the same length of time and Payne for one week. An appeal allowed the match against Vampires to be played, but it was unsuccessful and thus Clapham Rovers secured a walkover into the next round of the Amateur Cup.

Public Sympathy

The London FA's decision was to play a crucial part in Spurs' long-term history, but in the immediate aftermath they received an enormous amount of publicity and sympathy. The general consensus of opinion was that Spurs had been treated appallingly, the Association acting as if it were a headmaster slapping down a naughty schoolboy rather than the governing body of a growing sport. The incident generated a tremendous amount of goodwill towards Spurs. If the authorities could not see how London football was being held back, the public could. The ground re-opened for a London Senior Cup-tie and although Crusaders were not the most attractive of visitors, 2,000 paid their admission money.

In 1893 Woolwich Arsenal were elected as London's first representative in the Football League. As ambitious as their south London rivals, Millwall Athletic left the London FA in December 1893 after making the decision to openly pay their players, but they were reluctant to join the Football League because of the expenses they would incur in travelling to fulfil fixtures. More inclined to encourage their rivals to adopt the paid game and set up a new league, they called a meeting for January 1894 to which Spurs were not invited. Chatham, Clapton, Ilford, Luton Town, Reading and 2nd Battalion Scots Guards joined Millwall in resolving that a southern league was needed. They invited Casuals, Crouch End, Crusaders, Old Carthusians, Old Westminsters, Royal Ordnance Factories and Swindon Town to a further meeting. Only the last two attended, but the nine resolved to form the Southern League. Spurs and Southampton St Marys were great supporters of the plan and keen to join, but both were initially snubbed. When the Scots Guards withdrew, Southampton were invited to replace them, but even when it was decided to form a seven-club second division, Spurs were still excluded.

The increased interest in Spurs caused by the 'Payne's Boots Affair' may not have been enough to catapult them into the upper echelons of southern football, but it did attract the attentions of John Oliver. Disappointed at the failure of his Southern Alliance, he was still determined to influence the development of football in London but knew Westminster Criterion would never provide a suitable vehicle for his ambitions. A wealthy businessman, he threw in his lot with Spurs, taking on the president's role at the 1894 annual meeting. John Ripsher willingly stepped aside, having done all he could for the boys who had first turned to him for help and guidance. His invaluable service was recognised by his being appointed one of the club's Patrons, a position he held for several years.

Oliver Gets To Work

Oliver quickly made an impression, appointing Arthur Norris as the club's first professional trainer and paying for the erection of a stand. Spurs were now the only tenants of the Northumberland Park ground but thus far the only 'stand' of any description had consisted of a couple of wagons. The new structure was capable of accommodating over a hundred spectators and contained dressing room facilities. Part of it was blown away during a gale only weeks after it was erected but Oliver ensured it was soon repaired.

50 Greatest Players

JACK JULL   **Full back**

Joined Tottenham Hotspur: Founder member

Debut: 1882

Appearances: over 150   **Goals:** at least 24

Left Tottenham Hotspur: 1897 (retired)

Jack Jull was undoubtedly the first outstanding player in Spurs' history. A local lad, and son of a publican, he was a couple of years older than the other founder members of the club. This made him an obvious choice as captain, even though he missed some games because he attended a boarding school. He was capable of playing in any position, but settled at full back where his strength and fearlessness were put to best use in an age when forward lines consisted of six attackers. Most of his early team-mates gradually dropped out of the team, but Jull continued to turn out, becoming the first Spurs player to win representative honours when he played for Middlesex in 1891 and still playing the occasional game until 1897. He also played for Tottenham and London and was appointed club president in 1895. Later, he became a Southern League referee.

50 Greatest Players

STANLEY BRIGGS   Half back

Joined Tottenham Hotspur: January 1892 **From:** Tottenham FC

Debut: v Westminster Criterion, 23 January 1891

Appearances: 111   **Goals:** 8

Left Tottenham Hotspur: 1898   **For:** Clapton

At over six foot tall and weighing more than 14 stone, Stanley Briggs was a strapping young man whose football talent developed while at school in Folkestone. Returning to London he played for the Hermitage club that developed into Tottenham FC and was soon persuaded to throw in his lot with Spurs. Quickly made captain, he was probably the outstanding amateur half back in London – a ceaseless worker, commanding in defence and always a threat when pushing forward into attack. A great attraction to the paying public (as an amateur, he was available to play for other clubs), he turned out for Millwall Athletic and Woolwich Arsenal amongst many others, but refused numerous overtures to join the professional ranks. So opposed was he to the professional game that he refused to attend the meeting at which Spurs decided to adopt professionalism and soon wound down his career with Spurs, preferring to play for the still amateur Clapton. A regular for London and Middlesex, he never won international honours although in Germany in 1899 he did play for an FA team that many regarded as an unofficial England team.

Prior to the FA's acceptance of professionalism many clubs, notably those who founded the Football League, had circumvented the amateur rules by finding new recruits 'jobs' in their owners' or benefactors' factories and offices. One of Oliver's businesses was a carpet-making factory and he was always looking for new workers, especially if they were good footballers.

The combined efforts of Oliver and Norris soon had an effect. While Oliver enticed experienced players such as Charlie Ambler, Donald Goodall, Peter Hunter and Bill Julian, a former captain of Woolwich Arsenal, to Tottenham, Norris worked hard to improve the fitness of the amateur talent that still formed the basis of the club. His success was soon reflected in results. For the first time Spurs entered the FA Cup and sprang a major surprise by going all the way to the fourth qualifying round. West Herts, Wolverton and Clapton were all defeated, before Spurs went out to Luton Town in a replay. In the FA Amateur Cup, Spurs did even better. Old Harrovians were beaten 7-0, City Ramblers 6-1, Romford 8-0, London Welsh 4-2 and Beeston 2-0. Only when they came up against cup holders and eventual runners-up, Old Carthusians, in the second round proper, did Spurs exit the competition.

Spurs were on a definite upward curve but if they really wanted to join the elite one more hurdle had to be negotiated, perhaps the most difficult of all. Football had first been developed and then organised by the public schools and their Old Boys clubs. It was always a sport to them, nothing more than a physical pastime to fill a 'gentleman's leisure time'. They still controlled the game in the south and found the idea of anyone being paid to play sport abhorrent. Despite the success of the Football League, they could not appreciate that football was no longer theirs to control; that it was now the working man's game. Woolwich Arsenal had been the first London club to turn professional and were playing in the Second Division of the Football League. Millwall Athletic had followed and were first champions of the Southern League. Luton Town, New Brompton, Reading, Southampton St Marys and Swindon Town had all resolved to pay their players. If Spurs were to continue their progress they had to do likewise.

A Professional Club

Ever since the London FA's overreaction to Ernie Payne and his pair of boots, the idea of turning professional had not been far from the minds of those controlling Spurs' destiny, but John Oliver gave them added impetus. A special meeting was called for 16 December 1895 at the Eagle public house in Chesnut Road, but not before behind-the-scenes soundings had been taken. The whole committee was in favour, other clubs gave encouragement and most of the players gave the idea their support.

With Oliver in the chair there was only one resolution on the agenda; that the meeting should accept the committee's recommendation to adopt professionalism. It was proposed by Bobby Buckle, founder member, committeeman and secretary, one of the club's most respected stalwarts. Several members spoke in support, pointing out that paying players was the only way to attract the best talent, and as amateurs could not give total commitment to the club attendances were bound to fall. The work of the last 13 years would be wasted and the club would follow so many others into the football backwaters. Most of those in attendance were in favour, but there were some who were not happy with the proposal and were determined to have their say. Finance was the principal concern. Would gates increase enough to cover players' wages? Were there any plans to form a limited company? One member even asked if the committee were trying to hide something. Buckle admitted the club was £65 in debt but £60 of that was owed to the chairman. At times the debate was heated but when the vote was taken only one hand was raised in opposition. How much that

19

may have been down to Oliver's threat to resign as club president if the proposal was not accepted is unclear, but there can be no doubt the club could not afford to lose its benefactor, particularly if he were to demand the money owed him.

The decision taken, trainer Norris immediately made for Scotland, returning with Spurs' first two paid players, John Montgomery and J. Logan. Looking for new players in the middle of the season was not easy; any players worth having had already signed to other clubs and there was no way Spurs could afford to pay transfer fees. Several of the current players took the professional plunge, Charlie Ambler, Bob Clements and Ernie Payne included.

There were those who preferred to maintain their amateur status, amongst them Willie Almond, who had only been reinstated as an amateur on joining Spurs a few months earlier, after playing professionally for Millwall Athletic. The greatest loss, though, was without doubt, half back Stanley Briggs. Only 23, he was already an outstanding player who could have gone to the very top. However, he was totally opposed to professionalism, even refusing to attend the meeting at the Eagle. He remained with Spurs for the rest of the season and was even appointed captain for 1896-97, but was a committed amateur and soon ended his association with the club.

Numerous players were given the chance to impress, but this had an unsettling effect on the team. Two days before Mr Buckle had addressed the club meeting, Spurs had beaten Old St Stephens to qualify for the first round proper of the FA Cup. They returned from First Division Stoke firmly put in their place by a 0-5 defeat. They clearly had a long way to go if they were ever to challenge the established clubs. Valuable experience was gained, though, with many top clubs being enticed to Northumberland Park, and a new attendance record of 6,000 was set for Aston Villa's visit in April 1896.

Chapter Two: 1896-1908
The Southern League Years

Professionalism was only one step in John Oliver's plan to make Spurs a top club. He had always been a believer in competitive football and when the Football League invited applications to join the Second Division he lost no time in putting Spurs' name forward. At the league's meeting on 19 May 1896 Spurs were one of ten applicants. They finished bottom of the poll with only two votes. The decision was not surprising and might be regarded as showing that Oliver was naively over-ambitious. The struggling Woolwich Arsenal were still London's only Football League club and the time and expense of travelling to the capital made them unpopular with their league colleagues. They were hardly likely to vote for the prospect of a second trip to London each season.

Disappointed but not despairing, Oliver turned his attention to the Southern League. He had received much encouragement from the likes of Southampton St Marys, Millwall Athletic and Luton Town to make Spurs a professional club and now expected them to reward him for following their exhortations. They were desperate to make the Southern League a serious competitor to the Football League and recruiting an ambitious club like Spurs could do nothing but aid their cause. Anyway, the Southern League owed him a favour. He had, after all, donated the championship trophy when the league was formed. Two years earlier Spurs had not been considered good enough to even join the Second Division. It showed just how far they had come in such a short time that at the league's June meeting they were not merely elected to the Southern League but elected straight into the First Division.

With only 11 clubs in the First Division, 20 matches were not enough to fill a fixture list so Spurs also joined the United League. With the FA Cup, Wellingborough Charity Cup and several friendlies the paid players were certainly expected to earn their wages. A new trainer was secured in John Campbell and experienced professionals Bill Crump, James Devlin, Richard McElhaney, Jimmy Milliken and Willie Newbigging, the last four Scots, signed. The old players were not discarded; Spurs could not afford to replace them all with paid players. Apart from that, many of them were as good as their professional counterparts and had a commitment to the club that newcomers seldom possessed. To mark the latest step up, the red and blue colours Spurs had worn since 1890, which had given them the nickname of 'Tottenham Reds', were abandoned in favour of chocolate and gold, although quite why those colours were chosen is unclear.

Spurs began their competitive league career at Sheppey United. It was not a particularly auspicious start. Stanley Briggs pulled out at the last minute due to injury, and Charlie Ambler and Ly Burrows missed their train. Spurs tried to delay but with Sheppey threatening to claim the match Spurs kicked off with only nine men. By the time Ambler and Burrows arrived 20 minutes had been played and Spurs were a goal down. Crump pulled one back but Sheppey eased into a 3-1 lead before late goals from Milliken and Clements gave Spurs a draw. After losing to Wolverton in their next Southern League fixture, Spurs opened their United League campaign at Millwall Athletic. They lost 5-6 in an amazing game that they would probably have won had Spurs' captain Stanley Briggs not agreed to Millwall using a substitute when one of their number was injured. Briggs was roundly applauded for his sportsmanship, but there were some who pointed out that such an attitude conflicted with a professional game.

As the season progressed, the new players settled in and the team became more accustomed to competitive football, so Spurs' results improved. They finished a respectable fourth in the Southern League, but bottom of the United League, although that was regarded very much as a minor competition and many of the games were played towards the end of the season as the opportunity was given to give trials to possible recruits. In the FA Cup, Old St Stephens and Maidenhead were beaten before Spurs went out to Luton Town. A measure of success was found in the Wellingborough Charity Cup with Spurs getting through to the final.

The Arrival of Charles Roberts

On the playing side Spurs had no cause for complaint but financially the season was not a success. Friendly matches were essential to fill the calendar, gain experience and boost the club's profile but visitors, particularly well-known Football League clubs, demanded hefty guaranteed fees. All season tickets were sold before the season began, but the amount of paying spectators was not as high as hoped for and losses were sustained.

John Oliver's response was twofold. First, he called upon the services of Trooper C.D. Roberts of the Herts Yeomanry. He was a well-known fundraiser and immediately set about organising a military tournament at the Northumberland Park ground that was to turn in a profit of over £100. Second, he set about signing an entire new team. David Black, Joe Cullen, Jimmy Davidson, Sandy Hall, Jimmy Hartley, John L. Jones, Bill Joyce, Joe Knowles, Tom Meade, Bob Stormont and Bob Tannahill were all experienced pros, a cut above the earlier signings. Nine of the 11 were Scots, the exceptions being Meade and Jones. The latter signing, in particular, was a surprise for he was at the peak of his powers, a regular for Wales and one of the best half backs in the country. Oliver could not have made his ambitions clearer.

The influx of new players undoubtedly improved performances on the pitch with a corresponding improvement in final league placings. In the Southern League, Spurs finished third to Southampton and Bristol City: in the United League, second to Luton Town. Only the FA Cup proved a disappointment, Luton Town winning a thrilling game at Northumberland Park 4-3 in the second qualifying round. After that defeat, Arthur Norris was re-engaged as trainer with John Campbell reverting to groundsman. Luton's visits to Tottenham in 1897-98 were to prove quite eventful. In the United League fixture early in February, some of the crowd were incensed by the conduct of several Luton players (and by the referee allowing a Luton goal that was clearly punched home, then disallowing a perfectly legitimate late winner for Spurs). At the end of the game they ran on to the pitch and assaulted some of the visitors. As a result, the FA closed Northumberland Park for two weeks and Spurs were not allowed to play any game within a three-mile radius of the ground. Their Southern League meeting therefore had to take place at Millwall's East Ferry Road.

A Limited Company Formed

Once again, it was events off the pitch that were to be of greater importance. The club was still run by a committee, who worked for the club without pay and in their own time. A full-time employee was needed, someone who could run the club on a day-to-day basis and who knew all about football, both from a playing and administrative point of view. Thus it was that in February 1898 Frank Brettell was appointed as Spurs' first secretary-manager. Brettell had been both a player and served on the committee of Everton. When injury stopped him playing, he continued to be associated with Everton, but when they split and most of the club went off to Goodison Park, he remained at Anfield with Liverpool. In 1895 he joined Bolton Wanderers as secretary of the newly incorporated limited company and was regarded as having all the credentials Spurs needed.

At the same time as Spurs were securing Brettell's services, they were also considering plans to become a limited company. As a club any member could be held accountable for the club's liabilities. In practice, it was the committee who were most at risk and not surprisingly they were reluctant to take on the commitments they knew were needed. Although everything on the financial front looked rosy, limited liability would remove the fear of personal responsibility and attract investment. Charles Roberts, who was becoming increasingly influential at Spurs, was particularly in favour. At the Red Lion Hotel in Tottenham High Road on 2 March 1898, it again fell to Bobby Buckle to propose a resolution that was to prove pivotal to the club's future. Unlike the meeting in December 1895, there were no dissenters and it was quickly resolved to form the Tottenham Hotspur Football and Athletic Company Limited. Officially incorporated on 2 May 1898, John Oliver, Charles Roberts, Bobby Buckle, Ralph Bullock and John Thompson were elected as the company's first directors with Frank Brettell as the secretary.

Despite the undoubted enthusiasm for the flotation, it was not well received. Of 8,000 shares offered to the public, only 1,558 were initially taken up, although the figure did increase in later years. Almost a hundred years later the low subscription was to play a crucial role in events. It is quite ironic that one of the points Bobby Buckle emphasised in proposing the resolution was the members' personal liabilities. In particular, he commented that any individual member might be sued for compensation in the unlikely case of personal injuries being sustained through the collapse of one of the stands. A month later just such an event almost occurred. Claims that Northumberland Park could hold 30,000 people were put to the test at the United League fixture with Arsenal on Good Friday. With over 14,000 squeezed in, about 80 people climbed on the roof of a refreshment bar that promptly collapsed. Only five needed medical treatment, but it could have been much worse. The near disaster highlighted a new problem for Spurs: 14,000 was not even half the number that the club hoped to attract to games, so Northumberland Park was not big enough.

From Brettell to Cameron

The summer of 1898 saw another influx of new players at Tottenham, including Harry Erentz, James McNaught and Tom Smith, as Frank Brettell set about building a team. But results did not match expectations. Spurs finished third in both the United League and the Thames and Medway League, but slipped to a poor seventh in the Southern League as

Signed in 1898, John Cameron would become instrumental in Spurs' rise to national prominence.

Southampton won their third successive title. The vast number of games could not have helped. Entering three league competitions committed Spurs to 64 games and left precious little time for the FA Cup, which did at least provide some solace. Spurs beat Wolverton, Clapton in a replay and Luton Town (at last!) in a second replay in the qualifying rounds, but looked to be going out of the competition when a last-gasp goal gave them a 1-1 draw at home to Newton Heath. In the replay, though, they gave probably their finest performance in the competition to return with a 5-3 victory. Having knocked out a club from the Second Division of the Football League, they went one better in the next round, beating First Division Sunderland at home, but could not repeat the feat at Stoke, losing 1-4.

With Spurs unable to better a substantial offer from the reformed Portsmouth, Brettell left in February 1899. His replacement was something of a surprise. John Cameron was a fine footballer, but at only 26 still to reach his peak and he was expected to combine the secretary-manager's job with playing. Brettell was not the only mid-season departure. In November 1898, John Oliver stood down as chairman with Charles Roberts taking his place. In his four years leading Spurs, Oliver had done more than anyone to turn them from a local team playing for fun to potentially one of the top clubs in the country. Unfortunately, he perhaps gave too much of his time to Spurs and this contributed to his business interests getting into difficulty.

The Move to White Hart Lane

The summer of 1899 proved an exceptionally busy time for John Cameron. As secretary and a leading member of the Association Footballer's Union, (forerunner of the Professional Footballer's Association), he had excellent connections and soon used them, signing George Clawley, David Copeland, Ted Hughes, John Kirwan, Tom Morris, Tom Pratt and Sandy Tait. Much

Sandy Tait, whose fierce tackling earned him the nickname of 'Terrible Tait'.

of his time, though, was spent helping organise the building of, and relocation to, a brand new ground.

Ever since the collapse of the refreshment bar during the Woolwich Arsenal game, Spurs had known Northumberland Park was just not big enough and the search had been on for a suitable site to build the best ground in London. They eventually found it literally a matter of yards from Northumberland Park.

It was well-known that the brewers, Charringtons, had bought some nursery land off Tottenham High Road, intending to build a housing estate to provide custom for the White Hart. So it was a surprise when Charles Roberts heard that a new football club was moving to the site. He quickly approached the landlord of the White Hart, who used to run a public house near Millwall's ground, to see if there was any truth in the rumour. The landlord claimed he had never heard of Spurs, but if they wanted to move to the site he would have no objection as long as they could get the brewer's agreement. Within 24 hours Roberts and Bobby Buckle had approached Charringtons and had little difficulty persuading them to grant Spurs a lease. The only proviso was that Spurs should guarantee attendances of 1,000 for first team games and 500 for reserve fixtures, figures Roberts and Buckle knew could easily be met.

Signing the lease stretched Spurs to the limit financially. The ground was totally vacant, so a great deal of expense was going to be incurred turning it into a football arena, and they still had a five-year lease on Northumberland Park. Fortunately the landlord of Northumberland Park, not knowing of Spurs' plan to move, approached them offering 'a handsome sum' if Spurs would surrender the lease. He was surprised at how quickly the offer was accepted.

Over the summer months groundsman John Oliver worked miracles to prepare a playing surface, as terracing was installed and the old stands moved from Northumberland Park. By September, the ground was ready. Although public practice matches and a reserve game had already been played there, it was formally opened on the fourth of that month with 5,000 attending a friendly against Notts County, Charles Roberts performing the ceremonial kick-off. The ground was not given a name even though suggestions were invited. Gilpin Park was among the favourites, but none was ever adopted and it simply became known as White Hart Lane.

Flower of the South – Southern League Champions

From an opening day win at Millwall, Spurs looked as if they might at last lift a trophy. They dropped only three points in their opening 13 Southern League games – although two of their victories were later expunged when Brighton United and Cowes withdrew from the league – and the title race quickly settled down to a fight between Spurs, Southampton St Marys and Portsmouth. Early in the new year, Southampton were leading the table, but they then became distracted by their run to the FA Cup final, leaving Spurs and Frank Brettell's Portsmouth to fight it out. The fight went right to the last Saturday of the season with Spurs needing to win their final Southern League fixture at New Brompton to be sure of winning the title. Defeat would not hand the trophy to Portsmouth, for their last game was at Swindon Town two days later, but it would have left the Hampshire club favourites.

A great number of Spurs supporters travelled down to the Kent town where it was common knowledge Portsmouth had offered the New Brompton players a substantial bonus if they could win. From the start Spurs were the better team, but from one of their few attacks the home side took the lead. Three minutes after the restart John Cameron grabbed an equaliser and 20 minutes later David Copeland, who had scored Spurs' first goal of the season against Millwall, turned in a Sandy Tait free kick. At the final whistle, the visiting supporters invaded the pitch and carried the Spurs players shoulder high to the dressing rooms. When the Spurs players returned to Tottenham, they were met by an enormous crowd at Bruce Grove station, from where the Tottenham Town Band led a procession back to the club house in White Hart Lane. It was said at the time that such scenes had never been witnessed in Tottenham before, and so impressed were the players that they resolved to ensure the scenes were repeated in 1901, only then to celebrate the capture of the FA Cup.

Apart from winning the Southern League, Spurs were runners-up in the Southern District Combination. The only disappointment had come in the FA Cup. Exempt until the first round, they were beaten at Preston, whose white shirts and blue shorts they had adopted at the beginning of the season in tribute to the Lancashire club.

Previous close seasons had seen wholesale changes in Spurs' playing personnel. In 1900 there was only one significant change. John Cameron was determined to keep the players who had earned Spurs the title 'Flower of the South' together but centre forward Tom Pratt, complaining he could not settle in London, demanded more money. When Spurs refused to increase their offer, he returned to his previous club, Preston North End, with Spurs signing another former Preston player, Sandy Brown, as his replacement. Brown had spent 1899-1900 with Portsmouth, scoring 29 goals in senior matches.

FA Cup Winners

Spurs started the defence of their Southern League title poorly. Injuries, particularly to the crucial half back line, created havoc and they were soon out of the running as Southampton, Bristol City and Portsmouth pulled away from the rest. They eventually recovered to finish fifth, but it was not a league campaign to remember. Ted Hughes, John L. Jones and Tom Morris were all missing at one time or another, but the greatest loss was inside forward David Copeland. Out from the start of the season, it was only when he returned in January 1901 that Spurs began to show their true form, just in time for the team to fulfil its promise of securing the FA Cup.

Spurs began their quest for the 'little tin idol' with a home draw against Preston North End. The death of Queen Victoria delayed the game until February and Spurs seemed to have thrown the chance of revenge away as Preston scored midway through the first half. Spurs exerted continual pressure in the second half, but McBride in the Preston goal was outstanding and there were only nine minutes left when Brown managed to score an equaliser. For the replay Ted Hughes replaced the injured James McNaught and John L. Jones returned after injury. Spurs looked a different team as Cameron scored after six minutes and Brown added two more before half-time. Preston pulled one back, but Brown completed his hat-trick and a late goal from Tom Pratt simply flattered the home team.

The second round saw another Football League side, FA Cup holders Bury, attract a record crowd of 20,250 to White Hart Lane. Many were still finding their places when the visitors, second in the First Division, took a second-minute lead, but Spurs gave a performance full of commitment and skill to fight back. Goals in each half from Sandy Brown gave Spurs victory and even those sceptical journalists on the northern papers were impressed. They had never had much regard for clubs from the south, a view reinforced by Bury's comprehensive thrashing of Southampton in the 1900 final, but after watching two of Lancashire's finest outplayed, they had to admit that the south at last possessed a team that might bring the FA Cup back to its original home.

The third round paired Spurs with Reading, a strong, physical team renowned for overpowering more cultured opponents with their aggressive style of play. Around 3,000 expectant Spurs fans made their way to Elm Park but any thoughts that Spurs' superior skills would put Reading in their place were soon dispelled. The locals quickly took control, pinned Spurs back and took the lead after 15 minutes. Hard as Spurs tried they just could not get going. Only for ten minutes early in the second half did they get into the game and it was during this time that Irish winger John Kirwan nicked an equaliser with a snap shot that took the Reading keeper by surprise. As Reading re-asserted control, Spurs were forced to hang on grimly but it all looked to no avail as George Clawley failed to hold a shot. As the ball spun towards the net, Sandy Tait rushed back and punched it off the line. It looked a certain penalty, but the referee's view was obstructed and his linesman was convinced that Tait had not got to the ball. A goal-kick was given and Spurs hung on for a draw. The replay was as different from the first game as it could be. Copeland scored early on and two more goals from Brown gave Spurs an easy victory and a semi-final meeting with West Bromwich Albion.

Spurs had agreed to the semi-final taking place at Villa Park on Easter Monday. Aston Villa and Sheffield United had drawn the other semi-final two days earlier in Nottingham and, with Villa favourites to win the replay, their players were amongst a crowd of 46,000. If Albion hoped to gain an advantage from playing on their own doorstep they were disappointed, as thousands of Spurs' supporters made their way to Birmingham. Spurs were not at their best in the first half, but they were still far better than Albion and it was a considerable surprise that half-time arrived with no score. In the second half, Spurs really turned on the style and totally outclassed their opponents. Within five minutes of the restart, Brown had put Spurs ahead and by the 70th minute he had helped himself to two more. Pride was all the Throstles had to play for and for a while they threatened to pull one back, but with five minutes left Brown netted again to finish the scoring.

Three days later Sheffield United beat Aston Villa at Derby's Baseball Ground and went into the final as slight favourites. Man for man there was little difference between the teams, but United had nine internationals and the experience of playing in an FA Cup final only two years earlier. Interest in the game was enormous and a world record crowd of 114,815 made their way to Crystal Palace to see if Spurs could become the first southern club to win the cup since the Old Etonians in 1882 and the first Southern League team to do so. Not surprisingly, Spurs had the advantage of the majority of the crowd on their side but the was still a hefty contingent, perhaps 10,000 strong, to cheer on the 'Cutlers'.

Early on, expectations seemed to get the better of Spurs. They were clearly nervous as United had the better of the opening exchanges. It was ten minutes before they posed any threat but when Cameron was put through he was pulled up by the referee's whistle for offside. United continued to have the upper hand but it was still something of a surprise when, in the 12th minute, Priest caught Clawley unsighted and put United ahead. It was 20 minutes before Spurs got back on level terms, Brown getting to a free kick first and guiding his header past 'Fatty' Foulke in the United goal. There was no more scoring in the first half, but the second was barely five minutes old when Kirwan, Brown and Cameron combined to set the Spurs player-manager through. He could have gone for goal himself, but instead cut the ball back for Brown to unleash a glorious shot that hit the back of the net just under the crossbar. Spurs had little time to enjoy their lead or consolidate their position. Barely two minutes later came the defining moment of the game. Bert Lipsham, possibly offside, was allowed to escape down the left. George Clawley failed to hold his shot, but recovered to put the ball behind before Walter Bennett could get in a challenge. The linesman pointed for a corner but to the amazement of everyone referee Kingscott marched back to the centre circle, indicating a goal. So convinced was the official that the ball has crossed the line from Lipsham's initial effort, he refused to even consult his linesman. There was still the best part of 40 minutes left but Kingscott's decision had knocked Spurs back and even the United players seemed embarrassed to be on level terms. For the remainder of the game both teams tried their best, but few chances were created and so a replay was needed.

The general consensus was that Spurs had been the better team, their passing superior, their teamwork more effective than the United kick and rush style which relied so much on individual strengths. As for the disputed goal, the newspaper reporters complained that their position in the press box had made it impossible for them to form an opinion. There was no such problem for the crowd, who were certain the ball had not crossed the line. Even the uncommitted with a good view of the incident thought the referee had got it wrong, an opinion supported by newsreel film.

Everton's Goodison Park had already been selected for a replay seven days later but when Liverpool objected because they had a Football League game arranged for Anfield that day, the FA agreed to switch the replay to Burnden Park, Bolton. If proved an unfortunate decision. The Lancashire and Yorkshire Railway Company refused to offer cheap fares, with the result only 20,470 spectators attended. After the enormous crowd at the Crystal Palace the tradesmen of Bolton had prepared for another vast gathering. There was so much food left over that in some quarters the replay became known as the 'Pork Pie Final'! Those that did get to the game saw another polished performance by John Cameron's men. The only time they looked to be in trouble was after Priest had given United the lead, but in the second half their control was almost total and goals from Cameron, Tom Smith and Sandy Brown were no more than Spurs deserved.

PLAYER'S CIGARETTES

ERENTZ · TAIT · CLAWLEY · MORRIS · JONES · HUGHES · SMITH · KIRWAN · CAMERON · BROWN · COPELAND

ASSOCIATION CUP WINNERS
TOTTENHAM HOTSPUR. 1901

At the final whistle joyous scenes were witnessed as fans invaded the pitch and it took some time for John L. Jones to fight his way over to Lord Kinnaird and receive the cup. Those scenes were as nothing, though, compared to those that greeted Spurs' arrival at South Tottenham station early the next morning. The whole of Tottenham seemed to be waiting for the conquering heroes. With fireworks exploding and brass bands playing, fully 30,000 happy souls accompanied the two brakes (pulled by supporters unwilling to entrust the safety of their precious occupants to horses) back to the clubhouse in White Hart Lane.

Great Matches

FA CUP FINAL REPLAY　　　　　　Burnden Park, Bolton 27 April 1901

Sheffield United 1　**Tottenham Hotspur 3**　　　　Attendance 20,470
Priest　　　　　　　　Cameron
　　　　　　　　　　Smith
　　　　　　　　　　Brown

From the kick-off Spurs looked the better team, David Copeland and John Kirwan getting through only to be stopped by United's captain, 'Nudger' Needham. Copeland delayed when in with a chance and allowed Harry Johnston to dispossess him, and then Foulke made a good save when Copeland got his head to a Harry Erentz free-kick. For 25 minutes George Clawley hardly saw the ball as the Spurs forwards buzzed around the United goal, and when United did threaten he was easily capable of dealing with their weak efforts. Spurs were dominant but reluctant to shoot, seemingly intent on walking the ball into the net, rather than taking a half-chance. As the game wore on United were more in it, Needham in particular making his presence felt and leading from the front. Spurs should have been comfortably ahead, but with half-time approaching Needham got the better of Tom Morris and found Bert Lipsham. His pass put Fred Priest clear and he had no problem beating Clawley. Spurs threatened to wilt, but Erentz and Tait held them together and as the half-time whistle approached, Foulke was called upon to make two good saves. John Cameron changed Spurs' tactics at the start of the second half. No longer were wingers Kirwan and Tom Smith looking to go outside their men, now they were pushing in, exploiting the spaces behind the United half backs. Ten minutes had elapsed when a terrific pass from Sandy Tait released David Copeland. He rounded Thickett, played a one-two with Sandy Brown and then found Smith. His instant pass to Cameron was whipped, first time, past Foulke. For the next 20 minutes the teams were even, but as rain began to fall so Spurs took control, full backs Tait and Erentz snuffing out any threat, the half backs Tom Morris, Ted Hughes and Jack L. Jones running the show. Needham was forced deeper and deeper, but when he blocked Cameron's shot, the ball spun to Smith who rifled home to give Spurs the lead. There was never any danger of that being lost and with seven minutes left Sandy Brown's header from a corner sealed Spurs' first FA Cup triumph.

Tottenham Hotspur: Clawley, Erentz, Tait, Morris, Hughes, Jones, Smith, Cameron, Brown, Copeland, Kirwan.

Sheffield United: Foulke, Thickett, Boyle; Johnson, Morren, Needham, Bennett, Field, Hedley, Priest, Lipsham.

Referee: A.G. Kingscott.

Above: Action from the 1901 FA Cup Final at Crystal Palace. Over 100,000 spectators watch the teams kick off. Below: Sheffield United goalkeeper William 'Fatty' Foulke retrieves the ball as the Spurs players celebrate Sandy Brown's 32nd-minute goal. The match ended in a 2-2 draw, and a replay was needed to decide the winners.

John Cameron had built an excellent team in his short time as secretary-manager, a team that followed in the traditions of the early schoolboys, then amateurs, who had shaped the club from the very beginning. It was a team that reinforced the principles they had laid down and set new standards Spurs have always striven to follow. Cameron's team was one that played football the right way, one that relied on skill and ability, players talented in their own right but harnessed for the better good of the team. Many teams of the era relied on physical strength, long balls whacked out of defence, big men intimidating players of skill and hard tackling players who knew how to get the ball but not what to do with it. That was not the style of football that had first attracted crowds to watch a group of schoolboys on Tottenham Marshes. They had decided to follow Spurs because they wanted to see the game played with subtlety and beauty, players who wanted the ball, were comfortable with it and knew how to pass it around. Camerons's team possessed all those qualities. It was a team put together from all corners of the realm.

50 Greatest Players

JOHN L. JONES   Half back

Joined Tottenham Hotspur: May 1897   **From:** Sheffield United

Debut: v Sheppey United, 4 September 1897

Appearances: 162   **Goals:** 8

Left Tottenham Hotspur: May 1904   **For:** Watford

Honours Won with Tottenham Hotspur: Southern League Championship 1900, FA Cup winner 1901

The signing of 'Jack' Jones was a considerable surprise to the world of football but it illustrated perfectly the determination of the directors to make Spurs a power in the land. An inspirational leader, Jones had played for Rhuddlan, Bootle, Stockton and Grimsby Town. When he joined Sheffield United he soon established himself as an exceptional half back and automatic choice for his country. Jones was well-built and perhaps a little slow, but what he lacked in pace he compensated for with sound positional sense. He possessed first class passing skills and was the perfect link between his full back, inside forward and winger. Rarely absent from the first team, he was getting on for 40 when he left Spurs for Watford and then Worcester. He later played in exhibition games on a synthetic surface before becoming a cricket coach.

Goalkeeper George Clawley was born in the Potteries and started with Crewe Alexandra and Stoke before making his name with Southampton St Mary's. He helped Southampton win the Southern League in 1897 and 1898, but returned to Stoke, thus missing out on a hat-trick of titles. Cameron tempted him to Tottenham in the summer of 1899, but he missed most of his first season, and again a Southern League winner's medal, because of a broken leg. At 6ft 1ins (1.75m) he used his height to great advantage and was also comfortable dealing with long-range shots. His fumble at Reading could have seen Spurs out of the cup and, although it was the referee's mistake that gave Sheffield United their controversial equaliser at Crystal Palace, he was not blameless. However, he more than made up for those mistakes with some great performances throughout the cup run and finished his career with the Saints in 1907.

50 Greatest Players

SANDY BROWN Centre forward

Joined Tottenham Hotspur: May 1900 **From:** Portsmouth

Debut: v Millwall Athletic, 1 September 1900

Appearances: 57 **Goals:** 45

Left Tottenham Hotspur: May 1902 **For:** Portsmouth

Honours Won with Tottenham Hotspur: FA Cup winner 1901

The goal-scoring hero of the 1901 FA Cup success, Alexander Brown played for his native Glenbuck, Kilsyth Wanderers and Edinburgh St Bernards before making the move down to England with Preston North End. He made little impact in three years in Lancashire. However, after joining Portsmouth he really showed an eye for goal and Spurs' manager John Cameron had to beat off several other interested clubs to secure his signature, as he sought to strengthen the team that had just won the Southern League title. A pure and simple goalscorer, Brown did little work outside the box but when a scoring opportunity came along he sprang to life. He was strong and quite capable of hitting the ball with either foot, but for a player standing less than six feet tall scored a surprising number of goals with this head. Top-scorer in his two seasons with Spurs, he was surprisingly allowed to return to Portsmouth and later played for Middlesbrough, Luton Town and Kettering. In his time with Middlesbrough he won the Scottish cap he was deprived of with Spurs. He played against England in April 1902, but the match was subsequently declared 'unofficial'.

At full back Spurs had Harry Erentz and Sandy Tait. 'Tiger' Erentz was signed from Newton Heath in May 1898 and in six years with Spurs proved as solid and reliable as anyone could hope for. On leaving Spurs he joined Swindon Town, but a broken leg early in his time in Wiltshire forced him to retire from the game. In six years with Preston North End 'Terrible' Tait had earned a reputation as one of the best full backs in the game. An intimidating figure, he was fiercely competitive, an attribute that sometimes led to his undoubted skill being overlooked. If he had one weakness it was a lack of pace, but he made up for that with a fine sense of anticipation.

The half back line was Spurs' great strength. Formerly with Grantham Rovers and Gainsborough Trinity, right half Tom Morris had arrived at Spurs in May 1898. A ceaseless worker, he provided the defensive cover so important to allow his middle line colleague to get forward. He gave Spurs 14 years' great service as a player, followed by 30 more on the groundstaff. Centre half Ted Hughes was known to Cameron from his days in Everton reserves and was one of the first players Cameron approached on taking over as secretary-manager. So well did he perform in the cup run that he earned a recall to the Welsh team. At left half was the great Welsh international, John L. Jones, who formed the base of a solid triangle, with David Copeland and John Kirwan, that was so vital to Spurs' success.

Tom Smith was on the right wing, one of the fastest wingers around and also one of the strongest. He had joined Spurs from Preston North End in May 1898 and immediately impressed, not only with his pace, but also his ability to hit over telling crosses, crosses that were not only aimed at his centre forward but often pulled back to his onrushing inside forwards. Smith's shock retirement in the summer of 1902 was a blow that Spurs took some years to recover from. If Smith provided the pace then the guile was provided by John Kirwan on the opposite flank. An Irish international, he started with Southport and had a year with Everton before Cameron signed him. A frail but surprisingly tough figure, he was normally up against big, beefy opponents, but he was so tricky that if they were not dumped on their posteriors they were rarely able to get close enough to challenge him.

Cameron himself was at inside right where his great dribbling ability and precise passing were put to best use. He had played at centre forward with Ayr Parkhouse, Queens Park and Everton and never lost the striker's eye for goal. After the cup success he rapidly curtailed playing to concentrate on managing and, although he never repeated the success of his first two years in charge, it was still a surprise when he left in 1907. Another former centre forward, David Copeland, occupied the inside left position, forming one of

50 Greatest Players

SANDY TAIT   Full back

Joined Tottenham Hotspur: May 1899   **From:** Preston North End

Debut: v Millwall Athletic, 2 September 1899

Appearances: 242   **Goals:** 3

Left Tottenham Hotspur: May 1908   **For:** Leyton

Honours Won with Tottenham Hotspur: Southern League Championship 1900,

FA Cup winner 1901

Another of the many Scots signed around the turn of the century, Alexander Tait was one of the most committed and popular players during his time at Spurs. Famed for his sliding tackle, he was nicknamed 'Terrible Tait' for his ferocious tackling, He was one of 13 children and turned to football to escape a life down the pits. Starting out with Glenbuck Athletic, Ayr, Royal Albert and Rangers, he made his name with Motherwell before joining Preston North End in 1894. In five years with Preston he developed into one of the best full backs in the league and Preston were upset when John Cameron persuaded Tait to throw in his lot with Spurs. Enormously strong, Tait was not the quickest of players but he was always ahead of his opponents in speed of thought and made one of the most difficult of roles look easy. Captain in his latter days at White Hart Lane, he left after nine years' great service to join Leyton. He soon turned to managing the East London club and was later manager of Croydon Common.

the most potent left wing partnerships in the country with John Kirwan. Copeland was a native of Ayr and joined Spurs from Bedminster in May 1899. Forever probing, he provided the perfect support for Kirwan and it was a sad loss when the pair of them were enticed to the newly-formed Chelsea in 1905. The spearhead of Spurs' attack was another Scot: Alexander 'Sandy' Brown. He was the rough diamond in the team, not physically well-built or particularly cultured, but when a chance came he took it. His 15 goals in the cup run made him the hero and set a record that still stands.

Two major trophies in two seasons had established Spurs as the strongest team in the south and kindled hopes that at last a serious challenge could be mounted to the Football League clubs, but it was not to be. Rather it was Spurs' position that came under challenge, particularly from Southampton. There were few personnel changes in the summer of 1901 and Spurs began the 1901-02 season well with nine wins and one draw in their first 11 Southern League games. Southampton and Portsmouth had also started well and, just as in 1899-1900, the championship soon settled down to a three-way battle.

Action from White Hart Lane. Spurs take on Aston Villa in the third round of the FA Cup in March 1903. Southern League Spurs lost 3-2 to their Football League opponents.

For Spurs, it all fell apart around Christmas. The festive season began with a creditable, if disappointing, draw at Millwall but the really important results came on Christmas Day and Boxing Day. First Portsmouth snatched a 2-1 win at White Hart Lane, Spurs' first home defeat of the season, and then Spurs returned from what had became their annual Boxing Day visit to Southampton on the wrong end of a 0-1 scoreline. The results were not fatal, it was still too early in the season, but their two greatest rivals had shown that Spurs could be beaten. As if to prove the point Southampton then knocked Spurs out of the FA Cup in the first round, winning a second replay at Reading after two evenly contested games. Spurs continued to track Portsmouth and Southampton in the Southern League, but all realistic hope of a third successive trophy disappeared with a one-goal defeat at Portsmouth in March. They eventually finished second, five points adrift of Portsmouth, but at least ahead of Southampton thanks to a better goal average.

For the rest of their Southern League career Spurs did little of note. In 1903-04 they were runners-up, no mean feat when they won only one of their first nine games, but they were seven points behind Southampton who won the title for the sixth time in ten years. They were still playing attractive football, still pulling in the crowds, but the progress that had been so rapid now ground to a halt. Even the FA Cup provided few high spots.

In 1902-03 there were victories over West Bromwich Albion and Bristol City before Aston Villa won a thrilling third round tie 3-2 at White Hart Lane in front of almost 25,000 spectators.

The following season a great win at Everton in the first round had kindled memories of past glories and 32,000 people packed White Hart Lane for Aston Villa's second round visit, memories of the previous year's battle fresh in their minds and hopeful Spurs could turn the tables. The game was to be remembered for all the wrong reasons. So large was the crowd that to relieve some of the pressure, benches were put around the perimeter of the pitch. At half-time Villa were one up and as those on the benches stretched their legs on the pitch, so their seats were taken by those from behind. When the teams re-emerged the spectators who had left their seats were unable to return to their places and as the farce developed the referee abandoned the game. Spurs were dragged before the Football Association, fined £350 and ordered to replay the tie at Villa Park. A goal from John 'Bristol' Jones, signed from Bristol Rovers and so named to distinguish him from John L. Jones, gave Spurs a surprise victory but in the next round they went out to Football League champions Sheffield Wednesday.

50 Greatest Players

TED HUGHES   **Half back**

Joined Tottenham Hotspur: July 1899   **From:** Everton

Debut: v Brighton United, 7 October 1899

Appearances: 183   **Goals:** 11

Left Tottenham Hotspur: 1908   **For:** Clyde

Honours Won with Tottenham Hotspur: FA Cup winner 1901

Ted Hughes spent three years at Everton, despite making only eight league appearances. One of his club-mates was John Cameron, who obviously realised Hughes' value for he soon persuaded the Welshman to join him at White Hart Lane. Hughes took time to establish himself, the turning point coming when he replaced the injured James McNaught for the FA Cup third round replay with Preston North End in 1901. He kept his place for the rest of the cup run and performed so well that he earned a recall to the Welsh team. A ceaseless worker, good in the air and always backing up his forwards, Hughes went on to serve Spurs well, often at full back, collecting 12 caps to add to the two he had won with Everton, until the summer of 1908 when he moved to Clyde. He only stayed in Scotland for a month before returning south to run a public house in Enfield.

Great Managers – 1899-1907

JOHN CAMERON

Although only in charge for one season, Spurs first manager, Frank Brettell, left a legacy that was to lay the foundations for all that is good about the club. John Cameron had been a centre forward in his native Ayr, playing for Ayr Parkhouse and Queens Park before going to work in the Cunard offices in Liverpool where he signed as an amateur for Everton. Accepting professional terms he switched to inside forward but never fully established himself playing less than 50 senior games in three years. Brettell persuaded him to join Spurs in May 1898, a great dribbler like most Scottish forwards of the time, but intelligent enough to know that quick inter-passing was the most effective way forward. Cameron was one of the best at the passing game, sliding the ball for through for his winger or clipping it into the path of his centre forward. He was not a simple creator of goals though; he still possessed the centre forward's eye for a goal and was a regular scorer.

When Brettell resigned in February 1899, Spurs turned to Cameron as his replacement, giving him the manager-secretary's job to go with that of playing. Utilising to the full his contacts as secretary of the Association Footballer's Union he set about capturing the talent needed to turn Spurs into a power in the land, signing players of the calibre of Sandy Tait, David Copeland, Jack Kirwan and Sandy Brown. The results were immediate, the Southern League title in 1900 and the FA Cup a year later. Further trophies may have eluded Spurs, but Cameron kept them at the top of the southern tree, always challenging for trophies but more importantly establishing the entertaining type of football for which the club has become known. In March 1907 having decided he could do no more for Spurs, he resigned. He turned to football journalism for his living although that was punctuated by spells as a coach and manager of Ayr United.

'Differences with the Directorate'

Success was not everything in those days. Everybody wanted to win, of course, but providing entertainment, getting the crowds in and giving value for money was what mattered most. Football conducted its business in private, not through the media and, in public at least, John Cameron's position appeared to be under no threat. In 1906, Spurs even enticed the experienced Arthur Turner from Rotherham County to take on the secretarial responsibilities, so allowing Cameron to concentrate on playing matters. However, in March 1907 Cameron suddenly resigned, blaming 'differences with the directorate'. It was unfortunate the departure of such a highly popular person, a man who had done so much for Spurs, should be tinged with a touch of bitterness.

There were many applicants keen to take his place, but when his successor was named it was a considerable surprise. Fred Kirkham was a well-known referee from Preston. He had taken control of the 1902 and 1906 FA Cup finals and several internationals, but he was a commercial traveller, not a professional football man. He had not played the game and although he certainly knew how to control players for 90 minutes, doubts were expressed as to how he would handle day-to-day involvement with professional footballers. In his one season in charge Spurs dropped to seventh in the Southern League. It was their lowest placing in the competition, but no great surprise. Spurs had finished sixth for the last two seasons and fifth the year before, but Kirkham was not popular with players or supporters and had come in for a good deal of criticism. A settlement on his five-year contract was negotiated during the summer of 1908, just as Spurs were going through the most important few months of their history.

For some years Spurs had grown increasingly concerned at the conservative attitude of the Southern League, a competition that itself had grown and flourished despite the stubborn refusal of the footballing authorities to accept professionalism and regular competitive football. Now it was the once radical administrators who were holding back the game in London and the south, determined to hold on to their power at any cost. Chelsea and Clapton Orient had applied to join the Southern League in 1905, been refused and gone off to the more progressive Football League, keen to spread its power and set up a truly national competition. With the Southern League refusing proposals to join up with the Football League, Fulham, Southern League champions for two years, had defected in 1907.

The Football League was unquestionably the power in English football. It was attracting the best players, the best clubs, its tentacles were spreading and supporters were deserting the Southern League clubs for the better fare on offer at Football League grounds. For Spurs it all came to a head in February 1908. When director Morton Cadman reported that he had found no support for a proposal Spurs considered crucial to the future of the Southern League, Charles Roberts decided he had had enough. He announced Spurs would quit the Southern League at the end of the season and seek membership of the Football League. Champions Queens Park Rangers and Bradford Park Avenue soon followed suit. The Southern League, Millwall in particular who still regarded the competition as their child, were furious. The three 'rebels' were called upon to resign immediately. Bradford PA did, but when Spurs and QPR refused a rule change was bulldozed through giving the league power to expel them.

Charles Roberts was confident Spurs would win the ballot to join the Football League. They were up against three clubs seeking re-election,

Chesterfield, Grimsby Town and Lincoln City, plus Bradford PA, QPR and Boston United. Rangers could match Spurs for playing strength, they had just won the Southern League ten points ahead of Spurs, but none of their rivals could match Spurs for support, facilities or reputation. Both Football and Southern League meetings were set for 27 May 1908.

The small-minded attitude of the Southerners was perfectly exhibited when they advanced their meeting by 30 minutes to ensure the two clashed exactly. Rangers withdrew from the Football League ballot at the last minute, but, along with Spurs, were still expelled by the Southern League, who were apparently determined to teach Rangers a lesson, even if their replacements, Coventry City and Southend United, were nowhere near such attractive opponents. At the Football League meeting the votes were counted. Chesterfield and Grimsby Town got 23, Bradford PA 20, Lincoln City 18 and Spurs only 14, half of what they had been led to believe they could expect. The loyalty vote had obviously helped the three clubs seeking re-election and it was probably Bradford City's promotion to the First Division that removed the major obstacle to Bradford PA's election.

No matter the reasons, Spurs were rejected and they were now in a desperate situation. Charles Roberts was told they would be allowed back into the Southern League, but only in the Second Division. Roberts was not going to crawl back to the Southern League, Rangers did that and although they got back in the First Division, they were forced to play all their matches in midweek. For Spurs that would spell financial ruin and they would be better filling the calendar with friendly games. The only hope seemed to lie in the formation of a Third Division for the Football League. An advertisement for applicants appeared but the idea went no further. Hopes were only rekindled when Stoke, relegated from the First Division a year earlier, decided to withdraw from the Football League and agreed to throw their support behind Spurs as their replacements. The Football League called a special meeting for 29 June, but Spurs then received another setback as Stoke reversed their earlier decision and re-applied for membership. In the first ballot Spurs and Lincoln City got 17 votes each, Stoke six and Rotherham Town and Southport none. The second saw Spurs and Lincoln get 20 each. The final decision rested with the League Management Committee and they gave it to Spurs by five votes to three.

Despite their elevation to the country's premier league competition, Spurs decided not to replace Fred Kirkham. In future, team selection would be left to the directors.

Chapter Three: 1908-19
Early Football League Years

Spurs started their Football League career on 1 September 1908 with the most attractive fixture possible, a visit from FA Cup holders Wolverhampton Wanderers. A crowd of 20,000 saw Spurs win 3-0 with their first goal scored after six minutes by the famous amateur international and Spurs' director, Vivian Woodward. It was a great start and just a sample of what was to come. Spurs fully justified the Management Committee's decision to elect them, battling all season with Bolton Wanderers, West Bromwich Albion, Birmingham and Derby County to top the Second Division table. With three games left Albion were two points ahead of Bolton and Spurs, but Spurs' three games were all away from home. The odds seemed against them, but they won at Burnley and Bradford PA to take the battle into the final week of the season. Postponements meant the three contenders would not play their final match on the same day. In fact, they all had to visit Derby County for their last game. Albion went first and lost, Spurs followed, knowing victory or a draw of anything less than 2-2 would see them promoted. Defeat or a two-all draw would leave Spurs praying for Derby to beat Bolton. They settled for a 1-1 draw. Bolton beat Derby to take the title but it mattered little: after just one year Spurs were in the First Division.

Spurs celebrated promotion with a ground-breaking trip to South America for matches in Argentina and Uruguay. On the voyage home, one of the Spurs party used the ship's parrot as a prop when he dressed up as Long John Silver for a fancy dress contest. He was presented with the parrot as a souvenir. It was to remain at White Hart Lane for ten years.

The directors made few new signings for Spurs' entry into the top flight, despite the loss of their biggest star. Vivian Woodward had spent eight years with Spurs, developing into the best centre forward in the country, and his decision to quit the first class game to return to Chelmsford was a serious, and totally unexpected, blow to Spurs' hopes of making an impression. Without his major contribution, Spurs struggled from the start of the season. They may have been a big fish in the little pond of the Southern League, they may have been too good for the Second Division of the Football League, but they were now among the elite of English football. The step up was harder than

50 Greatest Players

VIVIAN WOODWARD Centre forward

Joined Tottenham Hotspur: March 1901   **From:** Chelmsford City

Debut: v Bristol City, 6 April 1901

Appearances: 156   **Goals:** 68

Left Tottenham Hotspur: May 1909   **For:** Chelmsford City

One of the outstanding players of his generation, Vivian Woodward was the epitome of the amateur centre forward, relying on skill and guile while most players in his position preferred pure brute strength. His game was not just about scoring goals, but also about bringing his team-mates into the game and creating chances. First joining Spurs in 1901, he did not play regularly until 1902-03, but by the end of that season he was playing for England at both amateur and full level. He went on to net 28 goals in 23 games at full level and played in 67 amateur internationals, captaining the United Kingdom teams that won the Olympic title in 1908 and 1912. Scorer of Spurs' first Football League goal and top scorer in their debut season, he announced he was leaving the first class game in the summer of 1909.

He returned to Chelmsford City, but then shocked Spurs by joining Chelsea in November. Although one of the most celebrated of players, he never won a domestic honour, refusing the chance to play for Chelsea in the 1915 FA Cup final, as it would have deprived Bob Thomson, whose goals had taken Chelsea to the final, of his place.

they had expected and they spent the entire season down near the bottom of the table. Without Woodward, scoring was their major problem. Although not a big scorer himself, Woodward set up chances for others and although Billy Minter chipped in his regular ration of goals he could not do it all on his own. Much as they looked around for a regular scorer, Spurs could find no one until December, and when they did manage to secure Percy Humphreys' transfer from Chelsea it was only thanks to Woodward. He had been persuaded to join Chelsea, a devastating blow to Spurs, but at least it meant they could afford to let Humphreys leave. Although Humphreys' goals kept Spurs out of the relegation spots, they were not able to pull away from the danger area. Come Chelsea's visit for the last match of the season, Spurs needed nothing less than a draw to send Chelsea down and avoid returning to the Second Division themselves. They got more than they needed: a 2-1 victory with goals from Minter and Humphreys.

Spurs retained their First Division place until the start of the Great War, but without ever really looking comfortable. They finished 12th in 1911-12, but spent most of their time in the lower reaches of the division, relegation often a threat. The club rarely ventured into the transfer market, the directors responding to criticism by saying they were not prepared to pay out over-inflated fees for players they did not consider any better than those already on the staff. It was not so easy to reply to suggestions that if the players were good enough, it must be the training and selection that were wrong, and eventually they realised that a professional manager was needed. In December 1912, the former Newcastle and Scotland half back Peter McWilliam was appointed. McWilliam soon identified players better than those he had inherited, signing Fanny Walden, Jimmy Banks and Tommy Clay and giving players like Arthur Grimsdell and Bert Bliss a real chance to show what they could do.

J. Walton: outside right in Spurs' first Football League season.

Invasion of the 'Gunners'

Poor results, though, soon became of secondary importance as Spurs' dominant position in North London came under threat. Ever since Spurs' elevation to the First Division their only rivals in London had been Woolwich Arsenal. The South Londoners had joined the Football League in 1893 and secured promotion to the First Division in 1904, but financially had always found life a struggle. In 1910 Fulham's Henry Norris had become involved with Woolwich Arsenal, planning to merge them with the Second Division Fulham to give him a First Division club playing at Craven Cottage. His plans had been thwarted by the Football League. The clubs could merge, but they would have to play in the Second Division. Norris decided Woolwich Arsenal were potentially the bigger, if only he could move them from Plumstead, so he concentrated his efforts on the South London club while retaining his interests in West London. Finding somewhere to transplant a football club was not easy, but eventually Norris identified a suitable site, the sports ground of St John's College of Divinity.

Still at Spurs in 1912, Tom Morris had been the only member of the 1901 FA Cup winning side to play in Spurs' first Football League game in 1908.

It was the perfect size for a football stadium, well situated in a residential area to provide a ready-made support and with good public transport facilities. It was also at Highbury, literally down the road from White Hart Lane.

As soon as stories of Norris' plans got out early in 1913, Spurs and Clapton Orient complained bitterly. Even Chelsea were up in arms but there was nothing they could do. The Football League were not happy with the idea, but their rules gave them no control over where a club was based. The rules were changed but only when it was too late. Local residents formed a 'defence committee' and Islington Borough Council voiced its opposition to Norris' proposal, but planning permission was not needed and the prospect of thousands flocking to the area every couple of weeks appealed to local businesses. Norris invested a large chunk of his not inconsiderable wealth in the venture and by September 1913 Highbury was open for business. Spurs had grown accustomed to being the only real choice for football fans in North London. They now had a real challenge to their position, but at least they had the advantage of being in the First Division while Arsenal were in the Second. That almost changed within a year as Spurs finished 1913-14 just above the relegation positions while Arsenal only missed promotion on goal average.

At the end of the season, Spurs accepted an invitation to tour Germany, Italy and Switzerland. It was perhaps an ill-advised decision. There were no problems in Italy or Switzerland, but in Germany the treatment they received was atrocious. Verbal and physical assaults by opponents and spectators were commonplace; referees ignored the laws and gave the home teams every advantage. Anti-British feelings were on the increase and Spurs were a convenient target. On their return home, Charles Roberts declared Spurs would never visit Germany again and, indeed, the club did not venture there until some years after his death. Some Spurs players did though, for within three months the Great War was declared and by the time it ended several of them had served at the front.

Bottom but not Relegated

With great enthusiasm for the war and claims the conflict would be over within weeks football was allowed to continue as normal, although in truth most clubs were hit by players joining up. Spurs had a terrible season. They started with just one win in the first 11 games, won only eight games all season and conceded 90 goals. They spent the entire season down near the bottom, scrambling for points with Notts County, Chelsea, Manchester United and Bolton. Right to the end they looked likely to escape, but only one point from their last four games, as Notts County collected six from the same number of matches and catapulted up the table, left Spurs rock bottom, a point below Chelsea. Even subsequent revelations that Manchester United's defeat of Liverpool had been fixed as part of a betting

50 Greatest Players

BOBBY STEEL   **Inside forward/Half back**

Joined Tottenham Hotspur: May 1908   **From:** Port Glasgow

Debut: v Wolverhampton Wanderers, 1 September 1908

Appearances: 246   **Goals:** 46

Left Tottenham Hotspur: 1919   **For:** Released

Like his brothers, Alex and Danny, Bobby Steel started his football career with his hometown club Newmilns before going on to greater things. He joined Spurs as they prepared for their first season in the Football League, having been playing for Port Glasgow, although Spurs had to pay the transfer fee to Greenock Morton with whom he had signed Scottish League forms. A hard-working inside forward with lovely passing skills, he was also an effective dribbler, making it difficult for opponents to know what to expect from him. He played regularly at inside left in his first five years with Spurs and then dropped back to centre half, filling the position vacated by brother Danny's departure. During the First World War he showed exceptional versatility playing at half back, anywhere in the forward line and even at full back. After the War, he was released and took up refereeing in the Southern League, before brother Alex persuaded him to join Gillingham. Bobby was later captain of the England bowls team.

With a shot like a cannonball, Bert Bliss was the leading scorer in 1914-15 and became the leading marksman again when hostilities ended.

scandal provided no consolation, for United had finished two points ahead of Spurs with a vastly superior goal average.

Spurs did not get to play in the Second Division immediately as the Football Association decided at the end of the season to suspend all football until the War was over. The government wanted the game to continue, albeit on a reduced scale and without interfering with more important activities, to provide at least some semblance of normality. Led by Henry Norris, the London clubs formed the London Football Combination and immediately ran into conflict with the Football League. Keen to maintain their control of the game, the League threatened any club that played in a competition it had not sanctioned with expulsion. The clubs and league seemed on a collision course until FA president, Sir Charles Clegg, intervened and made the league see sense.

The Combination ran throughout the rest of the War, Spurs' first game in the competition marking their first visit to Highbury. The competition was split into two parts in 1915-16, Spurs finishing sixth in the first and runners-up in the second. In September 1916, White Hart Lane was taken over by the Ministry of Munitions with the East Stand housing a rifle range and the rest of the ground being used to manufacture gas masks. Arsenal and Clapton Orient both offered Spurs a temporary home and for the rest of the War, Spurs split their 'home' games between Highbury and Orient's Homerton ground. In the last three seasons of the War, Spurs finished fourth, fourth and sixth, but this meant little. Spurs fared better than many clubs, who were not always able to fulfil their fixtures and when they did often had to put out very weak teams.

Chapter Four: 1919-39
The Inter-War Years

Arsenal's move to Spurs' territory had seriously damaged what had been a cordial relationship. If making Highbury available to Spurs during the War was intended to be a first step to healing the rift, Arsenal's immediate post-war conduct was to plunge the relationship to new depths. Not content with trying to steal Spurs' support, Henry Norris, now Sir Henry and an MP, set out to hijack Spurs' First Division place.

Preparing for the resumption of the pre-war league competition, the Football League decided to increase the number of First Division clubs to 22. Twice before the top division had been increased by two clubs. In 1898 promotion and relegation was decided by 'test matches'. After the 1898 test matches, with Burnley due to replace Blackburn Rovers and Stoke having seen off Newcastle's challenge, both Blackburn and Newcastle had been elected to the First Division. In 1905 Liverpool and Bolton Wanderers were promoted with the clubs they were due to replace, Bury and Notts County, retaining their place. Spurs had no reason to believe the same thing would not happen again: the Second Division's top two, Derby County and Preston North End, would be promoted, but the First Division's bottom two, Spurs and Chelsea, would not be relegated.

Norris was desperate to get Arsenal into the First Division. He had invested a huge amount of money and with the War's intervention needed to see a return. He could not trust to Arsenal winning promotion on the pitch, so he set about achieving it in the boardroom. Norris based his case on one simple fact; Arsenal had been members of the league longer than Spurs. That was true, but on that criteria Wolverhampton Wanderers and Birmingham had a better claim to promotion than Arsenal. Wolves had been founder members in 1888 and Birmingham had joined in 1892, whereas Arsenal had not become members until 1893. On playing performances Wolves had the better claim having finished third in Division Two in 1915. Birmingham had finished fifth and Arsenal sixth (although years later it was realised goal averages had been miscalculated and the positions should have been reversed). Behind the scenes, Norris beavered away to gain support for Arsenal, while Spurs did not take the challenge seriously, believing right was on their side.

Exactly how Norris managed to garner support for his case has never come out and it is probably too late now to hope it ever will. One certainty, though, is that it was only at the league meeting in March 1919 that Spurs realised just how much work he had put in. This became apparent almost as soon as the meeting began. When the First Division had been expanded in the past all the competing clubs were put in a ballot together and the top four were the winners. It was as simple as that. This time, Liverpool chairman and league President John McKenna suggested it would be different, and the meeting agreed that, because of the scandal surrounding the Liverpool-Manchester United game, Chelsea should be re-elected without a vote. He then proposed, and the meeting again agreed, that as Derby County and Preston North End had topped the Second Division in 1915, they should be promoted without a vote. That left just one place to be contested between Arsenal, Barnsley, Birmingham, Hull City, Spurs and Wolves, and only one vote for each of the member clubs to cast instead of their usual four. The biggest shock for the Spurs contingent, led by chairman Charles Roberts, was when McKenna made an impassioned speech supporting Arsenal's case. McKenna was a man of enormous influence and there seems little doubt the clubs took on board what he said. When the votes were counted Arsenal had 18; the other 24 were spread around the rest of the candidates with Spurs coming second on eight. There can be no logical reason for the league's decision, but there was nothing Spurs could do about it. They were as sick as their supporters, but not quite as sick as the parrot they had brought back from Argentina ten years earlier – it died, just days after the league meeting.

Winning Promotion – on the Pitch

Spurs felt genuine anger at the league's decision, but there was only one thing they could do – prove the injustice on the field of play. Peter McWilliam resumed his managerial duties and immediately set about reinforcing what remained of his pre-war squad. Jimmy Chipperfield, Bert Smith and Charlie Wilson, who had all played for Spurs in war-time competition were signed and the promising Jimmy Dimmock was promoted from the juniors. They started the 1919-20 season with a bang, winning 11 of their first 12 games and heading the table from beginning to end. Playing a free-flowing attacking game, they scored 102 goals while conceding just 32. With six draws and only four defeats, their 70 points set a record that stood for many years and left them six points ahead of Huddersfield Town. Well before the end of the season, McWilliam was planning for a First Division campaign, adding Jimmy Seed and Charlie Walters to an already exceptional squad.

The only disappointment in the season came in the FA Cup. After beating Bristol Rovers, West Stanley and West Ham United, White Hart Lane welcomed Aston Villa for a fourth round clash. It gave Spurs the chance to show what the First Division had missed because of the voting fiasco. Filled with confidence from their outstanding league form, Spurs felt sure they could beat Villa. A thrilling match ensued with Spurs proving the better team until captain Tommy Clay shaped to make an easy clearance. He totally muffed his kick and instead of sending it downfield, sliced it past a startled Bill Jacques for an own goal. Clay never forgot or forgave himself for the error. If Spurs had won he felt sure they would have gone on to lift the Cup instead of Villa.

FA Cup Winners Again

Winning the Second Division at a canter was one way of showing how wrong the league had been to promote Arsenal at Spurs' expense, but that alone was not enough. If Spurs really wanted to ridicule the decision they had to show they were capable of living with, if not beating, the best teams in the country.

The way they started the 1920-21 campaign, with only four points from their first six games, did not exactly inspire confidence, but as the season wore on so they grew more accustomed to the higher level. Slowly but surely, they settled to the task in hand and gradually moved up the table. They were never in with a chance of winning the title, but a final position of sixth – three places and three points above Arsenal – was more than satisfactory. The best performances came in the second half of the season, from the New Year on, just as the FA Cup trail began. It was here that Spurs would really make their point.

In the first round, Spurs were drawn at home to Third Division Bristol Rovers. A goal ahead within four minutes and four up by half-time, they sauntered to an easy 6-2 win. First Division rivals Bradford City were expected to prove a much tougher proposition in the second round, again at White Hart Lane, and so it proved with the scores level at half-time. In the second half, though, Jimmy Seed really turned on the style, netting a hat-trick to lead Spurs to a 4-0 victory. Another Third Division outfit, Southend United, provided the opposition in the third round, this time away from home. Spurs won 4-1, but it was their worst performance of the campaign. From the start Spurs appeared lethargic, content to let the home side make all the running and Southend duly scored first after just ten minutes. Spurs raised themselves to get an equaliser through Jimmy Cantrell, but then went back into their shell and let Southend exert all the pressure. A penalty was awarded against Bert Smith ten minutes before the break, but Spurs then had the touch of luck that all Cup-winners believe proves their name is on the trophy. The referee was not happy with Albert Fairclough's placing of the ball and moved it so he was satisfied it was on the spot. When Fairclough tried to adjust its position again the referee refused to let him. Clearly annoyed, Fairclough argued with the official but to no avail. He promptly gave the ball an almighty whack. It went well wide of the upright. Southend tore into Spurs at the resumption for the first 15 minutes, but Spurs again sat back and allowed the home team to blow themselves out. They then stepped up a gear to score three goals in the last half-hour.

A Chance For Revenge

It is amazing how often the luck of the draw gives a team beaten in the cup a chance for revenge the following year. That was exactly what happened to Spurs when the fourth round paired them with Aston Villa. Thoughts of the previous year's meeting, and in particular Tommy Clay's own goal, were fresh in the memory as almost 52,000 packed White Hart Lane to witness one of the best cup-ties ever seen there. A titanic battle was fought out as two evenly balanced teams put on a display of attacking play without equal. From the start both teams went forward, determined to get the upper hand

Jimmy Banks, whose quick thinking goal against Aston Villa took Spurs to the FA Cup semi-final.

but meeting defences equally as determined not to let their opponents take the advantage. It was a game that was to be talked about for years to come. Spurs won it with the only goal coming from Jimmy Banks in the 23rd minute. Jimmy Dimmock began the move with a run at the Villa defence from inside his own half. Jimmy Seed managed to get to the winger's cross first, but a Villa defender made a desperate challenge to prevent him getting a shot on target. The ball spun out to Banks, who hit a great shot past the Villa keeper, Sam Hardy. It was a goal fit to win a memorable match.

Spurs had to travel to Hillsborough for the semi-final meeting with Preston North End. It was the only match where Lady Luck seemed to be against them. Early in the first half, Banks collected a loose ball, advanced a few yards and hammered it into the net. He was not even allowed to begin celebrating as the referee called play back and awarded a free-kick to Spurs for a foul on Seed. Not long after this, a scramble in front of the Preston goal ended with the ball in the back of the net, but again Spurs' celebrations were cut short as the referee awarded Preston a free-kick. None of the players knew why and the official refused to let anyone in on the secret, even after the game. Not that the referee was the only one to blame for a lack of goals at half-time. Jimmy Dimmock had the best chance of the game, a few yards from goal and a gaping net in front of him, but excitement got the better of him and rather than just slipping the ball between the posts he decided to blast it. The crossbar was still shaking minutes later, but the ball was at the other end of the field.

Blatant Penalties

The fates continued to conspire against Spurs in the second half. First Banks was clearly chopped down in the box, and then a Preston defender handled the ball in full view of the 44,668 crowd. Both were blatant penalties, but not in the eyes of the referee. If Spurs thought they were up against 11 opponents and a man in black they did not let it get to them. They were determined to get to the final, redoubled their efforts and at last got the reward they deserved. Arthur Grimsdell and Jimmy Dimmock cut the Preston defence open, before Grimsdell set up Bert Bliss for one of his trademark drives. Bliss then added a second from another Grimsdell pass and Spurs could have gone on to grab another, before a defensive mix-up and deflection off Clay allowed Preston to pull one back. Even then Spurs never looked like losing and could have added to their score.

The other semi-final saw two Second Division teams in opposition. Wolverhampton Wanderers and Cardiff City drew 0-0 at Anfield, before Wolves triumphed 3-1 in an Old Trafford replay for the right to meet Spurs at Stamford Bridge. As the First Division side, Spurs were the clear favourites, but any advantages their superior skills were expected to give were negated even before the game started. Despite a downpour starting first thing in the morning, by 10.30am, a full five hours before kick-off, there were so many people queuing outside the ground that the police advised the gates should be opened early.

The rain ceased while the teams were presented to King George V and the Duke of York, but by the time the first whistle blew, much of the pitch was under water. It was not a surface on which any player could display his talents; keeping possession of the ball was difficult, but not as difficult as keeping their balance. Although the rain stopped during the game and

Great Matches

FA CUP FINAL   **Stamford Bridge, 23 April 1921**

Tottenham Hotspur 1 Wolverhampton Wanderers 0   **Attendance 72,805**
Dimmock

A one nil victory for Spurs was never a fair reflection of a game in which they were the masters from start to finish. Had it not been for the atrocious conditions, Spurs would have won the match by at least three or four goals. From the outset they set about mastering Wolves and the conditions with the passing game that had served them so well. Wolves were the more direct team, cutting out the midfield where the conditions were at their most treacherous, always looking to get the ball out to the wings or straight down the middle of the Spurs defence. Rarely did they get very far as Spurs centre half Charlie Walters was totally in command and having perhaps his best ever game for the club. Only twice did Wolves threaten. Little Sammy Brooks put across a perfect centre that Alex Hunter in the Spurs goal did well to cut out, as an unmarked centre forward lurked behind him, and then Brooks fired in a shot from an acute angle that Hunter again did well to block. At the other end Spurs were continually buzzing around the Wolves goal, but when they did create a clear-cut chance, the conditions would get the better of them or a Wolves defender would fling himself in the way.

Jimmy Seed never stopped working, probing inside and out, while Arthur Grimsdell controlled the midfield like the colossus he was and Tommy Clay gave a near-perfect display at full back. The only Spurs player who failed to live up to expectations was Jimmy Dimmock, and yet he got the only goal of the game in the 54th minute. Taking a pass from Bert Bliss he made for the Wolves goal but was dispossessed by Maurice Woodward. As Woodward hesitated, Dimmock recovered possession, took a couple of paces forward and then hit a low drive that skimmed across the surface and beat George at his far post. It was the most difficult of the few chances Dimmock had, but it was the one that wrote his name in Spurs' history.

Tottenham Hotspur: Hunter; Clay, McDonald; Smith, Walters, Grimsdell; Banks, Seed, Cantrell, Bliss, Dimmock.

Wolverhampton Wanderers: George; Woodward, Marshall; Gregory, Hodnett, Riley; Lea, Burrill, Edmonds, Potts, Brooks.

Referee: J. Davies.

the pitch began to dry out, the surface remained sodden and right to the end players were slipping and sliding everywhere. Today the match would be postponed, but in 1921 it just had to go ahead. Jimmy Dimmock's goal gave Spurs the trophy for the second time after a gap of 20 years and

PLAYER'S CIGARETTES

CLAY

McDONALD

HUNTER

SMITH

GRIMSDELL

WALTERS

DANES

DIMMOCK

SELD

CANTRELL

BLISS

ASSOCIATION CUP WINNERS
TOTTENHAM HOTSPUR. 1921

Arthur Grimsdell collected the cup from King George V. It was the first time the cup had been in southern hands since Spurs' last success. The conditions had not allow Spurs to exhibit their football at its best, but winning the cup meant Spurs would compete against the league champions for the FA Charity Shield and could show just how far they had come in the last 12 months. The title was won by Burnley who led Manchester City by a convincing five points. It could have been a lot more, but after securing the title they had eased up and collected only four points from their last six games. They had beaten Spurs 1-2 at White Hart Lane and 0-2 at Burnley at the end of October, but when they left White Hart Lane after the final match of the season, Spurs had secured their second trophy of the season 2-0, courtesy of goals from Jimmy Cantrell and Bert Bliss.

McWilliam's Team

The team that brought Spurs the Second Division title changed little to become the one that secured the FA Cup. Bill Jacques, at 5ft 10ins (1.68m) not exactly tall for a keeper but as strong as they come, had joined Spurs from Coventry City in May 1914. Ever-present in 1919-20, he played in the cup-ties against Bristol Rovers, Bradford City and Southend United, but was then injured and missed out on the rest of the games. He recovered his place early in 1921-22, but was later struck down by illness that led to his untimely death when only 37. His place for the rest of the Cup run was taken by Alex Hunter, signed from the Scottish amateurs, Queen's Park. A brave keeper, he was even shorter than Jacques at only 5ft 8ins (1.63m). Competent rather than spectacular, he was thrown in at the deep end with Bill Jacques' injury and, although he acquitted himself well, he was not really up to the top standard and left Spurs within a year of the final. At right back was Tommy Clay. Described as a 'treasure of a back', only Alf Ramsey would challenge him as the best player in that position Spurs have ever had. One of the few members of the team who cost a large fee (he was signed from Leicester Fosse in January 1914), he had it all. Great in the tackle, consistent, reliable and the master of positional play, he also had great passing ability, frequently turning defence into attack with raking passes straight to his target. He spent 15 years at White Hart Lane before helping nurture the young talent at Spurs' Northfleet nursery.

Clay's full back partner in the early days of the Second Division promotion campaign was John Pearson, who joined Spurs from Arbroath in February 1913. He played exactly half the league games before losing his place to Bob Brown who had arrived in the summer of 1919 from Thorneycrofts. Like Pearson, Brown was a dependable, solid player who did his job quietly but efficiently. Injury soon lost him his place early in 1920-21 and he was rarely able to get back in the team. When transfer-listed in April 1925 he could have joined several clubs, but decided to retire and become a butcher. Left back in the cup-winning team was Bob McDonald. Like Hunter he was picked up for nothing, being signed from another Scottish amateur club, Inverness Caledonians, in August 1919. Originally a right back, he was signed to understudy Clay but performed so well when Clay was injured he was switched to the left. He had a good turn of speed and was excellent at timing his tackles to make sure he got the ball.

The Half Back Line

Spurs' greatest strength was in the half back line. Right half Bert Smith was the workhorse, forever foraging, hunting down the ball, covering his full back one minute, supporting his winger the next. He had joined Huddersfield Town in 1913 as an inside forward but had few opportunities before the War began. Back in London on War service, he played several games for Spurs. Peter McWilliam realised he would be much better at half back than inside forward and secured his transfer. He gave Spurs great service for 11 years, playing for England and the Football League before starting a lengthy coaching career with the youngsters at Northfleet.

Left half was Arthur Grimsdell, one of the giants of Spurs' history. Signed from Watford in March 1912 as an 18-year-old, he was the epitome of the pre-war half back with skill, aggression, a never-say-die attitude and a flair for attacking. He defended when the need arose, but was at his best going forward, ploughing through the midfield, directing play and every now and then unleashing a fierce long-range shot. In 1919-20 Charlie Rance was the regular centre half. Another player Spurs signed from the amateur ranks, he had twice helped Clapton win the FA Amateur Cup before Spurs persuaded him to turn professional in July 1910. In many respects he retained his amateur attitude to the game with a cool commanding presence and a desire to always play football rather than just hammer the ball as far away as possible. He always seemed to be playing the game for the love of it, not for the money. He eventually lost his place midway through 1920-21 to yet another

Spurs' Arthur Grimsdell is tackled by Newcastle United's Billy Hampson in November 1922.

player McWilliam picked up without paying a fee. Charlie Walters was attracting a lot of attention at Oxford City when McWilliam persuaded him to join Spurs' amateur staff in December 1919 and he quickly joined the paid ranks. He developed rapidly, initially showing great defensive qualities, but then expanding his game to become the complete pivot. There was little to choose between Rance and Walters, except pace. Walters was one of the quickest half-backs around.

With a solid defence and a hard-working but skilful half back line, all any team needed was forwards with pace, power and trickery, and that was exactly what Spurs had. First choice right winger was the diminutive Fanny Walden, Spurs' most expensive signing at a record £1,700 from

Northampton Town. At 5ft 2ins (1.49m), he was one of the smallest players around, but in terms of trickery he was one of the biggest in the game. There was nothing he could not do with the ball, frequently showing in games the type of ball skills usually reserved for the training ground. Fast and elusive, even the biggest of full backs were given a torrid time by the little magician. Sadly for Walden and followers of the game, he was injured before the second round tie with Bradford City in 1921 and did not play again that season. His place went to Jimmy Banks, signed from Willington Athletic in December 1913. Banks was a play-anywhere forward, never quite good enough to make a position his own but always capable of doing a good job. He had displaced Billy Minter at inside right midway through 1919-20, but with the signing of Jimmy Seed found himself out of favour. With no natural replacement for Walden, Banks was tried out and although he was not in the same class, he proved a more than adequate deputy, adding a directness and unexpected goal-scoring knack that was never Walden's strongpoint.

Master Strategist

Billy Minter was a great servant to Spurs, joining the club from Reading in March 1908 and shouldering the main goal-scoring responsibility as Spurs established themselves in the Football League. He was getting on though and when Seed was signed, he became the club trainer. Jimmy Seed was one of the stars of the Cup run and was to go on to be one of the best inside forwards in the game for years. Discarded by Sunderland after being gassed in the trenches, he rebuilt his career with Mid-Rhondda before McWilliam moved in to sign him. A master strategist with excellent ball control, he was the fulcrum of the Spurs' attack, forever wanting the ball, probing for openings, making chances and snapping them up himself. His departure for Sheffield Wednesday in August 1927 was to prove one of the turning points in Spurs' early history.

Jimmy Cantrell was the regular centre forward, even though he was almost 39 by the time of the 1921 Cup final. Cantrell was signed from Notts County for a hefty fee in October 1912, as Spurs desperately sought some firepower to halt a miserable start to the season. It was never expected that, ten years later, he would still be leading the line, but he was not one of those big centre-forwards who relied on muscle. He was an intelligent ball-playing centre forward and relied on subtlety – much in the style of Vivian J Woodward. Not that he was afraid to go in where it hurt, far from it, he was frequently on the receiving end of some fearful challenges, but he always bounced back and let his skill do the damage.

50 Greatest Players

JIMMY CANTRELL   **Centre forward**

Joined Tottenham Hotspur: October 1912 **From:** Notts County

Debut: v Manchester United, 19 October 1912

Appearances: 176   **Goals:** 85

Left Tottenham Hotspur: October 1923   **For:** Sutton Town

Honours Won with Tottenham Hotspur: Division 2 Championship 1920; FA Cup winner 1921

After playing local junior football, Jimmy Cantrell spent four years with Aston Villa, but it was with Notts County that he flourished as a skilful, goalscoring centre forward. Unlike many of his contemporaries, he was not a bustling player, but one who relied on skill and guile. He joined Spurs in October 1912, only five days after scoring twice for Notts County at White Hart Lane in a game that was abandoned due to fog. A regular scorer, he was much like his predecessor Vivian Woodward, creating as many goals for his colleagues as he scored himself. Well into his thirties, and despite losing four years to the Great War, he led the line superbly in the team that ran away with the Second Division title in 1920 and collected an FA Cup winner's medal a year later. He played his last senior game in April 1923, just weeks before his 41st birthday (the oldest player to appear for Spurs in a Football League game). He left Spurs to return to Nottinghamshire with Sutton Town and later became a professional golfer.

On Cantrell's left was Bert Bliss, another little man at 5ft 6ins (1.58m), but famed for his blistering shooting. He was picked up from Willenhall Swifts in April 1912 at a cost of £50 and that was an *ex gratia* payment. Totally fearless, he adopted a shoot-on-sight policy and many a time the ball would end up miles from goal, but when he got a shot on target there were few keepers who could keep the ball out. He dovetailed perfectly with Grimsdell and Jimmy Dimmock, the three of them proving a never-ending threat to opposing defences. At outside right Dimmock was the only local born player. Signed as an amateur during the War and a professional in May 1919 as other clubs tried to secure his services, he was still only 20 when he played in the cup final. Scoring the only goal has ensured his place in the history books, but he was much more than just the man who won one cup final. He was a truly mesmeric figure, whether racing down the wing with his full back in hot pursuit, embarking on a long mazy dribble or cutting in for a wicked shot at goal. For ten years, he was the darling of the Spurs' crowd, the local boy turned local hero. It was only when age and weight slowed him down that he was allowed to leave White Hart Lane.

New Heights Attained

Spurs started 1921-22 in poor form and were soon languishing near the foot of the table, but from Christmas onwards they embarked on a fine run that eventually saw them reach their highest ever Football League position. They finished six points behind Liverpool and were never in with a chance of lifting the title, but runners-up was still the best any London club had managed since the Football League's formation. The turnaround in form also coincided with the start of their defence of the FA Cup. Brentford, Watford and Manchester City were overcome in the first three rounds and only a last-minute equaliser earned Cardiff City a White Hart Lane replay in the fourth round, when almost 54,000 witnessed Spurs win 2-1 to set up a semi-final with Preston North End.

50 Greatest Players

FANNY WALDEN Outside right

Joined Tottenham Hotspur: April 1912 **From:** Northampton Town

Debut: v Woolwich Arsenal, 19 April 1913

Appearances: 236 **Goals:** 25

Left Tottenham Hotspur: May 1926 **For:** Northampton Town

Honours Won with Tottenham Hotspur: Division 2 Championship 1920

At 5ft 2ins (1,49m) Fanny Walden was one of the smallest players ever to play for Spurs and it is perhaps surprising he should have started his career with Wellingborough Town and Northampton Town as a centre forward. Up against big, brawny defenders he developed the intricate dribbling skills that were later to serve him so well. His manager at Northampton was Herbert Chapman, who switched Walden to the right wing realising the damage his jinking runs could cause. When Chapman moved to Leeds City he was determined Walden would follow, but Spurs moved in with a then massive offer of £1,700 and secured his transfer. His trickery and outstanding ability to make even the biggest of defenders look foolish quickly made him a firm favourite with the Spurs crowd. He collected his first England cap in April 1914 and also played for the Football League. After the War his exciting wing play illuminated Spurs' run to the Second Division title but a cartilage injury deprived him of a FA Cup winner's medal in 1921. He continued to dazzle for Spurs until returning to Northampton in May 1926. A first class cricketer for Northants, he was later an umpire, reaching test match level.

As in 1921 the match was at Hillsborough, but this time it was the Lancashire club who won through to the final, in one of those games that find their own little niche in history. Jimmy Seed gave Spurs a first half lead, nothing more than they deserved, but in the second half Preston took control, having apparently been given champagne during the interval. After getting an equaliser the battle swayed from one end to the other. Spurs thought they had regained the advantage when a typical Bert Bliss thunderbolt almost broke the back of the net, but the referee had blown to stop play before the ball went in because he thought a Preston player was injured on the half-way line. Before Spurs could recover from the setback Preston grabbed the winner.

The semi-final proved the swansong of McWilliam's great team. As it broke up, Spurs slowly but surely began to slip backwards, becoming a middle of the table team, neither challenging for the title nor fighting against relegation. Only once did things look to be really improving, but Arthur Grimsdell broke his leg in October 1925 just as Spurs hit the top of the table. Without their great inspiration they tumbled towards the bottom, and although they finished 15th, they were only four points above the relegation zone. Even the FA Cup failed to provide any consolation, as they exited in a 0-2 defeat at Second Division Crystal Palace in 1924, one of the worst cup results the club had ever suffered.

The reason for the deterioration was quite simple; the players just were not good enough. Peter McWilliam worked valiantly to improve things, but his hands were tied by the directors, partly

Walter Alsford (right) is congratulated by Willie Hall (left) after winning his first England cap. The trainer George Hardy (with hat on) and forward Foster Headley (second right) look on.

61

50 Greatest Players

ARTHUR GRIMSDELL **Half back**

Joined Tottenham Hotspur: March 1912 **From:** Watford

Debut: v Bolton Wanderers, 20 April 1912

Appearances: 362 **Goals:** 27

Left Tottenham Hotspur: August 1929 **For:** Clapton Orient

Honours won with Tottenham Hotspur: Division Two Championship 1920; FA Cup winner 1921

Arthur Grimsdell was an England schoolboy star plucked from his hometown club for a hefty fee whilst still little more than a youth. He went on to became a star at senior level. Originally a centre half, the arrival of Peter McWilliam saw him switched to left half, where his natural attacking instincts could be put to greater benefit. Quick to join up for service in the First World War, the Army saw him develop into a strong, well-built and fiercely determined man. With never-ending energy, ease on the ball and an excellent long-range shot, he formed the cornerstone of the Spurs side throughout the 1920s and became an England regular.

Captain of the FA Cup winning team of 1921, a Tottenham team without Grimsdell was unthinkable and Spurs were far weaker when he was absent. This was well illustrated when he was injured in October 1925. Spurs were then top of the First Division, but without his inspirational qualities they tumbled down the table. Grimsdell collected eight England caps and played for the Football League before being released in August 1929 to take up the player-manager-secretary's role at Clapton Orient.

as a result of his own success. Spurs had never been a club to spend big money in the transfer market; they did not think it necessary. The players who served Spurs so well in the early 1920s had been secured by McWilliam in the immediate post-war period for little or no outlay. In the post-war chaos, he had been shrewd and fortunate enough to pick up some real bargains, but football had now recovered. There were some good players coming through the ranks, but not enough of them at the same time. McWilliam needed to bring top class players in, but the board would not sanction what they considered 'ludicrous fees'. He did get the purse strings loosened a few times, signing Jack Elkes for £1000 and England international Frank Osborne for £1,500, but one or two players were not enough.

McWilliam's frustration grew and came to a head in December 1926. In the middle of November, Spurs had hit top spot again, just the time to go out and reinforce the team, but the directors would not make the money available. Sensing McWilliam's dejection, Middlesbrough offered him £1,500

50 Greatest Players

TOMMY CLAY   Full back

Joined Tottenham Hotspur: January 1913 **From:** Leicester Fosse

Debut: v Oldham Athletic, 17 January 1914

Appearances: 353   **Goals:** 24

Left Tottenham Hotspur: June 1929   **For:** Northfleet

Honours won with Tottenham Hotspur: Division Two Championship 1920; FA Cup winner 1921

Tommy Clay was signed from Leicester Fosse after impressing in the two FA Cup third round ties of January 1913 and proved to be one of Peter McWilliam's most astute signings. A master full back, he combined great tackling ability and strength with tactical mastery and was particularly adept at exploiting the old offside rule. He was not, though, purely a defender, for he realised he had a responsibility to help set up attacks from deep and developed a passing game envied by many a half back or inside forward. Not for Clay the long boot out of defence. Although he was not averse to that when the situation demanded, he preferred a measured pass to a colleague and then to find space to provide support.

Captain of the Second Division winning side in 1920, he handed over the job to Arthur Grimsdell and so missed out on collecting the FA Cup in 1921. Clay won four England caps with Spurs and also represented the Football League. He gave Spurs 15 years' immaculate service, before taking on the player-coach job at their nursery club, Northfleet. In March 1921, Clay played a full league game in goal. With the regular goalies injured, Clay was given the keeper's jumper and kept a clean sheet as Spurs won at Sunderland.

a year to take over as their manager, a considerable increase on the £850 Spurs were paying him. McWilliam did not want to leave, but it was difficult to refuse such a big offer. He was prepared to stay if Spurs would increase his salary to £1,000 a year, but the directors refused. McWilliam quit. For the sake of £150 Spurs had lost one of the best managers around.

Goodbye Jimmy Seed, Hello Division Two

The directors' reluctance to spend money is illustrated by the appointment of McWilliam's successor. They knew that if they wanted to get a top man in they would have to pay more than the £1,000 McWilliam had asked for, but Billy Minter, club trainer and a loyal Spurs' man, would do the job for less. He took over from McWilliam in March 1927, but almost immediately made a mistake that was to have enormous ramifications for the club.

50 Greatest Players

JIMMY SEED   Inside forward

Joined Tottenham Hotspur: February 1920 **From:** Mid-Rhondda

Debut: v Wolverhampton Wanderers, 5 April 1920

Appearances: 256   **Goals:** 77

Left Tottenham Hotspur: August 1927   **For:** Sheffield
Wednesday

Honours won with Tottenham Hotspur: FA Cup winner 1921

If ever a player proved his football bosses wrong, Jimmy Seed was that player. Discarded by Sunderland after the First World War, because they thought he could never recover from the effects of a gas attack suffered in the trenches, Seed was allowed to move to the comparative football backwater of Mid-Rhondda. Peter McWilliam went to Rhondda to check out Ton Pentre's 'Darkie' Lowdell, but was so taken by Seed's performance, he immediately secured his transfer. Seed took to top class football with ease, masterminding Spurs' escape from the Second Division in 1920 and proving instrumental in their 1921 FA Cup success.

A delicate, probing inside forward, he linked well with his wing man, created many chances for his centre forward and also scored his fair share of goals. Another of Spurs' England internationals of the 1920s, Seed was surprisingly sidelined in 1927 when manager Billy Minter decide to build a team around the talents of Taffy O'Callaghan. Seed was allowed to move to a struggling Sheffield Wednesday, inspired them to a near miraculous escape from relegation at Spurs' expense and led them to successive Football League titles. He later moved into management having, in particular, great success at Charlton Athletic.

Jimmy Seed was injured in the third round FA Cup defeat at West Ham and was expected to be out for the rest of the season. John Blair was not an adequate replacement, so Minter promoted Taffy O'Callaghan, a 20-year-old with wonderful skills. He was clearly destined for the top, but he was young, would need time and could only benefit from playing with, not instead of, Seed. As it was Seed was fit to return for the last couple of matches, but O'Callaghan was preferred and Seed was then told his salary would be reduced from £8 a week to £7. He successfully applied for the manager's post at Aldershot, but Spurs refused to let him go, as there would be no transfer fee. However, when, weeks later, Sheffield Wednesday offered 'Darkie' Lowdell in exchange for Seed, Minter accepted.

Throughout the season Spurs occupied their now expected mid-table position. They got through to the sixth round of the FA Cup, but after a 1-6 hammering by Huddersfield Town, they just drifted along towards the end of the season. At Easter, Spurs had 35 points from an equal number of games and were 11 points ahead of Sheffield Wednesday who, with eight games left, seemed sure to go down. The Owls made Seed their captain and over Easter the former Lilywhite inspired Wednesday to two victories over Spurs, 3-1 at White Hart Lane and 4-2 at Hillsborough. After beating Arsenal, Spurs picked up only one point from their last four games and left for a tour to Holland looking certain of another mid-table finish.

50 Greatest Players

JIMMY DIMMOCK   Outside left

Joined Tottenham Hotspur: 1916 (amateur), May 1919 (professional)

From: Edmonton Ramblers

Debut: v Lincoln City, 4 October 1919

Appearances: 440   **Goals:** 112

Left Tottenham Hotspur: August 1931   **For:** Thames

Honours won with Tottenham Hotspur: Division 2 Championship 1920; FA Cup winner 1921

Jimmy Dimmock will always have a special place in Spurs' history as the scorer of the only goal in the 1921 FA Cup final, but he was far more than simply the 20-year old who won one game. He was one of the finest exponents of the winger's role, a player whose mere presence would add a few thousand to the crowd. A local lad, he first joined Spurs during the Great War from a junior club and was allowed to play 'on loan' for Clapton Orient, quickly showing the skills that were to enthral many a youngster. He rose to stardom as a youth of individual brilliance, but developed as a man into a crucial team player, although always with that 'little something' that made him stand out. Dimmock possessed every attribute a winger needed: pace, trickery, speed, balance, crossing ability, a fierce shot and, for good measure, a flair for showmanship.

It could only have been Spurs' poor performances in the 1920s that restricted him to only three England caps. Towards the end of his time at Spurs Dimmock put on weight depriving him of one of his most essential gifts, speed, and in 1931 he was allowed to move on to Thames. He played there for a year, spent 18 months at Clapton Orient and finished his career with a short spell at Ashford Town.

While they were away, every result conspired against them, and they returned to find seven clubs on 39 points. They had 38 with only Middlesbrough below them. Seventeen points from their last ten games had taken Sheffield Wednesday to safety, while Spurs were relegated. Seed went on to lead Wednesday to successive Football League championships while Spurs played Second Division football.

Prising Open the Purse Strings

Despite the shock of relegation, attitudes at White Hart Lane changed little. The criteria for signing new players was price and experience with the result that the few players secured – Tom Roberts, Randolph Galloway, Joe Scott and Harry Wilding – were cheap, but well past their best and soon on their way out. With Tommy Clay and Arthur Grimsdell fast approaching the end of their great careers, it was obvious an infusion of fresh talent was needed.

50 Greatest Players

TAFFY O'CALLAGHAN   Inside forward

Joined Tottenham Hotspur: 1924 (amateur),

September 1926 (professional)

From: Ebbw Vale Corinthians

Debut: v Everton, 15 February 1927

Appearances: 263   **Goals:** 98

Left Tottenham Hotspur: March 1935   **For:** Leicester City

Spotted by Spurs playing in his hometown, Eugene 'Taffy' O'Callaghan was to follow a well-trodden path to football fame. Signed as an amateur, he worked on the groundstaff, while Spurs arranged for him to play for Barnet, before moving on to the nursery club at Northfleet. A real will-o-the-wisp, he made the move up to White Hart Lane and was soon pushing for a first team place. Although slight of build, he had amazing stamina and allied to the deftest of touches soon displaced Jimmy Seed and became the darling of the crowds. His pin-point passing provided plenty of openings for George Hunt and Willie Hall, but O'Callaghan wasn't just a creator of chances, he knew how to finish them off himself. He had ten years at Spurs, winning 11 Welsh caps before moving to Leicester City, but returned to assist Spurs as a guest player during the Second World War. After the War, he signed for Fulham and was still working on their coaching staff when he died.

It took an FA Cup third round defeat at Reading, followed by a poor performance at Wolverhampton Wanderers that left Spurs just five places off the bottom, before action was at last taken. The defence was strengthened with the signing of Edwin Herod from Charlton, but it was the £5,500 paid out to secure former England centre forward, Ted Harper, from Sheffield Wednesday that really made the difference, 11 goals – at a goal a game – dragged Spurs to safety. The signing of one man, though, does not make a team and with Harper

Arthur Rowe in action in April 1934.

injured, Spurs again began a season badly and by November 1929 were at the wrong end of the table with 12 points from 15 games. Injuries did nothing to help, but discontent among Spurs supporters was rife and nothing Billy Minter tried would turn things round. The pressures were making Minter ill. He had a genuine love for the club, but felt he could do nothing more and so resigned.

It took until January for Percy Smith, manager of Bury, to be appointed Minter's successor. He started with two FA Cup-ties against Manchester City, a draw at White Hart Lane and a defeat in the replay, but did manage to quickly convince the board that money had to be spent. Within a month, he had signed two internationals, the Welsh winger Willie Davies and Northern Ireland centre forward Dick Rowley. Twelfth in Division Two was Spurs' lowest ever placing, but it was far better than had, at one time, seemed likely.

The cheque book remained open in the summer with Bert Hodgkinson, Bert Lyons and Alf Messer – all defenders – being signed. Smith also looked to the future, snapping up George Hunt, an exciting young centre forward from Chesterfield. Spurs opened the 1930-31 season in devastating style beating Reading 7-1 at White Hart Lane and going one better with an 8-1 defeat of Burnley, also at home, in the next game. It did not continue, of course, but was a sign that Smith was turning things round.

For almost the whole season, Spurs fought it out with Everton and West Bromwich Albion for the top two places. Spurs may well have secured second place to Everton were it not for an injury to Ted Harper. With eight games to play, Spurs were nine points behind Everton, but three ahead of Albion, who had a game in hand when they visited White Hart Lane. Harper, who had scored 34 goals in 28 league games, was out injured and the subsequent 2-2 draw was acceptable to both clubs. But Harper also missed the next five games and Spurs picked up only three points. Hunt deputised and scored three goals in the five games, but they were not enough. Harper returned for the penultimate game of the season, he and Hunt netting a pair each as Burnley were beaten, while Albion, who had defeated Spurs in the fourth round, were defeating Birmingham to lift the FA Cup. Five days later Albion beat Stoke City to secure second place.

Getting so close to promotion but failing at the last was a major disappointment. It might have been better to retain the squad that had done so well, but Smith continued to rebuild, players coming and going, newcomers being tried, but then rejected. The result was a season of inconsistency in 1931-32 as Spurs fell back to eighth. The policy of importing so many players now began to be questioned, particularly as Spurs began to reap the benefits of developing young talent. Some years earlier, Spurs had invested in making Northfleet a nursery club. Youngsters taken on the staff who were unlikely to get many games in the reserves were 'farmed out' to the Kent club, receiving coaching from former Spurs stalwarts, playing together regularly, and being educated into the Spurs style. It was an investment that over the years was to pay dividends, but already players like Wally Alsford, Joe Nicholls, Les Howe, Arthur Rowe and Tom Evans were beginning to come through.

Percy Smith's 'Greyhounds'

1932-33 started as if all the hard work Smith had put in would count for nought. Three points out of the first eight, six out of the first 16, left Spurs wallowing near the foot of the table. Smith knew things had to change

'Greyhound' George Hunt in full flow.

quickly. He dropped Jimmy Brain, Willie Davies and David Levene, calling up George Greenfield, Les Howe and Tommy Meads. The improvement was immediate. Preston were beaten 6-2 away, Burnley and Southampton 4-1 and 5-0 respectively at home, Millwall 4-1 away and Port Vale 4-0 at home. Spurs quickly moved up the table to challenge early leaders, Stoke City. They rarely managed to head the Potteries club, but had to see off threats from Bradford City, Bury, Nottingham Forest and finally Fulham before securing the runners-up spot and a return to the top flight. They were remarkably consistent, losing only two games in a run of 33, but too many games were drawn, particularly during a nerve-jangling end to the season. The biggest threat had come in December when George Greenfield broke his leg at Fulham. So much of Spurs' play went through the inside forward signed from Lea Bridge Gasworks that Smith immediately went out and signed Willie Hall from Notts County.

Smith's team, just like all Spurs teams of the past, played with skill and flair, but a new dimension had been added. They still kept the ball on the ground; they still looked to make progress with swift passing movements and the quick interchanging of players and positions. What was new was an abundance of pace, of little effect on its own, but devastating when

Spurs attack at the Paxton Road end in a 1-1 draw with Leicester City in April 1936.

combined with ball control and incisive passing. The forward line, in particular, contained some of the fastest players around: Jimmy McCormick, Taffy O'Callaghan, George Hunt, Willie Hall and Willie Evans. It earned them the nickname of the 'Greyhounds'. O'Callaghan and Hall at inside forward provided the ammunition for Hunt, firmly established as first choice centre forward, and he rewarded their great work with 33 goals, while on the right wing 20-year old Willie Evans, with searing pace and bullet like shooting, contributed 28.

The only attribute they lacked was height, as none of the forwards stood more than 5ft 8ins (1.63m), and many pundits thought this would lead to them being exposed in the First Division. They were soon proved wrong. Height made no difference to a game played at speed and by the end of November 1933, Spurs were top of the table ahead of Arsenal and Huddersfield Town. The one thing Spurs had no control over was the weather and as the pitches grew heavy so the 'Greyhounds' were slowed down. Christmas proved the crucial time with two games against Huddersfield. Spurs lost them both, 3-1 at home on Christmas Day and 2-0 away 24 hours later. They were never able to get back in the race and had to settle for third place, ten points adrift of Arsenal and seven behind Huddersfield.

The 1934-35 season proved a disaster for Spurs. They started with two draws in the first four games, were never able to get into the top half of the table and suffered one injury after another. Only Fred Channell and Bill Whatley played anything like a full season, all the other players suffering injury at one time or another. Even going out and signing new players did little good, Sam Bell and Andy Duncan both falling victim to the injury jinx. Spurs were rarely able to put out their strongest team, fielding the same 11 in successive games proved almost impossible and just finishing a game with 11 was regarded as a triumph. At the end of December, they were 16th, grateful there were teams doing just as badly. Then the injuries really began to take their toll; a run of 16 games without a win allowed everyone below to reel Spurs in. At the end of March they hit bottom and there they stayed. There was nothing Percy Smith could have done to save Spurs, but he had to accept the responsibility. In late April he resigned, complaining the directors had interfered in his team selections.

His replacement was West Ham's captain in the first Wembley FA Cup final, Jack Tresadern. He had been in charge of Crystal Palace for five years, years in which they had been around the top of Division Three (South) but without making the step up. He was to do little better at Spurs. He started well with victories in his first two games, and for the early part of the 1935-36 campaign Spurs were up with the leaders, but three successive defeats in Christmas week knocked them back. They did reach the sixth round of the FA Cup, seeing off Southend United, Huddersfield Town and Bradford Park Avenue before going out to Sheffield United, but if anything the cup games had a detrimental effect on league form, particularly at home. Spurs had always been strong on their own patch. Over the years it was results on their travels that had let them down, but losing six and drawing one of their last nine games at White Hart Lane was a handicap too great to overcome. The best feature of the season was the emergence of Johnny Morrison, another graduate of Northfleet. He was a raw, bustling centre forward similar in style to George Hunt, and eventually took Hunt's place scoring 28 goals in 38 matches.

League performances over the next two seasons were undistinguished, with Spurs hovering around the upper reaches of mid-table, never challenging to go up, never looking like relegation candidates. The FA Cup at least provided some distraction with the sixth round reached in each campaign. In 1937, Spurs put out Portsmouth and Plymouth Argyle before returning from their fifth round tie at Goodison Park with a 1-1 draw. The replay with Everton is one of those games that have gone down in White

50 Greatest Players

GEORGE HUNT   Centre forward

Joined Tottenham Hotspur: June 1930   **From:** Chesterfield

Debut: v Stoke City, 20 September 1930

Appearances: 198   **Goals:** 138

Left Tottenham Hotspur: October 1937   **For:** Arsenal

Rejected by Port Vale and Sheffield United, George Hunt was signed by Percy Smith from Chesterfield as Arsenal's Herbert Chapman dithered. At 5ft 8ins (1.63m) Hunt may have lacked height for a centre forward, but he more than made up for it with a terrier-like aggression that never gave opponents a moment's peace. The early 1930s side was made up of some wonderfully gifted players, but the great asset that earned it the nickname the 'Greyhounds' was its abundance of pace. Hunt was the perfect example, quick off the mark, tireless, muscular and with a determination to go in where it hurt in search of a goal. Replacing former England international Ted Harper, Hunt racked up 100 goals in only 132 games as Spurs escaped the Second Division and then went on to finish third in the top flight. Along the way, Hunt collected three England caps, but then injuries and the emergence of Johnny Morrison saw Hunt out of the team. He was surprisingly allowed to move to Arsenal and helped them secure the league title in 1938.

Hart Lane folklore. 1-3 down with six minutes left, Everton were awarded a penalty but the referee changed his decision when a linesman pointed out a foul throw by Joe Mercer. Reprieved, Johnny Morrison promptly scored his second of the game and in an amazing finale, Joe Meek grabbed an equaliser before Morrison completed his hat-trick with the winner. A great comeback, but Spurs were unable to repeat it in round six as Preston North End left Tottenham with a 3-1 victory after injuries to Arthur Rowe and Johnny Morrison tore the heart out of Spurs. 1938 saw Blackburn Rovers, New Brighton and Chesterfield defeated, before 75,038 spectators, a record crowd for White Hart Lane that will probably never be surpassed, saw Sunderland go into the semi-final thanks to a goal from Raich Carter.

The Return of Peter McWilliam

Tresadern's failure to lead Spurs out of the Second Division may have been forgiven if consolation had been found in the quality of football being played, but the fact was standards had fallen dramatically. Tresadern was not popular with the crowd and had done nothing to endear himself by the sale of favourites like Taffy O'Callaghan, who had gone to Leicester City, and George Hunt, remarkably allowed to move to Arsenal. Well before the end of 1937-38 it was an open secret that Tresadern's contract was not to be renewed and Peter McWilliam would be returning. Tresadern did not wait to be shown the door, making a successful last-minute application to manage Plymouth Argyle and telling Spurs he was leaving of his own choice. Barely had the ink dried on his resignation letter than McWilliam's return was announced.

McWilliam had experienced mixed results in seven years at Middlesbrough. After his arrival in February 1927, they had gone on to win the Second Division title, but had been relegated after just one season before bouncing back at the first attempt, again as champions. A period of consolidation followed, but by March 1934 further success seemed a distant dream and he was dismissed. He took to helping Arsenal as a scout in the North East, but when Spurs came calling, the chance to return to where he had enjoyed his greatest successes was too good to refuse.

Even before McWilliam had got his feet back under the table, hopes for improvement in 1938-39 were jolted by the departure of Jackie Gibbons. An aircraftsman in the RAF, Gibbons had been persuaded to sign for Spurs as an amateur in July 1937 and almost immediately formed a deadly partnership with Johnny Morrison, the pair of them contributing 43 of Spurs' 66 goals in the season. Unfortunately, he decided to accept the challenge of putting his talents to the test in the First Division with Brentford, a decision that left Spurs with a gaping hole to fill. McWilliam did not rush into the transfer market, though. In fact he made only one signing before the season began, testing promises that money would be available for acquisitions by paying out £9,500 to secure England full back Bert Sproston from Leeds United. It turned out to be a short-lived transfer. Sproston claimed to be unable to settle to life in London, but travelled up to Manchester for a game at Maine Road. He played, but rather than making his tenth league appearance for Spurs, it turned out to be his debut for City as before kick-off he was transferred to the home club.

Freddie Cox was promoted from the Northfleet nursery team in 1938 and scored on his debut.

50 Greatest Players

WILLIE EVANS   **Outside left**

Joined Tottenham Hotspur: May 1929 (amateur), May 1931 (professional)

From: Hayward Sports

Debut: v Swansea Town, 7 November 1931

Appearances: 195   **Goals:** 86

Left Tottenham Hotspur: May 1937   **For:** Fulham

His talent apparently overlooked by the Welsh clubs, Willie Evans was working down the pits when Spurs invited him to London as a 16-year old. Farmed out to the nursery clubs of Barnet and Haywards Sports, he developed well and was signed to the White Hart Lane professional staff as soon as possible. Within weeks, he was given his league debut and scored twice on his 19th birthday, thus announcing the arrival of a new star in North London. Evans had two great assets – speed and a remarkably powerful shot – and he put them both to great effect as Spurs secured promotion from Division Two in 1933. A regular for Wales, he looked to have a great career ahead of him, but was sadly injured at Villa on his 24th birthday. After one failed operation he was released, but Fulham took the gamble on another operation. Unfortunately it was not a success and at the age of 25 he was forced to retire from a game he, all too briefly, illuminated.

With war clouds gathering, McWilliam made no further forays into the transfer market, but rather, promoted players from Northfleet such as Ron Burgess, Bill Nicholson, Freddie Cox and Arthur Hitchins. It was rather appropriate McWilliam should have placed such faith in the players produced by the nursery club, for it was McWilliam who had first fostered the relationship with Northfleet back in the early 1920s. Throughout the last season of pre-war football, Spurs occupied a position in the middle of the Second Division. In terms of position it was a drop of three places on 1937-38, in terms of points secured it was an improvement, 47 against 44. Moreover, in terms of performance there was a marked improvement. As the season wore on, it could be seen he was getting the team to play in the style he firmly believed was the only way to ensure lasting success.

Having spent a year assessing the players at his disposal, McWilliam had identified some top quality youngsters at Northfleet and promoted Les Bennett, Ted Ditchburn and Les Medley to the staff. With the experience of former England inside forward Ronnie Dix, signed from Derby County, better times seemed about to dawn, but after only three league games World War Two was declared and league competition suspended for the duration.

Chapter Five: 1939-49
War and Reconstruction

The government was anxious football should continue despite the obvious difficulties and after a while the Football League organised emergency competitions. In 1939-40, Spurs participated in two sections of the Football League South, winning the second, and a League Cup competition. For 1940-41, the competition was restructured to provide far fewer games, so apart from the Football League War Cup, the FA was persuaded to sanction a London War Cup to provide extra games and revenue. Spurs lost to Brentford in the semi-final.

It was apparent from the very early days that football during the War was going to be something of a 'hit and miss' business. Player availability was uncertain to say the least. Juniors had to be called up, guest players were allowed and there were many instances of clubs appealing for members of the crowd to come forward and make up the numbers. London suffered particularly during the Blitz, with games delayed or called off due to air raids and stadiums suffering bomb damage. Some clubs even lost their stadiums entirely. Highbury was commandeered as a first aid post and air raid precaution centre with Arsenal moving to White Hart Lane. All clubs were losing money and there were several who decided it was better to totally shut down and hope to resume when hostilities ceased. One of the major problems was transport. It was all very well selecting a team but who would actually play was rarely known until kick-off, and this eventually caused a major rift between the London clubs and the Football League.

Full back Arthur Willis, a Spurs regular from the war years onwards. He would eventually win an England cap in 1951.

50 Greatest Players

WILLIE HALL   Inside forward

Joined Tottenham Hotspur: December 1932   **From:** Notts County

Debut: v Notts County, 20 December 1932

Appearances: 221   **Goals:** 29

Left Tottenham Hotspur: February 1944 (retired)

When Spurs lost George Greenfield, one of the outstanding young talents of his day, they moved quickly to snap up Willie Hall, another young starlet of whom much was expected. Discovered by County playing for the works team of Ransome & Miles, he had only been at Meadow Lane for two years, but had already led them to the championship of the Third Division (South). A non-stop midfield worker with an easy dribbling ability and passing perfection, Hall fitted into the Spurs' machine from the start, dovetailing particularly well with the flying Willie Evans and bustling George Hunt.

He made his England debut in December 1933, but then suffered with a series of injuries. When he was back playing regularly, he was soon picking up international honours again and, in November 1938, achieved the remarkable feat of scoring five times against Northern Ireland. A great servant to Spurs, he continued to play regularly during the Second World War, occupying any position required in times when it was difficult even to get 11 players together. A serious leg injury forced him to retire in February 1944 and eventually led to the amputation of both lower legs.

When the fixture list for 1941-42 was made available, many London clubs realised they just could not make the journeys demanded of them. When the Football League refused to make the changes that they had been told were essential, the London clubs formed their own London War League. The Football League took exception to this and decided that by forming their own competition the clubs had ceased to be members of the Football League.

Spurs finished fifth in the London War League in 1941-42. The FA had supported the London clubs and eventually brokered a peace deal that resulted in the Football League running a competition in almost exactly the format London had demanded for the rest of the War. Spurs finished second in the Football League South in 1942-43 and won it for the next two seasons.

The Football League originally intended to return to its pre-war format for 1945-46, but was soon forced to realise that it would take time to return to normality after such a lengthy and damaging conflict. The Football

League South continued, although now made up of clubs from the top two divisions rather than along strictly geographical lines.

Although nowhere near as many players lost their lives as in the Great War, much had changed in seven years. Players were that much older, many had seen no training, others were simply too old and a whole generation of youngsters had been unable to develop their skills. Spurs were lucky in some ways. Many of the players on their books in 1939 were young and full of promise, had seen plenty of football during their service careers and had gained vital experience. The club now had seasoned footballers rather than raw recruits. It was off the pitch that Spurs suffered losses. Chairman Charles Roberts had died in 1943 after guiding the club for over 40 years and Peter McWilliam decided he was too old to continue in management and retired.

Four Minutes from Wembley

In January 1946 Joe Hulme, a star of Arsenal's great side of the 1930s, was appointed Spurs manager and like managers throughout the country set about the job of rebuilding. Although Spurs had made a profit in the last few years of the War, money was still in short supply, but enough was found to enable Hulme to immediately replace the likes of Percy Hooper, Johnny Morrison, Fred Sargent and Willie Hall who, for one reason or another, were no longer available, with Charlie Rundle, Archie Hughes, George Foreman and Charlie Whitchurch.

In the main, though, Hulme concentrated on improving the players who had come through from Northfleet and the Tottenham Juniors. Spurs finished sixth, eighth and fifth under Hulme's guidance and, in 1948, got closer to their first visit to Wembley than they had ever managed before. After beating Bolton

Sonny Walters. The flying winger began to establish himself in the side in January 1949.

Wanderers, West Bromwich Albion, Leicester City and Southampton, they were drawn against Blackpool in the FA Cup semi-final at Villa Park.

For 65 minutes, Spurs were every bit the equal of their First Division rivals and then they stunned the favourites when Len Duquemin got the vital touch in a goalmouth scramble to put Spurs ahead. It was a lead they were to hold until four minutes from time when Stan Mortensen set out on a 30-yard run past four defenders. He ended up on the touchline, but somehow managed to get in a shot from an almost impossible angle that completely caught Ted Ditchburn out. The goal totally deflated Spurs and in extra-time time Blackpool took control with Mortensen scoring twice more. It was a result that did more than knock Spurs out of the cup. The run to the semi-final had seen league games postponed, leaving Spurs just off the top of the table, but with games in hand. Had they won those games they would have been well in the promotion frame but getting so near to the final knocked them sideways. Of their last 12 games they won only two and drew five.

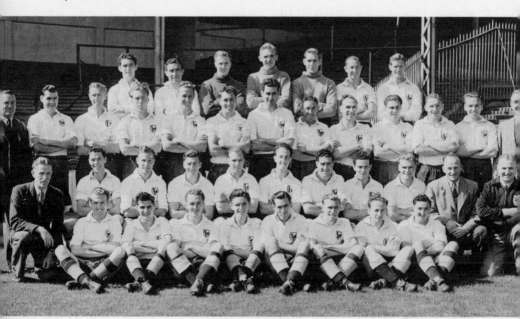

Tottenham Hotspur 1949-50 squad. From left. Back row: Rees, Ramsey, Hayhurst, Markham, Ditchburn, Burgess, Bennett. Third row: assistant manager J. Anderson, Duquemin, Buckingham, Robshaw, Brittan, Tickridge, Clarke, Cox, Medley, Rawlings, Nicholson, Gibbons, manager A. Rowe. Second row: trainer C. Poynton, Rundle, Ludford, Willis, Bailey, Gilberg, Withers, Henty, Walters, assistant trainer J. Coxford, assistant trainer J. Wallis. Front row: Cook, Elmes, Scarth, Harmer, Westwood, Adams, Kelly, Flint.

Chapter Six: 1949-58
From Rowe to Nicholson

Escaping the Second Division had become crucial to Spurs, and Hulme's failure to achieve that cost him his job in April 1949. In three years he had done a more than acceptable job, getting Spurs back on their feet, developing players and laying the foundations for future success, but he was not to reap the rewards of his work. Hulme had got together a fine set of players, players who individually were as good as he could hope for. All that was needed was a spark of genius to take them to heights Spurs players had never previously known.

The man to provide that spark was Arthur Rowe, a Spurs man to the core. Born in Tottenham, Rowe was first associated with Spurs as a schoolboy and went on to captain the club during the 1930s. A cultured centre half in an

New Tottenham manager Arthur Rowe starts work in August 1949.

age when the stopper style had become almost universally accepted, injury led to his retirement in April 1939. A deep thinker about the game in his playing days, he secured a coaching position in Hungary, but was unable to take it up when the War broke out. In the services he found himself managing the Army team and, when the war was over, was appointed manager of Chelmsford City. In four years he turned Chelmsford into one of the most entertaining non-league sides around, playing a brand of football that attracted many admirers. He was the obvious choice to take over from Hulme.

Les Bennett, Spurs' ever-present and top scorer in 1948-49.

As soon as he was installed, Rowe secured the transfer from Southampton of Alf Ramsey (a player Hulme had tried to sign but the deal had fallen through on transfer deadline day), and Billy Rees from Cardiff City. They were the only two additions to Hulme's squad, but the football Spurs were to play was totally different. Rowe was a firm believer in football being a simple game, all about having possession of the ball and keeping it. The best way to do that was by playing short, accurate passes, not trying to dribble past an opponent or hitting the ball over long distances into space. Of course, it was no good playing short passes to a man who was tightly marked; space had to be found and that meant players permanently on the move. Short passes did not need power; it was just a case of pushing the ball to a team-mate. Finding space simply meant running into a position where the ball could be safely received. 'Push and run' – it was as simple as that. All that was needed was players able to put the theory into practice. Fortunately, Rowe had players who were not only technically adept, they were also intelligent and immediately took to his way of playing.

The 1949-50 season opened with 4-1 defeats of Brentford and Plymouth Argyle. If Spurs were in danger of getting carried away by those results, Blackburn Rovers brought them back to reality with a 3-2 win at White Hart Lane, but Spurs then set off on a run that was to all but secure promotion. From the end of August to the end of December they played 22 games, dropping only four points, all of them in draws. At the turn of the year, they were ten points

An acrobatic Ted Ditchburn helps secure a 2-1 victory over Wolves in January 1951. The match attendance of 66,796 was White Hart Lane's biggest of the season.

ahead of nearest challengers, Sheffield Wednesday, and led the Second Division from start to finish. Promotion was secured with a 2-0 win at Queens Park Rangers on All Fools Day, the title six days later with a goalless draw against Hull City at White Hart Lane. There were six games left but with the hard work done Spurs eased up and lost four of their last five games. However, that was irrelevant, they were still nine points ahead of Sheffield Wednesday, Sheffield United and Southampton and were at last back in the top flight.

'Push and run' had set the game alight. Crowds flocked to see this new style of football, but could it have the same effect in the First Division? There was no reason why not. In the FA Cup they had met three First Division sides. They had beaten a struggling Stoke City in the third round, followed that up with a 5-1 hammering of Sunderland and only went out to Everton at Goodison Park after a dubious penalty decision.

League Champions at Last
After the first game against Blackpool at White Hart Lane there were real doubts. The visitors had clearly done their homework, worked out a way to counter the quick interchange of passing that Spurs relied on and went back to the seaside town with a 4-1 victory under their belts. In the next game,

at Bolton, Spurs were a goal down towards the end of the first half when Peter Murphy, a new signing and yet to fit into Rowe's system, scored after a 50-yard solo dribble. It gave Spurs confidence and in the second half, still playing the way Rowe favoured, Spurs scored three times to prove 'Push and run' could succeed against the best in the country. It took time but Spurs slowly got to grips with better quality opponents than they had met in Division Two.

At the end of September, they beat Aston Villa 3-2 at Villa Park and won their next seven games, including successive home victories over Stoke City by 6-1, Portsmouth 5-1 and Newcastle United. The Newcastle game saw possibly the finest performance given by a Spurs team in the First Division. The Geordies, including Jackie Milburn and George Robledo arrived at White Hart Lane second in the table, two points behind Arsenal. They left having been totally outclassed by a Spurs side missing captain Ron Burgess. Spurs scored seven without reply, ripping Newcastle apart time after time, while the visitors never even looked like threatening Ted Ditchburn's goal. That result more than any made Spurs serious title challengers and by the end of the year they were on top of the league for the first time in 25 years.

Over the next three months Manchester United emerged from a pack of chasing clubs to prove Spurs' only real threat but, by the middle of April, two points from the visit of a Huddersfield side desperate for points to lift them clear of relegation trouble would secure the title. Expectations were high, but the Terriers had already brought Spurs' eight-game winning run to an end in November and had knocked them out of the FA Cup in January. Sure enough, a third victory (this time by 2-0) saw the Yorkshire club thwart Spurs again. A point gained at Middlesbrough, left Spurs with two home games, against Sheffield Wednesday and Liverpool. Wednesday were also battling against relegation and drew confidence from Huddersfield's

Alf Ramsey: an instrumental figure in Rowe's 'push and run' team.

Ron Burgess beats Newcastle United's John Duncan to the ball in the 1951 Charity Shield at White Hart Lane. Spurs won the game 2-1.

success but, in a game marked only for the tension, a single goal from Len Duquemin was enough to make Spurs Football League champions for the first time.

Arthur Rowe's Team

Rowe's title-winning team showed the value of the Northfleet nursery which Peter McWilliam had instigated some 30 years earlier. Goalkeeper Ted Ditchburn was an outstanding prospect as a youngster, but had still spent a short time with Northfleet before moving up to White Hart Lane. Over six foot tall and a brilliant shot-stopper, he was the first line of attack in Rowe's master-plan, encouraged to throw the ball out to his full backs rather than punt it downfield. Arthur Willis had also spent some time at Northfleet. A quiet, neat defender, he made only two appearances in the Second Division winning side, but after replacing Charlie Withers kept his place on merit. Bill Nicholson, a terrier in the middle of the field with his covering and tackling, spent two years at Northfleet, a year longer than his wing half partner, Ron Burgess. Burgess was the heart of Rowe's team, an all-action, dynamo of a player recognised as the best in the country and a true great in Spurs' history. Les Bennett, tall and elegant, was another Northfleet graduate striding through midfield, creating chances and taking them himself, as was Les Medley, an outside left with pace and power who was also happy taking on his marker in one-on-one situations.

Northfleet was not the only club used to develop Spurs' stars of the future. Eddie Baily, perfectly suited to 'push and run' with his instant control and quick-thinking, and Sonny Walters, fast, direct and a natural opportunist, had both played for Finchley, after first being associated with Spurs through the Tottenham Juniors. Len Duquemin had arrived at Spurs from Guernsey, immediately after the War, and had not gone through the junior ranks. A great worker he was not a centre forward who scored vast numbers of goals, but a true team player linking the forward line and creating chances for his colleagues. The only regulars who had cost a transfer fee were Harry Clarke and Alf Ramsey. Clarke was a giant of a centre half signed from Lovells Athletic for a nominal fee, who was not merely a defender, but also quite happy in possession of the ball, with excellent distribution. Ramsey was one of the most cultured full backs of his age. A first class defender he worked perfectly with Nicholson and Walters, collecting Ditchburn's throw outs and starting attacks from his own area.

The Final Flings of a Great Team

'Push and run' had taken Spurs from the Second Division to the title, but Rowe realised it was not unbeatable and at the start of the 1951-52 season, admitted that he did not think Spurs could win the title in successive seasons. He was right, but if injuries had not played their part may have been proved wrong. Harry Clarke was injured before the campaign began and his replacement, Brian Farley, was crocked in an opening day defeat at Middlesbrough. Derek King played in the next two games, both victories, but he too got an injury and Bill Nicholson had to switch to centre half until Clarke was fit to return. With Eddie Baily and Sonny Walters also out, the instinctive passing that came with players who knew each other's game so well was absent and the free flowing football stuttered to a halt.

Never was that better illustrated than at St James Park at the beginning of September. Newcastle United still thirsted for revenge after their mauling the previous season and duly got it, sending Spurs home on the receiving end of a 2-7 scoreline. Still, Spurs were too good for most teams in the First Division and vied with Portsmouth, Arsenal and Manchester United for top spot for most of the season. Even after successive defeats at Manchester United and at home to Arsenal, sandwiching an FA Cup exit at Newcastle, they still remained near the top and it was only in the last few weeks that Manchester United pulled away to finish four points ahead of Spurs. At the end of the season both Spurs and Manchester United went on tour to North

Bill Nicholson: the ball-winner of the 1951 championship-winning side.

America. They met for two games in Toronto and New York. Spurs won both, 5-0 in the first and 7-1 in the second, to show that 'push and run' still had the beating of the best.

Football is, however, a game that never stands still. Rowe had given Spurs a period of success unprecedented in the club's history, but it could not last forever. 'Push and run' relied greatly on the players chosen to execute it knowing exactly what each other would do. That came from playing together for years. It was a style where every member of the team had their part to play and it was not easy for new players to come in and immediately find their feet. One weak link and the whole system could break down.

Ever Closer to a Wembley Debut

As age and injuries took their toll, Spurs slowed down and their football became more predictable, easier to overcome. The players who had done so well for three years were past their best and the reserves and new signings were just not of the same quality. This was obvious from early in 1952-53 as Spurs slipped back into mid-table, never in the hunt for the title. There was still, though, the FA Cup and the dream of a first Wembley visit, to provide a fitting epitaph for what had been a revolutionary brand of football. Not that anyone travelling back from Tranmere after the third round could ever have believed that Wembley might be a realistic target. Spurs had gone a goal down to their Third Division (North) opponents after 20 minutes and although they equalised 15 minutes into the second half there were many that thought they were lucky to escape with a draw.

Eddie Bailey: the 'Cheekie Chappie' of the 'push and run' side.

Any ideas of a famous giant-killing were soon banished in the replay two days later. Sid McClellan led the way with a hat-trick as Spurs well and truly put Tranmere in their place with a 9-1 victory.

In the fourth round Spurs were required to travel to their old cup foes Preston North End. Decimated by injuries, full back Charlie Withers was called up to play at outside left and amazed everyone by scoring both Spurs' goals in a two-all draw. Preston were beaten by the only goal of the game in the replay, giving Spurs a fifth round tie at Halifax Town. It was the draw nobody wanted, for Halifax had already beaten two First Division clubs, Cardiff City and Stoke City, but on a snow-covered pitch Spurs had their easiest game of the competition, winning 3-0. On the road again for the quarter-final, Spurs visited Birmingham City and earned another replay thanks to Les Bennett's goal. This time Spurs needed two replays to progress, drawing 2-2 with Birmingham at White Hart Lane before a Sonny Walters goal at Molineux earned them another visit to Birmingham for a Villa Park semi-final with Blackpool.

In 1948, Spurs had got within minutes of victory. This time they got within seconds. Bill Perry gave Blackpool a first half lead, but Len Duquemin grabbed an equaliser early in the second half. As the game wore on Spurs, even with Les Bennett little more than a passenger for the last half-hour, took control but a winner would not come and extra-time looked a certainty. With only seconds left, the referee gave a free-kick against Eddie Baily for handball. As he stood arguing with the referee, Blackpool took the kick and the ball ended up at the feet of Perry. Alf Ramsey moved in and quickly dispossessed him, but hesitated fractionally before deciding to pass the ball back to Ted Ditchburn. He slipped, mis-hit the ball and let Jackie Mudie in to whip the winner past a stranded Ditchburn. Spurs kicked off again, but barely had the ball moved than the final whistle went – once again, Spurs had missed out on a trip to Wembley.

A Great Manager Bows Out

Rowe's great team had now come to the end of its time and gradually began to break up. Les Medley was first to go, followed by Ron Burgess and Arthur Willis. Les Bennett was getting to the end of his career and Bill Nicholson knew it was time for him to call it a day and move on to something he loved, coaching. These were all great players and Rowe knew they had to be replaced, but that was easier said than done. He had set the highest of standards and was not prepared to see them lowered. He wanted only the best players for Spurs, but the best were rarely available, and when they were the fees demanded were exorbitant.

Rowe did manage to secure a replacement for Nicholson, but even that was at a price he was reluctant to pay and less than had originally been quoted. Danny Blanchflower was anxious to leave Aston Villa and was just the sort of player Rowe wanted, but Villa knew that not only were Spurs interested, so were Arsenal. They demanded a transfer fee of £40,000, a figure neither Spurs nor Arsenal were prepared to match. Rowe and the

50 Greatest Players

LES MEDLEY   Outside left

Joined Tottenham Hotspur: 1935 (amateur), February 1939 (professional)   **From:** Juniors

1948   **From:** Ulster United (Canada)

Debut: v Brentford, 5 January 1946

Appearances: 165   **Goals:** 46

Left Tottenham Hotspur: 1947   **For:** Toronto Greenbacks

1953 (retired)

Honours won with Tottenham Hotspur: Division 2 Championship 1950, Division 1 Championship 1951

A local lad, Spurs looked to have lost Medley's talents when he emigrated to Canada in November 1946 because his wife, whom he had met there while serving during the war, was homesick. He played for Toronto Greenbacks and Ulster United but, fortunately for Spurs, soon returned to form a devastating left side partnership in the 'push and run' side with Ron Burgess and Eddie Baily. Stocky and with good pace, Medley was a more than competent orthodox winger, but he rarely stuck to his line, wandering at will and popping up in the most unexpected positions. It was this unpredictability of his play that led to him finding so many openings and top-scoring in the 1950 Second Division Championship season. An England international and Spurs regular, Medley decided to retire in 1953 and returned to Canada, although he later coached in South Africa.

50 Greatest Players

RON BURGESS   Half back

Joined Tottenham Hotspur: May 1936 (amateur), August 1938
(professional)

From: Cwm Villa   **Debut:** v Norwich City, 4 February 1939

Appearances: 321   **Goals:** 16

Left Tottenham Hotspur: May 1954   **For:** Swansea Town

Honours won with Tottenham Hotspur: Division 2 Championship 1950,
Division 1 Championship 1951

Having been rejected by Spurs after a trial, Ron Burgess called in at
White Hart Lane to watch the 'A' team before heading back to Wales. They were a man
short and Burgess was asked to make up the numbers at half back, a position he had never
played in before. So well did he perform that it was to be almost 20 years before he
returned to Wales permanently, by which time he had become a true great, not just at Spurs
but of football in general. A human dynamo, he never stopped working, his natural instinct
pushing his men forward, but his football brain taking over when he needed to defend.

Ron Burgess provided the heart of Arthur Rowe's great 'push and run' side of the
early 1950s, captaining the team and leading by example. He also captained his
country, winning 32 caps, was the first Welshman to play for the Football League and
played for Great Britain against the Rest of Europe. After one of the finest careers a
footballer could hope for, he took to management with Swansea Town and Watford. At
Vicarage Road he did Spurs one more favour: nurturing a young goalkeeper by the name
of Pat Jennings who was later transferred to White Hart Lane.

Arsenal manager, Tom Whittaker, agreed that neither of them would offer
over £30,000 and if they offered the same, it would be up to the player to
decide which club he wanted to join. Both clubs put in bids of £28,000, but
after a particularly poor performance had allowed Everton to win 3-1 at
White Hart Lane in December 1954, Rowe increased Spurs' offer to £30,000.
Arsenal were not prepared to up their bid and Rowe got his man. Even he
was probably not to know that the record price for a half back he had
agreed to pay was to prove an absolute bargain.

Blanchflower arrived with Spurs only a point off the relegation positions,
but he had an immediate effect as Spurs climbed away from the strugglers.
Unfortunately, though, there was nothing even he could do to prevent Third
Division (North) York City dumping Spurs out of the FA Cup in the fourth
round. It was a clear sign of how far Spurs had fallen.

The pressures of trying to recreate the great days of 'push and run' took their toll on Rowe. He was passionate about Spurs, could not bear to see them struggle and blamed himself for every point dropped, every goal conceded. The worry made him ill and, in April 1955, he handed over team affairs to his assistant, Jimmy Anderson. His contract ran until January 1956, but almost immediately Rowe realised he would be away for some time so he resigned with Anderson taking on the manager's mantle on a permanent basis.

Jimmy Anderson – More than a Caretaker

Jimmy Anderson had been with Spurs for almost 50 years. He had joined the club in 1908 as a young player, did not make the grade, joined the coaching staff and worked as assistant to both Joe Hulme and Arthur Rowe. He knew the club and players inside out, but he was getting on in years and there was always the feeling he was just filling in until his new assistant, Bill Nicholson, was ready to step in.

Anderson knew big changes had to be made and results early in 1955-56 just showed that more money had to be spent, and spent quickly, if Spurs were not to return to the Second Division. After a 1-4 defeat at Portsmouth on 29 October 1955 Spurs were adrift at the foot of the table, only five points from 14 games. Anderson was reluctant to let Johnny Gavin go but the defence was in desperate need of strengthening and when Norwich City demanded the Irish winger in part-exchange for their big full-back, Maurice Norman, Anderson was almost forced to accept. Norman's arrival certainly tightened things up at the back, but the forward line was weak and in December 1955 he signed Bobby Smith from Chelsea. Two players do not make a team but they certainly make a difference and a team that seemed almost certain of relegation started to look like a team that might escape the drop.

A battle developed between Spurs, Huddersfield Town, Aston Villa and Sheffield United. Spurs' last three games of the season saw them meet both Huddersfield and Sheffield at home with a trip to Cardiff in between. Victory over Huddersfield would have made Spurs safe, but the Yorkshire club kept their hopes alive with a 1-2 victory. A point from a 0-0 draw at Ninian Park meant that Spurs should stay up, but Bobby Smith made certain with a hat-trick as Sheffield United were defeated in the last game and condemned to relegation with Huddersfield.

The 1955-56 league season had been one long struggle, but at least the FA Cup provided some welcome relief. After beating Midland League Boston United and Middlesbrough, Spurs banished the memory of the defeat at

Great Managers – 1949-55

ARTHUR ROWE

Tottenham born, Tottenham bred and Tottenham through and through – Arthur Rowe was born within a hefty clearance of White Hart Lane, grew up a Spurs supporter, captained the club back into the First Division and as manager led it to unknown success. Signed as an amateur he was farmed out to Cheshunt before working his way through the Northfleet nursery to the professional ranks. He was soon established as first choice centre half although he was unlike many of his contemporaries. Not for him the hurried boot downfield. He believed in playing football from the back, players passing their way out of trouble, defence used as a springboard for attack. For almost four years Rowe led Spurs from the back as promotion was secured and a challenge made for the league title. A serious knee injury in December 1934 saw Rowe out of action and in his absence Spurs plunged to relegation.

Rowe never fully recovered and when released in April 1939, having failed to recover from a cartilage operation, secured a coaching job in Hungary. The War prevented him taking up the job but he got some managerial experience with the Army team. After the War Rowe was appointed manager of Chelmsford City and took them to the Southern League title in his first season, fashioning them into an attractive, entertaining outfit.

On Joe Hulme's departure in May 1949 Rowe took over at Spurs, teaching the players his philosophy of how the game should be played. His maxim of 'Make it quick; make it simple' had an immediate effect, with the Second Division title in 1950 followed by Spurs first league title a year later. After the initial success, and with players getting old, the 'push and run' tactics became less effective. Rowe worked ceaselessly in the Spurs cause but the strains took their toll and in July 1955 he was forced to stand down. He was not out of football for long, scouting for West Bromwich Albion and managing Crystal Palace. Having led Palace out of Division Four in 1961 the pressures again built up and Rowe resigned, although he later acted as a consultant for both Orient and Millwall.

York by winning at Third Division (North) Doncaster Rovers. West Ham United provided the sixth round opposition and things did not bode well when the Second Division outfit took a 3-1 lead at White Hart Lane in front of over 69,000 spectators. Spurs fought back with goals from George Robb and Len Duquemin to salvage a draw and, in front of a packed house at Upton Park, a header from little Tommy Harmer and another goal from the ever-reliable Duquemin saw Spurs through.

The semi-final was again at Villa Park with the opposition provided by high-riding Manchester City, fourth in Division One. The two performances

50 Greatest Players

ALF RAMSEY   **Full back**

Joined Tottenham Hotspur: May 1949   **From:** Southampton

Debut: v Brentford, 20 August 1949

Appearances: 250   **Goals:** 24

Left Tottenham Hotspur: August 1955   **For:** Ipswich Town (manager)

Honours won with Tottenham Hotspur: Division 2 Championship 1950, Division 1 Championship 1951

Alf Ramsey looked to have missed out on a football career because of the Second World War but when he played for his battalion against Southampton they spotted his potential, quickly signed him up and moved him from centre half to full back. When peace returned he immediately made the right back spot his own and it took a hefty £21,000 fee for Spurs to secure his transfer in May 1949, the first signing by new manager Arthur Rowe and the last piece of the 'push and run' jigsaw. Ramsey was a magnificent full back, strong and quick with great positional sense. But more than that he was a great thinker and tactician, all the time looking to come up with new, innovative ways of playing the game. Captain of his country he more than anyone was responsible for taking Arthur Rowe's ideas from the training pitch and putting them into practice. Management was a natural progression for Ramsey and with Ipswich Town he took a bunch of average players, developed a playing style to suit and led them to the league title, before taking England to the pinnacle of the game with the World Cup success of 1966.

against West Ham had given Spurs a lot of confidence, particularly the way Tommy Harmer was playing. He was a genius of a player, but at 5ft 6ins (1.58m) and only eight-and-a-half stone, Anderson, like Arthur Rowe, had doubts about his ability to last the pace in the hurly burly of top flight football. Harmer had been outstanding at Doncaster and in the two games with West Ham, but just a week before the semi-final he had found the more physical approach of Portsmouth hard to overcome.

Conscious of the powerful play of Roy Paul in the City half back line, Anderson decided to leave out Harmer in favour of Dave Dunmore, normally a centre forward, but someone he thought would prove more of a handful for City. If Bill Leivers had not cleared Dunmore's shot off the line in the first few minutes he might have been right, but Spurs lacked cohesion, rarely threatened and were under pressure for most of the game. The only

50 Greatest Players

LEN DUQUEMIN   Centre forward

Joined Tottenham Hotspur: Janaury 1946 (amateur), September 1946 (professional)

From: Vauxbelet

Debut: v Sheffield Wednesday, 30 August 1947

Appearances: 308   **Goals:** 131

Left Totteham Hotspur: November 1958   **For:** Bedford Town

Honours won with Tottenham Hotspur: Division 2 Championship 1950, Division 1 Championship 1951

Recommended to Spurs after the Second World War by a supporter living in the Channel Islands, Len Duquemin was centre forward in the 'push and run' side of the early 1950s and one of the few players to notch over a hundred league goals for the club. His marvellous scoring record does nothing to reveal his true value, for Duquemin was far more than just a goalscorer. He was the ideal centre forward for the simple passing game Arthur Rowe advocated; a mobile, non-stop worker, good in the air, comfortable on the ball and always looking to drag his marker out of position to create openings for others. His unselfish work created as many goals for his team-mates as he scored himself. His great career at White Hart Lane was only brought to an end with the arrival of Bobby Smith and the 'Duke' then played for Bedford Town, Hastings United and Romford before he stopped playing completely to run a newsagents business in Northumberland Park and later a public house in Cheshunt.

goal came five minutes before the break when Bobby Johnstone headed in a cross from the left. With 20 minutes left Danny Blanchflower sent Maurice Norman forward as an extra centre forward. It made little difference, although Spurs should have had a penalty when City keeper Bert Trautmann, having saved a Dunmore shot, held George Robb's leg as the Spurs' forward pounced on the rebound. As there were only five minutes left a penalty might have made all the difference, but it could not hide the fact that City were the better team and deserved to win.

After what had been a tough first season in charge for Anderson, things took a mighty turn for the better in 1956-57. Anderson realised that in

Tommy Harmer he had a little genius and installed him as the midfield creator-in-chief, ably supported by the imaginative Danny Blanchflower and the more orthodox Tony Marchi. The only new signing was winger Terry Medwin from Swansea Town, but right from the start, Spurs looked a different team to the one that had struggled so much only 12 months earlier.

Three of the first four matches were won and after two defeats at Blackpool and Bolton Wanderers, a run of nine wins in ten games saw Spurs and Manchester United pulling away at the top of the table. United were an outstanding team and in any other season Spurs may well have taken the championship, but the 'Busby Babes' were head and shoulders above the opposition and rarely were Spurs able to get within a couple of points of them. They finished eight points adrift, but could have done better had their form not taken a dip after another FA Cup exit at the hands of a Third Division club, this time Bournemouth and Boscombe Athletic. The Southern section club, managed by former Spurs star Freddie Cox, pulled off the shock of the competition with a 3-1 fifth round win at Dean Court. After that six points were dropped in the next four league games to banish any thoughts of catching United.

Anderson's rebuilding was clearly on the right lines, but his plans suffered a jolt with the departure of Tony Marchi in the summer of 1957. The Edmonton-born half back was a schoolboy star who, as a 17-year old, had already made his Football League debut by the time he signed professional

George Robb seals a 5-1 victory over Manchester City at White Hart Lane in February 1958.

in June 1950. He eventually replaced Ron Burgess, although he was more like Bill Nicholson, defensively strong and covering for the attacking forays of his half back partner, Danny Blanchflower. From October 1954 he had established himself as an automatic choice and seemed destined to go on to great things until the Italians of Juventus made an offer for his services. The fee of £42,000 was reasonable compensation for Spurs but they would rather have had the player. However, in the age of the maximum wage the rewards of playing in the Italian League were too much for Marchi to turn down.

Marchi's steadying presence was missed from the start of the season as Spurs picked up only one point in their first four games and plummeted to the bottom of the table. Recovery was slow but a late season burst, coinciding with the signing of another Swansea Town winger, Cliff Jones, produced 14 points from the last eight games and pushed Spurs up to third, behind Wolverhampton Wanderers and Preston North End. Bobby Smith notched 36 league goals to equal the record set in 1930-31 by Ted Harper and it came as no surprise when Danny Blanchflower picked up the Footballer of the Year award.

Danny Blanchflower, Footballer of the Year 1958.

Chapter Seven: 1958-74
The Glory Years

The early months of 1958-59 yet again saw Spurs make a miserable start to a season. By 4 October they had nine points from 11 matches, just one off the bottom, and the pressures had started to get to Jimmy Anderson. Like his predecessor, Arthur Rowe, he was totally committed to the club but he had seen Rowe's health suffer and was not prepared to go through the same agonies himself. It was all getting too much for him and he resigned. He had done an excellent job in three years, halting the decline, taking Spurs back towards the top, if not to the summit, and laying the foundations for better things to come with some astute signings and the promotion of home-grown talent. His assistant, Bill Nicholson, was promoted, taking up the reins only a few hours before Spurs were due to meet Everton, one of the clubs a point below Spurs, at White Hart Lane.

Nicholson was already a legend at Spurs from his playing days, but the result of his first game was to lay the first brick in a legendary managerial career. Nicholson's first decision was to recall Tommy Harmer and the little man was inspired as he led Spurs to a 10-4 victory before an incredulous crowd just short of 38,000. Seven days later he was again the star as Spurs won 4-3 at Leicester, but any thoughts of a brave new world completely disappeared as reality set back in. Between the middle of October and the New Year Spurs slipped back, with 13 games yielding one win and two draws and they went into 1959 one point above Portsmouth and Aston Villa. The second half of the season was slightly better, at least in terms of league results, and Spurs managed to stumble on to finish 18th, thanks largely to Portsmouth and Villa being so much worse than their rivals. In the FA Cup, though, Spurs suffered another embarrassment, going out in the fifth round to yet another Third Division club, Norwich City, in a replay after a White Hart Lane draw.

Nicholson had only been manager for a few months but he had been at Spurs long enough to know that if the club was to go anywhere he desperately needed to sign new, top-class players; players with skill and finesse, stamina and determination, whom he could mould into a winning unit. He secured one of the best in March 1959 with the signing of Dave Mackay from Heart

Mel Hopkins (left) and Maurice Norman (right) challenge Nat Lofthouse. A struggling Spurs lost 4-1 to Bolton Wanderers at Burnden Park in March 1958.

of Midlothian, a rock of a man with an unquenchable thirst to win. At the end of the season Nicholson took Spurs off for a three-game tour to Russia. Spurs beat Moscow Torpedo and Dynamo Kiev before losing to a Russian Select XI, but the results were of little consequence. It was the fostering of that essential in any team game, team spirit, that later led Nicholson to regard the trip as his most important time with the players.

Almost There

Ever since Ted Ditchburn had begun to approach the twilight of his career, Spurs had searched for a suitable replacement. At times both John Hollowbread and Ron Reynolds had looked good enough to fill Ditchburn's shoes but Nicholson did not feel either of them were the top-notch keeper he needed. He wanted a goalkeeper who would be worth a couple of points a season, at least, and identified his man in Bill Brown of Dundee. Never afraid to back his judgement, Nicholson laid out £16,500 of Spurs' money to sign Brown in the summer of 1959

He immediately proved to be worth every penny as Spurs opened the season unbeaten in 12 games and led the First Division, but Nicholson was

50 Greatest Players

TED DITCHBURN   Goalkeeper

Joined Tottenham Hotspur: June 1938 (amateur),

May 1939 (professional)

From: Northfleet Paper Mills

Debut: v Birmingham City, 31 August 1946

Appearances: 453

Left Tottenham Hotspur: April 1959   **For:** Romford

Ted Ditchburn served Spurs for 20 years, clocking up over 450 senior appearances. If he had not lost seven of those years to the Second World War there can be no doubt he would have amassed a total not even Pat Jennings or Steve Perryman would have surpassed. Another of the players to progress through the Northfleet nursery, Ditchburn joined the White Hart Lane staff in May 1939 but his professional career was immediately brought to a stop by the outbreak of war. He played plenty of football in the services and was such an outstanding talent that by the time of his demob he had already represented England in two wartime internationals. Returning to Spurs he immediately claimed a first team place and for eight years was rarely absent from the line up.

Tall and commanding, Ditchburn had every attribute the last line of defence needed but he was more than just a stopper of goals. With Alf Ramsey he pioneered the quick throw out that made him the first line of attack. A truly great keeper, it was only competition from other world class number ones such as Frank Swift and Bert Williams that limited Ditchburn to six England appearances. When injuries finally took their toll and age began to creep up, Ditchburn left Spurs for Romford. After a short spell in management he ran a successful men's outfitters in Romford.

never a man to be satisfied. Immediately after overwhelming their nearest challengers, Wolverhampton Wanderers, 5-1 at White Hart Lane, he invested another £20,000 in the precocious talents of John White from Falkirk. White replaced Dave Dunmore but, at first, disrupting what had been a settled side looked to be a mistake as Spurs lost three games out of five. Dunmore was a big lad who took a lot of the weight off Bobby Smith up front, whereas White was an inside forward in the true meaning of the words, working away in the middle of the pitch, creating opportunities for others. Smith needed help so Nicholson signed Les Allen from Chelsea and switched White out to the right wing. Allen and Smith gelled instantly and Spurs got back to winning ways, moving four points ahead of Burnley and

50 Greatest Players

JOHNNY BROOKS   Inside forward

Joined Tottenham Hotspur: February 1952   **From:** Reading

Debut: v Stoke City, 6 April 1953

Appearances: 179   **Goals:** 51

Left Tottenham Hotspur: December 1960   **For:** Chelsea

As the 'push and run' side began to break up Johnny Brooks was signed from Reading to add something different to a midfield that opponents had begun to counter. A fine passer of the ball, Brooks also had great dribbling skills that enabled him to cut his way through a defence, whereas the team had been more used to making headway through quick incisive passing. At first it was difficult to harness Brooks' talents to these of the team but he slowly began to find his feet and with the departure of Eddie Baily became the main creative force in the team. He collected three England caps, and should have collected more, but he did not work well with Johnny Haynes. Prone to inconsistency, Brooks was often played on the wing where his natural body swerve and dribbling talents came to the fore but when Chelsea demanded Brooks as part of the deal for Les Allen to join Spurs, Nicholson decided to let him go. He later played for Brentford, Crystal Palace and in the non-league game.

hammering poor Crewe Alexandra 13-2 in an FA Cup fourth round replay, with Smith scoring four and Allen five. Spurs were favourites for the title but it all began to go wrong from the middle of March. Fulham and Luton Town left White Hart Lane with a point each, while Spurs lost at both Bolton Wanderers and Everton to leave the title race back in the melting pot. The three games over Easter were to be crucial with Chelsea away, followed by Manchester City and Chelsea at home. Then Spurs had to go to Molineux for what was expected to be the title decider. As it turned out the game at Wolves did decide the title but not in the way Spurs wanted. They started the run-in with a 3-1 success at Stamford Bridge but lost by the only goal to both Manchester City and Chelsea. They did pull off a remarkable 3-1 win over FA Cup finalists Wolves to prevent them doing the league and cup 'Double' but all that did was allow Burnley to take the championship and leave Spurs third.

So near and yet so far, but Bill Nicholson knew he had fashioned a team that was good enough to win the Football League. So did Danny Blanchflower. In fact he had even more faith in the men around him than his manager for on the eve of the 1960-61 season he told Spurs chairman Fred Bearman that Spurs were going to win the 'Double'. It was a feat Manchester United and Wolverhampton Wanderers had come so close to achieving it just seemed all the more impossible. Prophetic words or just a touch of the Irish blarney, Spurs set out to prove their captain right in double quick time.

The 'Double'

The season opened with a 2-0 win over Everton at White Hart Lane, followed by a 3-1 victory at Blackpool. Then Blackburn Rovers were beaten, as were Blackpool again, Manchester United, Bolton Wanderers twice, Arsenal, Leicester City, Aston Villa and Wolverhampton Wanderers. After 11 games Spurs had not dropped a point and were already pulling away from Sheffield Wednesday. Manchester City put the brakes on with a lucky 1-1 draw at Spurs but it was then back to winning ways as Nottingham Forest, Newcastle United, Cardiff City and Fulham all succumbed to what Stan Cullis described as the best team he had ever seen in the Football League. Only one team seemed capable of staying with Spurs, Sheffield Wednesday, and it was they who brought an opening 16-game unbeaten run to an end. Spurs had only managed to beat Wednesday on their own ground once, 24 years earlier, and with the Owls having won all their eight home league games many football fans, save those who followed Spurs, were hoping they could take the points. If not the title race would likely be over by Christmas. In a game of fast, furious, all-out attacking football Wednesday took the lead five minutes from the break but Maurice Norman equalised with a towering header moments before the half-time whistle. Spurs were on top for most of the second half but with 20 minutes left John Fantham scored to become the first player that season to hit a winning goal against Spurs.

A week later it was back to winning ways with a 6-0 defeat of Birmingham City and the start of another eight-match unbeaten run. Only defending champions, Burnley, managed to stop Spurs winning, coming back from 4-0 down to draw in an amazing game at White Hart Lane. By the end of the year Spurs were a full ten points ahead of Wolverhampton Wanderers. Only an incredible collapse could deprive them of the title as they turned their attention to the FA Cup.

Wembley At Last

Two goals from Les Allen and one from Terry Dyson, to give Spurs the best of five, saw off Charlton Athletic in the third round and Crewe Alexandra

50 Greatest Players

TOMMY HARMER   Inside forward

Joined Tottenham Hotspur: August 1945 (amateur), August 1948 (professional)
From: Finchley
Debut: v Bolton Wanderers, 8 September 1951
Appearances: 222   **Goals:** 51
Left Tottenham Hotspur: October 1960   **For:** Watford

'Harmer the Charmer' – three words that sum up little Tommy Harmer to perfection. At 5ft 6ins and 8st 9lbs, there was nothing to him, well not in physique. But in footballing talent the man was a giant. In his early career there were doubts as to whether he was strong enough to stand the rigours of hard-tackling opponents and heavy pitches and it took three years before Spurs decided to offer him professional terms. A supreme ball artist with a never-ending repertoire of trickery, Spurs need have had no worries about his ability withstand the physical side of the game. To tackle him opponents first had to get near enough and that was not easy. As for heavy pitches, Harmer just floated over them. It was only in 1956 that Harmer at last established a regular place in the team and for the next four years his talents made him the darling of White Hart Lane. Sadly, as Bill Nicholson sought to rebuild Spurs, Harmer found himself displaced by John White and, too good for reserve football, he was allowed to move to Watford. Nearing the twilight of his career he was transferred to Chelsea, an old head in a young team, and helped guide Chelsea back to the First Division.

improved on their performance 12 months earlier to escape White Hart Lane with nothing worse than a 5-1 scoreline in the fourth. Having won their League game at Villa Park, Spurs had to return to face Aston Villa in the fifth round but gave a magical performance to win 2-0 and set up a sixth round clash at Second Division Sunderland. Cliff Jones gave Spurs an early lead but instead of making the game safe they decided to give an exhibition of their skills, failed to take any of the many chances they created and paid the penalty when Sunderland equalised early in the second half. The goal gave the Wearsiders heart and Spurs' defence had to give its best performance of the season to secure a draw. In the replay Spurs made no mistake, winning 5-0 to earn a semi-final meeting with Burnley. Three times since the War

Spurs' dreams of a Wembley appearance had come to an end at Villa Park but there was no chance of that happening again. It took Spurs 30 minutes to get the first goal, Bobby Smith firing home after Jimmy Adamson had failed to cut out Les Allen's flick, and early in the second half Smith grabbed his second to make the Wembley dream a reality. Burnley fought hard and for long periods had Spurs on the back foot but in the last minute Cliff Jones broke away to finish the scoring.

A cup final place secure, attention now turned back to the league. The cup run had taken its toll with Spurs losing their next league game after the cup victories over Charlton, Crewe and Sunderland and only drawing after the defeat of Aston Villa. Having booked their Wembley place by beating Burnley, Spurs lost to Newcastle and drew at Fulham, allowing Sheffield Wednesday to move to within three points. Many pundits took this as evidence of the impossibility of the fabled 'Double'. If this was pressure then Spurs rode roughshod over it as they had so many opponents. Chelsea, Preston North End, Chelsea again and Birmingham City were all beaten to leave only Sheffield Wednesday in a position to overtake Spurs – and they were next on the guest list at White Hart Lane.

Wednesday arrived on 17 April 1961 having lost just once in 25 games, to Burnley in a FA Cup sixth round replay. Victory would give Spurs the title; a draw and mathematically they could still lose it. 61,205 crammed into White Hart Lane full of expectation, but on a night of muscle-tightening tension the skilful and fast flowing football that had served Spurs so well since August had to be set aside, replaced by passion and bravery. Wednesday knew their only hope lay in tearing into Spurs, disrupting the essential passing game of Blanchflower and White, pegging Mackay back in his own half. That was just what they did and got their reward on the half-hour mark when Don Megson volleyed home after a free-kick had rebounded back to him. All season Spurs had given their supporters something to crow about, now it was payback time. The fans were required to play their part and play it they did as the noise around the stadium grew into a deafening crescendo. They were almost silenced again as Keith Ellis hit the post but barely had he finished cursing his luck than Terry Dyson climbed above Megson to nod on Peter Baker's long clearance. The ball fell to Bobby Smith who showed amazing dexterity to flick the ball over Peter Swan with his right foot and smash it past Ron Springett with his left. Barely had play resumed than Maurice Norman ambled forward to connect with a Danny Blanchflower free-kick and set up Les Allen for what proved to be the championship winning goal. At the final whistle the pitch was flooded by a

Great Matches

FA CUP FINAL   **Wembley Stadium, 6 May 1961**

Tottenham Hotspur 2 Leicester City 0   **Attendance 100,000**
Smith
Dyson

Spurs were clearly suffering from nerves during the opening exchanges of the most important game in their history, although all their fears may have been banished had John White accepted a third-minute chance to put them ahead. Terry Dyson set up the opening after a defence-splitting pass by Dave Mackay but White blazed over the bar. Initially Leicester matched Spurs move for move but Spurs were gradually getting the better of things when Les Allen went in to challenge Len Chalmers. There was nothing dirty about the tackle but as the Leicester full back went down he badly twisted his knee and effectively was out of the game. With no substitutes Leicester were forced to re-shuffle, Chalmers moving out to the left wing.

For 50 minutes they kept Spurs at bay. Only once did Spurs break through, Cliff Jones' being wrongly called offside as he netted at the far post five minutes before half-time. Handicapped by Chalmers' injury, Leicester did remarkably well to hold out but after two or three near misses the breakthrough finally came in the 66th minute. Allen and White combined to release Dyson whose first time pass found Bobby Smith 15 yards from goal. With his back to goal, Smith killed the ball in an

Leicester keeper Gordon Banks is beaten as Terry Dyson fires home Spurs' second goal.

instant and swivelled to thump it past Gordon Banks. The burdens of expectation Spurs had been labouring under lifted and at last they began to play like the champions they were.

Ten minutes after the first goal, White found Smith out on the right wing. He chipped the ball right on to the forehead of an unmarked Terry Dyson and Spurs were two up, the game over, the 'Double' won.

Tottenham Hotspur: Brown; Baker, Henry; Blanchflower, Norman, Mackay; Jones, White, Smith, Allen, Dyson.

Leicester City: Banks; Chalmers, Norman; McLintock, King, Appleton; Riley, Walsh, McIlmoyle, Keyworth, Cheesebrough.

Referee: J. Kelly

Tottenham Hotspur, the first 'double' winners of the century, celebrate after their FA Cup victory. From left: Ron Henry, Bill Brown, Peter Baker, Cliff Jones, Danny Blanchflower, Terry Dyson, Les Allen, Bobby Smith and Maurice Norman.

sea of cheering fans who refused to leave until Blanchflower had led his men into the director's box to receive the plaudits they so richly deserved.

The first part of Blanchflower's prophecy to Fred Bearman fulfilled, Spurs eased up and lost two of their final three league games to finish eight points clear of Sheffield Wednesday. Such results mattered little; they had already set more than enough records. Eleven victories at the start of a season, unbeaten in the first 16 games, 31 victories, 16 away victories, 66 points secured, 33 points collected away from home, only 17 players used, the list went on. All that mattered now was Spurs' first visit to Wembley, where Leicester City were waiting for them, and the second leg of the 'Double'.

As a youngster Bill Nicholson had been bought up under the tutelage of Peter McWilliam, as an adult he had been at the core of Arthur Rowe's 'push and run' side. He was therefore steeped in the finest traditions of the Spurs style and the team he had shaped added to those traditions. It was a team that relied on playing the ball to feet, retaining possession, attacking from every position. It contained players of strength and determination like Mackay, Smith and Norman but they were in the team first and foremost because of the skills they possessed, not merely for their physical strength. Unlike his predecessors Nicholson had been allowed to import the players he believed were needed and had assembled a team of all the talents.

The Greatest Team in Spurs History

Bill Brown was a wonderful last line of defence; cool, unflappable and a magnificent shot-stopper. If a little suspect on crosses, he more than compensated with fine positional sense and a degree of agility that made a difficult job look easy. In front of him Maurice Norman was a giant of a man, dominant in the air but solid on the ground, putting to good use the ball control skills he had learned in his original full-back position. His reliability was a crucial factor in allowing his half-back partners the freedom to venture upfield, knowing that if attacks broke down Norman would always be there to cover for them. The unsung heroes of the team were full backs, Ron Henry and Peter Baker. Baker was a worthy successor to Alf Ramsey, if not as lauded as the England international. He was a solid, dependable defender who went about his job in a simple manner, jockeying his opponent before making a well-timed challenge, covering for Blanchflower's forward forays. He may not have grabbed the headlines but his team-mates knew exactly how valuable he was. Henry was similar, with his unfussy style masking a cool, calculating defender who knew exactly how to keep a winger quiet, when to nip in and pinch the ball and when to lay it off to an

Dave Mackay and Terry Medwin await the start of the 1962-63 season.

attacking colleague. The great strength of the team lay in midfield where Danny Blanchflower, Dave Mackay and John White strutted their stuff. Blanchflower, the captain, strolled through games, demanding the ball then hitting it long or playing it short, directing play, taking Nicholson's ideas on to the pitch and making them work. Alongside him John White, the 'Ghost', flitting here and there, popping up in the most unexpected places, a quick burst of speed taking him past opponents and endless stamina that had him working as hard in the last minute as the first.

Then there was Dave Mackay, heart and soul of the team, thundering around the pitch, tackling hard, forever urging his men forward, leading by example. On the right wing Cliff Jones flitted across the ground, searing pace leaving his marker for dead, before whipping in a dangerous cross or flinging himself at the ball with a prodigious leap and a total disregard for injury. Terry Dyson was on the left wing. A 5ft 3ins little terrier he may not have possessed the talent of many of his colleagues but he made up for any shortcomings in skill with his endless enthusiasm and hard work. He was always harrying and challenging, looking for the ball and proving a continual nuisance. Bobby Smith led the forward line, everything an English centre forward should be. Strong, brave and hard-working he put himself about, giving defenders as hard a time as anyone could, worrying goalkeepers with physical presence but a lot more skilful than he was given credit for. Alongside Smith was Les Allen, another hard-working unsung hero, always creating problems, taking the pressure off Smith and contributing a full measure of goals.

The Glory, Glory Nights Begin

Winning the 'Double' unquestionably made Spurs the best team in the country, but that was not enough for Bill Nicholson. He wanted his team to do even better and that meant moving up a level, meeting the best teams in Europe. The fast-flowing attacking football Nicholson preached would be put to the test in the European Cup.

Spurs' first European Cup match was a preliminary round first leg tie against Gornik Zabreze, in front of a 70,000 crowd in Poland. They approached the game just as they would any other match, taking the game to the home side, looking to overwhelm their opponents. Even when they went a goal down in eight minutes nothing changed, attack remained the order of the day. Only when they went four down immediately after the break did they realise there was a vast difference between the domestic game and international club football. They managed to pinch two late goals to make an impossible task in the second leg merely almost impossible. The second leg took place a week later and became the first of the 'glory, glory' nights for which White Hart Lane was to become famous. In a match of white-hot intensity they tore into the Poles like men possessed, were level on

A 'glory, glory' Night is well underway as Bobby Smith (out of picture) heads home Spurs' fifth goal. Terry Dyson (second left) and Les Allen (third left) hail his effort against Gornik.

aggregate within 20 minutes and 5-1 ahead by half-time. They went on to win 8-1 on the night. For the next round Spurs travelled to Holland to meet the Dutch champions, Feyenoord, without Mackay, Smith and Allen. They showed how much they had learned from their visit to Poland, playing a far more restrained game, counter-attacking when the chance arose and snatching two goals on the break to run out 3-1 winners. They settled for a comparatively comfortable 1-1 draw in the second leg and then concentrated on their domestic obligations as the second round was three months away.

Maurice Norman, a colossus of a defender.

The 1961-62 season had not started as well as Spurs would have liked but that was to be expected. With opponents raising their game against the best team in the country, retaining their title was never going to be easy, but Spurs were not helped by the demands of playing in Europe and injuries. By the time Feyenoord's challenge had been overcome Spurs had played 16 league games and suffered five defeats, only two less than in the whole of the previous season. Not that this was of any concern; they were only two points behind leaders Burnley and were soon to be reinforced by the best goalscorer in the game, Jimmy Greaves. Nicholson was never one to rest on his laurels and when he heard the former Chelsea striker was unhappy after just a few months in Italy he was quick to move in and laid out almost £100,000 to secure the one player he knew could improve the team. Greaves settled in immediately, finding the net with the amazing regularity that marked his career, but Burnley were not to be caught easily and by the time Spurs had to resume their European campaign Burnley had opened up a four-point gap.

The Czech champions, Dukla Prague, provided Spurs' next opposition in the European Cup. A single goal defeat on a snow-covered pitch in Prague left Spurs in confident mood for the return leg and, on another night when the crowd did their job as 12th man, two goals each from Dave Mackay and Les Allen took Spurs through to a semi-final with European Cup-holders Benfica. In the first leg at the Stadium of Light Benfica were at their imperious best while Spurs were suddenly stage-struck. A goal down after five minutes, Jimmy Greaves looked to have equalised within a minute but his strike was ruled out for offside and, although Greaves and Cliff Jones had chances to pull Spurs level, it was the home club who scored next. Bobby Smith did score early in the second half but Benfica snuffed out any Spurs comeback with a third, although Smith should have had a second in the last minute but his effort was ruled offside despite two Portuguese defenders standing on the goal-line.

Benfica's visit two weeks later was a night of which legends are made. Spurs threw everything at them in the opening minutes but were knocked back when Aguas strode through to give the visitors the lead. Spurs needed three to force a replay. They tore into Benfica and looked to have got the first, only for the linesman to again rule Greaves offside. Before half-time

Jimmy Greaves scored 37 league goals in 1962-63, including this one in a 4-2 victory over Manchester City at White Hart Lane.

Bobby Smith did pull one back and early in the second half a Danny Blanchflower penalty signalled a non-stop onslaught on the Benfica goal. With the crowd lifting Spurs to new heights they tried everything, but the nearest they got was a Dave Mackay shot that nearly broke the crossbar. Over the two games they had matched the European Cup holders and got a taste for European football.

While Spurs were concentrating on the European Cup, again their league results suffered with only one win in nine games. Burnley continued to maintain a healthy lead and were joined in the title fight by a new challenger from a surprising quarter. Ipswich Town, managed by Alf Ramsey, were competing in the First Division for the first time in their history and making a remarkable job of it. Spurs finished with a good run but it was not enough to overhaul Burnley who crumbled with one win in their last ten games, leaving the championship trophy on its way to Suffolk.

The FA Cup Retained

With no UEFA Cup, Spurs' only chance of further European football was to retain the FA Cup. In the third round they surrendered a 3-0 lead to Birmingham City and were somewhat fortunate to hang on for a draw before dispatching the Midlanders 4-2 in the replay. A visit to Plymouth Argyle followed, where Spurs put on an exhibition for the football outpost, winning 5-1. For the fifth round Spurs were again called upon to travel to Birmingham, this time for a meeting with West Bromwich Albion. They returned after a masterful performance with a 4-2 victory. Having knocked out two of Birmingham's senior clubs it was no surprise they should draw Aston Villa next, this time at White Hart Lane. It was no surprise either that, despite Villa's physical approach to the game, Spurs should win 2-0. The timing of the Hillsborough semi-final against Manchester United could not have been worse, four days before the second meeting with Benfica. If Spurs had their minds elsewhere it did not show as a fourth minute goal from Jimmy Greaves put them in control. Cliff Jones added a second midway through the first half and even when David Herd pulled one back, Spurs did not allow it to affect them for long, Terry Medwin quickly restoring the two-goal lead. As a warm-up for Benfica's meeting it was perfect; as a semi-final of the greatest cup competition in the world, it was a comparatively easy stroll.

Burnley may have finished a point ahead of Spurs in the league but Spurs had finished the campaign much the stronger and went into the final before the Queen and the Duke of Edinburgh as favourites.

Great Matches

FA CUP FINAL   **Wembley Stadium, London 5 May 1962**

Tottenham Hotspur 3   Burnley 1   Attendance 100,000
Greaves   Robson
Smith
Blanchflower (pen)

The Spurs team that returned to Wembley 364 days after the 'Double' had been won contained two changes from that which had permanently written Spurs name into history. Jimmy Greaves replaced Les Allen and little Terry Dyson had had to concede defeat in his battle with Terry Medwin for one of the winger's roles. Spurs should not have had any nerves after the events of May 1961 but if they did, they were banished within three minutes of the game's start when Greaves raced onto a pass from Bobby Smith. Twice he looked as if he had lost control but it was all part of Greaves' plan to throw three Burnley defenders off balance and before they could recover he had calmly placed the ball wide of Adam Blacklaw to give Spurs the lead.

Burnley did not take the setback lying down but set about retrieving the deficit, particularly looking to feed danger man John Connelly on the wing. Much as Burnley put the Spurs defence under dangerous pressure they seldom threatened until the 50th minute. Ray Pointer started the move in midfield and when Gordon Harris crossed the ball, Jimmy Robson turned it home from close range. Parity barely lasted 30 seconds though. From the resumption Spurs worked the ball down the left wing to John White. He hit in the perfect low cross. It was just out of Blacklaw's reach but too close for Tommy Cummings to risk deflecting into his own net. Bobby Smith was on the ball in an instant, swivelled and hammered it in. Burnley kept pressing but without any real threat until ten minutes from the end. Challenged by Cliff Jones, Blacklaw failed to hold a cross and Cummings could do nothing but handle Terry Medwin's shot on the line. Danny Blanchflower stepped up to take the penalty, sent Blacklaw the wrong way and for another 12 months the FA Cup was to remain in Tottenham.

Tottenham Hotspur: Brown; Baker, Henry; Blanchflower, Norman, Mackay; Medwin, White, Smith, Greaves, Jones.

Burnley: Blacklaw; Angus, Elder; Adamson, Cummings, Miller; Connelly, McIlroy, Pointer, Robson, Harris.

Referee: J. Finney.

Conquering Europe

Retaining the FA Cup qualified Spurs for the European Cup-Winners' Cup in 1962-63, and although Europe's champion clubs may not have been in the competition, there were still some top names to be overcome. One of those

Tottenham v Rangers, White Hart Lane, 1962. Maurice Norman (right) looks on as John White (left, hidden) forces the ball home for Spurs' second goal.

was Glasgow Rangers and when they were drawn to play Spurs in the first round the meeting was, perhaps inevitably, billed the 'Championship of Britain'. Of course that was inappropriate as neither club were champions but over the two games both teams certainly gave performances that merited such a description. The first leg was at White Hart Lane and Spurs won 5-2 with two goals from John White, one each from Les Allen and Maurice Norman and an own goal off Rangers' captain Bob Shearer. A three-goal advantage should have been enough to put Spurs through but they still had to face nearly 80,000 Scots in Glasgow. Rangers firmly believed they could still progress but it took only eight minutes for their hopes to be dashed as Jimmy Greaves all but sealed the game. Rangers did score twice but so did Bobby Smith to see Spurs through 8-4 on aggregate.

The first meeting with Rangers had taken place at the end of October, by which time Spurs were already top of the First Division with 22 points out of a possible 30. They had lost three games but had still managed to rattle up 54 goals, 19 more than any of their rivals. By the time of the second game Spurs had slipped back, picking up two points in the four games leading to the match at Ibrox and leaving them a point behind Burnley and three adrift of Everton. The gap was soon made up, though, and when the European competition resumed again in March Spurs were back in front, although

111

Despite many chances, like this header from Cliff Jones, Spurs were unable to overcome Benfica in the 1963 European Cup semi-final second leg.

they had surprisingly surrendered their grip on the FA Cup with a 0-3 defeat at White Hart Lane to Burnley in the third round. The weather in the early months of 1963 had been atrocious with many games postponed leaving a backlog of fixtures that was to prove costly.

In the second round of the Cup-Winners' Cup Spurs met the Czech side Slovan Bratislava. By the time of the first game the weather that had so decimated English football had spread to the continent and on a quagmire of a pitch Spurs had been lucky to escape with nothing worse than a 0-2 deficit. They were going to need the full roar of a White Hart Lane crowd to see them past the Czechs but for the first 30 minutes even the extra man the crowd provided did not seem enough. They failed to breach the Slovan defence and even looked more like conceding a goal on the break until Dave Mackay stepped up to drill home from the edge of the box. With one goal scored Spurs relaxed and eventually ran out comfortable 6-0 winners to reach their fourth semi-final in three years.

Before the meetings with OFK Belgrade, Spurs had to catch up on some of their league fixtures but another run of only two points from four games saw them slip behind Leicester City and Everton. They recovered with a marvellous 7-2 thrashing of Liverpool but their next game, against Everton at Goodison Park only four days before the first game with OFK, was crucial. They lost by the only goal to leave Everton favourites for the title and the Cup-Winners' Cup Spurs' best hope of another trophy.

In footballing terms OFK could not hope to match Spurs so they resorted to the physical approach and tried to kick Spurs out of the game. With players like Bobby Smith and Dave Mackay that was a big mistake. Whatever they dished out they were sure to get back with interest and so it proved when Mackay was brutally hacked down after 25 minutes. After Bobby Smith had 'sorted out' Mackay's assailant and the referee had sorted out the free-for-all that followed, Smith set up Tony Marchi's free kick for John White to score from 20 yards. The Yugoslavs equalised ten minutes later when a penalty was harshly given against Mackay and Spurs looked to be in real trouble ten minutes into the second half when Jimmy Greaves decided to get his own back on one of the Yugoslavs who had been kicking him all night. Unfortunately the referee's back was not turned and Greaves was sent off. The ten men left were determined that should not be the end of the game and midway through the second half Terry Dyson got the second. Spurs won the second leg 3-1 but it was not one of the most memorable nights. With Spurs having made sure of their place in the final early in the second half both teams decided to settle a few scores from the first leg and it was fortunate nobody was sent off.

The final was set for Rotterdam on 15 May 1963 with the opposition coming from the cup-holders, Atletico Madrid. Spurs lost at Maine Road four days earlier, the last nail in their Championship coffin, but worse still, both Dave Mackay and John White were injured. White recovered but not so Mackay. His loss was a big blow to Bill Nicholson, who pinned so much faith in the Scotsman, particularly as Danny Blanchflower was still not fully recovered from an injury sustained at Ibrox back in December. Tony Marchi was called up to replace Mackay but Nicholson's pre-match team-talk was downbeat, with him emphasising just how good Atletico were. It was left to Danny Blanchflower to give his own pep talk and make his team-mates realise they were every bit as good, if not better, than their Spanish opponents.

Bringing in New Talent
The 'Double', the FA Cup and now the European Cup-Winners' Cup in successive seasons – Spurs had set new standards but while setting standards is hard enough, maintaining them is even more difficult. Spurs started 1963-64 as if they would do just that but age and injuries began to

Great Matches

EUROPEAN CUP-WINNERS' CUP FINAL   Feyenoord Stadium, 15 May 1963

Tottenham Hotspur 5 Atletico Madrid 1   **Attendance 40,000**
Greaves 2   Collar (pen)
Dyson 2
White

Perhaps it was to prove to the manager just how good Spurs really could be that they put the Madrid defence under siege from the very first minute. Jimmy Greaves hit the post with a header from Terry Dyson's corner in the first few minutes but Spurs fans did not have to wait long for the breakthrough. There were barely 15 minutes on the clock when a sweet passing move that started with Danny Blanchflower saw Cliff Jones leave his full-back for dead. He whipped in an inviting cross towards the penalty spot and there was Greaves to half-volley home. There followed 20 minutes of sustained Spurs pressure before the second goal. Greaves beat the defence but his centre was allowed to go right across goal before Dyson picked the ball up and laid it into the path of John White, who calmly side-footed home from 20 yards. Little had been seen of the Spaniards as an attacking force in the first half but they knew they needed an early goal in the second period if they were not to surrender the trophy without a battle. They went at Spurs from the resumption and got their reward when Ron Henry could only stop a certain goal with his hand. Collar stepped up and gave Bill Brown no chance from the spot. The next 15 minutes belonged to Madrid as they tore into the Spurs defence searching desperately for an equaliser, but it was not to come. Instead Dyson, having the game of his life, got to a clearance first, beat his marker and lobbed the ball goalwards. Was it a cross or a shot? Who knows? All that matters is that the back-pedalling 'keeper could not get to the ball as it dipped just under his crossbar. At 3-1, the game was all over. Madrid were dispirited and for the last 20 minutes Spurs gave an exhibition. Greaves got his second from another Dyson cross and in the dying minutes Dyson finished things off with a 25 yarder after a terrific run at a retreating defence. Spurs were comfortable winners and the first English club to win a European competition.

Tottenham Hotspur: Brown; Baker, Henry; Blanchflower, Norman, Marchi; Jones, White, Smith, Greaves, Dyson.

Athletic Madrid: Madinabeytia; Rivilla, Rodrigues; Ramiro, Griffa, Glaria; Jones, Adelardo, Chuzo, Mendonca, Collar.

Referee: Van Leuwen (Holland).

take their toll. Terry Medwin had broken his leg on a summer tour of South Africa in 1963 and was not to recover, Danny Blanchflower had never fully recovered from the injury he sustained against Glasgow Rangers in

50 Greatest Players

DANNY BLANCHFLOWER   **Half back**

Joined Tottenham Hotspur: December 1954

From: Aston Villa

Debut: v Manchester City, 11 December 1954

Appearances: 384   **Goals:** 21

Left Tottenham Hotspur: June 1964 (retired)

Honours Won with Tottenham Hotspur: Division 1 Championship 1961; FA Cup winner 1961, 1962; European Cup-Winners' Cup winner 1963

One of the true giants of football, Danny Blanchflower had already built a reputation for himself with Glentoran, Barnsley and Aston Villa but moved onto a higher plain with his performances for Spurs. Arriving as the 'push and run' side broke up, Blanchflower replaced Bill Nicholson, led Spurs through an uncertain period of reconstruction and then to the heights of success as captain of the 'Double' winning side. He also skippered the team that won the FA Cup again in 1962 and the European Cup-Winners' Cup the following year. A half-back of immense talent, he knew his own strengths and played to them but was quick to size up an opponent and exploit his weaknesses.

If Blanchflower had a flaw it was a lack of pace but his superb positional play and tactical awareness more than compensated for that. An articulate Irishman, he had his own ideas about the game and often put them into practice, sometimes incurring the wrath of his manager but more often than not turning a game the Spurs way. Captain of his country, he won a record 56 caps, led Northern Ireland in their successful World Cup campaign of 1958 and collected the Player of the Award in both 1958 and 1961. A knee injury forced him to retire but after forging a career as a respected journalist he returned to football as manager of Northern Ireland and Chelsea.

December 1962 and was soon to retire, but the most crushing blow came in December 1963. Spurs had been drawn against Manchester United in the first round of the European Cup-Winners' Cup and a 2-0 win in the first leg looked to be enough to see them through. In the second leg they went a goal down early on but the contest was all but over after eight minutes when Dave Mackay broke his leg in a challenge with Noel Cantwell. With 11 men Spurs might have come back but as there were no substitutes in those days Spurs had to battle on with only ten men. Nevertheless, they almost took the tie to a third game (away goals did not count double at the time) but two minutes from time Bobby Charlton scored to give United a 4-1 win on the night, 4-3 on aggregate.

With the loss of Blanchflower and Mackay the heart was torn out of the team, but Bill Nicholson was quick to realise new blood was needed if he was to keep Spurs at the top and he moved into the transfer market, signing Alan Mullery, Laurie Brown and Jimmy Robertson. Fourth in the First Division was no disgrace but, along with an early FA Cup exit at the hands of Tommy Docherty's young Chelsea side, it was not good enough for Nicholson. In the summer of 1964 he signed Pat Jennings and Cyril Knowles and the nucleus of another great team looked to be in place, but just before the 1964-65 season kicked off he was dealt a devastating and cruel blow. Sheltering on a golf course at Crews Hill, Enfield, John White was struck by lightning. In an instant a wonderful footballer, still to reach the peak of his career, had been taken away from his family and his football club. With Blanchflower's retirement and Mackay still recovering from his broken leg, Nicholson had not only lost the heart of his team, for some time he lost its soul.

As if all this were not bad enough, further blows were dealt when Mackay broke his leg again in his comeback game for the reserves and Maurice Norman broke his in a meaningless friendly against a Hungarian Select XI.

50 Greatest Players

BOBBY SMITH   **Centre forward**

Joined Tottenham Hotspur: December 1955   **From:** Chelsea

Debut: v Luton Town, 24 December 1955

Appearances: 319   **Goals:** 210

Left Tottenham Hotspur: October 1964   **For:** Brighton & Hove Albion

Honours Won with Tottenham Hotspur: Division 1 Championship 1961; FA Cup winner 1961, 1962; European Cup-Winners' Cup Winner 1963

Bobby Smith may have been the epitome of the 'big, bustling English centre forward' but while he relished a hard physical battle his reputation as an aggressive battering ram should not be allowed to overshadow his footballing abilities. Many of his goals were the result of his physical attributes but an equal number were down to his speed off the mark and deft ball skills. A young star at Chelsea, he was struggling to escape their reserves when Jimmy Anderson moved to sign him as Spurs fought against relegation. He was an immediate success, finding the net regularly, equalling Ted Harper's record 36 league goals in 1957-58 and within five years surpassing George Hunt's total number of senior goals. Top scorer in the 'Double' winning side he went on to form a potent double act with Jimmy Greaves, both for Spurs and England until Bill Nicholson decided to pair Greaves with the younger Frank Saul. Smith moved to Brighton & Hove Albion where he was a great success and later played for Hastings and Banbury United.

50 Greatest Players

JOHN WHITE   Inside forward

Joined Tottenham Hotspur: October 1959 **From:** Falkirk

Debut: v Sheffield Wednesday, 17 October 1959

Appearances: 222   **Goals:** 48

Honours Won with Tottenham Hotspur: Division 1

Championship 1961; FA Cup winner 1961, 1962;

European Cup-Winners' Cup winner 1963

The 'Double' winning side was blessed with wonderful

footballers – the artistic Danny Blanchflower, swashbuckling

Dave Mackay, bulldozing Bobby Smith and mercurial Cliff

Jones, but holding it all together, making it all tick was John White, the master

playmaker. White was a slender figure, full of delicate skills and slide rule passes, but

appearances can be deceptive and within he possessed endless stamina and an

unexpected appetite for work. A £20,000 buy from Falkirk, he covered the ground

ceaselessly, forever probing for an opening, searching out any weakness in a defence and

gliding into goalscoring positions with a stealth that earned him the name the 'Ghost'. A

Scotland regular, there was no doubt White would go on to establish himself as one of the

true greats of British football. Sadly it was not to be. Apart from football, golf was the

passion of John White's short life and while sheltering from a storm on Crews Hill golf

course he was struck by lightning and killed. It was a tragic end to a wonderful career.

No team could ignore the loss of such crucial performers and for two years Spurs struggled to make their mark again, although always hovering around the top of the table. All the time Nicholson was working away, building again, searching for that next piece of silverware. Perhaps learning from his days under Arthur Rowe, Nicholson did not hold on to players he knew were past their best, no matter how much success they may have enjoyed under his guidance. Bill Brown, Bobby Smith, Les Allen and Terry Dyson were all allowed to move on, with top names like Alan Gilzean, Terry Venables and Mike England brought in. All cost big fees but Nicholson was determined Spurs would have only the best. He was also determined Spurs would continue to play in the style their supporters had been bought up on – players showing their skills and always looking to attack. It was all at odds with the way football was going after Alf Ramsey's team, more concerned with systems than players, had won the World Cup. The jigsaw fell into place for Nicholson again in 1966-67.

With England immediately settling in at centre half, Pat Jennings and Cyril Knowles maturing into top-class performers, Dave Mackay fully recovered from his twice-broken leg, Jimmy Greaves back to his best after a bout of hepatitis and Alan Gilzean proving the perfect foil for Greaves, Spurs started the season well. An early exit from the League Cup, a competition Spurs still treated with disdain despite the fact that the winners would go into the Fairs Cup, was disappointing but Spurs were interested in the major trophies. Spurs were leading the table by mid-October, but any hopes of lifting the title immediately disappeared with a run of five defeats and one draw, leaving Manchester United to battle it out with Liverpool and Nottingham Forest for the top honour. There was still the FA Cup, though, and once again the competition proved a good friend to Spurs.

Alan Mullery and Dave Mackay with the spoils of the 1967 FA Cup final.

Millwall were dismissed in a third round replay with Portsmouth soon following. In the fifth round Bristol City visited White Hart Lane and gave a stubborn performance that looked like earning a draw until they were awarded a penalty. Jennings saved Tony Ford's effort but referee Ken Burns decided he had moved too soon and ordered the kick to be retaken. Chris Crowe promptly blasted the ball wide. Was Spurs' name again on the Cup? Birmingham City were comprehensively beaten 6-0 in a sixth round replay after Spurs had battled to gain a draw at St Andrews and for the semi-final Spurs were paired with Nottingham Forest, Manchester United's remaining rivals for the league title, at Hillsborough. Forest were firm favourites but a typical piece of Greaves

Great Matches

FA CUP FINAL   **Wembley Stadium, 20 May 1967**

Tottenham Hotspur 2 Chelsea 1   **Attendance 100,000**
Robertson   Tambling
Saul

From the opening minutes of the game Spurs' role as favourites was fully justified as they set about the job in hand with the confidence of a team who knew the cup was as good as theirs. They attacked Chelsea from all angles but their opponents from West London showed a distinct lack of desire to go forward, presumably thinking they could take the sting out of Spurs' attacks before catching Spurs on the break. For most of the first half their tactics looked to have some merit but with barely a minute to go before half-time Alan Mullery surged at the Chelsea defence from midfield. His 25-yard shot was blocked by Alan Harris but the ball spun to Jimmy Robertson, loitering on the edge of the box, and his first-time shot winged its way past Peter Bonetti. The pattern of the second half was much the same as the first, with Spurs attacking and Chelsea relying on breakaways. A second goal was sure to give Spurs the Cup and it came with 20 minutes left. Dave Mackay hurled one of his famous long throws into the box, Jimmy Robertson got a touch at the near post and there was Frank Saul, controlling quickly then swivelling to hit home.

The game was all but over as Spurs contented themselves with a two-goal margin, happy just to pass the ball about and run the clock down. There were less than five minutes to go when, from a rare Chelsea attack, the ball was flung into the box by John Boyle. His cross was not aimed at anyone in particular, just the danger area, but Pat Jennings made his one mistake of the game as he missed the ball which struck Bobby Tambling on the head and rolled into the net. For the only time Chelsea were in the game but there was little time left and Spurs held on comfortably.

Tottenham Hotspur: Jennings, Kinnear, Knowles, Mullery, England, Mackay, Robertson, Greaves, Gilzean, Venables, Saul. Sub: (not used) Jones.

Chelsea: Bonetti, Harris A, McCreadie; Hollins, Hinton, Harris R, Cooke, Baldwin, Hateley, Tambling, Boyle. Sub: (not used) Kirkup.

Referee: K. Dagnall.

opportunism and a breakaway goal from the unsung Frank Saul gave Spurs the upper hand and, although Forest pulled one back, Spurs held on to set up the first all-London final of modern times.

The team Dave Mackay led up the Wembley steps as he collected his third winners' medal perfectly combined those crucial elements of youth and

As Spurs fall to a 3-1 defeat at Old Trafford in 1969, Cyril Knowles tackles Manchester United's Carlos Sartori. Alan Gilzean looks on.

experience. Pat Jennings, renowned for the massive size of his hands, was the established first choice between the sticks and already showing the calm re-assurance and lightning reflexes that were to make him the best number one in the world. In front of him was the man mountain, Mike England, dominant in the air, commanding on the floor. The full backs were Joe Kinnear and Cyril Knowles. Kinnear was just 19 and had only won a place in the team due to Phil Beal's broken arm but in the final he gave a mature performance that belied his tender years. Cyril Knowles was just one of the best left backs around, strong in the tackle, cool and skilful. There were few more exciting sights than Knowles rampaging on one of his overlapping runs down the wing before firing in an accurate cross. Alan Mullery wore the number four shirt that had been vacated by Danny Blanchflower. That was where all resemblance finished, as the two of them were as different as chalk and cheese. Mullery was a non-stop worker, forever foraging in midfield, organising and leading by example. Dave Mackay was back in his usual number six, a living legend, and his mere presence was an inspiration to Spurs. Terry Venables pulled the strings midfield, forever probing,

50 Greatest Players

CLIFF JONES   **Winger**

Joined Tottenham Hotspur: February 1958   **From:** Swansea Town

Debut: v Arsenal, 22 February 1958

Appearances: 380   **Goals:** 159

Left Tottenham Hotspur: October 1968   **For:** Fulham

Honours Won with Tottenham Hotspur: Division 1 Championship 1961; FA Cup winner 1961, 1962, 1967; European Cup-Winners' Cup winner 1963

For Spurs fans of the early 60s nothing was more thrilling than the sight of Cliff Jones speeding down the wing or soaring through the air to meet a cross. Spurs paid out £35,000, a record for a winger, to secure Jones' services from Swansea Town. But what a bargain he was. Speed, trickery, ball control, balance, bravery – some might say recklessness – he had it all. A broken leg early in his days at White Hart Lane might have hindered his career but he took it all in his stride, just as he did many a full backs flailing legs as he left them for dead and hared for goal. A member of the trophy-winning sides of the early 60s, he collected a third FA Cup winners' medal in 1967 as a non-playing substitute. As well as winning 59 caps for his country he played three times for the Football League finishing his career with Fulham, Wealdstone and Cambridge City.

playing short passes one minute, hitting the ball to the flanks the next. At centre-forward was the immaculate Alan Gilzean, week in, week out, giving a masterclass in the art of heading a football, and beside him the master goal scorer, Jimmy Greaves, always on the lookout for the little knock downs, ever ready for the half-chance. Jimmy Robertson occupied the outside-right position, a fast-raiding winger just as likely to cut inside for a shot as to beat his man on the outside before crossing. Frank Saul had won the battle with Cliff Jones to wear the number 11 shirt. A hard-working, under-appreciated player, Saul was happy to play in any of the forward positions. Although not as famed as many of his colleagues he could always be relied upon to give of his best and pop up with a crucial goal.

Bill Nicholson had enjoyed Spurs' European campaigns of the early 1960s and knew that, with the way football was developing, success in domestic competition was no longer enough. Any club that regarded itself as 'big' needed to be competing in Europe on a regular basis. Winning the FA Cup gave Spurs another shot at the European Cup-Winners' Cup but their campaign to win it in 1967-68 was a big disappointment. In the first round they returned from Yugoslavia with a 2-0 first leg advantage over Hadjuk Split. They won the second leg 4-3 but had allowed their opponents to come

50 Greatest Players

DAVE MACKAY Half back

Joined Tottenham Hotspur: March 1959 **From:** Heart of Midlothian

Debut: v Manchester City, 21 March 1959

Appearances: 321 **Goals:** 51

Left Tottenham Hotspur: July 1968 **For:** Derby County

Honours won with Tottenham Hotspur: Division 1 Championship 1961;
FA Cup winner 1961, 1962, 1967

To describe someone as the greatest player ever to appear for Spurs would be to burden them with a title most would find hard to bear but in Dave Mackay's case it would rest easy on his shoulders. A barrel-chested human dynamo, Mackay was the heart and soul of Spurs throughout the greatest period in its history. Famed for his bone-crushing tackles, Mackay was more than just a hard-tackling midfield destroyer though, he was a foootballer of the first order, comfortable in possession, creative, a fine passer of the ball and a cool finisher. The legend was already in place when Mackay broke his leg in December 1963 but was enhanced when he returned after breaking it again to lead Spurs to the FA Cup in 1967. As a reward for his service Mackay was allowed a cut-price transfer to Derby County in 1968 and led the Rams into the First Division, before embarking on a successful managerial career.

back after leading 3-0. With away goals now counting double they had been warned they had to kill off the opposition when they could. In the second round a rough, tough battle that saw Alan Mullery sent off with French centre forward Guy, ended with Spurs returning from Olympique Lyonnais a goal down. With the backing of the White Hart Lane crowd they were expected to go through with little difficulty and that seemed the case when they went in at half-time 2-0 ahead. Although the French fought back, Spurs maintained their two-goal advantage but failed to capitalise on a whole host of opportunities to finish the game off and with ten minutes left conceded a killer goal. They won 4-3 on the night but went out on the away goals rule.

Potentially the 1967 cup-winning squad looked to have the makings of another great team but it did not turn out that way. Martin Chivers was added at a record fee of £125,00 but was badly injured within eight months. Much as Nicholson tried Spurs had another couple of poor years by the standards he had set. In many respects this was out of his control as defensive football began to dominate the game; flair and style sacrificed on the altar of hard work. Success came to depend not only on the best players

50 Greatest Players

JIMMY GREAVES   **Inside forward**

Joined Tottenham Hotspur: December 1961

From: AC Milan

Debut: v Blackpool, 16 December 1961

Appearances: 381   **Goals:** 268

Left Tottenham Hotspur: March 1970   **For:** West Ham United

Honours won with Tottenham Hotspur: FA Cup winner 1962, 1967;

European Cup-Winners' Cup winner 1973

Simply the finest goalscorer in the history of football, Jimmy Greaves was the only player who could take the 'Double' winning side to even greater heights. As a boy Greaves was a goalscoring prodigy and seemed destined for Spurs but Chelsea nipped in to sign him as Jimmy Anderson was taking over from an ailing Arthur Rowe. In four years at Stamford Bridge he was a sensation and was lured to Italy where he suffered a traumatic few months before Bill Nicholson swooped to bring him home. For nine years he was the undoubted superstar of White Hart Lane, his natural predator's instincts, speed, ball control, quicksilver reflexes, coolness and eye for the half-chance breaking one Spurs scoring record after another: 37 league goals in 1962-63 – a season's best; 36 FA Cup goals and 220 league goals – both club records. His 44 goals was a record for England only beaten by Bobby Charlton and Gary Lineker who both played in far more than Greaves' 57 internationals. Greaves left Spurs in March 1970 as part of the deal that saw Martin Peters arrive from West Ham United but retired from the top-flight game after little more than a year.

---

demonstrating their abilities but also on players who were prepared to work hard, no matter how limited their talents. Spurs had to compete before they could allow their superior skills to shine through but there were those who could not adapt to a rapidly changing game. When a hard-working but limited Crystal Palace dumped Spurs out of the FA Cup in January 1970 Nicholson decided radical changes had to be made. Joe Kinnear, Cyril Knowles, Jimmy Greaves and Alan Gilzean were dropped, young home-produced talent given their chance. Results did not improve significantly, Kinnear, Knowles and Gilzean all got their places back, but Nicholson had made his point. Everybody knew now that if they were not prepared to work hard there was no place for them at White Hart Lane. The only departure was Jimmy Greaves, the greatest goalscorer in Spurs' history moving to West Ham as part of the £200,000 deal that saw Martin Peters arrive. It was not that Greaves was not prepared to pull his weight but he was a player who only came to life when a goal was in the offing, and such was Nicholson's desperation to sign Peters, he agreed to Greaves going when West Ham refused a deal if he was not included.

Midfield Strength

Peters was the epitome of the modern midfielder, skilful but hard-working, getting back to help out his defence but also supporting the strikers, coming through with late runs to snatch valuable goals. With Alan Mullery alongside him and the tenacious youngster Steve Perryman harrying opponents, Nicholson again had a solid midfield to provide a sound attacking base. Up front Chivers was now recovering from his injury problems and, with the subtle promptings of Peters and Alan Gilzean, began to flourish into the best central striker in the country. No matter what other clubs did, Spurs still concentrated on attacking, which often left the defence exposed to the counter-attack. It meant Spurs could not find the consistency needed for a sustained title challenge but when it came to knock-out competitions they were at their best.

In 1970-71 a place in the top half of the table was easily maintained with a serious challenge made in both the domestic cup competitions. In the FA Cup, Sheffield Wednesday, Carlisle United and Nottingham Forest were seen off and in the sixth round Spurs secured a hard fought goal-less draw at Anfield, a ground where they had not won since 1912. Spurs' record at Anfield may have been atrocious but one record they were proud of was not being beaten at home in a FA Cup replay since 1911. They lost that record thanks to Ray Clemence who gave an outstanding display in the Liverpool goal after his team had taken an early lead. Success was found, though, in the Football League Cup, a competition that had gained in importance with the final at Wembley and a place in Europe for the winners. Swansea City, Sheffield United, West Bromwich Albion and Coventry City were all beaten at White Hart Lane. In the two-legged semi-final Spurs were drawn against Second Division Bristol City. Spurs visited Ashton Gate for the first leg and came up against a battling City side who took a deserved lead and were only pegged back by Alan Gilzean's delicate header. If Spurs thought the hard work had been done they got a shock in the second leg as City played with a freedom sadly missing from their struggling league performances. They took the match to extra-time and it was only in the last few minutes that Martin Chivers and Jimmy Pearce got the all-important goals to see Spurs through. In the other semi-final Third Division Aston Villa surprisingly beat Manchester United. Spurs went into the final as firm favourites but twice before Third Division clubs had battled through to Wembley finals and each time, Queens Park Rangers in 1967 and Swindon Town in 1969, they had emerged triumphant.

Winning the Football League Cup added a new trophy to the Spurs Roll of Honour. Reaching the fifth round of the FA Cup was no disgrace and to cap it all Spurs finished third in the league. However the shine was taken off the season's efforts as deadly rivals Arsenal matched Spurs' achievement of winning the league and cup 'Double'. At least Spurs had the consolation of popular acclaim for the their greatest triumph whereas, while Arsenal earned respect for what they had done, it had been achieved with a far more cautious, indeed many would say boring, approach.

Spurs' first venture into the UEFA Cup pitched them against one of the minnows of European football, Keflavik from Iceland. They presented no barrier as Spurs won 15-1 on aggregate but in the second round they met much tougher opposition and only scraped through 1-0 against the French team, Nantes. In round three Spurs were drawn against Rapid Bucharest and it was thought they would need to be at their best to beat the Romanians, especially with the first leg at home. As it was a Martin Peters goal after only 20 seconds effectively killed off the visitors and Spurs went through on an aggregate of 5-0. After beating Rapid in December 1971 the UEFA Cup went into cold storage for three months but that did not mean Spurs could rest. Although Manchester United were well ahead in the Championship race, Spurs were in a pack of chasing clubs and there was still the Football League and FA Cups to play for.

In the League Cup, West Bromwich, Torquay, Preston and Blackpool had all been beaten and a week after returning from Bucharest Spurs had lost a thrilling semi-final first leg to Chelsea at Stamford Bridge by the odd goal in five. It was a deficit they were expected to make up in the return leg, but after another see-saw battle Cyril Knowles somehow managed to allow a weak Alan Hudson cross to slip under his foot with two minutes left to gift Chelsea an equaliser and a place in the final. In the FA Cup Spurs got through to the sixth round before going out to Leeds United.

There was still, though, the UEFA Cup and a fourth round meeting with another Romanian side, Unizale Textile Arad. Spurs did well to return from the first leg with a 2-0 advantage but in the second leg gave one of their poorest ever performances on the European stage. Perhaps still suffering from the FA Cup defeat to Leeds three days earlier, they were in command for practically the whole game but a goal would not come and when the factory side grabbed a goal in the 65th minute the nerves began to jangle.

Match-winner Martin Chivers runs at the Villa defence in the 1971 League Cup final.

It took a typical header from Alan Gilzean nine minutes from time to save Spurs' blushes and their unbeaten home record in European football.

The semi-final pairing against AC Milan gave Spurs their first UEFA Cup glamour tie. Spurs' success in the cups was now having an adverse effect with matches coming thick and fast. The first leg meeting at White Hart Lane was to be Spurs' eighth game in 19 days but the real problem was injuries. The situation was so bad, Bill Nicholson decided to recall club captain Alan Mullery from a loan spell at Fulham where he had gone to prove he had recovered from injury. Mullery gave one of his usual inspiring displays but the Italians were masters at sitting back, soaking up the pressure and then breaking out to grab a killer goal. That was exactly what they did after 25 minutes. Steve Perryman hit an equaliser through a ruck of players seven minutes later but for the rest of the game Milan gave a display of the cynical defensive football the Italians were famed for. Spurs did manage to win on the night with another Perryman goal from the edge of the box but the Italians had the all-important away goal and Spurs were given little chance in the second leg.

In the San Siro a fortnight later Spurs gave a performance to rank alongside any from the early 1960s. Alan Mullery scored with a 20-yard curler in the sixth minute and for the rest of the match Spurs were penned back in their own half under continual bombardment. Their defence was breached only once, by a Rivera penalty in the 68th minute, but as much as Milan attacked, Spurs held out for another result on which reputations are built.

Great Matches

LEAGUE CUP FINAL **Wembley Stadium, 27 February 1971**

Tottenham Hotspur 2 Aston Villa 0 **Attendance 100,000**
Chivers 2

Despite the gap in league standings there was precious little to choose between the two teams as Spurs started well in control, but the Villa defence stood firm and as the game wore on so Villa came more into it, pushing Spurs back and threatening to take the lead. Spurs were not their usual attacking force. Perhaps they were keeping something back for the following week's FA Cup-tie with Liverpool, perhaps they were afraid of losing to a lower division club as Arsenal had two years earlier. The longer the game wore on the more it became clear the first goal was going to be the decider. It almost came on the hour mark when a high ball was pumped into the Spurs box. Andy Lochhead, the Villa centre forward went up for it with Pat Jennings and Peter Collins, a young inexperienced centre half deputising for the injured Mike England. As Lochhead challenged, the wily old campaigner gave Collins a little nudge, just enough to knock Collins into Jennings but not serious enough to concede the foul. As the three players fell to the ground Lochhead got his foot to the ball and hooked it towards the empty net. He was wheeling away to celebrate when Steve Perryman appeared from nowhere to clear the ball off the line. The fright forced Spurs to attack and with 11 minutes left Jimmy Neighbour cut in from the left. His shot was parried by Villa 'keeper John Dunn but fell nicely for Martin Chivers to fire home. Any hopes Villa had of coming back were destroyed three minutes later as Chivers controlled a difficult bouncing ball, twisted round, held off three defenders and finished with aplomb.

Tottenham Hotspur: Jennings; Kinnear, Knowles; Mullery, Collins, Beal; Gilzean, Perryman, Chivers, Peters, Neighbour. Sub: (not used) Pearce

Aston Villa: Dunn; Bradley, Aitken; Godfrey, Turnbull, Tiler; McMahon, Rioch, Lochhead, Hamilton, Anderson. Sub: (not used) Gibson.

Referee: J. Finney.

The other semi-final had been between Wolves and Ferencvaros. A trip to Hungary was hoped for but it was Wolves who won through and for the first time two English clubs met in the final of a European competition. The proceedings had an air of familiarity about them and in many respects the first leg at Molineux, in particular, was much like an ordinary league game. Spurs had learned a lot from their meetings with AC Milan and although they were prepared to go forward whenever the opportunity arose, keeping a clean sheet was the order of the day. The match was remarkably even until 12 minutes into the second half when Mike England launched a free-kick to

Great Matches

UEFA CUP FINAL SECOND LEG　　　　　**White Hart Lane, 17 May 1972**

Tottenham Hotspur 1　Wolverhampton Wanderers 1　　　**Attendance 54,303**
Mullery　　　　　　　Wagstaffe
(Spurs won 3-2 on aggregate)

A goal up from the first leg, Spurs went into the second full of confidence and seemingly intent on finishing the contest in double quick time. They attacked from the outset with Alan Gilzean twice going close with headers, but it was 30 minutes before they got the goal that should have ensured the trophy. As Martin Peters shaped to take a free-kick the Wolves defence had eyes only for Martin Chivers and Gilzean. Peters curled the ball towards the near post where Alan Mullery suddenly appeared to hurl himself forward into a crowd of players. He just got his head to the ball to direct it into the net before colliding with Phil Parkes and knocking himself out.

Spurs were in control now, moving forward with menace. They should have added to their lead but the whole complexion of the game changed just before the interval. A Danny Hegan shot was charged down and Tony Wagstaffe blasted home off a post from 20 yards. The goal now gave Wolves the confidence and the second half was totally different from the first. Wolves piled forward and took control, fresh impetus being given by the appearance of Mike Bailey who had been absent since January. Spurs were forced to pull everybody back and resort to hammering the ball upfield at every opportunity. At times desperate measures were called for but, on the rare occasions Wolves did break through, Pat Jennings was there and no matter how much Wolves tried they just could not get past the big Irishman to force extra-time.

Tottenham Hotspur: Jennings; Kinnear, Knowles; Mullery, England, Beal; Gilzean, Perryman, Chivers, Peters, Pearce.

Wolverhampton Wanderers: Parkes; Shaw, Taylor; Munro, McAlle, McCalliog; Hibbitt (Bailey), Richards, Dougan (Curran), Wagstaffe.

Referee: L. van Ravens (Holland).

the edge of the Wolves box. Martin Chivers, who had been most restrained, got in front of his marker to power a header past Phil Parkes. Wolves were back on level terms within 15 minutes. As Spurs were lining up their defensive wall, John Richards slipped a free-kick to Jim McCalliog who beat a startled Pat Jennings. Spurs would certainly have been happy with the draw, but with just a few minutes to go Wolves powered forward looking for a winner. They left themselves exposed at the back and when Chivers collected Mullery's pass out of defence the big man moved forward a couple of paces before hitting a wonderful 40-yard volley into the top corner.

50 Greatest Players

ALAN MULLERY   Half back

Joined Tottenham Hotspur: March 1964   **From:** Fulham

Debut: v Manchester United, 21 March 1964

Appearances: 380   **Goals:** 30

Left Tottenham Hotspur: July 1972   **For:** Fulham

Honours won with Tottenham Hotspur: FA Cup winner 1967; League Cup winner 1971, UEFA Cup winner 1972

Whoever followed Danny Blanchflower into the Spurs number four shirt needed to be a strong character and in Alan Mullery Bill Nicholson found just the man. As a hard working, enthusiastic midfielder Mullery could not have been more different from his predecessor, relying on total commitment and hard work as opposed to Blanchflower's more sublime skills. It took time for Spurs fans to appreciate Mullery's qualities but he gradually won them over and went on to carve his own niche in Spurs' history. A member of the 1967 FA Cup winning team he became an England regular, took over from Dave Mackay as Spurs' captain and led the club to the 1971 League Cup. Loaned to Fulham in March 1972 as he recovered from injury, Mullery was recalled in an injury crisis, scored the crucial away goal that took Spurs to the 1972 UEFA Cup final and then scored the winning goal. At the end of the season Mullery returned to Fulham and later had a long career in management before becoming a television and radio pundit.

Spurs went into 1972-73 well established as a cup team, but went out of the FA Cup in a fourth round replay against Derby County in what was one of the most thrilling and incident-packed matches witnessed at White Hart Lane. With 15 minutes to go, a penalty from Mike England gave Spurs a 3-1 lead over the league champions in what had already proved an exciting match. Inspired by an awkward, gangling centre forward by the name of Roger Davies, Derby fought back to equalise, forced the tie into extra-time and then scored twice more to pull off a quite astonishing victory.

In the UEFA Cup, Lyn Oslo and Olympiakos Piraeus were easily overcome but Spurs found further progress much harder. Red Star Belgrade were beaten 2-1 on aggregate but in the fourth round Spurs found themselves up against it after the first leg meeting with Vitoria Setubal. They went to Portugal for the return with nothing better than a 1-0 lead, courtesy of a late strike from substitute Ray Evans, a full back thrown on at centre forward as Spurs searched desperately for a goal. The Portuguese wasted no time levelling the scores in the second leg and Spurs looked to have surrendered their grip on the trophy when the home team went ahead with a penalty. It was then that

Chivers blasted home a 35-yard free kick and Spurs went through on the away goals rule. In the semi-final Spurs met Liverpool and a 1-0 defeat at Anfield left Spurs favourites to make the final. An early second half goal from Martin Peters pulled Spurs level but as they threw everybody forward, searching for a winner, Liverpool equalised with a typical breakaway goal. Peters did get a second for Spurs but it was not enough and having been grateful for the away goals rule a month earlier, Spurs were now left cursing it.

It was the Football League Cup that again provided some reward for the season's efforts but not without a hard struggle. Huddersfield Town were comfortably seen off but it took three games for Spurs to overcome Second Division Middlesbrough in the third round. After knocking out Millwall, Spurs secured a draw at Anfield in the fifth round and demolished the league leaders in the first 15 minutes of the replay with one of their most exhilarating performances ever. Three goals without reply gave them an unassailable lead and although Liverpool pulled one back, Spurs were through to a semi-final with Wolves. As in the UEFA Cup final, the first leg was at Molineux and Spurs won 2-1, the goals coming from Chivers and John Pratt. The second leg should have been a formality but Spurs sat back and allowed Wolves to dominate. It was only after the visitors had taken the lead that Spurs came to life, but once Martin Peters had scored Spurs again relaxed and let John Richards grab a last-minute goal to force extra-time. Despite controlling the extra 30 minutes a third game looked likely when Chivers, again, popped up to score the crucial winning goal.

In the other semi-final Norwich City had beaten Chelsea 2-0 in the first leg at Stamford Bridge but the second leg had been abandoned due to fog with Norwich 3-2 ahead. The First Division newcomers won the third game 1-0 and the portents were good for an open, exciting final.

Another League Cup Victory

Unfortunately they went into the game with little belief they could win and apparently determined only not to be embarrassed. From the outset they fell back on defence, rarely attacked and left it to Spurs to provide the entertainment. Sadly Spurs were unable to rise to the challenge and the match proved one of the most tedious under the twin towers. The only goal of the game came in the 72nd minute. Martin Peters got his head to a long throw by Martin Peters and flicked the ball on to Alan Gilzean. The canny Scot slid the ball into the path of Mike England but his shot was charged down and as the ball fell to the edge of the box the danger seemed to be over. However Ralph Coates, on for the injured John Pratt, cracked a first time shot through a crowd of players and past Kevin Keelan in the Norwich goal. Only then did Norwich attack. The game opened up and Spurs could have had another but Keelan pulled off an excellent save to deny Chivers before being left helpless as Cyril Knowles hit the post with two minutes left. If only Norwich had shown earlier what they were capable of the match might have been memorable.

Collecting the League Cup meant Spurs had guaranteed their place in the UEFA Cup for 1973-74. Having gone out of the FA Cup, and with no chance of winning the title, the league was of secondary importance as Spurs concentrated on retaining the UEFA Cup until defeated by Liverpool. They slipped down the table to finish eighth. 1973-74 saw them drop a further three places and with early exits from both the domestic cup competitions there were clear warning signs that Spurs were on the slide, but these were overlooked as attention was again distracted by a run to the UEFA Cup final.

Even though they got through to the final it was obvious from the first round meetings with Grasshoppers of Zurich that all was not right. A 5-1 win in Switzerland may look good on paper but if Pat Jennings had not been on top form Spurs could easily have lost to the part-timers. Even in the return leg Spurs spent much of the evening a goal down, looking impotent and flattered by a 4-1 scoreline with all their goals coming in the last quarter. Aberdeen were beaten next and a definite improvement was seen in the victories over Dinamo Tbilisi and Cologne before a fine attacking performance in the first leg in Germany set up a comfortable semi-final win over Lokomotiv Leipzig.

The final was against Spurs' old European adversaries, Feyenoord, with the first leg at White Hart Lane. Determined to build a good lead for the return leg, Spurs attacked from the opening whistle. They created several chances but it was not until the 40th minute that Mike England got his head to a Ray Evans free kick to put Spurs ahead. The lead was short-lived as within four minutes van Hanegem curled a 20-yard free-kick round the wall and out of Jennings' reach for an equaliser. The Dutch took control and threatened to take Spurs' unbeaten home record in European games but on the hour another Evans free kick caused panic in the Dutch defence. Goalkeeper Treytel missed the ball completely and van Daele could do nothing but slice the ball into his own net. Spurs searched for the killer goal but as the final whistle loomed they began to settle for just the one goal lead. It was their undoing as, with only four minutes left, de Jong got on the end of a long clearance to level the scores again. Feyenoord had shown they were a top-class team and Spurs knew that if they were to win

50 Greatest Players

ALAN GILZEAN   **Centre forward**

Joined Tottenham Hotspur: December 1964   **From:** Dundee

Debut: v Everton, 22 December 1964

Appearances: 446   **Goals:** 134

Left Tottenham Hotspur: July 1974   **For:** Highland Park (South Africa)

Honours won with Tottenham Hotspur: FA Cup winner 1967; League Cup winner 1971, 1973; UEFA Cup winner 1972

The finest header of a ball seen at Spurs, Alan Gilzean was a long-time target of Bill Nicholson who had to show remarkable patience before prising the Scottish international away from Dundee. Gilzean added a new dimension to Spurs attacking play. While a top class goalscorer himself, he turned provider for first the quicksilver Jimmy Greaves and then the more bustling Martin Chivers. With his balding pate Gilzean looked deceptively older than he was but his cunning positional sense, deft control with head or foot and an appreciation of his colleagues' runs were allied to great physical strength. Reaching the veteran age at 36 he was allowed to move to South Africa but spent only three months before returning for a spell as manager of Stevenage Athletic.

the trophy they faced a real battle in Rotterdam. There was a battle but it was not of the type Spurs wanted.

In the opening exchanges Spurs gave as good as they got and a fascinating contest looked in prospect when Chris McGrath broke through after 20 minutes only for what appeared a good goal to be chalked off for offside. The decision upset many of the Spurs supporters on the terraces. Fuelled by a day of heavy drinking, they vented their anger on the home supporters and within no time a full-scale riot was underway, with the Dutch police wading in, batons flying. The match was allowed to continue, although few eyes, even those of the players, were focussed on events on the pitch. As half-time approached the authorities were beginning to get the situation under control but the violence was re-ignited three minutes before the break when Rijsbergen headed home. Any hopes Bill Nicholson had of re-organising his players were destroyed as he was forced to make loudspeaker appeals to the Spurs fans to end the fighting. By the time the match re-started many Spurs fans had fled the stadium and the second half was played out in an air of disbelief at the sickening scenes that had been witnessed. Ressel scored a second for Feyenoord six minutes from time to clinch the trophy but the result was immaterial. Of far more importance was the damage done to the reputations of Spurs and English football in general.

Chapter Eight: 1974-77
Decline and Relegation

The events of Rotterdam so shamed Spurs throughout the world that nobody complained when UEFA ordered their next two home European games to be played at least '250 kilometres' from White Hart Lane. It was a stiff financial penalty but the real damage was done months later.

For 16 years Bill Nicholson had managed Spurs, taking them to the greatest achievements in their history, setting records other clubs could only dream of emulating. He had built the greatest team British football had ever known, seen it begin to falter and built again to bring Spurs more glory. But football was a rapidly changing game; it was becoming more of a business than an entertainment, with money increasingly influential. Players were growing more and more powerful, fans more and more demanding. At the same time standards were slipping. It was not easy to find players that Nicholson thought were good enough for Spurs, let alone prepared to show the loyalty he demanded. On top of that Nicholson was a true football club manager, taking responsibility not just for the team but running the club from the top downwards. What he had witnessed in Rotterdam made him question whether it was all worthwhile. After tasting defeat in the opening four games of 1974-75 he decided it was not. He had had enough. He was burnt out and needed a break, so in August 1974 decided to resign. The board, players and supporters all tried to get Nicholson to change his decision, but his mind was made up. It was a sad end to a glorious managerial career, particularly when the board allowed him to just walk away without even listening to his views on his successor.

It was common knowledge Nicholson favoured Danny Blanchflower, despite the fact the 'Double' winning skipper's only involvement with the game since his retirement had been as a journalist. Nicholson knew they shared the same philosophy on how the game should be played, knew he would command the respect of the players and knew the fans would welcome home a living legend. The board, though, showed amazing arrogance, perhaps aware the outspoken Irishman would prove a challenge to their power. Knowing he would be amenable if approached to take the job, they decided to advertise the vacancy, confident that he would not

Great Managers – 1958-74

BILL NICHOLSON

Never can one man have given so much to one club as Bill Nicholson has given to Spurs. First signed as a 17-year-old, Nicholson played for Northfleet before signing professional in August 1938. Originally a full back, he made his league debut two months later and by the outbreak of War was a first choice. He returned at the cessation of hostilities to play at centre half, until the start of the 1947-48 season when Joe Hulme decided his ball-winning ability could be put to best use at right half.

As a player Nicholson was not blessed with extravagant skills. His was a simple game; first defending; second, winning the ball; then, laying it off to those with greater talent. An essential member of the 'push and run' team, he was selected for England against Portugal in May 1951. In almost 350 games for Spurs, he scored just six goals; for England, he scored with his first touch. Sadly that was to be his only cap. Injury forced him to withdraw from the next squad and he was never called up again.

As his playing career drew to a close Nicholson began coaching, working with Cambridge University, the England Under-23s and the Spurs first team under manager Jimmy Anderson. On Anderson's departure in October 1958, Nicholson was a natural successor and his managerial career got off to the best possible start with a 10-4 hammering of Everton. As a player Nicholson erred on the defensive, but as manager he he set about enhancing the Spurs tradition for fast-flowing, attractive and attacking football, signing players of flair and panache, building teams to win games by the brilliance of their play, not by stifling the opposition.

He created the 'Double' winning side of 1961, almost repeated the feat with the FA Cup winners of 1962 and then took Spurs to heights no British club had reached, winning the European Cup-Winners' Cup in 1963. As that team aged, he built again, creating the FA Cup winners of 1967, and then he rebuilt for a third time with the team that won the Football League Cup in 1971 and 1973 and the UEFA Cup in 1972. All his teams had one thing in common, they played beautiful football.

As the game changed in the 1970s, Nicholson became disenchanted – players' attitudes were changing, football was becoming more defensive, the values he prized so much were being cast aside. After a poor start to the 1974-75 season he decided to call it a day and resigned. He left White Hart Lane and was a scout for West Ham, until Keith Burkinshaw asked him to return in July 1976. As a consultant, he remained in the background, but was always available to help. In May 1991 he was appointed club president, a position he holds to this day. In 1975, he added an OBE to his CV. There is only one award missing now – a knighthood. Hopefully that will be put right soon, for no one deserves one more than the man who will always be 'Mr Tottenham Hotspur'. And that probably means more to Bill Nicholson than anything else.

Mr Tottenham Hotspur. Left: 1974, Bill Nicholson closing the gates on a great Tottenham era. Top right: as a key member of the 1950-51 championship-winning team. Bottom right: 1974, with Martin Chivers after Spurs' victory in the 1971 League Cup final.

50 Greatest Players

MIKE ENGLAND   Centre half

Joined Tottenham Hotspur: August 1966

From: Blackburn Rovers

Debut: v Leeds United, 20 August 1966

Appearances: 405   **Goals:** 20

Left Tottenham Hotspur: March 1975 (retired)

Honours won with Tottenham Hotspur: FA Cup winner 1967,

UEFA Cup winner 1972; League Cup winner 1973

The enforced retirement of Maurice Norman left an

enormous hole in the Spurs defence, but it was amply filled

by the £95,000 signing of the 6ft 2ins (1.85m) Welsh

international Mike England from Blackburn Rovers. An imposing figure, lean and hard,

England was primarily a 'stopper' style of centre half and his job was to win a bruising

battle with the opposing centre forward. That done, he could then display his sometimes

surprising control and passing ability, a legacy of his early football days in Wales when

he played at inside forward. A constant threat at corners (England had also played at

centre forward earlier in his career), he was frequently pushed forward when Spurs were

in desperate need of a goal. For nine years England, along with Pat Jennings, provided a

solid backbone to the Spurs defence and it was only when injuries began to take their

toll, that he decided to hang up his boots. He was soon to return, though, playing for

Seattle Sounders and Cardiff City before spending eight years as manager of Wales.

lower himself to apply for it. They were proved right, but were then placed
in a quandary when so few applications were received; most potential
applicants thinking the job would go to Blanchflower anyway. Even then
their choice came as a considerable surprise.

Terry Neill, Hull City manager and a former Arsenal captain, was one of
a new breed of managers always ready to oblige the press with a quote,
happy to express his views, and the direct opposite of the quiet, effective
manager the board had publicly announced they were looking for. In many
ways he was similar to Blanchflower, but with few of his attributes. He
arrived with Spurs lying bottom of the First Division and humiliatingly
dumped out of the League Cup, 0-4 at home, by newly-promoted
Middlesbrough. Publicly at least, Neill showed a relaxed attitude to Spurs'
problems, a fact that probably did little to endear him to an already
sceptical support. Like all new managers he quickly set about getting his

50 Greatest Players

MARTIN PETERS   Midfielder

Joined Tottenham Hotspur: March 1970

From: West Ham United

Debut: v Coventry City, 21 March 1970

Appearances: 266   **Goals:** 80

Left Tottenham Hotspur: March 1975   **For:** Norwich City

Honours won with Tottenham Hotspur: UEFA Cup winner 1972; League Cup winner 1971, 1973

A goalscoring hero of England's 1966 World Cup success, there is no more apt description of Martin Peters than that coined by Alf Ramsey – 'A player ten years ahead of his time'. Elegant and long striding, it took time to appreciate Peters' qualities. He was rarely involved in the hurly-burly of midfield play, seeming to know where the ball would break to and magically being there to collect it. He floated across the pitch, darting runs here and there taking him into space, from where a delicate pass could create an opening. He possessed a shrewd positional sense and perfected the art of the blind-side run, arriving in the box unannounced for a shot at goal or knockdown to a better placed colleague. Quiet and unassuming on the pitch, Peters was not the clenched fist type of captain, but led by example, letting his football do the talking. Spurs fans saw the best of Peters in his five years at the club, before he took a cut-price transfer to Norwich City, where he played for another five years.

own men around him, signing John Duncan and Don McAllister, and letting Martin Peters and Mike England leave. The changes had little effect, though, and the poor form shown under Nicholson continued, even the FA Cup failing to lift the gloom as Nottingham Forest won a third round replay at White Hart Lane.

By the middle of March 1975 relegation looked a very real possibility. Fortunately Carlisle United were out of their depth in the top flight and almost certain to go down, while Spurs were always just below Luton Town and Leicester City. Just when it was desperately needed Spurs suddenly hit form, winning four out of six games, including a victory over Chelsea that dragged the West Londoners into the relegation dogfight. Safety depended on the last match of the season, the visit of European Cup finalists Leeds United. Victory or a draw would see Spurs safe, and Luton and Chelsea down with Carlisle, but if Leeds won, it was Luton who would stay up. On

50 Greatest Players

CYRIL KNOWLES   Left back

Joined Tottenham Hotspur: May 1964   **From:** Middlesbrough

Debut: v Sheffield United, 22 August 1964

Appearances: 511   **Goals:** 17

Left Tottenham Hotspur: May 1976 (retired)

Honours won with Tottenham Hotspur: FA Cup winner 1967, UEFA Cup winner 1972, League Cup winner 1971, 1973

The great entertainers of football are always reckoned to be the midfield creators and goalscoring geniuses, but Cyril Knowles was a man who proved such ideas wrong. A winger in his early days, Knowles was rejected by Manchester United, but Middlesbrough saw he had the makings of a top-class full back and, after only 18 months at Ayresome Park, Bill Nicholson laid out £45,000 to secure his transfer. An effervescent character with a permanent smile on his face, Knowles had an aggressive determination that made him an ideal full back, but his attacking instincts were never far below the surface. An early exponent of the overlapping style of play, he was always ready and willing to support his colleagues and get forward. He would power down the wing before hitting an accurate cross into the middle for the likes of Gilzean, Chivers and Peters to feed off. Another of Spurs' England internationals, a knee injury led to an early retirement but he was not lost to football, proving an exceptional manager in the lower leagues with Darlington, Torquay United and Hartlepool United.

one of the most emotional nights White Hart Lane has witnessed, Cyril Knowles proved the hero, scoring twice and setting up another for Martin Chivers. Alfie Conn added a fourth after Leeds had scored, but even though the visitors pulled another goal back, there was no way the 50,000 Spurs fans were going to let their heroes slip. The scenes of celebration at the end were as great as any that had greeted cup or league success.

After 26 years of top-flight football, coming so close to relegation taught Spurs a salutary lesson. Although Neill's second season started almost as poorly as the previous one, a vast improvement in the second half saw a welcome rise to ninth in the league and a run to the semi-final of the League Cup. John Duncan was proving a valuable acquisition and home-produced youngsters like Keith Osgood, Chris Jones and Glenn Hoddle were beginning to make their mark. On the pitch there was promise for the future, but off it there were problems. Neill was never one to keep his views to himself. That was not a problem, but the manager was only too willing

Alfie Conn: a player of style in a time of struggle.

to make his feelings known through the media, and that was not popular with the board. From the time of his arrival at Spurs, some cynics had openly suggested Neill was just biding his time before replacing Bertie Mee in the Highbury hot seat. With Mee announcing his retirement in June 1976, the strained relationship between Neill and the Spurs board took on a new dimension and it was no surprise when Neill resigned, taking over at Highbury within the fortnight.

Finding a replacement for Neill proved surprisingly difficult with few applicants of sufficient stature. In the end, the board promoted first team coach, Keith Burkinshaw, a former coach at Newcastle United. Burkinshaw had only been at Spurs for 12 months and his managerial experience was limited to short spells in charge of Workington and Scunthorpe, but he was popular with the players, who had lobbied for his appointment. Burkinshaw, another Yorkshireman, was similar to Bill Nicholson – a quiet, unassuming character who got on with his job. He was a firm believer in attacking play, was innovative and never afraid to back his judgement. Although he was in sole charge of team affairs, he was not arrogant enough to think he didn't need help and immediately turned to the man who best knew what Spurs were all about. He persuaded Bill Nicholson to return as a consultant, a move that endeared him to the fans who knew they now had a manager with real feeling for the club.

Although Burkinshaw had all the support from players and supporters he could hope for, the one thing he lacked in his first season in charge was luck,

50 Greatest Players

MARTIN CHIVERS   Centre forward

Joined Tottenham Hotspur: January 1967

From: Southampton

Debut: v Sheffield Wednesday, 17 January 1968

Appearances: 373   **Goals:** 181

Left Tottenham Hotspur: July 1976   **For:** Servette

Honours won with Tottenham Hotspur: UEFA Cup winner 1972, League Cup winner 1971, 1973

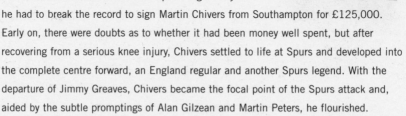

Bill Nicholson was never afraid to spend big money and he had to break the record to sign Martin Chivers from Southampton for £125,000. Early on, there were doubts as to whether it had been money well spent, but after recovering from a serious knee injury, Chivers settled to life at Spurs and developed into the complete centre forward, an England regular and another Spurs legend. With the departure of Jimmy Greaves, Chivers became the focal point of the Spurs attack and, aided by the subtle promptings of Alan Gilzean and Martin Peters, he flourished.

Big and strong, Chivers had a deceptive turn of pace; at times he looked lethargic, but once into his stride, few defenders could catch him. He possessed a vicious shot and an incredible long throw that created many goals. The scorer of both goals in the 1971 League Cup final, he followed that with the two first leg goals at Molineux that effectively won the 1972 UEFA Cup, one a 35-yard cannonball, the other a dipping header from the edge of the box. After almost nine years Chivers left Spurs for the Swiss club Servette and later ran a hotel in Brookmans Park.

particularly when it came to injuries. With Martin Chivers having departed, the burden of scoring goals was expected to fall upon John Duncan, but he was injured from the start of the season and rarely played. Ian Moores was signed, but when not injured proved a disappointment. Pat Jennings missed much of the season and even when John Gorman was signed to cover for the absent Don McAllister, he quickly succumbed to injury. Steve Perryman was pulled back from midfield into defence, but that only increased the burdens on a young and inexperienced Glenn Hoddle. Injuries apart, the simple fact of the matter was that Spurs were no longer good enough for the top flight, as evidenced by Second Division Cardiff City and Third Division Wrexham knocking them out of the FA and League Cups respectively. From the very start of the season Spurs had been amongst the strugglers, and when relegation was confirmed it came as no real shock.

Chapter Nine 1977-84
The Burkinshaw Years

Keith Burkinshaw's greatest coup: Argentinians Villa (left) and Ardiles (right) join Spurs.

Nobody connected with Spurs wanted to see them drop down a division, but for some it had been inevitable, and if the time was well used it might prove of benefit in the long term. Escaping the Second Division would not be easy, though. Spurs were still a big club, the club everybody wanted to beat, and although there were three promotion places to fight for Spurs were not so superior as to think they would automatically fill one. From the start of the 1977-78 campaign Spurs were up at the top with Bolton Wanderers, Southampton and Brighton & Hove Albion. The four clubs battled it out throughout the season but defeat at Brighton and a shock home defeat by Sunderland left Spurs needing three points from their last two games to go up. A last-gasp Steve Perryman goal gave Spurs victory over Hull City, leaving them to take one point from the final game at Southampton, for whom a draw would also secure promotion. If either team lost Brighton would pip them for third spot. In an almost unreal atmosphere, neither team made much pretence of trying to score, a clean sheet being the order of the day. That was what both teams got and with it the one point they needed.

50 Greatest Players

PAT JENNINGS   Goalkeeper

Joined Tottenham Hotspur: June 1964   **From:** Watford
August 1985   Arsenal
Debut: v Sheffield United, 22 August 1964
Appearances: 596   **Goals:** 1
Left Tottenham Hotspur: August 1977   **For:** Arsenal
June 1986 (retired)
Honours won with Tottenham Hotspur: FA Cup winner 1967, UEFA Cup
winner 1972, League Cup winner 1971, 1973

Simply the best. Not only the greatest goalkeeper to have worn the
Spurs jumper but the finest keeper the home countries have produced and at his peak
the best in the world. Spotted by Ron Burgess playing in an international youth tournament,
the former Gaelic footballer had only a year at Watford before Bill Nicholson secured his
transfer. It took a year or two for Jennings to settle down to the demands of the top
flight game but when he did he showed himself a keeper of outstanding ability. Tall and
commanding he controlled his penalty box, marshalling those in front of him and
inspiring with his own quiet, but supreme, confidence. A magnificent shot-stopper, he
excelled in one-on-one situations, dictating where his opponent should put the ball and
frequently getting to it. Northern Ireland's automatic choice, Jennings was surprisingly
allowed to leave in August 1977 when, with Spurs relegated, Keith Burkinshaw decided
to put his faith in the younger Barry Daines. It was a mistake Burkinshaw has never
been afraid to admit. Jennings continued to excel at Highbury but returned to Spurs in
1985 to keep fit for the 1986 World Cup finals.

The players who had secured promotion were little changed from those
that had been relegated and it was obvious that if Spurs were to make any
impact back at the top level, the squad needed strengthening. Various
targets were touted in the press but when manager Burkinshaw moved to
make signings he shocked not only Spurs fans but the whole of world
football. Argentina's success in the 1978 World Cup had largely been down
to a little midfield maestro by the name of Osvaldo Ardiles. When Burkinshaw
discovered he was available and keen to test himself in England, he moved
swiftly to persuade Ardiles that Spurs were the club for him. Ardiles was
keen on the idea, but concerned at uprooting his family and moving to a
new country where they would know nobody and be unable to speak the
language. His international colleague, Ricardo Villa, of whom little had

50 Greatest Players

JOHN PRATT   Midfielder

Joined Tottenham Hotspur: November 1965   **From:** School

Debut: v Arsenal, 24 March 1969

Appearances: 415   **Goals:** 49

Left Tottenham Hotspur: May 1980   **For:** Portland Timbers

Honours won with Tottenham Hotspur: League Cup winner 1973

Throughout his Spurs career John Pratt rarely got the credit his tenacious displays deserved. Forever foraging in midfield, Pratt may not have possessed the extravagant skills of a Martin Peters or Glenn Hoddle but without Pratt to win the ball for them they would not have had the stage on which to display their talents. He always gave 100% to the cause, and expected others to do likewise. Never one to hide, what he may have lacked in skill he more than made up for in whole-hearted commitment and even when things went wrong he never lost belief in his own ability. A frequent target of the 'boo-boys' it was only when he was not playing that his fighting qualities and willingness to battle, battle and battle again were fully appreciated. There can be no greater testament to his value to the team than the fact that he was a regular under Bill Nicholson, Terry Neill and Keith Burkinshaw. Released in May 1980 Pratt spent three years in America before returning to the coaching staff at White Hart Lane. A Spurs man through and through he rose to the position of assistant manager before departing along with Peter Shreeves.

been seen in the World Cup but whose reputation was well-known in football circles, was a good friend and also available for transfer. Burkinshaw agreed to sign the pair of them. At £725,000 they were not cheap and there was no certainty they could adapt to the English game, but it was a gamble well worth taking, and if nothing else a clear demonstration Spurs were determined to get right back to the very top.

That the two Argentinians, Ardiles in particular, were a resounding success is without question, but they were only two players and, apart from Glenn Hoddle and Steve Perryman, the players around them were not good enough to make a real impact. It was going to take time for Burkinshaw to fashion a team to complement their talents and for a couple of years Spurs had to be content with mid-table safety and runs to the sixth round of the FA Cup. The turning point came in the summer of 1980. In Hoddle and Ardiles, Burkinshaw had a midfield as good as any in the country. Steve

Perryman provided the experience in a young, hard-working defence. What was needed was someone up front to finish off the hard work. Burkinshaw signed two men to do the job, Steve Archibald and Garth Crooks. The pair of them gelled from the first minute but it was the promotion of Graham Roberts and Tony Galvin, two bargain signings from non-league clubs, in mid season that really turned Spurs back into a force to be reckoned with. Roberts added extra steel to the defence, forming a solid partnership with Paul Miller. On the wing Galvin added an extra dimension to Spurs' game with his non-stop shuttling back and forth, helping out in defence one minute, bursting past his full back the next.

Burkinshaw's First Success

The FA Cup was the only realistic target and Spurs fans were quick to point out that the year did end in a '1'. In the third round Spurs were drawn away to Queens Park Rangers. Few would have thought they would go far in the competition as a rather sterile contest ended in a goal-less draw, but after

winning the replay 3-1 and then beating Hull City and Coventry City, visions of Wembley began to appear less fanciful. This was all the more so when Spurs were drawn at home to Exeter City in the sixth round. The Third Division outfit put up a brave showing and at times a replay in the West Country, where Leicester City and Newcastle United had already seen their cup dreams shattered, did not seem out of the question. It needed Miller and Roberts to show their more famous colleagues how to do it in the latter stages with the goals

Signed in July 1980, Garth Crooks scored in his first three games and soon made his £600,000 transfer fee look a complete bargain.

Cockerel captain: Inspirational and skilful, Steve Perryman was the perfect skipper.

that took Spurs through to the semi-finals.

Spurs then met Wolverhampton Wanderers up at Hillsborough and took an early lead when Archibald slid home a cross from Galvin, but Kenny Hibbitt soon restored parity. Spurs were having all the play and it was no less than they deserved when Hoddle scored with a free kick from the edge of the box just before the interval. As was to be expected, Wolves pushed forward in the second half, but they rarely posed a threat and Spurs were just playing out time, waiting for the celebrations to begin. Then, with no more than 20 seconds to go, Hoddle tackled Hibbitt on the edge of his own box. The tackle looked perfectly timed, but even if it had been a foul it was well outside the box. Not so according to referee Clive Thomas, always one for the dramatic decision. To the surprise of the Wolves players and the despair of Spurs, the referee pointed to the spot. It was a decision television later proved to be wrong, but Willie Carr kept his composure and took the match into extra-time. A decider was never going to come in the extra 30 minutes as Spurs continued to complain at Thomas' decision and even Wolves seemed embarrassed to be given a second chance. The replay took place at Highbury and from the opening minutes it was clear Keith Burkinshaw had channelled the players' anger at being robbed of a Wembley stage into showing just how much better than Wolves they were. In charge from start to finish, Crooks scored two goals with Villa hitting a memorable third from 30 yards to ensure justice was done.

FA Cup final 1981: Ricky Villa scores the goal that made him a Wembley legend.

Not surprisingly Ardiles and Villa were the main focus of attention as the final with Manchester City approached. Spurs had all the flair and imagination and on Wembley's wide open spaces they were sure to prove too talented for the dogged workhorses City were portrayed to be. It was the 100th FA Cup final and in front of a worldwide audience Spurs were expected to win in style. As so often though, the final did not live up to expectations. City's great strength lay in their midfield quartet of Gow, Reid, MacKenzie and Power, perhaps not as talented as Hoddle, Ardiles and Villa but more than happy to make up for any lack of finesse with simple hard work. From the outset they took control, Gow shackling Ardiles, often crudely, Power and MacKenzie hunting Hoddle down, Villa looking lost. Without a supply from midfield Archibald and Crooks were isolated up front, Galvin rarely in the game.

City took the lead on 30 minutes when Hutchison twisted to head home Ranson's cross and Spurs were lucky not to go two down when MacKenzie's volley hit the post and rebounded clear. Desperate measures were needed and with 20 minutes left Villa was replaced by Garry Brooke, a tenacious little hustler who would give Spurs what Gow and co had given City. Villa was left to trudge down to the tunnel, a forlorn figure, head bowed, just wanting to get out of the spotlight. Whether it was Brooke's industry or Wembley's stamina-sapping pitch, Spurs at last began to get into the game. With ten minutes left, they were awarded a free kick on the

Great Matches

FA CUP FINAL REPLAY	Wembley Stadium, 14 May 1981
Tottenham Hotspur 3 Manchester City 2	Attendance 96,000

Villa 2   Reeves (pen)
Crooks   McKenzie

If the first match had not come up to expectations, the second was better and more dramatic than anyone could have imagined. Just seven minutes had elapsed when Corrigan parried Archibald's shot, only for the ball to drop perfectly for Villa. As he blasted it home Burkinshaw's decision not to drop him was already vindicated. City were level three minutes later when McKenzie, on the edge of the area, caught Hutchinson's knock down perfectly to volley past Milija Aleksic. It was a goal worthy of winning any Cup final but it simply inspired Spurs to greater heights. For the rest of the half they dominated City, Hoddle, Ardiles and Villa matching the City midfield for commitment, Crooks, Archibald and Galvin stretching the City back line, the Spurs defence solid and in control. A second goal was sure to come but when it did it was not Spurs that got it. Early in the second half City striker Dave Bennett burst between Paul Miller and Chris Hughton as he chased a long ball into the box. As the three of them tumbled to the floor referee Keith Hackett decided Miller and Hughton had brought Bennett down. Kevin Reeves had no difficulty from the penalty spot. It took 20 minutes for Spurs to get back on terms. Hoddle chipped a half-cleared corner back into the City box. Steve Archibald turned in a flash to knock the ball down and there was Garth Crooks, getting his toe to the ball and poking it past Corrigan. Extra-time was again looming when Ricky Villa took the ball off Galvin midway in the City half. There appeared no danger as he moved forward but suddenly the ball seemed tied to his laces as he swerved inside and outside the City defenders, drew Corrigan, dummied to shoot and then pushed his shot home. It was the finest goal even Wembley had ever seen. It was the goal that won the Cup.

Tottenham Hotspur: Aleksic, Hughton, Miller, Roberts, Villa, Perryman, Ardiles, Archibald, Galvin, Hoddle, Crooks. Sub (not used): Brooke.

Manchester City: Corrigan, Ranson, McDonald (Tueart), Reid, Power, Caton, Bennett, Gow, McKenzie, Hutchison, Reeves.

Referee: K. Hackett.

Glenn Hoddle, the most talented footballer of his generation.

edge of the area. Ardiles tapped it to Perryman who stopped it for Hoddle
to curl a shot at goal. The ball looked to be going well wide when
Hutchison half-broke from the wall, back turned to the ball. It hit him on
the arm and deflected over Joe Corrigan for the equaliser. Extra-time
brought no further scoring and for the first time Wembley was called upon
to host a replay.

In the five days leading up to the second game there was much speculation
about Ricky Villa. There was no denying he had been very poor in the first
game, letting down himself and his team-mates. There were many who
thought Brooke would be more suited to battle it out with City's midfield
but Keith Burkinshaw had other ideas. He had faith in the big Argentine, a
faith that was rewarded in full measure.

Cup Heartbreak

Winning their first trophy under Keith Burkinshaw gave Spurs tremendous confidence and set them off on another run of trophy-winning seasons, similar to ten and 20 years earlier. In 1981-82, their centenary season, they started the league campaign with two defeats in their first three games, but were soon moving towards the top of the table. It was only when cup-ties began to have an effect that they slipped out of the top few places, but with games in hand they could not be discounted. As the season neared its conclusion, the success Spurs had in the cup competitions began to have an effect. With a backlog of fixtures, injuries and inexperienced young reserves thrown in at the deep end, results began to dip. Liverpool and Ipswich Town pulled away and in the end Spurs had to settle for fourth, still their best position for ten years and enough to qualify for a UEFA Cup place.

The assault on the European Cup-Winners' Cup began with a stunning 6-1 aggregate defeat of Ajax, followed by a hard fought 2-1 success over the Irish side, Dundalk. In the third round a 2-0 first leg lead over Eintracht Frankfurt was wiped out in the first 15 minutes, but Glenn Hoddle grabbed a vital goal to see Spurs through to a semi-final meeting with Barcelona. The visit of the famous Spaniards for the first leg was eagerly anticipated, but proved a great disappointment. From the first minute it was clear they had

Backs to the wall. From left: Hoddle, Galvin, Villa and Crooks man the defence against Liverpool in the League Cup final.

little interest in playing football, their only desire to keep a clean sheet, and they were prepared to go to any lengths, most of them illegal, to achieve that. Even after Estella had been sent off for a particularly vicious foul on Galvin, and Olmo had caught Ray Clemence out with a speculative shot that the Spurs' keeper fumbled into the net, their attitude did not change. Graham Roberts did grab an equaliser three minutes from the end, but it was never going to be enough. Spurs made a great attempt in the Nou Camp to rescue the situation but the task was just beyond them.

Spurs got one step further in the League Cup, beating Manchester United 1-0 in both legs of the second round, then overcoming Wrexham, Fulham and Nottingham Forest at White Hart Lane. After a hard-fought goal-less draw in the first leg of the semi-final against West Bromwich Albion at the Hawthorns, a Mike Hazard goal proved enough in the return leg. By the

50 Greatest Players

RICKY VILLA   Midfielder

Joined Tottenham Hotspur: June 1978

From: Racing Club (Argentina)

Debut: v Nottingham Forest, 19 August 1978

Appearances: 181   **Goals:** 25

Left Tottenham Hotspur: June 1983

For: Fort Lauderdale Strikers

Honours won with Tottenham Hotspur: FA Cup winner 1981

For a player who arrived in such a blaze of publicity, Ricky Villa may not have had the greatest of careers at Spurs, but one moment of magic left a mark on the club's history that can never be erased. After traipsing to the tunnel in utter dejection following his substitution in the 1981 FA Cup final, Villa scored the first goal in the replay, but with the score level at 2-2 there were only minutes left when he got the ball midway in the Manchester City half. He set off on a mesmeric dribble, cutting one way then the other, beating one defender after another before dummying Joe Corrigan and shooting coolly into the net. It was the greatest goal ever seen at Wembley and an example of what might have been.

Signed along with Ardiles after the 1978 World Cup, Villa had all the physical attributes needed for the English game, together with typical South American flair, but niggling injuries and the fact his best position was already occupied by Glenn Hoddle meant he never fully settled. Often on the periphery, he may not have enjoyed the same success as his compatriot, but he will forever have a place in Spurs Hall of Fame.

Steve Archibald gives Spurs a tenth-minute lead in the 1982 League Cup final by slotting the ball past Bruce Grobbelaar. Mark Lawrensen and Phil Neal look on helplessly.

time of the final, the competition had been renamed the Milk Cup with a new trophy on offer to the winners. Spurs were unbeaten at Wembley and in any major domestic final, but knew they would do well to retain their record against the European Cup holders, Liverpool. Steve Archibald gave Spurs a tenth minute lead, but for the rest of the game they were under the cosh, penned back in their own half and clinging on, when Ronnie Whelan grabbed an equaliser with three minutes left. Spurs had got so near, but in extra-time they just had nothing left and further goals by Whelan and Ian Rush gave Liverpool the trophy.

The FA Cup Retained

Until beaten by Liverpool in March Spurs had been in the running for four trophies. Two months later they were out of the Cup-Winner's Cup and had

Ossie Ardiles, the little sorcerer, was missed by fans and the team when he left for Paris St Germain because of the Falklands conflict.

given up hope of catching Liverpool in the league. All that remained to prevent a season of endeavour finishing trophy-less was the FA Cup. At a time when Spurs were playing a cup-tie every week, they had struggled to overcome Arsenal, Leeds United and Aston Villa in the early rounds, all the victories coming by a solitary goal. The sixth round had Spurs travelling across London to meet Chelsea, a tough match seven days before the Milk Cup final. An end to end first half finished with Spurs a goal down but in the second they turned on the magic, sweeping down on the Chelsea defence with one flowing move after another. Archibald, Hoddle and Hazard all found the net and although Chelsea pulled one back to set up a grandstand finish, Spurs were through to another semi-final. They met Leicester City at Villa Park and comfortably overcame their Second Division opponents with a goal from Garth Crooks and a bizarre own goal from Ian Wilson.

Even before the celebrations were over, attention turned to who would be in Spurs' team for the final. Ossie Ardiles was needed at home in Argentina to prepare for the World Cup finals but Argentina's manager Cesar Menotti had already indicated he would release the little maestro if Spurs made it to Wembley again. Then all was thrown into doubt again only 24 hours before the semi-final when Argentine forces invaded the Falkland Islands. As the conflict in the South Pacific deepened, any hopes of Ardiles returning were quickly dashed. Ricky Villa had not been called up by Menotti, but when the big day came, Keith Burkinshaw decided he could not expose Villa to the pressures of playing in English football's biggest day while his countrymen were at war with Villa's adopted home.

Despite the loss of their talismen, Spurs were hot favourites to beat Queens Park Rangers, but a long hard season had clearly had its effect. Spurs were lethargic, lacking sharpness and penetration. Defensively they

Steve Archibald breaks the QPR offside trap in the 1982 FA Cup final.

were rarely troubled, but games are won by scoring goals and Spurs had little to offer up front; no spark, no moment of inspiration to turn the game. Extra-time approached with memories of March fresh in the minds, but when the final whistle blew the Spurs fans came to the fore. Against Liverpool the Spurs players had slumped to the floor in the period between the end of normal time and the beginning of extra-time, but they were not allowed to do so again. Exhorted to remain on their feet, Spurs were not to show Rangers how tired they were. Whether it made a difference or not Spurs started extra-time with added zest and got their reward after 11 minutes when a Glenn Hoddle shot was deflected past Peter Hucker by

Great Matches

FA CUP FINAL REPLAY   **Wembley Stadium, 27 May 1982**

Tottenham Hotspur 1 Queens Park Rangers 0   **Attendance 92,000**
Hoddle (pen)

After the first game hopes were high that, just as in the previous year, Spurs would turn on the style in the replay. They certainly started as if they intended to make up for Saturday's lacklustre showing and got an early reward when a swashbuckling run into the Rangers box by Graham Roberts was only brought to an end by Tony Currie's obvious trip. Glenn Hoddle's low shot from the spot went just inside the post as Peter Hucker dived the wrong way. That was about it for the first half. Spurs controlled the game without ever looking like getting a second, while Rangers' only threat came two minutes from half-time when Micklewhite forced the ball home, but play had already been called back for a free kick to Spurs.

In the second period, Rangers threw caution to the wind and attacked for practically the whole 45 minutes. Ray Clemence was called upon to make good saves from Simon Stainrod and Gary Waddock, Paul Miller cleared John Gregory's shot off the line and Gregory also saw his shot hit the top of the crossbar. Spurs were not totally impotent. Steve Archibald forced a good save out of Hucker and in the closing minutes hit the post, but overall Rangers had the better of the game. If their main goalscorer, Clive Allen, had not been injured in the first game it might have been a different story, but as it was Hoddle's penalty proved enough for Spurs to retain the trophy for another year.

Tottenham Hotspur: Clemence, Hughton, Miller; Price, Hazard (Brooke), Perryman, Roberts, Archibald, Galvin, Hoddle, Crooks.

Queens Park Rangers: Hucker, Fenwick, Gillard; Waddock, Hazell, Neill, Currie, Flanagan, Micklewhite (Burke), Stainrod, Gregory.

Referee: C. White.

Tony Currie's heel. Rangers threw everything forward in a desperate search for the equaliser and got their reward when Simon Stainrod's long throw was flicked on by Bob Hazell for Terry Fenwick to power a header home from only two yards out. For the second time in two years a replay was needed and again the venue was Wembley.

Spurs could be forgiven for two poor performances against Rangers. Over the year they had played 65 senior competitive games and had probably never played as badly as in the last two games of the season. Having got so close in four competitions, winning had become what mattered and much as Keith Burkinshaw wanted his team to entertain, the thought of ending the season empty-handed was too much to bear. It was an unusual attitude for Burkinshaw's team. He had achieved the almost impossible goal of a team that played attractive football but also got results. The defence was hard and uncompromising, built around Graham Roberts and Paul Miller, but with naturally attacking full backs in Chris Hughton and Steve Perryman. Garth Crooks and Steve Archibald were electric strikers, quick, skilful and hard-working. The jewel in the crown was the midfield duo of Ossie Ardiles and Glenn Hoddle. Ardiles was always there, flitting around, finding space, supporting his colleagues, playing neat little one-twos here and there. Hoddle was just the epitome of the perfect attacking midfielder. With poise, balance and perfect control, he could play the ball short or long, dribble past opponents or slide inch-perfect passes through. He invariably struck the ball perfectly, often scoring the most spectacular of goals.

Takeover

In 1982-83, Spurs were hard hit by the absence of their two crucial playmakers. Ardiles decided he could not return to England after the Falklands War and joined Paris St Germain on a year's loan. He returned much earlier than expected, but was almost immediately injured and spent the bulk of the season on the sidelines. Hoddle, too, suffered from injuries and was absent too often. An early exit from the European Cup-Winners' Cup was followed by an embarrassing Milk Cup exit at home to lowly Burnley and the FA Cup was surrendered in the fifth round at Everton. It was only a late season run in which 28 points were collected from the last 12 games that allowed Spurs to finish fourth in the league and qualify for the UEFA Cup.

Another problem Spurs faced in 1982-83 was one they had not encountered for many years – a severe lack of money. The building of the new West Stand had stretched the club to the limit; it left little money for buying players, split the board and led to the club being taken over. As a private company the board, which did not hold a majority of shares, could veto the transfer of shares, but it could not prevent shares, and with them voting rights, being sold.

Quietly, two wealthy property developers bought up shares and when former chairman, Sidney Wale, agreed to sell them his, the take-over was completed. Irving Scholar and Paul Bobroff found the club more in debt than they had expected, and the only solution was to attract outside funds, which meant floating the company on the Stock Exchange, the first football club ever to do so. This happened in October 1983. It put the club on a solid financial basis and was hailed as the future of football, but it was to create problems itself. Many of them were not to surface for a few years but the first came out within six months. The new owners had new ideas, particularly when it came to signing players and running the club on a day-to-day basis. That had been the preserve of Keith Burkinshaw and he decided that he could not work under the new regime. In April 1984, it was announced that Burkinshaw would be leaving at the end of the season. It was a great shock. Burkinshaw was the most successful Spurs manager since Bill Nicholson and was very popular with the supporters and players. They all wanted him to go out on a high note and as Spurs were already out of the FA Cup, Milk Cup and title race, all that remained was the UEFA Cup.

Gary Mabbutt signed from Bristol Rovers in 1982. His consistency and loyalty to the club made him an ideal captain.

Spurs were already in the semi-final, having beaten Drogheda United, Feyenoord, Bayern Munich and FK Austria Vienna. Apart from the Irish part-timers none of their matches had been exactly easy, but their best performance of the season had undoubtedly come against Feyenoord. The contest was billed as Glenn Hoddle against Johan Cruyff, but the Dutch also had a young Ruud Gullit in their team. In the first half of the first leg, Spurs had proved simply unstoppable, rattling in four goals

Great Managers – 1976-84

KEITH BURKINSHAW

As a player (a run-of-the-mill defensive half back), Keith Burkinshaw's career was what one might describe as undistinguished. In seven years with Liverpool, he made just one league appearance before joining Workington as player-manager. He then served Scunthorpe United for three years, sometimes as caretaker manager. When he stopped playing Burkinshaw joined the coaching staff of Newcastle United, rose to become first team coach and helped build an attacking team in the old Newcastle tradition, before being cruelly dismissed in 1975. Terry Neill immediately took him to Spurs where he quickly built a good relationship with players who respected his honesty and integrity. It was partly due to their support that he was given a chance as manager following Neill's departure in July 1976.

He stepped into an almost impossible job. Spurs were on the slide and there was nothing he could do to halt it. At the end of his first season they were relegated. Many managers would have walked away, but Burkinshaw was not like many managers. He was going to get Spurs back where they belonged. He put his faith in talented youngsters like Glenn Hoddle and Neil McNab, led Spurs back to the top flight at the first attempt and then shocked the world with his audacious signing of Ossie Ardiles and Ricky Villa. As the home-produced players came through, he added quality with the signing of players like Steve Archibald and Garth Crooks, always looking to build teams that played the 'Tottenham way', attacking and entertaining. He was rewarded with the FA Cup in 1981 and 1982 but, much like Bill Nicholson, disenchantment then set in. He did not like the way football was being taken over by businessmen, the way the game was changing with traditional supporters being replaced by people more interested in profits. In early 1984, Burkinshaw announced he would be leaving at the end of the season. His departure was crowned with the UEFA Cup, a trophy won by the players as much for him as for themselves. He later worked in Bahrain and Portugal and had short spells as manager of Gillingham and West Bromwich Albion.

without reply, Hoddle rising to new levels, creating three goals, and teaching the Dutch masters a few lessons. Although Feyenoord pulled two goals back another outstanding performance in Rotterdam put Spurs through 6-2 on aggregate. In the semi-final Spurs faced Hadjuk Split and lost the first leg in Yugoslavia by the odd goal in three. Back at White Hart Lane, the news of Burkinshaw's impending departure had just broken. The players were determined to see him off in style and Micky Hazard's sixth minute strike ensured another 'glory, glory' night.

In the final Spurs met Anderlecht who, after losing the first leg 0-2, had overcome Nottingham Forest in the other semi-final with a 3-0 victory on their own ground (a result that would later lead to allegations of corruption). At the time, though, Spurs only knew that in their own compact stadium, Anderlecht would be a real handful and even a one-goal defeat would be a great result. From the kick off Anderlecht pressed Spurs back in their own half, but with Paul Miller and Graham Roberts outstanding, the Belgians attacks were repulsed and Spurs slowly began to play their way into the game, often looking dangerous on the break. It was from a quick counter attack that Spurs won a corner on the hour mark. As

Gary Stevens heads goalwards in the UEFA Cup final at White Hart Lane.

Micky Hazard shaped to take the kick, Paul Miller made a late run into the area, was not picked up and scored with a firm header to put Spurs ahead. Anderlecht had been unbeaten on their own ground for ten years in European competition and Spurs looked like breaking that record until Morton Olsen managed to scramble home an equaliser with only five minutes left. Still, Spurs went into the second leg firm favourites.

Parks' save provided a dramatic end to Keith Burkinshaw's reign. There were few, if any, who were not sorry to see Burkinshaw leave, but he had made his decision and rejected all attempts to make him change his mind. Again many big name replacements were mentioned but when it came down to the final choice, it was someone closer to home who got the job. Peter Shreeve, originally youth team coach but latterly Burkinshaw's assistant and, again, a man popular with the players, was promoted.

Great Matches

UEFA CUP FINAL SECOND LEG **White Hart Lane, 23 May 1984**

Tottenham Hotspur 1 Anderlecht 1 **Attendance 46,258**
Roberts   Czerniatynski
After extra time (Spurs won 4-3 on penalties)

Already missing the injured Ray Clemence and Glenn Hoddle, Spurs had to go into the second leg without inspirational skipper Steve Perryman, who was suspended after collecting his second booking of the competition in the first leg. His experience would have proved invaluable as Anderlecht began the game determined to become the first club to retain the trophy.

For the first hour the visitors were on top and eventually got full reward for their attacking display when Morton Olsen set up Alex Czerniatynski for a beautifully taken goal. With young Ally Dick thrown on in a desperate attempt to salvage the game, Spurs began to pound the Anderlecht goal, but it was only when Ossie Ardiles was called from the bench that Spurs looked like finding a way through. In the 83rd minute, Steve Archibald brought a brilliant save out of Munaron. From the corner, Ardiles contrived to hit the bar from barely a yard out and for a moment it looked all up for Spurs. From the rebound, Graham Roberts managed to picked up the ball, storm his way through a crowded area and blast a shot into the net to earn his team another half-hour to breach the Belgian club's defence.

Both sides had opportunities to sew the game up in extra-time, but they were not taken and so the destiny of the cup went down to the cruel lottery of penalties. Graham Roberts scored from the first kick and Tony Parks then pulled off a splendid save from Morton Olsen to give Spurs the advantage. After Mark Falco, Gary Stevens and Steve Archibald had all seen their successful kicks matched by Anderlecht, Danny Thomas strode forward to take the kick that would seal the game. Everybody felt for him as Munaron dived to his left to keep the kick out. As an inconsolable Thomas was ushered back to the centre circle by Roberts and Archibald, a confident Arnor Gudjohnson passed him on the way to take his kick. It was then young Tony Parks' turn to write his name in the Spurs Hall of Fame, pulling off a brilliant save. Parks froze for a moment while he took in what he had done and then set off on his own mini lap of honour before being caught by his team-mates. For the team and the fans, Burkinshaw's departure added a tinge of sadness, but still the celebrations rang out through the night.

Tottenham Hotspur: Parks, Thomas, Hughton, Roberts, Miller (Ardiles), Mabbutt (Dick), Hazard, Archibald, Falco, Stevens, Galvin.

Anderlecht: Munaron, Grun, De Greef, Czernaitinski (Brylle), De Groote, Vercauteren, Vandereychen, Hofkens, Scifo, Olsen, Arnesen (Gudjohnson).

Referee: V. Roth (West Germany).

I'll be off then: Keith Burkinshaw with his leaving present.

Chapter Ten: 1984-91
From Shreeve to Venables

As soon as he was appointed, Shreeve signalled his intention to continue playing in the Nicholson/Burkinshaw style by signing Clive Allen and John Chiedozie, two exciting young forwards. Both looked to be top-class additions to the squad, and Spurs started the league campaign as if they meant to stay in the running. Depite a fourth round exit from the Milk Cup at the hands of Sunderland, come the Christmas matches, Spurs were leading the First Division. Liverpool knocked Spurs out of the FA Cup in round five to gain some revenge for Spurs' success in their Milk Cup clash, but it was the league and UEFA Cup that really mattered.

After beating SC Braga, Brugge and Bohemians of Prague, the UEFA Cup was put on the back burner for three months before a fourth round meeting with Real Madrid. It provided two games Steve Perryman will want to forget. In the first meeting it was his tragic own goal that finally saw Spurs lose their unbeaten home record in European games, and in the second leg, he was harshly sent off with 12 minutes to go and the game scoreless. There was still, though, the league to play for and with 13 games to go, the title race was between Spurs and Everton. Nine of Spurs' remaining fixtures were at White Hart Lane, making them slight favourites. They were undefeated in the four away games, making it even more ironic that it should be their home performances that should be their downfall. Aston Villa, Everton, Arsenal, Ipswich Town and Watford all left with the full three points, leaving Spurs to trail in a disappointing third to Everton and Liverpool.

Spurs had, at last, mounted a sustained challenge for English football's premier prize, but Shreeve's second season in charge saw early exits from the two cup competitions and a drop to tenth in the league. There was no consolation to be gained from Europe either, thanks to the action of Liverpool's fans in Heysel. With increasing demands for instant success, Shreeve was unceremoniously sacked and replaced by David Pleat, an innovative, attack-minded manager who had worked minor miracles with limited resources at Luton Town.

Pleat immediately set about re-shaping the team, releasing old favourites Mark Falco, Paul Miller and Graham Roberts and bringing in his own men

50 Greatest Players

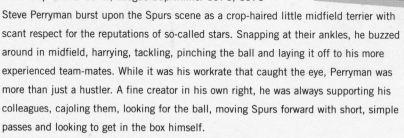

STEVE PERRYMAN   Midfield/Defender

Joined Tottenham Hotspur: July 1967 (apprentice),
January 1969 (professional)   **From:** School
Debut: v Sunderland, 27 September 1969
Appearances: 866   **Goals:** 39
Left Tottenham Hotspur: March 1986   **For:** Oxford United
Honours won with Tottenham Hotspur: FA Cup winner 1981, 1982;
UEFA Cup winner 1972; League Cup winner 1971, 1973

Steve Perryman burst upon the Spurs scene as a crop-haired little midfield terrier with scant respect for the reputations of so-called stars. Snapping at their ankles, he buzzed around in midfield, harrying, tackling, pinching the ball and laying it off to his more experienced team-mates. While it was his workrate that caught the eye, Perryman was more than just a hustler. A fine creator in his own right, he was always supporting his colleagues, cajoling them, looking for the ball, moving Spurs forward with short, simple passes and looking to get in the box himself.

Appointed captain following the departure of Martin Peters, Perryman moved back to play beside the centre half, exhibiting a fine ability to read the game before switching to full back. From there, he led Spurs to FA Cup success in 1981 and 1982. Perryman won a record number of England Under-23 caps, but only one at full level, a clear demonstration of how he sacrificed personal reward for the benefit of the team. One of the most loyal and consistent players in Spurs' history, Perryman eventually left Spurs in March 1986, returned as Ossie Ardiles' assistant before finding managerial success in the Japanese J League.

like Richard Gough, Mitchell Thomas, Steve Hodge and Nico Claesen. It meant spending heavily and a change in tactics that took some time for the players to adapt to. Eventually, they began to settle down with Clive Allen operating in front of a five-man midfield. A radical change, but with Allen on fire and a fluidity that saw danger coming from every position, there was as abundance of entertainment with results to match. Again an assault was made on all three trophies. In the Littlewoods Cup, Barnsley, Birmingham City, Cambridge United and West Ham United were beaten, giving Spurs a semi-final against Arsenal. The tie saw three titanic struggles that ended with an injury-time winner from David Rocastle in the White Hart Lane replay. Early league results did not help Spurs challenge for the title. They were always around the top, but the number of cup-ties left them off the

Chris Waddle took time to settle at White Hart Lane, but by the 1987 FA Cup final, he was the fans' favourite.

pace, although often with games in hand. It's points that matter, though, and when the final table was drawn up, Spurs could do no better than third.

Spurs' old friend, the FA Cup, was the nearest Pleat got to collecting some silverware. Scunthorpe United, Crystal Palace and Newcastle United were all safely negotiated in the early rounds and in the sixth round Wimbledon, fast becoming something of a bogey team, were put firmly in their place at Plough Lane. After seeing off one team that relied on the 'direct' style of play, Spurs met another, Watford, in the Villa Park semi-final. With Watford forced to call up a rookie keeper, an uneven contest ensued with Spurs easily winning through 4-1 to meet Coventry City in the final.

At Wembley, Spurs got off to the best possible start. Only two minutes had passed when a Chris Waddle cross found the head of Clive Allen, who notched his 49th goal of the season. In one of the most open and exciting finals for years, Dave Bennett equalised and even when Gary Mabbutt restored Spurs' lead, Coventry would not lie down. Keith Houchen grabbed another equaliser to take the game into extra-time before one of those memorable Wembley moments. Lloyd McGrath got clear down the right and hit over a near-post ball that Gary Mabbutt seemed to have covered. Just as he went to make the clearance the ball reared up, struck him on the thigh and looped over Ray Clemence for the winner.

The summer of 1987 saw the break up of the old guard continue with Glenn Hoddle making his long expected move to the continent and the

50 Greatest Players

GLENN HODDLE   Midfielder

Joined Tottenham Hotspur: April 1974 (apprentice), April 1975 (professional)

From: School

Debut: v Norwich City, 30 August 1975

Appearances: 494   **Goals:** 110

Left Tottenham Hotspur: July 1987   **For:** Monaco

Honours won with Tottenham Hotspur: FA Cup winner 1981, 1982

The most naturally talented midfielder of his or any other generation, Glenn Hoddle spent 12 years with Spurs, thrilling the fans with the range of his breathtaking talents. Spotted as a schoolboy, he rose through the ranks, marking his full debut with a wonderful long-range goal past England's Peter Shilton at Stoke in February 1976.

Tall and slim, Hoddle's mastery of the football was absolute. Capable of taking the ball down and controlling it in an instant, he could lay it off short, hit inch-perfect raking 50-yard passes or bamboozle opponents with a dip of his shoulder or a flick of his hips. A creator par excellence, he was also quite able to finish with a thunderous shot or delicate chip. Hoddle was an artist not a workhorse and although he collected 53 England caps in his career, he would have picked up twice that number were it not for England managers' pre-occupation with workrate. After 12 memorable years Hoddle moved to Monaco, delighting continental fans with the immense talents Spurs fans had been privileged to witness. An injury brought his career to an end and after proving his managerial abilities with Swindon Town, Chelsea, England and Southampton he returned to Spurs in March 2001, charged with rediscovering the exciting football for which Spurs have always been renowned.

departure of Tony Galvin. New recruits were secured in Chris Fairclough and Johnny Metgod, but soon Spurs were rocked by the departure of Richard Gough and, more damagingly, David Pleat. Tabloid stories about his private life had first arisen in the summer, but when they flared up again Pleat decided to resign. It was a sad and, in some respects, unnecessary end to an all-too short spell in charge and effectively ruined Spurs' season. Fortunately the perfect replacement was available. Terry Venables, a former Spurs' player who had enhanced an already blossoming reputation with four years in Barcelona, had just left the Catalan club. Immediately Pleat resigned, Spurs were in contact with Venables and terms were quickly agreed. Unfortunately, he had to tie up some loose ends in Spain and by the time he took control found a demoralised club on a rapid downward slope. There was little he could do in his first season as he found his feet, Spurs even going out of the FA Cup to Third Division Port Vale. Although never in the relegation zone, there were times when Spurs looked like being drawn into it and they were just grateful when a miserable season ended.

Venables really started to ring the changes in the summer of 1988, splashing out £2 million on the exciting young Geordie, Paul Gascoigne, and then paying £1.7 million for Paul Stewart. It was a sure sign of Venables' intent, but all counted for nought as the first game of the new season was postponed due to safety concerns about the partially rebuilt East Stand. With a two-point deduction and only one win in their first ten league games, Spurs were adrift at the foot of the table. The lost points were later restored, but the damage had been done and it was all compounded when Bradford City knocked Spurs out of the FA Cup in round three. It was only in the last third of the season that Spurs began to show any real form, a late season charge taking them up to sixth, a position that had been unthinkable at Christmas time. The one saving

50 Greatest Players

OSSIE ARDILES   **Midfielder**

Joined Tottenham Hotspur: June 1978   **From:** Huracan

Debut: v Nottingham Forest, 19 August 1978

Appearances: 315   **Goals:** 25

Left Tottenham Hotspur: August 1988   **For:** QPR

Honours won with Tottenham Hotspur: FA Cup winner 1981, UEFA Cup winner 1984

Ardiles joined Spurs after starring for Argentina in the 1978 World Cup. He was a magnificent midfielder with silky skills, wonderful touch, great vision, brilliant passing ability and a toughness that belied his slight frame. Cynics doubted his ability to withstand the rigours of English football, but he proved them all wrong, revelling in the English style, adapting his play and forming a magnificent pairing with Glenn Hoddle. The Falkland conflict caused him to miss the FA Cup success of 1982, but he returned from a loan spell with Paris St Germain and helped Spurs lift the UEFA Cup in 1984 and reach the FA Cup final in 1987. After a brief spell with Fort Lauderdale Strikers he managed Swindon Town, Newcastle United and West Bromwich Albion. But, when Spurs came calling, he could not pack his bags quickly enough. After a short but memorable spell as manager, Ardiles was sacked, but bounced back building a particularly successful career in Japan, managing Croatia Zagreb and then returning to Japan.

50 Greatest Players

CHRIS WADDLE   Winger/Midfielder

Joined Tottenham Hotspur: July 1985   **From:** Newcastle United

Debut: v Watford, 17 August 1985

Appearances: 177   **Goals:** 42

Left Tottenham Hotspur: July 1989   **For:** Olympique Marseille

Tall and willowy, Chris Waddle was a latecomer to football, only being picked up by Newcastle United after playing for Tow Law Town. He rapidly developed into the jewel in the Tyneside crown, particularly following the departure of Kevin Keegan.

He cost Spurs £590,000 and, at first, struggled to live up to the fee, but gradually he settled in, linking well with Glenn Hoddle and displaying some dazzling wing-play reminiscent of a bygone age. Able to beat his marker with either foot he could cut inside or out, fire over a tantalising cross, unleash a powerful shot or slip a delicate pass through a defence. With Hoddle's departure, Waddle moved into midfield, taking over as fulcrum of the Spurs attack and exhibiting a breadth of vision not always apparent out on the flank. Such was his impact that Marseille offered £4 million for his transfer, a figure even Spurs, especially with their unpublicised financial difficulties, could not refuse. He had three spectacular seasons in France, before returning to England with Sheffield Wednesday, later played for Bradford City, Sunderland and Burnley and was still turning on the magic for Worksop Town at 40.

grace was the form of Gascoigne. An instant hit with the supporters, he at least put a smile on their faces and showed enough promise for the fans to believe they at last had someone to follow in the footsteps of Glenn Hoddle.

In the summer of 1989 Venables signed the country's top striker, Gary Lineker, but lost the services of Chris Waddle. Realising their parlous financial position and surprised by Marseille's generous bid of £4 million, Spurs allowed the Geordie the opportunity to exhibit his prodigious skills on the continent. Lineker was disappointed. Playing with Waddle had been a major incentive to his own arrival at White Hart Lane. Again the season started badly and although the Littlewoods Cup semi-final was reached, it was Nottingham Forest who went on to Wembley. It took time to compensate for the loss of Waddle, but towards the end of the season Spurs again began to shine and finished third in the league.

Venables was a manager who relished wheeling and dealing in the transfer market, but prior to the start of the 1990-91 season he was surprisingly quiet. The reason was revealed soon after the season started. Spurs were in serious financial difficulty. So serious, they were even negotiating for media magnate-crook Robert Maxwell to buy into the club. Floating on the Stock Exchange had alleviated the money problems the club then had, but it had necessitated diversifying into related businesses. When the new businesses proved a failure, it meant the football club was left to dole out the subsidies not rake them in. At first, the news was not allowed to affect performances on the pitch and a reasonable start to the season was made with Spurs chasing Liverpool and Arsenal. However, as the rumour and speculation increased, results began to take a turn for the worse. While several saviours were mentioned none appeared willing to come forward and stories were rife that if bankruptcy was to be avoided, stars such as Gascoigne and Lineker would have to be sold.

Gazza's Cup – Well Almost

With league form suffering, the FA Cup took on added importance, not because of the hope of adding another trophy to the honours list, but because the money generated from a good run might make the difference between Spurs surviving or going to the wall. In the third round, Spurs beat Blackpool at Bloomfield Road, thanks to a Paul Stewart strike, and were drawn against Oxford United in the next round. Amid stories Venables was trying to put together a consortium to buy out the club, it was learned Gascoigne needed a hernia operation. Such was his importance to the team it was hoped he could be nursed through to the end of the season. Gascoigne scored twice to help beat Oxford, repeated the feat at Portsmouth and then grabbed the winner against Notts County in the sixth round to set up a semi-final with Arsenal. His injury had worsened, though, and an operation could not be put off any longer.

With many grounds undergoing major redevelopment in the aftermath of the Taylor report and such heavy demand for semi-final tickets, the FA decided only Wembley could provide a venue suitable for a clash of crucial importance to both clubs. Although an unpopular decision with the traditionalists, in truth the FA had little choice.

Arsenal were top of the table, clear favourites for the league title and to become the first club to pull off the 'Double' twice. Gascoigne was rushed back from his operation and took his place at Wembley. It was a gamble of enormous proportions, but one vindicated after only five minutes. Awarded a free kick 30 yards out, Gascoigne hit the ball with such power and swerve, David Seaman in the Arsenal goal did not see it until he picked it out of his net. Five minutes later, Gascoigne was at it again, linking perfectly with Paul Allen to create an opening Gary Lineker could not miss. Stung into action,

Great Matches

FA CUP FINAL   **Wembley Stadium, 18 May 1991**

Tottenham Hotspur 2   **Nottingham Forest 1**   **Attendance 80,000**
Stewart   Pearce
Walker (og)
After extra time

Paul Gascoigne had almost single-handedly taken Spurs to Wembley and even in the pre-match kick-about it was obvious he was more than well hyped-up for the game. Never a vicious player, but one who did sometimes let his enthusiasm run away with him, he caught Forest's Gary Parker with a chest high tackle in the first few minutes. It was the type of challenge he should have been booked for, but the referee decided a talking to was enough. It might have been better if a card had been shown and calmed Gascoigne down for, just ten minutes later, he produced a wild lunge on the edge of the Spurs box that scythed Gary Charles to the turf. Stuart Pearce took full advantage to blast the free kick through the Spurs wall and out of Erik Thorstvedt's reach, but Gascoigne's recklessness had done more than see his team go a goal down. As the teams lined up for the restart he crumpled to the ground seriously injured and was soon whisked off to hospital.

Without their talisman Spurs' heads might have dropped, but instead they raised their game determined to win the cup for 'Gazza'. Gary Lineker did get the ball in the net, but it was wrongly disallowed for offside. Minutes before the interval, Lineker was brought down by Crossley, but then the Forest keeper pulled off a great save from his penalty. Spurs seemed destined not to take the trophy, but ten minutes into the second half, Nayim and Paul Allen set up Paul Stewart to fire home from the edge of the Forest box. Spurs took control, but had to wait until four minutes into extra-time to take the lead. Nayim's corner was flicked on by Stewart and as Gary Mabbutt moved in to head home, Forest's Des Walker got there first – and gave Crossley no chance.

Spurs: Thorstvedt; Edinburgh, Van den Hauwe; Sedgley, Howells, Mabbutt; Stewart, Gascoigne (Nayim), Samways (Walsh), Lineker, Allen.

Nottingham Forest: Crossley; Charles, Pearce; Walker, Chettle, Keane; Crosby, Parker, Clough, Glover (Laws), Woan (Hodge).

Referee: R. Milford.

Arsenal retaliated and Alan Smith pulled a goal back just before the interval, but no matter what Arsenal tried in the second half the Spurs defence would not be breached again and when Lineker grabbed his second the improbable had been achieved. All that remained now was to beat Nottingham Forest in the final and that should not prove too difficult, after all the year did end in '1'.

Chapter Eleven: 1991-2001
Sugar is Sweet – and Bitter

Once the euphoria of winning the FA Cup had died down, attention again turned to Spurs' parlous financial situation. Gascoigne's injury, a cruciate ligament, had not only put him out of the game for months, it was also a big blow financially. The final was always destined to be his last game in a Spurs shirt; a move to Lazio agreed and all but delivered with the £8.5 million his sale was to bring in desperately needed. Venables had worked tirelessly to find the money to save Spurs and eventually his efforts were rewarded when he teamed up with computer multi-millionaire Alan Sugar. The partnership was regarded as the 'dream ticket', the talented football coach at the peak of his profession and the hard-dealing successful businessman. Not without problems, their take-over of the club went through, with Sugar taking on responsibility for the financial side of the business, Venables the overall football supremo.

Peter Shreeve returned to take charge of team affairs, but faced a difficult job with money still tight. Gordon Durie was signed, but early on he was the only major arrival. The team struggled from the start, although the semi-final of the Rumbelows League Cup and third round of the European Cup-Winners' Cup were reached, Spurs again found themselves too near the relegation zone and Shreeve abandoned the cultured passing style on which Spurs had always relied in favour of the more direct game preferred by some of football's lesser lights. It was not a popular move, even though it did have the desired result of staving off the dreaded drop. Shreeve only had a year in charge before Venables resumed control of team affairs.

With the financial situation having stabilised and Gascoigne's transfer to Lazio at last going through, Venables went on a spending spree, signing Darren Anderton, Neil Ruddock and Teddy Sheringham. As so often under Venables, though, Spurs started the season in poor form. Only when the FA Cup campaign started did they put together any sort of a run. It moved them up to finish eighth in the first Premier League table and took them to Wembley again for another FA Cup semi-final with Arsenal. This time it was the red half of North London that came out on top, Tony Adams getting the only goal in a game that reinforced Arsenal's 'lucky' reputation.

50 Greatest Players

GARY LINEKER   Striker

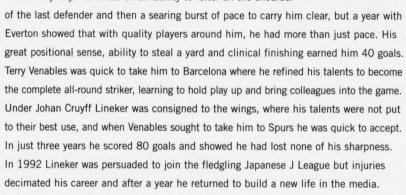

Joined Tottenham Hotspur: June 1989   **From:** Barcelona

Debut: v Luton Town, 19 August 1989

Appearances: 139   **Goals:** 80

Left Tottenham Hotspur: May 1992

For: Grampus Eight (Japan)

Honours won with Tottenham Hotspur: FA Cup winner 1991

England's master goalscorer of the 1980s, Gary Lineker was a lethal penalty box predator who started his career with his hometown club then travelled the world displaying his talents. Leicester's top-scorer for four successive years, in his early days he relied on an ability to loiter on the shoulder of the last defender and then a searing burst of pace to carry him clear, but a year with Everton showed that with quality players around him, he had more than just pace. His great positional sense, ability to steal a yard and clinical finishing earned him 40 goals. Terry Venables was quick to take him to Barcelona where he refined his talents to become the complete all-round striker, learning to hold play up and bring colleagues into the game. Under Johan Cruyff Lineker was consigned to the wings, where his talents were not put to their best use, and when Venables sought to take him to Spurs he was quick to accept. In just three years he scored 80 goals and showed he had lost none of his sharpness. In 1992 Lineker was persuaded to join the fledgling Japanese J League but injuries decimated his career and after a year he returned to build a new life in the media.

As the season's end approached thoughts turned to the future, but a boardroom storm then broke to throw the club back into an even more chaotic state than two years earlier.

Venables and Sugar had taken over the club as partners but when Venables was unable to take up a rights issue Sugar had gained control. Amid all sorts of allegations of illegal payments and other wrongdoing, Sugar sacked Venables. The dream ticket was torn in two and a battle royal between the two East End boys made good ensued that dragged the once proud name of Spurs through the mud and through the courts. The early rounds went to Sugar, and with Venables looking increasingly unlikely to return, Ossie Ardiles was appointed manager.

With the Sugar-Venables battle rarely off the front pages, let alone the sports pages, Ardiles took on a nigh impossible job. As the allegations flew

50 Greatest Players

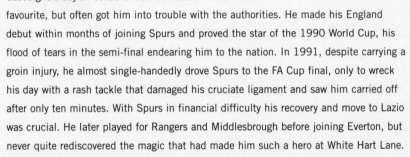

PAUL GASCOIGNE   **Midfielder**

Joined Tottenham Hotspur: July 1988   **From:** Newcastle United

Debut: v Newcastle United, 3 September 1988

Appearances: 112   **Goals:** 33

Left Tottenham Hotspur: June 1992   **For:** Lazio

Honours won with Tottenham Hotspur: FA Cup winner 1991

There can be few players who have made such an impression on Spurs in only three years as 'Gazza'. Signed from Newcastle for £2 million, the bubbling youngster was an individual talent who could cut through opposing defences with one judicious pass or a well-timed dribble with the ball almost glued to his boot.

Gascoigne's boyish sense of humour made him an instant favourite, but often got him into trouble with the authorities. He made his England debut within months of joining Spurs and proved the star of the 1990 World Cup, his flood of tears in the semi-final endearing him to the nation. In 1991, despite carrying a groin injury, he almost single-handedly drove Spurs to the FA Cup final, only to wreck his day with a rash tackle that damaged his cruciate ligament and saw him carried off after only ten minutes. With Spurs in financial difficulty his recovery and move to Lazio was crucial. He later played for Rangers and Middlesbrough before joining Everton, but never quite rediscovered the magic that had made him such a hero at White Hart Lane.

back and forth, with court hearings, players unhappy and a FA investigation, Ardiles was expected to keep the ship steady. Determined to impose his own beliefs from the outset, his reign did not start badly but the loss of star striker Sheringham due to injury proved a major setback. Performances suffered, results slumped and it was only a penultimate game victory over Oldham Athletic that saved Spurs from relegation.

It was a traumatic first season for Ardiles, but things got even worse during the close season. As a result of the Sugar-Venables feud Spurs were charged with making illegal payments to players. Despite co-operating fully with the authorities, Spurs were shocked to be fined £600,000 and banned from the FA Cup for a season. Even worse, though, was being deducted 12 points from the start of the 1994-95 season. With four teams to be relegated Spurs were certain to go down. The 12 points were reduced to six on appeal, but the fine was increased to £1.5 million and the FA Cup ban remained. Sugar was not satisfied and threatened to take the matter to the courts, but that would take time. In the meantime he provided the money for Ardiles to sign Ilie Dumitrescu, Gica Popescu and Jurgen Klinsmann. The signing of the three world stars showed Spurs really meant business and was almost as big a coup as it had been when Ardiles and Villa had signed for Spurs in 1978.

'The Famous Five'

Despite the points deduction still being in place, the 1994-95 season opened in an air of optimism. With Klinsmann and Dumitrescu joining Nicky Barmby, Teddy Sheringham and Darren Anderton, the 'famous five' were in place and a feast of attacking football was seen, some of the most exciting football Spurs had played for many years. Ardiles was a committed disciple of 'the beautiful game' and to him that meant passing football, all out attack and an emphasis on scoring goals. It was certainly a philosophy that provided plenty of excitement and entertainment but in modern football it was not enough. To be successful, great attacking play had to be allied to a solid defensive base but Ardiles spurned defence. It was to cost him his job. As results turned against Spurs so the fans turned against Ardiles and after being dumped out of the Coca-Cola Cup by Notts County, Sugar gave in to the demands of the more vociferous supporters and sacked Ardiles. It was a cruel move and one a more experienced football man would not have made.

Spurs did not have to wait long to find a replacement for Ardiles. Gerry Francis had recently left Queens Park Rangers and was soon recruited. A more pragmatic manager than Ardiles, he set about strengthening the defence and although the quality of football was not as stunning, results certainly began to improve and steady progress up the league table was made. Off the pitch matters also took a turn for the better. Sugar's pressure on the FA over the points deduction and FA Cup ban had resulted in the dispute being referred to arbitration. The three QCs who formed the arbitration panel decided the FA had exceeded its powers. Spurs got their six points back and were reinstated in the FA Cup, just in time for the third round.

After overcoming Altrincham and Sunderland, a Ronny Rosenthal hat-trick inspired an incredible comeback from two goals down to win a replay at Southampton and Jurgen Klinsmann then scored a late winner to beat Liverpool at Anfield in the sixth round. Spurs met Everton at Elland Road in the semi-final, but beset by injuries, were never in the game and were beaten 1-4. They continued to do well in the league though, seventh place far better than anyone could have hoped for when the season began.

Losing to Everton may have been a great disappointment, but an even greater loss followed when Klinsmann decided to take advantage of a release clause Sugar had naively allowed to be included in his contract and left for one last tilt at the Bundesliga title with Bayern Munich. He was followed out of the club by Nicky Barmby and Gica Popescu and soon the array of talent Ardiles had assembled was allowed to disperse. It was not replaced. Espousing dire forecasts for the future of football, and clearly taken aback by Klinsmann's departure, Sugar was not prepared to invest in top-class foreign stars as many of Spurs rivals were prepared to do. Francis, too, was not a man to sign the big names, preferring to surround himself with competent but not brilliant footballers, people he knew and trusted or could shape to play the way he liked.

Falling Behind

The result was a gradual but clear decline in performances and results. In 1995-96, Spurs finished eighth in the league and went out of both cup competitions in the early rounds. The following season they dropped to tenth,

50 Greatest Players

JURGEN KLINSMANN   **Striker**

Joined Tottenham Hotspur: July 1994   **From:** Monaco

December 1997 **From:** Sampdoria

Debut: v Sheffield Wednesday, 20 August 1994

Appearances: 68   **Goals:** 38

Left Tottenham Hotspur: May 1995   **For:** Bayern Munich

May 1998 (retired)

Jurgen Klinsmann arrived at Spurs with something of a reputation as a footballing mercenary and penalty box 'diver'. After two spells he left lauded as one of the finest strikers to have worn a Spurs shirt and a great ambassador for the club. From the moment of his debut goal followed by the exaggerated swallow dive, Klinsmann captured the hearts of anyone who appreciated a master craftsman at work. Prowling the forward line he possessed an almost animal-like cunning, eating up the yards with a gazelle-like grace, snapping up a goalscoring opportunity like a ravenous lion. Goals were his stock in trade but he also worked tirelessly to create openings. After one never to be forgotten season, he returned to Germany to lead Bayern Munich to the German title and then took his talents to Sampdoria. Injuries limited his effectiveness and with the World Cup coming up and Spurs struggling he returned to Spurs in December 1997. Lacking a little of the pace he relied upon, he still had the winning spirit, exalting his team-mates to ever higher levels of endeavour and helping banish the spectre of relegation.

50 Greatest Players

GARY MABBUTT   Midfielder/Defender

Joined Tottenham Hotspur: July 1982   **From:** Bristol Rovers

Debut: v Luton Town, 28 August 1982

Appearances: 619   **Goals:** 38

Left Tottenham Hotspur: June 1998   **For:** Released

Honours won with Tottenham Hotspur: FA Cup winner 1991; UEFA Cup winner 1984

A magnificent servant to Spurs, Gary Mabbutt was signed on Bill Nicholson's recommendation as a promising young midfielder, 'one for the future', but injuries dictated an early Spurs debut and from the outset Mabbutt was at home in the top flight. His non-stop running and hard tackling allied to quick, simple passing formed a solid base for Spurs to attack from with Mabbutt frequently foraying into the opposition box to finish moves off. Within three months of joining Spurs he was playing for England showing his great versatility by playing in defence. Defence proved to be his ultimate position. While not the tallest of players, he possessed a spring-heeled jump and allied to his man–marking and organisational qualities he was an outstanding defender. A broken leg early in the 1996-97 season could have ended Mabbutt's career but he fought back and only retired in 1998 after more than 600 appearances for Spurs. Fighting back was nothing new to Mabbutt though; he had done that from the age of 17 when he learned he was a diabetic.

went out of the FA Cup to Manchester United in the third round and were embarrassingly hammered 1-6 in the Coca-Cola Cup by Bolton. Perhaps remembering that he had acted too hastily in dismissing Ossie Ardiles, Sugar stuck by Gerry Francis when someone with a greater understanding of football, and Spurs in particular, might have shown him the door. Money was provided but with few exceptions little return achieved. More importantly though Spurs were falling further behind their rivals in terms of style. Under Francis the passing game for which they had always been renowned was sacrificed in favour of the long-ball style most clubs, particularly those looking to the future, had abandoned. With unrest on the terraces beginning to take a grip, Francis at last signed the type of player Spurs supporters wanted to see. In the summer of 1997, he secured the services of David Ginola but even then he tried to stifle the flamboyant Frenchman. Matters came to a head in November 1997. With Spurs down near the bottom and beaten 0-4 at Liverpool, Francis at last bowed to the inevitable and resigned.

To everybody's surprise Spurs did not appoint a well-known British manager, but followed many English clubs by appointing a foreign coach.

Stephen Carr quickly found a place in both the Spurs and the Republic of Ireland teams.

Unlike other English clubs, though, they did not go for a high profile name, but plucked a relative unknown from the obscurity of Swiss football. Christian Gross had done well with Grasshoppers of Zurich, taking them to the Swiss Cup, twice winning the league and leading them into Europe, but he was little known outside Switzerland. Not helped by the media with their headlines of 'Christian Who?', his lack of success in top level football and persistent exhortations that hard work would bring results, Gross had a hard time of it in his ten months at White Hart Lane. He arrived with Spurs languishing in 17th place in the league and spent the rest of the season working ceaselessly to lift them higher. With little money made available to him and a chairman reluctant to sanction the wages necessary to attract the best players, the season was one of continual struggle, memorable only for the silken skills of David Ginola and the return of Jurgen Klinsmann to help the relegation battle. Spurs finished three places higher than they were when Gross arrived, but while his commitment to the cause and understanding of what Spurs fans wanted could not be doubted, he never won the players over. When two of the first three matches of 1998-99 were lost he was relieved of his duties.

Director of Football, David Pleat, was put in temporary charge while Alan Sugar, often hinting he wanted to sell the club, took his time searching for who he wanted. Although frequently mentioned, when the new manager was unveiled it was still something of a surprise and, to many, proof that despite

Great Matches

WORTHINGTON CUP FINAL   **Wembley Stadium, 21 March 1999**

Tottenham Hotspur 1 Leicester City 0   **Attendance 77,892**
Nielsen

With Tim Sherwood and Mauricio Taricco cup-tied, George Graham drafted in Justin Edinburgh and Alan Nielsen, two players whose futures at White Hart Lane looked uncertain, but who were to play crucial roles in the day's events. From the kick-off both teams looked more concerned with not losing than winning and the game quickly settled down to little more than a midfield scrap. A spark of genius was desperately called for, but Rob Ullathorne closely shadowed David Ginola, the one true player of class on the pitch, with cover always available if Ginola did manage to escape his attentions.

In the first half there was barely a shot on target worth the name, the nearest either team came to scoring being a flicked header from Steffen Iversen easily held by Kasey Keller. The second half began the same way, but just after the hour mark the game at last came alive, although not in the way anybody wanted. Robbie Savage, snapping around in midfield in typical fashion, made a late, rash tackle on Edinburgh. As the full back jumped to his feet, arms waving, he caught Savage around the face, but there was no need for the Welshman to crumple to the ground as he did. It was a 'nothing' incident, but Edinburgh had raised his hands and the referee had no option but to send him off. With Spurs down to ten men, Leicester clearly had the advantage, but they failed to press it home and extra-time looked a certainty. Then, with only seconds remaining, Iversen took a pass from Ferdinand out on the right. Turning Walsh, Iversen hit a low centre across the six-yard box. Keller got his hand to it, but the ball popped up for Nielsen to dive in amongst a posse of Leicester defenders and head home.

Tottenham Hotspur: Walker, Carr, Edinburgh, Freund, Campbell, Vega, Anderton, Nielsen, Iversen, Ferdinand, Ginola (Sinton).

Leicester City: Keller, Ullathorne, Guppy, Elliott, Walsh, Taggart, Lennon, Izzet, Cottee, Savage (Zagorakis), Heskey (Marshall).

Referee: T. Heilbrun.

---

eight years in control Sugar had learned nothing about what Spurs meant. The new man was George Graham, a former player and manager of Arsenal. Having dismissed Terry Venables amid allegations of wrongdoing, Sugar had turned to a man banned from the game for a year for taking 'bungs' while in charge of Arsenal. It was an appointment that polarised Spurs supporters, some grateful that a man with a proven track record was in charge, others aghast that an advocate of defensive football should be in control of the club.

50 Greatest Players

DAVID GINOLA   Winger/ Midfielder

Joined Tottenham Hotspur: July 1997   **From:** Newcastle United

Debut: v Manchester United, 10 August 1997

Appearances: 127   **Goals:** 22

Left Tottenham Hotspur: August 2000   **For:** Aston Villa

Honours won with Tottenham Hotspur: League Cup winner 1999

The signing of David Ginola was a surprise to close followers of Spurs for he was not the type of player one would normally associate with Gerry Francis. Perhaps it was the fans' demands for a player of flair and elegance that forced Francis to pay £2.5 million for a player who could both delight and frustrate in a matter of seconds. Whatever the reasoning behind his signing, for three years Ginola was a beacon of light at an otherwise dark and dismal White Hart Lane. Not renowned for his hard work, Ginola only came to life when he had the ball, but he was an artist, not an artisan; he knew he was at his most effective going forward, not working back. With his long locks flowing there was no more exciting sight than Ginola bringing the ball under control with a trademark chest-trap, killing it instantly, dragging it back with his sole, then leaving his marker for dead with a burst of pace, before finishing with a cross or vicious shot. Even the arch pragmatist, George Graham, no matter how much he criticised Ginola, found it hard to leave him out. Graham at last got his way and sold Ginola to Aston Villa, but it was a decision he was never allowed to forget.

No matter what people thought of Graham's football philosophy, if he could help the club lift some silverware he might get the fans behind him, but he had to do that quickly. Spurs had already beaten Brentford in the second round of the Worthington Cup and soon accounted for Northampton Town, Liverpool and Manchester United, albeit playing with a team packed with reserves. Two dour battles with Wimbledon were settled by a Steffen Iversen goal in the semi-final and Spurs were through to a final with Leicester City.

Winning the Worthington Cup and getting Spurs back into Europe was as good a start as Graham could hope for, but it was going to take more than a hard fought, many would say, boring, victory in what had become a fourth rate competition to win Spurs followers over. Now, if the FA Cup could be captured as well things might be different. After beating Watford, Wimbledon and Leeds United, Graham's men had seen off Barnsley just five days before the Worthington Cup final. With only Newcastle United barring the way a quick return to Wembley seemed a definite possibility.

In the Old Trafford semi-final, Spurs were always second best. If they had been awarded a penalty when Dabizas blatantly handled a cross, the result might have been different, but two extra-time goals from Alan Shearer were no more than Newcastle deserved. Still, mid-table in the league was an improvement and there was always the UEFA Cup to look forward to.

Cup competitions had provided the highspots of Graham's first season in charge. In his second they were to provide the low points. In the UEFA Cup Spurs easily defeated Zimbru Chisinau in the first round first leg by 3-0 and then stifled the limited talents of the Moldovans in the second leg to secure a goal-less draw. In the second round a Steffen Iversen penalty gave Spurs a first leg lead over Kaiserslautern, but they should have had more and would have if they had really taken the game to the Germans. For the second leg Graham left David Ginola on the bench, a baffling decision when he was the one man who might conjure up a crucial away goal. As it was Spurs concentrated on defence, but on the occasions they did get forward it was clear that the German defence was less than secure. Had Spurs tried to win the game rather than hold on for the draw they would have done so, but in the last two minutes the Germans scored twice for a quite unexpected win. In the Worthington Cup Spurs beat Crewe Alexandra but were then humbled 1-4 by First Division Fulham, and in the FA Cup another inept performance saw them trounced 1-6 by Newcastle United in a third round replay. In the Premiership another mid-table position was the best Spurs could do.

One for the future: Simon Davies is already a regular for Wales.

Despite investing a club record £11 million in the talents of Sergei Rebrov, David Ginola was sold to Aston Villa and Spurs started the 2000-01 season with little expectation of making any real impression in the Premiership. Qualifying for the Champions League seemed a pipe-dream, the peak of Sugar and Graham's ambitions being to win a cup or finish high enough to make it into the UEFA Cup. One route to that was rapidly cut off when Birmingham City put Spurs out of the Worthington Cup on another of those nights that are best forgotten. Only the FA Cup remained and after scraping a late 1-0 win at Leyton

50 Greatest Players

TEDDY SHERINGHAM   **Striker**

Joined Tottenham Hotspur: August 1992 **From:** Nottingham Forest

                               May 2001 **From:** Manchester United

Debut: v Ipswich Town, 30 August 1992

Appearances: 197   **Goals:** 98

Left Spurs: June 1997   **For:** Manchester United

Throughout his career, Teddy Sheringham has stood out, not just as a goalscorer par excellence but as the all-round striker essential in the modern game. With supreme confidence in his ability, he has developed as the perfect link between midfield and attack, dropping back where his markers fear to follow and finding the space to carve out openings or to play measured one-twos that leave him advancing on goal.

  After starting with Millwall, Sheringham honed his talents with a year at Nottingham Forest, before Terry Venables signed him for Spurs, the team he supported as a boy. Top-scorer in his first two seasons at White Hart Lane, the arrival of Jurgen Klinsmann allowed Sheringham to display his immense talents, setting up chances for the mercurial German. When Klinsmann departed, Chris Armstrong was to benefit from Sheringham's razor sharp football brain. Unhappy with the Gerry Francis style of football that all too often left him watching the ball fly over his head, and eager to win some big trophies, Sheringham made his feelings known and was rewarded with a surprising cut-price move to Manchester United. At Old Trafford he collected all the trophies he could hope for, before Glenn Hoddle persuaded him to return to White Hart Lane.

Orient, Spurs looked to be out of that as they trailed 0-2 early in the second half at Charlton Athletic, before a remarkable turnaround saw them go through 4-2. Stockport County were then defeated, but before the sixth round clash with West Ham United, big changes were made off the field as Sugar at last sold a controlling interest in the club to the investment company ENIC.

  Sugar felt he had never received the credit he deserved for baling Spurs out of trouble in 1991, but football fans are renowned for their short memories. He had never managed to win them over with his brusque manner and was always viewed as a man who looked upon the club as a business venture rather than an object of affection. The new owners are also businessmen, but they are also long-standing supporters who know what the club means to those who pay for the privilege of watching the team play.

Sergei Rebrov, Spurs' record signing, in action for the Ukraine against England.

Return of the Prodigal

With the arrival of ENIC, stories were rife that George Graham's tenure as manager did not have long to go. Graham seemed to have ensured he would at least see the season out after a stunning 3-2 victory at Upton Park put Spurs into a FA Cup semi-final with Arsenal, but as a famous former Spurs player has oft been quoted as saying, 'football is a funny game'. The exact events are a matter of litigation, but just before the Old Trafford semi-final Graham was dismissed.

Initially it was expected David Pleat would again step in as caretaker manager, but only days before the most important match of Spurs' season, Hoddle took over. He had no time to influence events, but at least got a first hand view of how much work there was to do as Arsenal ran out easier winners than the 1-2 scoreline would suggest.

Hoddle had inherited a squad containing some good players, many of them young and with great potential, but lacking in depth and experience. Identifying the players he wanted was not difficult, but Hoddle was not helped by the way captain Sol Campbell toyed with the club before announcing he was going to take advantage of the Bosman decision and leave. It was a serious blow, made all the more painful when Campbell signed for Arsenal.

The Future

Glenn Hoddle is a man who knows Spurs. He supported the club as a boy, grew up at Spurs and has an affinity with the fans. He knows what it means to the fans and knows what the supporters want to see. Over the last few years Spurs have fallen behind the likes of Manchester United, Arsenal, Chelsea, Leeds United and Liverpool. They are a club who should be there challenging the best. If they are ever to do so again they could not have a better man to take them back to the top.

THE ESSENTIAL HISTORY OF
TOTTENHAM HOTSPUR

CLUB STATISTICS

The Tottenham Hotspur Directory

Origins

- Formed by a group of Tottenham schoolboy cricketers in 1882 to provide a winter pastime, the club took the name Hotspur Football Club from its cricket predecessor and for the first few years played friendly and minor cup games only.

- In 1892-93 the club played in league competition, the short-lived Southern Alliance, for the first time but then reverted to playing friendly games until, having turned professional in 1895, it was elected to the Southern League in 1896.

- In 1908 it was elected to the Second Division of the Football League and remained there until the formation of the Premier League in 1992

Honours

- Football League Champions: 1950-51, 1960-61

- Division Two (old) Champions: 1919-20, 1949-50

- Southern League Champions: 1899-1900

- FA Cup Winners: 1901, 1921, 1961, 1962, 1967, 1981, 1982, 1991

- League Cup winners: 1971, 1973

- Worthington Cup winners: 1999

- European Cup-Winners' Cup winners: 1963

- UEFA Cup winners: 1972, 1984

- FA Cup Runners-up 1987

- League (Milk) Cup Runners-up 1982

- FA Charity Shield winners: 1920-21, 1951-52, 1961-62, 1962-63, 1967-68 (joint), 1981-82 (joint), 1991-92 (joint).

League and Premiership Record

- Southern League 1896-1908

- Football League Division Two (old) 1908-09, 1919-20, 1928-33, 1935-50, 1977-78

- Football League Division One (old) 1909-15, 1920-28, 1933-35, 1950-77, 1978-92

- FA Premier League 1992-date

Records

- Highest attendance: 75,038 v Sunderland, FA Cup 6th Rd 5 March 1938

- Highest Football League/Premiership position: Champions 1950-51, 1960-61

- Record Football League/Premiership victory: 9-0 v Bristol Rovers, Football League Division Two, 22 October 1977

- Record Football League/Premiership defeat: 0-7 v Liverpool, Football League Division One, 2 September 1978

- Record Cup victory: 13-2 v Crewe Alexandra, FA Cup 4th rd rep, 3 February 1960

- Record Cup defeat: 0-5 v Stoke FA Cup 1st Rd, 1 February 1896; 1-6 v Huddersfield Town, FA Cup 6th Rd, 3 March 1928; 1-6 v Bolton Wanderers, Coca-Cola Cup 4th Rd, 27 November 1996; 1-6 v Newcastle United, FA Cup 3rd Rd rep, 23 December 1999

- Most Football League/Premiership points (2 for a win): 70, Football League Division Two 1919-20

- Most Football League/Premiership points (3 for a win): 77, Football League Division One 1984-85

Clive Allen in flight (with the help of Coventry City's Trevor Peake) in the 1987 FA Cup final. Allen scored a record 49 goals that season.

- Most Football League/Premiership goals: 115, Football League Division One 1960-61

- Record appearances (all competitive games): 862, (4) Steve Perryman

- Most goals for club (all competitive games): 268, Jimmy Greaves

- Most goals in one season (all competitive games): 49, Clive Allen 1986-87

- Most goals in one match (competitive games): 5 Ted Harper v Reading, Football League Division

Two, 30 August 1930; Alfie Stokes v Birmingham City, Football League Division One, 18 September 1957; Les Allen v Crewe Alexandra, FA Cup 4th Rd replay, 3 February 1960,

- Most capped player: Pat Jennings (Northern Ireland) 75

- Record transfer fee paid: £11,000,000 to Dynamo Kiev for Sergei Rebrov, May 2000

- Record transfer fee received: £5,500,000 from Lazio for Paul Gascoigne, June 1992

'You never know, you too could manage Spurs one day.' Terry Venables and George Graham share a joke before the 1991 FA Cup semi final.

Managers

- 1898-99 Frank Brettell
- 1899-1907 John Cameron
- 1907-08 Fred Kirkham
- 1912-27 Peter McWilliam
- 1927-29 Billy Minter
- 1930-35 Percy Smith
- 1935-38 Jack Tresadern
- 1938-42 Peter McWilliam
- 1942-46 Arthur Turner (secretary/manager)
- 1946-49 Joe Hulme
- 1949-55 Arthur Rowe
- 1955-58 Jimmy Anderson
- 1958-74 Bill Nicholson
- 1974-76 Terry Neill
- 1976-84 Keith Burkinshaw
- 1984-86 Peter Shreeve
- 1986-87 David Pleat
- 1987-91 Terry Venables
- 1991-92 Peter Shreeve
- 1992-93 Doug Livermore (First team coach)
- 1993-94 Ossie Ardiles
- 1994-97 Gerry Francis
- 1997-98 Christian Gross (Head coach)
- 1998-2001 George Graham
- 2001 - Glenn Hoddle

Club Information

- Address: Bill Nicholson Way, 748 High Road, Tottenham, London N17 0AP
- Tel: 020 8365 5000 Fax: 020 8365 5005
- email address: mail@tottenhamhotspur.co.uk
- Members office: 020 8365 5150
- Spurs ticket office: 08700 112222
- Ticket office recorded info: 09068 100505
- Spursline: 09068 100500
- Website: www.spurs.co.uk
- Mail order line: 020 8804 7888
- Ground capacity: 36,257
- Non-Executive Chairman: Daniel Levy
- Vice-Chairman: David Buchler
- Director of Football: David Pleat
- Club President: Bill Nicholson
- Year formed: 1882 as Hotspur FC, 1885 renamed Tottenham Hotspur FC
- Turned professional: 1895
- Limited Company, Tottenham Hotspur Football & Athletic Company, formed 1898
- Club nickname: Spurs
- Previous Grounds: 1882-1888 Tottenham Marshes, 1888-1899 Northumberland Park, 1899 to date White Hart Lane
- Colours: White shirts, navy shorts, navy socks
- Change Colours: Argentina blue shirts, white shorts, white socks

50 Greatest Players

Over the years, many wonderful players have turned out for Spurs. I have been fortunate to watch many of them but there are others who have played in the club's 119-year history that one can only learn about from contemporary reports. This makes selecting a Top 50 very difficult, especially since football has changed so much since the early days on Tottenham Marshes. Every reader will have his or her own opinion, but the following is my personal pecking order of the 50 greatest players selected for this book.

No.1 Dave Mackay (Half back) – 321 appearances, 51 goals. A mighty oak and the heart of the 'Double' side. A terrific tackler who battled for every inch of the midfield and never gave up. (see page 122).

No.2 Ron Burgess (Wing half) – 321 appearances, 16 goals. A human dynamo captain who dominated the half back line. He was forever exhorting the 'push and run' team to go forward. (see page 88).

No.3 Jack Jull (Full back) – at least 150 appearances, over 24 goals. Spurs' first captain was a strong and fearless defender (see page 17).

No.4 Arthur Grimsdell (Half back) – 362 appearances, 27 goals. Described as a complete player, he was an aggressive, determined wing half with a blistering long-range shot (see page 62).

No.5 Danny Blanchflower (Half back) – 384 appearances, 21 goals. The greatest attacking wing half of all time, an inspirational captain, faultless in his distribution and tactical nous. (see page 115).

No.6 Steve Perryman (Midfielder/Defender) – 866 appearances, 39 goals. A loyal captain, a fine tackler and a skilful midfield hustler. (see page 162).

No.7 Glenn Hoddle (Midfielder) – 494 appearances, 110 goals. Amazing ball control, visionary passing and a genius with a dead ball, he was the most creative English player ever seen. (see page 164).

No.8 Jimmy Greaves (Inside forward) – 381 appearances, 268 goals. The ultimate cool poacher was Spurs' greatest ever goalscorer. (see page 123).

No.9 Cliff Jones (Winger) – 380 appearances, 159 goals. The Welsh international was a lightning dribbler on either flank and was deadly in the area especially with his head. (see page 121).

No.10 Vivian Woodward (Centre forward) – 156 appearances, 68 goals. A cultured, elegant style set him apart from forwards of his time (see page 44).

No.11 Stanley Briggs (Half back) – 111 appearances, 8 goals. As stubborn an amateur as he was a defender, he taught the pros how to turn defence into attack (see page 18).

No.12 Pat Jennings (Goalkeeper) – 596 appearances, 1 goal. One of the greatest ever goalkeepers, confident, dominant and totally unflappable (see page 142).

No.13 Ossie Ardiles (Midfielder) – 315 appearances, 25 goals. The slight Argentinian was a gem. He gave total commitment, had magnificent control and his incisive passing made countless goals (see page 165).

No.14 Cyril Knowles (Left back) – 511 appearances, 17 goals. An overlapping full back, he brought great style to the art of defending, yearning to get forward and hitting accurate crosses (see page 138).

No.15 John White (Inside forward) – 222 appearances, 48 goals. Earning the nickname 'The Ghost' through his delicate and subtle play, White's tragic death was Spurs' great loss (see page 117).

No.16 Alan Gilzean (Forward) – 446 appearances, 134 goals. The Scottish international goalscorer was a renowned header of the ball, but was equally deft with his feet. Developed a masterly partnership with both Greaves and Chivers (see page 132).

No.17 Alf Ramsey (Right back) – 250 appearances, 24 goals. England's greatest manager was cool and clinical in defence and a dead-ball expert upfield (see page 91).

No.18 Martin Chivers (Centre Forward) – 373 appearances, 181 goals. 'Big Chiv' had more to subtlety to his armoury than his fierce shots and long throws suggested. His goals won the 1971 League Cup and a year later set up Spurs' UEFA Cup victory against Wolves (see page 140).

No.19 Ted Ditchburn (Goalkeeper) – 453 appearances. Tall, commanding international keeper with swift, pin-point distribution (see page 97).

No.20 Jimmy Dimmock (Outside left) – 440 appearances, 112 goals. The England winger's mazy dribbles and touch-line trickery won the hearts of the White Hart Lane faithful. (see page 65).

No.21 Alan Mullery (Half back) – 380 appearances, 30 goals. Industry, stamina and the occasional stunning goal won round the Spurs' faithful and earned him England caps (see page 129).

No.22 Willie Evans (Outside left) – 195 appearances, 86 goals. Remarkable pace and a powerful shot saw the Welsh international become one of the stars of Spurs' 'Greyhounds' (see page 74).

No.23 John L. Jones (Left half) – 162 appearances,

8 goals. The most skilful player of his time. Skipper of the 1901 FA Cup winning team, 'Jack' Jones would often operate as a sixth forward (see page 34).

No.24 Tommy Harmer (Inside forward) – 222 appearances, 51 goals. Slight of build, but his flicks and tricks bedazzled the crowd (see page 100).

No.25 Bobby Smith (Centre forward) – 319 appearance, 210 goals. A typical old-fashioned forward who had strength and determination to browbeat defenders, but he had that something extra – a touch of class (see page 116).

No.26 Gary Mabbutt (Midfielder/Defender) – 619 appearances, 38 goals. Honest endeavour allied to precise tackling and passing made him a modern Spurs' hero. (see page 174).

No.27 Jimmy Cantrell (Centre forward) – 176 appearances, 85 goals. A dainty player who eschewed the power game for skill and guile, but still hit the net regularly. (see page 59).

No.28 Tommy Clay (Full back) – 352 appearances, 24 goals. A hard-tackling full back who believed in building play once he had won the ball. (see page 63).

No.29 Jimmy Seed (Inside forward) – 256 appearances, 77 goals. An intelligent player with excellent vision and a great shot, he was capped five times for England (see page 64).

No.30 Les Medley (Left winger) – 165 appearances, 46 goals. Free-roaming goal-scoring winger who could cut inside to add variety to the 1950s side's attacks (see page 87).

No.31 Sandy Tait (Full back) – 242 appearances, 3 goals. Nicknamed 'Terrible Tait' for his ferocious tackling, but he could play a bit too. (see page 37).

No.32 Martin Peters (Midfielder) – 266 appearances, 80 goals. Sir Alf Ramsey said he was '10 years ahead of his time'. Ever elegant in his midfield play, Peters' blind-side goals were his Spurs and England trademark (see page 137).

No.33 Paul Gascoigne (Midfielder) – 112 appearances, 33 goals. Spurs had the best of the wayward genius' talents, especially in the 1991 FA Cup run. Audacious, brilliant and foolhardy, he was a one-off. (see page 171).

No.34 Mike England (Centre half) – 405 appearances, 20 goals. Lean and strong, the Welsh international was a rock at the back (see page 136).

No.35 Sandy Brown (Centre forward) – 57 appearances, 45 goals. The original Spurs poacher had an amazing goalscoring record with the club. Devastating in the area, he would whip in any half chance. (see page 35).

No.36 Taffy O'Callaghan (Inside forward) – 263 appearances, 98 goals. An excellent passer of the ball who set 'the greyhounds' off, but also knew where the net was (see page 66).

No.37 Fanny Walden (Outside righ) – 236 appearances, 25 goals. One of the smallest players of all time, Walden's dribbling skills ensured the little winger became a Spurs' hero. (see page 60).

No.38 George Hunt (Centre forward) – 198 appearances, 138 goals. An England international, his aggression and pace left both defenders and crowds gasping. (see page 72).

No.39 Ted Hughes (Half back) – 183 appearances, 11 goals. A tireless worker with a great shot, he helped Spurs to the 1901 FA Cup final and played for Wales for eight years (see page 39).

No.40 John Pratt (Midfielder) – 415 appearances, 49 goals. Hard-working and tenacious, he was an essential bulwark for the flair players (see page 143).

No.41 Jurgen Klinsmann (Striker) – 68 appearances, 38 goals. A World Cup-winning goalscorer and team-player, who linked particularly well with Sheringham. His great charm won over the nation (see page 173).

No.42 Ricky Villa (Midfielder) – 181 appearances, 25 goals. Capable of brilliance, his incredible FA Cup final goal will be replayed forever (see page 150).

No.43 Bobby Steel (Inside forward/Half back) – 246 appearances, 46 goals. A good tackler, dribbler and passer, he had the required skills to be a valuable player in any position (see page 47).

No.44 Len Duquemin (Centre forward) – 308 appearances, 131 goals. More than just a goalscorer, 'the Duke' was also an unselfish player, whose passes brought his team-mates into the game (see page 92).

No.45 Teddy Sheringham (Striker) – 197 appearances, 98 goals. A fantastic thinking footballer who links play and hits the net. Teddy has the caps, the medals and the goals to prove it. (see page 179).

No.46 Gary Lineker (Striker) – 139 appearances, 80 goals. Joined Spurs at his peak. A predator in the area, his scoring rate with Spurs shows why he was one of England's greatest scorers (see page 170).

No.47 Chris Waddle (Winger/Midfielder) – 177 appearances, 42 goals. Supremely gifted player, whose ease on the ball belied his effort and talent. Even when the team struggled, his silky skills lit up White Hart Lane (see page 166).

No.48 David Ginola (Midfielder) – 127 appearances, 22 goals. Beautiful in looks and footballing philosophy, the Frenchman's flair and posturing made him the fans' anti-Graham idol (see page 177).

No.49 Johnny Brooks (Inside forward) – 179 appearances, 51 goals. An England international with superb dribbling and passing skills (see page 98).

No.50 Willie Hall (Inside forward) – 221 appearances, 29 goals. All-round ability that brought out the best in those around him (see page 76).

Results and Tables 1885-2001

The following pages include details of every senior competitive match played by Tottenham Hotspur since their first venture into the London Association Cup in 1885. From 1896 each season has its own page and is dated at the top. League matches appear first, followed by individual cup competitions. The opponents played at home are written in capital letters and appear in upper and lower case for away games. The date of the match, the score, the Tottenham Hotspur goalscorers and the match attendance are also included. Full league and cup appearances and goalscorers are featured separately. The final league table is included at the bottom of each page as well as a Fact File which notes particularly interesting facts and figures for the season as well as any notable transfers etc. In both the League and Cup Appearances and Goalscorers tables the category 'other' includes matches in the FA Charity Shield, the Screen Sport Super Cup and the Texaco Cup.

Key:
1Q – first qualifying round etc;
PRd – Preliminary Round;
Rd1 – first round; Rd2 – second round etc;
1L – 1st leg; 2L – 2nd leg;
R – replay;
2R – second replay;
QF – quarter-final; SF – semi-final;
SF/1L – semi-final first leg etc;
DF – divisional fina;l
F – final;
aet – after extra time.

Season 1885-86

London Association Cup

Oct 17	ST ALBANS	(Rd1) W	5-2
Nov 7	CASUALS	(Rd2) L	0-8

Season 1886-87

London Association Cup

Oct 16	Upton Park	(Rd1) L	0-6

East End Cup

Dec 18	PHOENIX	(Rd1) W	6-0
Jan 15	PARK	(Rd2) W	2-0
Feb 19	ST LUKES	(Rd3) W	2-1
Mar 26	LONDON CALEDONIANS	(SF) W	1-0
Apr 16	LONDON CALEDONIANS	(R) L	0-1

Season 1887-88

London Senior Cup

Oct 8	Hendon	(Rd1) L	0-6

Season 1888-89

London Senior Cup

Oct 13	OLD ETONIANS	(Rd1) L	2-8

Middlesex Senior Cup

Jan 10	CIVIL ENGINEERS	(Rd1) D	0-0
Jan 19	Civil Engineers	(R) L	1-4

Season 1889-90

London Senior Cup

Nov 2	Old St Marks	(Rd2) L	0-4

Middlesex Senior Cup

Jan 18	Old St Stephens	(Rd1) W	4-2
Feb 11	CLAPTON	(Rd2) L	2-4

Season 1890-91

London Senior Cup

Nov 1	Queens Park Rangers	(PRd2) D	1-1
Nov 8	QUEENS PARK RANGERS	(R) W	2-1
Nov 22	BARKING	(PRd3) W	2-0
Jan 24	Barnes	(Rd1) W	1-0
Jan 31	Millwall Athletic	(Rd2) L	1-5

Middlesex Senior Cup

Feb 7	ORION GYMNASIUM	(Rd1) W	7-1
Feb 14	CLAPTON	(Rd2) L	U

Season 1891-92

London Senior Cup

Oct 10	CALEDONIAN ATHLETIC	(Rd1) W	4-3
Oct 31	Hampstead	(Rd2) W	3-2
Nov 21	City Ramblers	(Rd3) L	1-4

Middlesex Senior Cup

Dec 5	Minerva	(Rd2) L	0-2

Luton Charity Cup

Nov 7	COLDSTREAM GUARDS	(Rd1) D	3-3
Nov 14	COLDSTREAM GUARDS*	(R) W	7-2
Dec 19	1st Scots Guards	(Rd2) L	0-4

*played at home by mutual consent

Season 1892-93

Southern Alliance

Sep 24	Polytechnic	W	2-1
Oct 15	Old St Stephens	L	0-3
Nov 5	Windsor and Eton	W	2-1
Nov 19	ERITH	W	3-2
Jan 14	Erith	L	1-2

Jan 21	Slough	D	3-3
Feb 4	SLOUGH	W	5-2
Feb 11	POLYTECHNIC	D	2-2
Feb 25	UPTON PARK	W	1-0
Mar 4	WINDSOR AND ETON	W	5-2
Mar 25	OLD ST STEPHENS	L	1-2
Apr 8	Upton Park	W	4-1

London Senior Cup

Dec 3	Polytechnic	(Rd3) D	2-2
Dec 17	POLYTECHNIC	(R) W	3-0
Jan 28	CASUALS	(Rd4) L	0-1

Wolverton & District Charity Cup

Apr 15	Smethwick*	(SF) L	0-2

played at Wolverton

Season 1893-94

FA Amateur Cup

Nov 11	VAMPIRES	(Rd1) W	3-1

London Senior Cup

Oct 21	OLD ST MARKS	(Rd1) D	0-0
Oct 28	OLD ST MARKS*	(R) L	1-6

played at home by mutual consent

Middlesex Senior Cup

Jan 13	3RD GRENADIER GUARDS	(Rd1) D	1-1
Jan 20	3RD GRENADIER GUARDS*	(R) L	0-2

played at home by mutual consent

London Charity Cup

Dec 9	CRUSADERS	(Rd1) L	2-5

Wolverton & District Charity Cup

Jan 27	CHESHAM	(Rd1) D	2-2
Feb 24	Chesham	(R) W	3-1
Mar 10	Smethwick*	(SF) L	0-1

played at Wolverton

Season 1894-95

FA Cup

Oct 13	WEST HERTS	(QRd1) W	3-2
Nov 3	WOLVERTON	(QRd2) W	5-3
Nov 24	Clapton	(QRd3) W	4-0
Dec 15	LUTON TOWN	(QRd4) D	2-2
Dec 19	Luton Town	(R) L	0-4

FA Amateur Cup

Oct 20	OLD HARROVIANS	(QRd1) W	7-0
Nov 10	CITY RAMBLERS	(QRd2) W	6-1
Dec 1	Romford	(QRd3) W	8-0
Dec 22	LONDON WELSH	(DF) D	1-1
Jan 5	LONDON WELSH	(R) D	3-3
Jan 19	London Welsh	(2R) W	4-2
Feb 23	BEESTON	(Rd1) W	2-0
Mar 16	OLD CARTHUSIANS	(Rd2) L	0-5

London Senior Cup

Jan 26	LONDON WELSH	(Rd1) W	5-0
Mar 2	Old Westminsters	(Rd2) D	3-3
Mar 9	OLD WESTMINSTERS	(R) L	4-5

London Charity Cup

Dec 8	CRUSADERS	(Rd1) W	4-2
Mar 21	Old Carthusians	(Rd2) L	0-3

Season 1895-96

FA Cup

Oct 12	Luton Town	(Rd1Q) W	2-1
Nov 2	Vampires	(Rd2Q) L	2-4
Nov 16	VAMPIRES*	(R) W	2-1
Nov 23	Ilford	(Rd3Q) W	5-1
Dec 14	OLD ST STEPHENS	(Rd4Q) W	2-1
Feb 1	Stoke	(Rd1) L	0-5

match replayed due to incorrect pitch markings

London Charity Cup

Nov 9	Old Westminsters	(Rd1) W	2-1

White Hart Lane in 1978. It has been Spurs home since 1899.

Season 1896-97

Southern League Division One

DATE	OPPONENTS	SCORE	GOALSCORERS	ATTENDANCE
Sep 5	Sheppey United	D 3-3	Crump, Milliken, Clements	2,000
Sep 12	Wolverton	L 0-1		1,000
Oct 3	Gravesend United	W 3-1	Newbigging, Clements, Payne	1,600
Oct 10	CHATHAM	L 2-3	Milliken, Payne	5,000
Oct 17	GRAVESEND UNITED	W 4-0	McElhaney, Milliken 2, Clements	3,000
Oct 24	Royal Ordnance*	W 2-1	Almond, Payne	500
Oct 31	Chatham	W 2-1	McElhaney, Milliken	5,000
Nov 7	SHEPPEY UNITED	W 3-2	McElhaney, Clements, Payne	3,000
Nov 14	SWINDON TOWN	W 3-1	Devlin, Milliken, Newbigging	2,000
Nov 28	MILLWALL ATHLETIC	L 1-3	Fleming	6,000
Dec 5	Reading	L 1-2	Payne	3,500
Dec 25	Millwall Athletic	W 4-0	McElhaney, Clements 2, Payne	6,000
Jan 9	Swindon Town	L 0-1		2,000
Feb 13	NORTHFLEET	W 5-0	Robertson, Clements 3, Stirling o.g.	3,000
Feb 20	New Brompton	L 1-2	Clements	2,000
Mar 6	Northfleet	L 0-2		2,000
Mar 20	READING	D 4-4	Almond, McElhaney, Wilson, Clements	4,000
Mar 27	NEW BROMPTON	W 2-0	Wilson, Clements	2,000
Mar 29	Southampton St Marys	D 1-1	Clements	3,000
Apr 1	WOLVERTON	W 2-0	McElhaney, Crump	2,000
Apr 8	SOUTHAMPTON ST MARYS	D 2-2	Wilson, Clements	3,000

* result not included in final table due to Royal Ordnances resignation from League

FA Cup

Dec 12	OLD ST STEPHENS	(1Q) W 4-0	Newbigging, Clements2, Payne	1,500
Jan 6	MAIDENHEAD	(2Q) W 6-0	Crump 2, McElhaney, Newbigging 2, Payne	2,000
Jan 16	Luton Town	(3Q) L 0-3		5,000

Wellingborough Charity Cup

Nov 19	GRAVESEND UNITED	(PRd) W 3-2	Almond, Fleming 2	1,000
Dec 16	Wolverton	(Rd1) W 2-0	McElhaney, Lanham	
Apr 5	Rushden **	(SF) W 2-1†	McElhaney (pen), Clements	1,000
Apr 29	Wellingborough	(F) L 0-2		

**played at Wellingborough
† after extra-time

League and Cup Appearances

PLAYER	LEAGUE	CUP COMPETITION		TOTAL
		FA CUP	WC	
Allen	4		2	6
Almond	16	3	1	20
Ambler	20	3	3	26
Briggs	6	1	3	10
Brown			1	1
Burrows	17	3	1	21
Clements	21	3	3	27
Collins	2			2
Crump	20	2	4	26
Devlin	21	3	3	27
Fleming	2		1	3
Hatfield	1		1	2
Hunter			1	1
Lanham	2		1	3
Mair	2		1	3
Markham	3			3
McElhaney	19	3	3	25
Milliken	19	3	4	26
Montgomery	21	3	3	28
Newbigging	10	3	3	16
Payne	19	3	1	23
Robertson	1		1	2
Wilson	5			5

Goalscorers

PLAYER	LEAGUE	CUP COMPETITION		TOTAL
		FA CUP	WC	
Clements	14	2	1	17
McElhaney	6	1	2	9
Payne	6	2		8
Milliken	6			6
Newbigging	2	3		5
Crump	2	2		4
Almond	2		1	3
Fleming	1		2	3
Wilson	3			3
Devlin	1			1
Lanham			1	1
Robertson	1			1
Opp's o.gs.	1			1

Fact File

The Wellingborough Charity Cup was the first competition in which Spurs reached the final.

MANAGER: None

CAPTAIN: Stanley Briggs

TOP SCORER: Bob Clements

BIGGEST WIN: 6-0 v Maidenhead (H), 6 January 1897, FA Cup 2nd Qualifying Round

HIGHEST ATTENDANCE: 6,000 v Millwall Athletic, 28 November 1896, Southern League Division One

MAJOR TRANSFERS IN: Willie Newbigging from Lanark County, Jimmy Milliken from St Mirren, Richard McElhaney from Celtic, Harry Crump from Hereford Thistle, Jimmy Devlin from Airdrie

Final Southern League Division One Table

		P	W	D	L	F	A	Pts
1	SOUTHAMPTON ST M	20	15	5	0	63	18	35
2	MILLWALL A	20	13	5	2	63	24	31
3	CHATHAM	20	13	1	6	54	29	27
4	TOTTENHAM HOTSPUR	20	9	4	7	43	29	22
5	GRAVESEND U	20	9	4	7	35	34	22
6	SWINDON T	20	8	3	9	33	37	19
7	READING	20	8	3	9	31	49	19
8	NEW BROMPTON	20	7	2	11	32	42	16
9	NORTHFLEET	20	5	4	11	24	46	14
10	SHEPPEY UNITED	20	5	1	14	34	47	11
11	WOLVERTON	20	2	0	18	17	74	4

Season 1897-98

Southern League Division One

DATE	OPPONENTS	SCORE		GOALSCORERS	ATTENDANCE
Sep 4	Sheppey United	D	1-1	Joyce	2,000
Sep 18	SOUTHAMPTON	W	2-0	Davidson 2	6,000
Sep 25	MILLWALL ATHLETIC	W	7-0	Tannahill, Davidson, Meade 3, Joyce, Black	10,000
Oct 2	New Brompton	L	0-1		4,000
Oct 9	GRAVESEND UNITED	W	2-0	Hartley 2	2,000
Oct 23	Southampton	L	1-4	Tannahill	10,000
Nov 6	Reading	D	3-3	Tannahill, Joyce, Black	4,000
Nov 13	BRISTOL CITY	D	2-2	Burrows, Black	9,000
Nov 27	Bristol City	L	1-3	Joyce	4,000
Dec 18	Wolverton	W	2-1	Joyce, Stormont	1,500
Jan 15	NORTHFLEET	W	4-0	Hartley, Joyce 3	2,000
Jan 22	WOLVERTON	W	7-1	Davidson 2, Joyce 4, Hartley	3,000
Jan 29	Chatham	L	2-4	Black, Joyce	2,500
Feb 5	Swindon Town	L	0-3		4,000
Feb 19	Northfleet	W	3-1	Joyce 2, Black	2,000
Feb 26	READING*	D	1-1	Jones	5,500
Mar 5	Gravesend United	W	2-1	Hartley 2	3,000
Mar 19	SHEPPEY UNITED	W	4-0	Joyce 4	2,800
Apr 2	NEW BROMPTON	W	3-1	Joyce, Black 2	4,000
Apr 9	CHATHAM	W	2-1	Hartley, Black	3,000
Apr 11	SWINDON TOWN	W	2-0	Meade, Stormont	5,000
Apr 16	Millwall Athletic	L	1-3	Meade	3,000

* played at Millwall

FA Cup

Oct 30	2nd Coldstream Guards **	(1QR) W	7-0	Hall, Crump, Meade 2, Joyce, Stormont, Black	4,000
Nov 20	Luton Town	(2QR) L	3-4	Joyce 2, Black	12,000

** drawn away but played at home by mutual consent

League and Cup Appearances

PLAYER	LEAGUE	CUP COMPETITION FA CUP	TOTAL
Ambler	1		1
Black	20	2	22
Briggs	1		1
Burrows	10	2	12
Crump	11	2	13
Cullen	21	2	23
Davidson	17		17
Downie	7		7
Hall	21	2	23
Hartley	15	1	16
Jones	20	2	22
Joyce	19	2	21
Knowles	19	1	20
Madden	2		2
Meade	10	1	11
Montgomery	15	1	16
Stormont	22	2	24
Tannahill	11	2	13

Goalscorers

PLAYER	LEAGUE	CUP COMPETITION FA CUP	TOTAL
Joyce	20	3	23
Black	8	2	10
Hartley	7		7
Meade	5	2	7
Davidson	5		5
Stormont	2	1	3
Tannahill	3		3
Burrows	1		1
Crump		1	1
Hall		1	1
Jones	1		1

Fact File

When John L Jones played for Wales against Ireland in February 1898 he became the first Spurs player to win an international cap.

MANAGER: None

CAPTAIN: John L Jones

TOP SCORER: Bill Joyce

BIGGEST WIN: 7-0 v Millwall Athletic (H), 25 September 1897, Southern League Division One; 7-0 v Coldstream Guards (A), 30 October 1897, FA Cup 1st Qualifying Round

HIGHEST ATTENDANCE: 12,000 v Luton Town, 20 November 1897, FA Cup 2nd Qualifying Round

MAJOR TRANSFERS IN: David Black from Burnley, Joe Cullen from Celtic, Jimmy Davidson from Burnley, Sandy Hall from Dundee, Jimmy Hartley from Burnley, John L Jones from Sheffield United, Bill Joyce from Bolton Wanderers, Tom Meade from Woolwich Arsenal, Bob Stormont from Dundee, Bob Tannahill from Bolton Wanderers

MAJOR TRANSFERS OUT: Willie Almond to Millwall Athletic, Lycurgus Burrows to Sheffield United, James Devlin to Woolwich Arsenal, Richard McElhaney to Swindon Town, Jimmy Milliken to Clyde

Final Southern League Division One Table

		P	W	D	L	F	A	Pts
1	SOUTHAMPTON ST M	22	18	1	3	53	18	37
2	BRISTOL C	22	13	7	2	67	33	33
3	TOTTENHAM HOTSPUR	22	12	4	6	52	31	28
4	CHATHAM	22	12	4	6	50	34	28
5	READING	22	8	7	7	39	31	23
6	NEW BROMPTON	22	9	4	9	37	37	22
7	SHEPPEY UNITED	22	10	1	11	40	49	21
8	GRAVESEND U	22	7	6	9	28	39	20
9	MILLWALL ATH	22	8	2	12	48	45	18
10	SWINDON T	22	7	2	13	36	48	16
11	NORTHFLEET	22	4	3	15	29	60	11
12	WOLVERTON	22	3	1	18	28	82	7

Season 1898-99

Southern League Division One

DATE	OPPONENTS	SCORE	GOALSCORERS	ATTENDANCE
Sep 10	BEDMINSTER	D 1-1	Cameron	5,000
Sep 17	SHEPPEY UNITED	W 3-2	Cameron 3	4,500
Sep 24	WARMLEY *	W 7-1	Smith 3, McKay, Joyce 3	4,000
Oct 8	CHATHAM	W 2-0	Smith, Cameron	10,000
Oct 22	Millwall Athletic	L 2-4	Smith 2	14,000
Nov 5	READING	W 3-0	McKay, Cameron, Bradshaw	12,000
Nov 26	Royal Artillery	W 3-2	Joyce 3	5,000
Dec 3	Bristol City	L 1-2	Joyce	6,000
Dec 17	Sheppey United	L 2-3	McKay, Penney o.g.	900
Dec 24	Warmley *	W 5-1	Smith, Hartley, Joyce, Cameron, Bradshaw	2,000
Dec 26	Southampton	D 1-1	Smith	16,000
Dec 31	Swindon Town	L 3-4	Cameron 3	6,000
Jan 7	ROYAL ARTILLERY	W 1-0	McKay	3,500
Jan 14	Gravesend United	L 2-4	Joyce 2	3,500
Jan 21	Brighton United	W 1-0	Bradshaw	2,000
Feb 4	Reading	L 0-2		3,000
Feb 18	BRISTOL CITY	W 3-2	McKay, Hartley, Bradshaw	6,000
Mar 13	New Brompton	D 1-1	Joyce	3,000
Mar 18	NEW BROMPTON	W 3-0	Smith 2, Rule	3,000
Mar 25	BRIGHTON UNITED	L 1-3	Joyce	2,500
Mar 31	SOUTHAMPTON	L 0-1		8,500
Apr 1	GRAVESEND UNITED	W 3-0	Joyce, Leech 2	4,000
Apr 3	SWINDON TOWN	D 1-1	Cameron	4,500
Apr 8	Chatham	L 0-1		3,000
Apr 15	Bedminster	L 0-1		1,500
Apr 22	MILLWALL ATHLETIC	W 3-1	Joyce, Cameron, Bradshaw	7,000

* results not included in final table due to Warmley's resignation from League

FA Cup

Oct 29	WOLVERTON	(1Q) W 4-0	McKay, Joyce, Cameron, Bradshaw	3,000
Nov 19	Clapton	(2Q) D 1-1	Bradshaw	7,000
Nov 23	CLAPTON	(R) W 2-1	Cameron 2	2,500
Dec 10	LUTON TOWN	(3Q) D 1-1	Joyce	12,000
Dec 14	Luton Town	(R) D 1-1	Meade	4,000
Dec 19	Luton Town †	(2R) W 2-0	Cameron, Bradshaw	8,000
Jan 28	NEWTON HEATH	(Rd1) D 1-1	Joyce	13,721
Feb 1	Newton Heath	(R) W 5-3	Jones, McNaught, Smith, Hartley, Joyce	6,000
Feb 11	SUNDERLAND	(Rd2) W 2-1	Cameron, Bradshaw	12,371
Feb 25	Stoke	(Rd3) L 1-4	Bradshaw	25,000

† played at Tufnell Park, London

League and Cup Appearances

PLAYER	LEAGUE	CUP COMPETITION FA CUP	TOTAL
Ambler	1		1
Atherton	2		2
Bradshaw	24	9	33
Cain	24	10	34
Cameron	25	9	34
Cullen	22	10	32
Downie	4		4
Erentz	24	9	33
Hall	3		3
Hartley	3	2	5
Jones	16	10	26
Joyce	21	10	31
Leech	4		4
McKay	18	9	27
McNaught	21	8	29
Meade	5	1	6
Melia	13	3	16
Payne	1		1
Rule	3		3
Smith	26	10	36
Stormont	23	10	33
Waller	3		3

Goalscorers

PLAYER	LEAGUE	CUP COMPETITION FA CUP	TOTAL
Smith	10	1	11
Bradshaw	5	5	10
Joyce	14	4	18
Cameron	12	5	17
McKay	5	1	6
Hartley	2	1	3
Leech	2		2
Jones		1	1
McNaught		1	1
Meade		1	1
Rule	1		1
Opp's o.gs.	1		1

Fact File

White Hart Lane was opened on 3 September 1899, with a friendly match against Notts County. Spurs won 4-1.

MANAGER: Frank Brettell until February 1899 then John Cameron
CAPTAIN: John L Jones
TOP SCORER: Bill Joyce
BIGGEST WIN: 7-1 v Warmley (H), 24 September 1898, Southern League Division One
HIGHEST ATTENDANCE: 25,000 v Stoke, 25 February 1899, FA Cup 3rd Round
MAJOR TRANSFERS IN: Harry Bradshaw from Liverpool, Bob Cain from Sheffield United, John Cameron from Everton, Harry Erentz from Newton Heath, Kenny McKay from Sheffield United, Jimmy McNaught from Newton Heath, Jimmy Melia from Sheffield Wednesday, Tom Smith from Preston North End
MAJOR TRANSFERS OUT: David Black to Woolwich Arsenal, Harry Crump to Luton Town, Jimmy Davidson to Brighton United, Joe Knowles to South Shields, Jock Montgomery to Notts County, Bob Tannahill to Millwall Athletic

Final Southern League Division One Table

		P	W	D	L	F	A	Pts
1	SOUTHAMPTON	24	15	5	4	54	24	35
2	BRISTOL CITY	24	15	3	6	55	12	33
3	MILLWALL A	24	12	6	6	59	35	30
4	CHATHAM	24	10	8	6	32	23	28
5	READING	24	9	8	7	31	24	26
6	NEW BROMPTON	24	10	5	9	38	30	25
7	TOTTENHAM HOTSPUR	24	10	4	10	40	36	24
8	BEDMINSTER	24	10	4	10	35	39	24
9	SWINDON T	24	9	5	10	43	49	23
10	BRIGHTON U	24	9	2	13	37	48	20
11	GRAVESEND U	24	7	5	12	42	52	19
12	SHEPPEY U	24	5	3	16	23	53	13
13	ROYAL ARTILLERY	24	4	4	16	17	60	12

Season 1899-1900

Southern League Division One

DATE	OPPONENTS	SCORE	GOALSCORERS	ATTENDANCE
Sep 2	Millwall Athletic	W 3-1	Copeland, Kirwan 2	12,000
Sep 9	QUEENS PARK RANGERS	W 1-0	Smith	11,000
Sep 16	Chatham	W 3-2	Morris, Pratt, Kirwan	4,000
Sep 23	READING	W 2-1	Smith 2	9,000
Oct 2	GRAVESEND UNITED	W 4-0	Pratt, Copeland 2, Cameron	1,800
Oct 7	BRIGHTON UNITED *	W 6-1	Jones, Copeland 2, Kirwan 3	6,000
Oct 14	Bedminster	L 1-2	Copeland	3,000
Nov 4	THAMES IRONWORKS	W 7-0	Morris 2, Pratt 3, Copeland, Kirwan	7,000
Dec 2	Swindon Town	W 2-0	Pratt, Cameron	3,000
Dec 9	BRISTOL CITY	D 2-2	Copeland, Kirwan	5,000
Dec 16	Cowes *	W 6-1	Smith 2, Pratt, Copeland 3	500
Dec 25	PORTSMOUTH	W 3-0	Pratt, Copeland, Kirwan	14,000
Dec 26	Southampton	L 1-3	Cameron	9,000
Dec 30	MILLWALL ATHLETIC	W 2-1	Cameron, Pratt	10,000
Jan 6	Queens Park Rangers	D 0-0		8,000
Jan 13	CHATHAM	W 2-1	Smith, Pratt (pen)	4,500
Jan 20	Reading	W 1-0	Cameron	2,000
Feb 3	Sheppey United	W 4-1	Cameron, Pratt 2, Morris	2,000
Feb 10	Brighton United *	W 3-0	Pratt (1 pen) 3	1,800
Feb 17	BEDMINSTER	W 5-2	Pratt 3, Kirwan 2	7,000
Feb 24	Bristol Rovers	D 2-2	Copeland, Hyde	3,000
Mar 3	Portsmouth	L 0-1		7,000
Mar 10	Thames Ironworks	D 0-0		9,000
Mar 19	BRISTOL ROVERS	W 5-1	Morris, Cameron 2, Stormont, Kirwan	3,000
Mar 24	NEW BROMPTON	W 1-0	Pratt	5,000
Mar 31	Gravesend United	W 6-2	Cameron 2, Pratt 2, Copeland 2	2,000
Apr 7	SWINDON TOWN	W 3-0	Smith, Pratt, Copeland	7,000
Apr 13	SOUTHAMPTON	W 2-0	Cameron 2	15,000
Apr 14	Bristol City	L 0-3		4,000
Apr 16	SHEPPEY UNITED	W 3-0	Hyde, Pratt, Kirwan	4,500
Apr 28	New Brompton	W 2-1	Cameron, Copeland	3,000

* results not included in final table due to Brighton United's and Cowes' resignation from League

FA Cup

Jan 27	Preston North End	L 0-1		15,000

League and Cup Appearances

PLAYER	LEAGUE	CUP COMPETITION FA CUP	TOTAL
Cameron	29	1	30
Clawley	8		8
Copeland	27	1	28
Erentz	18	1	19
Haddow	22	1	23
Hughes	3		3
Hyde	6		6
Jones	19		19
Kirwan	29	1	30
McNaught	26	1	27
Melia	13		13
Morris	23	1	24
Pratt	29	1	30
Raby	2		2
Rule	4		4
Smith	27	1	28
Stormont	24	1	25
Tait	31	1	32
Waller	1		1

Goalscorers

PLAYER	LEAGUE	CUP COMPETITION FA CUP	TOTAL
Pratt	23		23
Copeland	17		17
Cameron	13		13
Kirwan	13		13
Smith	7		7
Morris	5		5
Hyde	2		2
Jones	1		1
Stormont	1		1

Fact File

Apart from winning the Southern League, Spurs finished second in the Southern District Combination.

MANAGER: John Cameron
CAPTAIN: Jimmy McNaught
TOP SCORER: Tom Pratt
BIGGEST WIN: 7-0 v Thames Ironworks (H), 4 November 1899, Southern League Division One
HIGHEST ATTENDANCE: 15,000 v Preston North End, 27 January 1900, FA Cup; 15,000 v Southampton, 13 April 1900, Southern League Division One
MAJOR TRANSFERS IN: George Clawley from Southampton, David Copeland from Bedminster, Ted Hughes from Everton, Jack Kirwan from Everton, Tom Morris from Gainsborough Trinity, Tom Pratt from Preston North End, Sandy Tait from Preston North End
MAJOR TRANSFERS OUT: Harry Bradshaw to Thames Ironworks, Bob Cain to Albion Rovers, Bill Joyce to Thames Ironworks, Kenny McKay to Thames Ironworks

Final Southern League Division One Table

		P	W	D	L	F	A	Pts
1	TOTTENHAM HOTSPUR	28	20	4	4	67	26	44
2	PORTSMOUTH	28	20	1	7	58	27	41
3	SOUTHAMPTON	28	17	1	10	70	33	35
4	READING	28	15	2	11	41	28	32
5	SWINDON T	28	15	2	11	50	42	32
6	BEDMINSTER	28	13	2	13	44	45	28
7	MILLWALL A	28	12	3	13	36	37	27
8	QPR	28	12	2	14	49	57	26
9	BRISTOL C	28	9	7	12	43	47	25
10	BRISTOL R	28	11	3	14	46	55	25
11	NEW BROMPTON	28	9	6	13	39	49	24
12	GRAVESEND U	28	10	4	14	38	58	24
13	CHATHAM	28	10	3	15	38	58	23
14	THAMES IRONWORKS	28	8	5	15	30	45	21
15	SHEPPEY U	28	3	7	18	24	66	13

The Essential History of Tottenham Hotspur

Season 1900-01

Southern League Division One

DATE	OPPONENTS	SCORE	GOALSCORERS	ATTENDANCE
Sep 1	MILLWALL ATHLETIC	L 0-3		13,400
Sep 15	CHATHAM *	W 5-0	Smith, Cameron, Brown 3	3,000
Sep 22	Bristol City	D 1-1	Stormont	9,000
Sep 29	SWINDON TOWN	W 2-0	Smith, Stormont	7,000
Oct 6	Watford	L 1-2	Brown	7,000
Oct 20	Queens Park Rangers	L 1-2	Brown	5,000
Oct 27	WEST HAM UNITED	D 0-0		5,000
Nov 10	New Brompton	W 2-1	Cameron, Brown	3,000
Nov 24	Reading	L 1-3	Morris	5,000
Dec 1	KETTERING TOWN	W 1-0	Morris	4,000
Dec 15	Millwall Athletic	W 2-1	Cameron, Brown	8,000
Dec 25	PORTSMOUTH	W 4-1	Smith, Brown, Jones JL, Kirwan	12,000
Dec 26	Southampton	L 1-3	Cameron	10,000
Jan 12	Swindon Town	D 1-1	Brown	2,500
Jan 19	WATFORD	W 7-0	Smith, Brown, Jones JL 2, Kirwan 2, Cother o.g.	3,200
Jan 26	BRISTOL ROVERS	W 4-0	Morris (pen), Cameron, Copeland 2	6,000
Feb 16	West Ham United	W 4-1	Brown, Stormont 2, Hyde	5,000
Mar 2	NEW BROMPTON	W 2-1	Brown, Copeland	4,500
Mar 9	Bristol Rovers	L 0-1		5,000
Mar 16	READING	W 1-0	Hughes	5,000
Mar 30	QUEENS PARK RANGERS	W 4-1	Copeland 2, Kirwan, Hyde	4,000
Apr 3	Gravesend United	L 1-2	Stormont	5,000
Apr 5	SOUTHAMPTON	W 1-0	Hughes	12,000
Apr 6	BRISTOL CITY	W 1-0	Burton	5,000
Apr 24	Portsmouth	L 0-4		3,000
Apr 25	LUTON TOWN	W 3-2	Melia, Moffatt 2	4,000
Apr 27	GRAVESEND UNITED	W 5-0	Burton, Fortnum, Woodward 2, Hyde (pen)	5,000
Apr 29	Luton Town	W 4-2	Hawley 2, Moffatt, Kirwan	4,000
Apr 30	Kettering Town	D 1-1	Jones AE	4,000

* result not included in final table due to Chatham's resignation from League

FA Cup

Feb 9	PRESTON NORTH END	(Rd1) D 1-1	Brown	15,223
Feb 13	Preston North End	(Rd2) W 4-2	Brown 3, Cameron	6,000
Feb 23	BURY	(Rd3) W 2-1	Brown 2	20,250
Mar 23	Reading	(Rd4) D 1-1	Kirwan	14,417
Mar 28	READING	(R) W 3-0	Brown 2, Copeland	11,600
Apr 8	West Bromwich Albion **	(SF) W 4-0	Brown 4	46,000
Apr 20	Sheffield United†	(F) D 2-2	Brown 2	114,815
Apr 27	Sheffield United††	(R) W 3-1	Smith, Brown, Cameron	20,470

** played at Villa Park, Birmingham
† played at Crystal Palace, London
†† played at Burnden Park, Bolton

League and Cup Appearances

PLAYER	LEAGUE	CUP COMPETITION FA CUP	TOTAL
Anson	4		4
Berry	1		1
Brown	20	8	28
Buckingham	6		6
Burton	4		4
Cameron	21	8	29
Clawley	25	8	33
Copeland	9	8	17
Erentz	20	8	28
Fortnum	2		2
Haddow	4		4
Hawley	3		3
Hudson	1		1
Hughes	18	7	25
Hyde	10		10
Jones AE	8		8
Jones JL	17	7	24
Kirwan	19	8	27
McNaught	20	1	21
Melia	11		11
Moffatt	6		6
Moles	2		2
Morris	19	8	27
Pangbourne	2		2
Smith	17	8	25
Stevens	3		3
Stormont	23	1	24
Tait	22	8	30
Woodward	2		2

Goalscorers

PLAYER	LEAGUE	CUP COMPETITION FA CUP	TOTAL
Brown	12	15	27
Cameron	5	2	7
Copeland	5	1	6
Kirwan	5	1	6
Smith	4	1	5
Stormont	5		5
Hyde	3		3
Jones JL	3		3
Moffatt	3		3
Morris	3		3
Burton	2		2
Hawley	2		2
Hughes	2		2
Woodward	2		2
Fortnum	1		1
Jones AE	1		1
Melia	1		1
Opp's o.gs.	1		1

Fact File

Sandy Brown's 15 goals in the FA Cup remains a record to this day.

MANAGER: John Cameron

CAPTAIN: Jimmy McNaught/John L Jones

TOP SCORER: Sandy Brown

BIGGEST WIN: 7-0 v Watford (H), 19 January 1901, Southern League Division One

HIGHEST ATTENDANCE: 114,815 v Sheffield United, 20 April 1901, FA Cup Final

MAJOR TRANSFERS IN: Sandy Brown from Portsmouth

MAJOR TRANSFERS OUT: Tom Pratt to Preston North End

Final Southern League Division One Table

		P	W	D	L	F	A	Pts
1	SOUTHAMPTON	28	18	5	5	58	26	41
2	BRISTOL C	28	17	5	6	54	27	39
3	PORTSMOUTH	28	17	4	7	56	32	38
4	MILLWALL A	28	17	2	9	55	32	36
5	TOTTENHAM HOTSPUR	28	16	4	8	55	33	36
6	WEST HAM U	28	14	5	9	40	28	33
7	BRISTOL R	28	14	4	10	46	35	32
8	QPR	28	11	4	13	43	48	26
9	READING	28	8	8	12	24	25	24
10	LUTON TOWN	28	11	2	15	43	49	24
11	KETTERING	28	7	9	12	33	46	23
12	NEW BROMPTON	28	7	5	16	34	51	19
13	GRAVESEND	28	6	7	15	32	85	19
14	WATFORD	28	6	4	18	24	52	16
15	SWINDON T	28	3	8	17	19	47	14

Season 1901-02

Southern League Division One

DATE	OPPONENTS	SCORE	GOALSCORERS	ATTENDANCE
Sep 7	MILLWALL ATHLETIC	W 2-0	Cameron, Brown	27,000
Sep 14	QUEENS PARK RANGERS	W 2-0	Cameron, Copeland	9,000
Sep 21	Reading	D 1-1	Morris (pen)	8,000
Oct 5	Bristol Rovers	W 2-1	Smith, Brown	7,000
Oct 12	NEW BROMPTON	W 3-1	Brown, Kirwan 2	7,324
Oct 19	Northampton Town	L 1-3	Smith	5,000
Oct 26	WATFORD	W 8-1	Cameron 2, Brown 3, Copeland 2, Kirwan	7,500
Nov 2	West Ham United	W 1-0	Jones	14,000
Nov 9	Wellingborough	W 1-0	Brown	4,500
Nov 23	Swindon Town	W 3-1	Morris, Cameron 2	3,000
Dec 7	Kettering Town	W 2-0	Cameron, Kirwan	1,200
Dec 21	Millwall Athletic	D 1-1	Kirwan	4,000
Dec 25	PORTSMOUTH	L 1-2	Cameron	14,000
Dec 26	Southampton	L 0-1		11,000
Dec 28	Queens Park Rangers	W 3-0	Brown 3	13,000
Jan 4	READING	W 4-2	Hughes, Cameron, Copeland, Kirwan	8,500
Jan 18	BRISTOL ROVERS	W 1-0	Cameron	6,000
Feb 1	NORTHAMPTON TOWN	W 1-0	Kirwan	3,000
Feb 8	Watford	W 3-0	Brown 2, Copeland	2,500
Feb 15	WEST HAM UNITED	L 1-2	Copeland	9,000
Feb 22	WELLINGBOROUGH	W 3-0	Brown, Copeland 2	6,000
Mar 8	SWINDON TOWN	W 7-1	Cameron, Brown 3, Copeland 2, Kirwan	4,000
Mar 15	Brentford	L 1-2	Smith	11,000
Mar 22	KETTERING TOWN	W 4-0	Smith, Copeland 3	3,000
Mar 28	SOUTHAMPTON	D 2-2	Hughes, Kirwan	21,300
Mar 29	Luton Town	D 0-0		3,000
Mar 31	Portsmouth	L 0-1		13,400
Apr 5	New Brompton	D 0-0		5,000
Apr 12	LUTON TOWN	D 0-0		
Apr 26	BRENTFORD	W 3-0	Morris (pen), Brown 2	3,000

FA Cup

Jan 25	SOUTHAMPTON	(Rd1) D 1-1	Copeland	25,000
Jan 29	Southampton	(R) D 2-2	Hughes 2	12,036
Feb 3	Southampton *	(2R) L 1-2	Kirwan	10,000

* played at Elm Park, Reading

League and Cup Appearances

PLAYER	LEAGUE	CUP COMPETITION FA CUP	TOTAL
Barlow	2		2
Brown	26	3	29
Burton	3		3
Cameron	25	3	28
Clawley	20		20
Copeland	29	3	32
Erentz	30	3	33
Fitchie	1		1
Gilhooley	10	2	12
Griffiths	9	3	12
Haig-Brown	2		2
Hughes	24	3	27
Hyde	2		2
Jones	25	3	28
Kirwan	28	3	31
McNaught	16	3	19
Moles	1		1
Morris	25		25
Smith	23	1	24
Stevenson	1		1
Tait	26	3	29
Woodward	2		2

Goalscorers

PLAYER	LEAGUE	CUP COMPETITION FA CUP	TOTAL
Brown	18		18
Copeland	13	1	14
Cameron	11		11
Kirwan	9	1	10
Hughes	2	2	4
Smith	4		4
Morris	3		3
Jones	1		1

Fact File

As well as finishing second in the Southern League Spurs, were also runners-up in the Western and London Leagues.

MANAGER: John Cameron

CAPTAIN: John L Jones

TOP SCORER: Sandy Brown

BIGGEST WIN: 8-1 v Watford (H), 26 October 1901, Southern League Division One

HIGHEST ATTENDANCE: 27,000 v Millwall Athletic, 7 September 1901, Southern League Division One

MAJOR TRANSFERS IN: John Barlow from Reading, Fred Griffiths from Millwall

MAJOR TRANSFERS OUT: Fred Griffiths to Preston North End, Jimmy Melia to Preston North End, Bob Stormont to Brentford

Final Southern League Division One Table

		P	W	D	L	F	A	Pts
1	PORTSMOUTH	30	20	7	3	67	24	47
2	TOTTENHAM HOTSPUR	30	18	6	6	61	22	42
3	SOUTHAMPTON	30	18	6	6	71	28	42
4	WEST HAM U	30	17	6	7	45	28	40
5	READING	30	16	7	7	57	24	39
6	MILLWALL A	30	13	6	11	48	31	32
7	LUTON TOWN	30	11	10	9	31	35	32
8	KETTERING	30	12	5	13	44	39	29
9	BRISTOL R	30	12	5	13	43	39	29
10	NEW BROMPTON	30	10	7	13	39	38	27
11	NORTHAMPTON	30	11	5	14	53	64	27
12	QPR	30	8	7	15	34	56	23
13	WATFORD	30	9	4	17	36	60	22
14	WELLINGBOROUGH	30	9	4	17	34	72	22
15	BRENTFORD	30	7	6	17	34	61	20
16	SWINDON T	30	2	3	25	17	93	7

Season 1902-03

Southern League Division One

DATE	OPPONENTS	SCORE	GOALSCORERS	ATTENDANCE
Sep 6	QUEENS PARK RANGERS	D 0-0		13,000
Sep 20	WELLINGBOROUGH	W 6-1	Morris, Jones J, Cameron, Copeland, Kirwan, Dartnell o.g.	8,000
Sep 27	Bristol Rovers	L 2-3	Jones J 2	12,000
Oct 4	NORTHAMPTON TOWN	W 2-0	Morris (pen), Copeland	7,000
Oct 11	Watford	W 2-1	Houston 2	4,000
Oct 18	BRENTFORD	W 3-1	Burton J, Morris, Jones J	5,000
Oct 25	Millwall Athletic	L 0-2		8,000
Nov 1	WEST HAM UNITED	D 1-1	Copeland	9,000
Nov 22	SWINDON TOWN	W 2-0	Gilhooley, Kirwan	5,500
Dec 6	LUTON TOWN	D 1-1	Gilhooley	4,500
Dec 20	Queens Park Rangers	W 4-0	Hughes, Woodward 2, Kirwan	7,000
Dec 25	PORTSMOUTH	D 2-2	Dryburgh, Warner	23,000
Dec 26	Southampton	W 1-0	Kirwan	12,000
Jan 3	Wellingborough	W 2-0	Warner, Kirwan	3,000
Jan 5	NEW BROMPTON	W 3-1	Tait (pen), Warner, Copeland	3,000
Jan 10	BRISTOL ROVERS	W 3-0	Warner 2, Woodward	11,000
Jan 17	Northampton Town	L 1-3	Woodward	4,000
Jan 24	WATFORD	D 1-1	Kirwan	6,000
Jan 31	Brentford	D 1-1	Copeland	4,000
Feb 14	West Ham United	L 0-1		10,000
Mar 14	KETTERING TOWN	W 4-0	Hughes (1 pen) 2, Dryburgh, Warner	7,000
Mar 21	Luton Town	L 0-3		6,000
Mar 28	READING	W 2-0	Warner, Copeland	4,000
Apr 4	Reading	D 0-0		5,000
Apr 10	SOUTHAMPTON	W 2-1	Warner, Copeland	20,000
Apr 11	New Brompton	L 0-3		4,000
Apr 13	Portsmouth	L 0-2		12,000
Apr 14	MILLWALL ATHLETIC	W 2-0	Cameron, Copeland	8,000
Apr 22	Swindon Town	L 0-2		3,000
Apr 25	Kettering Town	L 0-1		2,000

FA Cup

Feb 7	WEST BROMWICH ALBION (Rd1)	D 0-0		25,641
Feb 11	West Bromwich Albion	(R) W 2-0	Dryburgh (pen), Woodward	35,000
Feb 21	BRISTOL CITY	(Rd2) W 1-0	Woodward	18,750
Mar 7	ASTON VILLA	(Rd3) L 2-3	Woodward, Copeland	24,500

League and Cup Appearances

PLAYER	LEAGUE	CUP COMPETITION FA CUP	TOTAL
Barlow	4		4
Brown	14		14
Burton	15		15
Cameron	14	4	18
Chalmers	4		4
Clawley	29	4	33
Copeland	28	3	31
Dryburgh	16	4	20
Erentz	24		24
Fredericks	1		1
Gilhooley	7	1	8
Haig-Brown	2		2
Houston	9		9
Hughes	18	4	22
Jones J	8		8
Jones JL	15	4	19
Kirwan	26	4	30
Morris	25	4	29
Tait	25	4	29
Warner	19		19
Watson	14	4	18
Williams	1		1
Woodward	12	4	16

Goalscorers

PLAYER	LEAGUE	CUP COMPETITION FA CUP	TOTAL
Copeland	8	1	9
Warner	8		8
Woodward	4	3	7
Kirwan	6		6
Jones J	4		4
Dryburgh	2	1	3
Hughes	3		3
Morris	3		3
Cameron	2		2
Gilhooley	2		2
Houston	2		2
Burton	1		1
Tait	1		1
Opp's o.gs.	1		1

Fact File

Spurs were undefeated in Southern League games at White Hart Lane, dropping only five points.

MANAGER: John Cameron

CAPTAIN: John J Jones

TOP SCORER: David Copeland

BIGGEST WIN: 6-1 v Wellingborough (H), 20 September 1902, Southern League Division One

HIGHEST ATTENDANCE: 35,000 v West Bromwich Albion, 11 February 1903, FA Cup 1st Round replay

MAJOR TRANSFERS IN: Charles Brown from Everton, Jimmy Chalmers from Watford, William Dryburgh from Cowdenbeath, Bob Houston from Heart of Midlothian, John "Bristol" Jones from Bristol Rovers, Alf Warner from Notts County, John Watson from Everton, Charlie Williams from Manchester City

MAJOR TRANSFERS OUT: Sandy Brown to Portsmouth

Final Southern League Division One Table

		P	W	D	L	F	A	Pts
1	SOUTHAMPTON	30	20	8	2	83	20	48
2	READING	30	19	7	4	72	30	45
3	PORTSMOUTH	30	17	7	6	69	32	41
4	TOTTENHAM HOTSPUR	30	14	7	9	47	31	35
5	BRISTOL R	30	13	8	9	46	34	34
6	NEW BROMPTON	30	11	11	8	37	35	33
7	MILLWALL A	30	14	3	13	52	37	31
8	NORTHAMPTON T	30	12	6	12	39	48	30
9	QPR	30	11	6	13	34	42	28
10	WEST HAM U	30	9	10	11	35	49	28
11	LUTON TOWN	30	10	7	13	43	44	27
12	SWINDON T	30	10	7	13	38	46	27
13	KETTERING	30	8	11	11	33	40	27
14	WELLINGBOROUGH	30	11	3	16	36	56	25
15	WATFORD	30	6	4	20	35	87	16
16	BRENTFORD	30	2	1	27	16	84	5

Season 1903-04

Southern League Division One

DATE	OPPONENTS	SCORE	GOALSCORERS	ATTENDANCE
Sep 5	Fulham	D 0-0		10,000
Sep 12	MILLWALL	L 0-1		16,000
Sep 14	Brentford	D 0-0		4,000
Sep 19	Queens Park Rangers	L 0-2		6,000
Sep 26	PLYMOUTH ARGYLE	L 0-2		8,000
Oct 3	Reading	D 2-2	Jones J, Jones JL	6,000
Oct 10	WELLINGBOROUGH	W 1-0	Jones J	9,000
Oct 17	Bristol Rovers	L 0-1		8,000
Oct 24	BRIGHTON & HOVE ALBION	D 2-2	Woodward, Chalmers	8,000
Nov 7	NORTHAMPTON TOWN	W 2-1	Morris (pen), Jones J	8,000
Nov 21	WEST HAM UNITED	W 2-1	Jones J, Kirwan	8,000
Dec 5	Luton Town	L 2-3	Jones J (pen), Copeland	6,000
Dec 19	Kettering Town	D 3-3	Woodward 2, Copeland	5,000
Dec 25	PORTSMOUTH	D 1-1	Jones J (pen)	20,000
Dec 26	Southampton	L 0-1		12,000
Jan 2	FULHAM	W 1-0	Warner	10,000
Jan 9	Millwall	W 1-0	Woodward	1,000
Jan 16	QUEENS PARK RANGERS	D 2-2	Jones J 2	10,000
Jan 23	Plymouth Argyle	W 3-1	Brearley 2, Copeland	10,000
Jan 30	READING	W 7-4	Warner, Jones J, Woodward 3, Copeland 2	8,000
Feb 13	BRISTOL ROVERS	W 5-1	Warner, Jones J (pen), Woodward 2, Kirwan	10,000
Feb 22	SWINDON TOWN	W 1-0	Walton	7,000
Mar 12	BRENTFORD	D 1-1	Jones J	5,000
Mar 19	West Ham United	W 2-0	Walton 2	8,000
Mar 26	Swindon Town	D 0-0		3,000
Apr 1	SOUTHAMPTON	W 2-1	Jones J, Woodward	21,300
Apr 2	LUTON TOWN	D 1-1	Turner	10,000
Apr 4	Portsmouth	L 0-1		11,000
Apr 5	NEW BROMPTON	W 1-0	Morris	6,000
Apr 9	New Brompton	W 1-0	Kirwan	10,000
Apr 13	Brighton & Hove Albion	W 2-1	Warner, Kirwan	8,000
Apr 16	KETTERING TOWN	W 5-1	Turner 4, Brearley	4,000
Apr 25	Northampton Town	W 1-0	Copeland	3,000
Apr 30	Wellingborough	D 3-3	Jones J 3	3,000

FA Cup

Feb 6	Everton	(Rd1)	W 2-1	Woodward, Balmer o.g.	25,000
Feb 20	ASTON VILLA *	(Rd2)	L 0-1		32,000
Feb 25	Aston Villa	(R)	W 1-0	Jones J	30,000
Mar 5	SHEFFIELD WEDNESDAY	(Rd3)	D 1-1	Jones J	15,500
Mar 10	Sheffield Wednesday	(R)	L 0-2		32,000

* abandoned after 20 minutes due to crowd overflow

League and Cup Appearances

PLAYER	LEAGUE	CUP COMPETITION FA CUP	TOTAL
Berry	3		3
Brearley	17	2	19
Brown	2		2
Burton J	3		3
Burton O	17		17
Cameron	3		3
Chalmers	6		6
Copeland	32	5	37
Erentz	16		16
Gilhooley	1		1
Hughes	24	5	29
Jones J	24	5	29
Jones JL	19	5	24
Kirwan	28	5	33
Leach-Lewis	2		2
Mapley	5		5
McConnachie	6		6
McNaught	14		14
Mearns	5		5
Milton	1		1
Morris	22	3	25
Quinn	1		1
Tait	25	5	30
Turner	6		6
Walton	10		10
Warner	19	5	24
Watson	17	5	22
Williams	29	5	34
Woodward	17	5	22

Goalscorers

PLAYER	LEAGUE	CUP COMPETITION FA CUP	TOTAL
Jones J	15	2	17
Woodward	10	1	11
Copeland	6		6
Turner	5		5
Kirwan	4		4
Warner	4		4
Brearley	3		3
Walton	3		3
Morris	2		2
Chalmers	1		1
Jones J L	1		1
Opp's o.gs.		1	1

Fact File

Spurs were runners-up in the Southern and London Leagues but won the Western League title.

MANAGER: John Cameron

CAPTAIN: John L Jones

TOP SCORER: John Jones

BIGGEST WIN: 5-1 v Bristol Rovers (H), 13 February 1904, Southern League Division One; 5-1 v Kettering Town (H), 16 April 1904, Southern League Division One

HIGHEST ATTENDANCE: 32,000 v Aston Villa, 20 February 1904, FA Cup 2nd Round; 32,000 v Sheffield Wednesday, 10 March 1904, FA Cup 3rd Round replay

MAJOR TRANSFERS IN: John Brearley from Everton, Joe Walton from Preston North End

MAJOR TRANSFERS OUT: George Clawley to Southampton

Final Southern League Division One Table

		P	W	D	L	F	A	Pts
1	SOUTHAMPTON	34	22	6	6	75	30	50
2	TOTTENHAM HOTSPUR	34	16	11	7	54	37	43
3	BRISTOL R	34	17	8	9	66	42	42
4	PORTSMOUTH	34	17	8	9	41	38	42
5	QPR	34	15	11	8	53	37	41
6	READING	34	14	13	7	48	35	41
7	MILLWALL	34	16	8	10	64	42	40
8	LUTON TOWN	34	14	12	8	38	33	40
9	PLYMOUTH A	34	13	10	11	44	34	36
10	SWINDON T	34	10	11	13	30	42	31
11	FULHAM	34	9	12	13	33	34	30
12	WEST HAM U	34	10	7	17	38	43	27
13	BRENTFORD	34	9	9	16	34	48	27
14	WELLINGBOROUGH	34	11	5	18	44	63	27
15	NORTHAMPTON T	34	10	7	17	36	69	27
16	NEW BROMPTON	34	6	13	15	26	43	25
17	BRIGHTON & HA	34	6	12	16	45	79	24
18	KETTERING	34	6	7	21	30	78	19

The Essential History of Tottenham Hotspur

Southern League Division One

DATE	OPPONENTS	SCORE	GOALSCORERS	ATTENDANCE
Sep 3	FULHAM	L 0-1		17,000
Sep 10	Watford	W 1-0	Walton	7,000
Sep 17	PLYMOUTH ARGYLE	W 2-0	Stansfield, Woodward	25,000
Sep 24	West Ham United	D 0-0		13,000
Oct 1	READING	L 1-3	Copeland	13,000
Oct 8	Bristol Rovers	L 1-3	Hughes	11,000
Oct 15	NORTHAMPTON TOWN	L 0-1		12,000
Oct 29	BRENTFORD	D 1-1	Stansfield	9,800
Nov 5	Queens Park Rangers	W 2-1	Morris, Brearley	12,000
Nov 12	MILLWALL	W 1-0	Warner	2,000
Nov 19	Brighton & Hove Albion	D 1-1	Bull	9,000
Nov 26	Luton Town	L 0-1		8,000
Dec 3	SWINDON TOWN	W 6-3	Morris (pen), Walton 2, Glen, O'Hagan 2	10,000
Dec 10	New Brompton	D 1-1	Woodward	6,000
Dec 17	WELLINGBOROUGH	W 8-0	Morris (pen), Brearley, Walton 2, Woodward, Glen 3	5,000
Dec 26	Southampton	D 1-1	Kirwan	14,000
Dec 27	PORTSMOUTH	D 1-1	Woodward	28,000
Dec 31	Fulham	L 0-1		9,000
Jan 7	WATFORD	W 2-0	Tait (pen), Woodward	8,000
Jan 21	WEST HAM UNITED	W 1-0	Kirwan	14,000
Jan 28	Reading	L 2-3	Brearley, Glen	1,000
Feb 11	Northampton Town	W 3-0	Hughes, O'Hagan 2	8,000
Feb 25	Brentford	D 0-0		6,000
Mar 4	QUEENS PARK RANGERS	W 5-1	Stansfield 2, Woodward, Glen 2	7,000
Mar 11	Millwall	W 2-0	Woodward, Glen	5,000
Mar 18	BRIGHTON & HOVE ALBION	D 1-1	Chapman	7,000
Mar 25	LUTON TOWN	W 1-0	O'Hagan	7,000
Apr 1	Swindon Town	L 1-2	Stansfield	7,000
Apr 5	Plymouth Argyle	L 1-2	Walton	8,000
Apr 8	NEW BROMPTON	W 2-0	Copeland, Glen	6,000
Apr 15	Wellingborough	W 1-0	Glen	3,000
Apr 21	SOUTHAMPTON	L 1-2	Kirwan	27,000
Apr 24	Portsmouth	L 2-3	Bull, Chapman	10,000
Apr 29	BRISTOL ROVERS	W 1-0	George	10,000

FA Cup

Feb 4	Middlesbrough	(Rd1)	D 1-1	Glen	25,000
Feb 9	MIDDLESBROUGH	(R)	W 1-0	O'Hagan	18,000
Feb 18	NEWCASTLE UNITED	(Rd2)	D 1-1	Walton	19,013
Feb 22	Newcastle United	(R)	L 0-4		26,755

League and Cup Appearances

PLAYER	LEAGUE	CUP COMPETITION FA CUP	TOTAL
Berry	9	1	10
Brearley	19	4	23
Bull	26	3	29
Burton	7		7
Chapman	5		5
Copeland	19		19
Eggett	27	4	31
Freeborough	1		1
George	4		4
Glen	18	4	22
Hughes	17	2	19
Kirwan	25	3	28
McCurdy	12		12
McNaught	7		7
Morris	28	4	32
Murray	9	1	10
O'Hagan	12	3	15
Stansfield	22	1	23
Swann	2		2
Tait	25	4	29
Walton	19	3	22
Warner	9		9
Watson	25	3	28
Williams	7		7
Woodward	20	4	24

Goalscorers

PLAYER	LEAGUE	CUP COMPETITION FA CUP	TOTAL
Glen	10	1	11
Walton	6	1	7
Woodward	7		7
O'Hagan	5	1	6
Stansfield	5		5
Brearley	3		3
Kirwan	3		3
Morris	3		3
Bull	2		2
Chapman	2		2
Copeland	2		2
Hughes	2		2
George	1		1
Tait	1		1
Warner	1		1

Fact File

Spurs undertook their first foreign tour in May 1905, playing seven games in Austria, Hungary and Czechoslovakia including two against Everton.

MANAGER: John Cameron

CAPTAIN: Sandy Tait

TOP SCORER: Alex Glen

BIGGEST WIN: 8-0 v Wellingborough (H), 17 December 1904, Southern League Division One

HIGHEST ATTENDANCE: 28,000 v Portsmouth, 27 December 1904, Southern League Division One

MAJOR TRANSFERS IN: Walter Bull from Notts County, Herbert Chapman from Northampton Town, John Eggett from West Ham United, Charlie O'Hagan from Everton, Harry Stansfield from Stockport County

MAJOR TRANSFERS OUT: John L Jones to Watford

Final Southern League Division One Table

		P	W	D	L	F	A	Pts
1	Bristol R	34	20	8	6	74	36	48
2	Reading	34	18	7	9	57	38	43
3	Southampton	34	18	7	9	54	40	43
4	Plymouth A	34	18	5	11	57	39	41
5	Tottenham Hotspur	34	15	8	11	53	34	38
6	Fulham	34	14	10	10	46	34	38
7	QPR	34	14	8	12	51	46	36
8	Portsmouth	34	16	4	14	61	56	36
9	New Brompton	34	11	11	12	40	41	33
10	West Ham U	34	12	8	14	48	42	32
11	Brighton & HA	34	13	6	15	44	45	32
12	Northampton T	34	12	8	14	43	54	32
13	Watford	34	14	3	17	41	44	31
14	Brentford	34	10	9	15	33	38	29
15	Millwall	34	11	7	16	38	47	29
16	Swindon T	34	12	5	17	41	59	29
17	Luton Town	34	12	3	19	45	54	27
18	Wellingborough	34	5	3	26	25	104	13

Season 1905-06

Southern League Division One

DATE	OPPONENTS	SCORE	GOALSCORERS	ATTENDANCE
Sep 2	Reading	D 1-1	Kyle	12,000
Sep 9	WATFORD	W 1-0	Kyle	8,000
Sep 16	Brighton & Hove Albion	L 0-2		9,000
Sep 23	WEST HAM UNITED	W 2-0	Chapman 2	14,000
Sep 30	Fulham	D 0-0		25,000
Oct 7	QUEENS PARK RANGERS	W 2-1	Chapman, Kyle	13,000
Oct 14	Bristol Rovers	W 2-0	Tait (pen), Chapman	10,000
Oct 21	NEW BROMPTON	W 6-0	Walton 2, Chapman 2, Kyle, Glen	15,000
Nov 4	SWINDON TOWN	W 2-1	Morris, Kyle	10,000
Nov 11	Millwall	L 1-2	Kyle	10,000
Nov 18	LUTON TOWN	W 1-0	Woodward	22,000
Nov 25	NORTHAMPTON TOWN	W 2-0	Bull, Carrick	13,000
Dec 2	Brentford	W 3-0	Walton, Chapman 2	10,000
Dec 16	Plymouth Argyle	L 1-2	Morris (pen)	10,000
Dec 25	PORTSMOUTH	W 3-1	Chapman, Kyle, Carrick	33,000
Dec 26	Southampton	L 0-1		12,000
Dec 30	READING	W 1-0	Glen (pen)	12,000
Jan 6	Watford	D 0-0		5,000
Jan 20	BRIGHTON & HOVE ALBION	W 3-1	Bull, Walton, Woodward	10,000
Jan 27	West Ham United	W 1-0	Kyle	18,000
Feb 10	Queens Park Rangers	D 0-0		10,000
Feb 12	FULHAM	L 0-1		18,000
Feb 17	BRISTOL ROVERS	D 2-2	Walton, Carrick	4,000
Mar 5	New Brompton	L 0-1		6,000
Mar 10	Swindon Town	L 0-2		3,000
Mar 17	MILLWALL	W 3-1	Shackleton, Brearley, Carrick	12,000
Mar 24	Luton Town	L 0-2		10,000
Mar 31	Northampton Town	D 0-0		6,000
Apr 7	BRENTFORD	W 4-1	Berry, Chapman, Leach 2	8,000
Apr 13	SOUTHAMPTON	D 1-1	Chapman	22,000
Apr 14	Norwich City	L 1-4	Woodward	12,000
Apr 16	Portsmouth	L 0-1		12,000
Apr 17	NORWICH CITY	W 3-0	Stansfield, Woodward 2	15,000
Apr 21	PLYMOUTH ARGYLE	L 0-1		8,000

FA Cup

DATE	OPPONENTS		SCORE	GOALSCORERS	ATTENDANCE
Jan 13	BURNLEY	(Rd1)	W 2-0	Woodward, Kyle	20,000
Feb 3	READING	(Rd2)	W 3-2	Bull, Walton, Kyle	26,000
Feb 24	BIRMINGHAM	(Rd3)	D 1-1	Kyle	28,000
Feb 28	Birmingham	(R)	L 0-2		34,000

League and Cup Appearances

PLAYER	LEAGUE	CUP COMPETITION FA CUP	TOTAL
Berry	6		6
Brearley	16		16
Bull	30	4	34
Burton	6		6
Carrick	15	4	19
Chaplin	2		2
Chapman	28	1	29
Darnell	10		10
Eggett	34	4	38
Freeborough	1		1
George	1		1
Glen	14	4	18
Hughes	22	4	26
Kyle	25	4	29
Leach	2		2
Morris	32	4	36
Murray	12		12
O'Hagan	7		7
Page	1		1
Shackleton	3		3
Stansfield	7		7
Tait	27	4	31
Walton	21	4	25
Watson	33	4	37
Whyman	7		7
Woodward	12	3	15

Goalscorers

PLAYER	LEAGUE	CUP COMPETITION FA CUP	TOTAL
Chapman	11		11
Kyle	8	3	11
Walton	5	1	6
Woodward	5	1	6
Carrick	4		4
Bull	2	1	3
Glen	2		2
Leach	2		2
Morris	2		2
Berry	1		1
Brearley	1		1
Shackleton	1		1
Stansfield	1		1
Tait	1		1

Fact File

In March 1906 Chris Carrick and Peter Kyle were suspended for a breach of the club's training rules and never played for the first team again.

MANAGER: John Cameron

CAPTAIN: Sandy Tait

TOP SCORERS: Herbert Chapman and Peter Kyle

BIGGEST WIN: 6-0 v New Brompton (H), 21 October 1905, Southern League Division One

HIGHEST ATTENDANCE: 34,000 v Birmingham, 28 February 1906, FA Cup 3rd Round replay

MAJOR TRANSFERS IN: Chris Carrick from West Ham United, John Chaplin from Dundee, Jabez Darnell from Northampton Town, John Shackleton from Darlington, Jack Whitbourne from Sunderland

MAJOR TRANSFERS OUT: David Copeland to Chelsea, Jack Kirwan to Chelsea, Bill McCurdy to New Brompton, Charlie Williams to Norwich City.

Final Southern League Division One Table

		P	W	D	L	F	A	Pts
1	FULHAM	34	19	12	3	44	15	50
2	SOUTHAMPTON	34	19	7	8	58	39	45
3	PORTSMOUTH	34	17	9	8	61	35	43
4	LUTON TOWN	34	17	7	10	64	40	41
5	TOTTENHAM HOTSPUR	34	16	7	11	46	29	39
6	PLYMOUTH A	34	16	7	11	52	33	39
7	NORWICH C	34	13	10	11	46	38	36
8	BRISTOL R	34	15	5	14	56	56	35
9	BRENTFORD	34	14	7	13	43	52	35
10	READING	34	12	9	13	53	46	33
11	WEST HAM U	34	14	5	15	42	39	33
12	MILLWALL	34	11	11	12	38	41	33
13	QPR	34	12	7	15	58	44	31
14	WATFORD	34	8	10	16	38	57	26
15	SWINDON T	34	8	9	17	31	52	25
16	BRIGHTON & HA	34	9	7	18	30	55	25
17	NEW BROMPTON	34	7	8	19	20	62	22
18	NORTHAMPTON T	34	8	5	21	32	79	2

Season 1906-07

Southern League Division One

DATE	OPPONENTS	SCORE	GOALSCORERS	ATTENDANCE
Sep 1	WEST HAM UNITED	L 1-2	Dow	16,000
Sep 5	Watford	D 1-1	Hewitt	4,000
Sep 8	Bristol Rovers	W 3-2	Bull, Eames, Dow	10,000
Sep 15	Swindon Town	D 0-0		6,000
Sep 22	NORWICH CITY	D 2-2	Walton, Hewitt	16,000
Sep 24	FULHAM	W 5-1	Walton, Hewitt, Reid 2, Dow	13,000
Sep 29	Luton Town	W 2-0	Bull, Hewitt	10,000
Oct 6	CRYSTAL PALACE	W 3-0	Walton, Reid 2	20,000
Oct 13	Brentford	D 2-2	Reid (1 pen) 2	8,000
Oct 27	Leyton	D 1-1	Woodward	15,000
Oct 29	Fulham	L 1-2	Stansfield	20,000
Nov 3	PORTSMOUTH	D 1-1	Reid	20,000
Nov 10	New Brompton	W 1-0	Woodward	6,000
Nov 17	PLYMOUTH ARGYLE	W 4-2	Hewitt 2, Reid 2	20,000
Nov 24	Brighton & Hove Albion	L 0-2		8,000
Dec 1	READING	W 2-0	Hewitt, Reid	10,000
Dec 15	NORTHAMPTON TOWN	W 6-0	Walton 2, Hewitt (1 pen) 2, Eames, Reid	7,000
Dec 22	Queens Park Rangers	L 1-3	Morris	15,000
Dec 25	MILLWALL	W 3-1	Hewitt, Chapman, Reid	20,000
Dec 26	Southampton	L 1-2	Reid	8,000
Dec 29	West Ham United	L 2-4	Woodward, Reid	13,000
Jan 5	BRISTOL ROVERS	W 4-0	Chapman, Woodward 2, Pickett	12,000
Jan 19	SWINDON TOWN	W 3-0	Hewitt, Walton, Whyman	7,000
Jan 26	Norwich City	L 0-5		5,000
Feb 9	Crystal Palace	W 1-0	Pickett	8,000
Feb 16	BRENTFORD	W 2-1	Chapman, Pickett	15,000
Mar 2	LEYTON	D 0-0		14,000
Mar 9	Portsmouth	L 1-3	Woodward	12,000
Mar 16	NEW BROMPTON	W 2-0	Walton, Reid	6,000
Mar 23	Plymouth Argyle	D 0-0		5,000
Mar 25	LUTON TOWN	L 1-2	Stansfield	9,000
Mar 29	SOUTHAMPTON	W 2-0	Woodward, Reid	20,000
Mar 30	BRIGHTON & HOVE ALBION	W 3-0	Walton, Walker, Pickett	12,000
Apr 1	Millwall	L 0-2		12,000
Apr 6	Reading	L 0-2		8,000
Apr 13	WATFORD	D 0-0		9,000
Apr 20	Northampton Town	L 0-2		8,000
Apr 27	QUEENS PARK RANGERS	W 2-0	Reid (1 pen) 2	7,000

FA Cup

Jan 12	HULL CITY	(Rd1)	D 0-0		27,033
Jan 17	Hull City	(R)	D 0-0*		18,000
Jan 21	HULL CITY **	(2R)	W 1-0	Chapman	20,000
Feb 2	BLACKBURN ROVERS	(Rd2)	D 1-1	Walton	24,963
Feb 7	Blackburn Rovers	(R)	D 1-1†	Reid	29,900
Feb 11	Blackburn Rovers ††	(2R)	W 2-1	Walton, Reid	18,000
Feb 23	Notts County	(Rd3)	L 0-4		25,000

* abandoned after ten minutes of extra-time due to bad light – result stood
** played at home by mutual consent
† after extra time
†† played at Villa Park

MANAGER: John Cameron until March then Fred Kirkham

CAPTAIN: Sandy Tait

TOP SCORER: Jimmy Reid

BIGGEST WIN: 6-0 v Northampton Town (H), 15 December 1906, Southern League Division 1

HIGHEST ATTENDANCE: 29,900 v Blackburn Rovers, 7 February 1907, FA Cup 2nd Round replay

MAJOR TRANSFERS IN: George Badenoch from Watford, William Dow from Bury, Walter Eames from Watford, Charlie Hewitt from Middlesbrough, Billy Jones from Bristol City, Arthur Pickett from Workington, Jimmy Reid from Watford, Matt Reilly from Notts County, Danny Steel from Rangers

MAJOR TRANSFERS OUT: William Berry to Manchester United, Chris Carrick to Reading, Alex Glen to Southampton, Willie Murray to Leeds City, Charlie O'Hagan to Middlesbrough, John Shackleton to Bury

League and Cup Appearances

PLAYER	LEAGUE	CUP COMPETITION FA CUP	TOTAL
Badenoch	1		1
Berry	1		1
Brearley	18	2	20
Bull	28	7	35
Burton	4		4
Chaplin	34		34
Chapman	10	6	16
Darnell	2	1	3
Dow	9		9
Eames	7		7
Eggett	5		5
Hewitt	30	5	35
Hughes	25	6	31
Jones	8		8
McDiarmid	7		7
Morris	33	7	40
Pickett	15		15
Reid	26	7	33
Reilly	19	7	26
Stansfield	11	5	16
Steel	6		6
Tait	24	7	31
Walker	10		10
Walton	34	7	41
Watson	12	7	19
Whitbourne	14		14
Whyman	3		3
Wilkinson	2		2
Woodward	20	3	23

Goalscorers

PLAYER	LEAGUE	CUP COMPETITION FA CUP	TOTAL
Reid	18	2	20
Hewitt	11		11
Walton	8	2	10
Woodward	7		7
Chapman	3	1	4
Pickett	4		4
Dow	3		3
Bull	2		2
Eames	2		2
Stansfield	2		2
Morris	1		1
Walker	1		1
Whyman	1		1

Fact File

After he had signed for Spurs, Liverpool offered Middlesbrough £400 for Charlie Hewitt. He wanted to join the Merseysiders but the FA ordered him to honour his Spurs' contract.

Final Southern League Division One Table

		P	W	D	L	F	A	Pts
1	FULHAM	38	20	13	5	58	32	53
2	PORTSMOUTH	38	22	7	9	64	36	51
3	BRIGHTON & HA	38	18	9	11	53	43	45
4	LUTON TOWN	38	18	9	11	52	52	45
5	WEST HAM U	38	15	14	9	60	41	44
6	TOTTENHAM HOTSPUR	38	17	9	12	63	45	43
7	MILLWALL	38	18	6	14	71	50	42
8	NORWICH C	38	15	12	11	57	48	42
9	WATFORD	38	13	16	9	46	43	42
10	BRENTFORD	38	17	8	13	57	56	42
11	SOUTHAMPTON	38	13	9	16	49	56	35
12	READING	38	14	6	18	57	47	34
13	LEYTON	38	11	12	15	38	60	34
14	BRISTOL R	38	12	9	17	55	54	33
15	PLYMOUTH A	38	10	13	15	43	50	33
16	NEW BROMPTON	38	12	9	17	47	59	33
17	SWINDON T	38	11	11	16	43	54	33
18	QPR	38	11	10	17	47	55	32
19	CRYSTAL P	38	8	9	21	46	66	25
20	NORTHAMPTON T	38	5	9	24	29	88	19

Season 1907-08

Southern League Division One

DATE	OPPONENTS	SCORE	GOALSCORERS	ATTENDANCE
Sep 2	Queens Park Rangers	D 3-3	Walton, Pass, McNair	6,000
Sep 7	West Ham United	D 1-1	McNair	10,000
Sep 14	QUEENS PARK RANGERS	W 3-2	Bull, Darnell, Pass	20,000
Sep 21	NEW BROMPTON	W 2-1	McNair 2	16,000
Sep 28	Swindon Town	L 0-1		5,000
Oct 5	CRYSTAL PALACE	L 1-2	Stansfield	18,000
Oct 12	Luton Town	L 1-3	McNair	7,000
Oct 19	BRIGHTON & HOVE ALBION	D 1-1	Morris o.g.	12,000
Oct 26	Portsmouth	W 2-1	Seeburg 2	10,000
Nov 2	BRADFORD	D 0-0		20,000
Nov 9	Millwall	W 2-1	Woodward 2	8,000
Nov 16	BRENTFORD	W 1-0	Reid	12,000
Nov 23	Bristol Rovers	D 0-0		8,000
Nov 30	LEYTON	W 1-0	Woodward	12,000
Dec 7	Reading	L 1-3	Middlemiss	5,000
Dec 14	WATFORD	W 5-0	Steel, Woodward 2, Middlemiss, Hitch o.g.	9,000
Dec 21	Norwich City	L 1-2	Middlemiss	5,000
Dec 25	NORTHAMPTON TOWN	W 2-0	Woodward 2	25,000
Dec 26	Southampton	D 1-1	Walker	18,000
Dec 28	Northampton Town	L 1-2	Pass	9,000
Jan 4	WEST HAM UNITED	W 3-2	Pass, Payne, Pickett	13,000
Jan 18	New Brompton	W 2-1	Woodward, Bull	5,000
Jan 20	PLYMOUTH ARGYLE	L 0-1		10,000
Jan 25	SWINDON TOWN	W 1-0	Reid	10,000
Feb 8	LUTON TOWN	L 1-2	Walker	11,000
Feb 12	Crystal Palace	W 2-0	Pass, Pickett	8,000
Feb 15	Brighton & Hove Albion	L 0-2		3,000
Feb 29	Bradford	W 2-1	Seeburg, Middlemiss	7,000
Mar 7	MILLWALL	L 1-2	Minter	20,000
Mar 14	Brentford	L 0-3		6,000
Mar 21	BRISTOL ROVERS	L 1-2	Woodward	11,000
Mar 28	Leyton	W 5-2	Woodruff 2, Woodward, Seeburg, Bidmead o.g.	12,000
Apr 4	READING	W 2-0	Minter 2	8,000
Apr 6	PORTSMOUTH	L 2-3	Middlemiss, Phillips o.g.	6,000
Apr 11	Watford	D 2-2	Woodruff, Minter	5,000
Apr 17	SOUTHAMPTON	W 3-0	Seeburg, Payne, Middlemiss	22,000
Apr 18	NORWICH CITY	W 3-0	Payne, Middlemiss 2	10,000
Apr 20	Plymouth Argyle	L 0-1		8,000

FA Cup

Jan 1	Everton	(Rd1) L 0-1		21,000

League and Cup Appearances

PLAYER	LEAGUE	CUP COMPETITION FA CUP	TOTAL
Brewster	1		1
Bull	21	1	22
Burton	31	1	32
Chaplin	30	1	31
Coquet	6		6
Cousins	2		2
Darnell	22		22
Dixon	5		5
Gray	15	1	16
Hughes	1		1
Manning	33	1	34
McNair	15	1	16
Middlemiss	25		25
Minter	9		9
Morris	31	1	32
Pass	18	1	19
Payne	7		7
Pickett	13		13
Reid	10		10
Seeburg	15		15
Stansfield	8		8
Steel	26	1	27
Tait	1		1
Walker	14	1	15
Walton	18		18
Watson	3		3
Whitbourne	5		5
Whyman	8		8
Woodruff	5		5
Woodward	20	1	21

Goalscorers

PLAYER	LEAGUE	CUP COMPETITION FA CUP	TOTAL
Woodward	10		10
Middlemiss	8		8
McNair	5		5
Pass	5		5
Seeburg	5		5
Minter	4		4
Payne	3		3
Woodruff	3		3
Bull	2		2
Pickett	2		2
Reid	2		2
Walker	2		2
Darnell	1		1
Stansfield	1		1
Steel	1		1
Walton	1		1
Opp's o.gs.			4

Fact File

In June 1907, centre forward Vivian Woodward was appointed a director of the club.

MANAGER: Fred Kirkham

CAPTAIN: Danny Steel

TOP SCORER: Vivian Woodward

BIGGEST WIN: 5-0 v Watford (H), 14 December 1907, Southern League Division One

HIGHEST ATTENDANCE: 25,000 v Northampton Town, 25 December 1907, Southern League Division One

MAJOR TRANSFERS IN: Ernie Coquet from Reading, James Gray from Rangers, Gordon Manning from Preston North End, Willie McNair from Falkirk, Herbert Middlemiss from Stockport County, Billy Minter from Reading, Jimmy Pass from Stockport County

MAJOR TRANSFERS OUT: George Badenoch to Northampton Town, John Brearley to Crystal Palace, Herbert Chapman to Northampton Town, Walter Eames to New Brompton, John Eggett to Croydon Common, Charlie Hewitt to Liverpool, Matt Reilly to Shelbourne

Final Southern League Division One Table

		P	W	D	L	F	A	Pts
1	QPR	38	21	9	8	82	57	51
2	PLYMOUTH A	38	19	11	8	50	31	49
3	MILLWALL	38	19	8	11	49	32	46
4	CRYSTAL P	38	17	10	11	54	51	44
5	SWINDON T	38	16	10	12	55	40	42
6	BRISTOL R	38	16	10	12	59	56	42
7	TOTTENHAM HOTSPUR	38	17	7	14	59	48	41
8	NORTHAMPTON T	38	15	11	12	50	41	41
9	PORTSMOUTH	38	17	6	15	63	52	40
10	WEST HAM U	38	15	10	13	47	48	40
11	SOUTHAMPTON	38	16	6	16	51	60	38
12	READING	38	15	6	17	55	50	36
13	BRADFORD PARK A	38	12	12	14	53	54	36
14	WATFORD	38	12	10	16	47	59	34
15	BRENTFORD	38	14	5	19	49	52	33
16	NORWICH C	38	12	9	17	46	49	33
17	BRIGHTON & HA	38	12	8	18	46	59	32
18	LUTON TOWN	38	12	6	20	33	56	30
19	LEYTON	38	8	11	19	51	73	27
20	NEW BROMPTON	38	9	7	22	44	75	25

Season 1908-09

Football League Division Two

DATE	OPPONENTS	SCORE	GOALSCORERS	ATTENDANCE
Sep 1	WOLVERHAMPTON WANDERERS	W 3-0	Morris, Woodward 2	20,000
Sep 5	Leeds City	L 0-1		20,000
Sep 12	BARNSLEY	W 4-0	Walton, Woodward, Middlemiss 2	20,000
Sep 19	BOLTON WANDERERS	W 2-1	Minter, Middlemiss	25,000
Sep 26	Hull City	L 0-1		12,000
Oct 3	DERBY COUNTY	D 0-0		25,000
Oct 10	Blackpool	D 1-1	Steel R	6,000
Oct 17	CHESTERFIELD	W 4-0	Walton, Minter 2, Steel R	14,000
Oct 24	Glossop North End	D 1-1	Minter	3,000
Oct 31	STOCKPORT COUNTY	D 0-0		16,000
Nov 7	West Bromwich Albion	L 0-3		20,000
Nov 14	BIRMINGHAM	W 4-0	Woodward 2, Middlemiss 2	25,000
Nov 21	Gainsborough Trinity	W 2-0	Steel R, Middlemiss	6,000
Nov 28	GRIMSBY TOWN	W 2-0	Woodward 2	14,000
Dec 5	Fulham	W 3-2	Minter 2, Steel R	35,000
Dec 12	BURNLEY	W 4-2	Minter, Woodward 2, Steel R	10,000
Dec 19	Bradford	W 2-0	Minter, Woodward	5,000
Dec 25	Oldham Athletic	L 0-1		24,000
Dec 26	OLDHAM ATHLETIC	W 3-0	Minter, Woodward, Middlemiss	40,000
Dec 28	Wolverhampton Wanderers	L 0-1		9,000
Jan 2	LEEDS CITY	W 3-0	Minter 2, Middlemiss	16,000
Jan 9	Barnsley	D 1-1	Minter	7,000
Jan 23	Bolton Wanderers	W 1-0	Steel R	24,000
Jan 30	HULL CITY	D 0-0		21,000
Feb 13	BLACKPOOL	W 4-1	Minter, Steel R, Middlemiss 2	15,000
Feb 27	GLOSSOP NORTH END	D 3-3	McFarlane, Steel R 2	12,000
Mar 6	Stockport County	W 3-1	Minter, Steel R, Middlemiss	5,000
Mar 8	Chesterfield	W 3-1	Woodward, Middlemiss 2	5,000
Mar 13	WEST BROMWICH ALBION	L 1-3	Woodruff	35,000
Mar 20	Birmingham	D 3-3	Steel D, Woodward, Steel R	8,000
Mar 27	GAINSBOROUGH TRINITY	D 1-1	Woodward	15,000
Apr 3	Grimsby Town	W 2-1	Minter, McFarlane	5,000
Apr 9	CLAPTON ORIENT	L 0-1		33,000
Apr 10	FULHAM	W 1-0	Woodward	22,000
Apr 12	Clapton Orient	D 0-0		20,000
Apr 17	Burnley	W 2-1	Woodward 2	8,000
Apr 24	BRADFORD	W 3-0	Curtis, Minter, Woodward	20,000
Apr 28	Derby County	D 1-1	Steel R	9,000

FA Cup

DATE	OPPONENTS		SCORE	GOALSCORERS	ATTENDANCE
Jan 16	Manchester City	(Rd1)	W 4-3	Morris (pen), Minter 2, Steel R	20,000
Feb 6	FULHAM	(Rd2)	W 1-0	Steel R	33,008
Feb 20	BURNLEY	(Rd3)	D 0-0		21,838
Feb 24	Burnley	(R)	L 1-3	Coquet (pen)	30,000

League and Cup Appearances

PLAYER	LEAGUE	CUP COMPETITION FA CUP	TOTAL
Boreham	8		8
Brough	1	1	2
Bull	12		12
Burton	33	4	37
Coquet	37	4	41
Curtis	2		2
Darnell	37	4	41
Hewitson	30	4	34
Leslie	2		2
Massey	1		1
McFarlane	16		16
Middlemiss	38	4	42
Minter	34	4	38
Morris	24	3	27
Morton	2		2
Seeburg	1		1
Steel D	38	4	42
Steel R	37	4	41
Walton	24	4	28
Wilkes	6		6
Woodruff	9		9
Woodward	26	4	30

Goalscorers

PLAYER	LEAGUE	CUP COMPETITION FA CUP	TOTAL
Minter	16	2	18
Woodward	18		18
Steel R	12	2	14
Middlemiss	13		13
McFarlane	2		2
Morris	1	1	2
Walton	2		2
Coquet		1	1
Curtis	1		1
Steel D	1		1
Woodruff	1		1

Fact File

Goalkeeper for Spurs on their Football League debut, Bob Hewitson, had also kept goal for Oldham Athletic 12 months earlier when they made their Football League bow.

MANAGER: None

CAPTAIN: Danny Steel

TOP SCORERS: Billy Minter and Vivian Woodward

BIGGEST WIN: 4-0 v Barnsley (H), 12 September 1908, Football League Division Two; 4-0 v Chesterfield (H), 17 October 1908, Football League Division Two; 4-0 v Birmingham (H), 14 November 1908, Football League Division Two

HIGHEST ATTENDANCE: 40,000 v Oldham Athletic, 26 December 1908, Football League Division Two

MAJOR TRANSFERS IN: Frank Bentley from Stoke, Fred Boreham from Leyton, Joe Brough from Stoke, Bob Hewitson from Oldham Athletic, Tom Leslie from Vale of Clyde, Doug MacFarlane from Burnley, Bobby Steel from Port Glasgow, Fred Wilkes from Reading

MAJOR TRANSFERS OUT: John Chaplin to Dundee, Ted Hughes to Clyde, Jimmy Pass to New Brompton, Harry Stansfield to Luton Town

Final Division Two Table

		P	W	D	L	F	A	Pts
1	BOLTON W	38	24	4	10	59	28	52
2	TOTTENHAM HOTSPUR	38	20	11	7	67	32	51
3	WBA	38	19	13	6	56	27	51
4	HULL CITY	38	19	6	13	63	39	44
5	DERBY COUNTY	38	16	11	11	55	41	43
6	OLDHAM A	38	17	6	15	55	43	40
7	WOLVERHAMPTON W	38	14	11	13	56	48	39
8	GLOSSOP NE	38	15	8	15	57	53	38
9	GAINSBOROUGH TRINITY	38	15	8	15	49	70	38
10	FULHAM	38	13	11	14	58	48	37
11	BIRMINGHAM	38	14	9	15	58	61	37
12	LEEDS CITY	38	14	7	17	43	53	35
13	GRIMSBY T	38	14	7	17	41	54	35
14	BURNLEY	38	13	7	18	51	58	33
15	CLAPTON O	38	12	9	17	37	49	33
16	BRADFORD	38	13	6	19	51	59	32
17	BARNSLEY	38	11	10	17	48	57	32
18	STOCKPORT CO	38	14	3	21	39	71	31
19	CHESTERFIELD	38	11	8	19	37	67	30
20	BLACKPOOL	38	9	11	18	46	68	29

Season 1909-10

Football League Division One

DATE	OPPONENTS	SCORE	GOALSCORERS	ATTENDANCE
Sep 1	Sunderland	L 1-3	Morris	10,000
Sep 4	Everton	L 2-4	Minter, Middlemiss	20,000
Sep 11	MANCHESTER UNITED	D 2-2	Steel R (2 pen) 2	32,275
Sep 18	Bradford City	L 1-5	Tull	25,000
Sep 25	SHEFFIELD WEDNESDAY	W 3-0	Steel D, Curtis, Minter	24,000
Oct 2	Bristol City	D 0-0		20,000
Oct 9	BURY	W 1-0	Middlemiss	30,000
Oct 16	MIDDLESBROUGH	L 1-3	Middlemiss	23,000
Oct 30	NOTTS COUNTY	L 1-3	Minter	23,000
Nov 6	Newcastle United	L 0-1		26,000
Nov 13	LIVERPOOL	W 1-0	Middlemiss	22,000
Nov 20	Aston Villa	L 2-3	Minter, Steel R	25,000
Nov 22	Preston North End	L 1-4	Steel R	
Nov 27	SHEFFIELD UNITED	W 2-1	Minter, Steel R (pen)	26,000
Dec 4	Woolwich Arsenal	L 0-1		18,000
Dec 11	BOLTON WANDERERS	D 1-1	Minter	20,000
Dec 18	Chelsea	L 1-2	Minter	50,000
Dec 25	NOTTINGHAM FOREST	D 2-2	Humphreys 2	30,000
Dec 27	Nottingham Forest	D 2-2	Steel R, Middlemiss	22,300
Jan 1	Blackburn Rovers	L 0-2		15,000
Jan 8	EVERTON	W 3-0	Steel R, Middlemiss 2	24,000
Jan 22	Manchester United	L 0-5		8,000
Jan 29	BRADFORD CITY	D 0-0		22,000
Feb 12	BRISTOL CITY	W 3-2	Minter, Humphreys, Middlemiss	25,000
Feb 26	Middlesbrough	L 3-4	Minter 2, Steel R	5,000
Mar 5	PRESTON NORTH END	W 2-1	Minter, Humphreys	25,000
Mar 12	Notts County	L 0-3		15,000
Mar 14	Sheffield Wednesday	D 1-1	Steel D	3,000
Mar 19	NEWCASTLE UNITED	L 0-4		25,000
Mar 25	SUNDERLAND	W 5-1	Curtis, Humphreys 2, Steel R, Middlemiss	35,000
Mar 26	Liverpool	L 0-2		15,000
Mar 28	BLACKBURN ROVERS	W 4-0	Minter 3, Humphreys	23,000
Apr 2	ASTON VILLA	D 1-1	Humphreys	34,000
Apr 9	Sheffield United	D 1-1	Humphreys	10,000
Apr 16	WOOLWICH ARSENAL	D 1-1	Curtis	39,800
Apr 20	Bury	L 1-3	Humphreys	4,000
Apr 23	Bolton Wanderers	W 2-0	Humphreys 2	3,000
Apr 30	CHELSEA	W 2-1	Minter, Humphreys	35,000

FA Cup

Jan 15	Plymouth Argyle	(Rd1) W 1-1	Humphreys	10,200
Jan 19	Plymouth Argyle	(R) W 7-1	Minter, Humphreys 3, Steel R, Middlemiss 2	17,000
Feb 5	Chelsea	(Rd2) W 1-0	Humphreys	31,766
Feb 19	Swindon Town	(Rd3) L 2-3	Minter, Steel R	11,818

League and Cup Appearances

PLAYER	LEAGUE	CUP COMPETITION FA CUP	TOTAL
Bentley	19	2	1
Boreham	12		12
Brown	1		1
Brown	8		8
Burton	4		4
Coquet	27	4	31
Curtis	37	4	41
Darnell	25	2	27
Drabble	1		1
Elkin	8	2	10
Harris	7		7
Humphreys	20	4	24
Joyce	23	4	27
Kennedy	2		2
Kerry	1		1
Leslie	7	2	9
Lunn	2		2
Lyle	1		1
McFarlane	5		5
Middlemiss	36	4	40
Minter	38	4	42
Morris	26	4	30
Newman	1		1
Steel A	1		1
Steel D	36	4	40
Steel R	38	4	42
Tull	7		7
Wilkes	23		23
Woodruff	2		2

Goalscorers

PLAYER	LEAGUE	CUP COMPETITION FA CUP	TOTAL
Humphreys	13	5	18
Minter	15	2	17
Middlemiss	9	2	11
Steel R	9	2	11
Curtis	3		3
Steel D	2		2
Morris	1		1
Tull	1		1

Fact File

On 29 January Spurs fielded three brothers, Alex, Bobby and Danny Steel, in a Football League game for the only time in the club's history.

MANAGER: None

CAPTAIN: Danny Steel

TOP SCORER: Percy Humphreys

BIGGEST WIN: 7-1 v Plymouth Argyle (A), 19 January 1910, FA Cup 1st Round replay

HIGHEST ATTENDANCE: 50,000 v Chelsea, 18 December 1909, Football League Division One

MAJOR TRANSFERS IN: John Curtis from Gainsborough Trinity, Percy Humphries from Chelsea, John Joyce from Millwall, Tommy Lunn from Wolverhampton Wanderers, Walter Tull from Clapton

MAJOR TRANSFERS OUT: Joe Brough to Burslem Port Vale, Bob Hewitson to Croydon Common, Joe Walton to Sheffield United, Vivian Woodward to Chelmsford City

Final Division One Table

		P	W	D	L	F	A	Pts
1	Aston Villa	38	23	7	8	84	42	53
2	Liverpool	38	21	6	11	78	57	48
3	Blackburn R	38	18	9	11	73	55	45
4	Newcastle U	38	19	7	12	70	56	45
5	Manchester U	38	19	7	12	69	61	45
6	Sheffield U	38	16	10	12	62	41	42
7	Bradford C	38	17	8	13	64	47	42
8	Sunderland	38	18	5	15	66	51	41
9	Notts Co	38	15	10	13	67	59	40
10	Everton	38	16	8	14	51	56	40
11	Sheffield W	38	15	9	14	60	63	39
12	Preston NE	38	15	5	18	52	58	35
13	Bury	38	12	9	17	62	66	33
14	Nottingham F	38	11	11	16	54	72	33
15	Tottenham H	38	11	10	17	53	69	32
16	Bristol C	38	12	8	18	45	60	32
17	Middlesbrough	38	11	9	18	56	73	31
18	Woolwich A	38	11	9	18	37	67	31
19	Chelsea	38	11	7	20	47	70	29
20	Bolton W	38	9	6	23	44	71	24

Season 1910-11

Football League Division One

DATE	OPPONENTS	SCORE	GOALSCORERS	ATTENDANCE
Sep 1	Everton	L 0-1		22,000
Sep 3	SHEFFIELD WEDNESDAY	W 3-1	Darnell, Steel R, Middlemiss	29,200
Sep 10	Bristol City	W 2-0	Humphreys, Middlemiss	20,000
Sep 17	NEWCASTLE UNITED	L 1-2	Minter	36,000
Sep 24	Oldham Athletic	L 0-2		14,000
Oct 1	Middlesbrough	L 0-2		20,000
Oct 8	PRESTON NORTH END	D 1-1	Minter	24,000
Oct 15	Notts County	L 0-1		14,000
Oct 22	MANCHESTER UNITED	D 2-2	Minter, Humphreys	28,000
Oct 29	Liverpool	W 2-1	Minter, Humphreys	12,000
Nov 5	BURY	W 5-0	Curtis, Minter, Humphreys 2, Middlemiss	20,000
Nov 12	Sheffield United	L 0-3		10,000
Nov 19	ASTON VILLA	L 1-2	Humphreys	28,000
Nov 26	Sunderland	L 0-4		12,000
Dec 3	WOOLWICH ARSENAL	W 3-1	Darnell, Minter, Humphreys	16,000
Dec 10	Bradford City	L 0-3		10,000
Dec 17	BLACKBURN ROVERS	D 2-2	McTavish R 2	16,000
Dec 24	Nottingham Forest	W 2-1	Minter, McTavish R	10,000
Dec 26	NOTTINGHAM FOREST	L 1-4	Minter	35,000
Dec 27	MANCHESTER CITY	D 1-1	Tull	28,000
Dec 31	Sheffield Wednesday	L 1-2	Minter	25,000
Jan 3	Manchester City	L 1-2	Kennedy	10,000
Jan 7	BRISTOL CITY	W 3-2	Minter 3	18,000
Jan 21	Newcastle United	D 1-1	Minter	22,000
Feb 11	Preston North End	L 0-2		10,000
Feb 13	MIDDLESBROUGH	W 6-2	Minter, Humphreys, Steel R 3, Forman	8,000
Feb 18	NOTTS COUNTY	W 3-0	Minter, Humphreys, Steel R	26,000
Feb 25	Aston Villa	L 0-4		17,000
Mar 4	LIVERPOOL	W 1-0	Minter	25,000
Mar 11	Bury	L 1-2	Steel R	10,000
Mar 15	Manchester United	L 2-3	Birnie, Humphreys	13,000
Mar 18	SHEFFIELD UNITED	W 2-1	Humphreys, Steel R	18,000
Mar 27	OLDHAM ATHLETIC	W 2-0	Minter, Steel R	7,000
Apr 1	SUNDERLAND	D 1-1	Minter	26,000
Apr 8	Woolwich Arsenal	L 0-2		24,853
Apr 15	BRADFORD CITY	W 2-0	Minter, Steel R	30,000
Apr 17	EVERTON	L 0-1		20,000
Apr 22	Blackburn Rovers	L 0-3		14,000

FA Cup

Jan 14	MILLWALL	(Rd1) W 2-1	Minter, Carmichael o.g.	21,464
Feb 4	Blackburn Rovers	(Rd2) D 0-0		25,000
Feb 9	BLACKBURN ROVERS	(R) L 0-2		26,946

League and Cup Appearances

PLAYER	LEAGUE	CUP COMPETITION FA CUP	TOTAL
Bentley	18	3	19
Birnie	4		4
Brown	4		4
Bulling	2		2
Collins	25	3	28
Coquet	12		12
Crompton	5	2	7
Curtis	30	3	33
Darnell	38	3	41
Elkin	18		18
Forman	2		2
Gosnell	5	2	7
Humphreys	24	1	25
Joyce	4		4
Kennedy	7		7
Leslie	1		1
Lunn	34	3	37
McTavish J	8	1	9
McTavish R	10	1	11
Middlemiss	29		29
Minter	39	3	42
Morris	11		11
Newman	2		2
Rance	11		11
Steel D	26	3	29
Steel R	29	2	31
Tull	3		3
Wilkes	19	3	22

Goalscorers

PLAYER	LEAGUE	CUP COMPETITION FA CUP	TOTAL
Minter	19	1	20
Humphreys	11		11
Steel R	9		9
McTavish R	3		3
Middlemiss	3		3
Darnell	2		2
Birnie	1		1
Curtis	1		1
Forman	1		1
Kennedy	1		1
Tull	1		1
Opp's o.gs.		1	1

Fact File

Spurs originally played their league game at home to Oldham Athletic on 28 January. But the match was abandoned at half-time due to fog with the score at 1-1. The match was replayed on 27 March.

MANAGER: None

CAPTAIN: Danny Steel

TOP SCORER: Billy Minter

BIGGEST WIN: 5-0 v Bury (H), 5 November 1910, Football League Division One

HIGHEST ATTENDANCE: 36,000 v Newcastle United, 17 September 1910, Football League Division One

MAJOR TRANSFERS IN: Tom Collins from Heart of Midlothian, Bob McTavish from Falkirk, Charlie Rance from Clapton

MAJOR TRANSFERS OUT: Fred Boreham to Leyton

Final Division One Table

		P	W	D	L	F	A	Pts
1	MANCHESTER U	38	22	8	8	72	40	52
2	ASTON V	38	22	7	9	69	41	51
3	SUNDERLAND	38	15	15	8	67	48	45
4	EVERTON	38	19	7	12	50	36	45
5	BRADFORD CITY	38	20	5	13	51	42	45
6	SHEFFIELD W	38	17	8	13	47	48	42
7	OLDHAM A	38	16	9	13	44	41	41
8	NEWCASTLE U	38	15	10	13	61	43	40
9	SHEFFIELD U	38	15	8	15	49	43	38
10	WOOLWICH A	38	13	12	13	41	49	38
11	NOTTS CO	38	14	10	14	37	45	38
12	BLACKBURN R	38	13	11	14	62	54	37
13	LIVERPOOL	38	15	7	16	53	53	37
14	PRESTON NE	38	12	11	15	40	49	35
15	Tottenham Hotspur	38	13	6	19	52	63	32
16	MIDDLESBROUGH	38	11	10	17	49	63	32
17	MANCHESTER C	38	9	13	16	43	58	31
18	BURY	38	9	11	18	43	71	29
19	BRISTOL C	38	11	5	22	43	66	27
20	NOTTINGHAM F	38	9	7	22	55	75	25

Season 1911-12

Football League Division One

DATE	OPPONENTS	SCORE	GOALSCORERS	ATTENDANCE
Sep 2	Everton	D 2-2	McTavish J, Young	25,000
Sep 4	SHEFFIELD WEDNESDAY	W 3-1	Minter, Young 2	20,000
Sep 9	WEST BROMWICH ALBION	W 1-0	Minter	30,000
Sep 16	Sunderland	D 1-1	Steel R	16,000
Sep 23	BLACKBURN ROVERS	L 0-2		37,820
Sep 30	Sheffield Wednesday	L 0-4		15,000
Oct 7	BURY	W 2-1	Minter 2	18,000
Oct 14	Middlesbrough	L 0-2		15,000
Oct 21	NOTTS COUNTY	D 2-2	Minter, Middlemiss	25,000
Oct 28	PRESTON NORTH END	W 6-2	Newman 3, Minter, Middlemiss 2	20,000
Nov 4	Manchester United	W 2-1	Minter, Middlemiss	26,000
Nov 11	LIVERPOOL	W 2-0	Minter, Middlemiss	23,000
Nov 18	Aston Villa	D 2-2	Steel R 2	30,000
Nov 25	NEWCASTLE UNITED	L 1-2	Newman	37,541
Dec 2	Sheffield United	W 2-1	Steel R, Middlemiss	11,000
Dec 9	OLDHAM ATHLETIC	W 4-0	McTavish J, Minter, Steel R, Middlemiss	20,000
Dec 16	Bolton Wanderers	L 0-1		20,000
Dec 23	BRADFORD CITY	L 2-3	Steel R 2	30,000
Dec 25	WOOLWICH ARSENAL	W 5-0	Darnell, McTavish J, Minter 2, Middlemiss	47,109
Dec 26	Woolwich Arsenal	L 1-3	Minter	20,000
Dec 30	EVERTON	L 0-1		24,500
Jan 20	SUNDERLAND	D 0-0		17,000
Jan 27	Blackburn Rovers	D 0-0		14,000
Feb 10	Bury	L 1-2	Elliott	6,000
Feb 17	MIDDLESBROUGH	W 2-1	Minter, Steel R	22,000
Feb 24	Notts County	D 2-2	Minter 2	10,000
Mar 2	Preston North End	W 1-0	Minter	5,000
Mar 13	West Bromich Albion	L 0-2		12,000
Mar 16	Liverpool	W 2-1	Newman, Mason	15,000
Mar 23	ASTON VILLA	W 2-1	Middlemiss 2	19,000
Mar 30	Newcastle United	L 0-2		21,000
Apr 5	Manchester City	L 1-2	Newman	39,800
Apr 6	SHEFFIELD UNITED	D 1-1	Middlemiss (pen)	26,000
Apr 8	MANCHESTER CITY	L 0-2		20,000
Apr 9	MANCHESTER UNITED	D 1-1	Bliss	14,000
Apr 13	Oldham Athletic	L 1-2	Elliott	6,000
Apr 20	BOLTON WANDERERS	W 1-0	Minter	18,000
Apr 27	Bradford City	L 0-3		8,000

FA Cup

Jan 13	West Bromwich Albion	(Rd1)	L	0-3	22,000

League and Cup Appearances

PLAYER	LEAGUE	CUP COMPETITION FA CUP	TOTAL
Bentley	1		1
Bliss	5		5
Bowering	7		7
Brittan	26	1	27
Collins	33	1	34
Crompton	3		3
Curtis	9		9
Darnell	34	1	35
Elliott	5		5
Forman	6		6
Grimsdell	2		2
Humphreys	1		1
Joyce	4		4
Kennedy	4		4
Lightfoot	21		21
Lunn	34	1	35
Mason	7		7
McTavish	30	1	31
Middlemiss	32	1	33
Minter	35	1	36
Morris	2		2
Newman	19	1	20
Rance	17	1	18
Steel D	28	1	29
Steel R	31	1	32
Tattersall	2		2
Webster	6		6
Wilkes	9		9
Young	5		5

Goalscorers

PLAYER	LEAGUE	CUP COMPETITION FA CUP	TOTAL
Minter	17		17
Middlemiss	11		11
Steel R	8		8
Newman	6		6
McTavish	3		3
Young	3		3
Elliott	2		2
Bliss	1		1
Darnell	1		1
Mason	1		1

Fact File

Spurs met Woolwich Arsenal in a friendly at the Park Royal ground in West London on 29 April with the procceds going to the *Daily Mail* Titanic fund.

MANAGER: None

CAPTAIN: Danny Steel

TOP SCORER: Billy Minter

BIGGEST WIN: 5-0 v Woolwich Arsenal (H), 25 December 1911, Football League Division One

HIGHEST ATTENDANCE: 47,109 v Woolwich Arsenal, 25 December 1911, Football League Division One

MAJOR TRANSFERS IN: Bert Bliss from Willenhall Swifts, Charlie Brittan from Northampton Town, Arthur Grimsdell from Watford, Alex Young from Everton

MAJOR TRANSFERS OUT: Ernie Coquet to Burslem Port Vale, Percy Humphries to Leicester Fosse, Walter Tull to Northampton Town

Final Division One Table

		P	W	D	L	F	A	Pts
1	BLACKBURN R	38	20	9	9	60	43	49
2	EVERTON	38	20	6	12	46	42	46
3	NEWCASTLE U	38	18	8	12	64	50	44
4	BOLTON W	38	20	3	15	54	43	43
5	SHEFFIELD W	38	16	9	13	69	49	41
6	ASTON VILLA	38	17	7	14	76	63	41
7	MIDDLESBROUGH	38	16	8	14	56	45	40
8	SUNDERLAND	38	14	11	13	58	51	39
9	WBA	38	15	9	14	43	47	39
10	WOOLWICH A	38	15	8	15	55	59	38
11	BRADFORD C	38	15	8	15	46	50	38
12	TOTTENHAM HOTSPUR	38	14	9	15	53	53	37
13	MANCHESTER U	38	13	11	14	45	60	37
14	SHEFFIELD U	38	13	10	15	63	56	36
15	MANCHESTER C	38	13	9	16	56	58	35
16	NOTTS CO	38	14	7	17	46	63	35
17	LIVERPOOL	38	12	10	16	49	55	34
18	OLDHAM A	38	12	10	16	46	54	34
19	PRESTON NE	38	13	7	18	40	57	33
20	BURY	38	6	9	23	32	59	21

Season 1912-13

Football League Division One

DATE	OPPONENTS	SCORE	GOALSCORERS	ATTENDANCE
Sep 2	EVERTON	L 0-2		22,000
Sep 7	SHEFFIELD WEDNESDAY	L 2-4	Tattersall, Middlemiss	28,000
Sep 14	Blackburn Rovers	L 1-6	Minter	25,000
Sep 21	DERBY COUNTY	L 1-2	Collins (pen)	25,000
Sep 28	Sunderland	D 2-2	Bliss, Middlemiss	8,000
Oct 5	Middlesbrough	D 1-1	Minter	18,000
Oct 19	Manchester United	L 0-2		12,000
Oct 26	ASTON VILLA	D 3-3	Cantrell 2, Middlemiss	18,000
Nov 2	Liverpool	L 1-4	Minter	15,000
Nov 4	NOTTS COUNTY	L 0-3		11,000
Nov 9	BOLTON WANDERERS	L 0-1		23,000
Nov 16	Sheffield United	L 0-4		12,000
Nov 23	NEWCASTLE UNITED	W 1-0	Cantrell	26,000
Nov 30	Oldham Athletic	L 1-4	Middlemiss	12,000
Dec 7	CHELSEA	W 1-0	Tattersall	36,771
Dec 14	Woolwich Arsenal	W 3-0	Cantrell 2, Steel	13,000
Dec 21	BRADFORD CITY	W 2-1	Cantrell, Middlemiss	20,000
Dec 25	Manchester City	D 2-2	Cantrell, Middlemiss	30,000
Dec 26	MANCHESTER CITY	W 4-0	Minter, Cantrell 3	20,000
Dec 28	Sheffield Wednesday	L 1-2	Tattersall	15,000
Jan 1	Everton	W 2-1	Minter 2	30,000
Jan 4	BLACKBURN ROVERS	L 0-1		33,000
Jan 18	Derby County	L 0-5		10,000
Jan 25	SUNDERLAND	L 1-2	Minter	31,000
Feb 8	MIDDLESBROUGH	W 5-3	Minter 2, Elliott 2, Middlemiss	24,000
Feb 15	Notts County	W 1-0	Bliss	12,000
Feb 22	SHEFFIELD UNITED	W 1-0	Weir	25,000
Mar 1	Aston Villa	L 0-1		27,000
Mar 8	LIVERPOOL	W 1-0	Middlemiss	20,000
Mar 15	Bolton Wanderers	L 0-2		25,000
Mar 21	WEST BROWMICH ALBION	W 3-1	Cantrell, Bliss 2	34,000
Mar 24	West Bromwich Albion	L 1-4	Middlemiss	20,000
Mar 29	Newcastle United	L 0-3		20,000
Mar 31	MANCHESTER UNITED	D 1-1	Minter	12,762
Apr 5	OLDHAM ATHLETIC	W 1-0	Bliss	20,000
Apr 12	Chelsea	L 0-1		50,500
Apr 19	WOOLWICH ARSENAL	D 1-1	Minter	20,000
Apr 26	Bradford City	L 1-3	Cantrell	10,000

FA Cup

Jan 11	BLACKPOOL	(Rd1) D 1-1	Rance	18,677
Jan 16	BLACKPOOL *	(R) W 6-1	Tattersall 2, Cantrell 2, Steel, Middlemiss	16,926
Feb 1	Reading	(Rd2) L 0-1		17,794

* played at home as Blackpool sold replay rights

League and Cup Appearances

PLAYER	LEAGUE	CUP COMPETITION FA CUP	TOTAL
Bliss	18		18
Brittan	14	1	15
Cantrell	25	3	28
Collins	28	2	30
Curtis	4		4
Darnell	4		4
Elliott	6		6
Grimsdell	25	3	28
Jones	7		7
Joyce	20	2	22
Lightfoot	15		15
Lunn	16	1	17
Middlemiss	38	3	41
Minter	37	3	40
Newman	3		3
Rance	32	3	35
Steel	19	3	22
Tate	2		2
Tattersall	30	3	33
Upton	2		2
Walden	1		1
Webster	34	3	37
Weir	34	3	37
Young	4		4

Goalscorers

PLAYER	LEAGUE	CUP COMPETITION FA CUP	TOTAL
Cantrell	12	2	14
Minter	11		11
Middlemiss	9	1	10
Bliss	5		5
Tattersall	3	2	5
Elliott	2		2
Steel	1	1	2
Collins	1		1
Rance		1	1
Weir	1		1

Fact File

Ten defeats and three draws – Spurs' worst ever start to a season.

MANAGER: None until December 1912 then Peter McWilliam

CAPTAIN: Tom Collins

TOP SCORER: Jimmy Cantrell

BIGGEST WIN: 6-1 v Blackpool (H), 16 January 1913, FA Cup 1st Round replay

HIGHEST ATTENDANCE: 50,500 v Chelsea, 12 April 1913, Football League Division One

MAJOR TRANSFERS IN: Jimmy Cantrell from Notts County, Fanny Walden from Northampton Town

MAJOR TRANSFERS OUT: Frank Bentley to Brentford, Ernie Bowering to Fulham, Danny Steel to Third Lanark

Final Division One Table

		P	W	D	L	F	A	Pts
1	SUNDERLAND	38	25	4	9	86	43	54
2	ASTON VILLA	38	19	12	7	86	52	50
3	SHEFFIELD W	38	21	7	10	75	55	49
4	MANCHESTER U	38	19	8	11	69	43	46
5	BLACKBURN R	38	16	13	9	79	43	45
6	MANCHESTER C	38	18	8	12	53	37	44
7	DERBY CO	38	17	8	13	69	66	42
8	BOLTON W	38	16	10	12	62	63	42
9	OLDHAM A	38	14	14	10	50	55	42
10	WBA	38	13	12	13	57	50	38
11	EVERTON	38	15	7	16	48	54	37
12	LIVERPOOL	38	16	5	17	61	45	37
13	BRADFORD C	38	12	11	15	50	60	35
14	NEWCASTLE U	38	13	8	17	47	47	34
15	SHEFFIELD U	38	14	6	18	56	70	34
16	MIDDLESBROUGH	38	11	10	17	55	69	32
17	TOTTENHAM HOTSPUR	38	12	6	20	45	72	30
18	CHELSEA	38	11	6	21	51	73	28
19	NOTTS CO	38	7	9	22	28	56	23
20	ARSENAL	38	3	12	23	26	74	18

Season 1913-14

Football League Division One

DATE	OPPONENTS	SCORE	GOALSCORERS	ATTENDANCE
Sep 1	Sheffield United	W 4-1	Walden, Minter, Bauchop 2	16,000
Sep 6	Chelsea	W 3-1	Grimsdell, Cantrell 2	65,000
Sep 8	SHEFFIELD UNITED	W 2-1	Cantrell 2	26,000
Sep 13	DERBY COUNTY	D 1-1	Cantrell	40,000
Sep 20	Oldham Athletic	L 0-3		18,000
Sep 27	MANCHESTER CITY	W 3-1	Minter 2, Cantrell	30,513
Oct 4	Manchester United	L 1-3	Middlemiss	39,000
Oct 11	BRADFORD CITY	D 0-0		30,000
Oct 18	Burnley	L 1-3	Cantrell	22,000
Oct 25	BLACKBURN ROVERS	D 3-3	Minter, Cantrell, Middlemiss	46,128
Nov 1	Preston North End	W 2-1	Bauchop, Bliss	14,000
Nov 8	SUNDERLAND	L 1-4	Cantrell	36,000
Nov 15	Newcastle United	L 0-2		23,000
Nov 22	EVERTON	W 4-1	Bauchop, Bliss 2, Middlemiss	22,000
Nov 29	Liverpool	L 1-2	Cantrell	21,000
Dec 6	WEST BROMWICH ALBION	W 3-0	Bauchop 2, Bliss	24,000
Dec 13	Aston Villa	D 3-3	Walden, Cantrell, Bliss	30,000
Dec 20	SHEFFIELD WEDNESDAY	D 1-1	Walden	22,000
Dec 26	MIDDLESBROUGH	L 0-1		37,055
Dec 27	CHELSEA	L 1-2	Fleming	29,355
Jan 1	Bolton Wanderers	L 0-3		30,000
Jan 3	Derby County	L 0-4		10,000
Jan 17	OLDHAM ATHLETIC	W 3-1	Lightfoot, Sparrow 2	25,000
Jan 24	Manchester City	L 1-2	Sparrow	30,000
Feb 7	MANCHESTER UNITED	W 2-1	Minter, Cantrell	28,000
Feb 14	Bradford City	L 1-2	Cantrell	18,000
Feb 23	BURNLEY	W 2-0	Walden (pen), Bliss	15,000
Feb 28	Blackburn Rovers	D 1-1	Walden	25,000
Mar 7	PRESTON NORTH END	W 1-0	Cantrell	25,000
Mar 14	Sunderland	L 0-2		10,000
Mar 21	NEWCASTLE UNITED	D 0-0		20,000
Mar 28	Everton	D 1-1	Sparrow	15,000
Apr 4	LIVERPOOL	D 0-0		19,800
Apr 10	BOLTON WANDERERS	W 3-0	Joyce, Cantrell, Bliss	39,020
Apr 11	West Bromwich Albion	D 1-1	Cantrell	15,000
Apr 13	Middlesbrough	L 0-6		22,000
Apr 18	ASTON VILLA	L 0-2		22,000
Apr 25	Sheffield Wednesday	L 0-2		12,000

FA Cup

Jan 10	Leicester City	(Rd1) D 5-5	Walden, Minter, Cantrell, Bliss 2	9,454
Jan 15	LEICESTER CITY	(R) W 2-0	Walden, Bliss	20,252
Jan 31	Manchester City	(Rd2) L 1-2	Bliss	36,256

League and Cup Appearances

PLAYER	LEAGUE	CUP COMPETITION FA CUP	TOTAL
Banks	12		12
Bauchop	10		10
Bliss	29	3	32
Bowler	3		3
Cantrell	33	2	35
Cartwright	13	2	15
Clay	15		15
Collins	15	3	18
Crowl	1		1
Darnell	1		1
Elliott	1		1
Fleming	8		8
Gemmell		1	1
Grimsdell	37	3	40
Joyce	17	2	19
King	19	1	20
Lightfoot	2	3	5
Middlemiss	34	3	37
Minter	16	2	18
Newman	5	1	6
Oliver	2		2
Sparrow	3		3
Steel	37	3	40
Tate	2		2
Tattersall	7		7
Walden	30	3	33
Webster	33	1	34
Weir	33		33

Goalscorers

PLAYER	LEAGUE	CUP COMPETITION FA CUP	TOTAL
Cantrell	16	1	17
Bliss	7	4	11
Walden	5	2	7
Bauchop	6		6
Minter	5	1	6
Sparrow	4		4
Middlemiss	3		3
Fleming	1		1
Grimsdell	1		1
Joyce	1		1
Lightfoot	1		1

Fact File

Spurs had new neighbours this season. Arsenal's new stadium at Highbury opened in September 1913.

MANAGER: Peter McWilliam

CAPTAIN: Tom Collins

TOP SCORER: Jimmy Cantrell

BIGGEST WIN: 4-1 v Sheffield United (A), 1 September 1913, Football League Division One; 4-1 v Everton (H), 22 November 1913, Football League Division One

HIGHEST ATTENDANCE: 65,000 v Chelsea, 6 September 1913, Football League Division One

MAJOR TRANSFERS IN: Jimmy Banks from Willington Athletic, Tommy Clay from Leicester Fosse, Arthur King from Aberdeen

MAJOR TRANSFERS OUT: Charlie Brittan to Cardiff City, Tommy Lunn to Stockport County

Final Division One Table

		P	W	D	L	F	A	Pts
1	BLACKBURN R	38	20	11	7	78	42	51
2	ASTON VILLA	38	19	6	13	65	50	44
3	MIDDLESBROUGH	38	19	5	14	77	60	43
4	OLDHAM A	38	17	9	12	55	45	43
5	WBA	38	15	13	10	46	42	43
6	BOLTON W	38	16	10	12	65	52	42
7	SUNDERLAND	38	17	6	15	63	52	40
8	CHELSEA	38	16	7	15	46	55	39
9	BRADFORD C	38	12	14	12	40	40	38
10	SHEFFIELD U	38	16	5	17	63	60	37
11	NEWCASTLE U	38	13	11	14	39	48	37
12	BURNLEY	38	12	12	14	61	53	36
13	MANCHESTER C	38	14	8	16	51	53	36
14	MANCHESTER U	38	15	6	17	52	62	36
15	EVERTON	38	12	11	15	46	55	35
16	LIVERPOOL	38	14	7	17	46	62	35
17	TOTTENHAM HOTSPUR	38	12	10	16	50	62	34
18	SHEFFIELD W	38	13	8	17	53	70	34
19	PRESTON NE	38	12	6	20	52	69	30
20	DERBY CO	38	8	11	19	55	71	27

Season 1914-15

Football League Division One

DATE	OPPONENTS	SCORE	GOALSCORERS	ATTENDANCE
Sep 2	EVERTON	L 1-3	Cantrell	9,000
Sep 5	CHELSEA	D 1-1	Cantrell	26,000
Sep 12	Bradford City	D 2-2	Bliss 2	10,000
Sep 19	BURNLEY	L 1-3	Bliss	25,000
Sep 26	Manchester City	L 1-2	Sparrow	13,000
Sep 28	WEST BROMWICH ALBION	W 2-0	Clay (pen), Fleming	8,500
Oct 3	Newcastle United	L 0-4		12,000
Oct 10	MIDDLESBROUGH	D 3-3	Lightfoot, Walden, Cantrell	15,000
Oct 17	Sheffield United	D 1-1	Bliss	20,000
Oct 24	ASTON VILLA	L 0-2		25,000
Oct 31	Liverpool	L 2-7	Clay (pen), Bliss	12,000
Nov 7	BRADFORD	W 3-0	Cantrell, Bliss 2	14,000
Nov 14	Oldham Athletic	L 1-4	Bliss	10,000
Nov 21	MANCHESTER UNITED	W 2-0	Clay (pen), Cantrell	11,000
Nov 28	Bolton Wanderers	L 2-4	Clay (pen), Cantrell	8,000
Dec 5	BLACKBURN ROVERS	L 0-4		14,000
Dec 12	Notts County	W 2-1	Cantrell, Bliss	8,000
Dec 19	SUNDERLAND	L 0-6		5,000
Dec 25	Sheffield Wednesday	L 2-3	Minter, Bliss	26,000
Dec 26	SHEFFIELD WEDNESDAY	W 6-1	Steel, Sparrow, Bliss 4	8,000
Jan 1	Everton	D 1-1	Bliss	17,000
Jan 2	Chelsea	D 1-1	Middlemiss	31,000
Jan 16	BRADFORD CITY	D 0-0		12,000
Jan 23	Burnley	L 1-3	Cantrell	4,000
Feb 13	Middlesbrough	L 5-7	Cantrell 4, Bliss	8,000
Feb 20	NOTTS COUNTY	W 2-0	Weir, Iremonger o.g.	12,000
Feb 27	Aston Villa	L 1-3	Bliss	16,000
Mar 10	LIVERPOOL	D 1-1	Minter	12,000
Mar 13	Bradford	L 1-5	Minter	9,000
Mar 15	MANCHESTER CITY	D 2-2	Minter, Sparrow	6,000
Mar 20	OLDHAM ATHLETIC	W 1-0	Middlemiss	14,000
Mar 27	Manchester United	D 1-1	Minter	7,000
Apr 2	NEWCASTLE UNITED	D 0-0		18,000
Apr 3	BOLTON WANDERERS	W 4-2	Cantrell, Bliss 3	11,000
Apr 6	West Bromwich Albion	L 2-3	Steel, Cantrell	6,000
Apr 10	Blackburn Rovers	L 1-4	Bliss	10,000
Apr 17	SHEFFIELD UNITED	D 1-1	Fleming	7,500
Apr 24	Sunderland	L 0-5		10,000

FA Cup

Jan 9	SUNDERLAND	(Rd1) W 2-1	Walden, Bliss	17,000
Jan 30	Norwich City	(Rd2) L 2-3	Cantrell, Lansdale o.g.	9,758

League and Cup Appearances

PLAYER	LEAGUE	CUP COMPETITION FA CUP	TOTAL
Banks	5		5
Bliss	33	2	35
Cantrell	26	1	27
Clay	38	2	40
Collins	12		12
Darnell	11		11
Eadon	5		5
Fleming	11		11
Grimsdell	8		8
Jacques	28	2	30
Joyce	5		5
Lightfoot	23	2	25
Lowe	2		2
Middlemiss	33	2	35
Minter	26	2	28
Pearson	17	2	19
Rance	3		3
Sparrow	15	1	16
Steel	36	2	38
Tattersall	5		5
Walden	38	2	40
Webster	9		9
Weir	29	2	31

Goalscorers

PLAYER	LEAGUE	CUP COMPETITION FA CUP	TOTAL
Bliss	21	1	22
Cantrell	14	1	15
Minter	5		5
Clay	4		4
Sparrow	3		3
Fleming	2		2
Middlemiss	2		2
Steel	2		2
Walden	1	1	2
Lightfoot	1		1
Weir	1		1
Opp's o.gs.	1	1	2

Fact File

Spurs looked as though they would escape relegation until they lost three of their last four games.

MANAGER: Peter McWilliam

CAPTAIN: Danny Steel

TOP SCORER: Bert Bliss

BIGGEST WIN: 6-1 v Sheffield Wednesday (H), 26 December 1914, Football League Division One

HIGHEST ATTENDANCE: 31,000 v Chelsea, 2 January 1915, Football League Division One

MAJOR TRANSFERS IN: Bill Jacques from Coventry City, John Pearson from Arbroath

MAJOR TRANSFERS OUT: Arthur King to Belfast Celtic

Final Division One Table

		P	W	D	L	F	A	Pts
1	EVERTON	38	19	8	11	76	47	46
2	OLDHAM A	38	17	11	10	70	56	45
3	BLACKBURN R	38	18	7	13	83	61	43
4	BURNLEY	38	18	7	13	61	47	43
5	MANCHESTER C	38	15	13	10	49	39	43
6	SHEFFIELD U	38	15	13	10	49	41	43
7	SHEFFIELD W	38	15	13	10	61	54	43
8	SUNDERLAND	38	18	5	15	81	72	41
9	BRADFORD	38	17	7	14	69	65	41
10	WBA	38	15	10	13	49	43	40
11	BRADFORD C	38	13	14	11	55	49	40
12	MIDDLESBROUGH	38	13	12	13	62	44	38
13	LIVERPOOL	38	14	9	15	65	75	37
14	ASTON VILLA	38	13	11	14	62	72	37
15	NEWCASTLE U	38	11	10	17	46	48	32
16	NOTTS COUNTY	38	9	13	16	41	57	31
17	BOLTON W	38	11	8	19	68	84	30
18	MANCHESTER U	38	9	12	17	46	62	30
19	CHELSEA	38	8	13	17	51	65	29
20	TOTTENHAM HOTSPUR	38	8	12	18	57	90	28

Season 1919-20

Football League Division Two

DATE	OPPONENTS	SCORE	GOALSCORERS	ATTENDANCE
Aug 30	Coventry City	W 5-0	Grimsdell, Bliss 2, Chipperfield 2	15,000
Sep 1	LEICESTER CITY	W 4-0	Clay (pen), Cantrell 2, Bliss	21,060
Sep 6	COVENTRY CITY	W 4-1	Grimsdell, Cantrell, Bliss, Chipperfield	30,610
Sep 11	Leicester City	W 4-2	Clay (pen), Minter, Cantrell, Bliss	20,000
Sep 13	SOUTH SHIELDS	W 2-0	Cantrell, Bliss	33,172
Sep 20	South Shields	W 3-0	Wilson 3	20,000
Sep 27	LINCOLN CITY	W 6-1	Grimsdell, Minter, Wilson, Bliss 2, Chipperfield	35,000
Oct 4	Lincoln City	D 1-1	Goodman	7,000
Oct 11	CLAPTON ORIENT	W 2-1	Minter, Bliss	44,268
Oct 18	Clapton Orient	W 4-0	Minter, Bliss 3	32,644
Oct 27	Port Vale	W 1-0	Cantrell	17,000
Nov 1	PORT VALE	W 2-0	Smith, Bliss	28,603
Nov 8	Bury	L 1-2	Wilson	12,000
Nov 15	BURY	W 2-1	Bliss, Chipperfield	32,000
Nov 22	Nottingham Forest	D 1-1	Chipperfield	18,000
Nov 29	NOTTINGHAM FOREST	W 5-2	Walden, Cantrell, Bliss 2, Dimmock	28,000
Dec 6	Fulham	W 4-1	Grimsdell, Minter, Cantrell, Bliss	30,000
Dec 13	FULHAM	W 4-0	Walden, Minter 2, Bliss	38,000
Dec 20	Barnsley	L 0-3		12,000
Dec 25	HULL CITY	W 4-0	Grimsdell (pen), Cantrell, Bliss 2	40,008
Dec 26	Hull City	W 3-1	Cantrell, Dimmock, Bell o.g.	28,000
Dec 27	BARNSLEY	W 4-0	Grimsdell, Banks, Cantrell, Bliss	43,071
Jan 3	Stockport County	W 2-1	Bliss, Dimmock	15,000
Jan 17	STOCKPORT COUNTY	W 2-0	Walden, Bliss	38,000
Jan 24	Huddersfield Town	D 1-1	Bliss	27,000
Feb 7	Blackpool	W 1-0	Walden	10,000
Feb 14	BLACKPOOL	D 2-2	Banks, Wilson	40,000
Feb 16	HUDDERSFIELD TOWN	W 2-0	Grimsdell, Wilson	35,000
Feb 25	Bristol City	W 2-1	Bliss 2	12,000
Feb 28	BRISTOL CITY	W 2-0	Grimsdell, Cantrell	38,000
Mar 13	West Ham United	L 1-2	Grimsdell (pen)	25,691
Mar 20	ROTHERHAM COUNTY	W 2-0	Smith, Cantrell	28,000
Mar 22	WEST HAM UNITED	W 2-0	Cantrell, Dimmock	26,000
Mar 27	Rotherham County	D 1-1	Grimsdell (pen)	18,000
Apr 2	WOLVERHAMPTON WANDERERS	W 4-2	Cantrell, Bliss 3	38,000
Apr 3	STOKE	W 2-0	Grimsdell, Dimmock	36,000
Apr 5	Wolverhampton Wanderers	W 3-1	Grimsdell 2, Cantrell	25,000
Apr 10	Stoke	W 3-1	Seed, Cantrell 2	12,000
Apr 17	GRIMSBY TOWN	W 3-1	Grimsdell, Bliss 2	32,000
Apr 24	Grimsby Town	L 0-2		10,000
Apr 26	BIRMINGHAM	D 0-0		30,000
May 1	Birmingham	W 1-0	Seed	39,000

FA Cup

Jan 10	Bristol Rovers	(Rd1) W 4-1	Cantrell 3, Bliss	17,000
Jan 31	WEST STANLEY	(Rd2) W 4-0	Banks, Wilson 2, Bliss	35,527
Feb 21	WEST HAM UNITED	(Rd3) W 3-0	Grimsdell, Wilson 2	47,642
Mar 6	ASTON VILLA	(Rd4) L 0-1		52,179

FA Charity Shield

May 15	WEST BROMWICH ALBION	L 0-2		36,000

Fact File

Twelve wins in the opening 13 games set the foundation for Spurs return to their rightful place in the top flight.

MANAGER: Peter McWilliam

CAPTAIN: Arthur Grimsdell

TOP SCORER: Bert Bliss

BIGGEST WIN: 6-1 v Lincoln City (H), 27 September 1919, Football League Division Two

HIGHEST ATTENDANCE: 52,179 v Aston Villa, 6 March 1920, FA Cup

MAJOR TRANSFERS IN: Jimmy Chipperfield from Luton Town, Alex Lindsay from Raith Rovers, Jimmy Seed from Mid-Rhondda,

MAJOR TRANSFERS OUT: Bobby Steel to Gillingham, Fred Webster to Brentford

League and Cup Appearances

PLAYER	LEAGUE	CUP COMPETITION FA CUP	OTHER	TOTAL
Archibald	13	1	1	15
Banks	18	4	1	23
Bliss	42	4	1	47
Brown	20	4	1	25
Cantrell	29	2	1	32
Castle	2			2
Chipperfield	15			15
Clay	27	3	1	31
Dimmock	27	4	1	32
Elliott	1			1
Goodman	16	1		17
Grimsdell	37	4	1	42
Jacques	42	4	1	47
Lindsay	3			3
Lorimer	4			4
Lowe	1			1
McDonald	1			1
Middlemiss	4			4
Minter	20			20
Pearson	21			21
Rance	26	3		29
Sage	1			1
Seed	5		1	6
Skinner	3			3
Smith	40	4	1	45
Walden	31	4		35
Walters	1			1
Wilson	12	2		14

Goalscorers

PLAYER	LEAGUE	CUP COMPETITION FA CUP	OTHER	TOTAL
Bliss	31	2		33
Cantrell	18	3		21
Grimsdell	14	1		15
Wilson	7	4		11
Minter	7			7
Chipperfield	6			6
Dimmock	5			5
Walden	4			4
Banks	2	1		3
Clay	2			2
Seed	2			2
Smith	2			2
Goodman	1			1
Opp's o.gs.	1			1

Final Division Two Table

		P	W	D	L	F	A	Pts
1	TOTTENHAM HOTSPUR	42	32	6	4	102	32	70
2	HUDDERSFIELD T	42	28	8	6	97	38	64
3	BIRMINGHAM	42	24	8	10	85	34	56
4	BLACKPOOL	42	21	10	11	65	47	52
5	BURY	42	20	8	14	60	44	48
6	FULHAM	42	19	9	14	61	50	47
7	WEST HAM U	42	19	9	14	47	40	47
8	BRISTOL C	42	13	17	12	46	43	43
9	GATESHEAD	42	15	12	15	58	48	42
10	STOKE	42	18	6	18	60	54	42
11	HULL CITY	42	18	6	18	78	72	42
12	BARNSLEY	42	15	10	17	61	48	40
13	PORT VALE*	42	16	8	18	59	62	40
14	LEICESTER C	42	15	10	17	41	61	40
15	CLAPTON O	42	16	6	20	51	59	38
16	STOCKPORT CO	42	14	9	19	52	61	37
17	ROTHERHAM CO	42	13	8	21	51	83	34
18	NOTTINGHAM F	42	11	9	22	43	73	31
19	WOLVERHAMPTON W	42	10	10	22	55	80	30
20	COVENTRY C	42	9	11	22	35	73	29
21	LINCOLN C	42	9	9	24	44	101	27
22	GRIMSBY T	42	10	5	27	34	75	25

*Leeds City were expelled from the league after eight games. Their results were inherited by Port Vale who took their place.

Season 1920-21

Football League Division One

Aug 28	BLACKBURN ROVERS	L 1-2	Bliss	47,345
Aug 30	Derby County	D 2-2	Clay (pen), Bliss	18,628
Sep 4	Blackburn Rovers	D 1-1	Seed	40,000
Sep 6	DERBY COUNTY	W 2-0	Seed, Bliss	26,142
Sep 11	Aston Villa	L 2-4	Walden, Dimmock	55,000
Sep 18	ASTON VILLA	L 1-2	Bliss	42,000
Sep 25	Manchester United	W 1-0	Grimsdell	52,000
Oct 2	MANCHESTER UNITED	W 4-1	Walden 2, Seed 2	34,600
Oct 9	CHELSEA	W 5-0	Wilson, Bliss 3, Dimmock	47,000
Oct 16	Chelsea	W 4-0	Wilson 2, Bliss, Dimmock	76,000
Oct 23	BURNLEY	L 1-2	Banks	39,661
Oct 30	Burnley	L 0-2		40,000
Nov 6	OLDHAM ATHLETIC	W 5-1	Grimsdell 2, Seed 2, Bliss	27,824
Nov 13	Oldham Athletic	W 5-2	Seed 2, Wilson 2, Bliss	15,000
Nov 20	PRESTON NORTH END	L 1-2	Walden	33,338
Nov 27	Preston North End	L 1-4	Smith	20,000
Dec 4	SHEFFIELD UNITED	W 4-1	Walden, Wilson 2, Dimmock	23,500
Dec 11	Sheffield United	D 1-1	Dimmock	25,000
Dec 18	BOLTON WANDERERS	W 5-2	Seed, Cantrell, Bliss 2, Dimmock	33,000
Dec 25	Newcastle United	D 1-1	Cantrell	30,000
Dec 27	NEWCASTLE UNITED	W 2-0	Bliss, Dimmock	54,500
Jan 1	Bolton Wanderers	L 0-1		45,000
Jan 15	ARSENAL	W 2-1	Cantrell, Bliss	39,221
Jan 22	Arsenal	L 2-3	Smith, Cantrell	60,600
Feb 3	BRADFORD	W 2-0	Cantrell, Bliss	20,000
Feb 5	Bradford	D 1-1	Dimmock	18,000
Feb 12	MANCHESTER CITY	W 2-0	Cantrell, Dimmock	32,000
Feb 23	West Bromwich Albion	L 1-3	Seed	16,000
Feb 26	WEST BROMWICH ALBION	W 1-0	Bliss	38,000
Mar 9	Manchester City	L 0-2		30,000
Mar 12	EVERTON	W 2-0	Archibald, Seed	30,000
Mar 25	Liverpool	D 1-1	Bliss	40,000
Mar 26	Sunderland	W 1-0	Seed	35,000
Mar 28	LIVERPOOL	W 1-0	Smith	35,000
Apr 2	SUNDERLAND	D 0-0		35,000
Apr 9	Bradford City	L 0-1		15,000
Apr 16	BRADFORD CITY	W 2-0	Wilson 2	30,000
Apr 25	Huddersfield Town	L 0-2		28,000
Apr 27	Everton	D 0-0		23,000
Apr 30	HUDDERSFIELD TOWN	W 1-0	Banks	35,000
May 2	Middlesbrough	L 0-1		10,000
May 7	MIDDLESBROUGH	D 2-2	Banks, Cantrell	25,000

FA Cup

Jan 8	BRISTOL ROVERS	(Rd1) W 6-2	Clay (pen), Smith, Walden, Seed, Cantrell, Bliss	35,175
Jan 29	BRADFORD CITY	(Rd2) W 4-0	Banks, Seed 3	39,048
Feb 19	Southend United	(Rd3) W 4-1	Banks, Seed, Cantrell, Bliss	11,600
Mar 5	ASTON VILLA	(Rd4) W 1-0	Banks	51,991
Mar 19	Preston North End *	(SF) W 2-1	Bliss	44,668
Apr 23	Wolverhampton Wanderers †	(F) W 1-0	Dimmock	72,805

* played at Hillsborough, Sheffield
† played at Stamford Bridge, London

FA Charity Shield

May 16	BURNLEY	W 2-0	Cantrell, Bliss	18,000

League and Cup Appearances

PLAYER	LEAGUE	CUP COMPETITION FA CUP	OTHER	TOTAL
Archibald	6			6
Banks	21	5	1	27
Bliss	36	6	1	43
Brown	2			2
Cantrell	23	6	1	30
Castle	3			3
Clay	35	6	1	42
Dimmock	41	6	1	48
Forster	7			7
Grimsdell	38	6	1	45
Hunter	11	3	1	15
Jacques	30	3		33
Lindsay	5			5
Lowe	5			5
McDonald	36	6	1	43
Pearson	5			5
Rance	14			14
Seed	36	6	1	43
Skinner	2			2
Smith	36	6	1	43
Thompson	3			3
Walden	22	1		23
Walters	25	6	1	32
Wilson	20			20

Goalscorers

PLAYER	LEAGUE	CUP COMPETITION FA CUP	OTHER	TOTAL
Bliss	17	4	1	22
Seed	12	5		17
Cantrell	7	2	1	10
Dimmock	9	1		10
Wilson	9			9
Banks	3	3		6
Walden	5	1		6
Smith	3	1		4
Grimsdell	3			3
Clay	1	1		2
Archibald	1			1

Fact File

Spurs had four players in the England team against Scotland in April 1921, Bert Bliss, Jimmy Dimmock, Arthur Grimsdell and Bert Smith.

Final Division One Table

		P	W	D	L	F	A	Pts
1	BURNLEY	42	23	13	6	79	36	59
2	MANCHESTER C	42	24	6	12	70	50	54
3	BOLTON W	42	19	14	9	77	53	52
4	LIVERPOOL	42	18	15	9	63	35	51
5	NEWCASTLE U	42	20	10	12	66	45	50
6	TOTTENHAM HOTSPUR	42	19	9	14	70	48	47
7	EVERTON	42	17	13	12	66	55	47
8	MIDDLESBROUGH	42	17	12	13	53	53	46
9	ARSENAL	42	15	14	13	59	63	44
10	ASTON VILLA	42	18	7	17	63	70	43
11	BLACKBURN R	42	13	15	14	57	59	41
12	BLACKBURN R	42	14	13	15	57	42	41
13	MANCHESTER U	42	15	10	17	64	68	40
14	WBA	42	13	14	15	54	58	40
15	BRADFORD C	42	12	15	15	61	63	39
16	PRESTON NE	42	15	9	18	61	65	39
17	HUDDERSFIELD T	42	15	9	18	42	49	39
18	CHELSEA	42	13	13	16	48	58	39
19	OLDHAM A	42	9	15	18	49	86	33
20	SHEFFIELD U	42	6	18	18	42	68	30
21	DERBY CO	42	5	16	21	32	58	26
22	BRADFORD	42	8	8	26	43	76	24

MANAGER: Peter McWilliam

CAPTAIN: Arthur Grimsdell

TOP SCORER: Bert Bliss

BIGGEST WIN: 5-0 v Chelsea (H), 9 October 1920, Football League Division One

HIGHEST ATTENDANCE: 76,000 v Chelsea, 16 October 1920, Football League Division One

MAJOR TRANSFERS IN: Alex Hunter from Queens Park

MAJOR TRANSFERS OUT: Herbert Middlemiss to Queens Park Rangers, Charlie Rance to Derby County

Season 1921-22

Football League Division One

Aug 27	Cardiff City	W 1-0	Banks	50,000
Aug 29	BOLTON WANDERERS	L 1-2	Thompson	31,771
Sep 3	CARDIFF CITY	W 4-1	Clay (pen), Thompson 2, Dimmock	35,000
Sep 5	Bolton Wanderers	L 0-1		40,000
Sep 10	MIDDLESBROUGH	L 2-4	Clay (pen), Bliss	34,882
Sep 17	Middlesbrough	D 0-0		20,000
Sep 24	ASTON VILLA	W 3-1	Clay (pen), Seed, Bliss	47,017
Oct 1	Aston Villa	L 1-2	Dimmock	40,000
Oct 8	MANCHESTER UNITED	D 2-2	Wilson 2	36,113
Oct 15	Manchester United	L 1-2	Dimmock	40,000
Oct 22	LIVERPOOL	L 0-1		31,593
Oct 29	Liverpool	D 1-1	Dimmock	25,000
Nov 5	NEWCASTLE UNITED	W 4-0	Grimsdell, Seed 3	34,448
Nov 12	Newcastle United	W 2-0	Seed, Lindsay	20,000
Nov 19	BURNLEY	D 1-1	Seed	45,000
Nov 26	Burnley	L 0-1		25,000
Dec 3	SHEFFIELD UNITED	W 2-1	Clay (pen), Skinner	27,321
Dec 10	Sheffield United	L 0-1		27,000
Dec 17	CHELSEA	D 0-0		44,035
Dec 24	Chelsea	W 2-1	Bliss 2	54,000
Dec 26	BRADFORD CITY	W 1-0	Clay (pen)	34,483
Dec 27	Bradford City	W 4-0	Seed, Wilson 2, Thompson	25,000
Dec 31	PRESTON NORTH END	W 5-0	Seed, Wilson 2, Thompson, Dimmock	28,097
Jan 14	Preston North End	W 2-1	Walden, Cantrell	20,000
Jan 21	West Bromwich Albion	L 0-3		20,000
Jan 30	WEST BROMWICH ALBION	W 2-0	Clay (pen), Wilson	30,000
Feb 4	Manchester City	D 3-3	Wilson, Bliss 2	20,000
Feb 11	MANCHESTER CITY	W 3-1	Grimsdell, Bliss, Dimmock	43,000
Feb 25	EVERTON	W 2-0	Wilson, Dimmock	34,871
Mar 11	SUNDERLAND	W 1-0	Thompson	41,003
Mar 15	Everton	D 0-0		30,000
Mar 18	HUDDERSFIELD TOWN	W 1-0	Skinner	36,187
Mar 27	Huddersfield Town	D 1-1	Lindsay	16,000
Apr 1	Birmingham	W 3-0	Clay (pen), Seed, Roulsen o.g.	34,000
Apr 5	Sunderland	L 0-2		37,000
Apr 8	BIRMINGHAM	W 2-1	Lindsay, Jones o.g.	19,638
Apr 14	OLDHAM ATHLETIC	W 3-1	Clay (pen), Cantrell 2	34,881
Apr 15	ARSENAL	W 2-0	Grimsdell, Seed	40,394
Apr 17	Oldham Athletic	L 0-1		31,343
Apr 22	Arsenal	L 0-1		42,000
Apr 29	BLACKBURN ROVERS	W 2-1	Walden, Wilson	24,559
May 6	Blackburn Rovers	D 1-1	Wilson	25,000

FA Cup

Jan 7	Brentford	(Rd1) W 2-0	Seed, Cantrell	12,964
Jan 28	WATFORD	(Rd2) W 1-0	Bliss	47,660
Feb 18	MANCHESTER CITY	(Rd3) W 2-1	Wilson, Bliss	53,810
Mar 4	Cardiff City	(Rd4) D 1-1	Seed	55,000
Mar 9	CARDIFF CITY	(R) W 2-1	Wilson, Dimmock	53,626
Mar 25	Preston North End *	(SF) L 1-2	Seed	50,095

* played at Hillsbrough, Sheffield

League and Cup Appearances

PLAYER	LEAGUE	CUP COMPETITION FA CUP	TOTAL
Archibald	5		5
Banks	11		11
Blake	8		8
Bliss	23	6	29
Cantrell	13	1	14
Clay	37	6	43
Dimmock	42	6	48
Forster	4		4
Grimsdell	35	6	41
Handley	1		1
Hunter	12		12
Jacques	22	6	28
Lindsay	16		16
Lorimer	1		1
Lowe	12	1	13
McDonald	40	6	46
Pearson	3		3
Seed	36	6	42
Skinner	16		16
Smith	25	6	31
Thompson	18		18
Walden	28	6	34
Walters	33	5	38
Wilson	21	5	26

Goalscorers

PLAYER	LEAGUE	CUP COMPETITION FA CUP	TOTAL
Seed	10	3	13
Wilson	11	2	13
Bliss	7	2	9
Clay	8		8
Dimmock	7	1	8
Thompson	6		6
Cantrell	3	1	4
Grimsdell	3		3
Lindsay	3		3
Skinner	2		2
Walden	2		2
Banks	1		1
Opp's o.gs.	2		2

Fact File

Second place represented Spurs highest ever finish in the Football League.

MANAGER: Peter McWilliam

CAPTAIN: Arthur Grimsdell

TOP SCORERS: Jimmy Seed and Charlie Wilson

BIGGEST WIN: 5-0 v Preston North End (H), 31 December 1921, Football League Division One

HIGHEST ATTENDANCE: 55,000 v Cardiff City, 4 March 1922, FA Cup 4th Round

MAJOR TRANSFERS IN: Bert Blake from Mid-Rhondda

MAJOR TRANSFERS OUT: Hugh Lorimer to Dundee

Final Division One Table

		P	W	D	L	F	A	Pts
1	LIVERPOOL	42	22	13	7	63	36	57
2	TOTTENHAM HOTSPUR	42	21	9	12	65	39	51
3	BURNLEY	42	22	5	15	72	54	49
4	CARDIFF C	42	19	10	13	61	53	48
5	ASTON VILLA	42	22	3	17	74	55	47
6	BOLTON W	42	20	7	15	68	59	47
7	NEWCASTLE U	42	18	10	14	59	45	46
8	MIDDLESBROUGH	42	16	14	12	79	69	46
9	CHELSEA	42	17	12	13	40	43	46
10	MANCHESTER C	42	18	9	15	65	70	45
11	SHEFFIELD U	42	15	10	17	59	54	40
12	BLACKBURN R	42	16	8	18	60	37	40
13	WBA	42	15	10	17	51	63	40
14	HUDDERSFIELD T	42	15	9	18	53	54	39
15	BLACKBURN R	42	13	12	17	54	57	38
16	PRESTON NE	42	13	12	17	42	65	38
17	ARSENAL	42	15	7	20	47	56	37
18	BIRMINGHAM C	42	15	7	20	48	60	37
19	OLDHAM A	42	13	11	18	38	50	37
20	EVERTON	42	12	12	18	57	55	36
21	BRADFORD C	42	11	10	21	48	72	32
22	MANCHESTER U	42	8	12	22	41	73	28

Season 1922-23

Football League Division One

Aug 26	CARDIFF CITY	D	1-1	Cantrell	43,168
Sep 2	Cardiff City	W	3-2	Smith, Seed, Bliss	50,000
Sep 4	EVERTON	W	2-0	Seed, Bliss	24,262
Sep 9	BURNLEY	L	1-3	Cantrell	39,434
Sep 16	Burnley	W	1-0	Bliss	20,000
Sep 23	ARSENAL	L	1-2	Lindsay	40,582
Sep 30	Arsenal	W	2-0	Dimmock 2	55,000
Oct 7	Aston Villa	L	0-2		50,000
Oct 14	ASTON VILLA	L	1-2	Seed	43,252
Oct 21	WEST BROMWICH ALBION	W	3-1	Skinner, Walden, Brooks	26,188
Oct 28	West Bromwich Albion	L	1-5	Seed	23,000
Nov 4	LIVERPOOL	L	2-4	Clay (pen), Grimsdell	35,068
Nov 11	Liverpool	D	0-0		29,000
Nov 18	NEWCASTLE UNITED	L	0-1		30,300
Nov 25	Newcastle United	D	1-1	Lindsay	25,000
Dec 2	NOTTINGHAM FOREST	W	2-1	Seed, Dimmock	25,252
Dec 9	Nottingham Forest	W	1-0	Seed	15,000
Dec 16	Chelsea	D	0-0		50,000
Dec 23	CHELSEA	W	3-1	Smith, Seed 2	33,068
Dec 25	SHEFFIELD UNITED	W	2-1	Cantrell, Handley	45,000
Dec 26	Sheffield United	L	0-2		42,000
Dec 30	Middlesbrough	L	0-2		8,000
Jan 1	Everton	L	1-3	Lindsay	20,000
Jan 6	MIDDLESBROUGH	W	2-0	Walden, Handley	35,000
Jan 20	Oldham Athletic	W	3-0	Grimsdell, Lindsay, Dimmock	9,000
Jan 27	OLDHAM ATHLETIC	W	3-0	Clay (2 pens) 2, Lindsay	24,843
Feb 10	Blackburn Rovers	L	0-1		6,000
Feb 14	BLACKBURN ROVERS	W	2-0	Lindsay 2	10,000
Feb 17	BOLTON WANDERERS	L	0-1		30,000
Mar 3	MANCHESTER CITY	W	3-1	Walden, Seed, Handley	27,963
Mar 14	Manchester City	L	0-3		25,000
Mar 17	Stoke	D	0-0		30,000
Mar 24	STOKE	W	3-1	Lindsay, Handley, Dimmock	20,000
Mar 30	PRESTON NORTH END	D	1-1	Handley	30,865
Mar 31	Sunderland	L	0-2		18,000
Apr 2	Preston North End	L	0-2		22,000
Apr 7	SUNDERLAND	L	0-1		23,571
Apr 11	Bolton Wanderers	W	2-0	Cantrell, Dimmock	15,000
Apr 14	Birmingham	L	1-2	Lindsay	15,000
Apr 21	BIRMINGHAM	W	2-0	Lindsay 2	16,335
Apr 28	Huddersfield Town	L	0-1		15,000
May 5	HUDDERSFIELD TOWN	D	0-0		17,000

FA Cup

Jan 13	WORKSOP TOWN	(Rd1)	D 0-0		23,928
Jan 15	WORKSOP TOWN *	(R)	W 9-0	Seed, Lindsay 4, Handley 3, Dimmock	23,122
Feb 3	MANCHESTER UTD	(Rd2)	W 4-0	Lindsay, Handley 3	38,333
Feb 24	Cardiff City	(Rd3)	W 3-2	Seed, Lindsay, Handley	54,000
Mar 10	DERBY COUNTY	(Rd4)	L 0-1		50,349

* played at home by mutual consent

League and Cup Appearances

PLAYER	LEAGUE	CUP COMPETITION FA CUP	TOTAL
Banks	2		2
Barnett	2		2
Blake	36	5	41
Bliss	8		8
Brooks	7		7
Brown	12	4	16
Cantrell	10		10
Clay	34	4	38
Dimmock	42	5	47
Forster	12		12
Grimsdell	40	5	45
Handley	30	5	35
Hartley	1		1
Jacques	1		1
Lindsay	34	5	39
Lowe	14	5	19
Maddison	5		5
McDonald	17		17
Pearson	1	1	2
Ross	6		6
Seed	36	5	41
Sharp	2		2
Skinner	15	1	16
Smith	32	5	37
Thompson	2		2
Walden	30	5	35
Walters	29		29
Wilson	2		2

Goalscorers

PLAYER	LEAGUE	CUP COMPETITION FA CUP	TOTAL
Lindsay	11	6	17
Handley	5	7	12
Seed	9	2	11
Dimmock	6	1	7
Cantrell	4		4
Bliss	3		3
Clay	3		3
Walden	3		3
Grimsdell	2		2
Smith	2		2
Brooks	1		1
Skinner	1		1

Fact File

At the end of the season, the Park Lane End was covered at a cost of £3,000, giving total covered accommodation for 45,000 spectators.

MANAGER: Peter McWilliam

CAPTAIN: Arthur Grimsdell

TOP SCORER: Alex Lindsay

BIGGEST WIN: 9-0 v Worksop Town (H), 15 January 1923, FA Cup 1st Round replay

HIGHEST ATTENDANCE: 54,000 v Cardiff City, 24 February 1923, FA Cup 3rd Round

MAJOR TRANSFERS IN: Sammy Brooks from Wolverhampton Wanderers, Buchanan Sharp from Chelsea

MAJOR TRANSFERS OUT: Bert Bliss to Clapton Orient, Alex Hunter to Wigan Borough, Charlie Wilson to Huddersfield Town

Final Division One Table

		P	W	D	L	F	A	Pts
1	LIVERPOOL	42	26	8	8	70	31	60
2	BLACKBURN R	42	22	10	10	72	54	54
3	HUDDERSFIELD T	42	21	11	10	60	32	53
4	NEWCASTLE U	42	18	12	12	45	37	48
5	EVERTON	42	20	7	15	63	59	47
6	ASTON VILLA	42	18	10	14	64	51	46
7	WBA	42	17	11	14	58	49	45
8	MANCHESTER C	42	17	11	14	50	49	45
9	CARDIFF C	42	18	7	17	73	59	43
10	SHEFFIELD U	42	16	10	16	68	64	42
11	ARSENAL	42	16	10	16	61	62	42
12	TOTTENHAM HOTSPUR	42	17	7	18	50	38	41
13	BOLTON W	42	14	12	16	50	58	40
14	BLACKBURN R	42	14	12	16	47	62	40
15	BURNLEY	42	16	6	20	58	59	38
16	PRESTON NE	42	13	11	18	60	64	37
17	BIRMINGHAM C	42	13	11	18	41	57	37
18	MIDDLESBROUGH	42	13	10	19	57	63	36
19	CHELSEA	42	9	18	15	45	53	36
20	NOTTINGHAM F	42	13	8	21	41	70	34
21	STOKE	42	10	10	22	47	67	30
22	OLDHAM A	42	10	10	22	35	65	30

Season 1923-24

Football League Division One

Aug 25	PRESTON NORTH END	W 2-0	Lindsay, Handley	33,405
Aug 27	Chelsea	W 1-0	Lindsay	40,000
Sep 1	Preston North End	D 2-2	Handley, Dimmock	16,000
Sep 3	CHELSEA	L 0-1		31,996
Sep 8	MIDDLESBROUGH	W 2-1	Lindsay 2	32,772
Sep 15	Middlesbrough	W 1-0	Lindsay	25,000
Sep 22	BOLTON WANDERERS	D 0-0		35,012
Sep 29	Bolton Wanderers	L 1-3	Lindsay	25,000
Oct 6	Notts County	D 0-0		19,000
Oct 13	NOTTS COUNTY	L 1-3	Elkes	28,503
Oct 20	Sunderland	L 0-1		20,000
Oct 27	SUNDERLAND	D 1-1	Lindsay	24,840
Nov 3	Nottingham Forest	D 0-0		18,000
Nov 10	NOTTINGHAM FOREST	W 3-0	Lindsay, Elkes, Handley	23,831
Nov 17	Arsenal	D 1-1	Seed	50,000
Nov 24	ARSENAL	W 3-0	Lindsay 2, Elkes	31,624
Dec 1	WEST BROMWICH ALBION	D 0-0		23,048
Dec 8	West Bromwich Albion	L 1-4	Seed	23,000
Dec 15	BLACKBURN ROVERS	W 2-1	Lindsay, Elkes	19,471
Dec 22	Blackburn Rovers	W 1-0	Lindsay	15,000
Dec 25	HUDDERSFIELD TOWN	W 1-0	Lindsay	44,274
Dec 26	Huddersfield Town	L 1-2	Handley	29,000
Dec 29	BIRMINGHAM	D 1-1	Lindsay	24,414
Jan 1	Manchester City	L 0-1		24,000
Jan 5	Birmingham	L 2-3	Thompson, Elkes	25,000
Jan 19	NEWCASTLE UNITED	W 2-0	Poynton, Elkes	25,649
Jan 26	Newcastle United	D 2-2	Clay (pen), Osborne	27,000
Feb 9	West Ham United	D 0-0		30,000
Feb 16	CARDIFF CITY	D 1-1	Smith	32,478
Mar 1	SHEFFIELD UNITED	L 1-2	Dimmock	25,925
Mar 8	Sheffield United	L 2-6	Lindsay, Elkes	25,000
Mar 15	Aston Villa	D 0-0		30,000
Mar 22	ASTON VILLA	L 2-3	Lindsay, Elkes	28,771
Mar 29	Liverpool	L 0-1		22,000
Apr 5	LIVERPOOL	D 1-1	Grimsdell	22,470
Apr 7	Cardiff City	L 1-2	Lindsay	25,000
Apr 12	EVERTON	L 2-5	Walden, Lindsay	14,606
Apr 19	Everton	L 2-4	Lindsay, Raitt o.g.	20,000
Apr 21	MANCHESTER CITY	W 4-1	Elkes, Lindsay, Hargreaves 2	11,739
Apr 22	WEST HAM UNITED	L 0-1		18,153
Apr 26	Burnley	D 2-2	Hargreaves, Elkes	50,000
May 3	BURNELY	W 1-0	Elkes	20,000

FA Cup

Jan 12	Crystal Palace	(Rd1) L 0-2		17,000

League and Cup Appearances

PLAYER	LEAGUE	CUP COMPETITION FA CUP	TOTAL
Barnett	2		2
Blake	7		7
Brooks	3		3
Brown	3		3
Clay	40	1	41
Dimmock	25		25
Elkes	37	1	38
Forster	35	1	36
Grimsdell	27	1	28
Handley	22	1	23
Hargreaves	7		7
Lindsay	39	1	40
Lowe	22	1	23
Maddison	35	1	36
McDonald	3		3
Osborne	12		12
Poynton	10		10
Ross	1		1
Sage	7		7
Seed	21		21
Skinner	2		2
Smith	41	1	42
Thompson	7	1	8
Walden	34	1	35
Walters	15		15
White	5		5

Goalscorers

PLAYER	LEAGUE	CUP COMPETITION FA CUP	TOTAL
Lindsay	20		20
Elkes	11		11
Handley	4		4
Hargreaves	3		3
Dimmock	2		2
Seed	2		2
Clay	1		1
Grimsdell	1		1
Osborne	1		1
Poynton	1		1
Smith	1		1
Thompson	1		1
Walden	1		1
Opp's o.gs.	1		1

Fact File

League Champions Huddersfield Town were managed by former Spurs inside forward Herbert Chapman.

MANAGER: Peter McWilliam
CAPTAIN: Arthur Grimsdell
TOP SCORER: Alex Lindsay
BIGGEST WIN: 4-1 v Manchester City (H), 21 April 1924, Football League Division One
HIGHEST ATTENDANCE: 50,000 v Arsenal, 17 November 1923, Football League Division One; 50,000 v Burnley, 26 April 1924, Football League Division One
MAJOR TRANSFERS IN: Jack Elkes from Southampton, Frank Osborne from Fulham
MAJOR TRANSFERS OUT: Jimmy Banks to Norwich City, Jimmy Cantrell to Sutton Town

Final Division One Table

		P	W	D	L	F	A	Pts
1	HUDDERSFIELD T	42	23	11	8	60	33	57
2	CARDIFF C	42	22	13	7	61	34	57
3	BLACKBURN R	42	22	9	11	71	54	53
4	BOLTON W	42	18	14	10	68	34	50
5	SHEFFIELD U	42	19	12	11	69	49	50
6	ASTON VILLA	42	18	13	11	52	37	49
7	EVERTON	42	18	13	11	62	53	49
8	BLACKBURN R	42	17	11	14	46	50	45
9	NEWCASTLE U	42	17	10	15	60	54	44
10	NOTTS COUNTY	42	14	14	14	44	49	42
11	MANCHESTER C	42	15	12	15	54	71	42
12	LIVERPOOL	42	15	11	16	49	48	41
13	WEST HAM U	42	13	15	14	40	43	41
14	BIRMINGHAM C	42	13	13	16	41	49	39
15	TOTTENHAM HOTSPUR	42	12	14	16	50	56	38
16	WBA	42	12	14	16	51	62	38
17	BURNLEY	42	12	12	18	55	60	36
18	PRESTON NE	42	12	10	20	52	67	34
19	ARSENAL	42	12	9	21	40	63	33
20	NOTTINGHAM F	42	10	12	20	42	64	32
21	CHELSEA	42	9	14	19	31	53	32
22	MIDDLESBROUGH	42	7	8	27	37	60	22

213

Season 1924-25

Football League Division One

DATE	OPPONENTS	SCORE	GOALSCORERS	ATTENDANCE
Aug 30	BOLTON WANDERERS	W 3-0	Clay (pen), Lindsay, Hargreaves	42,000
Sep 3	Birmingham	W 2-0	Seed, Dimmock	20,000
Sep 6	Notts County	D 0-0		20,000
Sep 8	West Bromwich Albion	L 0-2		17,000
Sep 13	EVERTON	D 0-0		35,039
Sep 20	Sunderland	L 1-4	Lindsay	30,000
Sep 22	WEST BROMWICH ALBION	L 0-1		16,281
Sep 27	CARDIFF CITY	D 1-1	Elkes	38,324
Oct 4	Preston North End	W 3-0	Seed 2, Dimmock	20,000
Oct 11	BURNLEY	D 1-1	Handley	23,508
Oct 18	Leeds United	L 0-1		25,000
Oct 25	Arsenal	L 0-1		51,000
Nov 1	ASTON VILLA	L 1-3	Handley	19,054
Nov 8	Huddersfield Town	W 2-1	Thompson, Seed	18,000
Nov 10	MANCHESTER CITY	D 1-1	Smith	10,781
Nov 15	BLACKBURN ROVERS	W 5-0	Seed 2, Elkes 3	30,000
Nov 22	West Ham United	D 1-1	Elkes	30,000
Nov 29	SHEFFIELD UNITED	W 4-1	Seed, Hargreaves, Elkes, Handley	24,483
Dec 6	Newcastle United	D 1-1	Elkes	28,000
Dec 13	LIVERPOOL	D 1-1	Hargreaves	25,604
Dec 20	Nottingham Forest	L 0-1		15,000
Dec 25	BURY	D 1-1	Elkes (pen)	35,716
Dec 27	Bolton Wanderers	L 0-3		18,000
Jan 1	Bury	L 2-5	Seed 2	18,000
Jan 3	NOTTS COUNTY	D 1-1	Elkes	23,933
Jan 17	Everton	L 0-1		30,000
Jan 24	SUNDERLAND	W 1-0	Seed	26,696
Feb 7	PRESTON NORTH END	W 2-0	Seed, Lane	35,000
Feb 14	Burnley	W 4-1	Clay (pen), Thompson, Seed, Lane	18,000
Feb 28	ARSENAL	W 2-0	Elkes, Dimmock	29,457
Mar 7	Aston Villa	W 1-0	Lane	25,000
Mar 9	LEEDS UNITED	W 2-1	Seed, Lane	8,000
Mar 14	HUDDERSFIELD TOWN	L 1-2	Lane	35,000
Mar 18	Cardiff City	W 2-0	Seed 2	31,126
Mar 21	Blackburn Rovers	D 1-1	Thompson	15,000
Mar 28	WEST HAM UNITED	D 1-1	Seed	29,321
Apr 4	Sheffield United	L 0-2		20,000
Apr 10	BIRMINGHAM	L 0-1		30,411
Apr 11	NEWCASTLE UNITED	W 3-0	Lane, Dimmock 2	23,144
Apr 18	Liverpool	L 0-1		12,000
Apr 25	NOTTINGHAM FOREST	W 1-0	Seed	20,000
May 2	Manchester City	L 0-1		10,000

FA Cup

Jan 10	NORTHAMPTON TOWN	(Rd1) W 3-0	Seed, Lindsay, Elkes	32,718
Jan 31	BOLTON WANDERERS	(Rd2) D 1-1	Seed	52,635
Feb 4	Bolton Wanderers	(R) W 1-0	Lane	51,774
Feb 21	BLACKBURN ROVERS	(Rd3) D 2-2	Lane, Dimmock	54,521
Feb 26	Blackburn Rovers	(R) L 1-3	Dimmock	48,000

League and Cup Appearances

PLAYER	LEAGUE	CUP COMPETITION FA CUP	TOTAL
Clay	21	4	25
Dimmock	29	4	33
Elkes	33	5	38
Forster	21	1	22
Grimsdell	14	4	18
Handley	14		14
Hargreaves	20		20
Hinton	42	5	47
Lane	17	4	21
Lindsay	18	1	19
Lowe	6		6
McDonald	12	4	16
Osborne	23	2	25
Poynton	24	1	25
Sage	1		1
Seed	41	5	46
Sharp	1		1
Skinner	34	4	38
Skitt	27	5	32
Smith	37	2	39
Thompson	20	4	24
Walters	2		2
White	5		5

Goalscorers

PLAYER	LEAGUE	CUP COMPETITION FA CUP	TOTAL
Seed	17	2	19
Elkes	10	1	11
Lane	6	2	8
Dimmock	5	2	7
Handley	3		3
Hargreaves	3		3
Lindsay	2	1	3
Thompson	3		3
Clay	2		2
Smith	1		1

Fact File

Spurs spent May 1925 in Switzerland, scoring 29 goals while conceding only two in seven games.

MANAGER: Peter McWilliam
CAPTAIN: Arthur Grimsdell
TOP SCORER: Jimmy Seed
BIGGEST WIN: 5-0 v Blackburn Rovers (H), 15 November 1924, Football League Division One
HIGHEST ATTENDANCE: 54,521 v Blackburn Rovers, 21 February 1925, FA Cup 3rd Round
MAJOR TRANSFERS IN: Bill Hinton from Bolton Wanderers
MAJOR TRANSFERS OUT: Geordie Maddison to Hull City

Final Division One Table

		P	W	D	L	F	A	Pts
1	HUDDERSFIELD T	42	21	16	5	69	28	58
2	WBA	42	23	10	9	58	34	56
3	BOLTON W	42	22	11	9	76	34	55
4	LIVERPOOL	42	20	10	12	63	55	50
5	BURY	42	17	15	10	54	51	49
6	NEWCASTLE U	42	16	16	10	61	42	48
7	BLACKBURN R	42	19	10	13	64	51	48
8	BIRMINGHAM	42	17	12	13	49	53	46
9	NOTTS COUNTY	42	16	13	13	42	31	45
10	MANCHESTER C	42	17	9	16	76	68	43
11	CARDIFF C	42	16	11	15	56	51	43
12	Tottenham Hotspur	42	15	12	15	52	43?	42
13	WEST HAM U	42	15	12	15	62	60	42
14	SHEFFIELD U	42	13	13	16	55	63	39
15	ASTON VILLA	42	13	13	16	58	71	39
16	BLACKBURN R	42	11	13	18	53	66	35
17	EVERTON	42	12	11	19	40	60	35
18	LEEDS UNITED	42	11	12	19	46	59	34
19	BURNLEY	42	11	12	19	46	75	34
20	ARSENAL	42	14	5	23	46	58	33
21	PRESTON NE	42	10	6	26	37	74	26
22	NOTTINGHAM F	42	6	12	24	29	65	24

Season 1925-26

Football League Division One

DATE	OPPONENTS	SCORE	GOALSCORERS	ATTENDANCE
Aug 29	Arsenal	W 1-0	Dimmock	53,183
Aug 31	Sheffield United	W 3-2	Osborne 2, Hargreaves	18,743
Sep 5	MANCHESTER CITY	W 1-0	Seed	35,594
Sep 7	SHEFFIELD UNITED	W 3-2	Seed 2, Dimmock	21,978
Sep 12	Everton	D 1-1	Dimmock	37,506
Sep 14	CARDIFF CITY	L 1-2	Elkes	26,716
Sep 19	HUDDERSFIELD TOWN	D 5-5	Clay (pen), Osborne, Elkes 2, Dimmock	20,880
Sep 21	Cardiff City	W 1-0	Dimmock	20,698
Sep 26	Sunderland	L 0-3		30,700
Oct 3	BLACKBURN ROVERS	W 4-2	Dimmock, Osborne 2, Thompson	35,645
Oct 10	Bury	L 0-3		19,759
Oct 17	Manchester United	D 0-0		26,496
Oct 24	LIVERPOOL	W 3-1	Osborne 3	29,952
Oct 31	Leicester City	L 3-5	Osborne 3	28,076
Nov 7	WEST HAM UNITED	W 4-2	Osborne 3, Elkes	35,259
Nov 14	Newcastle United	L 1-3	Seed	23,391
Nov 21	BOLTON WANDERERS	L 2-3	Osborne, Elkes	26,792
Nov 28	Notts County	L 2-4	Elkes, Dimmock	12,191
Dec 5	ASTON VILLA	D 2-2	Osborne, Elkes	28,821
Dec 12	Burnley	W 2-1	Osborne, Dimmock	18,592
Dec 19	LEEDS UNITED	W 3-2	Thompson, Osborne, Elkes	19,200
Dec 25	Birmingham	L 1-3	Clay (pen)	29,586
Dec 26	BIRMINGHAM	W 2-1	Seed, Osborne	44,429
Jan 2	ARSENAL	D 1-1	Thompson	43,221
Jan 16	Manchester City	D 0-0		25,244
Jan 23	EVERTON	D 1-1	Thompson	22,805
Feb 6	SUNDERLAND	L 0-2		31,434
Feb 13	Blackburn Rovers	L 2-4	Osborne, Dimmock	21,584
Feb 20	BURY	W 4-2	Lindsay 2, Osborne 2	33,023
Feb 27	MANCHESTER UNITED	L 0-1		25,466
Mar 3	Huddersfield Town	L 1-2	Elkes	13,005
Mar 6	Liverpool	D 0-0		26,355
Mar 13	LEICESTER CITY	L 1-3	Osborne	23,911
Mar 20	West Ham United	L 1-3	Osborne	29,423
Mar 25	NEWCASTLE UNITED	W 1-0	Dimmock	11,774
Apr 2	WEST BROMWICH ALBION	W 3-2	Seed, Dimmock 2	27,914
Apr 3	Bolton Wanderers	D 1-1	Osborne	21,364
Apr 5	West Bromwich Albion	L 0-1		15,365
Apr 10	NOTTS COUNTY	W 4-0	Roe, Elkes, Dimmock 2	17,892
Apr 17	Aston Villa	L 0-3		11,774
Apr 24	BURNLEY	L 0-2		21,211
May 1	Leeds United	L 1-4	Elkes	16,158

FA Cup

Jan 9	WEST HAM UNITED	(Rd3)	W 5-0	Osborne 2, Dimmock 3	49,800
Jan 30	MANCHESTER UTD	(Rd4)	D 2-2	Thompson, Lindsay	43,653
Feb 3	Manchester United	(R)	L 0-2		46,929

League and Cup Appearances

PLAYER	LEAGUE	CUP COMPETITION FA CUP	TOTAL
Bann	8		8
Britton	9		9
Clay	34	3	37
Dimmock	40	3	43
Elkes	32	3	35
Forster	42	3	45
Grimsdell	13		13
Handley	2		2
Hargreaves	7		7
Hinton	15	2	17
Kaine	11	1	12
Lane	4		4
Lindsay	24	3	27
Lowe	2		2
Osborne	39	1	40
Roe	3		3
Sage	4		4
Seed	31	2	33
Skinner	15	1	16
Skitt	36	3	39
Smith B	38	3	41
Smith J	7		7
Thompson	35	3	38
Walters	1		1
White	10	2	12

Goalscorers

PLAYER	LEAGUE	CUP COMPETITION FA CUP	TOTAL
Osborne	25	2	27
Dimmock	14	3	17
Elkes	11		11
Seed	6		6
Thompson	4	1	5
Lindsay	2	1	3
Clay	2		2
Hargreaves	1		1
Roe	1		1

Fact File

At the beginning of October Spurs topped the First Division for the first time in their history.

MANAGER: Peter McWilliam

CAPTAIN: Arthur Grimsdell/Tommy Clay

TOP SCORER: Frank Osborne

BIGGEST WIN: 5-0 v West Ham United (H), 9 January 1926, FA Cup 3rd Round

HIGHEST ATTENDANCE: 53,183 v Arsenal, 29 August 1925, Football League Division One

MAJOR TRANSFERS IN: Jock Britton from Dundee, Bill Kaine from West Ham United, Jimmy Smith from Rosyth Recreation

MAJOR TRANSFERS OUT: Harry Hargreaves to Burnley

Final Division One Table

		P	W	D	L	F	A	Pts
1	HUDDERSFIELD T	42	23	11	8	92	60	57
2	ARSENAL	42	22	8	12	87	63	52
3	BLACKBURN R	42	21	6	15	96	80	48
4	BURY	42	20	7	15	85	77	47
5	SHEFFIELD U	42	19	8	15	102	82	46
6	ASTON VILLA	42	16	12	14	86	76	44
7	LIVERPOOL	42	14	16	12	70	63	44
8	BOLTON W	42	17	10	15	75	76	44
9	MANCHESTER U	42	19	6	17	66	73	44
10	NEWCASTLE U	42	16	10	16	84	75	42
11	EVERTON	42	12	18	12	72	70	42
12	BLACKBURN R	42	15	11	16	91	65	41
13	WBA	42	16	8	18	79	78	40
14	BIRMINGHAM	42	16	8	18	66	81	40
15	TOTTENHAM HOTSPUR	42	15	9	18	66	79	39
16	CARDIFF C	42	16	7	19	61	76	39
17	LEICESTER C	42	14	10	18	70	80	38
18	WEST HAM U	42	15	7	20	63	76	37
19	LEEDS UNITED	42	14	8	20	64	76	36
20	BURNLEY	42	13	10	19	85	108	36
21	MANCHESTER C	42	12	11	19	89	100	35
22	NOTTS COUNTY	42	13	7	22	54	74	33

Season 1926-27

Football League Division One

DATE	OPPONENTS	SCORE	GOALSCORERS	ATTENDANCE
Aug 28	EVERTON	W 2-1	Blair, Osborne	28,324
Aug 30	SHEFFIELD WEDNESDAY	W 7-3	Elkes 2, Thompson, Blair, Osborne, Seed, Dimmock	19,726
Sep 4	Blackburn Rovers	L 0-1		21,964
Sep 6	LEICESTER CITY	D 2-2	Dimmock 2	19,461
Sep 11	HUDDERSFIELD TOWN	D 3-3	Thompson, Blair 2	29,516
Sep 13	Leicester City	D 2-2	Lane, Dimmock	24,928
Sep 18	Sunderland	L 2-3	Blair 2	17,459
Sep 25	WEST BROMWICH ALBION	W 3-0	Blair, Osborne, Seed	31,236
Oct 2	Bury	D 0-0		16,581
Oct 9	BIRMINGHAM	W 6-1	Blair 2, Roe 2, Seed, Dimmock	29,392
Oct 16	SHEFFIELD UNITED	W 3-1	Osborne 2, Seed	29,656
Oct 23	Derby County	L 1-4	Handley	20,325
Oct 30	BOLTON WANDERERS	W 1-0	Handley	29,999
Nov 6	Aston Villa	W 3-2	Seed 2, Dimmock	19,496
Nov 13	CARDIFF CITY	W 4-1	Osborne 2, Handley, Dimmock	15,350
Nov 20	Burnley	L 0-5		17,957
Nov 27	NEWCASTLE UNITED	L 1-3	Dimmock	33,325
Dec 4	Leeds United	D 1-1	Dimmock	24,470
Dec 11	LIVERPOOL	L 1-2	Blair	26,640
Dec 18	Arsenal	W 4-2	Seed, Osborne 2, Handley	49,429
Dec 25	MANCHESTER UNITED	D 1-1	Dimmock	37,287
Dec 27	Manchester United	L 1-2	Handley	50,665
Dec 28	Sheffield Wednesday	L 1-3	Dimmock	35,529
Jan 15	Everton	W 2-1	Blair, Dimmock	35,986
Jan 22	BLACKBURN ROVERS	D 1-1	Handley	14,323
Jan 29	Huddersfield Town	L 0-2		15,147
Feb 5	SUNDERLAND	L 0-2		32,506
Feb 12	West Bromwich Albion	L 0-5		15,388
Feb 19	BURY	W 1-0	Dimmock (pen)	19,759
Feb 26	Birmingham	L 0-1		21,145
Mar 5	Sheffield United	D 3-3	O'Callaghan 2, Sanders	21,732
Mar 12	DERBY COUNTY	W 3-2	O'Callaghan, Roe, Dimmock	26,556
Mar 19	Bolton Wanderers	D 2-2	Sanders, Dimmock	17,762
Mar 26	ASTON VILLA	L 0-1		30,614
Apr 2	Cardiff City	W 2-1	O'Callaghan, Handley	13,384
Apr 9	BURNLEY	W 4-1	O'Callaghan, Sanders 2, Dimmock	15,481
Apr 15	WEST HAM UNITED	L 1-3	Handley	42,010
Apr 16	Newcastle United	L 2-3	Sanders, Dimmock	32,151
Apr 18	West Ham United	W 2-1	Handley, Dimmock	21,354
Apr 23	LEEDS UNITED	W 4-1	Sanders 2, Handley, Dimmock (pen)	17,745
Apr 30	Liverpool	L 0-1		15,756
May 7	ARSENAL	L 0-4		29,555

FA Cup

DATE	OPPONENT		SCORE	GOALSCORERS	ATTENDANCE
Jan 8	West Ham United	(Rd3)	L 2-3	Handley, Dimmock	44,417

League and Cup Appearances

PLAYER	LEAGUE	CUP COMPETITION FA CUP	TOTAL
Barnett	1		1
Bellamy	1		1
Blair	24	1	25
Britton	18		18
Clay	16	1	17
Dimmock	41	1	42
Elkes	40	1	41
Forster	35		35
Grimsdell	2		2
Handley	24	1	25
Lane	4		4
Lindsay	37	1	38
Lowe	1		1
Nicholls	1		1
O'Callaghan	13		13
Osborne	34		34
Poynton	31	1	32
Richardson	2		2
Roe	3		3
Sanders	12		12
Seed	23	1	24
Skitt	22		22
Smith	24	1	25
Smith	23	1	24
Thompson	30	1	31

Goalscorers

PLAYER	LEAGUE	CUP COMPETITION FA CUP	TOTAL
Dimmock	19	1	20
Blair	11		11
Handley	10	1	11
Osborne	9		9
Sanders	7		7
Seed	7		7
O'Callaghan	5		5
Roe	3		3
Elkes	2		2
Thompson	2		2
Lane	1		1

Fact File

Peter McWilliam handed in his notice in December to accept Middlesbrough's offer of £1,500 a year. He was only earning £850 a year at Spurs.

MANAGER: Peter McWilliam until February then Billy Minter

CAPTAIN: Arthur Grimsdell/Jack Elkes

TOP SCORER: Jimmy Dimmock

BIGGEST WIN: 6-1 v Birmingham (H), 9 October 1926, Football League Division One

HIGHEST ATTENDANCE: 50,665 v Manchester United, 27 December 1926, Football League Division One

MAJOR TRANSFERS IN: John Blair from Third Lanark, Joe Nicholls from Grenadier Guards

MAJOR TRANSFERS OUT: Charlie Walters to Fulham

Final Division One Table

		P	W	D	L	F	A	Pts
1	NEWCASTLE U	42	25	6	11	96	58	56
2	HUDDERSFIELD T	42	17	17	8	76	60	51
3	BLACKBURN R	42	21	7	14	98	70	49
4	BOLTON W	42	19	10	13	84	62	48
5	BURNLEY	42	19	9	14	91	80	47
6	WEST HAM U	42	19	8	15	86	70	46
7	LEICESTER C	42	17	12	13	85	70	46
8	SHEFFIELD U	42	17	10	15	74	86	44
9	LIVERPOOL	42	18	7	17	69	61	43
10	ASTON VILLA	42	18	7	17	81	83	43
11	ARSENAL	42	17	9	16	77	86	43
12	DERBY CO	42	17	7	18	86	54	41
13	TOTTENHAM HOTSPUR	42	16	9	17	76	78	41
14	CARDIFF C	42	16	9	17	55	65	41
15	MANCHESTER U	42	13	14	15	52	64	40
16	SHEFFIELD W	42	15	9	18	75	92	39
17	BIRMINGHAM	42	17	4	21	64	73	38
18	BLACKBURN R	42	15	8	19	77	96	38
19	BURY	42	12	18	68	77	36	
20	EVERTON	42	12	10	20	64	90	34
21	LEEDS UNITED	42	11	8	23	69	88	30
22	WBA	42	11	8	23	65	86	30

Season 1927-28

Football League Division One

DATE	OPPONENTS	SCORE		GOALSCORERS	ATTENDANCE
Aug 27	BIRMINGHAM	W	1-0	O'Callaghan	37,408
Aug 31	Middlesbrough	L	1-3	Dimmock (pen)	29,113
Sep 3	Newcastle United	L	1-4	O'Callaghan	41,038
Sep 10	HUDDERSFIELD TOWN	D	2-2	Lindsay (pen), Dimmock	27,983
Sep 12	MIDDLESBROUGH	W	4-2	Blair 3, Dimmock (pen)	19,219
Sep 17	Portsmouth	L	0-3		26,115
Sep 22	LEICESTER CITY	W	2-1	Osborne, Blair	9,436
Sep 24	Manchester United	L	0-3		13,952
Oct 1	EVERTON	L	1-3	Townley	7,716
Oct 8	Cardiff City	L	1-2	Townley	21,811
Oct 15	BLACKBURN ROVERS	D	1-1	Osborne	23,020
Oct 22	SUNDERLAND	W	3-1	Osborne, Dimmock 2	19,039
Oct 29	Derby County	D	1-1	Grimsdell	15,963
Nov 5	WEST HAM UNITED	W	5-3	Handley, O'Callaghan 2, Osborne, Elkes	35,099
Nov 12	Aston Villa	W	2-1	Osborne 2	30,759
Nov 19	SHEFFIELD UNITED	D	2-2	Osborne, Elkes	19,147
Dec 3	BURNLEY	W	5-0	Handley, O'Callaghan, Osborne 2, Dimmock	20,404
Dec 10	Bury	W	2-1	O'Callaghan 2	12,204
Dec 17	LIVERPOOL	W	3-1	Osborne, Elkes 2	21,234
Dec 24	Leicester City	L	1-6	Handley	19,987
Dec 26	Bolton Wanderers	L	1-4	Elkes	25,229
Dec 31	Birmingham	L	2-3	O'Callaghan, Womack o.g.	11,603
Jan 2	Arsenal	D	1-1	O'Callaghan	13,518
Jan 7	NEWCASTLE UNITED	W	5-2	Osborne 4, Dimmock	34,731
Jan 21	Huddersfield Town	L	2-4	O'Callaghan, Osborne	17,892
Feb 4	MANCHESTER UNITED	W	4-0	O'Callaghan, Armstrong 2, Dimmock	23,545
Feb 6	BOLTON WANDERERS	L	1-2	Armstrong	18,183
Feb 11	Everton	W	5-3	O'Callaghan 4, Dimmock	29,149
Feb 25	Blackburn Rovers	L	1-2	O'Callaghan	20,890
Mar 5	CARDIFF CITY	W	1-0	Dimmock	15,559
Mar 10	DERBY COUNTY	L	1-2	Armstrong	22,458
Mar 17	West Ham United	D	1-1	Osborne	33,908
Mar 19	PORTSMOUTH	L	0-3		12,829
Mar 24	ASTON VILLA	W	2-1	Grimsdell (pen), Lindsay	21,537
Mar 28	Sunderland	D	0-0		9,244
Mar 31	Sheffield United	L	1-3	Handley	17,495
Apr 6	SHEFFIELD WEDNESDAY	L	1-3	Lindsay	26,432
Apr 7	ARSENAL	W	2-0	O'Callaghan 2	39,193
Apr 10	Sheffield Wednesday	L	2-4	O'Callaghan, Osborne	15,900
Apr 14	Burnley	D	2-2	Osborne, Dimmock	10,906
Apr 21	BURY	L	1-4	Lindsay	15,618
Apr 28	Liverpool	L	0-2		31,780

FA Cup

DATE	OPPONENTS		SCORE		GOALSCORERS	ATTENDANCE
Jan 14	Bristol City	(Rd3)	W	2-1	O'Callaghan, Osborne	36,260
Jan 28	OLDHAM ATHLETIC	(Rd4)	W	3-0	Handley, O'Callaghan, Dimmock	36,828
Feb 18	Leicester City	(Rd5)	W	3-0	O'Callaghan 2, Dimmock	47,296
Mar 3	Huddersfield Town	(Rd6)	L	1-6	O'Callaghan	52,390

League and Cup Appearances

PLAYER	LEAGUE	CUP COMPETITION FA CUP	TOTAL
Armstrong	11	4	15
Austin	1		1
Barnett	5		5
Bellamy	4		4
Blair	5		5
Britton	13		13
Clay	16	3	19
Dimmock	38	4	42
Elkes	22		22
Evans	3		3
Forster	32	2	34
Grimsdell	35	4	39
Handley	26	4	30
Hartley	2		2
Helliwell	2		2
Lindsay	19	1	20
Lowdell	34	4	38
Nicholls	3		3
O'Callaghan	42	4	46
Osborne	31	3	34
Poynton	14		14
Richardson	24	3	27
Sanders	1		1
Skitt	38	4	42
Smith	8		8
Spiers	26	4	30
Thompson	4		4
Townley	3		3

Goalscorers

PLAYER	LEAGUE	CUP COMPETITION FA CUP	TOTAL
O'Callaghan	19	5	24
Osborne	18	1	19
Dimmock	11	2	13
Elkes	5		5
Handley	4	1	5
Armstrong	4		4
Blair	4		4
Lindsay	4		4
Grimsdell	2		2
Townley	2		2
Opp's o.gs.	1		1

Fact File

Peter McWilliam had signed Jimmy Seed after spotting him play for Mid-Rhondda having gone along to watch Darkie Lowdell. When Seed joined Sheffield Wednesday, Lowdell moved in the other direction in part-exchange.

MANAGER: Billy Minter

CAPTAIN: Arthur Grimsdell

TOP SCORER: Taffy O'Callaghan

BIGGEST WIN: 5-0 v Burnley (H), 3 December 1927, Football League Division One

HIGHEST ATTENDANCE: 52,390 v Huddersfield Town, 3 March 1928, FA Cup 6th Round

MAJOR TRANSFERS IN: Darkie Lowdell from Sheffield Wednesday, Sid Helliwell from Reading, Cyril Spiers from Aston Villa

MAJOR TRANSFERS OUT: John Blair to Sheffield United, Harry Lowe to Fulham, Jimmy Seed to Sheffield Wednesday

Final Division One Table

		P	W	D	L	F	A	Pts
1	EVERTON	42	20	13	9	102	66	53
2	HUDDERSFIELD T	42	22	7	13	91	68	51
3	LEICESTER C	42	18	12	12	96	72	48
4	DERBY CO	42	17	10	15	96	83	44
5	BURY	42	20	4	18	80	80	44
6	CARDIFF C	42	17	10	15	70	80	44
7	BOLTON W	42	16	11	15	81	66	43
8	ASTON VILLA	42	17	9	16	78	73	43
9	NEWCASTLE U	42	15	13	14	79	81	43
10	ARSENAL	42	13	15	14	82	86	41
11	BIRMINGHAM	42	13	15	14	70	75	41
12	BLACKBURN R	42	16	9	17	66	47	41
13	SHEFFIELD U	42	15	10	17	79	86	40
14	SHEFFIELD W	42	13	13	16	81	78	39
15	BLACKBURN R	42	15	9	18	74	76	39
16	LIVERPOOL	42	13	13	16	84	87	39
17	WEST HAM U	42	14	11	17	81	88	39
18	MANCHESTER U	42	16	7	19	72	80	39
19	BURNLEY	42	16	7	19	82	98	39
20	PORTSMOUTH	42	16	7	19	66	90	39
21	TOTTENHAM HOTSPUR	42	15	8	19	74	86	38
22	MIDDLESBROUGH	42	11	15	16	81	88	37

Season 1928-29

Football League Division Two

DATE	OPPONENTS	SCORE	GOALSCORERS	ATTENDANCE
Aug 25	OLDHAM ATHLETIC	W 4-1	Elkes, Roberts 2, Osborne	33,173
Aug 27	MIDDLESBROUGH	L 2-5	Osborne, Dimmock	23,990
Sep 1	Southampton	D 1-1	Galloway	22,574
Sep 8	WOLVERHAMPTON WANDERERS	W 3-2	Galloway, Hartley, Scott	26,018
Sep 15	Notts County	L 0-2		23,304
Sep 22	MILLWALL	W 2-1	Osborne 2	47,073
Sep 29	Port Vale	L 1-2	Osborne	12,502
Oct 6	HULL CITY	W 4-1	Scott, Osborne, Elkes 2	28,737
Oct 13	Bradford	L 1-4	Osborne	22,688
Oct 20	GRIMSBY TOWN	W 2-1	Scott, O'Callaghan	22,218
Oct 27	Stoke City	L 0-2		15,333
Nov 3	CLAPTON ORIENT	W 2-1	Elkes 2	33,382
Nov 10	Swansea Town	L 0-4		6,936
Nov 17	NOTTINGHAM FOREST	W 2-1	Wilding, Osborne	23,384
Nov 24	Bristol City	L 1-2	Crompton	13,937
Dec 1	BARNSLEY	W 2-0	Osborne, Elkes	18,951
Dec 8	Chelsea	D 1-1	Armstrong	45,840
Dec 15	BLACKPOOL	L 1-2	Dimmock	15,729
Dec 22	West Bromwich Albion	L 2-3	Crompton, O'Callaghan	12,609
Dec 25	READING	D 2-2	O'Callaghan, Dimmock	28,344
Dec 26	Reading	L 3-4	Osborne 2, Dimmock	23,730
Dec 29	Oldham Athletic	L 1-3	Osborne	12,833
Jan 1	Middlesbrough	L 0-3		25,145
Jan 5	SOUTHAMPTON	W 3-2	Poynton (pen), O'Callaghan, Osborne	15,962
Jan 19	Wolverhampton Wanderers	L 2-4	Osborne, Dimmock	11,956
Jan 26	NOTTS COUNTY	W 3-0	O'Callaghan, Elkes 2	16,946
Feb 2	Millwall	L 1-5	Thompson	18,974
Feb 9	PORT VALE	W 4-2	Barnett, Osborne 2, Dimmock	21,342
Feb 23	BRADFORD	W 3-2	O'Callaghan, Dimmock 2	19,910
Mar 2	Grimsby Town	L 0-2		13,850
Mar 9	STOKE CITY	W 1-0	O'Callaghan	26,760
Mar 16	Clapton Orient	W 3-2	Harper, Dimmock 2	37,615
Mar 23	SWANSEA TOWN	D 1-1	Harper	25,109
Mar 29	Preston North End	D 2-2	Elkes, Dimmock	19,216
Mar 30	Nottingham Forest	D 2-2	Harper, Elkes	8,504
Apr 1	PRESTON NORTH END	W 2-0	O'Callaghan, Elkes	23,125
Apr 6	BRISTOL CITY	D 1-1	Harper	22,396
Apr 13	Barnsley	L 1-4	Scott	8,449
Apr 15	Hull City	D 1-1	Harper	4,139
Apr 20	CHELSEA	W 4-1	O'Callaghan, Harper 3	24,356
Apr 27	Blackpool	D 2-2	Harper, Dimmock	8,744
May 4	WEST BROMWICH ALBION	W 2-0	Harper 2	15,789

FA Cup

Jan 3	Reading	(Rd3) L 0-2		26,137

League and Cup Appearances

PLAYER	LEAGUE	CUP COMPETITION FA CUP	TOTAL
Armstrong	12	1	13
Bann	4		4
Barnett	6		6
Bellamy	9		9
Cable	2		2
Clay	5		5
Crompton	8		8
Dimmock	30	1	31
Elkes	27		27
Evans	2		2
Forster	33	1	34
Galloway	3		3
Grimsdell	11		11
Handley	1		1
Harper	11		11
Hartley	3		3
Helliwell	6	1	7
Herod	13		13
Knight	1		1
Lindsay	6	1	7
Lowdell	39		39
Nicholls	11		11
O'Callaghan	36	1	37
Osborne	33	1	34
Poynton	23	1	24
Richardson	12		12
Roberts	4		4
Scott	12		12
Skitt	29	1	30
Smith	10		10
Smy	4		4
Spiers	31	1	32
Thompson	13	1	14
Wilding	12		2

Goalscorers

PLAYER	LEAGUE	CUP COMPETITION FA CUP	TOTAL
Osborne	16		16
Dimmock	12		12
Elkes	11		11
Harper	11		11
O'Callaghan	9		9
Scott	4		4
Crompton	2		2
Galloway	2		2
Roberts	2		2
Armstrong	1		1
Barnett	1		1
Hartley	1		1
Poynton	1		1
Thompson	1		1
Wilding	1		1

Fact File

The 4,139 spectators at Hull in April was the smallest crowd to watch Spurs in a Football League game since the Great War.

MANAGER: Billy Minter

CAPTAIN: Arthur Grimsdell/Matt Forster

TOP SCORER: Frank Osborne

BIGGEST WIN: 4-1 v Oldham Athletic (H), 25 August 1928, Football League Division Two; 4-1 v Hull City (H), 6 October 1928, Football League Division Two; 4-1 v Chelsea (H), 20 April 1929, Football League Division Two

HIGHEST ATTENDANCE: 47,073 v Millwall, 22 September 1928, Football League Division Two

MAJOR TRANSFERS IN: Tommy Cable from Leyton, Ted Harper from Sheffield Wednesday, Edwin Herod from Brentford, Tom Roberts from Preston North End, Joe Scott from Barnsley, Harry Wilding from Chelsea

MAJOR TRANSFERS OUT: Jimmy Townley to Brighton & Hove Albion

Final Division Two Table

		P	W	D	L	F	A	Pts
1	MIDDLESBROUGH	42	22	11	9	92	57	55
2	GRIMSBY T	42	24	5	13	97	61	53
3	BRADFORD	42	22	4	16	88	70	48
4	SOUTHAMPTON	42	17	14	11	74	60	48
5	NOTTS COUNTY	42	19	9	14	78	65	47
6	STOKE C	42	17	12	13	74	51	46
7	WBA	42	19	8	15	80	79	46
8	BLACKPOOL	42	19	7	16	92	76	45
9	CHELSEA	42	17	10	15	64	65	44
10	TOTTENHAM HOTSPUR	42	17	9	16	75	81	43
11	NOTTINGHAM F	42	15	12	15	71	70	42
12	HULL CITY	42	13	14	15	58	63	40
13	PRESTON NE	42	15	9	18	78	79	39
14	MILLWALL	42	16	7	19	71	86	39
15	READING	42	15	9	18	63	86	39
16	BARNSLEY	42	16	6	20	69	66	38
17	WOLVERHAMPTON W	42	15	7	20	77	81	37
18	OLDHAM A	42	16	5	21	54	75	37
19	SWANSEA A	42	13	10	19	62	75	36
20	BRISTOL C	42	13	10	19	58	72	36
21	PORT VALE	42	15	4	23	71	86	34
22	CLAPTON O	42	12	8	22	45	72	32

Season 1929-30

Football League Division Two

DATE	OPPONENTS	SCORE	GOALSCORERS	ATTENDANCE
Aug 31	Bradford	L 1-2	Dimmock	18,771
Sep 2	Millwall	W 5-2	Osborne, O'Callaghan, Cook, Dimmock 2	22,297
Sep 7	BARNSLEY	W 2-1	O'Callaghan, Cook	26,056
Sep 14	Blackpool	L 2-3	O'Callaghan, Smy	14,913
Sep 21	BURY	D 2-2	Crompton, Osborne	25,051
Sep 23	MILLWALL	D 1-1	O'Callaghan	16,629
Sep 28	Chelsea	L 0-3		46,770
Oct 5	NOTTINGHAM FOREST	D 1-1	Cook	22,332
Oct 9	STOKE CITY	W 3-1	Osborne 3	8,545
Oct 12	Oldham Athletic	L 0-2		18,265
Oct 19	Wolverhampton Wanderers	L 0-3		26,591
Oct 26	BRADFORD CITY	D 1-1	Osborne	17,349
Nov 2	Swansea Town	W 1-0	Harper	8,961
Nov 9	CARDIFF CITY	L 1-2	Meads	23,071
Nov 16	Preston North End	L 0-4		10,687
Nov 23	BRISTOL CITY	W 2-1	Harper, Dimmock	11,863
Nov 30	Notts County	W 1-0	Harper	10,294
Dec 7	READING	D 0-0		11,522
Dec 14	Charlton Athletic	L 0-1		17,350
Dec 21	HULL CITY	D 2-2	Harper 2	9,103
Dec 25	SOUTHAMPTON	W 3-2	Osborne (pen), Harper 2	26,564
Dec 26	Southampton	L 0-1		25,203
Dec 28	BRADFORD	D 1-1	Dimmock	20,726
Jan 4	Barnsley	L 0-2		5,870
Jan 18	BLACKPOOL	W 6-1	Meads, Harper 3, Cook, Dimmock	24,956
Jan 25	Bury	L 1-2	Cook	13,192
Feb 1	CHELSEA	D 3-3	Thompson, Harper, Cook	33,623
Feb 8	Nottingham Forest	D 0-0		9,833
Feb 15	OLDHAM ATHLETIC	W 2-1	Poynton (pen), Cook	35,516
Feb 22	WOLVERHAMPTON WANDERERS	W 4-2	Thompson, Rowley 3	29,341
Mar 1	Bradford City	W 2-0	Cook, Bellamy	16,642
Mar 8	SWANSEA TOWN	W 3-0	Davies 2, Rowley	30,331
Mar 15	Cardiff City	L 0-1		15,404
Mar 22	PRESTON NORTH END	W 1-0	Osborne	29,108
Mar 29	Bristol City	L 0-1		10,935
Apr 5	NOTTS COUNTY	W 2-0	Cook, Bellamy	17,848
Apr 12	Reading	L 0-3		11,183
Apr 18	WEST BROMWICH ALBION	L 0-2		25,228
Apr 19	CHARLTON ATHLETIC	W 3-0	Harper 2, Smy	15,814
Apr 21	West Bromwich Albion	L 3-4	Osborne, Harper, Finch o.g.	13,989
Apr 26	Hull City	L 0-2		6,396
May 3	Stoke City	L 0-1		6,560

FA Cup

Jan 11	MANCHESTER CITY	(Rd3) D 2-2	Osborne, Cook	37,000
Jan 15	Manchester City	(R) L 1-4	Thompson	37,716

League and Cup Appearances

PLAYER	LEAGUE	CUP COMPETITION FA CUP	TOTAL
Armstrong	5		5
Bellamy	12		12
Cable	34	2	36
Cook	32	2	34
Crompton	7		7
Davies	14		14
Dimmock	32	2	34
Evans	3		3
Forster	15		15
Harper	19	2	21
Hartley	1		1
Herod	41	2	43
Illingworth	9	2	11
Lindsay	10	2	12
Lowdell	13		13
Meads	33		33
O'Callaghan	10		10
Osborne	32	2	34
Poynton	16		16
Reddish	3		3
Rowley	9		9
Scott	5		5
Skitt	37	2	39
Smy	7		7
Spiers	42	2	44
Thompson	21	2	23

Goalscorers

PLAYER	LEAGUE	CUP COMPETITION FA CUP	TOTAL
Harper	14		14
Cook	9	1	10
Osborne	9	1	10
Dimmock	6		6
O'Callaghan	4		4
Rowley	4		4
Thompson	2	1	3
Bellamy	2		2
Davies	2		2
Meads	2		2
Smy	2		2
Crompton	1		1
Poynton	1		1
Opp's o.gs.	1		1

Fact File

Twelfth in the Second Division was Spurs' lowest ever Football League placing.

MANAGER: Billy Minter until November then Percy Smith

CAPTAIN: Darkie Lowdell/Jimmy Dimmock/Cecil Poynton

TOP SCORER: Ted Harper

BIGGEST WIN: 6-1 v Blackpool (H), 18 January 1930, Football League Division Two

HIGHEST ATTENDANCE: 46,770 v Chelsea, 28 September 1929, Football League Division Two

MAJOR TRANSFERS IN: Billy Cook from Aston Villa, Willie Davies from Notts County, Tommy Meads from Reading, Dick Rowley from Southampton

MAJOR TRANSFERS OUT: Tommy Clay to Northfleet, Jack Elkes to Middlesbrough, Arthur Grimsdell to Clapton Orient

Final Division Two Table

		P	W	D	L	F	A	Pts
1	BLACKPOOL	42	27	4	11	98	67	58
2	CHELSEA	42	22	11	9	74	46	55
3	OLDHAM A	42	21	11	10	90	51	53
4	BRADFORD	42	19	12	11	91	70	50
5	BURY	42	22	5	15	78	67	49
6	WBA	42	21	5	16	105	73	47
7	SOUTHAMPTON	42	17	11	14	77	76	45
8	CARDIFF C	42	18	8	16	61	59	44
9	WOLVERHAMPTON W	42	16	9	17	77	79	41
10	NOTTINGHAM F	42	13	15	14	55	69	41
11	STOKE C	42	16	8	18	74	72	40
12	TOTTENHAM HOTSPUR	42	15	9	18	59	40	39
13	CHARLTON A	42	14	11	17	59	63	39
14	MILLWALL	42	12	15	15	57	73	39
15	SWANSEA T	42	14	9	19	57	61	37
16	PRESTON NE	42	13	11	18	65	80	37
17	BARNSLEY	42	14	8	20	56	71	36
18	BRADFORD C	42	12	12	18	60	77	36
19	READING	42	12	11	19	54	67	35
20	BRISTOL C	42	13	9	20	61	83	35
21	HULL CITY	42	14	7	21	51	78	35
22	NOTTS COUNTY	42	9	15	18	54	70	33

Season 1930-31

Football League Division Two

DATE	OPPONENTS	SCORE	GOALSCORERS	ATTENDANCE
Aug 30	READING	W 7-1	Harper 5, Cook, Dimmock	25,484
Sep 1	BURNLEY	W 8-1	Davies, O'Callaghan 2, Harper 2, Cook 3	23,518
Sep 6	Wolverhampton Wanderers	L 1-3	Cook	24,990
Sep 8	Preston North End	L 1-2	Harper	17,031
Sep 13	BRADFORD	W 3-2	Harper, Cook, Dimmock	18,828
Sep 15	PRESTON NORTH END	D 0-0		18,793
Sep 20	Stoke City	L 1-2	Cook	10,252
Sep 27	MILLWALL	W 4-1	O'Callaghan, Harper, Smy, Dimmock	37,106
Oct 4	Oldham Athletic	W 2-1	Davies, Harper	15,559
Oct 11	NOTTINGHAM FOREST	W 2-1	O'Callaghan, Harper	34,238
Oct 18	BURY	W 3-1	Harper, Cook, Dimmock	32,856
Oct 25	Everton	L 2-4	Smy 2	25,265
Nov 1	CHARLTON ATHLETIC	W 5-0	O'Callaghan, Harper 3, Smy	24,544
Nov 8	Bradford City	L 0-2		13,710
Nov 15	SWANSEA TOWN	D 1-1	Lyons (pen)	20,211
Nov 22	West Bromwich Albion	W 2-0	Harper 2	17,923
Nov 29	PORT VALE	W 5-0	Harper 4, Cook	23,609
Dec 6	Plymouth Argyle	L 0-2		24,549
Dec 13	BRISTOL CITY	W 4-1	Messer, Rowley 2, Cook	21,464
Dec 20	Barnsley	W 1-0	Bellamy	7,294
Dec 25	SOUTHAMPTON	L 1-3	O'Callaghan	36,652
Dec 26	Southampton	W 3-0	Davies, O'Callaghan, Rowley	22,408
Dec 27	Reading	W 2-1	Davies, O'Callaghan	16,571
Jan 3	WOLVERHAMPTON WANDERERS	W 1-0	Cook	26,221
Jan 17	Bradford	L 1-4	Harper	15,229
Jan 26	STOKE CITY	W 3-0	Lyons (pen), Messer, Harper	10,927
Jan 31	Millwall	W 3-2	Harper, Bellamy 2	27,899
Feb 7	OLDHAM ATHLETIC	W 4-0	Harper 3, Cook	27,708
Feb 14	Nottingham Forest	D 2-2	Harper 2	14,196
Feb 21	Bury	L 0-2		7,776
Mar 7	Charlton Athletic	L 0-1		18,060
Mar 14	BRADFORD CITY	W 3-1	Harper 2, Smailes	32,976
Mar 16	EVERTON	W 1-0	Harper	30,205
Mar 21	Swansea Town	W 2-1	Harper, Smailes	9,876
Mar 28	WEST BROMWICH ALBION	D 2-2	O'Callaghan, Smailes	49,921
Apr 3	CARDIFF CITY	D 2-2	Hunt, Cook	41,547
Apr 4	Port Vale	L 0-3		14,290
Apr 6	Cardiff City	D 0-0		6,666
Apr 11	PLYMOUTH ARGYLE	D 1-1	Hunt	33,546
Apr 18	Bristol City	L 1-2	Hunt	15,149
Apr 25	BARNSLEY	W 4-2	Harper 2, Hunt 2	20,762
May 2	Burnley	L 0-1		10,077

FA Cup

Jan 10	PRESTON NORTH END	(Rd3)	W 3-1	Harper, Cook, Dimmock	36,549
Jan 24	West Bromwich Albion	(Rd4)	L 0-1		40,850

League and Cup Appearances

PLAYER	LEAGUE	CUP COMPETITION FA CUP	TOTAL
Alsford	14		14
Bellamy	17		17
Cable	4		4
Cook	31	2	33
Davies	42	2	44
Dimmock	13	2	15
Harper	30	2	32
Herod	3		3
Hodgkinson	39	2	41
Howe	3		3
Hunt	9		9
Lyons	37	2	39
Meads	41	2	43
Messer	39	2	41
O'Callaghan	37	1	38
Osborne	6		6
Poynton	5		5
Rowley	8		8
Scott	1		1
Skitt	24	2	26
Smailes	11		11
Smy	6		6
Spiers	42	2	44
Thompson		1	1

Goalscorers

PLAYER	LEAGUE	CUP COMPETITION FA CUP	TOTAL
Harper	36	1	37
Cook	13	1	14
O'Callaghan	9		9
Dimmock	4	1	5
Hunt	5		5
Davies	4		4
Smy	4		4
Bellamy	3		3
Rowley	3		3
Smailes	3		3
Lyons	2		2
Messer	2		2

Fact File

Ted Harper's 36 Football League goals was to remain Spurs' record for over 30 years.

MANAGER: Percy Smith

CAPTAIN: Tommy Meads

TOP SCORER: Ted Harper

BIGGEST WIN: 8-1 v Burnley (H), 1 September 1930, Football League Division Two

HIGHEST ATTENDANCE: 49,921 v West Bromwich Albion, 28 March 1931, Football League Division Two

MAJOR TRANSFERS IN: George Hunt from Chesterfield, Bert Lyons from Clapton Orient, Alf Messer from Reading

MAJOR TRANSFERS OUT: Alex Lindsay to Thames

Final Division Two Table

		P	W	D	L	F	A	Pts
1	EVERTON	42	28	5	9	121	66	61
2	WBA	42	22	10	10	83	49	54
3	TOTTENHAM HOTSPUR	42	22	7	13	88	55	51
4	WOLVERHAMPTON W	42	21	5	16	84	67	47
5	PORT VALE	42	21	5	16	67	61	47
6	BRADFORD	42	18	10	14	97	66	46
7	PRESTON NE	42	17	11	14	83	64	45
8	BURNLEY	42	17	11	14	81	77	45
9	SOUTHAMPTON	42	19	6	17	74	62	44
10	BRADFORD C	42	17	10	15	61	63	44
11	STOKE C	42	17	10	15	64	71	44
12	OLDHAM A	42	16	10	16	61	44	42
13	BURY	42	19	3	20	75	82	41
14	MILLWALL	42	16	7	19	71	80	39
15	CHARLTON A	42	15	9	18	59	86	39
16	BRISTOL C	42	15	8	19	54	82	38
17	NOTTINGHAM F	42	14	9	19	80	85	37
18	PLYMOUTH A	42	14	8	20	76	84	36
19	BARNSLEY	42	13	9	20	59	79	35
20	SWANSEA T	42	12	10	20	51	74	34
21	READING	42	12	6	24	72	96	30
22	CARDIFF C	42	8	9	25	47	87	25

Season 1931-32

Football League Division Two

DATE	OPPONENTS	SCORE	GOALSCORERS	ATTENDANCE
Aug 29	Wolverhampton Wanderers	L 0-4		23,267
Aug 31	PRESTON NORTH END	W 4-0	Davies, O'Callaghan, Hunt 2	22,104
Sep 5	BRADFORD	D 3-3	Meads, O'Callaghan, Rowley (pen)	27,108
Sep 7	Southampton	L 1-2	O'Callaghan	13,566
Sep 12	Manchester United	D 1-1	Rowley	9,557
Sep 14	SOUTHAMPTON	W 5-2	Meads 2, Brain, O'Callaghan, Bellamy	19,217
Sep 19	BARNSLEY	W 4-2	Brain, O'Callaghan 2, Bellamy	28,585
Sep 26	NOTTINGHAM FOREST	L 1-3	Hunt	25,128
Oct 3	Chesterfield	L 2-4	Brain, Bellamy	15,192
Oct 10	BURNLEY	D 1-1	Harper	28,877
Oct 17	Notts County	L 1-3	Rowley	13,397
Oct 24	PLYMOUTH ARGYLE	L 0-1		22,863
Oct 31	Bristol City	D 1-1	Hunt	9,129
Nov 7	SWANSEA TOWN	W 6-2	Davies 2, Hunt, O'Callaghan, Evans W 2	20,834
Nov 14	Bury	D 1-1	Mills o.g.	7,628
Nov 21	PORT VALE	W 9-3	Lyons (pen), Colquhoun, Davies 3, Brain 2, Hunt 2	22,226
Nov 28	Millwall	W 2-1	Hunt 2	28,424
Dec 5	BRADFORD CITY	L 1-5	Evans W	26,622
Dec 12	Leeds United	L 0-1		15,689
Dec 19	OLDHAM ATHLETIC	W 3-2	Hunt, O'Callaghan 2	10,339
Dec 25	Charlton Athletic	L 0-1		36,469
Dec 26	CHARLTON ATHLETIC	W 5-2	Davies, Brain, Hunt 3	26,417
Jan 2	WOLVERHAMPTON WANDERERS	D 3-3	Hunt 3	25,122
Jan 16	Bradford	L 1-2	O'Callaghan	12,596
Jan 23	MANCHESTER UNITED	W 4-1	Davies 2, Hunt, O'Callaghan	19,139
Jan 30	Barnsley	L 2-3	Hunt, O'Callaghan	5,852
Feb 6	Nottingham Forest	W 3-1	Brain 2, O'Callaghan	10,487
Feb 13	CHESTERFIELD	D 3-3	Davies, Hunt, Evans W	21,591
Feb 20	Burnley	L 0-2		7,517
Feb 27	NOTTS COUNTY	W 2-0	O'Callaghan 2	20,481
Mar 5	Plymouth Argyle	L 1-4	Davies	18,903
Mar 12	BRISTOL CITY	W 2-1	Davies, Greenfield	15,178
Mar 19	Swansea Town	D 1-1	Evans T (pen)	11,357
Mar 25	STOKE CITY	D 3-3	Evans T (pen), Hunt, O'Callaghan	26,503
Mar 26	BURY	D 0-0		20,822
Mar 28	Stoke City	D 2-2	Greenfield, Evans W	15,042
Apr 2	Port Vale	W 3-1	Hunt, Greenfield 2	7,682
Apr 9	MILLWALL	W 1-0	Evans T (pen)	22,495
Apr 16	Bradford City	L 0-2		12,740
Apr 23	LEEDS UNITED	W 3-1	O'Callaghan, Hunt, Greenfield	17,285
Apr 30	Oldham Athletic	W 2-1	Hunt 2	5,963
May 7	Preston North End	L 0-2		5,900

FA Cup

Jan 9	SHEFFIELD WEDNESDAY	(Rd3) D 2-2	Hunt, Evans W	41,511
Jan 13	Sheffield Wednesday	(R) L 1-3	Hunt (pen)	30,000

League and Cup Appearances

PLAYER	LEAGUE	CUP COMPETITION FA CUP	TOTAL
Alsford	10		10
Bellamy	12		12
Brain	32	2	34
Cable	2		2
Colquhoun	36	2	38
Davies	38	2	40
Evans	12	2	14
Evans	28	2	30
Felton	10		10
Greenfield	12		12
Harper	3		3
Hodgkinson	17		17
Hunt	37	2	39
Lyons	17	1	18
Marshall	1		1
Meads	27		27
Messer	11		11
Moran	12		12
Nicholls	2		2
O'Callaghan	34	2	36
Poynton	25	2	27
Reddish	3	1	4
Rowe	29	2	31
Rowley	7		7
Smailes	5		5
Spiers	17	2	19
Taylor	23		23

Goalscorers

PLAYER	LEAGUE	CUP COMPETITION FA CUP	TOTAL
Hunt	24	2	26
O'Callaghan	17		17
Davies	12		12
Brain	8		8
Evans W	5	1	6
Greenfield	5		5
Bellamy	3		3
Evans T	3		3
Meads	3		3
Rowley	3		3
Colquhoun	1		1
Harper	1		1
Lyons	1		1
Opp's o.gs.	1		1

Fact File

New signing Jimmy Brain had scored on his debut for Arsenal against Spurs in October 1924.

MANAGER: Percy Smith

CAPTAIN: Tommy Meads/Jimmy Brain

TOP SCORER: George Hunt

BIGGEST WIN: 9-3 v Port Vale (H), 21 November 1931, Football League Division Two

HIGHEST ATTENDANCE: 41,511 v Sheffield Wednesday, 9 January 1932, FA Cup 3rd Round

MAJOR TRANSFERS IN: Jimmy Brain from Arsenal, Bill Felton from Manchester City, Jack Moran from Wigan Borough

MAJOR TRANSFERS OUT: Jimmy Dimmock to Thames, Ted Harper to Preston North End, Frank Osborne to Southampton, Harry Skitt to Chester

Final Division Two Table

		P	W	D	L	F	A	Pts
1	WOLVERHAMPTON W	42	24	8	10	115	49	56
2	LEEDS UNITED	42	22	10	10	78	54	54
3	STOKE C	42	19	14	9	69	48	52
4	PLYMOUTH A	42	20	9	13	100	66	49
5	BURY	42	21	7	14	70	58	49
6	BRADFORD	42	21	7	14	72	63	49
7	BRADFORD C	42	16	13	13	80	61	45
8	TOTTENHAM HOTSPUR	42	16	11	15	87	78	43
9	MILLWALL	42	17	9	16	61	61	43
10	CHARLTON A	42	17	9	16	61	66	43
11	NOTTINGHAM F	42	16	10	16	77	72	42
12	MANCHESTER U	42	17	8	17	71	58	42
13	PRESTON NE	42	16	10	16	75	77	42
14	SOUTHAMPTON	42	17	7	18	66	77	41
15	SWANSEA T	42	16	7	19	73	75	39
16	NOTTS COUNTY	42	13	12	17	75	75	38
17	CHESTERFIELD	42	13	11	18	64	86	37
18	OLDHAM A	42	13	10	19	62	84	36
19	BURNLEY	42	13	9	20	59	87	35
20	PORT VALE	42	13	7	22	58	89	33
21	BARNSLEY	42	12	9	21	55	91	33
22	BRISTOL C	42	6	11	25	39	78	23

Season 1932-33

Football League Division Two

DATE	OPPONENTS	SCORE	GOALSCORERS	ATTENDANCE
Aug 27	CHARLTON ATHLETIC	W 4-1	Hunt 2, Evans W 2	34,263
Aug 29	Nottingham Forest	L 1-3	Hunt	9,906
Sep 3	Stoke City	L 0-2		12,366
Sep 5	NOTTINGHAM FOREST	D 0-0		13,757
Sep 10	MANCHESTER UNITED	W 6-1	Brain, Hunt 2, O'Callaghan, Evans W (1 pen) 2	23,333
Sep 17	Bury	L 0-1		11,602
Sep 24	Grimsby Town	L 2-3	Hunt 2	9,597
Oct 1	OLDHAM ATHLETIC	D 1-1	Hunt	20,435
Oct 8	Preston North End	W 6-2	Colquhoun, O'Callaghan, Hunt, Greenfield, Evans W 2	6,368
Oct 15	BURNLEY	W 4-1	Howe, Hunt, Greenfield, Evans W	26,097
Oct 22	SOUTHAMPTON	W 5-0	O'Callaghan 3, Hunt, Evans W	24,778
Oct 29	Millwall	W 4-1	Howe, O'Callaghan, Greenfield, Evans W	32,301
Nov 5	PORT VALE	W 4-0	O'Callaghan 2, Hunt, Evans W (pen)	33,071
Nov 12	Lincoln City	D 2-2	Howe, Greenfield	11,654
Nov 19	CHESTERFIELD	W 4-1	O'Callaghan, Evans W (1 pen) 3	24,584
Nov 26	Bradford City	W 1-0	Hunt	18,351
Dec 3	SWANSEA TOWN	W 7-0	O'Callaghan, Hunt 2, Greenfield 2, Evans W (2 pen)	31,993
Dec 10	Fulham	D 2-2	Hunt 2	42,111
Dec 17	WEST HAM UNITED	D 2-2	O'Callaghan, Hunt	45,129
Dec 24	Notts County	L 0-3		16,355
Dec 26	Bradford	D 3-3	Howe, O'Callaghan, Evans W (pen)	25,318
Dec 27	BRADFORD	W 2-0	Hunt, Evans W	48,478
Dec 31	Charlton Athletic	W 3-0	Hunt 2, Evans W	26,666
Jan 7	STOKE CITY	W 3-2	Davies, Hunt 2	43,711
Jan 21	Manchester United	L 1-2	Evans W	20,661
Feb 1	BURY	W 2-1	Hunt 2	19,836
Feb 4	GRIMSBY TOWN	W 4-3	O'Callaghan, Hunt, Evans W 2	33,395
Feb 11	Oldham Athletic	W 5-1	O'Callaghan, Hunt 3, Hall	5,412
Feb 18	PRESTON NORTH END	D 1-1	Hunt	41,209
Mar 4	Southampton	D 1-1	Hunt	11,806
Mar 11	MILLWALL	W 2-1	Evans W (1 pen) 2	50,299
Mar 18	Port Vale	D 1-1	Evans W (pen)	14,588
Mar 25	LINCOLN CITY	W 3-2	Brain, Hunt, Evans W (pen)	33,930
Apr 1	Chesterfield	D 1-1	Morrison	10,630
Apr 8	BRADFORD CITY	D 1-1	Allen	32,202
Apr 14	PLYMOUTH ARGYLE	D 0-0		44,483
Apr 15	Swansea Town	W 2-0	Howe, Evans W	14,590
Apr 17	Plymouth Argyle	D 2-2	Howe 2	21,461
Apr 22	FULHAM	D 0-0		44,312
Apr 24	Burnley	D 1-1	Hunt	11,353
Apr 29	West Ham United	L 0-1		31,706
May 6	NOTTS COUNTY	W 3-1	Evans T, Evans W (1 pen) 2	28,015

FA Cup

Jan 14	Oldham Athletic	(Rd3) W 6-0	O'Callaghan, Hunt 3, Evans W, Brunskill o.g.	16,662
Jan 28	Luton Town	(Rd4) L 0-2		17,213

MANAGER: Percy Smith

CAPTAIN: Bill Felton

TOP SCORER: George Hunt

BIGGEST WIN: 7-0 v Swansea Town (H), 3 December 1932, Football League Division Two

HIGHEST ATTENDANCE: 50,299 v Millwall, 11 March 1933, Football League Division Two

MAJOR TRANSFERS IN: Willie Hall from Notts County, Jimmy McCormick from Chesterfield

MAJOR TRANSFERS OUT: Tommy Cable to Southampton, Bert Lyons to Colwyn Bay

League and Cup Appearances

PLAYER	LEAGUE	CUP COMPETITION FA CUP	TOTAL
Allen	1		1
Alsford	2		2
Bellamy	3		3
Brain	12		12
Colquhoun	29	2	31
Davies	15	2	17
Evans T	16		16
Evans W	42	2	44
Felton	41	2	43
Greenfield	13		13
Hall	21	2	23
Howe	18		18
Hunt	41	2	43
Levene	5	2	7
McCormick	9		9
Meads	35	2	37
Morrison	1		1
Nicholls	37	2	39
O'Callaghan	32	2	34
Poynton	4	1	5
Rowe	41		41
Taylor	5		5
Whatley	39	1	40

Goalscorers

PLAYER	LEAGUE	CUP COMPETITION FA CUP	TOTAL
Hunt	33	3	36
Evans W	28	1	29
O'Callaghan	14	1	15
Howe	7		7
Greenfield	6		6
Brain	2		2
Allen	1		1
Colquhoun	1		1
Davies	1		1
Evans T	1		1
Hall	1		1
Morrison	1		1
Opp's o.gs.		1	1

Fact File

Spurs lost four of their first seven League games but only three of their last 35.

Final Division Two Table

		P	W	D	L	F	A	Pts
1	STOKE C	42	25	6	11	78	39	56
2	TOTTENHAM HOTSPUR	42	20	15	7	96	51	55
3	FULHAM	42	20	10	12	78	65	50
4	BURY	42	20	9	13	84	59	49
5	NOTTINGHAM F	42	17	15	10	67	59	49
6	MANCHESTER U	42	15	13	14	71	68	43
7	MILLWALL	42	16	11	15	59	57	43
8	BRADFORD	42	17	8	17	77	71	42
9	PRESTON NE	42	16	10	16	74	70	42
10	SWANSEA T	42	19	4	19	50	54	42
11	BRADFORD C	42	14	13	15	65	61	41
12	SOUTHAMPTON	42	18	5	19	66	40	41
13	GRIMSBY T	42	14	13	15	79	84	41
14	PLYMOUTH A	42	16	9	17	63	67	41
15	NOTTS COUNTY	42	15	10	17	67	78	40
16	OLDHAM A	42	15	8	19	67	80	38
17	PORT VALE	42	14	10	18	66	79	38
18	LINCOLN C	42	12	13	17	72	87	37
19	BURNLEY	42	11	14	17	67	79	36
20	WEST HAM U	42	13	9	20	75	93	35
21	CHESTERFIELD	42	12	10	20	61	84	34
22	CHARLTON A	42	12	7	23	60	91	31

Season 1933-34

Football League Division One

DATE	OPPONENTS	SCORE	GOALSCORERS	ATTENDANCE
Aug 26	Sheffield United	D 0-0		16,583
Aug 28	WOLVERHAMPTON WANDERERS	W 4-0	O'Callaghan 2, Hunt 2	20,953
Sep 2	ASTON VILLA	W 3-2	O'Callaghan, Hunt, Evans W (pen)	44,974
Sep 4	Wolverhampton Wanderers	L 0-1		20,510
Sep 9	Leicester City	W 3-1	McCormick 3	26,112
Sep 16	ARSENAL	D 1-1	Felton (pen)	56,612
Sep 23	LIVERPOOL	L 0-3		33,080
Sep 30	Chelsea	W 4-0	O'Callaghan, Hunt 3	67,454
Oct 7	SUNDERLAND	W 3-1	Hunt, Hall W, Evans W	44,235
Oct 14	Portsmouth	W 1-0	O'Callaghan	25,679
Oct 21	Everton	D 1-1	Evans W	35,082
Oct 28	MIDDLESBROUGH	W 2-0	O'Callaghan, Hunt	35,800
Nov 4	West Bromwich Albion	W 2-1	Howe, Evans W	32,292
Nov 11	NEWCASTLE UNITED	W 4-0	Hunt 2, Evans W 2	41,379
Nov 18	Leeds United	D 0-0		19,681
Nov 25	DERBY COUNTY	L 1-2	O'Callaghan	41,469
Dec 2	Manchester City	L 0-2		38,021
Dec 9	BIRMINGHAM	W 3-2	Howe, Hunt 2	26,142
Dec 16	Sheffield Wednesday	L 1-2	Howe	17,232
Dec 23	BLACKBURN ROVERS	W 4-1	Howe, Hall W, Evans W 2	28,001
Dec 25	HUDDERSFIELD TOWN	L 1-3	Hall W	53,959
Dec 26	Huddersfield Town	L 0-2		32,501
Dec 30	SHEFFIELD UNITED	W 4-1	Hunt 4	23,894
Jan 1	Blackburn Rovers	L 0-1		19,955
Jan 6	Aston Villa	W 5-1	Meads, McCormick 2, Howe, Hunt	35,296
Jan 20	LEICESTER CITY	L 0-1		31,393
Jan 31	Arsenal	W 3-1	Howe, Evans W (1 pen) 2	68,674
Feb 3	Liverpool	L 1-3	Hunt	30,809
Feb 10	CHELSEA	W 2-1	Hunt, Evans W (pen)	39,652
Feb 21	Sunderland	L 0-6		16,105
Feb 24	PORTSMOUTH	D 0-0		26,921
Mar 3	EVERTON	W 3-0	Hunt 3	26,121
Mar 10	Middlesbrough	D 1-1	Evans W	11,832
Mar 17	WEST BROMWICH ALBION	W 2-1	O'Callaghan, Evans W (pen)	26,393
Mar 24	Newcastle United	W 3-1	Hunt 3	25,246
Mar 30	STOKE CITY	D 0-0		32,912
Mar 31	LEEDS UNITED	W 5-1	McCormick, Hunt 3, Evans W	29,547
Apr 2	Stoke City	L 0-2		32,665
Apr 7	Derby County	L 3-4	McCormick, O'Callaghan, Evans W (pen)	14,244
Apr 14	MANCHESTER CITY	W 5-1	O'Callaghan 2, Hunt 2, Evans W	24,576
Apr 21	Birmingham	L 0-2		24,576
Apr 28	SHEFFIELD WEDNESDAY	W 4-3	McCormick 2, Hunt 2	20,322

FA Cup

Jan 13	EVERTON	(Rd3)	W 3-0	Howe, Hunt, Evans W	45,637
Jan 27	WEST HAM UNITED	(Rd4)	W 4-1	Hunt 2, Evans W 2	51,747
Feb 17	ASTON VILLA	(Rd5)	L 0-1		44,365

League and Cup Appearances

PLAYER	LEAGUE	CUP COMPETITION FA CUP	TOTAL
Alsford	13	2	15
Bellamy	5		5
Bolan	1		1
Channell	22	3	25
Colquhoun	13	2	15
Day	3		3
Evans T	26	1	27
Evans W	36	3	39
Felton	22		22
Hall A	2		2
Hall W	42	3	45
Hedley	1		1
Howe	10	3	13
Hunt	40	3	43
McCormick	40	3	43
Meads	30	1	31
Nicholls	42	3	45
O'Callaghan	32		32
Rowe	42	3	45
Whatley	40	3	43

Goalscorers

PLAYER	LEAGUE	CUP COMPETITION FA CUP	TOTAL
Hunt	32	3	35
Evans W	16	3	19
O'Callaghan	11		11
McCormick	9		9
Howe	6	1	7
Hall W	3		3
Felton	1		1
Meads	1		1

Fact File

Alf Day was plucked from Spurs reserves in November 1933 to make his debut for Wales without playing even one Football League game.

MANAGER: Percy Smith

CAPTAIN: Bill Felton/Arthur Rowe

TOP SCORER: George Hunt

BIGGEST WIN: 5-1 v Aston Villa (A), 6 January 1934, Football League Division One; 5-1 v Leeds United (H), 31 March 1934, Football League Division One; 5-1 v Manchester City (H), 14 April 1935, Football League Division One

HIGHEST ATTENDANCE: 68,674 v Arsenal, 31 January 1934, Football League Division One

MAJOR TRANSFERS IN: Foster Hedley from Chester

MAJOR TRANSFERS OUT: Willie Davies to Swansea Town

Final Division One Table

		P	W	D	L	F	A	Pts
1	ARSENAL	42	25	9	8	75	47	59
2	HUDDERSFIELD T	42	23	10	9	90	61	56
3	TOTTENHAM HOTSPUR	42	21	7	14	79	56	49
4	DERBY CO	42	17	11	14	68	54	45
5	MANCHESTER C	42	17	11	14	65	72	45
6	BLACKBURN R	42	16	12	14	81	56	44
7	WBA	42	17	10	15	78	70	44
8	BLACKBURN R	42	18	7	17	74	81	43
9	LEEDS UNITED	42	17	8	17	75	66	42
10	PORTSMOUTH	42	15	12	15	52	55	42
11	SHEFFIELD W	42	16	9	17	62	67	41
12	STOKE C	42	15	11	16	58	44	41
13	ASTON VILLA	42	14	12	16	78	75	40
14	EVERTON	42	12	16	14	62	63	40
15	WOLVERHAMPTON W	42	14	12	16	74	86	40
16	MIDDLESBROUGH	42	16	7	19	68	80	39
17	LEICESTER C	42	14	11	17	59	74	39
18	LIVERPOOL	42	14	10	18	79	87	38
19	CHELSEA	42	14	8	20	67	69	36
20	BIRMINGHAM	42	12	12	18	54	56	36
21	NEWCASTLE U	42	10	14	18	68	77	34
22	SHEFFIELD U	42	12	7	23	58	101	31

Season 1934-35

Football League Division One

DATE	OPPONENTS	SCORE	GOALSCORERS	ATTENDANCE
Aug 25	EVERTON	D 1-1	Hall GW	50,586
Aug 27	PRESTON NORTH END	L 1-2	Evans W	24,961
Sep 1	Huddersfield Town	D 0-0		13,941
Sep 3	Preston North End	L 0-1		25,936
Sep 8	WOLVERHAMPTON WANDERERS	W 3-1	McCormick, Hunt G, Hall GW	37,114
Sep 15	Chelsea	W 3-1	O'Callaghan, Hunt G, Evans W	46,715
Sep 22	ASTON VILLA	L 0-2		42,088
Sep 29	Derby County	L 1-2	Hunt G	15,459
Oct 6	LEICESTER CITY	D 2-2	Hedley, Frame o.g.	37,409
Oct 13	Sunderland	W 2-1	Hunt G, Hall GW	28,204
Oct 20	Arsenal	L 1-5	Hunt G	70,544
Oct 27	PORTSMOUTH	W 4-1	Bolan, Howe, Hunt G 2	33,461
Nov 3	Manchester City	L 1-3	Evans W	28,802
Nov 10	MIDDLESBROUGH	W 3-1	Howe, Hunt G, Evans W	25,761
Nov 17	West Bromwich Albion	L 0-4		20,416
Nov 24	SHEFFIELD WEDNESDAY	W 3-2	McCormick, Evans W (1 pen) 2	25,103
Dec 1	Birmingham	L 1-2	O'Callaghan	20,546
Dec 8	STOKE CITY	W 3-2	O'Callaghan, Hunt G, Bellamy	31,082
Dec 15	Liverpool	L 1-4	O'Callaghan	24,688
Dec 22	LEEDS UNITED	D 1-1	Evans W	23,662
Dec 25	Grimsby Town	L 0-3		19,706
Dec 26	GRIMSBY TOWN	W 2-1	Hall A 2	45,512
Dec 29	Everton	L 2-5	McCormick, Hall A	25,851
Jan 1	Blackburn Rovers	L 0-1		12,083
Jan 5	HUDDERSFIELD TOWN	D 0-0		35,523
Jan 19	Wolverhampton Wanderers	L 2-6	McCormick, Evans W	28,209
Jan 30	CHELSEA	L 1-3	Hunt D	28,121
Feb 2	Aston Villa	L 0-1		36,973
Feb 9	DERBY COUNTY	D 2-2	McCormick 2	42,941
Feb 23	SUNDERLAND	D 1-1	Channell	44,886
Mar 6	ARSENAL	L 0-6		47,714
Mar 9	Portsmouth	D 1-1	Evans W (pen)	11,687
Mar 16	MANCHESTER CITY	D 0-0		43,572
Mar 23	Middlesbrough	L 1-3	Hunt G	14,625
Mar 28	Leicester City	L 0-6		13,061
Mar 30	WEST BROMWICH ALBION	L 0-1		29,161
Apr 6	Sheffield Wednesday	L 0-4		12,158
Apr 13	BIRMINGHAM	D 1-1	Bell	27,190
Apr 19	BLACKBURN ROVERS	W 1-0	Bell	31,101
Apr 20	Stoke City	L 1-4	Hunt D	11,574
Apr 27	LIVERPOOL	W 5-1	Bolan, Hunt D, Evans W 3	15,613
May 4	Leeds United	L 3-4	Bolan, Morrison, Hunt D	7,668

FA Cup

Jan 12	MANCHESTER CITY	(R3) W 1-0	Evans W	48,983
Jan 26	NEWCASTLE UNITED	(Rd4) W 2-0	Hunt G 2	61,195
Feb 16	BOLTON WANDERERS	(Rd5) D 1-1	Evans W	70,347
Feb 20	Bolton Wanderers	(R) D 1-1	Hunt G	47,453
Feb 25	Bolton Wanderers*	(2R) L 0-2		26,692

* played at Villa Park, Birmingham

League and Cup Appearances

PLAYER	LEAGUE	CUP COMPETITION FA CUP	TOTAL
Alsford	21	5	26
Bell	8		8
Bellamy	7	3	10
Bolan	9		9
Brain	1		1
Burgon	4		4
Channell	41	5	46
Colquhoun	3		3
Day	9	1	10
Duncan	6		6
Evans T	28	4	32
Evans W	32	4	36
Fullwood	2		2
Goldsmith	1		1
Greenfield	6		6
Hall A	12	5	17
Hall GW	18		18
Hedley	3	1	4
Hooper	3		3
Howe	32	5	37
Hunt D	12	2	14
Hunt G	30	3	33
Illingworth	1		1
Jones	8		8
King	1		1
Levene	3		3
McCormick	28	5	33
Meads	18		18
Morrison	2	1	3
Nicholls	21		21
O'Callaghan	16	1	17
Phypers	2		2
Rowe	18		18
Sargent	1		1
Taylor	18	5	23
Whatley	37	5	42

Goalscorers

PLAYER	LEAGUE	CUP COMPETITION FA CUP	TOTAL
Evans W	12	2	14
Hunt G	10	3	13
McCormick	6		6
Hunt D	4		4
O'Callaghan	4		4
Bolan	3		3
Hall A	3		3
Hall GW	3		3
Bell	2		2
Howe	2		2
Bellamy	1		1
Channell	1		1
Hedley	1		1
Morrison	1		1
Opp's o.gs.	1		1

Fact File

Following Arthur Rowe's injury three wins in 24 games plunged Spurs to relegation.

MANAGER: Percy Smith

CAPTAIN: Arthur Rowe/Tom Evans/Wally Alsford

TOP SCORER: Willie Evans

BIGGEST WIN: 5-1 v Liverpool (H), 27 April 1934, Football League Division One

HIGHEST ATTENDANCE: 70,544 v Arsenal, 20 October 1934, Football League Division One

MAJOR TRANSFERS IN: Sam Bell from Luton Town, Archie Burgon from Grantham Town, Andy Duncan from Hull City

MAJOR TRANSFERS OUT: Bill Felton to Altrincham, Taffy O'Callaghan to Leicester City

Final Division One Table

		P	W	D	L	F	A	Pts
1	ARSENAL	42	23	12	7	115	46	58
2	BLACKBURN R	42	19	16	7	90	51	54
3	SHEFFIELD W	42	18	13	11	70	64	49
4	MANCHESTER C	42	20	8	14	82	67	48
5	GRIMSBY T	42	17	11	14	78	60	45
6	DERBY CO	42	18	9	15	81	66	45
7	LIVERPOOL	42	19	7	16	85	88	45
8	EVERTON	42	16	12	14	89	88	44
9	WBA	42	17	10	15	83	83	44
10	STOKE C	42	18	6	18	71	70	42
11	PRESTON NE	42	15	12	15	62	67	42
12	CHELSEA	42	16	9	17	73	56	41
13	ASTON VILLA	42	14	13	15	74	88	41
14	PORTSMOUTH	42	15	10	17	71	72	40
15	BLACKBURN R	42	14	11	17	66	78	39
16	HUDDERSFIELD T	42	14	10	18	76	71	38
17	WOLVERHAMPTON W	42	15	8	19	88	94	38
18	LEEDS UNITED	42	13	12	17	75	92	38
19	BIRMINGHAM C	42	13	10	19	63	81	36
20	MIDDLESBROUGH	42	10	14	18	70	90	34
21	LEICESTER C	42	12	9	21	61	86	33
22	TOTTENHAM HOTSPUR	42	10	10	22	54	93	30

Season 1935-36

Football League Division Two

DATE	OPPONENTS	SCORE	GOALSCORERS	ATTENDANCE
Aug 31	Bradford City	W 1-0	Hunt D	14,359
Sep 2	HULL CITY	W 3-1	McCormick, Howe, Hunt D	25,603
Sep 7	NEWCASTLE UNITED	L 1-2	Howe	47,442
Sep 9	Hull City	L 0-1		9,616
Sep 14	Sheffield United	D 1-1	Morrison	14,879
Sep 16	BARNSLEY	W 3-0	Duncan, Morrison 2	14,930
Sep 21	Manchester United	D 0-0		34,718
Sep 28	PORT VALE	W 5-2	Howe 2, Morrison 3	32,872
Oct 5	Fulham	W 2-1	Duncan, Evans W	37,298
Oct 12	BURNLEY	W 5-1	Howe, Morrison 2, Hall GW, Evans W	34,483
Oct 19	BRADFORD	W 4-0	Morrison 2, Hall GW, Evans W	37,796
Oct 26	Leicester City	L 1-4	Morrison	24,721
Nov 2	SWANSEA TOWN	W 7-2	Fullwood (pen), Morrison 2, Hall GW 3, Evans W	36,121
Nov 9	West Ham United	D 2-2	Morrison 2	40,245
Nov 16	BURY	W 4-3	McCormick, Morrison, Hall GW, Evans W	32,176
Nov 23	Southampton	L 0-2		21,333
Nov 30	BLACKPOOL	W 3-1	Duncan, Morrison, Cardwell o.g.	35,031
Dec 7	Nottingham Forest	L 1-4	Edrich	9,232
Dec 14	NORWICH CITY	W 2-1	McCormick, Morrison	29,204
Dec 21	Doncaster Rovers	L 1-2	Morrison	20,131
Dec 25	PLYMOUTH ARGYLE	L 1-2	Morrison	34,510
Dec 26	Plymouth Argyle	L 1-2	Bell	34,426
Dec 28	BRADFORD CITY	W 4-0	Howe (pen), Duncan, Evans W 2	28,518
Jan 4	Newcastle United	W 4-1	Morrison, Bell, Evans W 2	35,389
Jan 18	SHEFFIELD UNITED	D 1-1	Evans W	35,534
Feb 1	Port Vale	W 5-1	Sargent, Morrison 3, Evans W	10,770
Feb 5	MANCHESTER UNITED	D 0-0		20,085
Feb 8	FULHAM	D 2-2	Sargent, Evans W	45,277
Feb 22	Bradford	W 5-2	Sargent 2, Morrison, Hunt G, Evans W	6,987
Mar 4	NOTTINGHAM FOREST	D 1-1	Hunt G	14,700
Mar 7	Bury	D 1-1	Bell	6,012
Mar 14	WEST HAM UNITED	L 1-3	Hunt G	57,417
Mar 21	Swansea Town	D 1-1	Sargent	12,498
Mar 28	SOUTHAMPTON	W 8-0	Meek 3, Hunt G (1 pen) 3, Evans W 2	28,907
Apr 4	Blackpool	W 4-2	Hunt G 3, Cardwell o.g.	11,044
Apr 10	CHARLTON ATHLETIC	D 1-1	Duncan	55,866
Apr 11	LEICESTER CITY	D 1-1	Hunt G	35,286
Apr 13	Charlton Athletic	L 1-2	Hunt G	46,713
Apr 18	Norwich City	L 0-1		23,952
Apr 20	Burnley	D 0-0		8,567
Apr 25	DONCASTER ROVERS	W 3-1	Meek 2, Duncan	15,093
May 2	Barnsley	D 0-0		9,271

FA Cup

Jan 11	SOUTHEND UNITED	(Rd3)	D 4-4	Sargent 2, Morrison 2	48,839
Jan 15	Southend United	(R)	W 2-1	Sargent, Evans W	23,634
Jan 25	HUDDERSFIELD TOWN	(Rd4)	W 1-0	Howe	64,149
Feb 15	Bradford	(Rd5)	D 0-0		24,053
Feb 17	BRADFORD	(R)	W 2-1	Hunt G 2	35,492
Feb 29	Sheffield United	(Rd6)	L 1-3	Morrison	22,295

Fact File

Former Spurs' player Len Bolan scored in both games as Third Division (South) Southend United almost beat Spurs to pull off the shock of the FA Cup third round.

MANAGER: Jack Tresadern

CAPTAIN: Arthur Rowe

TOP SCORER: John Morrison

BIGGEST WIN: 8-0 v Southampton (H), 28 March 1936, Football League Division Two

HIGHEST ATTENDANCE: 64,149 v Huddersfield Town, 25 January 1936, FA Cup 4th Round

MAJOR TRANSFERS IN: Joe Meek and Ralph Ward from Bradford

MAJOR TRANSFERS OUT: Jimmy Brain to Kings Lynn, Tom Meads to Notts County

League and Cup Appearances

PLAYER	LEAGUE	CUP COMPETITION FA CUP	TOTAL
Alsford	14	2	16
Bell	5	1	6
Buckingham	16	2	18
Channell	32	6	38
Day	1		1
Duncan	24	3	27
Edrich	9		9
Evans T	8		8
Evans W	33	6	39
Fullwood	12	1	13
Grice	7		7
Hall, A	4		4
Hall BAC	1		1
Hall GW	32	5	37
Hooper	21	1	22
Howe	33	6	39
Hunt D	4		4
Hunt G	15	3	18
Jones	10		10
McCormick	21		21
Meek	10		10
Morrison	32	6	38
Nicholls	7		7
Phypers	26	3	29
Rowe	28	6	34
Sargent	16	6	22
Taylor	14	5	19
Ward	8		8
Whatley	19	4	23

Goalscorers

PLAYER	LEAGUE	CUP COMPETITION FA CUP	TOTAL
Morrison	25	3	28
Evans W	15	1	16
Hunt G	11	2	13
Sargent	5	3	8
Howe	6	1	7
Duncan	6		6
Hall GW	6		6
Meek	5		5
McCormick	3		3
Bell	3		3
Hunt D	2		2
Edrich	1		1
Fullwood	1		1
Opp's o.gs.	2		2

Final Division Two Table

		P	W	D	L	F	A	Pts
1	MANCHESTER U	42	22	12	8	85	43	56
2	CHARLTON A	42	22	8	9	85	58	55
3	SHEFFIELD U	42	20	8	10	79	50	52
4	WEST HAM U	42	22	8	12	90	68	52
5	TOTTENHAM HOTSPUR	42	18	13	11	91	55	49
6	LEICESTER C	42	19	10	13	79	57	48
7	PLYMOUTH A	42	20	8	14	47	57	48
8	NEWCASTLE U	42	20	6	16	88	79	46
9	FULHAM	42	15	14	13	76	52	44
10	BLACKPOOL	42	18	7	17	60	72	43
11	NORWICH CITY	42	17	9	16	72	65	43
12	BRADFORD C	42	15	13	14	55	41	43
13	SWANSEA TOWN	42	15	9	18	67	76	39
14	BURY	42	13	12	17	66	84	38
15	BURNLEY	42	12	13	17	50	59	37
16	BRADFORD	42	14	9	19	62	84	37
17	SOUTHAMPTON	42	14	9	19	47	65	37
18	DONCASTER R	42	14	9	19	51	71	37
19	NOTTINGHAM F	42	12	11	19	69	76	35
20	BARNSLEY	42	12	9	21	54	80	33
21	PORT VALE	42	12	8	22	56	106	32
22	HULL CITY	42	5	10	27	47	111	20

Season 1936-37

Football League Division Two

DATE	OPPONENTS	SCORE	GOALSCORERS	ATTENDANCE
Aug 29	West Ham United	L 1-2	Morrison	31,906
Aug 31	Blackpool	D 0-0		23,875
Sep 5	NORWICH CITY	L 2-3	Hunt G, Edrich	32,767
Sep 12	Newcastle United	W 1-0	Morrison	28,314
Sep 14	LEICESTER CITY	W 4-2	Morrison 2, Bell, Evans W	17,913
Sep 19	BRADFORD	W 5-1	Morrison 4, Evans W	33,177
Sep 21	BLACKPOOL	L 1-2	Morrison	16,308
Sep 26	Barnsley	L 0-1		12,024
Oct 3	SHEFFIELD UNITED	D 2-2	Morrison, Edrich	34,522
Oct 10	Burnley	L 1-3	Morrison	22,447
Oct 17	SOUTHAMPTON	W 4-0	McCormick, Morrison 2, Hall GW	26,335
Oct 24	Swansea Town	L 1-2	Meek	15,545
Oct 31	BRADFORD CITY	W 5-1	Ward, Meek, Morrison 3	16,653
Nov 7	Aston Villa	D 1-1	Morrison	37,220
Nov 14	CHESTERFIELD	W 5-1	Hunt G (2 pen) 3, Morrison, Miller	30,054
Nov 28	PLYMOUTH ARGYLE	L 1-3	Hunt G	32,305
Dec 5	Coventry City	L 0-1		27,395
Dec 12	DONCASTER ROVERS	W 2-0	McCormick, Hunt G	16,844
Dec 19	Fulham	D 3-3	Ward (pen), Morrison, Miller	20,495
Dec 25	Blackburn Rovers	W 4-0	Meek, Morrison 2, Miller	26,756
Dec 26	WEST HAM UNITED	L 2-3	Meek, Miller	34,190
Dec 28	BLACKBURN ROVERS	W 5-1	McCormick, Miller 4	16,135
Jan 2	Norwich City	W 3-2	Morrison 3	13,131
Jan 9	NEWCASTLE UNITED	L 0-1		30,505
Jan 23	Bradford	L 2-3	Meek 2	7,481
Feb 3	BARNSLEY	W 3-0	Meek, Duncan, Edrich	11,097
Feb 6	Sheffield United	L 2-3	McCormick, Morrison	22,838
Feb 13	BURNLEY	W 3-0	McCormick, Morrison, Miller	30,283
Feb 24	Southampton	L 0-1		5,226
Feb 27	SWANSEA TOWN	W 3-1	Duncan 3	26,346
Mar 10	Bradford City	D 2-2	Meek, Hunt G	6,050
Mar 13	ASTON VILLA	D 2-2	Meek, Miller	35,652
Mar 20	Chesterfield	W 3-1	McCormick 3	13,621
Mar 26	Bury	L 3-5	Hunt G, Duncan, Miller	12,748
Mar 27	NOTTINGHAM FOREST	W 2-1	Hunt G 2	23,801
Mar 29	BURY	W 2-0	Duncan, Miller	27,642
Apr 3	Plymouth Argyle	D 2-2	Morrison, Duncan	19,158
Apr 10	COVENTRY CITY	W 3-1	Ward (pen), Duncan 2	18,515
Apr 17	Doncaster Rovers	D 1-1	Morrison	3,560
Apr 21	Nottingham Forest	L 0-3		14,687
Apr 24	FULHAM	D 1-1	Alexander	21,133
May 1	Leicester City	L 1-4	Morrison	22,761

FA Cup

Jan 16	Portsmouth	(Rd3) W 5-0	Morrison 3, Duncan, Miller	32,665
Jan 30	PLYMOUTH ARGYLE	(Rd4) W 1-0	McCormick	42,430
Feb 20	Everton	(Rd5) D 1-1	McCormick	57,149
Feb 22	EVERTON	(R) W 4-3	Meek, Morrison 3	46,972
Mar 6	PRESTON NORTH END	(Rd6) L 1-3	Duncan	71,913

League and Cup Appearances

PLAYER	LEAGUE	CUP COMPETITION FA CUP	TOTAL
Alexander	9		9
Alsford	7		7
Bell	2		2
Blyth	11		11
Brown	4		4
Buckingham	25	5	30
Duncan	29	5	34
Edrich	11		11
Evans T	1		1
Evans W	7		7
Fullwood	5		5
Grice	22	5	27
Hall A	1		1
Hall J	39	5	44
Hall GW	19		19
Hooper	3		3
Howe	28		28
Hunt D	1		1
Hunt G	13		13
Ludford	1		1
McCormick	35	5	40
Meek	28	5	33
Miller	23	5	28
Morrison	32	5	37
Page	15		15
Phypers	2		2
Ringrose	10		10
Rowe	15	5	20
Ward	32	5	37
Whatley	32	5	37

Goalscorers

PLAYER	LEAGUE	CUP COMPETITION FA CUP	TOTAL
Morrison	29	6	35
Miller	12	1	13
Duncan	9	2	11
Hunt G	10		10
McCormick	8	2	10
Meek	9	1	10
Edrich	3		3
Ward	3		3
Evans W	2		2
Alexander	1		1
Bell	1		1
Hall GW	1		1

Fact File

After England's cricket tour of 1937 Bill Edrich decided to give up football to concentrate on the summer game. He became one of England's greatest cricketers.

MANAGER: Jack Tresadern

CAPTAIN: Arthur Rowe/Ralph Ward/Bill Whatley

TOP SCORER: John Morrison

BIGGEST WIN: 5-0 v Portsmouth (A), 16 January 1937, FA Cup 3rd Round

HIGHEST ATTENDANCE: 71,913 v Preston North End, 6 March 1937, FA Cup 6th Round

MAJOR TRANSFERS IN: Stan Alexander from Millwall, Jack Hall from Manchester United, Les Miller from Sochaux

MAJOR TRANSFERS OUT: Joe Nicholls to Bristol Rovers

Final Division Two Table

		P	W	D	L	F	A	Pts
1	LEICESTER C	42	24	8	10	89	57	56
2	BLACKPOOL	42	24	7	11	88	53	55
3	BURY	42	22	8	12	74	55	52
4	NEWCASTLE U	42	22	5	15	80	56	49
5	PLYMOUTH A	42	18	13	11	71	53	49
6	WEST HAM U	42	19	9	12	73	55	49
7	SHEFFIELD U	42	18	10	14	66	54	46
8	COVENTRY C	42	17	17	14	66	54	45
9	ASTON VILLA	42	16	12	14	82	70	44
10	TOTTENHAM HOTSPUR	42	17	9	16	88	66	43
11	FULHAM	42	15	13	14	71	61	43
12	BLACKBURN R	42	16	10	16	70	53	42
13	BURNLEY	42	16	10	16	57	61	42
14	BARNSLEY	42	16	9	17	50	64	41
15	CHESTERFIELD	42	16	8	18	84	89	40
16	SWANSEA T	42	15	7	20	50	65	37
17	NORWICH CITY	42	14	8	20	63	71	36
18	NOTTINGHAM F	42	12	10	20	68	90	34
19	SOUTHAMPTON	42	11	12	19	53	77	34
20	BRADFORD	42	12	9	21	52	88	33
21	BRADFORD C	42	9	12	21	54	94	30
22	DONCASTER R	42	7	10	25	30	84	24

Season 1937-38

Football League Division Two

DATE	OPPONENTS	SCORE	GOALSCORERS	ATTENDANCE
Aug 28	COVENTRY CITY	D 0-0		32,519
Aug 30	BURNLEY	W 4-0	Ward (pen), Morrison 3	13,766
Sep 4	Nottingham Forest	L 1-3	Sargent	16,478
Sep 6	Burnley	L 1-2	Miller	11,287
Sep 11	NEWCASTLE UNITED	D 2-2	Sargent, Morrison	25,577
Sep 16	Sheffield Wednesday	W 3-0	Sargent, Morrison, Gibbons	13,263
Sep 18	Luton Town	W 4-2	Sargent, Morrison 2, Miller	23,788
Sep 25	BARNSLEY	W 3-0	Hall GW, Gibbons, Miller	26,417
Oct 2	Stockport County	L 2-3	Hall GW, Morrison	19,069
Oct 9	MANCHESTER UNITED	L 0-1		31,189
Oct 16	Fulham	L 1-3	Sargent	29,556
Oct 23	PLYMOUTH ARGYLE	W 3-2	Sargent, Morrison, Jeffrey	22,734
Oct 30	Chesterfield	D 2-2	Ward (pen), Morrison	16,092
Nov 6	SWANSEA TOWN	W 2-0	Gibbons 2	22,328
Nov 13	Norwich City	L 1-2	Gibbons	19,019
Nov 20	WEST HAM UNITED	W 2-0	Sargent, Gibbons	47,000
Nov 27	Bradford	L 1-3	Gibbons	10,794
Dec 4	ASTON VILLA	W 2-1	Hall GW, Morrison	37,238
Dec 11	Southampton	L 1-2	Gibbons	17,718
Dec 18	BLACKBURN ROVERS	W 3-1	Grice, Lyman 2	20,251
Dec 25	Bury	W 2-1	Morrison, Gibbons	13,659
Dec 27	BURY	L 1-3	Gibbons	40,901
Jan 1	Coventry City	L 1-2	Duncan	24,336
Jan 15	NOTTINGHAM FOREST	W 3-0	Sargent, Hall GW, Gibbons	21,288
Jan 29	LUTON TOWN	W 3-0	Morrison, Lyman 2	29,806
Feb 2	Newcastle United	L 0-1		11,249
Feb 5	Barnsley	D 1-1	Sargent	13,327
Feb 19	Manchester United	W 1-0	Sargent	34,631
Feb 23	STOCKPORT COUNTY	W 2-0	Howe 2	11,049
Feb 26	FULHAM	D 1-1	Morrison	34,097
Mar 9	Plymouth Argyle	D 2-2	Morrison, Duncan	15,724
Mar 12	CHESTERFIELD	W 2-0	Sargent, Miller	20,915
Mar 19	Swansea Town	L 2-3	Meek, Gibbons	10,656
Mar 26	NORWICH CITY	W 4-0	Ward, Sargent, Morrison 2	18,431
Apr 2	West Ham United	W 3-1	Sargent, Gibbons, Miller	30,031
Apr 9	BRADFORD	W 2-1	Morrison 2	17,967
Apr 15	SHEFFIELD UNITED	L 1-2	Howe	23,162
Apr 16	Aston Villa	L 0-2		53,730
Apr 18	Sheffield United	L 0-1		45,305
Apr 23	SOUTHAMPTON	W 5-0	Ward (pen), Sargent, Morrison 3	15,982
Apr 30	Blackburn Rovers	L 1-2	Howe	7,088
May 7	SHEFFIELD WEDNESDAY	L 1-2	Sargent	13,367

FA Cup

Jan 8	BLACKBURN ROVERS	(Rd3) W 3-2	Sargent, Gibbons 2	35,576
Jan 22	New Brighton	(Rd4) D 0-0		13,029
Jan 26	NEW BRIGHTON	(R) W 5-2	Morrison 2, Gibbons 2, Lyman	36,004
Feb 12	Chesterfield	(Rd5) D 2-2	Gibbons, Miller	30,561
Feb 16	CHESTERFIELD	(R) W 2-1	Sargent, Morrison	36,994
Mar 5	SUNDERLAND	(Rd6) L 0-1		75,038

League and Cup Appearances

PLAYER	LEAGUE	CUP COMPETITION FA CUP	TOTAL
Buckingham	29	5	34
Duncan	13		13
Fullwood	15		15
Gibbons	27	6	33
Grice	17	3	20
Hall A	7		7
Hall J	12		12
Hall GW	29	6	35
Hitchins	10	3	13
Hooper	30	6	36
Howe	33	4	37
Jeffrey	1		1
Ludford	1		1
Lyman	24	4	28
McCormick	3		3
Meek	7		7
Miller	16	2	18
Morrison	39	6	45
Page	23		23
Rowe	9	3	12
Sargent	42	6	48
Spelman	8		8
Ward	42	6	48
Whatley	25	6	31

Goalscorers

PLAYER	LEAGUE	CUP COMPETITION FA CUP	TOTAL
Morrison	22	3	25
Sargent	15	2	17
Gibbons	13	5	18
Miller	5	1	6
Lyman	4	1	5
Hall GW	4		4
Howe	4		4
Ward	4		4
Duncan	2		2
Grice	1		1
Jeffrey	1		1
Meek	1		1

Fact File

FA Cup holders Sunderland drew a crowd of 75,038 to White Hart Lane for the FA Cup 6th round, a record unlikely to ever be surpassed.

MANAGER: Jack Tresadern
CAPTAIN: Bill Whatley/Willie Hall
TOP SCORER: John Morrison
BIGGEST WIN: 5-0 v Southampton (H), 23 April 1938, Football League Division Two
HIGHEST ATTENDANCE: 75,038 v Sunderland, 5 March 1938, FA Cup 6th Round
MAJOR TRANSFERS IN: Colin Lyman from Northampton Town
MAJOR TRANSFERS OUT: Sam Bell to Southend United, Tom Evans to West Bromwich Albion, Willie Evans to Fulham

Final Division Two Table

		P	W	D	L	F	A	Pts
1	ASTON VILLA	42	25	7	10	73	35	57
2	MANCHESTER U	42	22	9	11	82	50	53
3	SHEFFIELD U	42	22	9	11	73	56	53
4	COVENTRY C	42	20	12	10	66	45	52
5	TOTTENHAM HOTSPUR	42	19	6	17	76	54	44
6	BURNLEY	42	17	10	15	54	54	44
7	BRADFORD	42	17	9	16	69	56	43
8	FULHAM	42	16	11	15	61	57	43
9	WEST HAM U	42	14	14	14	53	52	42
10	BURY	42	18	5	19	63	60	41
11	CHESTERFIELD	42	16	9	17	63	63	41
12	LUTON TOWN	42	15	10	17	89	72	40
13	PLYMOUTH A	42	14	12	16	57	65	40
14	NORWICH CITY	42	14	11	17	56	75	39
15	SOUTHAMPTON	42	15	9	18	55	77	39
16	BLACKBURN R	42	14	10	18	71	80	38
17	SHEFFIELD W	42	14	10	18	49	56	38
18	SWANSEA T	42	13	12	17	45	73	38
19	NEWCASTLE U	42	14	8	20	51	58	36
20	NOTTINGHAM F	42	14	8	20	47	60	36
21	BARNSLEY	42	11	14	17	50	64	36
22	STOCKPORT CO	42	11	9	22	43	70	31

The Essential History of Tottenham Hotspur

Season 1938-39

Football League Division Two

DATE	OPPONENTS	SCORE	GOALSCORERS	ATTENDANCE
Aug 27	Southampton	W 2-1	Sargent, Hall GW	22,653
Aug 29	SHEFFIELD WEDNESDAY	D 3-3	Howe, Hall GW 2	28,133
Sep 3	COVENTRY CITY	W 2-1	Morrison, Lyman	39,982
Sep 10	Nottingham Forest	L 1-2	Hall GW	18,594
Sep 12	SHEFFIELD UNITED	D 2-2	Morrison, Hall A	21,323
Sep 17	NEWCASTLE UNITED	W 1-0	Whatley (pen)	39,694
Sep 24	West Bromwich Albion	L 3-4	Hall GW, Morrison, Hall A	24,996
Oct 1	NORWICH CITY	W 4-1	Hall GW, Hall A 2, Lyman	30,055
Oct 8	Luton Town	D 0-0		21,061
Oct 15	FULHAM	W 1-0	Lyman	46,679
Oct 22	Blackburn Rovers	L 1-3	Lyman	18,136
Oct 29	WEST HAM UNITED	W 2-1	Lyman 2	51,170
Nov 5	Manchester City	L 0-2		47,998
Nov 12	BRADFORD	D 2-2	Spelman, Ludford	24,132
Nov 19	Swansea Town	D 1-1	Cox	13,172
Nov 26	CHESTERFIELD	D 2-2	Whatley (pen), Ludford	24,434
Dec 3	Tranmere Rovers	W 2-0	Hall A 2	12,043
Dec 10	MILLWALL	W 4-0	Ward (pen), Cox, Hall GW, Hall A	47,278
Dec 17	Bury	L 1-3	Hall A	5,723
Dec 24	SOUTHAMPTON	D 1-1	Ward (pen)	9,454
Dec 26	Burnley	L 0-1		15,629
Dec 27	BURNLEY	W 1-0	Duncan	30,276
Dec 31	Coventry City	L 0-4		19,499
Jan 14	NOTTINGHAM FOREST	W 4-1	Sargent, Hall A, Duncan, Miller	19,091
Jan 28	WEST BROMWICH ALBION	D 2-2	Sargent, Morrison	38,190
Feb 4	Norwich City	W 2-1	Buckingham, Ludford	15,347
Feb 11	LUTON TOWN	L 0-1		30,704
Feb 18	Fulham	L 0-1		26,466
Feb 25	BLACKBURN ROVERS	W 4-3	Sargent, Morrison 2, Miller	22,709
Mar 1	Newcastle United	W 1-0	Hall A	18,503
Mar 4	West Ham United	W 2-0	Hall GW, Duncan	20,832
Mar 11	MANCHESTER CITY	L 2-3	Hitchins, Hall GW	27,426
Mar 18	Bradford	D 0-0		8,202
Mar 25	SWANSEA TOWN	W 3-0	Burgess, Morrison 2	17,478
Apr 1	Chesterfield	L 1-3	Spelman	15,285
Apr 7	PLYMOUTH ARGYLE	W 1-0	Miller	33,621
Apr 8	TRANMERE ROVERS	W 3-1	Ward (pen), Morrison, Miller	19,229
Apr 10	Plymouth Argyle	W 1-0	Ludford	15,230
Apr 15	Millwall	L 0-2		33,428
Apr 22	BURY	W 4-3	Ludford 2, Duncan 2	16,279
Apr 29	Sheffield Wednesday	L 0-1		27,639
May 6	Sheffield United	L 1-6	Miller	38,460

FA Cup

Jan 7	WATFORD	(Rd3) W 7-1	Ward (pen), Sargent, Hall W 2, Duncan, Miller 2	34,896
Jan 21	West Ham United	(Rd4) D 3-3	Sargent, Morrison, Duncan	42,716
Jan 30	WEST HAM UNITED	(R) D 1-1	Sargent	50,798
Feb 2	West Ham United *	(2R) L 1-2	Morrison	50,468

* played at Highbury, London

League and Cup Appearances

PLAYER	LEAGUE	CUP COMPETITION FA CUP	TOTAL
Buckingham	41	4	45
Burgess	17		17
Cox	9		9
Duncan	21	2	23
Grice	1		1
Hall A	24	2	26
Hall J	2		2
Hall GW	40	4	44
Hitchins	25	4	29
Hooper	40	4	44
Howe	8		8
Ludford	10		10
Lyman	22	2	24
McCormick	1		1
Meek		1	1
Miller	17	2	19
Morrison	27	3	30
Nicholson	8		8
Page	17		17
Sargent	34	4	38
Spelman	20	4	24
Sproston	9		9
Tomkin	2		2
Ward	33	4	37
Whatley	34	4	38

Goalscorers

PLAYER	LEAGUE	CUP COMPETITION FA CUP	TOTAL
Hall GW	9	2	11
Morrison	9	2	11
Hall A	10		10
Duncan	5	2	7
Miller	5	2	7
Sargent	4	3	7
Ludford	6		6
Lyman	6		6
Ward	3	1	4
Cox	2		2
Spelman	2		2
Whatley	2		2
Buckingham	1		1
Burgess	1		1
Hitchins	1		1
Howe	1		1

Fact File

Bert Sproston travelled to Manchester with Spurs for the game with City on 5 November. He played, but not for Spurs. Prior to the match he was transferred to the Maine Road club.

MANAGER: Peter McWilliam

CAPTAIN: Willie Hall

TOP SCORER: Willie Hall and John Morrison

BIGGEST WIN: 7-1 v Watford (H), 7 January 1939, FA Cup 3rd Round

HIGHEST ATTENDANCE: 51,170 v West Ham United, 29 October 1938, Football League Division Two

MAJOR TRANSFERS IN: Bert Sproston from Leeds United

MAJOR TRANSFERS OUT: Jim Fullwood to Reading, Bert Sproston to Manchester City

Final Division Two Table

		P	W	D	L	F	A	Pts
1	BLACKBURN R	42	25	5	12	94	60	55
2	SHEFFIELD U	42	20	14	8	69	41	54
3	SHEFFIELD W	42	21	11	10	88	59	53
4	COVENTRY C	42	21	8	13	62	45	50
5	MANCHESTER C	42	21	7	14	96	72	49
6	CHESTERFIELD	42	20	9	13	69	52	49
7	LUTON TOWN	42	22	5	15	82	66	49
8	TOTTENHAM HOTSPUR	42	19	9	14	67	62	47
9	NEWCASTLE U	42	18	10	14	61	48	46
10	WBA	42	18	9	15	89	72	45
11	WEST HAM U	42	17	10	15	70	52	44
12	FULHAM	42	17	10	15	61	46	44
13	MILLWALL	42	14	14	14	64	53	42
14	BURNLEY	42	15	9	18	50	56	39
15	PLYMOUTH A	42	15	8	19	49	55	38
16	BURY	42	12	13	17	65	74	37
17	BRADFORD	42	12	11	19	61	82	35
18	SOUTHAMPTON	42	13	9	20	56	82	35
19	SWANSEA T	42	11	12	19	50	83	34
20	NOTTINGHAM F	42	10	11	21	49	82	31
21	NORWICH CITY	42	13	5	24	50	91	31
22	TRANMERE R	42	6	5	31	39	99	17

Season 1945-46

Football League South

DATE	OPPONENTS	SCORE	GOALSCORERS	ATTENDANCE
Aug 25	WOLVERHAMPTON WANDERERS	L 1-4	Broadis	33,852
Sep 1	Wolverhampton Wanderers	L 2-4	Ward (pen), Lyman	24,899
Sep 8	West Ham United	D 1-1	Burgess	26,437
Sep 12	LEICESTER CITY	W 6-2	Burgess 2, McCormick, Hall A, Ludford 2	13,294
Sep 15	WEST HAM UNITED	L 2-3	Gibbons 2	34,342
Sep 22	West Bromwich Albion	L 0-5		24,433
Sep 29	WEST BROMWICH ALBION	W 4-2	Acquroff 2, Lyman 2	31,403
Oct 6	Birmingham City	L 0-8		21,608
Oct 13	BIRMINGHAM CITY	L 0-1		30,589
Oct 20	Swansea Town	L 2-4	Stevens, Gibbons	16,985
Oct 27	SWANSEA TOWN	W 3-1	Hall A, Gibbons 2	20,407
Nov 3	BRENTFORD	W 1-0	Gibbons	28,603
Nov 10	Brentford	W 3-1	Hall A 2, Gibbons	19,270
Nov 17	Chelsea	W 2-1	Dix, Lyman	35,343
Nov 24	CHELSEA	W 3-2	Broadis 2, Gibbons	43,717
Dec 1	MILLWALL	W 5-1	Ward (pen), Gibbons 3, Dix	34,807
Dec 8	Millwall	L 2-3	Burgess, Gibbons	24,143
Dec 15	Southampton	L 2-3	Ward (pen), Lyman	13,935
Dec 22	SOUTHAMPTON	W 4-3	Ward (pen), Gibbons 2, Lyman	17,932
Dec 25	DERBY COUNTY	L 2-5	Broadis 2	33,700
Dec 26	Derby County	L 0-2		30,823
Dec 29	Leicester City	L 0-4		15,330
Jan 12	Luton Town	L 1-3	Skinner	9,528
Jan 19	LUTON TOWN	L 2-3	Burgess, Lyman	13,108
Jan 26	COVENTRY CITY	W 2-0	Burgess, Whitchurch	17,632
Feb 2	Aston Villa	L 1-5	Burgess	30,736
Feb 9	Arsenal *	D 1-1	Blair	38,927
Feb 16	ARSENAL	W 2-0	Hall A, Whitchurch	44,510
Feb 20	ASTON VILLA	W 3-0	Jinks 2, Whitchurch	19,300
Feb 23	CHARLTON ATHLETIC	W 2-1	Skinner, Dix	37,743
Mar 9	Fulham	D 1-1	Whitchurch	30,000
Mar 16	FULHAM	L 1-3	Dix (pen)	23,211
Mar 23	PLYMOUTH ARGYLE	W 2-0	Foreman 2	20,789
Mar 30	Plymouth Argyle	W 1-0	Foreman	25,000
Apr 6	Portsmouth	W 1-0	Medley	22,000
Apr 13	PORTSMOUTH	W 2-0	Foreman 2	23,000
Apr 17	Charlton Athletic	L 0-1		10,000
Apr 19	NOTTINGHAM FOREST	W 3-2	Ludford, Foreman, Medley	23,955
Apr 20	Newport County	W 4-1	Foreman 4	16,000
Apr 22	Nottingham Forest	W 2-0	Foreman, Medley	18,474
Apr 27	NEWPORT COUNTY	W 1-0	Foreman	15,223
May 4	Coventry City	W 1-0	Foreman	11,446

* played at White Hart Lane, London

FA Cup

Jan 5	BRENTFORD	(Rd3/1L) D 2-2	Burgess, Hall A	30,202
Jan 10	Brentford	(Rd3/2L) L 0-2		21,050

Fact File

Eight goals in five games as a guest in 1944-45 persuaded Spurs to secure George Foreman's transfer after the War.

Final Football League South Table

		P	W	D	L	F	A	Pts
1	Birmingham C	42	28	5	9	96	45	61
2	Aston Villa	42	25	11	6	106	58	61
3	Charlton A	42	25	10	7	92	45	60
4	Derby Co	42	24	7	11	101	62	55
5	WBA	42	22	8	12	104	69	52
6	Wolverhampton W	42	20	11	11	75	48	51
7	West Ham U	42	20	11	11	94	76	51
8	Fulham	42	20	10	12	93	73	50
9	Tottenham Hotspur	42	22	3	17	78	81	47
10	Chelsea	42	19	6	17	92	80	44
11	Arsenal	42	16	11	15	76	73	43
12	Millwall	42	17	8	17	79	105	42
13	Coventry C	42	15	10	17	70	69	40
14	Brentford	42	14	10	18	82	72	38
15	Nottingham F	42	12	13	17	72	73	37
16	Southampton	42	14	9	19	97	105	37
17	Swansea T	42	15	7	20	90	112	37
18	Luton Town	42	13	7	22	60	92	33
19	Portsmouth	42	11	6	25	66	87	28
20	Leicester C	42	8	7	27	57	101	23
21	Newport Co	42	9	2	31	52	125	20
22	Plymouth A	42	3	8	25	39	120	14

League and Cup Appearances

PLAYER	LEAGUE	CUP COMPETITION FA CUP	TOTAL
Acquroff	2		2
Adams	1	1	2
Beasley	2		2
Bennett	11		11
Blair	2		2
Broadis	9		9
Buckingham	19	1	20
Burgess	37	2	39
Ditchburn	2		2
Dix	26	2	28
Ford	3		3
Foreman	10		10
Gibbons	21		21
Hall A	24	2	26
Hall F	6		6
Hall J	9		9
Hughes	27	2	29
Joslin	4		4
Ludford	30	2	32
Lyman	21	2	23
McCormick	3		3
Medley	17	1	18
Nicholson	11		11
Page	16	1	17
Rundle	3		3
Sargent	2		2
Skinner	11		11
Smith	4		4
Stevens	14		14
Walters	2		2
Ward	26	2	28
Whitchurch	17		17
White	25	2	27
Willis	32	2	34

The following players made one appearance this season; Baily, Chisholm, Cox, Duquemin, Ferrier, Fletcher, Garwood, Gilberg, Howe, Howshall, Jinks, Morrison, Young.

Goalscorers

PLAYER	LEAGUE	CUP COMPETITION FA CUP	TOTAL
Gibbons	14		14
Foreman	13		13
Burgess	7	1	8
Lyman	7		7
Hall A	5	1	6
Broadis	5		5
Dix	4		4
Ward	4		4
Whitchurch	4		4
Ludford	3		3
Medley	3		3
Acquroff	2		2
Jinks	2		2
Skinner	2		2
Blair	1		1
McCormick	1		1
Stevens	1		1

MANAGER: Joe Hulme from January

CAPTAIN: Ralph Ward/Ron Burgess

TOP SCORER: Jack Gibbons

BIGGEST WIN: 6-2 v Leicester City (H), 12 September 1945, Football League South

HIGHEST ATTENDANCE: 44,510 v Arsenal, 16 February 1946, Football League South

MAJOR TRANSFERS IN: George Foreman from West Ham United, Archie Hughes from Huddersfield Town, Charlie Rundle from West Ham United

MAJOR TRANSFERS OUT: Jimmy McCormick to Fulham

Season 1946-47

Football League Division Two

DATE	OPPONENTS	SCORE	GOALSCORERS	ATTENDANCE
Aug 31	BIRMINGHAM CITY	L 1-2	Foreman	51,256
Sep 7	West Bromwich Albion	L 2-3	Bennett, Medley	34,970
Sep 9	SOUTHAMPTON	W 2-1	Rundle, Bennett	22,153
Sep 14	NEWCASTLE UNITED	D 1-1	Bennett	52,213
Sep 19	Newport County	W 4-2	Ludford, Whitchurch, Bennett, Dix	18,169
Sep 21	Swansea Town	W 2-0	Bennett 2	22,934
Sep 28	MANCHESTER CITY	D 0-0		55,253
Oct 5	BURNLEY	D 1-1	Medley	44,351
Oct 7	NEWPORT COUNTY	W 3-1	Foreman 2, Medley	14,540
Oct 12	Barnsley	W 3-1	Burgess, Foreman, Medley	24,494
Oct 19	West Ham United	D 2-2	Bennett, Foreman	34,341
Oct 26	SHEFFIELD WEDNESDAY	W 2-0	Cox, Bennett	33,251
Nov 2	Fulham	D 1-1	Foreman	40,762
Nov 9	BURY	W 2-1	Burgess, Stevens	38,684
Nov 16	Luton Town	L 2-3	Bennett, Foreman	26,362
Nov 23	PLYMOUTH ARGYLE	W 2-1	Bennett, Foreman	40,795
Nov 30	Leicester City	D 1-1	Foreman	34,543
Dec 7	CHESTERFIELD	L 3-4	Ludford, Cox 2	38,654
Dec 14	Millwall	W 3-0	Rundle 2, Foreman	20,937
Dec 21	BRADFORD	D 3-3	Foreman 2, Dix (pen)	24,779
Dec 25	Coventry City	L 1-3	Burgess	23,307
Dec 26	COVENTRY CITY	D 0-0		44,311
Dec 28	Birmingham City	L 0-1		44,171
Jan 4	WEST BROMWICH ALBION	W 2-0	Burgess, Walters	40,537
Jan 18	Newcastle United	L 0-1		62,876
Jan 27	SWANSEA TOWN	W 3-1	Bennett, Dix, Whitchurch	6,292
Feb 1	Manchester City	L 0-1		41,645
Feb 18	Burnley	D 0-0		28,462
Mar 1	Sheffield Wednesday	L 1-5	Rundle	23,144
Mar 8	FULHAM	D 1-1	Bennett	27,715
Mar 22	LUTON TOWN	W 2-1	Cox, Dix	36,160
Mar 29	Plymouth Argyle	W 4-3	Bennett 2, Foreman 2	22,525
Apr 4	NOTTINGHAM FOREST	W 2-0	Burgess, Rundle	29,176
Apr 5	LEICESTER CITY	W 2-1	Rundle 2	37,843
Apr 7	Nottingham Forest	D 1-1	Bennett	30,656
Apr 12	Chesterfield	D 0-0		14,802
Apr 19	MILLWALL	W 2-1	Rundle, Brolly o.g.	34,311
Apr 26	Bradford	L 1-2	Rundle	11,371
May 3	Bury	W 2-1	Cox, Rundle	13,063
May 10	Southampton	L 0-1		12,884
May 17	WEST HAM UNITED	D 0-0		37,503
June 7	BARNSLEY	D 1-1	Dix (pen)	17,575

FA Cup

Jan 11	STOKE CITY	(Rd3) D 2-2	Ludford, Bennett	65,681
Jan 15	Stoke City	(R) L 0-0		38,631

League and Cup Appearances

PLAYER	LEAGUE	CUP COMPETITION FA CUP	TOTAL
Baily	1		1
Bennett	38	2	40
Buckingham	27	2	29
Burgess	40	2	42
Cox	25		25
Ditchburn	41	2	43
Dix	31	2	33
Foreman	36	2	38
Gilberg	1		1
Hall	8		8
Hughes	1		1
Jones	1		1
Joseph	1		1
Ludford	41	2	43
Medley	10		10
Nicholson	39	2	41
Rundle	18		18
Skinner	1		1
Stevens	30	2	32
Tickridge	14		14
Trailor	1		1
Walters	1	2	3
Whitchurch	8		8
Willis	37	2	39
Woodward	11		11

Goalscorers

PLAYER	LEAGUE	CUP COMPETITION FA CUP	TOTAL
Bennett	15	1	16
Foreman	14		14
Rundle	10		10
Burgess	5		5
Cox	5		5
Dix	5		5
Medley	4		4
Ludford	2	1	3
Whitchurch	2		2
Stevens	1		1
Walters	1		1
Opp's o.gs.	1		1

Fact File

With few exceptions, the same fixture list was used as had been set for the expunged 1939-40 season.

MANAGER: Joe Hulme
CAPTAIN: Ron Burgess
TOP SCORER: Les Bennett
BIGGEST WIN: 3-0 v Millwall (A), 14 December 1946, Football League Division Two
HIGHEST ATTENDANCE: 65,681 v Stoke City, 11 January 1947, FA Cup 3rd Round
MAJOR TRANSFERS IN: Ernie Jones from Swansea Town
MAJOR TRANSFERS OUT: Andy Duncan to Chelmsford City, Colin Lyman to Port Vale, Roy White to Bradford

Final Division Two Table

		P	W	D	L	F	A	Pts
1	MANCHESTER C	42	26	10	6	78	35	62
2	BURNLEY	42	22	14	6	65	29	58
3	BIRMINGHAM C	42	25	5	12	74	33	55
4	CHESTERFIELD	42	18	14	10	58	44	50
5	NEWCASTLE U	42	19	10	13	95	62	48
6	TOTTENHAM HOTSPUR	42	17	14	11	65	53	48
7	WBA	42	20	8	14	88	75	48
8	COVENTRY C	42	16	13	13	66	59	45
9	LEICESTER C	42	18	7	17	69	64	43
10	BARNSLEY	42	17	8	17	84	86	42
11	NOTTINGHAM F	42	15	10	17	69	74	40
12	WEST HAM U	42	16	8	18	70	76	40
13	LUTON TOWN	42	16	7	19	71	73	39
14	SOUTHAMPTON	42	15	9	18	69	76	39
15	FULHAM	42	15	9	18	63	74	39
16	BRADFORD	42	14	11	17	65	77	39
17	BURY	42	12	12	18	80	78	36
18	MILLWALL	42	14	8	20	56	79	36
19	PLYMOUTH A	42	14	5	23	79	96	33
20	SHEFFIELD W	42	12	8	22	67	88	32
21	SWANSEA TOWN	42	11	7	24	55	83	29
22	NEWPORT CO	42	10	3	29	61	133	23

Season 1947-48

Football League Division Two

DATE	OPPONENTS	SCORE	GOALSCORERS	ATTENDANCE
Aug 23	West Browmich Albion	L 0-1		32,521
Aug 27	Bury	L 0-2		16,391
Aug 30	SHEFFIELD WEDNESDAY	W 5-1	Jordan 2, Duquemin, Bennett 2	36,751
Sep 1	BURY	D 2-2	Duquemin, Jones	29,635
Sep 6	Cardiff City	W 3-0	Duquemin 2, Bennett	48,894
Sep 8	West Ham United	D 1-1	Jordan	25,732
Sep 13	BRADFORD	W 3-1	Jordan, Duquemin 2	44,004
Sep 15	WEST HAM UNITED	D 2-2	Jordan, Bennett	33,415
Sep 20	Nottingham Forest	L 0-1		26,202
Sep 27	DONCASTER ROVERS	W 2-0	Jordan 2	46,011
Oct 4	Southampton	D 1-1	Duquemin	23,860
Oct 11	Barnsley	L 1-2	Duquemin	24,715
Oct 18	PLYMOUTH ARGYLE	W 2-0	Duquemin, Bennett	35,249
Oct 25	Luton Town	D 0-0		26,496
Nov 1	BRENTFORD	W 4-0	Baily, Duquemin 3	42,362
Nov 8	Leicester City	W 3-0	Cox, Stevens 2	34,426
Nov 15	LEEDS UNITED	W 3-1	Burgess, Baily, Duquemin	41,563
Nov 22	Fulham	W 2-0	Duquemin, Stevens	36,147
Nov 29	COVENTRY CITY	W 2-1	Bennett, Stevens	41,843
Dec 6	Newcastle United	L 0-1		57,950
Dec 13	BIRMINGHAM CITY	L 1-2	Baily	53,730
Dec 20	WEST BROMWICH ALBION	D 1-1	Cox	40,219
Dec 25	CHESTERFIELD	W 3-0	Baily, Duquemin, Bennett	44,863
Dec 27	Chesterfield	L 1-3	Burgess	19,495
Jan 3	Sheffield Wednesday	L 0-1		47,902
Jan 17	CARDIFF CITY	W 2-1	Cox (pen), Jordan	57,386
Jan 31	Bradford	W 2-0	Cox, Jordan	20,807
Feb 14	Doncaster Rovers	D 1-1	Woodward	24,033
Feb 21	SOUTHAMPTON	D 0-0		29,784
Mar 6	Plymouth Argyle	D 1-1	Bennett	32,049
Mar 15	BARNSLEY	L 0-3		31,969
Mar 20	Brentford	L 0-2		31,297
Mar 26	Millwall	D 0-0		42,288
Mar 27	LEICESTER CITY	D 0-0		33,108
Mar 29	MILLWALL	W 3-2	Jordan (pen), Duquemin, Jones	31,339
Apr 3	Leeds United	W 3-1	Rundle, Baily, Flint	24,891
Apr 5	LUTON TOWN	L 0-1		23,807
Apr 10	FULHAM	L 0-2		32,490
Apr 12	NOTTINGHAM FOREST	L 0-3		18,569
Apr 17	Coventry City	D 1-1	Barratt o.g.	18,262
Apr 24	NEWCASTLE UNITED	D 1-1	Opponent o.g.	44,164
May 1	Birmingham City	D 0-0		35,569

FA Cup

Jan 10	Bolton Wanderers	(Rd3)	W 2-0*	Duquemin 2	37,075
Jan 24	WEST BROMWICH ALBION	(Rd4)	W 3-1	Cox, Duquemin 2	71,853
Feb 7	LEICESTER CITY	(Rd5)	W 5-2	Cox (pen), Jordan 3, South o.g.	69049
Feb 28	Southampton	(Rd6)	W 1-0	Bennett	28,425
Mar 13	Blackpool †	(SF)	L 1-3*	Duquemin	70,687

* after extra time. † played at Villa Park, Birmingham

League and Cup Appearances

PLAYER	LEAGUE	CUP COMPETITION FA CUP	TOTAL
Baily	22	5	27
Bennett	35	2	37
Buckingham	41	5	46
Burgess	32	4	36
Chisholm	2		2
Cox	34	5	39
Ditchburn	41	5	46
Dix	5		5
Duquemin	36	5	41
Flint	5		5
Gilberg	1		1
Hughes	1		1
Jones	19	1	20
Jordan	24	3	27
Ludford	8	2	10
Medley	2	1	3
Nicholson	38	5	43
Rundle	6		6
Stevens	22	3	25
Tickridge	38	5	43
Trailor	10	1	11
Walters	1		1
Willis	3		3
Withers	1		1
Woodward	35	3	38

Goalscorers

PLAYER	LEAGUE	CUP COMPETITION FA CUP	TOTAL
Duquemin	16	5	21
Jordan	10	3	13
Bennett	8	1	9
Cox	4	2	6
Baily	5		5
Stevens	4		4
Burgess	2		2
Jones	2		2
Flint	1		1
Rundle	1		1
Woodward	1		1
Opp's o.gs.	2	1	3

Fact File

Spurs were only four minutes away from their first visit to Wembley when Stanley Matthews beat four defenders to set up Blackpool's equaliser in the FA Cup semi-final at Villa Park.

MANAGER: Joe Hulme

CAPTAIN: Ron Burgess

TOP SCORER: Len Duquemin

BIGGEST WIN: 5-1 v Sheffield Wednesday (H), 30 August 1947, Football League Division Two

HIGHEST ATTENDANCE: 71,853 v West Bromwich Albion, 24 January 1948, FA Cup 4th Round

MAJOR TRANSFERS IN: None

MAJOR TRANSFERS OUT: George Skinner to Gillingham, Charlie Whitchurch to Southend United

Final Division Two Table

		P	W	D	L	F	A	Pts
1	Birmingham C	42	22	15	5	55	24	59
2	Newcastle U	42	24	8	10	72	41	56
3	Southampton	42	21	10	11	71	53	52
4	Sheffield W	42	20	11	11	66	53	51
5	Cardiff C	42	18	11	13	61	58	47
6	West Ham U	42	16	14	12	55	53	46
7	WBA	42	18	9	15	63	58	45
8	Tottenham Hotspur	42	15	14	13	56	43	44
9	Leicester C	42	16	11	15	60	57	43
10	Coventry C	42	14	13	15	59	52	41
11	Fulham	42	15	10	17	47	46	40
12	Barnsley	42	15	10	17	62	53	40
13	Luton Town	42	14	12	16	56	59	40
14	Bradford	42	16	8	18	68	72	40
15	Brentford	42	13	14	15	44	61	40
16	Chesterfield	42	16	7	19	54	55	39
17	Plymouth Argyle	42	9	20	13	40	58	38
18	Leeds United	42	14	8	20	62	72	36
19	Nottingham F	42	12	11	19	54	60	35
20	Bury	42	9	16	17	58	73	34
21	Doncaster R	42	9	11	22	40	66	29
22	Millwall	42	9	11	22	44	74	29

The Essential History of Tottenham Hotspur

Season 1948-49

Football League Division Two

DATE	OPPONENTS	SCORE	GOALSCORERS	ATTENDANCE
Aug 21	SHEFFIELD WEDNESDAY	W 3-2	Baily, Duquemin, Jones	51,265
Aug 23	Coventry City	L 0-2		21,110
Aug 28	Lincoln City	D 0-0		19,540
Aug 30	COVENTRY CITY	W 4-0	Cox, Duquemin 2, Jones	31,768
Sep 4	CHESTERFIELD	W 4-0	Cox, Baily 2, Jones	46,804
Sep 8	Leeds United	D 0-0		33,793
Sep 11	West Bromwich Albion	D 2-2	Duquemin, Bennett	32,279
Sep 13	LEEDS UNITED	D 2-2	Cox, Jones	37,640
Sep 18	BURY	W 3-1	Duquemin, Bennett, Jones	60,442
Sep 25	West Ham United	L 0-1		38,132
Oct 2	BLACKBURN ROVERS	W 4-0	Baily, Bennett 2, Jones	53,721
Oct 9	Cardiff City	W 1-0	Jones	56,018
Oct 16	QUEENS PARK RANGERS	W 1-0	Baily	69,718
Oct 23	Luton Town	D 1-1	Baily	24,859
Oct 30	BRADFORD	W 5-1	Burgess 2, Duquemin, Bennett, Jones	47,955
Nov 6	Southampton	L 1-3	Jones	28,800
Nov 13	BARNSLEY	W 4-1	Bennett, Duquemin, Baily 2	48,989
Nov 20	Grimsby Town	D 1-1	Cox	15,863
Dec 4	Fulham	D 1-1	Nicholson	36,247
Dec 11	PLYMOUTH ARGYLE	W 3-0	Baily, Duquemin, Boyd o.g.	41,910
Dec 18	Sheffield Wednesday	L 1-3	Baily	40,256
Dec 25	Leicester City	W 2-1	Burgess, Bennett	30,949
Dec 27	LEICESTER CITY	D 1-1	Rundle	49,411
Jan 1	LINCOLN CITY	L 1-2	Jones	33,218
Jan 15	Chesterfield	L 0-1		15,861
Jan 22	WEST BROMWICH ALBION	W 2-0	Baily, Jones	62,566
Feb 5	Bury	D 1-1	Bennett	17,679
Feb 12	NOTTINGHAM FOREST	W 2-1	Duquemin, Bennett	37,599
Feb 19	WEST HAM UNITED	D 1-1	Bennett	62,980
Feb 26	Blackburn Rovers	D 1-1	Jones	20,262
Mar 5	CARDIFF CITY	L 0-1		51,183
Mar 12	Queens Park Rangers	D 0-0		25,416
Mar 19	LUTON TOWN	W 2-1	Bennett 2	41,839
Mar 26	Bradford	D 1-1	Duquemin	13,304
Apr 2	SOUTHAMPTON	L 0-1		69,265
Apr 9	Barnsley	L 1-4	Bennett	16,796
Apr 15	BRENTFORD	W 2-0	Bennett, Medley	39,050
Apr 16	GRIMSBY TOWN	W 5-2	Bennett 2, Duquemin 2, Medley	29,808
Apr 18	Brentford	D 1-1	Walters	19,004
Apr 23	Nottingham Forest	D 2-2	Nicholson, Duquemin	27,126
Apr 30	FULHAM	D 1-1	Duquemin	50,133
May 7	Plymouth Argyle	W 5-0	Duquemin, Bennett 3, Medley	23,927

FA Cup

Jan 8	Arsenal	(Rd3) L 0-3		47,314

League and Cup Appearances

PLAYER	LEAGUE	CUP COMPETITION FA CUP	TOTAL
Baily	41		41
Bennett	42	1	43
Buckingham	25	1	26
Burgess	40	1	41
Clarke	10		10
Cox	31	1	32
Ditchburn	42	1	43
Duquemin	37		37
Garwood	2		2
Gilberg		1	1
Jones	35	1	36
Ludford	10		10
Medley	6		6
Nicholson	41	1	42
Rundle	4	1	5
Stevens	2		2
Tickridge	41	1	42
Toulouse	2		2
Walters	12		12
Willis	10		10
Withers	12		12
Woodward	17	1	18

Goalscorers

PLAYER	LEAGUE	CUP COMPETITION FA CUP	TOTAL
Bennett	19		19
Duquemin	15		15
Jones	12		12
Baily	11		11
Cox	4		4
Burgess	3		3
Medley	3		3
Nicholson	2		2
Rundle	1		1
Walters	1		1
Opp's o.gs.	1		1

Fact File

Joe Hulme did not attend the FA Cup tie at his former club Arsenal. He preferred to watch the reserves at White Hart Lane.

MANAGER: Joe Hulme

CAPTAIN: Ron Burgess

TOP SCORER: Les Bennett

BIGGEST WIN: 5-0 v Plymouth Argyle (A), 7 May 1949, Football League Division Two

HIGHEST ATTENDANCE: 69,718 v Queens Park Rangers, 16 October 1948, Football League Division Two

MAJOR TRANSFERS IN: Harry Clarke from Lovells Athletic

MAJOR TRANSFERS OUT: Archie Hughes to Blackburn Rovers, Johnny Jordan to Juventus

Final Division Two Table

		P	W	D	L	F	A	PTS
1	FULHAM	42	24	9	9	77	37	57
2	WBA	42	24	8	10	69	39	56
3	SOUTHAMPTON	42	23	9	10	69	36	55
4	CARDIFF C	42	19	13	10	62	47	51
5	TOTTENHAM HOTSPUR	42	17	16	9	72	44	50
6	CHESTERFIELD	42	15	17	10	51	45	47
7	WEST HAM U	42	18	10	14	56	58	46
8	SHEFFIELD W	42	15	13	14	63	56	43
9	BARNSLEY	42	14	12	16	62	61	40
10	LUTON TOWN	42	14	12	16	55	57	40
11	GRIMSBY TOWN	42	15	10	17	72	76	40
12	BURY	42	17	6	19	67	49	40
13	QPR	42	14	11	17	44	62	39
14	BLACKBURN R	42	15	8	19	53	63	38
15	LEEDS UNITED	42	12	13	17	55	63	37
16	COVENTRY C	42	15	7	20	55	64	37
17	BRADFORD PA	42	13	11	18	65	78	37
18	BRENTFORD	42	11	14	17	42	53	36
19	LEICESTER C	42	10	16	16	62	79	36
20	PLYMOUTH A	42	12	12	18	49	64	36
21	NOTTINGHAM F	42	14	7	21	50	54	35
22	LINCOLN C	42	8	12	22	53	91	28

Season 1949-50

Football League Division Two

DATE	OPPONENTS	SCORE	GOALSCORERS	ATTENDANCE
Aug 20	Brentford	W 4-1	Bennett, Duquemin, Medley 2	32,702
Aug 22	PLYMOUTH ARGYLE	W 4-1	Ramsey (pen), Bennett, Baily, Medley	41,882
Aug 27	BLACKBURN ROVERS	L 2-3	Walters 2	53,016
Aug 31	Plymouth Argyle	W 2-0	Bennett, Baily	24,828
Sep 3	Cardiff City	W 1-0	Medley	42,629
Sep 5	SHEFFIELD WEDNESDAY	W 1-0	Duquemin	37,697
Sep 10	LEEDS UNITED	W 2-0	Bennett, Baily	48,274
Sep 17	BURY	W 3-1	Nicholson, Duquemin, Baily	54,438
Sep 24	Leicester City	W 2-1	Walters, Duquemin	36,846
Oct 1	BRADFORD	W 5-0	Ramsey (pen), Walters, Bennett, Medley 2	54,905
Oct 8	Southampton	D 1-1	Walters	30,240
Oct 15	COVENTRY CITY	W 3-1	Bennett, Duquemin 2	54,375
Oct 22	Luton Town	D 1-1	Walters	27,319
Oct 29	BARNSLEY	W 2-0	Duquemin, Baily	54,856
Nov 5	West Ham United	W 1-0	Walters	31,734
Nov 12	SHEFFIELD UNITED	W 7-0	Walters 3, Duquemin 2, Medley 2	54,193
Nov 19	Grimsby Town	W 3-2	Ramsey, Bennett, Medley	22,482
Nov 26	QUEENS PARK RANGERS	W 3-0	Nicholson, Bennett 2	62,783
Dec 3	Preston North End	W 3-1	Bennett, Duquemin, Medley	35,501
Dec 10	SWANSEA TOWN	W 3-1	Bennett, Duquemin 2	50,758
Dec 17	BRENTFORD	D 1-1	Baily	49,297
Dec 24	Blackburn Rovers	W 2-1	Scarth, Medley	33,078
Dec 26	CHESTERFIELD	W 1-0	Ramsey (pen)	61,879
Dec 27	Chesterfield	D 1-1	Scarth	26,341
Dec 31	CARDIFF CITY	W 2-0	Rees, Baily	59,780
Jan 14	Leeds United	L 0-3		50,476
Jan 21	Bury	W 2-1	Walters, Bennett	27,386
Feb 4	LEICESTER CITY	L 0-2		60,595
Feb 18	Bradford	W 3-1	Duquemin 2, Rees	20,287
Feb 25	SOUTHAMPTON	W 4-0	Rees, Duquemin, Medley 2	70,302
Mar 4	Coventry City	W 1-0	Medley	36,320
Mar 11	LUTON TOWN	D 0-0		53,145
Mar 18	Barnsley	L 0-2		22,346
Mar 25	WEST HAM UNITED	W 4-1	Walters 2, Bennett, Medley	51,124
Apr 1	Queens Park Rangers	W 2-0	Baily, Medley	29,771
Apr 7	HULL CITY	D 0-0		66,889
Apr 8	PRESTON NORTH END	W 3-2	Walters, Bennett, Medley	49,170
Apr 10	Hull City	L 0-1		38,345
Apr 15	Sheffield United	L 1-2	Medley	41,419
Apr 22	GRIMSBY TOWN	L 1-2	Duquemin	46,423
Apr 29	Swansea Town	L 0-1		16,417
May 6	Sheffield Wednesday	D 0-0		50,777

FA Cup

Jan 7	Stoke City	(Rd3) W 1-0	Baily		47,000
Jan 28	SUNDERLAND	(Rd4) W 5-1	Walters 2, Bennett 2, Medley		66,246
Feb 11	Everton	(Rd5) L 0-1			72,921

League and Cup Appearances

PLAYER	LEAGUE	CUP COMPETITION FA CUP	TOTAL
Baily	40	3	43
Bennett	35	2	37
Burgess	39	3	42
Clarke	42	3	45
Cook	3		3
Ditchburn	42	3	45
Duquemin	40	2	42
Ludford	4		4
Marchi	2		2
Medley	42	3	45
Nicholson	39	3	42
Ramsey	41	3	44
Rees	11	2	13
Scarth	4		4
Tickridge	1		1
Walters	35	3	38
Willis	2		2
Withers	40	3	43

Goalscorers

PLAYER	LEAGUE	CUP COMPETITION FA CUP	TOTAL
Medley	18	1	19
Bennett	14	2	16
Duquemin	16		16
Walters	14	2	16
Baily	8	1	9
Ramsey	4		4
Rees	3		3
Nicholson	2		2
Scarth	2		2

Fact File

Spurs were presented with the Second Division Championship Shield after the home game with Grimsby Town – which they had lost!

MANAGER: Arthur Rowe

CAPTAIN: Ron Burgess

TOP SCORER: Les Medley

BIGGEST WIN: 7-0 v Sheffield United (H), 12 November 1949, Football League Division Two

HIGHEST ATTENDANCE: 72,921 v Everton, 11 February 1950, FA Cup 5th Round

MAJOR TRANSFERS IN: Alf Ramsey from Southampton, Billy Rees from Cardiff City

MAJOR TRANSFERS OUT: Freddie Cox to Arsenal, Ernie Jones to Southampton

Final Division Two Table

		P	W	D	L	F	A	Pts
1	TOTTENHAM HOTSPUR	42	27	7	8	81	35	61
2	SHEFFIELD W	42	18	16	8	67	48	52
3	SHEFFIELD U	42	19	14	9	68	49	52
4	SOUTHAMPTON	42	19	14	9	64	48	52
5	LEEDS UNITED	42	17	13	12	54	45	47
6	PRESTON NE	42	18	9	15	60	49	45
7	HULL CITY	42	17	11	14	64	72	45
8	SWANSEA T	42	17	9	16	53	49	43
9	BRENTFORD	42	15	13	14	44	49	43
10	CARDIFF C	42	16	10	16	41	44	42
11	GRIMSBY T	42	16	8	18	74	73	40
12	COVENTRY C	42	13	13	16	55	47	39
13	BARNSLEY	42	13	13	16	64	67	39
14	CHESTERFIELD	42	15	9	18	43	47	39
15	LEICESTER C	42	12	15	15	55	65	39
16	BLACKBURN R	42	14	10	18	55	60	38
17	LUTON TOWN	42	10	18	14	41	51	38
18	BURY	42	14	9	19	60	65	37
19	WEST HAM U	42	12	12	18	53	61	36
20	QPR	42	11	12	19	40	57	34
21	PLYMOUTH A	42	8	16	18	44	65	32
22	BRADFORD	42	10	11	21	51	77	31

Season 1950-51

Football League Division One

DATE	OPPONENTS	SCORE	GOALSCORERS	ATTENDANCE
Aug 19	BLACKPOOL	L 1-4	Baily	65,978
Aug 23	Bolton Wanderers	W 4-1	Walters, Murphy, Duquemin, Medley	21,745
Aug 26	Arsenal	D 2-2	Burgess, Walters	63,638
Aug 28	BOLTON WANDERERS	W 4-2	o.g., Duquemin 2, Baily	44,246
Sep 2	Charlton Athletic	D 1-1	Ramsey (pen)	61,480
Sep 6	Liverpool	L 1-2	Medley	39,015
Sep 9	MANCHESTER UNITED	W 1-0	Walters	60,621
Sep 16	Wolverhampton Wanderers	L 1-2	Chatham o.g.	55,364
Sep 23	SUNDERLAND	D 1-1	Baily	59,190
Sep 30	Aston Villa	W 3-2	Murphy, Duquemin, Medley	36,538
Oct 7	BURNLEY	W 1-0	Medley	46,518
Oct 14	Chelsea	W 2-0	Walters, Duquemin	65,992
Oct 21	STOKE CITY	W 6-1	Walters, Bennett 2, Duquemin 2, Medley	54,124
Oct 28	West Bromwich Albion	W 2-1	Walters, Medley	44,543
Nov 4	PORTSMOUTH	W 5-1	Walters, Duquemin, Baily 3	66,402
Nov 11	Everton	W 2-1	Baily, Medley	47,125
Nov 18	NEWCASTLE UNITED	W 7-0	Ramsey (pen), Walters, Bennett, Baily, Medley 3	70,336
Nov 25	Huddersfield Town	L 2-3	Nicholson, Walters	39,519
Dec 2	MIDDLESBROUGH	D 3-3	Ramsey (pen), Walters, Duquemin	61,148
Dec 9	Sheffield Wednesday	D 1-1	Bennett	44,367
Dec 16	Blackpool	W 1-0	Duquemin	22,203
Dec 23	ARSENAL	W 1-0	Baily	54,898
Dec 25	Derby County	D 1-1	Murphy	32,301
Dec 26	DERBY COUNTY	W 2-1	McClellan 2	59,885
Dec 30	CHARLTON ATHLETIC	W 1-0	Walters	54,667
Jan 13	Manchester United	L 1-2	Baily	45,104
Jan 20	WOLVERHAMPTON WANDERERS	W 2-1	Walters, McClellan	66,796
Feb 3	Sunderland	D 0-0		56,817
Feb 17	ASTON VILLA	W 3-2	Ramsey (pen), Baily, Medley	47,842
Feb 24	Burnley	L 0-2		33,047
Mar 3	CHELSEA	W 2-1	Burgess, Wright	59,449
Mar 10	Stoke City	D 0-0		24,236
Mar 17	WEST BROMWICH ALBION	W 5-0	Bennett, Duquemin 3, Baily	45,353
Mar 23	Fulham	W 1-0	Murphy	47,391
Mar 24	Portsmouth	D 1-1	Uphill	49,716
Mar 26	FULHAM	W 2-1	Bennett, Murphy	51,862
Mar 31	EVERTON	W 3-0	Walters, Bennett, Murphy	46,651
Apr 7	Newcastle United	W 1-0	Walters	41,241
Apr 14	HUDDERSFIELD TOWN	L 0-2		55,014
Apr 21	Middlesbrough	D 1-1	Murphy	36,689
Apr 28	SHEFFIELD WEDNESDAY	W 1-0	Duquemin	46,645
May 5	LIVERPOOL	W 3-1	Walters, Murphy 2	49,072

FA Cup

Jan 6	Huddersfield Town	(Rd3) L 0-2		25,390

League and Cup Appearances

PLAYER	LEAGUE	CUP COMPETITION FA CUP	TOTAL
Baily	40	1	41
Bennett	25	1	26
Brittan	8		8
Burgess	35	1	36
Clarke	42	1	43
Ditchburn	42	1	43
Duquemin	33	1	34
McClellan	7		7
Medley	35	1	36
Murphy	25		25
Nicholson	41	1	42
Ramsey	40	1	41
Scarth	1		1
Tickridge	1		1
Uphill	2		2
Walters	40	1	41
Willis	39	1	40
Wither	4		4
Wright	2		2

Goalscorers

PLAYER	LEAGUE	CUP COMPETITION FA CUP	TOTAL
Walters	15		15
Duquemin	14		14
Baily	12		12
Medley	11		11
Murphy	9		9
Bennett	7		7
Ramsey	4		4
McClellan	3		3
Burgess	2		2
Nicholson	1		1
Uphill	1		1
Wright	1		1
Opp's o.gs.	2		2

Fact File

Bill Nicholson made his England debut against Portugal at Goodison Park in May 1951. He scored with his first kick but it was to be his only full cap.

MANAGER: Arthur Rowe

CAPTAIN: Ron Burgess

TOP SCORER: Sonny Walters

BIGGEST WIN: 7-0 v Newcastle United (H), 18 November 1950, Football League Division One

HIGHEST ATTENDANCE: 70,336 v Newcastle United, 18 November 1950, Football League Division One

MAJOR TRANSFERS IN: Peter Murphy from Coventry City

MAJOR TRANSFERS OUT: Sid Tickridge to Chelsea

Final Division One Table

		P	W	D	L	F	A	Pts
1	TOTTENHAM HOTSPUR	42	25	10	7	82	44	60
2	MANCHESTER U	42	24	8	10	74	40	56
3	BLACKPOOL	42	20	10	12	79	53	50
4	NEWCASTLE U	42	18	13	11	62	53	49
5	ARSENAL	42	19	9	14	73	56	47
6	MIDDLESBROUGH	42	18	11	13	76	65	47
7	PORTSMOUTH	42	16	15	11	71	68	47
8	BOLTON W	42	19	7	16	64	61	45
9	LIVERPOOL	42	16	11	15	53	59	43
10	BURNLEY	42	14	14	14	48	43	42
11	DERBY CO	42	16	8	18	81	75	40
12	BLACKBURN R	42	12	16	14	63	54	40
13	STOKE C	42	13	14	15	50	59	40
14	WOLVERHAMPTON W	42	15	8	19	74	61	38
15	ASTON VILLA	42	12	13	17	66	68	37
16	WBA	42	13	11	18	53	61	37
17	CHARLTON A	42	14	9	19	63	80	37
18	FULHAM	42	13	11	18	52	68	37
19	HUDDERSFIELD T	42	15	6	21	64	92	36
20	CHELSEA	42	12	8	22	53	65	32
21	SHEFFIELD W	42	12	8	22	64	83	32
22	EVERTON	42	12	8	22	48	86	32

Season 1951-52

Football League Division One

DATE	OPPONENTS	SCORE	GOALSCORERS	ATTENDANCE
Aug 18	Middlesbrough	L 1-2	Bennett	44,004
Aug 20	FULHAM	W 1-0	Medley	48,766
Aug 25	WEST BROMWICH ALBION	W 3-1	Bennett 2, Medley	51,544
Aug 29	Fulham	W 2-1	Bennett, McClellan	33,920
Sep 1	Newcastle United	L 2-7	Scarth, Bennett	52,541
Sep 3	Burnley	D 1-1	Bennett	27,045
Sep 8	BOLTON WANDERERS	W 2-1	Bennett, Edwards o.g.	61,838
Sep 10	BURNLEY	D 1-1	Ramsey (pen)	35,948
Sep 15	Stoke City	W 6-1	Ramsey (pen), Walters, Bennett, McClellan, Medley 2	27,154
Sep 22	MANCHESTER UNITED	W 2-0	Bennett, Medley	70,882
Sep 29	Arsenal	D 1-1	Murphy	72,164
Oct 6	MANCHESTER CITY	L 1-2	Bennett	58,163
Oct 13	Derby County	L 2-4	Bennett, McClellan	27,495
Oct 20	ASTON VILLA	W 2-0	Bennett, Duquemin	49,247
Oct 27	Sunderland	W 1-0	Walters	50,513
Nov 3	WOLVERHAMPTON WANDERERS	W 4-2	Ramsey (pen), Walters, Bennett, Duquemin	61,626
Nov 10	Huddersfield Town	D 1-1	Duquemin	30,259
Nov 17	CHELSEA	W 3-2	Nicholson, Bennett, Duquemin	48,985
Nov 24	Portsmouth	L 0-2		46,815
Dec 1	LIVERPOOL	L 2-3	Walters, Bennett	51,342
Dec 8	Blackpool	L 0-1		14,821
Dec 15	MIDDLESBROUGH	W 3-1	Bennett, Murphy 2	37,781
Dec 22	West Bromwich Albion	L 1-3	Murphy	29,962
Dec 25	Charlton Athletic	W 3-0	Medley, Bennett, Robb	37,711
Dec 26	CHARLTON ATHLETIC	L 2-3	Walters, Murphy	49,350
Dec 29	NEWCASTLE UNITED	W 2-1	Walters, Medley	55,219
Jan 5	Bolton Wanderers	D 1-1	Harmer	46,354
Jan 19	STOKE CITY	W 2-0	Duquemin, Harmer	45,976
Jan 26	Manchester United	L 0-2		42,668
Feb 9	ARSENAL	L 1-2	Walters	66,438
Feb 16	Manchester City	D 1-1	Walters	39,080
Feb 23	PRESTON NORTH END	W 1-0	Harmer	49,193
Mar 1	DERBY COUNTY	W 5-0	Walters, Bennett, Duquemin, Adams, Mozley o.g.	44,388
Mar 8	Aston Villa	W 3-0	Walters, Duquemin 2	56,475
Mar 15	SUNDERLAND	W 2-0	Bennett, Duquemin	51,745
Mar 22	Wolverhampton Wanderers	D 1-1	Baily	45,343
Apr 2	HUDDERSFIELD TOWN	W 1-0	Duquemin	22,396
Apr 12	PORTSMOUTH	W 3-1	Duquemin, Baily 2	66,988
Apr 14	Preston North End	D 1-1	Ramsey (pen)	36,525
Apr 19	Liverpool	D 1-1	Duquemin	36,898
Apr 26	BLACKPOOL	W 2-0	Ramsey, Baily	45,991
Apr 30	Chelsea	W 2-0	Bennett, Medley	46,574

FA Cup

Jan 12	Scunthorpe United	(Rd3) W 3-0	Baily, Duquemin 2	22,652
Feb 2	NEWCASTLE UNITED	(Rd4) W 0-3		69,009

FA Charity Shield

Sep 24	NEWCASTLE UNITED	W 2-1	Bennett, Murphy	27,660

Fact File

At the end of the season, Spurs and Manchester United toured America. They met twice, in Toronto and New York, with Spurs beating the League Champions 5-0 and 7-1.

MANAGER: Arthur Rowe

CAPTAIN: Ron Burgess

TOP SCORER: Les Bennett

BIGGEST WIN: 6-1 v Stoke City (A), 15 September 1951, Football League Division One

HIGHEST ATTENDANCE: 72,164 v Arsenal, September 29 1951, Football League Division One

MAJOR TRANSFERS IN: None

MAJOR TRANSFERS OUT: Peter Murphy to Birmingham City

League and Cup Appearances

PLAYER	LEAGUE	CUP COMPETITION FA CUP	OTHER	TOTAL
Adams	5			5
Baily	30	2		32
Bennett	35		1	36
Brittan	6			6
Burgess	40	2	1	43
Clarke	33	2	1	36
Ditchburn	42	2	1	45
Duquemin	25	2	1	28
Farley	1			1
Harmer	13	2		15
King	2			2
McClellan	12			12
Les Medley	34	2	1	37
Murphy	13		1	14
Nicholson	37	2	1	40
Ramsey	38	2		40
Robb	1			1
Robshaw	1			1
Scarth	2			2
Uphill	2			2
Walters	37	2	1	40
Wetton	7			7
Willis	17		1	18
Withers	29	2	1	32

Goalscorers

PLAYER	LEAGUE	CUP COMPETITION FA CUP	OTHER	TOTAL
Bennett	20		1	21
Duquemin	12	2		14
Walters	10			10
Medley	8			8
Murphy	5		1	6
Baily	4	1		5
Ramsey	5			5
Harmer	3			3
McClellan	3			3
Adams	1			1
Nicholson	1			1
Robb	1			1
Scarth	1			1
Opp's o.gs.	2			2

Final Division One Table

		P	W	D	L	F	A	Pts
1	MANCHESTER U	42	23	11	8	95	52	57
2	TOTTENHAM HOTSPUR	42	22	9	11	76	51	53
3	ARSENAL	42	21	11	10	80	61	53
4	PORTSMOUTH	42	20	8	14	68	58	48
5	BOLTON W	42	19	10	13	65	61	48
6	ASTON VILLA	42	19	9	14	79	70	47
7	PRESTON NE	42	17	12	13	74	54	46
8	NEWCASTLE U	42	18	9	15	98	73	45
9	BLACKPOOL	42	18	9	15	64	64	45
10	CHARLTON A	42	17	10	15	68	63	44
11	LIVERPOOL	42	12	19	11	57	61	43
12	BLACKBURN R	42	15	12	15	70	57	42
13	WBA	42	14	13	15	74	77	41
14	BURNLEY	42	15	10	17	56	63	40
15	MANCHESTER C	42	13	13	16	58	61	39
16	WOLVERHAMPTON W	42	12	14	16	73	73	38
17	DERBY CO	42	15	7	20	63	80	37
18	MIDDLESBROUGH	42	15	6	21	64	88	36
19	CHELSEA	42	14	8	20	52	72	36
20	STOKE C	42	12	7	23	49	88	31
21	HUDDERSFIELD T	42	10	8	24	49	82	28
22	FULHAM	42	8	11	23	58	77	27

Season 1952-53

Football League Division One

DATE	OPPONENTS	SCORE	GOALSCORERS	ATTENDANCE
Aug 23	WEST BROMWICH ALBION	L 3-4	Ramsey (pen), Bennett, Duquemin	56,552
Aug 27	MANCHESTER CITY	W 1-0	Duquemin	33,621
Aug 30	Newcastle United	D 1-1	McClellan	59,629
Sep 1	Manchester City	D 3-3	Ramsey (pen), McClellan, Robb	41,113
Sep 6	CARDIFF CITY	W 2-1	McClellan, Duquemin	62,150
Sep 10	Liverpool	L 1-2	Baily	49,869
Sep 13	Sheffield Wednesday	L 0-2		42,136
Sep 15	LIVERPOOL	W 3-1	Groves 2, Harmer	37,319
Sep 20	ARSENAL	L 1-3	Harmer	69,247
Sep 27	BURNLEY	W 2-1	Duquemin, Medley	43,031
Oct 4	Preston North End	L 0-1		28,108
Oct 11	Derby County	D 0-0		27,696
Oct 18	BLACKPOOL	W 4-0	Ramsey (pen), Duquemin, Baily 2	53,928
Oct 25	Chelsea	L 1-2	Ramsey (pen)	62,688
Nov 1	MANCHESTER UNITED	L 1-2	Walters	44,285
Nov 8	Portsmouth	L 1-2	Uphill	40,462
Nov 15	BOLTON WANDERERS	D 1-1	Bennett	31,442
Nov 22	Aston Villa	W 3-0	Bennett, Duquemin, Dicker	32,265
Nov 29	SUNDERLAND	D 2-2	Bennett, Duquemin	45,980
Dec 6	Wolverhampton Wanderers	D 0-0		37,062
Dec 13	CHARLTON ATHLETIC	W 2-0	Walters, Bennett	35,684
Dec 20	West Bromwich Albion	L 1-2	Dicker	18,698
Dec 25	MIDDLESBROUGH	W 7-1	Bennett 4, Duquemin 2, Baily	36102
Dec 27	Middlesbrough	W 4-0	Walters, Bennett, Duquemin, Bilciss o.g.	23,265
Jan 3	NEWCASTLE UNITED	W 3-2	Burgess 2, Duquemin	52,648
Jan 17	Cardiff City	D 0-0		36,423
Jan 24	SHEFFIELD WEDNESDAY	W 2-1	Walters, Baily	43,241
Feb 7	Arsenal	L 0-4		69,051
Feb 17	Burnley	L 2-3	Baily, Duquemin	13,771
Feb 21	PRESTON NORTH END	D 4-4	Walters, Duquemin 3	50,070
Mar 7	Blackpool	L 0-2		26,796
Mar 12	DERBY COUNTY	W 5-2	Bennett, Hollis, McClellan 2, Robb	13,933
Mar 14	CHELSEA	L 2-3	Willis (pen), Bennett	47,903
Mar 25	Manchester United	L 2-3	Walters, McClellan	20,215
Mar 28	PORTSMOUTH	D 3-3	Duquemin 2, Harmer	38,636
Apr 3	STOKE CITY	W 1-0	Harmer	35,606
Apr 4	Bolton Wanderers	W 3-2	McClellan, Stokes, Duquemin	40,185
Apr 6	Stoke City	L 0-2		25,346
Apr 11	ASTON VILLA	D 1-1	McClellan	39,217
Apr 18	Sunderland	L 1-4	Walters	24,953
Apr 25	WOLVERHAMPTON WANDERERS	W 3-2	Ramsey (pen), Bennett 2	48,136
Apr 30	Charlton Athletic	L 2-3	Ramsey, Walters	9,269

FA Cup

Jan 10	Tranmere Rovers	(Rd3) D 1-1	Bennett	21,537
Jan 12	TRANMERE ROVERS	(R) W 9-1	McClellan 3, Duquemin 2, Hollis 2, Baily 2	31,541
Jan 31	Preston North End	(Rd4) D 2-2	Withers 2	34,956
Feb 4	PRESTON NORTH END	(R) W 1-0	Duquemin	55,601
Feb 14	Halifax Town	(Rd5) W 3-0	Bennett 2, Duquemin	36,995
Feb 28	Birmingham City	(Rd6) D 1-1	Bennett	52,348
Mar 4	BIRMINGHAM CITY	(R) D 2-2*	Bennett, Duquemin	59,543
Mar 9	Birmingham City **	(R2) W 1-0	Walters	50,801
Mar 21	Blackpool†	(SF) L 1-2	Duquemin	68,221

*after extra time. **played at Molineux, Wolverhampton. † played at Villa Park, Birmingham

Fact File

This time Spurs were only ten seconds away from Wembley when Blackpool got their winner, but at least that paved the way for the 'Matthews Final'.

MANAGER: Arthur Rowe

CAPTAIN: Ron Burgess

TOP SCORER: Len Duquemin

BIGGEST WIN: 9-1 v Tranmere Rovers (H), 12 January 1953, FA Cup 3rd Round replay

HIGHEST ATTENDANCE: 69,247 v Arsenal, 20 September 1952, Football League Division One

MAJOR TRANSFERS IN: Johnny Brooks from Reading, Roy Hollis from Norwich City

League and Cup Appearances

PLAYER	LEAGUE	CUP COMPETITION FA CUP	TOTAL
Adams	1		1
Baily	30	9	39
Baker	1		1
Bennett	30	8	38
Brittan	9	4	13
Brooks	1		1
Burgess	30	7	37
Clarke	31	6	37
Dicker	10		10
Ditchburn	42	9	51
Duquemin	38	9	47
Gibbins	1	3	4
Groves	3		3
Grubb	2		2
Harmer	17		17
Hollis	3	1	4
Hopkins	2		2
King	10		10
Marchi	5		5
McClellan	17	2	19
Medley	21	6	27
Nicholson	31	7	38
Ramsey	37	9	46
Robb	6		6
Stokes	2		2
Uphill	2		2
Walters	26	8	34
Wetton	12		12
Willis	27	5	32
Withers	15	6	21

Goalscorers

PLAYER	LEAGUE	CUP COMPETITION FA CUP	TOTAL
Duquemin	18	6	24
Bennett	14	5	19
McClellan	8	3	11
Walters	8	1	9
Baily	6	2	8
Ramsey	6		6
Harmer	4		4
Hollis	1	2	3
Burgess	2		2
Dicker	2		2
Groves	2		2
Robb	2		2
Withers		2	2
Medley	1		1
Stokes	1		1
Uphill	1		1
Willis	1		1
Opp's o.gs.	1		1

Final Division One Table

		P	W	D	L	F	A	Pts
1	ARSENAL	42	21	12	9	97	64	54
2	PRESTON NE	42	21	12	9	85	60	54
3	WOLVERHAMPTON W	42	19	13	10	86	63	51
4	WBA	42	21	8	13	66	60	50
5	CHARLTON A	42	19	11	12	77	63	49
6	BURNLEY	42	18	12	12	67	52	48
7	BLACKPOOL	42	19	9	14	71	70	47
8	MANCHESTER U	42	18	10	14	69	72	46
9	BLACKBURN R	42	15	13	14	68	82	43
10	TOTTENHAM HOTSPUR	42	15	11	16	78	69	41
11	ASTON VILLA	42	14	13	15	63	61	41
12	CARDIFF C	42	14	10	16	54	39	40
13	MIDDLESBROUGH	42	14	11	17	70	77	39
14	BOLTON W	42	15	9	18	61	69	39
15	PORTSMOUTH	42	14	10	18	74	83	38
16	NEWCASTLE U	42	14	9	19	59	70	37
17	LIVERPOOL	42	14	8	20	61	82	36
18	SHEFFIELD W	42	12	11	19	62	72	35
19	CHELSEA	42	12	11	19	56	66	35
20	MANCHESTER C	42	14	7	21	72	87	35
21	STOKE C	42	12	10	20	53	66	34
22	DERBY CO	42	11	10	21	59	74	32

Season 1953-54

Football League Division One

DATE	OPPONENTS	SCORE	GOALSCORERS	ATTENDANCE
Aug 19	ASTON VILLA	W 1-0	Parkes o.g.	50,202
Aug 22	Sheffield Wednesday	L 1-2	Walters	38,114
Aug 26	CHARLTON ATHLETIC	W 3-1	Baily, Robb 2	48,035
Aug 29	MIDDLESBROUGH	W 4-1	Walters, Bennett, Duquemin, Robb	44,911
Sep 3	Charlton Athletic	W 1-0	Groves	37,609
Sep 5	West Bromwich Albion	L 0-3		42,959
Sep 7	Burnley	L 2-4	Walters, Robb	34,280
Sep 12	LIVERPOOL	W 2-1	Ramsey, Walters	47,535
Sep 16	BURNLEY	L 2-3	Duquemin 2	30,472
Sep 19	Newcastle United	W 3-1	Walters, Baily, Robb	53,056
Sep 26	MANCHESTER UNITED	D 1-1	Duquemin	52,837
Oct 3	Bolton Wanderers	L 0-2		39,842
Oct 10	ARSENAL	L 1-4	Robb	69,821
Oct 17	Cardiff City	L 0-1		41,083
Oct 24	MANCHESTER CITY	W 3-0	Duquemin, Robb 2	37,577
Oct 31	Sunderland	L 3-4	Walters, Duquemin, Robb	38,345
Nov 7	CHELSEA	W 2-1	Walters, Baily	44,795
Nov 14	Blackpool	L 0-1		19,667
Nov 21	HUDDERSFIELD TOWN	W 1-0	Duquemin	42,503
Nov 28	Sheffield United	L 2-5	Walters, Bennett	31,337
Dec 5	WOLVERHAMPTON WANDERERS	L 2-3	Bennett, Duquemin	48,164
Dec 12	Aston Villa	W 2-1	Walters, Baily	27,480
Dec 19	SHEFFIELD WEDNESDAY	W 3-1	Baker, Duquemin, Curtis o.g.	25,957
Dec 25	PORTSMOUTH	D 1-1	Brooks	36,502
Dec 26	Portsmouth	D 1-1	Walters	36,677
Jan 2	Middlesbrough	L 0-3		35,141
Jan 16	WEST BROMWICH ALBION	L 0-1		48,812
Jan 23	Liverpool	D 2-2	Walters, Lock o.g.	43,592
Feb 6	NEWCASTLE UNITED	W 3-0	Walters, Robb 2	35,798
Feb 13	Manchester United	L 0-2		37,289
Feb 27	Arsenal	W 3-0	Walters, Robb 2	64,311
Mar 3	BOLTON WANDERERS	W 3-2	Walters, Stokes, Dunmore	16,720
Mar 6	CARDIFF CITY	L 0-1		45,248
Mar 17	Manchester City	L 1-4	Marchi	9,984
Mar 20	SUNDERLAND	L 0-3		39,393
Mar 27	Chelsea	L 0-1		49,315
Apr 3	BLACKPOOL	D 2-2	Baily, Robb	43,870
Apr 10	Huddersfield Town	W 5-2	Hutchinson, Brooks, Harmer, Robb 2	26,232
Apr 16	Preston North End	L 1-2	Harmer	24,521
Apr 17	SHEFFIELD UNITED	W 2-1	Ramsey (pen), Brittan	35,105
Apr 19	PRESTON NORTH END	L 2-6	Bennett, Dunmore	30,206
Apr 24	Wolverhampton Wanderers	L 0-2		44,055

FA Cup

Jan 9	Leeds United	(Rd3) D 3-3	Walters, Bennett 2	41,645
Jan 13	LEEDS UNITED	(R) W 1-0	Bennett	35,023
Jan 30	Manchester City	(Rd4) W 1-0	Bennett	51,182
Feb 20	Hull City	(Rd5) D 1-1	Bennett	46,839
Feb 24	HULL CITY	(R) W 2-0	Walters, Baily	52,934
Mar 13	West Bromwich Albion	(Rd6) L 0-3		51,049

League and Cup Appearances

PLAYER	LEAGUE	CUP COMPETITION FA CUP	TOTAL
Baily	33	6	39
Baker	4		4
Bennett	26	6	32
Brittan	3		3
Brooks	18		18
Burgess	24	5	29
Clarke	41	6	47
Ditchburn	39	6	45
Dunmore	10		10
Duquemin	27	6	33
Groves	1		1
Harmer	6		6
Hopkins	2		2
Hutchinson	5		5
King	2		2
Marchi	8		8
McClellan	5		5
Nicholson	30	6	36
Owen	1		1
Ramsey	37	6	43
Reynolds	3		3
Robb	37	6	43
Stokes	2		2
Walters	37	6	43
Wetton	21	1	22
Willis	9	6	15
Withers	31		31

Goalscorers

PLAYER	LEAGUE	CUP COMPETITION FA CUP	TOTAL
Robb	16		16
Walters	14	2	16
Bennett	4	5	9
Duquemin	9		9
Baily	5	1	6
Brooks	2		2
Dunmore	2		2
Harmer	2		2
Ramsey	2		2
Baker	1		1
Brittan	1		1
Groves	1		1
Hutchinson	1		1
Marchi	1		1
Stokes	1		1
Opp's o.gs.	3		3

Fact File

Ted Ditchburn's absence from the team that played Sunderland in March 1954 brought to an end his run of 247 consecutive League appearances.

MANAGER: Arthur Rowe

CAPTAIN: Ron Burgess/Bill Nicholson

TOP SCORER: George Robb and Sonny Walters

BIGGEST WIN: 5-2 v Huddersfield Town (A), 10 April 1954, Football League Division One

HIGHEST ATTENDANCE: 69,821 v Arsenal, 10 October 1953, Football League Division One

MAJOR TRANSFERS IN: Dave Dunmore from York City

MAJOR TRANSFERS OUT: None

Final Division One Table

		P	W	D	L	F	A	Pts
1	WOLVERHAMPTON W	42	25	7	10	96	56	57
2	WBA	42	22	9	11	86	38	53
3	HUDDERSFIELD T	42	20	11	11	78	61	51
4	MANCHESTER U	42	18	12	12	73	58	48
5	BOLTON W	42	18	12	12	75	60	48
6	BLACKPOOL	42	19	10	13	80	69	48
7	BURNLEY	42	21	4	17	78	67	46
8	CHELSEA	42	16	12	14	74	68	44
9	CHARLTON A	42	19	6	17	75	77	44
10	CARDIFF C	42	18	8	16	51	71	44
11	PRESTON NE	42	19	5	18	87	58	43
12	ARSENAL	42	15	13	14	75	70	43
13	ASTON VILLA	42	16	9	17	70	68	41
14	PORTSMOUTH	42	14	11	17	81	89	39
15	NEWCASTLE U	42	14	10	18	72	77	38
16	TOTTENHAM HOTSPUR	42	16	5	21	65	76	37
17	MANCHESTER C	42	14	9	19	62	77	37
18	BLACKBURN R	42	18	8	16	86	50	44
19	SHEFFIELD W	42	15	6	21	70	91	36
20	SHEFFIELD U	42	11	11	20	69	90	33
21	MIDDLESBROUGH	42	10	10	22	60	91	30
22	LIVERPOOL	42	9	10	23	68	97	28

Season 1954-55

Football League Division One

DATE	OPPONENTS	SCORE	GOALSCORERS	ATTENDANCE
Aug 21	Aston Villa	W 4-2	Dowsett, Bennett 2, Baily	44,193
Aug 25	WOLVERHAMPTON WANDERERS	W 3-2	Dunmore 3	47,776
Aug 28	SUNDERLAND	L 0-1		53,646
Aug 30	Wolverhampton Wanderers	L 2-4	Walters, Robb	37,384
Sep 4	Arsenal	L 0-2		53,971
Sep 8	MANCHESTER UNITED	L 0-2		35,162
Sep 11	Sheffield Wednesday	D 2-2	McClellan, Baily	34,047
Sep 15	Manchester United	L 1-2	McClellan	31,041
Sep 18	PORTSMOUTH	D 1-1	McClellan	37,404
Sep 25	Blackpool	L 1-5	Ramsey (pen)	34,626
Oct 2	CHARLTON ATHLETIC	L 1-4	Brooks	33,105
Oct 9	WEST BROMWICH ALBION	W 3-1	Ramsey (pen), McClellan 2	45,547
Oct 16	Newcastle United	D 4-4	Baily 2, McClellan 2	45,306
Oct 23	PRESTON NORTH END	W 3-1	Ramsey (pen), McClellan, Dunmore	42,863
Oct 30	Sheffield United	L 1-4	Dunmore	24,084
Nov 6	CARDIFF CITY	L 0-2		38,805
Nov 13	Chelsea	L 1-2	Gavin	52,961
Nov 20	LEICESTER CITY	W 5-1	Gavin 2, Baily, Robb 2	27,874
Nov 27	Burnley	W 2-1	Gavin, Baily	21,973
Dec 4	EVERTON	L 1-3	Baily	31,554
Dec 11	Manchester City	D 0-0		27,052
Dec 18	ASTON VILLA	D 1-1	Baily	28,131
Dec 25	Bolton Wanderers	W 2-1	Dunmore, Robb	25,978
Dec 27	BOLTON WANDERERS	W 2-0	Baily, Brooks	41,063
Jan 1	Sunderland	D 1-1	Dunmore	49,884
Jan 15	ARSENAL	L 0-1		36,263
Jan 22	SHEFFIELD WEDNESDAY	W 7-2	Gavin 2, Brooks 2, Duquemin, Baily, Robb	26,315
Feb 5	Portsmouth	W 3-0	Gavin 2, Duquemin	27,539
Feb 12	BLACKPOOL	W 3-2	Baily, Robb 2	47,386
Mar 5	MANCHESTER CITY	D 2-2	Duquemin 2	35,358
Mar 12	Preston North End	L 0-1		24,344
Mar 19	SHEFFIELD UNITED	W 5-0	Gavin 4, Brooks	26,678
Mar 26	Cardiff City	W 2-1	Duquemin, Robb	14,461
Apr 2	CHELSEA	L 2-4	Duquemin 2	53,159
Apr 9	Everton	L 0-1		42,219
Apr 11	HUDDERSFIELD TOWN	D 1-1	Brooks	23,332
Apr 12	Huddersfield Town	L 0-1		23,580
Apr 16	BURNLEY	L 0-3		23,555
Apr 23	Leicester City	L 0-2		23,908
Apr 27	West Bromwich Albion	W 2-1	Brooks, Baily	16,617
Apr 30	NEWCASTLE UNITED	W 2-1	Gavin, Stokoe o.g.	37,262
May 5	Charlton Athletic	W 2-1	Walters, Duquemin	12,318

FA Cup

Jan 3	Gateshead	(Rd3)	W 2-0	Brooks 2	18,842
Jan 29	PORT VALE	(Rd4)	W 4-2	Gavin, Duquemin, Brooks 2	50,684
Feb 19	York City	(Rd5)	L 1-3	Robb	21,000

League and Cup Appearances

PLAYER	LEAGUE	CUP COMPETITION FA CUP	TOTAL
Baily	41	3	44
Baker	8		8
Bennett	6		6
Blanchflower	22	3	25
Brittan	10		10
Brooks	31	3	34
Clarke	36	3	39
Ditchburn	16		16
Dowsett	1		1
Dunmore	22	1	23
Duquemin	19	2	21
Dyson	1		1
Gavin	29	2	31
Harmer	5		5
Henry	1		1
Hopkins	32	3	35
King	5		5
Marchi	32	3	35
McClellan	11		11
Nicholson	10		10
Ramsey	33	3	36
Reynolds	26	3	29
Robb	36	3	39
Walters	7	1	8
Wetton	5		5
Withers	11		11
Woods	6		6

Goalscorers

PLAYER	LEAGUE	CUP COMPETITION FA CUP	TOTAL
Gavin	13	1	14
Baily	12		12
Brooks	7	4	11
Duquemin	8	1	9
Robb	8	1	9
McClellan	8		8
Dunmore	7		7
Ramsey	3		3
Bennett	2		2
Walters	2		2
Dowsett	1		1
Opp's o.gs.	1		1

Fact File

Spurs met Accrington Stanley for the only time in November 1954. A friendly, the match was abandoned after 52 minutes due to torrential rain.

MANAGER: Arthur Rowe

CAPTAIN: Alf Ramsey/Danny Blanchflower

TOP SCORER: Johnny Gavin

BIGGEST WIN: 7-2 v Sheffield Wednesday (H), 22 January 1955, Football League Division One

HIGHEST ATTENDANCE: 53,971 v Arsenal, 4 September 1954, Football League Division One

MAJOR TRANSFERS IN: Danny Blanchflower from Aston Villa, Johnny Gavin from Norwich City

MAJOR TRANSFERS OUT: Les Bennett to West Ham United, Ron Burgess to Swansea Town, Arthur Willis to Swansea Town

Final Division One Table

		P	W	D	L	F	A	Pts
1	CHELSEA	42	20	12	10	81	57	52
2	WOLVERHAMPTON W	42	19	10	13	89	70	48
3	PORTSMOUTH	42	18	12	12	74	62	48
4	BLACKBURN R	42	15	18	9	64	54	48
5	MANCHESTER U	42	20	7	15	84	74	47
6	ASTON VILLA	42	20	7	15	72	73	47
7	MANCHESTER C	42	18	10	14	76	69	46
8	NEWCASTLE U	42	17	9	16	89	77	43
9	ARSENAL	42	17	9	16	69	63	43
10	BURNLEY	42	17	9	16	51	48	43
11	EVERTON	42	16	10	16	62	68	42
12	HUDDERSFIELD T	42	14	13	15	63	58	41
13	SHEFFIELD U	42	17	7	18	70	86	41
14	PRESTON NE	42	16	8	18	83	64	40
15	CHARLTON A	42	15	10	17	76	75	40
16	Tottenham Hotspur	42	16	8	18	72	73	40
17	WBA	42	16	8	18	76	96	40
18	BOLTON W	42	13	13	16	62	69	39
19	BLACKPOOL	42	14	10	18	60	64	38
20	CARDIFF C	42	13	11	18	62	76	37
21	LEICESTER C	42	12	11	19	74	86	35
22	SHEFFIELD W	42	8	10	24	63	100	26

Season 1955-56

Football League Division One

DATE	OPPONENTS	SCORE	GOALSCORERS	ATTENDANCE
Aug 20	BURNLEY	L 0-1		33,178
Aug 24	Manchester United	D 2-2	Gavin (pen), Stokes	28,713
Aug 27	Luton Town	L 1-2	Gavin	21,143
Aug 31	MANCHESTER UNITED	L 1-2	Clarke	27,453
Sep 3	CHARLTON ATHLETIC	L 2-3	Clarke, Brooks	33,198
Sep 5	Sheffield United	L 0-2		19,692
Sep 10	ARSENAL	W 3-1	Stokes 2, Baily	51,029
Sep 17	Everton	L 1-2	Walters	42,851
Sep 24	NEWCASTLE UNITED	W 3-1	Clarke, Stokes 2	41,096
Oct 1	Birmingham City	L 0-3		31,320
Oct 8	BOLTON WANDERERS	L 0-3		35,237
Oct 15	Chelsea	L 0-2		48,195
Oct 22	SUNDERLAND	L 2-3	Brooks, Robb	36,396
Oct 29	Portsmouth	L 1-4	Robb	26,018
Nov 5	CARDIFF CITY	D 1-1	Brooks	34,368
Nov 12	Manchester City	W 2-1	McClellan, Dunmore	24,094
Nov 19	WOLVERHAMPTON WANDERERS	W 2-1	McClellan, Robb	51,363
Nov 26	Aston Villa	W 2-0	Clarke, McClellan	23,836
Dec 3	BLACKPOOL	D 1-1	Brooks	51,336
Dec 10	Huddersfield Town	L 0-1		11,094
Dec 17	Burnley	L 0-2		20,346
Dec 24	LUTON TOWN	W 2-1	Brooks, Duquemin	41,168
Dec 26	WEST BROMWICH ALBION	W 4-1	Norman, Brooks, Duquemin 2	32,430
Dec 27	West Bromwich Albion	L 0-1		31,381
Dec 31	Charlton Athletic	W 2-1	Duquemin, Robb	37,872
Jan 14	Arsenal	W 1-0	Robb	60,606
Jan 21	EVERTON	D 1-1	Robb	37,119
Feb 4	Newcastle United	W 2-1	Robb, Duquemin	29,597
Feb 11	BIRMINGHAM CITY	L 0-1		26,141
Feb 25	CHELSEA	W 4-0	Marchi, Brooks 2, Smith	46,767
Mar 10	PORTSMOUTH	D 1-1	Smith	44,314
Mar 21	Bolton Wanderers	L 2-3	Smith, Robb	10,942
Mar 24	MANCHESTER CITY	W 2-1	Brooks (pen), Smith	31,622
Mar 30	PRESTON NORTH END	L 0-4		39,441
Mar 31	Sunderland	L 2-3	McClellan 2	22,311
Apr 2	Preston North End	D 3-3	Harmer (1pen) 2, Ryden	26,699
Apr 7	ASTON VILLA	W 4-3	McClellan, Harmer, Smith, Brooks	36,235
Apr 14	Blackpool	W 2-0	McClellan, Smith	19,257
Apr 18	Wolverhampton Wanderers	L 1-5	Harmer (pen)	29,890
Apr 21	HUDDERSFIELD TOWN	L 1-2	Harmer (pen)	36,387
Apr 23	Cardiff City	D 0-0		19,684
Apr 28	SHEFFIELD UNITED	W 3-1	Smith 3	32,612

FA Cup

Jan 7	BOSTON UNITED	(Rd3) W 4-0	Duquemin, Smith 2, Robb	46,185
Jan 28	MIDDLESBROUGH	(Rd4) W 3-1	Norman, Dunmore, Robb	41,895
Feb 18	Doncaster Rovers	(Rd5) W 2-0	Brooks, Smith	30,436
Mar 3	WEST HAM UNITED	(Rd6) D 3-3	Harmer (pen), Duquemin, Robb	69,118
Mar 8	West Ham United	(R) W 2-1	Harmer, Duquemin	34,911
Mar 17	Manchester City *	(SF) L 0-1		69,788

* played at Villa Park, Birmingham

League and Cup Appearances

PLAYER	LEAGUE	CUP COMPETITION FA CUP	TOTAL
Baily	18		18
Baker	5		5
Blanchflower	40	6	46
Brittan	1		1
Brooks	39	6	45
Clarke	39	6	45
Ditchburn	14		14
Dulin	6	1	7
Dunmore	10	2	12
Duquemin	17	6	23
Dyson	3		3
Gavin	3		3
Harmer	10	3	13
Henry	1		1
Hopkins	41	6	47
Marchi	42	6	48
McClellan	16		16
Norman	27	6	33
Reynolds	28	6	34
Robb	41	6	47
Ryden	3		3
Smith	21	6	27
Stokes	11		11
Walley	2		2
Walters	14		14
Withers	10		10

Goalscorers

PLAYER	LEAGUE	CUP COMPETITION FA CUP	TOTAL
Smith	10	3	13
Brooks	10	1	11
Robb	7	3	10
Duquemin	5	3	8
Harmer	5	2	7
McClellan	7		7
Stokes	5		5
Clarke	4		4
Dunmore	1	1	2
Gavin	2		2
Norman	1	1	2
Baily	1		1
Marchi	1		1
Ryden	1		1
Walters	1		1

Fact File

Spurs' game with Boston United was the first time they had played an FA Cup tie partially under floodlights. Previously all ties from the Third Round on had to be completed in daylight.

MANAGER: Jimmy Anderson

CAPTAIN: Danny Blanchflower

TOP SCORER: Bobby Smith

BIGGEST WIN: 4-0 v Chelsea (H), 25 February 1956, Football League Division One

HIGHEST ATTENDANCE: 69,788 v Manchester City, 17 March 1956, FA Cup Semi-final

MAJOR TRANSFERS IN: Maurice Norman from Norwich City, John Ryden from Accrington Stanley, Bobby Smith from Chelsea

MAJOR TRANSFERS OUT: Eddie Baily to Port Vale, Johnny Gavin to Norwich City

Final Division One Table

		P	W	D	L	F	A	Pts
1	MANCHESTER U	42	25	10	7	83	51	60
2	BLACKPOOL	42	20	9	13	86	62	49
3	WOLVERHAMPTON W	42	20	9	13	89	65	49
4	MANCHESTER C	42	18	10	14	82	69	46
5	ARSENAL	42	18	10	14	60	61	46
6	BIRMINGHAM C	42	18	9	15	75	57	45
7	BURNLEY	42	18	8	16	64	54	44
8	BOLTON W	42	18	7	17	71	58	43
9	BLACKBURN R	42	17	9	16	80	95	43
10	LUTON TOWN	42	17	8	17	66	64	42
11	NEWCASTLE U	42	17	7	18	85	70	41
12	PORTSMOUTH	42	16	9	17	78	70	41
13	WBA	42	18	5	19	58	70	41
14	CHARLTON A	42	17	6	19	75	81	40
15	EVERTON	42	15	10	17	55	69	40
16	CHELSEA	42	14	11	17	64	77	39
17	CARDIFF C	42	15	9	18	55	69	39
18	TOTTENHAM HOTSPUR	42	15	7	20	61	71	37
19	PRESTON NE	42	14	8	20	73	72	36
20	ASTON VILLA	42	11	13	18	52	69	35
21	HUDDERSFIELD T	42	14	7	21	54	83	35
22	SHEFFIELD U	42	12	9	21	63	77	33

Season 1956-57

Football League Division One

DATE	OPPONENTS	SCORE	GOALSCORERS	ATTENDANCE
Aug 18	Preston North End	W 4-1	Medwin 2, Brooks 2	22,752
Aug 22	Manchester City	D 2-2	Medwin, Brooks	32,718
Aug 25	LEEDS UNITED	W 5-1	Blanchflower, Medwin, Smith, Brooks, Robb	51,212
Aug 29	MANCHESTER CITY	W 3-2	Medwin, Harmer (pen), Smith	33,443
Sep 1	Bolton Wanderers	L 0-1		30,889
Sep 3	Blackpool	L 1-4	Brooks	28,460
Sep 8	WOLVERHAMPTON WANDERERS	W 4-1	Smith 2, Brooks 2	62,592
Sep 15	Aston Villa	W 4-2	Harmer, Smith, Stokes, Robb	43,947
Sep 22	LUTON TOWN	W 5-0	Harmer (pen), Stokes, Robb 2, Dunne o.g.	58,960
Sep 29	Sunderland	W 2-0	Smith, Stokes	41,657
Oct 6	Chelsea	W 4-2	Stokes 3, Robb	55,788
Oct 13	CARDIFF CITY	W 5-0	Stokes 2, Robb 3	52,429
Oct 20	Arsenal	L 1-3	Smith	60,588
Oct 27	BURNLEY	W 2-0	Medwin, Harmer	49,154
Nov 3	Portsmouth	W 3-2	Smith, Brooks, Wilson o.g.	31,903
Nov 10	NEWCASTLE UNITED	W 3-1	Smith 2, Robb	51,722
Nov 17	Sheffield Wednesday	L 1-4	Harmer (pen)	32,115
Nov 24	MANCHESTER UNITED	D 2-2	Harmer (pen), Robb	57,724
Dec 1	Birmingham City	D 0-0		38,035
Dec 8	WEST BROMWICH ALBION	D 2-2	Harmer, Smith	36,098
Dec 15	PRESTON NORTH END	D 1-1	Medwin	29,748
Dec 25	EVERTON	W 6-0	Medwin 2, Harmer (pen), Smith 2, Stokes	27,761
Dec 26	Everton	D 1-1	Robb	20,172
Dec 29	BOLTON WANDERERS	W 4-0	Dyson, Harmer (pen), Smith, Robb	42,030
Jan 12	Wolverhampton Wanderers	L 0-3		42,416
Jan 19	ASTON VILLA	W 3-0	Smith, Stokes 2	38,934
Feb 2	Luton Town	W 3-1	Duquemin, Stokes, Robb	22,586
Feb 9	SUNDERLAND	W 5-2	Harmer, Smith, Stokes 2, Anderson o.g.	52,104
Feb 20	CHELSEA	L 3-4	Medwin, Harmer (pen), Stokes	20,849
Mar 2	Leeds United	D 1-1	Stokes	33,895
Mar 9	West Bromwich Albion	D 1-1	Stokes	30,602
Mar 13	ARSENAL	L 1-3	Medwin	64,555
Mar 16	PORTSMOUTH	W 2-0	Smith, Mansell o.g.	36,110
Mar 23	Newcastle United	D 2-2	Medwin, Stokes	37,955
Mar 30	SHEFFIELD WEDNESDAY	D 1-1	Harmer	34,485
Apr 6	Manchester United	D 0-0		60,583
Apr 13	BIRMINGHAM CITY	W 5-1	Medwin, Harmer (pen), Dunmore 2, Dyson	33,512
Apr 19	Charlton Athletic	D 1-1	Brooks	27,793
Apr 20	Cardiff City	W 3-0	Dunmore, Brooks, Dyson	25,181
Apr 22	CHARLTON ATHLETIC	W 6-2	Medwin, Harmer 2, Smith, Brooks, Robb	25,579
Apr 27	BLACKPOOL	W 2-1	Harmer (1pen) 2	49,878
Apr 29	Burnley	L 0-1		12,048

FA Cup

Jan 5	LEICESTER CITY	(Rd3) W 2-0	Blanchflower, Robb	56,492
Jan 26	CHELSEA	(Rd4) W 4-0	Medwin, Harmer, Smith, Stokes	66,398
Feb 16	Bournemouth	(Rd5) L 1-3	Medwin	25,892

Fact File

FA Cup conquerors Bournemouth and Boscombe Athletic were managed by former Spurs winger Freddie Cox.

MANAGER: Jimmy Anderson

CAPTAIN: Harry Clarke/Tony Marchi

TOP SCORER: Bobby Smith and Alfie Stokes

BIGGEST WIN: 6-0 Everton (H), 25 December 1956, Football League Division One

HIGHEST ATTENDANCE: 66,398 v Chelsea, 26 January 1957, FA Cup 4th Round

MAJOR TRANSFERS IN: Terry Medwin from Swansea Town

MAJOR TRANSFERS OUT: Sid McClellan to Portsmouth

League and Cup Appearances

PLAYER	LEAGUE	CUP COMPETITION FA CUP	TOTAL
Baker	38	3	41
Blanchflower	39	3	42
Brittan	1		1
Brooks	23		23
Clarke	21		21
Ditchburn	29	3	32
Dulin	1		1
Dunmore	5		5
Duquemin	2		2
Dyson	8	1	9
Harmer	42	3	45
n Henry	1		1
Hopkins	35	3	38
Marchi	42	3	45
Medwin	37	2	39
Norman	16		16
Reynolds	13		13
Robb	37	3	40
Ryden	15	3	18
Smith	33	3	36
Stokes	21	3	24
Walley	2		2
Wilkie	1		1

Goalscorers

PLAYER	LEAGUE	CUP COMPETITION FA CUP	TOTAL
Smith	18	1	19
Stokes	18	1	19
Harmer	17	1	18
Medwin	14	2	16
Robb	14	1	15
Brooks	11		11
Dunmore	3		3
Dyson	3		3
Blanchflower	1	1	2
Duquemin	1		1
Opp's o.gs.	4		4

Final Division One Table

		P	W	D	L	F	A	Pts
1	MANCHESTER U	42	28	8	6	103	54	64
2	TOTTENHAM HOTSPUR	42	22	12	8	104	56	56
3	PRESTON NE	42	23	10	9	84	56	56
4	BLACKPOOL	42	22	9	11	93	65	53
5	ARSENAL	42	21	8	13	85	69	50
6	WOLVERHAMPTON W	42	20	8	14	94	70	48
7	BURNLEY	42	18	10	14	56	50	46
8	LEEDS UNITED	42	15	14	13	72	63	44
9	BOLTON W	42	16	12	14	65	65	44
10	ASTON VILLA	42	14	15	13	65	55	43
11	WBA	42	14	14	14	59	61	42
12	BIRMINGHAM C	42	15	9	18	69	42	39
13	CHELSEA	42	13	13	16	73	73	39
14	SHEFFIELD W	42	16	6	20	82	88	38
15	EVERTON	42	14	10	18	61	79	38
16	LUTON TOWN	42	14	9	19	58	76	37
17	NEWCASTLE U	42	14	8	20	67	87	36
18	MANCHESTER C	42	13	9	20	78	88	35
19	PORTSMOUTH	42	10	13	19	62	92	33
20	BLACKBURN R	42	12	8	22	67	88	32
21	CARDIFF C	42	10	9	23	53	88	29
22	CHARLTON A	42	9	4	29	62	120	22

Season 1957-58

Football League Division One

DATE	OPPONENTS	SCORE	GOALSCORERS	ATTENDANCE
Aug 24	CHELSEA	D 1-1	Stokes	52,580
Aug 28	Portsmouth	L 1-5	Smith	33,479
Aug 31	Newcastle United	L 1-3	Smith	37,742
Sep 49	PORTSMOUTH	L 3-5	Harmer (pen), Brooks, Dulin	35,813
Sep 79	BURNLEY	W 3-1	Dunmore 2, Dulin	40,108
Sep 11	Birmingham City	D 0-0		26,485
Sep 14	Preston North End	L 1-3	Stokes	23,364
Sep 18	BIRMINGHAM CITY	W 7-1	Harmer (pen), Stokes 5, Dyson	35,292
Sep 21	SHEFFIELD WEDNESDAY	W 4-2	Medwin, Smith 2, Dyson	39,954
Sep 28	Manchester City	L 1-5	Brannigan o.g.	22,497
Oct 2	Wolverhampton Wanderers	L 0-4		36,024
Oct 5	NOTTINGHAM FOREST	L 3-4	Medwin, Harmer, Brooks	51,429
Oct 12	ARSENAL	W 3-1	Medwin 2, Smith	60,671
Oct 19	Bolton Wanderers	L 2-3	Smith, Robb	20,381
Oct 26	LEEDS UNITED	W 2-0	Medwin, Smith	33,860
Nov 2	Sunderland	D 1-1	Brooks	36,091
Nov 9	EVERTON	W 3-1	Brooks, Smith, Harmer (pen)	39,999
Nov 16	Aston Villa	D 1-1	Smith	28,390
Nov 23	LUTON TOWN	W 3-1	Medwin 2, Brooks	41,242
Nov 30	Manchester United	W 4-3	Smith 3, Blanchflower o.g.	43,307
Dec 7	LEICESTER CITY	L 1-4	Brooks	27,855
Dec 14	Blackpool	W 2-0	Smith 2	14,938
Dec 21	Chelsea	W 4-2	Medwin, Harmer, Smith 2	39,747
Dec 26	WOLVERHAMPTON WANDERERS	W 1-0	Smith	58,393
Dec 28	NEWCASTLE UNITED	D 3-3	Norman, Harmer (pen), Stokes	51,649
Jan 11	Burnley	L 0-2		25,927
Jan 18	PRESTON NORTH END	D 3-3	Medwin, Brooks (pen), Smith	43,941
Feb 1	Sheffield Wednesday	L 0-2		22,966
Feb 8	MANCHESTER CITY	W 5-1	Smith 3, Brooks, Robb	37,539
Feb 15	Nottingham Forest	W 2-1	Brooks, Robb	32,334
Feb 22	Arsenal	D 4-4	Harmer (1 pen) 2, Smith 2	59,116
Mar 8	Leeds United	W 2-1	Smith 2	23,429
Mar 12	BOLTON WANDERERS	W 4-1	Brooks, Smith 3	22,978
Mar 15	SUNDERLAND	L 0-1		40,751
Mar 22	Luton Town	D 0-0		22,384
Mar 29	ASTON VILLA	W 6-2	Medwin 2, Smith 4	34,102
Apr 4	WEST BROMWICH ALBION	D 0-0		56,166
Apr 5	Everton	W 4-3	Smith 2, Clayton 2	30,149
Apr 7	West Bromwich Albion	W 2-0	Medwin, Clayton	26,556
Apr 12	MANCHESTER UNITED	W 1-0	Harmer (pen)	59,836
Apr 19	Leicester City	W 3-1	Medwin, Smith, Jones	37,234
Apr 26	BLACKPOOL	W 2-1	Medwin, Smith	37,632

FA Cup

Jan 4	LEICESTER CITY	(Rd3) W 4-0	Medwin, Smith 2, Stokes	42,716
Jan 25	SHEFFIELD UNITED	(Rd4) L 0-3		51,136

League and Cup Appearances

PLAYER	LEAGUE	CUP COMPETITION FA CUP	TOTAL
Baker	18		18
Bing	1		1
Blanchflower	40	2	42
Brittan	3		3
Brooks	25	1	26
Clayton	5		5
Ditchburn	26	2	28
Dulin	3		3
Dunmore	5		5
Dyson	12	2	14
Harmer	40	2	42
Henry	15		15
Hills	21	2	23
Hopkins	26	2	28
Iley	19		19
Ireland	1		1
Jones	10		10
Medwin	39	2	41
Norman	33	2	35
Reynold	16		16
Robb	15		15
Ryden	35	2	37
Smith	38	2	40
Stokes	15	1	16
Walley	1		1

Goalscorers

PLAYER	LEAGUE	CUP COMPETITION FA CUP	TOTAL
Smith	36	2	38
Medwin	14	1	15
Brooks	10		10
Harmer	9		9
Stokes	8	1	9
Clayton	3		3
Robb	3		3
Dulin	2		2
Dunmore	2		2
Dyson	2		2
Jones	1		1
Norman	1		1
Opp's o.gs.	2		2

Fact File

Bobby Smith equalled Ted Harper's 1931 record of 36 Football League goals in a season.

MANAGER: Jimmy Anderson

CAPTAIN: John Ryden

TOP SCORER: Bobby Smith

BIGGEST WIN: 7-1 v Birmingham City (H), 18 September 1957, Football League Division One

HIGHEST ATTENDANCE: 60,671 v Arsenal, 12 October 1957, Football League Division One

MAJOR TRANSFERS IN: Jim Iley from Sheffield United, Cliff Jones from Swansea Town

MAJOR TRANSFERS OUT: Tony Marchi to Juventus

Final Division One Table

		P	W	D	L	F	A	Pts
1	WOLVERHAMPTON W	42	28	8	6	103	47	64
2	PRESTON NE	42	26	7	9	100	51	59
3	TOTTENHAM HOTSPUR	42	21	9	12	93	77	51
4	WBA	42	18	14	10	92	70	50
5	MANCHESTER C	42	22	5	15	104	100	49
6	BURNLEY	42	21	5	16	80	74	47
7	BLACKPOOL	42	19	6	17	80	67	44
8	LUTON TOWN	42	19	6	17	69	63	44
9	MANCHESTER U	42	16	11	15	85	75	43
10	NOTTINGHAM F	42	16	10	16	69	63	42
11	CHELSEA	42	15	12	15	83	79	42
12	ARSENAL	42	16	7	19	73	64	39
13	BIRMINGHAM C	42	14	11	17	76	89	39
14	ASTON VILLA	42	16	7	19	73	86	39
15	BOLTON W	42	14	10	18	65	87	38
16	EVERTON	42	14	11	18	65	75	37
17	LEEDS UNITED	42	14	9	19	51	63	37
18	LEICESTER C	42	14	5	23	91	112	33
19	NEWCASTLE U	42	12	8	22	73	81	32
20	PORTSMOUTH	42	12	8	22	73	88	32
21	BLACKBURN R	42	10	12	20	54	97	32
22	SHEFFIELD W	42	12	7	23	69	92	31

Season 1958-59

Football League Division One

DATE	OPPONENTS	SCORE	GOALSCORERS	ATTENDANCE
Aug 23	BLACKPOOL	L 2-3	Smith, Brooks	57,043
Aug 27	Chelsea	L 2-4	Medwin, Smith	59,203
Aug 30	Blackburn Rovers	L 0-5		41,830
Sep 3	CHELSEA	W 4-0	Medwin 3, Robb	50,299
Sep 6	NEWCASTLE UNITED	L 1-3	Medwin	41,805
Sep 10	Nottingham Forest	D 1-1	Smith	26,097
Sep 13	Arsenal	L 1-3	Clayton	65,565
Sep 17	NOTTINGHAM FOREST	W 1-0	Sharpe	39,431
Sep 20	Manchester United	D 2-2	Smith 2	62,277
Sep 27	WOLVERHAMPTON WANDERERS	W 2-1	Smith, Clayton	48,563
Oct 4	Portsmouth	D 1-1	Stokes	26,402
Oct 11	EVERTON	W10-4	Ryden, Medwin, Harmer, Smith 4, Stokes 2, Robb	37,794
Oct 18	Leicester City	W 4-3	Harmer (pen), Smith, Stokes 2	31,509
Oct 25	LEEDS UNITED	L 2-3	Iley, Smith	38,691
Nov 1	Manchester City	L 1-5	Smith	30,601
Nov 8	BOLTON WANDERERS	D 1-1	Smith	39,820
Nov 15	Luton Town	W 2-1	Dunmore, Medwin	23,592
Nov 22	BIRMINGHAM CITY	L 0-4		28,708
Nov 29	West Bromwich Albion	L 3-4	Dunmore, Smith 2	21,753
Dec 6	PRESTON NORTH END	L 1-2	Smith	31,806
Dec 13	Burnley	L 1-3	Stokes	17,047
Dec 20	Blackpool	D 0-0		12,939
Dec 25	West Ham United	L 1-2	Smith	26,178
Dec 26	WEST HAM UNITED	L 1-4	Stokes	43,817
Jan 3	BLACKBURN ROVERS	W 3-1	Harmer (pen), Smith, Dunmore	39,522
Jan 17	Newcastle United	W 2-1	Dunmore 2	32,503
Jan 31	ARSENAL	L 1-4	Smith	60,241
Feb 7	MANCHESTER UNITED	L 1-3	Norman	48,401
Feb 21	PORTSMOUTH	D 4-4	Smith 2, Clayton, Jones (pen)	27,237
Feb 28	Everton	L 1-2	Jones	36,782
Mar 2	Wolverhampton Wanderers	D 1-1	Harmer	30,437
Mar 7	LEICESTER CITY	W 6-0	Blanchflower, Medwin 4, Dunmore	30,561
Mar 14	Leeds United	L 1-3	Norman	17,010
Mar 21	MANCHESTER CITY	W 3-1	Medwin, Smith, Jones (pen)	34,493
Mar 27	ASTON VILLA	W 3-2	Medwin, Smith, Jones	45,059
Mar 28	Bolton Wanderers	L 1-4	Clayton	21,384
Mar 30	Aston Villa	D 1-1	Norman	34,354
Apr 4	LUTON TOWN	W 3-0	Medwin, Smith, Brooks	37,093
Apr 8	BURNLEY	D 2-2	Smith 2	32,296
Apr 11	Birmingham City	L 1-5	Jones (pen)	20,557
Apr 18	WEST BROMWICH ALBION	W 5-0	Smith 4, Brooks	36,805
Apr 25	Preston North End	D 2-2	Smith, Brooks	20,323

FA Cup

DATE	OPPONENTS		SCORE	GOALSCORERS	ATTENDANCE
Jan 10	WEST HAM UNITED	(Rd3)	W 2-0	Smith, Jones	56,252
Jan 24	NEWPORT COUNTY	(Rd4)	W 4-1	Smith 2, Dunmore 2	50,561
Feb 14	NORWICH CITY	(Rd5)	D 1-1	Jones	67,633
Feb 18	Norwich City	(Rd6)	L 0-1		38,000

League and Cup Appearances

PLAYER	LEAGUE	CUP COMPETITION FA CUP	TOTAL
Baker	36	4	40
Blanchflower	36	1	37
Brooks	25	3	28
Clayton	11	1	12
Ditchburn	2		2
Dodge	5	4	9
Dunmore	13	3	16
Dyson	7		7
Harmer	35	3	38
Henry	8		8
Hills	7		7
Hollowbread	40	4	44
Hopkins	34	4	38
Iley	34	4	38
Ireland	2		2
Jones	22	4	26
Mackay	4		4
Medwin	35	1	36
Norman	35	4	39
Robb	9		9
Ryden	10		10
Sharpe	2		2
Smith	36	4	40
Stokes	14		14

Goalscorers

PLAYER	LEAGUE	CUP COMPETITION FA CUP	TOTAL
Smith	32	3	35
Medwin	14		14
Dunmore	6	2	8
Jones	5	2	7
Stokes	7		7
Brooks	4		4
Clayton	4		4
Harmer	4		4
Norman	3		3
Robb	2		2
Blanchflower	1		1
Iley	1		1
Ryden	1		1
Sharpe	1		1

Fact File

The ten goals against Everton remains the only time Spurs have scored double figures in a Football League game.

MANAGER: Jimmy Anderson until October then Bill Nicholson

CAPTAIN: Bobby Smith/Danny Blanchflower

TOP SCORER: Bobby Smith

BIGGEST WIN: 10-4 v Everton (H), 11 October 1958, Football League Division One

HIGHEST ATTENDANCE: 67,633 v Norwich City, 14 February 1959, FA Cup 5th Round

MAJOR TRANSFERS IN: Dave Mackay from Heart of Midlothian

MAJOR TRANSFERS OUT: None

Final Division One Table

		P	W	D	L	F	A	Pts
1	WOLVERHAMPTON W	42	28	5	9	110	49	61
2	MANCHESTER U	42	24	7	11	103	66	55
3	ARSENAL	42	21	8	13	88	68	50
4	BOLTON W	42	20	10	12	79	66	50
5	WBA	42	18	13	11	88	68	49
6	WEST HAM U	42	21	6	15	85	70	48
7	BURNLEY	42	19	10	13	81	70	48
8	BLACKPOOL	42	18	11	13	66	49	47
9	BIRMINGHAM C	42	20	6	16	84	68	46
10	BLACKBURN R	42	17	10	15	76	70	44
11	NEWCASTLE U	42	17	7	18	80	80	41
12	PRESTON NE	42	17	7	18	70	69	41
13	NOTTINGHAM F	42	17	6	19	71	74	40
14	CHELSEA	42	18	4	20	77	98	40
15	LEEDS UNITED	42	15	9	18	57	74	39
16	EVERTON	42	17	4	21	71	87	38
17	LUTON TOWN	42	13	13	17	68	71	37
18	TOTTENHAM HOTSPUR	42	13	10	19	85	95	36
19	LEICESTER C	42	11	10	21	67	98	32
20	MANCHESTER C	42	11	9	22	64	95	31
21	ASTON VILLA	42	11	8	23	58	87	30
22	PORTSMOUTH	42	6	9	27	64	112	21

Season 1959-60

Football League Division One

DATE	OPPONENTS	SCORE	GOALSCORERS	ATTENDANCE
Aug 22	Newcastle United	W 5-1	Brooks 2, Jones 3	40,782
Aug 26	WEST BROMWICH ALBION	D 2-2	Medwin, Smith R	54,114
Aug 29	BIRMINGHAM CITY	D 0-0		45,243
Sep 2	West Bromwich albion	W 2-1	Harmer, Smith R	35,924
Sep 5	Arsenal	D 1-1	Medwin	60,791
Sep 9	WEST HAM UNITED	D 2-2	Smith R, Jones	58,909
Sep 12	Manchester United	W 5-1	Mackay, Harmer, Smith R 2, Dunmore	55,641
Sep 14	West Ham United	W 2-1	Marchi, Smith R	36,831
Sep 19	PRESTON NORTH END	W 5-1	Mackay, Smith R, Dunmore, Jones 2	51,776
Sep 26	Leicester City	D 1-1	Jones (pen)	34,445
Oct 3	BURNLEY	D 1-1	Medwin	42,717
Oct 10	WOLVERHAMPTON WANDERERS	W 5-1	Smith R 4, Jones	59,344
Oct 17	Sheffield Wednesday	L 1-2	White	37,623
Oct 24	NOTTINGHAM FOREST	W 2-1	Smith R 2	52,002
Oct 31	Manchester City	W 2-1	Mackay, Jones	45,506
Nov 7	BOLTON WANDERERS	L 0-2		41,909
Nov 14	Luton Town	L 0-1		22,528
Nov 21	EVERTON	W 3-0	Jones (pen), Harris o.g., King o.g.	39,432
Nov 28	Blackpool	D 2-2	Mackay, Smith R	17,085
Dec 5	BLACKBURN ROVERS	W 2-1	Medwin, Bray o.g.	37,130
Dec 12	Fulham	D 1-1	Jones (pen)	36,772
Dec 19	NEWCASTLE UNITED	W 4-0	Blanchflower, Norman, White, Jones	32,824
Dec 26	Leeds United	W 4-2	Harmer, Smith R, Allen 2	36,037
Dec 28	LEEDS UNITED	L 1-4	Mackay	54,170
Jan 2	Birmingham City	W 1-0	Allen	27,558
Jan 16	ARSENAL	W 3-0	Smith R, Allen 2	58,962
Jan 23	MANCHESTER UNITED	W 2-1	Smith R 2	62,602
Feb 6	Preston North End	D 1-1	Mackay	33,039
Feb 13	LEICESTER CITY	L 1-2	Smith R	33,504
Feb 27	Blackburn Rovers	W 4-1	Mackay, Smith R, Allen, Jones	29,228
Mar 1	Burnley	L 0-2		32,992
Mar 5	SHEFFIELD WEDNESDAY	W 4-1	White, Jones 3	53,822
Mar 12	Nottingham Forest	W 3-1	Mackay, White, Allen	35,291
Mar 19	FULHAM	D 1-1	Mackay	52,189
Mar 26	Bolton Wanderers	L 1-2	Mackay	31,106
Apr 2	LUTON TOWN	D 1-1	Jones	39,462
Apr 9	Everton	L 1-2	Jones	57,959
Apr 15	Chelsea	W 3-1	Smith R 3	67,819
Apr 16	MANCHESTER CITY	L 0-1		49,767
Apr 18	CHELSEA	L 0-1		37,200
Apr 23	Wolverhampton Wanderers	W 3-1	Jones, Smith R, Mackay	56,283
Apr 30	BLACKPOOL	W 4-1	Blanchflower, Jones, White, Smith R	49,823

FA Cup

Jan 9	Newport County	(Rd3) W 4-0	Blanchflower, Smith R, Allen 2	22,655
Jan 30	Crewe Alexandra	(Rd4) D 2-2	Allen, Jones	20,000
Feb 3	CREWE ALEXANDRA	(R) W13-2	Harmer, Smith R 4, Allen 5, Jones (1 pen) 3	64,365
Feb 20	BLACKBURN ROVERS	(Rd5) L 1-3	Jones	54,745

League and Cup Appearances

PLAYER	LEAGUE	CUP COMPETITION FA CUP	TOTAL
Allen	15	4	19
Baker	41	3	44
Blanchflower	40	4	44
Brooks	4		4
Brown	40	4	44
Clayton	1		1
Dodge	1		1
Dunmore	10		10
Dyson	6		6
Harmer	37	4	41
Henry	25	4	29
Hills	1	1	2
Hollowbread	2		2
Hopkins	14		14
Jones	38	4	42
Mackay	38	3	41
Marchi	14	1	15
Medwin	26		26
Norman	39	4	43
Smith J	1		1
Smith R	40	4	44
White	28	4	32
Worley	1		1

Goalscorers

PLAYER	LEAGUE	CUP COMPETITION FA CUP	TOTAL
Smith R	25	5	30
Jones	20	5	25
Allen	7	8	15
Mackay	11		11
White	5		5
Harmer	3	1	4
Medwin	4		4
Blanchflower	2	1	3
Brooks	2		2
Dunmore	2		2
Marchi	1		1
Norman	1		1
Opp's o.gs.	3		3

Fact File

Spurs' record score in a competitive game remains the 13-2 FA Cup 4th Round reply win over Crewe Alexandra.

MANAGER: Bill Nicholson

CAPTAIN: Danny Blanchflower

TOP SCORER: Bobby Smith

BIGGEST WIN: 13-2 v Crewe Alexandria (H), 3 February 1960, FA Cup 4th Round replay

HIGHEST ATTENDANCE: 67,819 v Chelsea, 15 April 1960, Football League Division One

MAJOR TRANSFERS IN: Les Allen from Chelsea, John Smith from West Ham United, John White from Falkirk, Bill Brown from Dundee

MAJOR TRANSFERS OUT: Johnny Brooks to Chelsea, Ted Ditchburn to Romford, John Dunmore to West Ham United, Jim Iley to Nottingham Forest, Alfie Stokes to Fulham

Final Division One Table

		P	W	D	L	F	A	Pts
1	BURNLEY	42	24	7	11	85	61	55
2	WOLVERHAMPTON W	42	24	6	12	106	67	54
3	TOTTENHAM HOTSPUR	42	24	11	10	86	50	53
4	WBA	42	19	11	12	83	57	49
5	SHEFFIELD W	42	19	11	12	80	59	49
6	BOLTON W	42	20	8	14	59	51	48
7	MANCHESTER U	42	19	7	16	102	80	45
8	NEWCASTLE U	42	18	8	16	82	78	44
9	PRESTON NE	42	16	12	14	79	76	44
10	FULHAM	42	17	10	15	73	80	44
11	BLACKPOOL	42	15	10	17	59	71	40
12	LEICESTER C	42	13	13	16	66	60	39
13	ARSENAL	42	15	9	18	68	80	39
14	WEST HAM U	42	16	6	20	75	91	38
15	EVERTON	42	13	11	18	73	78	37
16	MANCHESTER C	42	17	3	22	78	84	37
17	BLACKBURN R	42	16	5	21	60	70	37
18	CHELSEA	42	14	9	19	76	91	37
19	BIRMINGHAM C	42	13	10	19	63	80	36
20	NOTTINGHAM F	42	13	9	20	50	74	35
21	LEEDS UNITED	42	12	10	20	65	92	34
22	LUTON TOWN	42	9	12	21	50	73	30

Season 1960-61

Football League Division One

DATE	OPPONENTS	SCORE	GOALSCORERS	ATTENDANCE
Aug 20	EVERTON	W 2-0	Smith R, Allen	50,393
Aug 22	Blackpool	W 3-1	Medwin, Dyson 2	27,656
Aug 27	Blackburn Rovers	W 4-1	Smith R 2, Allen, Dyson	26,819
Aug 31	BLACKPOOL	W 3-1	Smith R 3	45,684
Sep 3	MANCHESTER UNITED	W 4-1	Smith R, Allen 2	55,442
Sep 7	Bolton Wanderers	W 2-1	White, Allen	41,565
Sep 10	Arsenal	W 3-2	Saul, Allen, Dyson	59,868
Sep 14	BOLTON WANDERERS	W 3-1	Blanchflower (pen), Smith R 2	43,559
Sep 17	Leicester City	W 2-1	Smith R 2	30,129
Sep 24	ASTON VILLA	W 6-2	Mackay, White 2, Smith R, Allen, Dyson	61,356
Oct 1	Wolverhampton Wanderers	W 4-0	Blanchflower, Jones, Allen, Dyson	52,829
Oct 10	MANCHESTER CITY	D 1-1	Smith R	58,916
Oct 15	Nottingham Forest	W 4-0	Mackay, Jones 2, White	37,248
Oct 29	Newcastle United	W 4-3	Norman, Jones, White, Smith R	51,369
Nov 2	CARDIFF CITY	W 3-2	Blanchflower (pen), Medwin, Dyson	47,605
Nov 5	FULHAM	W 5-1	Jones 2, White, Allen 2	56,270
Nov 12	Sheffield Wednesday	L 1-2	Norman	53,988
Nov 19	BIRMINGHAM CITY	W 6-0	Jones 2, White, Smith R (pen), Dyson 2	46,010
Nov 26	West Bromwich Albion	W 3-1	Smith R 2, Allen	39,017
Dec 3	BURNLEY	D 4-4	Norman, Mackay, Jones 2	58,737
Dec 10	Preston North End	W 1-0	White	21,657
Dec 17	Everton	W 3-1	Mackay, White, Allen	61,052
Dec 24	WEST HAM UNITED	W 2-0	White, Dyson	54,930
Dec 26	West Ham United	W 3-0	White, Allen, Brown o.g.	34,351
Dec 31	BLACKBURN ROVERS	W 5-2	Blanchflower, Smith R 2, Allen 2	48,742
Jan 16	Manchester United	L 0-2		65,535
Jan 21	ARSENAL	W 4-2	Blanchflower (pen), Smith R, Allen 2	65,251
Feb 4	LEICESTER CITY	L 2-3	Blanchflower (pen), Allen	53,627
Feb 11	Aston Villa	W 2-1	Smith R, Dyson	50,786
Feb 22	WOLVERHAMPTON WANDERERS	D 1-1	Smith R	62,261
Feb 25	Manchester City	W 1-0	Medwin	40,278
Mar 11	Cardiff City	L 2-3	Allen, Dyson	45,463
Mar 22	NEWCASTLE UNITED	L 1-2	Allen	46,470
Mar 25	Fulham	D 0-0		38,536
Mar 31	CHELSEA	W 4-2	Jones 2, Saul, Allen	65,032
Apr 1	PRESTON NORTH END	W 5-0	Jones 3, White, Saul	46,325
Apr 3	CHELSEA	W 3-2	Norman, Smith R, Medwin	57,103
Apr 8	Birmingham City	W 3-2	White, Smith R, Allen	40,961
Apr 17	SHEFFIELD WEDNESDAY	W 2-1	Smith R, Allen	61,205
Apr 22	Burnley	L 2-4	Baker, Smith R	28,991
Apr 26	NOTTINGHAM FOREST	W 1-0	Medwin	35,743
Apr 29	WEST BROMWICH ALBION	L 1-2	Smith R	52,054

FA Cup

Jan 7	CHARLTON ATHLETIC	(Rd3)	W 3-2	Allen 2, Dyson	54,969
Jan 28	CREWE ALEXANDRIA	(Rd4)	W 5-1	Mackay, Jones, Smith R, Allen, Dyson	53,721
Feb 18	Aston Villa	(Rd5)	W 2-0	Jones, Neil o.g.	65,474
Mar 4	SUNDERLAND	(Rd6)	D 1-1	Jones	61,236
Mar 8	Sunderland	(R)	W 5-0	Mackay, Smith R, Allen, Dyson 2	64,797
Mar 18	Burnley *	(SF)	W 3-0	Jones, Smith R 2	69,968
May 6	Leicester City †	(F)	W 2-0	Smith R, Dyson	100,000

* played at Villa Park, Birmingham. † played at Wembley, London

League and Cup Appearances

PLAYER	LEAGUE	CUP COMPETITION FA CUP	TOTAL
Allen	42	7	49
Baker	41	7	48
Barton	1		1
Blanchflower	42	7	49
Brown	41	7	48
Dyson	40	7	47
Henry	42	7	49
Hollowbread	1		1
Jones	29	6	35
Mackay	37	7	44
Marchi	6		6
Medwin	14	1	15
Norman	41	7	48
Saul	6		6
Smith J	1		1
Smith R	36	7	43
White	42	7	49

Goalscorers

PLAYER	LEAGUE	CUP COMPETITION FA CUP	TOTAL
Smith R	28	5	33
Allen	23	4	27
Jones	15	4	19
Dyson	12	5	17
White	13		13
Blanchflower	6		6
Mackay	4	2	6
Medwin	5		5
Norman	4		4
Saul	3		3
Baker	1		1
Opp's o.gs.	1	1	2

Fact File

Just as ten years earlier, Spurs secured the Football League title by defeating Sheffield Wednesday at White Hart Lane.

Final Division One Table

		P	W	D	L	F	A	Pts
1	TOTTENHAM HOTSPUR	42	31	4	7	115	55	66
2	SHEFFIELD W	42	23	12	7	78	47	58
3	WOLVERHAMPTON W	42	25	7	10	103	75	57
4	BURNLEY	42	22	7	13	102	77	51
5	EVERTON	42	22	6	14	87	69	50
6	LEICESTER C	42	18	9	15	87	70	45
7	MANCHESTER U	42	18	9	15	88	76	45
8	BLACKBURN R	42	15	13	14	77	76	43
9	ASTON VILLA	42	17	9	16	78	77	43
10	WBA	42	18	5	19	67	71	41
11	ARSENAL	42	15	11	16	77	85	41
12	CHELSEA	42	15	7	20	98	85	37
13	MANCHESTER C	42	13	11	18	79	90	37
14	NOTTINGHAM F	42	14	9	19	62	78	37
15	CARDIFF C	42	13	11	18	60	85	37
16	WEST HAM U	42	13	10	19	77	88	36
17	FULHAM	42	14	8	20	72	95	36
18	BOLTON W	42	12	11	19	58	73	35
19	BIRMINGHAM C	42	14	6	22	62	84	34
20	BLACKPOOL	42	12	9	21	68	73	33
21	NEWCASTLE U	42	11	10	21	86	109	32
22	PRESTON NE	42	10	10	22	43	71	30

MANAGER: Bill Nicholson

CAPTAIN: Danny Blanchflower

TOP SCORER: Bobby Smith

BIGGEST WIN: 6-0 v Birmingham City (H), 19 November 1960, Football League Division One

HIGHEST ATTENDANCE: 100,000 v Leicester City, 6 May 1961, FA Cup Final

MAJOR TRANSFERS IN: None

MAJOR TRANSFERS OUT: Tommy Harmer to Watford

Season 1961-62

Football League Division One

DATE	OPPONENTS	SCORE	GOALSCORERS	ATTENDANCE
Aug 19	Blackpool	W 2-1	Jones, Smith R	29,023
Aug 23	WEST HAM UNITED	D 2-2	Dyson 2	50,434
Aug 26	ARSENAL	W 4-3	Allen, Dyson 3	59,371
Aug 28	West Ham United	L 1-2	Allen	36,274
Sep 2	CARDIFF CITY	W 3-2	Blanchflower (pen), Jones, Smith R	37,834
Sep 4	Sheffield United	D 1-1	White	32,902
Sep 9	Manchester United	L 0-1		57,135
Sep 16	WOLVERHAMPTON WANDERERS	W 1-0	Mackay	45,334
Sep 23	Nottingham Forest	L 0-2		40,875
Sep 30	ASTON VILLA	W 1-0	Dyson	38,099
Oct 9	Bolton Wanderers	W 2-1	Allen, Clayton	24,726
Oct 14	MANCHESTER CITY	W 2-0	Medwin, White	40,561
Oct 21	Ipswich Town	L 2-3	Jones 2	28,778
Oct 28	BURNLEY	W 4-2	Jones 2, Saul, Clayton	56,772
Nov 4	Everton	L 0-3		54,234
Nov 11	FULHAM	W 4-2	Jones, White 2, Mackay	35,662
Nov 18	Sheffield Wednesday	D 0-0		43,085
Nov 25	LEICESTER CITY	L 1-2	White	41,745
Dec 2	West Bromwich Albion	W 4-2	Medwin, White, Allen, Howe o.g.	28,701
Dec 9	BIRMINGHAM CITY	W 3-1	Allen 2, Mackay	32,509
Dec 16	BLACKPOOL	W 5-2	Allen 2, Greaves 3	42,734
Dec 23	Arsenal	L 1-2	Mackay	63,440
Dec 26	Chelsea	W 2-0	Greaves, Jones	51,282
Dec 30	CHELSEA	W 5-2	Mackay, Allen, Jones 3	44,630
Jan 13	Cardiff City	D 1-1	Mackay	33,606
Jan 20	MANCHESTER UNITED	D 2-2	Greaves 2	55,225
Feb 3	Wolverhampton Wanderers	L 1-3	White	45,687
Feb 10	NOTTINGHAM FOREST	W 4-2	Medwin, Smith R, Jones 2	42,710
Feb 21	Aston Villa	D 0-0		49,892
Feb 24	BOLTON WANDERERS	D 2-2	Smith R, Greaves	36,470
Mar 3	Manchester City	L 2-6	Greaves 2	31,706
Mar 14	IPSWICH TOWN	L 1-3	Greaves	51,098
Mar 17	Burnley	D 2-2	Greaves, Jones	46,810
Mar 24	EVERTON	W 3-1	Jones, White, Greaves	47,343
Apr 7	SHEFFIELD WEDNESDAY	W 4-0	Clayton, Saul, Greaves 2	40,846
Apr 9	SHEFFIELD UNITED	D 3-3	Blanchflower (pen), Smith R, Greaves	49,030
Apr 17	Fulham	D 1-1	Greaves	43,355
Apr 20	BLACKBURN ROVERS	W 4-1	Medwin, Smith R, Jones, Greaves	55,183
Apr 21	WEST BROMWICH ALBION	L 1-2	Saul	53,512
Apr 23	Blackburn Rovers	W 1-0	Greaves	23,301
Apr 28	Birmingham City	W 3-2	Mackay, Greaves 2	29,614
Apr 30	Leicester City	W 3-2	Mackay, Medwin, Greaves	23,929

FA Cup

Jan 6	Birmingham City	(Rd3) D 3-3	Greaves 2, Jones	46,096
Jan 10	BIRMINGHAM CITY	(R) W 4-2	Medwin 2, Allen, Greaves	62,917
Jan 27	Plymouth Argyle	(Rd4) W 5-1	Medwin, White, Greaves 2, Jones	40,040
Feb 17	West Bromwich Albion	(Rd5) W 4-2	Smith R 2, Greaves	53,539
Mar 10	ASTON VILLA	(Rd6) W 2-0	Blanchflower, Jones	64,000
Mar 31	Manchester United *	(SF) W 3-1	Medwin, Greaves, Jones	65,000
May 5	Burnley †	(F) W 3-1	Blanchflower (pen), Smith R, Greaves	100,000

* played at Hillsbrough, Sheffield. † played at Wembley, London

European Cup

Sep 13	Gornik Zabreze	(PRd/1L) L 2-4	Jones, Dyson	70,000
Sep 20	GORNIK ZABREZE	(PRd/2L) W 8-1	Blanchflower, Jones 3, White, Smith R 2, Dyson	56,737
Oct 1	Feyenoord	(Rd1/1L) W 3-1	Saul 2, Dyson	61,719
Nov 15	FEYENOORD	(Rd1/2L) D 1-1	Dyson	62,144
Feb 14	Dukla Prague	(Rd2/1L) L 0-1		64,000
Feb 26	DUKLA PRAGUE	(Rd2/2L) W 4-1	Mackay 2, Smith R, Jones	55,388
Mar 21	Benfica	(SF/1L) L 1-3	Smith R	86,000
Apr 5	BENFICA	(SF/2L) W 2-1	Blanchflower (pen), Smith R	64,448

FA Charity Shield

Aug 12	FA XI		W 3-2	Smith R, Allen 2	36,593

Fact File

A crowd of 12,907 watched Spurs, reserves at Plymouth Argyle in December. Jimmy Greaves scored twice on his debut in Spurs colours.

League and Cup Appearances

PLAYER	LEAGUE	CUP COMPETITION		OTHER	TOTAL
		FA CUP	EC		
Allen	23	3	2	1	29
Baker	36	7	8	1	52
Barton	2				2
Blanchflower	39	7	8	1	55
Brown	35	7	8	1	51
Clayton	7		1		8
Collins	2				2
Dyson	23		4	1	28
Greaves	22	7	2		31
Henry	41	7	8	1	57
Hollowbread	7				7
Hopkins	5				5
Jones	38	7	8	1	54
Mackay	26	7	7	1	41
Marchi	21		5		26
Medwin	20	7	3		30
Norman	40	7	8	1	56
Saul	8		2		10
Smith J	5				5
Smith R	26	4	6	1	37
White	36	7	8	1	52

Goalscorers

PLAYER	LEAGUE	CUP COMPETITION		OTHER	TOTAL
		FA CUP	EC		
Greaves	21	9			30
Jones	16	4	4		24
Smith R	6	3	6	1	16
Allen	9	1		2	12
Mackay	8		2		10
Dyson	6		4		10
White	8	1	1		10
Medwin	5	4			9
Blanchflower	2	2	2		6
Saul	3		2		5
Clayton	3				3
Opp's o.gs.	1				1

MANAGER: Bill Nicholson

CAPTAIN: Danny Blanchflower

TOP SCORER: Jimmy Greaves

BIGGEST WIN: 8-1 v Gornik Zabreze, 20 September 1961, European Cup Preliminary Round 2nd Leg

HIGHEST ATTENDANCE: 100,000 v Burnley, 5 May 1962, FA Cup Final at Wembley

MAJOR TRANSFERS IN: Jimmy Greaves from AC Milan

MAJOR TRANSFERS OUT: None

Final Division One Table

		P	W	D	L	F	A	Pts
1	Ipswich T	42	24	8	10	93	67	56
2	Burnley	42	21	11	10	101	67	53
3	Tottenham Hotspur	42	21	10	11	88	69	52
4	Everton	42	20	11	11	88	54	51
5	Sheffield U	42	19	9	14	61	69	47
6	Sheffield W	42	20	6	16	72	58	46
7	Aston Villa	42	18	8	16	65	56	44
8	West Ham U	42	17	10	15	76	82	44
9	WBA	42	15	13	14	83	67	43
10	Arsenal	42	16	11	15	71	72	43
11	Bolton W	42	16	10	16	62	66	42
12	Manchester C	42	17	7	18	78	70	41
13	Blackpool	42	15	11	16	70	75	41
14	Leicester C	42	17	6	19	72	71	40
15	Manchester U	42	15	9	18	72	75	39
16	Blackburn R	42	14	11	17	50	58	39
17	Birmingham C	42	14	10	18	65	81	38
18	Wolverhampton W	42	13	10	19	73	86	36
19	Nottingham F	42	13	10	19	63	79	36
20	Fulham	42	13	7	22	66	74	33
21	Cardiff C	42	9	14	19	50	81	32
22	Chelsea	42	9	10	23	63	94	28

Season 1962-63

Football League Division One

DATE	OPPONENTS	SCORE	GOALSCORERS	ATTENDANCE
Aug 18	BIRMINGHAM CITY	W 3-0	Blanchflower (pen), Greaves, Jones	51,140
Aug 20	Aston Villa	L 1-2	Medwin	55,630
Aug 25	West Ham United	W 6-1	Medwin, White, Greaves 2, Jones, Lyall o.g.	32,527
Aug 29	ASTON VILLA	W 4-2	White, Greaves 2, Jones	55,650
Sep 1	MANCHESTER CITY	W 4-2	Blanchflower (pen), Medwin, Greaves, Jones	48,758
Sep 8	Blackpool	W 2-1	Norman, Allen	31,786
Sep 12	WOLVERHAMPTON WANDERERS	L 1-2	White	61,412
Sep 15	BLACKBURN ROVERS	W 4-1	Medwin, White, Allen, Taylor o.g.	43,014
Sep 19	Wolverhampton Wanderers	D 2-2	Greaves 2	48,166
Sep 22	Sheffield United	L 1-3	Greaves	38,355
Sep 29	NOTTINGHAM FOREST	W 9-2	Medwin, White, Allen (pen), Greaves 4, Jones 2	49,075
Oct 6	ARSENAL	D 4-4	Mackay, White, Jones 2	61,749
Oct 13	West Bromwich Albion	W 2-1	Marchi, Jones	32,753
Oct 24	MANCHESTER UNITED	W 6-2	Medwin 2, Greaves 3, Jones	51,314
Oct 27	Leyton Orient	W 5-1	Medwin, White, Allen, Jones, Bishop o.g.	30,967
Nov 3	LEICESTER CITY	W 4-0	Blanchflower (pen), Medwin, Greaves 2	52,361
Nov 10	Fulham	W 2-0	Mackay, Jones	39,961
Nov 17	SHEFFIELD WEDNESDAY	D 1-1	Mackay	42,390
Nov 24	Burnley	L 1-2	Greaves	44,478
Dec 1	EVERTON	D 0-0		60,626
Dec 8	Bolton Wanderers	L 0-1		20,737
Dec 15	Birmingham City	W 2-0	Smith R, Greaves	36,623
Dec 22	WEST BROMWICH ALBION	D 4-4	Smith J, Mackay 3	44,650
Dec 26	IPSWICH TOWN	W 5-0	Smith R, Greaves 3, Jones	34,822
Jan 19	BLACKPOOL	W 2-0	Greaves 2	25,710
Feb 23	Arsenal	W 3-2	Marchi, Smith R, Jones	59,980
Mar 2	WEST BROMWICH ALBION	W 2-1	Smith R 2	41,193
Mar 9	Manchester United	W 2-0	Saul, Jones	53,416
Mar 16	Ipswich Town	W 4-2	Saul, Greaves (1 pen) 2, Jones	23,679
Mar 23	Leicester City	D 2-2	Smith R, Greaves	41,622
Mar 27	LEYTON ORIENT	W 2-0	Smith R, Greaves (pen)	40,260
Mar 30	BURNLEY	D 1-1	Greaves	46,536
Apr 8	Sheffield Wednesday	L 1-3	McAnearney o.g.	43,368
Apr 12	Liverpool	L 2-5	Jones, Dyson	54,463
Apr 13	FULHAM	D 1-1	Greaves	45,951
Apr 15	LIVERPOOL	W 7-2	Jones 2, Saul, Greaves (1 pen) 4	53,727
Apr 20	Everton	L 0-1		67,650
Apr 27	BOLTON WANDERERS	W 4-1	Marchi, Greaves, White, Smith R	40,965
May 4	SHEFFIELD UNITED	W 4-2	Jones, Saul, Greaves, Dyson	42,886
May 11	Manchester City	L 0-1		27,784
May 18	Nottingham Forest	D 1-1	Allen	27,995
May 20	Blackburn Rovers	L 0-3		22,867

FA Cup

Jan 16	BURNLEY	L 0-3		32,756

European Cup-Winners' Cup

Oct 31	GLASGOW RANGERS	(Rd1/1L)	W 5-2	Norman, White 2, Allen, Shearer o.g.	58,859
Dec 11	Glasgow Rangers	(Rd1/2L)	W 3-2	Smith R 2, Greaves	80,000
Mar 5	Slovan Bratislava	(Rd2/1L)	L 0-2		32,000
Mar 14	SLOVAN BRATISLAVA	(Rd2/2L)	W 6-0	Mackay, White, Smith R, Greaves 2, Jones	61,504
Apr 24	OFK Belgrade	(SF/1L)	W 2-1	White, Dyson	45,000
May 1	OFK BELGRADE	(SF/2L)	W 3-1	Mackay, Jones, Smith R	59,736
May 15	Athletico Madrid *	(F)	W 5-1	White, Greaves 2, Dyson 2	40,000

* played at Feyenoord Stadium, Rotterdam

FA Charity Shield

Aug 11	Ipswich Town	W 5-1	Medwin, White, Smith R, Greaves 2	20,179

MANAGER: Bill Nicholson

CAPTAIN: Danny Blanchflower

TOP SCORER: Jimmy Greaves

BIGGEST WIN: 9-2 v Nottingham Forest (H), 29 September 1962, Football League Division One

HIGHEST ATTENDANCE: 80,000 v Rangers, 11 December 1962, European Cup-Winners' Cup 1st Round 2nd leg

---

League and Cup Appearances

PLAYER	LEAGUE	CUP COMPETITION		OTHER	TOTAL
		FA CUP	ECWC		
Allen	25		1		26
Baker	33	1	6	1	41
Blanchflower	24		4	1	29
Brown	40	1	7	1	49
Clayton	3				3
Dyson	13	1	3		17
Greaves	41	1	6	1	49
Henry	42	1	7	1	51
Hollowbread	2				2
Hopkins	9		1		10
Jones	37	1	6	1	45
Mackay	37	1	6	1	45
Marchi	22		5		27
Medwin	26		2	1	29
Norman	38	1	7	1	47
Piper	1				1
Saul	10		2		12
Smith J	7	1	1		9
Smith R	15	1	6	1	23
White	37	1	7	1	46

Goalscorers

PLAYER	LEAGUE	CUP COMPETITION		OTHER	TOTAL
		FA CUP	ECWC		
Greaves	37		5	2	44
Jones	20		2		22
White	8		5	1	14
Smith R	8		4	1	13
Medwin	9			1	10
Mackay	6		2		8
Allen	5		1		6
Dyson	2		3		5
Saul	4				4
Blanchflower	3				3
Marchi	3				3
Norman	1		1		2
Smith J	1				1
Opp's o.gs.	4		1		5

Fact File

Jimmy Greaves was originally credited with one of the goals against Rangers on 31 October 1962. It was only after close study of the film in 1987 that the goal was debited from Greaves and credited to John White.

Final Division One Table

		P	W	D	L	F	A	Pts
1	EVERTON	42	25	11	6	84	42	61
2	TOTTENHAM HOTSPUR	42	23	9	10	111	62	55
3	BURNLEY	42	22	10	10	78	57	54
4	LEICESTER C	42	20	12	10	79	53	52
5	WOLVERHAMPTON W	42	20	10	12	93	65	50
6	SHEFFIELD W	42	19	10	13	77	63	48
7	ARSENAL	42	18	10	14	86	77	46
8	LIVERPOOL	42	17	10	15	71	59	44
9	NOTTINGHAM F	42	17	10	15	67	69	44
10	SHEFFIELD U	42	16	12	14	58	60	44
11	BLACKBURN R	42	15	12	15	79	71	42
12	WEST HAM U	42	14	12	16	73	69	40
13	BLACKPOOL	42	13	14	15	58	64	40
14	WBA	42	16	7	19	71	79	39
15	ASTON VILLA	42	15	8	19	62	68	38
16	FULHAM	42	14	10	18	50	71	38
17	IPSWICH T	42	12	11	19	59	78	35
18	BOLTON W	42	15	5	22	55	75	35
19	MANCHESTER U	42	12	10	20	67	81	34
20	BIRMINGHAM C	42	10	13	19	63	90	33
21	MANCHESTER C	42	10	11	21	58	102	31
22	LEYTON ORIENT	42	6	9	27	37	81	21

Season 1963-64

Football League Division One

DATE	OPPONENTS	SCORE	GOALSCORERS	ATTENDANCE
Aug 24	Stoke City	L 1-2	Smith R	40,638
Aug 28	Wolverhampton Wanderers	W 4-1	Smith R 2, Greaves (1 pen) 2	41,488
Aug 31	NOTTINGHAM FOREST	W 4-1	Jones, Greaves 3	49,407
Sep 4	WOLVERHAMPTON WANDERERS	W 4-3	Norman, White, Dyson 2	51,851
Sep 7	Blackburn Rovers	L 2-7	Mackay, Greaves	20,949
Sep 14	BLACKPOOL	W 6-1	Jones, White, Smith R, Greaves 3	38,138
Sep 16	Aston Villa	W 4-2	Jones, Greaves 2, Dyson	36,643
Sep 21	Chelsea	W 3-0	Baker, Smith R, Shellito o.g.	57,401
Sep 28	WEST HAM UNITED	W 3-0	Mackay, Jones, Brown o.g.	51,667
Oct 2	BIRMINGHAM CITY	W 6-1	White, Smith R, Greaves (1 pen) 3, Dyson	37,649
Oct 5	Sheffield United	D 3-3	Smith R, Greaves, Dyson	33,606
Oct 15	Arsenal	D 4-4	Mackay, Smith R 2, Greaves	67,857
Oct 19	LEICESTER CITY	D 1-1	Jones	50,521
Oct 26	Everton	L 0-1		65,386
Nov 2	FULHAM	W 1-0	Greaves	42,023
Nov 9	Manchester United	L 1-4	Gregg o.g.	57,513
Nov 16	BURNLEY	W 3-2	Norman, Smith R 2	42,222
Nov 23	Ipswich Town	W 3-2	Marchi, Dyson 2	25,014
Nov 30	SHEFFIELD WEDNESDAY	D 1-1	Smith R	39,378
Dec 7	Bolton Wanderers	W 3-1	Greaves, Dyson, Farrimond o.g.	18,394
Dec 14	STOKE CITY	W 2-1	Greaves 2	36,776
Dec 21	Nottingham Forest	W 2-1	Jones, Greaves	23,888
Dec 26	West Bromwich Albion	D 4-4	Jones, Smith R, Greaves 2	37,189
Dec 28	WEST BROMWICH ALBION	L 0-2		47,863
Jan 11	BLACKBURN ROVERS	W 4-1	Greaves 3, Dyson	43,953
Jan 18	Blackpool	W 2-0	Greaves, Martin o.g.	13,955
Jan 25	ASTON VILLA	W 3-1	Possee, Greaves, Dyson	36,394
Feb 1	CHELSEA	L 1-2	Greaves	51,007
Feb 8	West Ham United	L 0-4		36,838
Feb 15	SHEFFIELD UNITED	D 0-0		30,833
Feb 22	ARSENAL	W 3-1	Jones 2, Greaves (pen)	57,261
Feb 29	Birmingham City	W 2-1	Jones, Greaves (pen)	28,433
Mar 7	EVERTON	L 2-4	Allen, Dyson	41,926
Mar 21	MANCHESTER UNITED	L 2-3	Brown L, Greaves (pen)	56,292
Mar 27	LIVERPOOL	L 1-3	Norman	57,022
Mar 28	Fulham	D 1-1	Greaves	30,388
Mar 30	Liverpool	L 1-3	Mullery	52,904
Apr 4	IPSWICH TOWN	W 6-3	Jones 3, White 2, Robertson	25,115
Apr 13	Sheffield Wednesday	L 0-2		26,628
Apr 18	BOLTON WANDERERS	W 1-0	Greaves	32,507
Apr 21	Burnley	L 2-7	Jones, Greaves	16,660
Apr 25	Leicester City	W 1-0	White	26,441

FA Cup

Jan 4	CHELSEA	(Rd3)	D 1-1	Dyson	49,382
Jan 8	Chelsea	(R)	L 0-2		70,123

European Cup-Winners' Cup

Dec 3	MANCHESTER UNITED	(Rd1/1L)	W 2-0	Mackay, Dyson	57,447
Dec 10	Manchester United	(Rd1/2L)	L 1-4	Greaves	48,639

MANAGER: Bill Nicholson

CAPTAIN: Danny Blanchflower/Tony Marchi

TOP SCORER: Jimmy Greaves

BIGGEST WIN: 6-1 v Blackpool (H), 14 September 1963, Football League Division One; 6-1 v Birmingham City, 2 October 1963, Football League Division One

HIGHEST ATTENDANCE: 70,123 v Chelsea, 8 January 1964, FA Cup 3rd Round replay

MAJOR TRANSFERS IN: Laurie Brown from Arsenal, Alan Mullery from Fulham, Jimmy Robertson from St Mirren

MAJOR TRANSFERS OUT: John Smith to Coventry City

League and Cup Appearances

PLAYER	LEAGUE	CUP COMPETITION		TOTAL
		FA CUP	ECWC	
Allen	8	1		9
Baker	35	2	2	39
Barton	1			
Beal	16	2		
Blanchflower	15			15
Brown L	9			9
Brown W	27		2	29
Clayton	1	2		3
Dyson	39	2	2	43
Greaves	41	2	2	45
Henry	29		2	31
Hollowbread	15	2		17
Hopkins	19	2		21
Jones	39	2	2	43
Mackay	17		2	19
Marchi	21	1	2	24
Mullery	9			9
Norman	42	2	2	46
Possee	1			1
Robertson	3			3
Saul	2			2
Smith J	7	1		8
Smith R	26	1	2	29
White	40		2	42

Goalscorers

PLAYER	LEAGUE	CUP COMPETITION		TOTAL
		FA CUP	ECWC	
Greaves	35		1	36
Jones	14			14
Dyson	11	1	1	13
Smith R	13			13
White	6			6
Mackay	3		1	4
Norman	3			3
Allen	1			1
Baker	1			1
Brown L	1			1
Marchi	1			1
Mullery	1			1
Possee	1			1
Robertson	1			1
Opp's o.g.s.	5			5

Fact File

Alan Mullery was expected to make his England debut on the summer tour to South America. On the morning of departure he ricked his neck while shaving and was forced to withdraw from the squad.

Final Division One Table

		P	W	D	L	F	A	Pts
1	LIVERPOOL	42	26	5	11	92	45	57
2	MANCHESTER U	42	23	7	12	90	62	53
3	EVERTON	42	21	10	11	84	64	52
4	TOTTENHAM HOTSPUR	42	22	7	13	97	81	51
5	CHELSEA	42	20	10	12	72	56	50
6	SHEFFIELD W	42	19	11	12	84	67	49
7	BLACKBURN R	42	18	10	14	89	65	46
8	ARSENAL	42	17	11	14	90	82	45
9	BURNLEY	42	17	10	15	71	64	44
10	WBA	42	16	11	15	70	61	43
11	LEICESTER C	42	16	11	15	61	58	43
12	SHEFFIELD U	42	16	11	15	61	64	43
13	NOTTINGHAM F	42	16	9	17	64	68	41
14	WEST HAM U	42	14	12	16	69	74	40
15	FULHAM	42	13	13	16	58	65	39
16	WOLVERHAMPTON W	42	12	15	15	70	80	39
17	STOKE C	42	14	10	18	77	78	38
18	BLACKPOOL	42	13	9	20	52	73	35
19	ASTON VILLA	42	11	12	19	62	71	34
20	BIRMINGHAM C	42	11	7	24	54	92	29
21	BOLTON W	42	10	8	24	48	80	28
22	IPSWICH T	42	9	7	26	56	121	25

The Essential History of Tottenham Hotspur

Football League Division One

DATE	OPPONENTS	SCORE	GOALSCORERS	ATTENDANCE
Aug 22	SHEFFIELD UNITED	W 2-0	Greaves, Saul	45,724
Aug 25	Burnley	D 2-2	Greaves, Saul	21,661
Aug 29	Everton	L 1-4	Jones	55,148
Sep 2	BURNLEY	W 4-1	Saul 3, Dyson	42,326
Sep 5	BIRMINGHAM CITY	W 4-1	Robertson, Greaves, Dyson, Foster o.g.	34,809
Sep 9	Stoke City	L 0-2		36,329
Sep 12	West Ham United	L 2-3	Greaves (1 pen) 2	36,730
Sep 16	STOKE CITY	W 2-1	Greaves, Saul	34,821
Sep 19	WEST BROMWICH ALBION	W 1-0	Greaves	36,993
Sep 26	Manchester United	L 1-4	Robertson	53,362
Sep 28	Blackpool	D 1-1	Jones	26,436
Oct 5	FULHAM	W 3-0	Norman, Greaves, Saul	32,908
Oct 10	ARSENAL	W 3-1	Robertson, Greaves, Saul	55,959
Oct 17	Leeds United	L 1-3	Greaves	41,464
Oct 24	CHELSEA	D 1-1	Jones	52,927
Oct 31	Leicester City	L 2-4	Greaves, Allen	29,167
Nov 7	SUNDERLAND	W 3-0	Robertson, Greaves, Jones	36,677
Nov 14	Wolverhampton Wanderers	L 1-3	Brown L	28,728
Nov 21	ASTON VILLA	W 4-0	Mullery, Robertson, Greaves, Dyson	29,724
Nov 28	Liverpool	D 1-1	Greaves	41,198
Dec 5	SHEFFIELD WEDNESDAY	W 3-2	Greaves (1 pen) 2, Megson o.g.	24,019
Dec 12	Sheffield United	D 3-3	Greaves, Saul 2	19,325
Dec 19	EVERTON	D 2-2	Greaves 2	41,994
Dec 26	Nottingham Forest	W 2-1	Gilzean, Jones	42,056
Dec 28	NOTTINGHAM FOREST	W 4-0	Robertson, Greaves, Gilzean, Dyson	56,693
Jan 2	Birmingham City	L 0-1		33,833
Jan 16	WEST HAM UNITED	W 3-2	Greaves 2, Dyson	50,054
Jan 23	West Bromwich Albion	L 0-2		23,718
Feb 6	MANCHESTER UNITED	W 1-0	Henry	58,639
Feb 13	Fulham	L 1-4	Greaves	27,708
Feb 23	Arsenal	L 1-3	Gilzean	48,637
Feb 27	LEEDS UNITED	D 0-0		42,350
Mar 10	Chelsea	L 1-3	Gilzean	51,390
Mar 13	BLACKPOOL	W 4-1	Mullery, Robertson, Greaves, Jones	27,257
Mar 20	Sunderland	L 1-2	Greaves	44,394
Mar 27	WOLVERHAMPTON WANDERERS	W 7-4	Clayton, Allen, Gilzean 2, Jones 3	25,974
Apr 3	Aston Villa	L 0-1		24,930
Apr 9	LIVERPOOL	W 3-0	Saul, Low, Gilzean	28,441
Apr 16	BLACKBURN ROVERS	W 5-2	Greaves 2, Gilzean 3	36,497
Apr 17	Sheffield Wednesday	L 0-1		21,843
Apr 19	Blackburn Rovers	L 1-3	Jones	14,026
Apr 24	LEICESTER CITY	W 6-2	Greaves (1 pen) 2, Gilzean, Jones 3	32,427

FA Cup

Jan 9	Torquay United	(Rd3)	D 3-3	Norman, Gilzean 2	20,000
Jan 18	TORQUAY UNITED	(R)	W 5-1	Robertson, Greaves 3, Gilzean	55,081
Jan 30	IPSWICH TOWN	(Rd4)	W 5-0	Greaves (1 pen) 3, Gilzean 2	43,992
Feb 20	Chelsea	(Rd5)	L 0-1		63,205

League and Cup Appearances

PLAYER	LEAGUE	CUP COMPETITION FA CUP	TOTAL
Allen	6		6
Baker	3		3
Beal	8		8
Brown L	16		16
Brown B	19	4	23
Clayton	15	3	18
Dyson	32	3	35
Gilzean	20	4	24
Greaves	41	4	45
Henry	41	4	45
Jennings	23		23
Jones	39	4	43
Knowles	38	4	42
Low	6		6
Marchi	17	2	19
Mullery	42	4	46
Norman	30	4	34
Possee	1		1
Robertson	36	4	40
Saul	23		23
Weller	6		6

Goalscorers

PLAYER	LEAGUE	CUP COMPETITION FA CUP	TOTAL
Greaves	29	6	35
Gilzean	11	5	16
Jones	13		13
Saul	11		11
Robertson	7	1	8
Dyson	5		5
Allen	2		2
Mullery	2		2
Norman	1	1	2
Brown	1		1
Clayton	1		1
Henry	1		1
Low	1		1
Opp's o.gs.	2		2

Fact File

In November Spurs played a Scotland XI in a memorial match for John White. Alan Gilzean scored twice as the Scots won 6-2 with Tom White, John's brother, guesting for Spurs and scoring once.

MANAGER: Bill Nicholson

CAPTAIN: Ron Henry

TOP SCORER: Jimmy Greaves

BIGGEST WIN: 5-0 v Ipswich Town, 30 January 1965, FA Cup 4th Round

HIGHEST ATTENDANCE: 63,205 v Chelsea, 20 February 1965, FA Cup 5th Round

MAJOR TRANSFERS IN: Alan Gilzean from Dundee, Pat Jennings from Watford, Cyril Knowles from Middlesbrough

MAJOR TRANSFERS OUT: Mel Hopkins to Brighton & Hove Albion

Final Division One Table

		P	W	D	L	F	A	Pts
1	MANCHESTER U	42	26	9	7	89	39	61
2	LEEDS UNITED	42	26	9	7	83	52	61
3	CHELSEA	42	24	8	10	89	54	56
4	EVERTON	42	17	15	10	69	60	49
5	NOTTINGHAM F	42	17	13	12	71	67	47
6	TOTTENHAM HOTSPUR	42	19	7	16	87	71	45
7	LIVERPOOL	42	17	10	15	67	73	44
8	SHEFFIELD W	42	16	11	15	57	55	43
9	WEST HAM U	42	19	4	19	82	71	42
10	BLACKBURN R	42	16	10	16	83	79	42
11	STOKE C	42	16	10	16	67	66	42
12	BURNLEY	42	16	10	16	70	57	42
13	ARSENAL	42	17	7	18	69	75	41
14	WBA	42	13	13	16	70	65	39
15	BLACKBURN R	42	14	9	19	64	74	37
16	ASTON VILLA	42	16	5	21	57	82	37
17	BLACKPOOL	42	12	11	19	67	78	35
18	LEICESTER C	42	11	13	18	69	85	35
19	SHEFFIELD U	42	12	11	19	50	64	35
20	FULHAM	42	11	12	19	60	78	34
21	WOLVERHAMPTON W	42	13	4	25	59	89	30
22	BIRMINGHAM C	42	8	11	23	64	96	27

Season 1965-66

Football League Division One

DATE	OPPONENTS	SCORE	GOALSCORERS	ATTENDANCE
Aug 25	LEICESTER CITY	W 4-2	Knowles, Possee, Greaves, Robertson	39,876
Aug 27	BLACKPOOL	W 4-0	Clayton, Gilzean, Greaves 2	36,882
Sep 1	Leicester City	D 2-2	Possee, Greaves (pen)	28,463
Sep 4	Fulham	W 2-0	Mackay, Clayton	28,718
Sep 8	LEEDS UNITED	W 3-2	Mackay, Greaves 2	48,156
Sep 11	ARSENAL	D 2-2	Gilzean, Saul	53,962
Sep 15	Leeds United	L 0-2		41,920
Sep 18	LIVERPOOL	W 2-1	Clayton, Gilzean	46,925
Sep 25	Aston Villa	L 2-3	Norman, Robertson	29,856
Oct 6	SUNDERLAND	W 3-0	Mackay, Clayton, Greaves	37,364
Oct 9	Everton	L 1-3	Mullery	40,022
Oct 16	MANCHESTER UNITED	W 5-1	Johnson, Clayton, Gilzean, Greaves, Robertson	58,051
Oct 23	Newcastle United	D 0-0		42,430
Oct 30	WEST BROMWICH ALBION	W 2-1	Greaves 2	43,658
Nov 6	Nottingham Forest	L 0-1		29,611
Nov 13	SHEFFIELD WEDNESDAY	L 2-3	Mackay (pen), Saul	30,422
Nov 20	Northampton Town	W 2-0	Mackay, Saul	17,611
Nov 27	STOKE CITY	D 2-2	Gilzean, Robertson	26,406
Dec 4	Burnley	D 1-1	Clayton	19,509
Dec 11	CHELSEA	W 4-2	Gilzean 2, Jones 2	42,299
Dec 18	Manchester United	L 1-5	Jones	39,511
Dec 27	SHEFFIELD UNITED	W 1-0	Gilzean	45,766
Dec 28	Sheffield United	W 3-1	Saul, Jones 2	24,787
Jan 1	EVERTON	D 2-2	Knowles, Saul	34,953
Jan 8	Chelsea	L 1-2	Mackay (pen)	48,529
Jan 15	NEWCASTLE UNITED	D 2-2	Knowles, Weller	27,490
Jan 29	BLACKBURN ROVERS	W 4-0	Saul, Gilzean 2, Greaves (pen)	34,573
Feb 5	Blackpool	D 0-0		13,103
Feb 19	FULHAM	W 4-3	Saul, Jones 3	32,244
Mar 8	Arsenal	D 1-1	Possee	51,824
Mar 12	Liverpool	L 0-1		50,760
Mar 19	ASTON VILLA	D 5-5	Brown L, Robertson, Greaves, Saul, Gilzean	28,371
Mar 26	Sunderland	L 0-2		27,828
Apr 2	NOTTINGHAM FOREST	L 2-3	Robertson, Clayton	27,593
Apr 8	WEST HAM UNITED	L 1-4	Gilzean	50,635
Apr 9	Sheffield Wednesday	D 1-1	Clayton	17,456
Apr 16	NORTHAMPTON TOWN	D 1-1	Greaves (pen)	29,749
Apr 23	Stoke City	W 1-0	Greaves (pen)	19,112
Apr 25	West Ham United	L 0-2		32,232
Apr 30	BURNLEY	L 0-1		29,337
May 7	West Bromwich Albion	L 1-2	Clayton	22,586
May 9	Blackburn Rovers	W 1-0	Greaves	7,256

FA Cup

DATE	OPPONENTS		SCORE	GOALSCORERS	ATTENDANCE
Jan 22	MIDDLESBROUGH	(Rd3)	W 4-0	Mackay (1 pen) 2, Saul 2	37,349
Feb 12	BURNLEY	(Rd4)	W 4-3	Gilzean 3, Saul	50,611
Mar 5	Preston North End	(Rd5)	L 1-2	Greaves	36,792

League and Cup Appearances

PLAYER	LEAGUE	CUP COMPETITION FA CUP	TOTAL
Beal	21	3	24
Brown L	37	3	40
Brown B	20		20
Clayton	38	3	41
Collins	2		2
Gilzean	40	3	43
Greaves	29	2	31
Henry	1		1
Hoy	5		5
Jennings	22	3	25
Johnson	9 (1)		9 (1)
Jones	9	2	11 (1)
Kinnear	8		8
Knowles	41	3	44
Low	0 (1)		0 (1)
Mackay	41	2	43
Mullery	40	3	43
Norman	16		16
Pitt	1		1
Possee	16		16
Robertson	34	3	37
Saul	26	3	29
Venables	1		1
Weller	5		5

Goalscorers

PLAYER	LEAGUE	CUP COMPETITION FA CUP	TOTAL
Greaves	15	1	16
Gilzean	12	3	15
Saul	8	3	11
Clayton	9		9
Jones	8		8
Mackay	6	2	8
Robertson	6		6
Knowles	3		3
Possee	3		3
Brown L	1		1
Johnson	1		1
Mullery	1		1
Norman	1		1
Weller	1		1 (

Fact File

Roy Low became Spurs' first Football League substitute when he replaced Derek Possee against Arsenal on September 11 1965.

MANAGER: Bill Nicholson

CAPTAIN: Dave Mackay

TOP SCORER: Jimmy Greaves

BIGGEST WIN: 5-1 v Manchester United, 16 October 1965, Football League Division One

HIGHEST ATTENDANCE: 58,051 v Manchester United, 16 October 1965, Football League Division One

MAJOR TRANSFERS IN: Terry Venables from Chelsea

MAJOR TRANSFERS OUT: Les Allen to Queens Park Rangers, Terry Dyson to Fulham, Tony Marchi to Cambridge City

Final Division One Table

		P	W	D	L	F	A	Pts
1	LIVERPOOL	42	26	9	7	79	34	61
2	LEEDS UNITED	42	23	9	10	79	38	55
3	BURNLEY	42	24	7	11	79	47	55
4	MANCHESTER U	42	18	15	9	84	59	51
5	CHELSEA	42	22	7	13	65	53	51
6	WBA	42	19	12	11	91	69	50
7	LEICESTER C	42	21	7	14	80	65	49
8	TOTTENHAM HOTSPUR	42	16	12	14	75	66	44
9	SHEFFIELD U	42	16	11	15	56	59	43
10	STOKE C	42	15	12	15	65	64	42
11	EVERTON	42	15	11	16	56	62	41
12	WEST HAM U	42	15	9	18	70	57	39
13	BLACKPOOL	42	14	9	19	55	65	37
14	ARSENAL	42	12	13	17	62	75	37
15	NEWCASTLE U	42	14	9	19	50	63	37
16	ASTON VILLA	42	15	6	21	69	80	36
17	SHEFFIELD W	42	14	8	20	56	66	36
18	NOTTINGHAM F	42	14	8	20	56	72	36
19	BLACKBURN R	42	14	8	20	51	72	36
20	FULHAM	42	14	7	21	67	85	35
21	NORTHAMPTON T	42	10	13	19	55	92	33
22	BLACKBURN R	42	8	4	30	57	88	20

Season 1966-67

Football League Division One

DATE	OPPONENTS	SCORE	GOALSCORERS	ATTENDANCE
Aug 20	LEEDS UNITED	W 3-1	Mullery, Greaves, Gilzean	43,844
Aug 24	Stoke City	L 0-2		34,683
Aug 27	Newcastle United	W 2-0	Mackay, Robertson	35,780
Aug 31	STOKE CITY	W 2-0	Greaves (pen), Gilzean	37,908
Sep 3	ARSENAL	W 3-1	Greaves 2, Jones	56,271
Sep 6	Sheffield United	L 1-2	Greaves (pen)	21,650
Sep 10	MANCHESTER UNITED	W 2-1	Greaves, Gilzean	56,295
Sep 17	Burnley	D 2-2	Greaves, Saul	25,184
Sep 24	NOTTINGHAM FOREST	W 2-1	Mullery, Greaves	34,405
Oct 1	Fulham	W 4-3	Robertson, Greaves, Gilzean, Venables	28,628
Oct 8	Manchester City	W 2-1	Gilzean 2	32,551
Oct 15	BLACKPOOL	L 1-3	Knowles	36,459
Oct 26	Chelsea	L 0-3		54,191
Oct 29	ASTON VILLA	L 0-1		31,014
Nov 5	Blackpool	D 2-2	Gilzean 2	16,524
Nov 12	WEST HAM UNITED	L 3-4	Greaves (pen), Gilzean, Venables	57,157
Nov 19	Sheffield Wednesday	L 0-1		32,376
Nov 26	SOUTHAMPTON	W 5-3	Mullery, Mackay, Greaves (pen), Jones 2	35,736
Dec 3	Sunderland	W 1-0	Gilzean	32,733
Dec 10	LEICESTER CITY	W 2-0	Rodrigues o.g., Greaves	41,089
Dec 17	Leeds United	L 2-3	Greaves, Gilzean	29,852
Dec 26	West Bromwich Albion	L 0-3		37,969
Dec 27	WEST BROMWICH ALBION	D 0-0		39,129
Dec 31	NEWCASTLE UNITED	W 4-0	Mackay, Greaves 2, Venables	27,948
Jan 7	Arsenal	W 2-0	Robertson, Gilzean	49,851
Jan 14	Manchester United	L 0-1		57,365
Jan 21	BURNLEY	W 2-0	Greaves, Jones	42,187
Feb 4	Nottingham Forest	D 1-1	Greaves	41,822
Feb 11	FULHAM	W 4-2	Greaves, Gilzean, Jones 2	43,961
Feb 25	MANCHESTER CITY	D 1-1	Robertson	33,832
Mar 4	Aston Villa	D 3-3	Mullery, England, Gilzean	31,718
Mar 18	CHELSEA	D 1-1	Greaves	49,553
Mar 22	Everton	W 1-0	Greaves	50,108
Mar 25	Leicester City	W 1-0	Robertson	27,711
Mar 27	EVERTON	W 2-0	Mullery, Gilzean	46,917
Apr 1	LIVERPOOL	W 2-1	Greaves 2	53,135
Apr 15	SHEFFIELD WEDNESDAY	W 2-1	Saul 2	36,062
Apr 22	Southampton	W 1-0	Gilzean	30,285
May 3	SUNDERLAND	W 1-0	Greaves (pen)	33,936
May 6	Liverpool	D 0-0		40,845
May 9	West Ham United	W 2-0	Greaves, Gilzean	35,758
May 13	SHEFFIELD UNITED	W 2-0	Greaves, Saul	44,912

FA Cup

Jan 28	Millwall	(Rd3) D 0-0		41,260
Feb 1	MILLWALL	(R) W 1-0	Gilzean	58,189
Feb 18	PORTSMOUTH	(Rd4) W 3-1	Greaves, Gilzean 2	57,910
Mar 11	BRISTOL CITY	(Rd5) W 2-0	Greaves (1 pen) 2	54,610
Apr 8	Birmingham City	(Rd6) D 0-0		51,500
Apr 12	BIRMINGHAM CITY	(R) W 6-0	Greaves 2, Gilzean, Venables 2, Saul	52,304
Apr 29	Nottingham Forest *	(SF) W 2-1	Greaves, Saul	55,000
May 20	Chelsea †	(F) W 2-1	Robertson, Saul	100,000

* played at Hillsbrough, Sheffield. † played at Wembley, London

League Cup

Sep 14	West Ham United	(Rd2) L 0-1		34,068

League and Cup Appearances

PLAYER	LEAGUE	CUP COMPETITION		TOTAL
		FA CUP	LC	
Beal	26	1	1	28
Bond			0 (1)	0 (1)
Brown	1			1
Clayton	6 (3)	1		7 (3)
England	42	8		50
Gilzean	40	8	1	49
Greaves	38	8	1	47
Jennings	41	8	1	50
Jones	20	4	0 (1)	24 (1)
Kinnear	19 (1)	7	1	27 (1)
Knowles	42	8	1	51
Low	0 (1)			0 (1)
Mackay	39	8		47
Mullery	39	8	1	48
Robertson	40	8	1	49
Saul	20 (2)	4	1	25 (2)
Venables	41	8	1	50
Weller	8 (2)			8 (2)

Goalscorers

PLAYER	LEAGUE	CUP COMPETITION		TOTAL
		FA CUP	LC	
Greaves	25	6		31
Gilzean	17	4		21
Saul	4	3		7
Jones	6			6
Robertson	5	1		6
Mullery	5			5
Venables	3	2		5
Mackay	3			3
England	1			1
Knowles	1			1
Opp's o.g.s.	1			1

Fact File

Unused substitute Cliff Jones became the first player to collect an FA Cup winners' medal without actually playing.

Final Division One Table

		P	W	D	L	F	A	Pts
1	MANCHESTER U	42	24	12	6	84	45	60
2	NOTTINGHAM F	42	23	10	9	64	41	56
3	TOTTENHAM HOTSPUR	42	24	8	10	71	48	56
4	LEEDS UNITED	42	22	11	9	62	42	55
5	LIVERPOOL	42	19	13	10	64	47	51
6	EVERTON	42	19	10	13	65	46	48
7	ARSENAL	42	16	14	12	58	47	46
8	LEICESTER C	42	18	8	16	78	71	44
9	CHELSEA	42	15	14	13	67	62	44
10	SHEFFIELD U	42	16	10	16	52	59	42
11	SHEFFIELD W	42	14	13	15	56	47	41
12	STOKE C	42	17	7	18	63	44	41
13	WBA	42	16	7	19	77	73	39
14	BURNLEY	42	15	9	18	66	76	39
15	MANCHESTER C	42	12	15	15	43	52	39
16	WEST HAM U	42	14	8	20	80	84	36
17	BLACKBURN R	42	14	8	20	58	72	36
18	FULHAM	42	11	12	19	71	83	34
19	SOUTHAMPTON	42	14	6	22	74	92	34
20	NEWCASTLE U	42	12	9	21	39	81	33
21	ASTON VILLA	42	11	7	24	54	85	29
22	BLACKPOOL	42	6	9	27	41	76	21

MANAGER: Bill Nicholson

CAPTAIN: Dave Mackay

TOP SCORER: Jimmy Greaves

BIGGEST WIN: 6-0 v Birmingham City (H), 12 April 1967, FA Cup 6th Round

HIGHEST ATTENDANCE: 100,000 v Chelsea, 20 May 1967, FA Cup Final

MAJOR TRANSFERS IN: Dennis Bond from Watford, Mike England from Blackburn Rovers

MAJOR TRANSFERS OUT: Laurie Brown to Norwich City, Bill Brown to Northampton Town

Season 1967-68

Football League Division One

DATE	OPPONENTS	SCORE	GOALSCORERS	ATTENDANCE
Aug 19	Leicester City	W 3-2	Kinnear, England, Saul	32,552
Aug 23	EVERTON	D 1-1	Gilzean	53,809
Aug 26	WEST HAM UNITED	W 5-1	Mullery, Greaves (1 pen) 2, Saul, Jones	55,831
Aug 29	Everton	W 1-0	Saul	57,790
Sep 2	Burnley	L 1-5	Greaves	23,337
Sep 6	WOLVERHAMPTON WANDERERS	W 2-1	Robertson, Greaves	44,408
Sep 9	SHEFFIELD WEDNESDAY	W 2-1	Gilzean, Saul	43,317
Sep 16	Arsenal	L 0-4		62,936
Sep 23	Manchester United	L 1-3	Gilzean	58,779
Sep 30	SUNDERLAND	W 3-0	Greaves 2, Todd o.g.	36,017
Oct 7	SHEFFIELD UNITED	D 1-1	Greaves	33,233
Oct 14	Coventry City	W 3-2	Greaves 2, Jones	38,008
Oct 25	NOTTINGHAM FOREST	D 1-1	Greaves	40,928
Oct 28	Stoke City	L 1-2	Venables	27,144
Nov 4	LIVERPOOL	D 1-1	Jones	47,682
Nov 11	Southampton	W 2-1	Robertson, Gilzean	29,902
Nov 18	CHELSEA	W 2-0	Gilzean, Jones	53,981
Nov 25	West Bromwich Albion	L 0-2		29,033
Dec 2	NEWCASTLE UNITED	D 1-1	Gilzean	34,494
Dec 9	Manchester City	L 1-4	Greaves	35,792
Dec 16	LEICESTER CITY	L 0-1		26,036
Dec 23	West Ham United	L 1-2	Robertson	32,122
Dec 26	FULHAM	D 2-2	Jones 2	36,274
Dec 30	Fulham	W 2-1	Robertson, Jones	30,051
Jan 17	Sheffield Wednesday	W 2-1	Chivers, Greaves	31,610
Jan 20	ARSENAL	W 1-0	Gilzean	57,885
Feb 3	MANCHESTER UNITED	L 1-2	Chivers	57,690
Feb 10	Sunderland	W 1-0	Jones	31,735
Feb 26	Sheffield United	L 2-3	Greaves, Chivers	27,008
Mar 1	WEST BROMWICH ALBION	D 0-0		31,318
Mar 16	Nottingham Forest	D 0-0		37,707
Mar 23	STOKE CITY	W 3-0	England, Robertson, Jones	29,530
Mar 30	BURNLEY	W 5-0	England, Greaves 2, Venables, Jones	26,494
Apr 6	SOUTHAMPTON	W 6-1	Mullery, Greaves (1 pen) 2, Chivers, Jones, Hollywood o.g.	41,834
Apr 12	LEEDS UNITED	W 2-1	Greaves, Chivers	56,587
Apr 13	Chelsea	L 0-2		53,049
Apr 17	Leeds United	L 0-1		48,933
Apr 20	COVENTRY CITY	W 4-2	Mackay, Greaves 2, Jones	36,175
Apr 27	Newcastle United	W 3-1	Gilzean, Chivers 2	30,281
Apr 29	Liverpool	D 1-1	Greaves	41,688
May 4	MANCHESTER CITY	L 1-3	Greaves (pen)	51,242
May 11	Wolverhampton Wanderers	L 1-2	Greaves	40,929

FA Cup

Jan 27	Manchester Utd	(Rd3)	D 2-2	Chivers 2	63,500
Jan 31	MANCHESTER UTD	(R)	W 1-0	Robertson	57,200
Feb 17	PRESTON NORTH END	(Rd4)	W 3-1	Greaves 2, Chivers	47,088
Mar 9	LIVERPOOL	(Rd5)	D 1-1	Greaves	54,005
Mar 12	Liverpool	(R)	L 1-2	Jones	53,658

European Cup-Winners' Cup

Sep 20	Hadjuk Split	(Rd1/1L)	W 2-0	Robertson, Greaves	25,000
Sep 27	HADJUK SPLIT	(Rd1/2L)	W 4-3	Robertson 2, Gilzean, Venables	38,623
Nov 29	Olympique Lyon	(Rd2/1L)	L 0-1		10,997
Dec 13	OLYMPIQUE LYON	(Rd2/2L)	W 4-3	Greaves (1 pen) 2, Gilzean, Jones	41,895

FA Charity Shield

Aug 12	Manchester United		D 3-3	Jennings, Robertson, Saul	54,106

MANAGER: Bill Nicholson

CAPTAIN: Dave Mackay

TOP SCORER: Jimmy Greaves

BIGGEST WIN: 6-1 v Southampton, 6 April 1968, Football League Division One

HIGHEST ATTENDANCE: 63,500 v Manchester United, 27 January 1968, FA Cup 3rd Round

MAJOR TRANSFERS IN: Martin Chivers from Southampton

MAJOR TRANSFERS OUT: None

League and Cup Appearances

PLAYER	LEAGUE	CUP COMPETITION		OTHER	TOTAL
		FA CUP	ECWC		
Beal	34 (1)		4	2	40 (1)
Bond	5 (1)		1		6 (1)
Chivers	18	5			23
Clayton	1 (1)				1 (1)
England	31	5	2	1	39
Gilzean	32 (2)	5	4	1	42 (2)
Greaves	39	4	4	1	48
Hoy	5		2		7
Jennings	42	5	4	1	52
Jones	27 (3)	1 (3)		3	31 (6)
Kinnear	29 (1)	3	4	1	37 (1)
Knowles	42	5	4	1	52
Mackay	29	5	2	1	37
Mullery	41	5	3	1	50
Robertson	33 (1)	3	4	1	41 (1)
Saul	17 (2)		1	1	19 (2)
Venables	35 (1)	3 (1)	4	1	43 (2)
Want	2		2		4

Goalscorers

PLAYER	LEAGUE	CUP COMPETITION		OTHER	TOTAL
		FA CUP	ECWC		
Greaves	23	3	3		29
Jones	12	1	1		14
Chivers	7	3			10
Gilzean	8		2		10
Robertson	5	1	3	1	10
Saul	4			1	5
England	3				3
Venables	2		1		3
Mullery	2				2
Jennings				1	1
Kinnear	1				1
Mackay	1				1
Opp's o.gs.	2				2

Fact File

Pat Jennings scored in the FA Charity Shield against Manchester United with a punt downfield from his own penalty box.

Final Division One Table

		P	W	D	L	F	A	Pts
1	MANCHESTER C	42	26	6	10	86	43	58
2	MANCHESTER U	42	24	8	10	89	55	56
3	LIVERPOOL	42	22	11	9	71	40	55
4	LEEDS UNITED	42	22	9	11	71	41	53
5	EVERTON	42	23	6	13	67	40	52
6	CHELSEA	42	18	12	12	62	68	48
7	TOTTENHAM HOTSPUR	42	19	9	14	70	59	47
8	WBA	42	17	12	13	75	62	46
9	ARSENAL	42	17	10	15	60	56	44
10	NEWCASTLE U	42	13	15	14	54	67	41
11	NOTTINGHAM F	42	14	11	17	52	64	39
12	WEST HAM U	42	14	10	18	73	69	38
13	LEICESTER C	42	13	12	17	64	69	38
14	BURNLEY	42	14	10	18	64	71	38
15	BLACKBURN R	42	13	11	18	51	61	37
16	SOUTHAMPTON	42	13	11	18	66	83	37
17	WOLVERHAMPTON W	42	14	8	20	66	75	36
18	STOKE C	42	14	7	21	50	73	35
19	SHEFFIELD W	42	11	12	19	51	63	34
20	COVENTRY C	42	9	15	18	51	71	33
21	SHEFFIELD U	42	11	10	21	49	70	32
22	FULHAM	42	10	7	25	56	98	27

The Essential History of Tottenham Hotspur

Season 1968-69

Football League Division One

DATE	OPPONENTS	SCORE	GOALSCORERS	ATTENDANCE
Aug 10	ARSENAL	L 1-2	Greaves	56,280
Aug 17	Everton	W 2-0	Greaves, Chivers	56,570
Aug 21	WEST BROMWICH ALBION	D 1-1	Gilzean	35,746
Aug 24	SHEFFIELD WEDNESDAY	L 1-2	England	30,542
Aug 28	Manchester United	L 1-3	Greaves	62,649
Aug 31	Chelsea	D 2-2	Jones, Greaves	48,412
Sep 7	BURNLEY	W 7-0	Jones 2, Robertson, Greaves (1 pen) 3, Chivers	30,167
Sep 14	West Ham United	D 2-2	Greaves, Gilzean	35,802
Sep 17	Coventry City	W 2-1	Chivers, Gilzean	40,950
Sep 21	NOTTINGHAM FOREST	W 2-1	Jones, Greaves	37,386
Sep 28	Newcastle United	D 2-2	Mullery, Pearce	30,469
Oct 5	LEICESTER CITY	W 3-2	Greaves 3	36,622
Oct 9	MANCHESTER UNITED	D 2-2	Jones, Gilzean	56,205
Oct 12	Manchester City	L 0-4		38,019
Oct 19	LIVERPOOL	W 2-1	Greaves 2	44,122
Oct 26	Ipswich Town	W 1-0	Gilzean	30,251
Nov 2	STOKE CITY	D 1-1	Greaves	33,308
Nov 9	Leeds United	D 0-0		38,995
Nov 16	SUNDERLAND	W 5-1	Greaves 4, England	29,072
Nov 23	Southampton	L 1-2	Greaves	27,384
Dec 7	Wolverhampton Wanderers	L 0-2		30,846
Dec 14	MANCHESTER CITY	D 1-1	England	28,462
Dec 21	Liverpool	L 0-1		43,843
Jan 11	Stoke City	D 1-1	Jenkins	21,729
Jan 18	LEEDS UNITED	D 0-0		42,396
Jan 29	Queens Park Rangers	W 3-2	Beal, Gilzean, Jenkins	38,766
Feb 1	Sunderland	D 0-0		22,251
Feb 15	QUEENS PARK RANGERS	D 1-1	Greaves	30,013
Feb 22	WOLVERHAMPTON WANDERERS	D 1-1	Morgan	35,912
Mar 8	EVERTON	D 1-1	Morgan	44,882
Mar 18	IPSWICH TOWN	D 2-2	Knowles, Greaves (pen)	21,608
Mar 22	CHELSEA	W 1-0	Johnson	47,349
Mar 24	Arsenal	L 0-1		43,972
Mar 29	Burnley	D 2-2	Johnson, Pearce	14,547
Apr 2	NEWCASTLE UNITED	L 0-1		22,528
Apr 4	COVENTRY CITY	W 2-0	Johnson, Pearce	35,034
Apr 7	West Bromwich Albion	L 3-4	Knowles, Greaves (1 pen) 2	24,173
Apr 12	Nottingham Forest	W 2-0	Greaves, Gilzean	22,920
Apr 19	WEST HAM UNITED	W 1-0	Greaves	50,970
Apr 22	SOUTHAMPTON	W 2-1	Greaves, Morgan	29,201
Apr 29	Leicester City	L 0-1		35,833
May 12	Sheffield Wednesday	D 0-0		28,582

FA Cup

Jan 4	Walsall	(Rd3)	W 1-0	Greaves	18,779
Jan 25	WOLVERHAMPTON W	(Rd4)	W 2-1	Johnson, Greaves	48,985
Feb 12	ASTON VILLA	(Rd5)	W 3-2	England, Greaves (1 pen) 2	49,986
Mar 1	Manchester City	(Rd6)	L 0-1		48,872

League Cup

Sep 4	Aston Villa	(Rd2)	W 4-1	Jones, Chivers 3	24,775
Sep 25	EXETER CITY	(Rd3)	W 6-3	Greaves 3, Pearce 2, Venables	25,798
Oct 16	PETERBOROUGH UNITED	(Rd4)	W 1-0	Greaves	28,378
Oct 30	SOUTHAMPTON	(Rd5)	W 1-0	Collins	35,198
Nov 20	Arsenal	(SF/1L)	L 0-1		55,237
Dec 4	ARSENAL	(SF/2L)	D 1-1	Greaves	55,923

League and Cup Appearances

PLAYER	LEAGUE	CUP COMPETITION		TOTAL
		FA CUP	LC	
Beal	39	4	6	49
Bond	2		2 (1)	4 (1)
Chivers	10		1	11
Collins	22 (3)	4	3 (1)	29 (4)
England	36	4	5	45
Evans	5 (1)			5 (1)
Gilzean	37	4	6	47
Greaves	42	4	6	52
Jenkins	10 (1)	2 (1)		12 (4)
Jennings	42	4	6	52
Johnson	13 (3)	3	1	17 (3)
Jones	6 (1)		1	7 (1)
Kinnear	24	1	6	31
Knowles	36 (1)	4	5	45 (1)
Morgan	13			13
Mullery	41	4	6	51
Pearce	24 (3)	2	5	31 (3)
Pratt	8 (1)			8 (1)
Robertson	8 (3)		1	9 (3)
Venables	37	4	5	46
Want	7 (1)		1	8 (1)

Goalscorers

PLAYER	LEAGUE	CUP COMPETITION		TOTAL
		FA CUP	LC	
Greaves	27	4	5	36
Gilzean	7			7
Chivers	3		3	6
Jones	5		1	6
Pearce	3		2	5
England	3	1		4
Johnson	3	1		4
Morgan	3			3
Jenkins	2			2
Knowles	2			2
Beal	1			1
Collins			1	1
Mullery	1			1
Robertson	1			1
Venables			1	1

Fact File

In his last full season at the club Jimmy Greaves topped the scorers chart as he had for every season since he joined in 1961-62.

Final Division One Table

		P	W	D	L	F	A	Pts
1	LEEDS UNITED	42	27	13	2	66	26	67
2	LIVERPOOL	42	25	11	6	63	24	61
3	EVERTON	42	21	15	6	77	36	57
4	ARSENAL	42	22	12	8	56	27	56
5	CHELSEA	42	20	10	12	73	53	50
6	TOTTENHAM HOTSPUR	42	14	17	11	61	51	45
7	SOUTHAMPTON	42	16	13	13	57	48	45
8	WEST HAM U	42	13	18	11	66	50	44
9	NEWCASTLE U	42	15	14	13	61	55	44
10	WBA	42	16	11	15	64	67	43
11	MANCHESTER U	42	15	12	15	57	53	42
12	IPSWICH T	42	15	11	16	59	53	41
13	MANCHESTER C	42	15	10	17	64	55	40
14	BURNLEY	42	15	9	18	55	82	39
15	SHEFFIELD W	42	10	16	16	41	54	36
16	WOLVERHAMPTON W	42	10	15	17	41	58	35
17	BLACKBURN R	42	11	12	19	43	67	34
18	NOTTINGHAM F	42	10	13	19	45	57	33
19	STOKE C	42	9	15	18	40	63	33
20	COVENTRY C	42	10	11	21	46	64	31
21	LEICESTER C	42	9	12	21	39	68	30
22	QPR	42	4	10	28	39	95	18

MANAGER: Bill Nicholson

CAPTAIN: Alan Mullery

TOP SCORER: Jimmy Greaves

BIGGEST WIN: 7-0 v Burnley (H), 7 September 1968, Football League Division One

HIGHEST ATTENDANCE: 62,649 v Manchester United, 28 August 1968, Football League Division One

MAJOR TRANSFERS IN: David Jenkins from Arsenal, Roger Morgan from Queens Park Rangers

MAJOR TRANSFERS OUT: Cliff Jones to Fulham, Dave Mackay to Derby County, Jimmy Robertson to Arsenal

Season 1969-70

Football League Division One

DATE	OPPONENTS	SCORE	GOALSCORERS	ATTENDANCE
Aug 9	Leeds United	L 1-3	Greaves	35,804
Aug 13	BURNLEY	W 4-0	Collins, Pearce, Greaves, Chivers	35,920
Aug 16	LIVERPOOL	L 0-2		50,474
Aug 19	Burnley	W 2-0	Collins, Pearce	19,485
Aug 23	Crystal Palace	W 2-0	Pearce, Chivers	39,494
Aug 27	CHELSEA	D 1-1	Pearce	47,661
Aug 30	IPSWICH TOWN	W 3-2	Mullery, Greaves, Gilzean	33,333
Sep 6	West Ham United	W 1-0	Pearce	40,561
Sep 13	MANCHESTER CITY	L 0-3		41,644
Sep 16	Arsenal	W 3-2	Chivers, Gilzean, Pratt	55,280
Sep 20	Derby County	L 0-5		41,826
Sep 27	SUNDERLAND	L 0-1		30,523
Oct 4	Southampton	D 2-2	Greaves, Gilzean	23,901
Oct 7	Liverpool	D 0-0		46,518
Oct 11	WOLVERHAMPTON WANDERERS	L 0-1		36,736
Oct 18	NEWCASTLE UNITED	W 2-1	Greaves 2	33,287
Oct 25	Stoke City	D 1-1	Gilzean	19,569
Nov 1	SHEFFIELD WEDNESDAY	W 1-0	Morgan	31,656
Nov 8	Nottingham Forest	D 2-2	Pearce, Greaves	24,034
Nov 15	WEST BROMWICH ALBION	W 2-0	Chivers, Morgan	28,340
Nov 22	Manchester United	L 1-3	Chivers	53,053
Dec 6	Coventry City	L 2-3	England, Gilzean	28,443
Dec 13	Manchester City	D 1-1	Johnson	29,216
Dec 20	WEST HAM UNITED	L 0-2		28,375
Dec 26	CRYSTAL PALACE	W 2-0	Mullery, Perryman	32,845
Dec 27	Ipswich Town	L 0-2		24,658
Jan 10	DERBY COUNTY	W 2-1	Greaves, Morgan	38,645
Jan 17	Sunderland	L 1-2	Morgan	13,993
Jan 31	SOUTHAMPTON	L 0-1		27,693
Feb 7	Wolverhampton Wanderers	D 2-2	Chivers 2	27,295
Feb 14	LEEDS UNITED	D 1-1	Cooper o.g.	41,723
Feb 21	STOKE CITY	W 1-0	Mullery	29,976
Feb 28	Newcastle United	W 2-1	Pearce, Chivers	34,827
Mar 11	EVERTON	L 0-1		27,764
Mar 14	Everton	L 2-3	Gilzean, Bond (pen)	51,533
Mar 21	COVENTRY CITY	L 1-2	Peters	34,942
Mar 27	NOTTINGHAM FOREST	W 4-1	Gilzean 2, Chivers 2	36,947
Mar 28	West Bromwich Albion	D 1-1	Peters	24,890
Mar 30	Sheffield Wednesday	W 1-0	Mullery	30,340
Apr 4	Chelsea	L 0-1		44,925
Apr 13	MANCHESTER UNITED	W 2-1	Gilzean, Chivers	41,808
May 2	ARSENAL	W 1-0	Gilzean	46,969

FA Cup

Jan 3	Bradford City	(Rd3) D 2-2	Greaves, Morgan	23,000
Jan 7	BRADFORD CITY	(R) W 5-0	Pearce 2, Greaves 2, Morgan	36,039
Jan 24	CRYSTAL PALACE	(Rd4) D 0-0		43,948
Jan 28	Crystal Palace	(R) L 0-1		45,980

League Cup

Sep 3	Wolverhampton Wanderers	(Rd2) L 0-1		34,017

League and Cup Appearances

PLAYER	LEAGUE	CUP COMPETITION		TOTAL
		FA CUP	LC	
Beal	29 (2)	4	1	34 (2)
Bond	12			12
Chivers	27 (4)	1 (2)	1	29 (6)
Collins	16 (2)		1	17 (2)
England	36	4	1	41
Evans	15 (1)			15 (1)
Gilzean	34 (2)	4		38 (2)
Greaves	28	4	1	33
Hancock	1			1
Jenkins	1 (2)			1 (2)
Jennings	41	4	1	46
Johnson	5	1		6
Kinnear	9	4		13
Knowles	33	4	1	38
Morgan	37	4	1	42
Mullery	41	4	1	46
Naylor	3			3
Pearce	25 (6)	2 (2)	1	28 (8)
Perryman	23	4		27
Peters	7			7
Pratt	12		0 (1)	12 (1)
Want	26 (3)		1	27 (3)
Woolcott	1			1

Goalscorers

PLAYER	LEAGUE	CUP COMPETITION		TOTAL
		FA CUP	LC	
Chivers	11			11
Greaves	8	3		11
Gilzean	10			10
Pearce	7	2		9
Morgan	4	2		6
Mullery	4			4
Collins	2			2
Peters	2			2
Bond	1			1
England	1			1
Johnson	1			1
Perryman	1			1
Pratt	1			1
Opp's o.gs.	1			1

Fact File

Spurs Football League game against Everton on 17 December was abandoned after 29 minutes when the White Hart Lane floodlights failed. The match was replayed on 11 March.

MANAGER: Bill Nicholson

CAPTAIN: Alan Mullery

TOP SCORER: Martin Chivers and Jimmy Greaves

BIGGEST WIN: 5-0 v Bradford City (H), 7 January 1970, FA Cup 3rd Round replay

HIGHEST ATTENDANCE: 53,053 v Manchester United, 22 November 1969, Football League Division One

MAJOR TRANSFERS IN: Martin Peters from West Ham United

MAJOR TRANSFERS OUT: Jimmy Greaves to West Ham United

Final Division One Table

		P	W	D	L	F	A	Pts
1	EVERTON	42	29	8	5	72	34	66
2	LEEDS UNITED	42	21	15	6	84	49	57
3	CHELSEA	42	21	13	8	70	50	55
4	DERBY CO	42	22	9	11	64	37	53
5	LIVERPOOL	42	20	11	11	65	42	51
6	COVENTRY C	42	19	11	12	58	48	49
7	NEWCASTLE U	42	17	13	12	57	35	47
8	MANCHESTER U	42	14	17	11	66	61	45
9	STOKE C	42	15	15	12	56	52	45
10	MANCHESTER C	42	16	11	15	55	48	43
11	TOTTENHAM HOTSPUR	42	17	9	16	54	55	43
12	ARSENAL	42	12	18	12	51	45	42
13	WOLVERHAMPTON W	42	12	16	14	55	57	40
14	BURNLEY	42	12	15	15	56	61	39
15	NOTTINGHAM F	42	10	18	14	50	71	38
16	WBA	42	14	9	19	58	66	37
17	WEST HAM U	42	12	12	18	51	60	36
18	IPSWICH T	42	10	11	21	40	63	31
19	SOUTHAMPTON	42	6	17	19	46	67	29
20	CRYSTAL P	42	6	15	21	34	68	27
21	BLACKBURN R	42	6	14	22	30	68	26
22	SHEFFIELD W	42	8	9	25	40	71	25

Season 1970-71

Football League Division One

DATE	OPPONENTS	SCORE	GOALSCORERS	ATTENDANCE
Aug 15	WEST HAM UNITED	D 2-2	Gilzean 2	53,640
Aug 19	LEEDS UNITED	L 0-2		39,927
Aug 22	Wolverhampton Wanderers	W 3-0	Mullery, Chivers, Morgan	23,896
Aug 25	Southampton	D 0-0		27,149
Aug 29	COVENTRY CITY	W 1-0	Chivers	27,103
Sep 1	Huddersfield Town	D 1-1	Chivers	26,701
Sep 5	Arsenal	L 0-2		48,931
Sep 12	BLACKPOOL	W 3-0	Mullery (pen), Peters 2	19,894
Sep 19	Crystal Palace	W 3-0	Mullery, Chivers 2	41,308
Sep 26	MANCHESTER CITY	W 2-0	Gilzean, Chivers	42,490
Oct 3	Derby County	D 1-1	Peters	36,007
Oct 10	LIVERPOOL	W 1-0	Peters	44,547
Oct 17	West Ham United	D 2-2	Mullery, England	42,322
Oct 24	STOKE CITY	W 3-0	Gilzean, Chivers 2	36,238
Oct 31	Nottingham Forest	W 1-0	Chivers	25,301
Nov 7	BURNLEY	W 4-0	Gilzean, Perryman, Chivers 2	30,524
Nov 14	Chelsea	W 2-0	Mullery, Pearce	61,277
Nov 21	NEWCASTLE UNITED	L 1-2	Chivers	38,873
Nov 28	Everton	D 0-0		44,301
Dec 5	MANCHESTER UNITED	D 2-2	Gilzean, Peters	55,693
Dec 12	West Bromwich Albion	L 1-3	Chivers	26,584
Dec 19	WOLVERHAMPTON WANDERERS	D 0-0		30,544
Jan 9	Leeds United	W 2-1	Chivers 2	43,867
Jan 16	SOUTHAMPTON	L 1-3	Chivers	39,486
Jan 30	EVERTON	W 2-1	Gilzean, Chivers	42,105
Feb 6	Manchester United	L 1-2	Peters	38,416
Feb 17	WEST BROMWICH ALBION	D 2-2	Mullery (pen), Gilzean	22,695
Feb 20	Newcastle United	L 0-1		31,718
Mar 10	NOTTINGHAM FOREST	L 0-1		21,697
Mar 13	CHELSEA	W 2-1	Chivers, Peters	49,292
Mar 20	Burnley	D 0-0		16,376
Mar 23	Ipswich Town	W 2-1	Gilzean, Peters	21,718
Apr 3	Coventry City	D 0-0		22,947
Apr 7	DERBY COUNTY	W 2-1	Chivers, Pearce	25,627
Apr 10	IPSWICH TOWN	W 2-0	Chivers, Morris o.g.	28,708
Apr 12	Blackpool	D 0-0		16,541
Apr 17	Liverpool	D 0-0		46,363
Apr 24	CRYSTAL PALACE	W 2-0	Perryman, Blyth o.g.	28,619
Apr 28	HUDDERSFIELD TOWN	D 1-1	Chivers	18,959
May 1	Manchester City	W 1-0	Perryman	19,761
May 3	ARSENAL	L 0-1		51,992
May 5	Stoke City	W 1-0	Peters	14,019

FA Cup

Jan 2	SHEFFIELD WEDNESDAY	(Rd3) W 4-1	Mullery (pen), Gilzean 2, Peters	34,170
Jan 23	Carlisle United	(Rd4) W 3-2	Gilzean, Peters, Neighbour	25,369
Feb 13	NOTTINGHAM FOREST	(Rd5) W 2-1	Gilzean, Chivers	46,366
Mar 6	Liverpool	(Rd6) D 0-0		54,731
Mar 16	LIVERPOOL	(R) L 0-1		56,283

League Cup

Sep 9	SWANSEA CITY	(Rd2) W 3-0	Perryman, Peters, Morgan	15,848
Oct 7	SHEFFIELD UNITED	(Rd3) W 2-1	Chivers, Pearce	23,559
Oct 28	WEST BROMWICH ALBION	(Rd4) W 5-0	Gilzean 2, Peters 3	31,598
Nov 18	COVENTRY CITY	(Rd5) W 4-1	Gilzean, Chivers 3	31,864
Dec 16	Bristol City	(SF/1L) D 1-1	Gilzean	30,201
Dec 23	BRISTOL CITY	(SF/2L) W 2-0	Chivers, Pearce	29,982
Feb 27	Aston Villa *	(F) W 2-0	Chivers 2	100,000

* played at Wembley, London

Texaco Cup

Sep 16	DUNFERMLINE ATHLETIC	(Rd1/1L) W 4-0	England, Chivers 3	16,388
Sep 29	Dunfermline Athletic	(Rd1/2L) W 3-0	Chivers, Peters 2	9,000
Oct 21	MOTHERWELL	(Rd2/1L) W 3-2	Chivers, Peters 2	19,670
Nov 3	Motherwell	(Rd2/2L) L 1-3	Pearce	22,688

MANAGER: Bill Nicholson

CAPTAIN: Alan Mullery

TOP SCORER: Martin Chivers

BIGGEST WIN: 5-0 v West Bromwich Albion (H), 28 October 1970, Football League Cup 4th Round

HIGHEST ATTENDANCE: 100,000 v Aston Villa, 27 February 1971, Football League Cup Final

League and Cup Appearances

PLAYER	LEAGUE	CUP COMPETITION		OTHER	TOTAL
		FA CUP	LC		
Beal	32	4	7	3	46
Bond	1 (1)				1 (1)
Chivers	42	5	7	4	58
Collins	26	4	1		31
England	22		6	4	32
Evans	7				7
Gilzean	38	3	7	4	52
Hancock	2		1	2	5
Jennings	40	5	6	2	53
Johnson	0 (3)				0 (3)
Kinnear	35	5	7	4	51
Knowles	38	5	6	3	52
Morgan	8		2	2	12
Mullery	41	5	7	4	57
Naylor	3 (1)	2		2	7 (1)
Neighbour	12 (5)	5	2 (1)	0 (1)	19 (7)
Pearce	23 (10)		3 (3)	2 (2)	28 (15)
Perryman	42	5	6	3	56
Peters	42	5	7	4	58
Pratt	4 (2)	2	1		7 (2)
Want	4	1	1		6

Goalscorers

PLAYER	LEAGUE	CUP COMPETITION		OTHER	TOTAL
		FA CUP	LC		
Chivers	21	1	7	5	34
Peters	9	2	4	4	19
Gilzean	9	4	4		17
Mullery	6	1			7
Pearce	2		2	1	5
Perryman	3		1		4
England	1			1	2
Morgan	1		1		2
Neighbour		1			1
Opp's o.gs.	2				2

Fact File

Liverpool were the first club to win an FA Cup replay at White Hart Lane since Blackburn Rovers in 1911.

Final Division Two Table

		P	W	D	L	F	A	Pts
1	ARSENAL	42	29	7	6	71	29	65
2	LEEDS UNITED	42	27	10	5	72	30	64
3	TOTTENHAM HOTSPUR	42	19	14	9	54	33	52
4	WOLVERHAMPTON W	42	22	8	12	64	54	52
5	LIVERPOOL	42	17	17	8	42	24	51
6	CHELSEA	42	18	15	9	52	42	51
7	SOUTHAMPTON	42	17	12	13	56	44	46
8	MANCHESTER U	42	16	11	15	65	66	43
9	DERBY CO	42	16	10	16	56	54	42
10	COVENTRY C	42	16	10	16	37	38	42
11	MANCHESTER C	42	12	17	13	47	42	41
12	NEWCASTLE U	42	14	13	15	44	33	41
13	STOKE CITY	42	12	13	17	44	48	37
14	EVERTON	42	12	13	17	54	60	37
15	HUDDERSFIELD T	42	11	14	17	40	49	36
16	NOTTINGHAM F	42	14	8	20	42	61	36
17	WBA	42	10	15	17	58	75	35
18	CRYSTAL P	42	12	11	19	39	57	35
19	IPSWICH T	42	12	10	20	42	48	34
20	WEST HAM U	42	10	14	18	47	60	34
21	BURNLEY	42	7	13	22	29	63	27
22	BLACKPOOL	42	4	15	23	34	66	23

Season 1971-72

Football League Division One

DATE	OPPONENTS	SCORE	GOALSCORERS	ATTENDANCE
Aug 14	Wolverhampton Wanderers	D 2-2	Chivers, Gilzean	30,495
Aug 18	NEWCASTLE UNITED	D 0-0		42,715
Aug 21	HUDDERSFIELD TOWN	W 4-1	Chivers 2, Gilzean 2	33,260
Aug 25	Leeds United *	D 1-1	Gilzean	25,099
Aug 28	Manchester City	L 0-4		33,683
Sep 4	LIVERPOOL	W 2-0	Chivers, Peters	50,124
Sep 11	Sheffield United	D 2-2	Peters, Gilzean	41,663
Sep 18	CRYSTAL PALACE	W 3-0	Mullery, Chivers, Peters (pen)	37,239
Sep 25	Coventry City	L 0-1		26,517
Oct 2	IPSWICH TOWN	W 2-1	Chivers, Peters	33,562
Oct 9	Derby County	D 2-2	Pearce, Chivers	35,744
Oct 16	WOLVERHAMPTON WANDERERS	W 4-1	Neighbour, Chivers 2, Gilzean	36,582
Oct 23	NOTTINGHAM FOREST	W 6-1	Mullery, Chivers, Peters (1 pen) 2, Pearce 2	35,846
Oct 30	Stoke City	L 0-2		28,540
Nov 6	EVERTON	W 3-0	Pratt, Chivers 2	40,005
Nov 13	Manchester United	L 1-3	Chivers	54,058
Nov 20	WEST BROMWICH ALBION	W 3-2	England, Gilzean 2	31,895
Nov 24	ARSENAL	D 1-1	Chivers	52,884
Nov 27	Chelsea	L 0-1		52,581
Dec 4	SOUTHAMPTON	W 1-0	Gilzean	31,351
Dec 11	Leicester City	W 1-0	Peters	30,721
Dec 18	Liverpool	D 0-0		43,409
Dec 27	WEST HAM UNITED	L 0-1		53,868
Jan 1	Crystal Palace	D 1-1	Chivers	35,571
Jan 8	MANCHESTER CITY	D 1-1	Peters	36,470
Jan 22	Newcastle United	L 1-3	Gilzean	30,113
Jan 29	LEEDS UNITED	W 1-0	Chivers	46,774
Feb 12	Nottingham Forest	W 1-0	Peters	20,209
Feb 19	STOKE CITY	W 2-0	Chivers 2	32,841
Mar 1	Everton	D 1-1	Peters	21,601
Mar 4	MANCHESTER UNITED	W 2-0	Perryman, Chivers	54,814
Mar 11	DERBY COUNTY	L 0-1		36,310
Mar 25	SHEFFIELD UNITED	W 2-0	Gilzean, Chivers	30,984
Mar 28	Huddersfield Town	D 1-1	Pearce	16,123
Mar 31	COVENTRY CITY	W 1-0	Chivers	32,542
Apr 1	West Ham United	L 0-2		30,763
Apr 3	Ipswich Town	L 1-2	Chivers	24,302
Apr 8	West Bromwich Albion	D 1-1	Chivers	20,862
Apr 15	CHELSEA	W 3-0	Chivers 2, Coates	45,799
Apr 22	Southampton	D 0-0		24,914
Apr 29	LEICESTER CITY	W 4-3	Knowles (1 pen) 2, England, Pearce	19,631
May 11	Arsenal	W 2-0	Mullery, Coates	42,038

* played at Boothferry Park, ?

FA Cup

Jan 15	CARLISLE UNITED	(Rd3) D 1-1	Gilzean	33,702
Jan 18	Carlisle United	(R) W 3-1	Gilzean, Chivers 2	21,560
Feb 5	ROTHERHAM UNITED	(Rd4) W 2-0	Gilzean, Peters	36,903
Feb 26	Everton	(Rd5) W 2-0	Gilzean, Peters	50,511
Mar 18	Leeds United	(Rd6) L 1-2	Pratt	43,937

League Cup

Sep 8	West Bromwich Albion	(Rd2) W 1-0	Pearce	26,185
Oct 6	Torquay United	(Rd3) W 4-1	Pearce, Chivers 2, Peters (pen)	20,213
Oct 27	PRESTON NORTH END	(Rd4) D 1-1†	Chivers	30,338
Nov 8	Preston North End	(R) W 2-1	Perryman, Chivers	27,239
Nov 17	BLACKPOOL	(Rd5) W 2-0	Chivers, Peters	30,099
Dec 22	Chelsea	(SF/1L) L 2-3	Naylor, Chivers	43,330
Jan 5	CHELSEA	(SF/2L) D 2-2	Chivers, Peters (pen)	52,755

† after extra-time

UEFA Cup

Sep 14	Keflavik	(Rd1/1L) W 6-1	Mullery 2, Coates, Gilzean 3	18,000
Sep 28	KEFLAVIK	(Rd1/2L) W 9-0	Knowles, Coates, Perryman, Chivers 3, Holder, Gilzean 2	23,818
Oct 20	FC Nantes	(Rd2/1L) D 0-0		20,033
Nov 2	FC NANTES	(Rd2/2L) W 1-0	Peters	32,630
Dec 8	RAPID BUCHAREST	(Rd3/1L) W 3-0	Chivers, Peters	30,702
Dec 15	Rapid Bucharest	(Rd3/2L) W 2-0	Chivers, Pearce	12,000
Mar 7	UT Arad	(Rd4/1L) W 2-0	England, Morgan	20,000
Mar 21	UT ARAD	(Rd4/2L) D 1-1	Gilzean	30,253
Apr 5	AC MILAN	(SF/1L) W 2-1	Perryman 2	42,064
Apr 19	AC Milan	(SF/2L) D 1-1	Mullery	68,482
May 3	WOLVERHAMPTON W	(F/1L) W 2-1	Chivers 2	38,362
May 17	Wolverhampton Wanderers	(F/2L) D 1-1	Mullery	54,303

League and Cup Appearances

PLAYER	LEAGUE	CUP COMPETITION			TOTAL
		FA CUP	LC	UEFA	
Beal	32	5	7	10	54
Chivers	39	5	7	11	62
Coates	32	3 (1)	5	9	49 (1)
Collins	6 (1)	0 (1)	0 (1)	1 (1)	7 (4)
Daines	1				1
England	38	5	7	11	61
Evans	22	4	5	6	37
Gilzean	38	5	4	11	58
Holder	4 (2)			0 (1)	4 (3)
Jennings	41	5	7	12	65
Kinnear	20 (1)	1	2	6	29 (1)
Knowles	34	4	7	12	57
Morgan	8 (2)	2		2 (1)	12 (3)
Mullery	18		3	7	28
Naylor	12	1	1	2 (2)	16 (2)
Neighbour	12 (2)	2	2 (1)	3 (1)	19 (4)
Pearce	9 (6)	0 (1)	3 (2)	0 (5)	12 (14)
Perryman	39	5	6	12	62
Peters	35	5	7	12	59
John Pratt	15 (8)	2	4	5 (1)	26 (9)
Souness				0 (1)	0 (1)
Want	7	1			8

Goalscorers

PLAYER	LEAGUE	CUP COMPETITION			TOTAL
		FA CUP	LC	UEFA	
Chivers	25	2	7	8	42
Gilzean	11	4		6	21
Peters	10	2	3	2	17
Pearce	5		2	1	8
Mullery	3			4	7
Perryman	1		1	3	5
Coates	2			2	4
England	2			1	3
Knowles	2			1	3
Pratt	1	1			2
Holder	1				1
Morgan	1				1
Naylor	1				1
Neighbour	1				1

MANAGER: Bill Nicholson

CAPTAIN: Alan Mullery

TOP SCORER: Martin Chivers

BIGGEST WIN: 9-0 v Keflavik (H), 28 September 1971, UEFA Cup 1st Round 2nd leg

HIGHEST ATTENDANCE: 68,482 v AC Milan, 19 April 1972, UEFA Cup Semi-final 2nd leg

MAJOR TRANSFERS IN: Ralph Coates from Burnley

Final Division One Table

		P	W	D	L	F	A	Pts
1	DERBY CO	42	24	10	8	69	33	58
2	LEEDS UNITED	42	24	9	9	73	31	57
3	LIVERPOOL	42	24	9	9	64	30	57
4	MANCHESTER C	42	23	11	8	77	45	57
5	ARSENAL	42	22	8	12	58	40	52
6	TOTTENHAM HOTSPUR	42	19	13	10	63	42	51
7	CHELSEA	42	18	12	12	58	49	48
8	MANCHESTER U	42	19	10	13	69	61	48
9	WOLVERHAMPTON W	42	18	11	13	65	57	47
10	SHEFFIELD U	42	17	12	13	61	60	46
11	NEWCASTLE U	42	15	11	16	49	52	41
12	LEICESTER C	42	13	13	16	41	46	39
13	IPSWICH T	42	11	16	15	39	53	38
14	WEST HAM U	42	12	12	18	47	51	36
15	EVERTON	42	9	18	15	37	48	36
16	WBA	42	12	11	19	42	54	35
17	STOKE C	42	10	15	17	39	56	35
18	COVENTRY C	42	9	15	18	44	67	33
19	SOUTHAMPTON	42	12	7	23	52	80	31
20	CRYSTAL P	42	8	13	21	39	65	29
21	NOTTINGHAM F	42	8	9	25	47	81	25
22	HUDDERSFIELD T	42	6	13	23	27	59	25

The Essential History of Tottenham Hotspur

Season 1972-73

Football League Division One

DATE	OPPONENTS	SCORE	GOALSCORERS	ATTENDANCE
Aug 12	COVENTRY CITY	W 2-1	Peters 2	33,884
Aug 16	West Bromwich Albion	W 1-0	Peters	19,175
Aug 19	Wolverhampton Wanderers	L 2-3	Pratt, Peters	24,238
Aug 23	BIRMINGHAM CITY	W 2-0	Chivers, Coates	30,798
Aug 26	LEEDS UNITED	D 0-0		41,191
Aug 30	Newcastle United	W 1-0	Kinnear	27,912
Sep 2	Ipswich Town	D 1-1	Peters (pen)	23,140
Sep 9	CRYSTAL PALACE	W 2-1	England, Peters (pen)	28,545
Sep 16	Manchester City	L 1-2	Peters	31,755
Sep 23	WEST HAM UNITED	W 1-0	Lampard o.g.	51,291
Sep 30	Derby County	L 1-2	Perryman	32,133
Oct 7	STOKE CITY	W 4-3	Pratt 2, Gilzean, Coates	31,951
Oct 14	Norwich City	L 1-2	Chivers	34,445
Oct 21	CHELSEA	L 0-1		47,429
Oct 28	Manchester United	W 4-1	Peters 4	52,497
Nov 4	Birmingham City	D 0-0		38,504
Nov 11	WEST BROMWICH ALBION	D 1-1	Chivers	25,875
Nov 18	Leicester City	W 1-0	Chivers	22,707
Nov 25	LIVERPOOL	L 1-2	Chivers	45,497
Dec 2	Southampton	D 1-1	Chivers	16,486
Dec 9	ARSENAL	L 1-2	Peters	47,515
Dec 16	Everton	L 1-3	Neighbour	31,129
Dec 23	SHEFFIELD UNITED	W 2-0	Perryman, Chivers	19,877
Dec 26	West Ham United	D 2-2	Peters, Pearce	37,397
Jan 6	Leeds United	L 1-2	Gilzean	32,404
Jan 20	IPSWICH TOWN	L 0-1		33,014
Jan 27	Crystal Palace	D 0-0		44,536
Feb 10	MANCHESTER CITY	L 2-3	Chivers 2	30,944
Feb 17	Coventry City	W 1-0	Pratt	26,854
Feb 24	EVERTON	W 3-0	Gilzean, Chivers, Pearce	27,427
Mar 10	NORWICH CITY	W 3-0	Chivers (1 pen) 2, Pearce	25,088
Mar 14	Stoke City	D 1-1	Pearce	23,351
Mar 24	MANCHESTER UNITED	D 1-1	Chivers	50,017
Mar 31	Liverpool	D 1-1	Gilzean	48,477
Apr 3	Chelsea	W 1-0	Pratt	25,536
Apr 7	SOUTHAMPTON	L 1-2	Peters	23,693
Apr 14	Arsenal	D 1-1	Chivers	50,863
Apr 18	DERBY COUNTY	W 1-0	McFarland o.g.	22,659
Apr 21	LEICESTER CITY	D 1-1	Gilzean	23,312
Apr 28	NEWCASTLE UNITED	W 3-2	Chivers (1 pen) 2, Peters	21,721
Apr 30	WOLVERHAMPTON WANDERERS	D 2-2	Coates, Collins	16,942
May 2	Sheffield United	L 2-3	Collins, Chivers (pen)	20,716

FA Cup

Jan 13	Margate	(Rd3) W 6-0	Knowles, Pratt, Pearce, Chivers 2, Peters	8,500
Feb 3	Derby County	(Rd4) D 1-1	Chivers	37,895
Feb 7	DERBY COUNTY	(R) L 3-5*	England (pen), Gilzean, Chivers	52,736

League Cup

Sep 6	HUDDERSFIELD TOWN	(Rd2) W 2-1	Gilzean, Chivers	21,422
Oct 3	Middlesbrough	(Rd3) D 1-1	Pearce	23,822
Oct 11	MIDDLESBROUGH	(R) D 0-0*		19,256
Oct 30	MIDDLESBROUGH	(R2) W 2-1	Gilzean, Peters	19,287
Nov 1	MILLWALL	(Rd4) W 2-0	Perryman, Peters	28,904
Dec 4	Liverpool	(Rd5) D 1-1	Peters	48,677
Dec 6	LIVERPOOL	(R) W 3-1	Pratt, Chivers 2	34,565
Dec 20	Wolverhampton W	(SF/1L) W 2-1	Pratt, Peters	28,327
Dec 30	WOLVERHAMPTON W	(SF/2L) D 2-2	Chivers, Peters	41,653
Mar 3	Norwich City †	(F) W 1-0	Coates	100,000

*after extra time. † played at Wembley, London

UEFA Cup

Sep 13	Lyn Oslo	(Rd1/1L) W 6-3	Pratt, Gilzean 2, Chivers 2, Peters	10,770
Sep 27	LYN OSLO	(Rd1/2L) W 6-0	Chivers 3, Pearce, Coates 2	21,109
Oct 25	OLYMPIAKOS PIRAEUS	(Rd2/1L) W 4-0	Pearce 2, Chivers, Coates	27,815
Nov 8	Olympiakos Piraeus	(Rd2/2L) L 0-1		35,000
Nov 29	RS BELGRADE	(Rd3/1L) W 2-0	Gilzean, Chivers	23,958
Dec 13	RS Belgrade	(Rd3/2L) L 0-1		70,000
Mar 7	VITORIA SETUBAL	(Rd4/1L) W 1-0	Evans	30,469
Mar 21	Vitoria Setubal	(Rd4/2L) L 1-2	Chivers	30,000
Apr 10	Liverpool	(SF/1L) L 0-1		42,174
Apr 25	LIVERPOOL	(SF/2L) W 2-1	Peters 2	46,919

Fact File

In October Spurs met Feyenoord in a testimonial for Jimmy Greaves, the first player to be honoured in such a way since the turn of the century. The great man scored within three minutes.

League and Cup Appearances

PLAYER	LEAGUE	CUP COMPETITION			TOTAL
		FA CUP	LC	UEFA	
Beal	24	2	3	6	35
Chivers	38	3	10	10	61
Clarke	0 (1)				0 (1)
Coates	29 (3)	3	4 (3)	7	43 (6)
Collins	7				7
Daines	2				2
Dillon	8		1	1	10
England	31	3	10	10	54
Evans	23 (1)	2	6	5 (3)	36 (4)
Gilzean	35	3	8	9	55
Holder			0 (1)		0 (1)
Jennings	40	3	10	10	63
Kinnear	24	1	4	6	35
Knowles	35	3	10	10	58
Naylor	14 (2)	1	7 (1)	3 (3)	25 (6)
Neighbour	6 (1)		0 (1)	0 (1)	6 (3)
Pearce	27 (8)	0 (3)	9 (1)	8 (2)	44 (14)
Perryman	41	3	10	10	64
Peters	41	3	8	8	60
Pratt	37 (1)	3	10	7	57 (1)

Goalscorers

PLAYER	LEAGUE	CUP COMPETITION			TOTAL
		FA CUP	LC	UEFA	
Chivers	17	4	4	8	33
Peters	15	1	5	3	24
Gilzean	5	1	2	3	11
Pearce	4	1	1	3	9
Pratt	5	1	2	1	9
Coates	3		1	3	7
Perryman	2		1		3
Collins	2				2
England	1	1			2
Evans	1			1	1
Kinnear	1				1
Knowles		1			1
Neighbour	1				1
Opp's o.gs.	2				2

MANAGER: Bill Nicholson

CAPTAIN: Alan Mullery/Martin Peters

TOP SCORER: Martin Chivers

BIGGEST WIN: 6-0 v Lyn Oslo (H), 27 September 1972, UAF Cup 1st Round 2nd leg; 6-0 v Margate (A), 13 January 1973, FA Cup 3rd Round

HIGHEST ATTENDANCE: 100,000 v Norwich City, 3 March 1973, Football League Cup Final

MAJOR TRANSFERS OUT: Alan Mullery to Fulham

Final Division One Table

		P	W	D	L	F	A	Pts
1	LIVERPOOL	42	25	10	7	72	42	60
2	ARSENAL	42	23	11	8	57	43	57
3	LEEDS UNITED	42	21	11	10	71	45	53
4	IPSWICH T	42	17	14	11	55	45	48
5	WOLVERHAMPTON W	42	18	11	13	66	54	47
6	WEST HAM U	42	17	12	13	67	53	46
7	DERBY CO	42	19	8	15	56	54	46
8	TOTTENHAM HOTSPUR	42	16	13	13	58	48	45
9	NEWCASTLE U	42	16	13	13	60	51	45
10	BIRMINGHAM C	42	15	12	15	53	54	42
11	MANCHESTER C	42	15	11	16	57	60	41
12	CHELSEA	42	13	14	15	49	41	40
13	SOUTHAMPTON	42	11	18	13	47	52	40
14	SHEFFIELD U	42	15	10	17	51	59	40
15	STOKE C	42	14	10	18	61	56	38
16	LEICESTER C	42	10	17	15	40	46	37
17	EVERTON	42	13	11	18	41	49	37
18	MANCHESTER U	42	12	13	17	44	60	37
19	COVENTRY C	42	13	9	20	40	55	35
20	NORWICH CITY	42	11	10	21	36	63	32
21	CRYSTAL P	42	9	12	21	41	58	30
22	WBA	42	9	10	23	38	62	28

Season 1973-74

Football League Division One

DATE	OPPONENTS	SCORE	GOALSCORERS	ATTENDANCE
Aug 25	Coventry City	L 0-1		25,094
Aug 28	Birmingham City	W 2-1	Peters 2	37,754
Sep 1	LEEDS UNITED	L 0-3		42,091
Sep 5	BURNLEY	L 2-3	Knowles, Chivers	25,543
Sep 8	West Ham United	W 1-0	Chivers	30,888
Sep 11	Burnley	D 2-2	Holder, Peters	25,158
Sep 15	SHEFFIELD UNITED	L 1-2	Chivers	26,350
Sep 22	Liverpool	L 2-3	Chivers, Peters	42,901
Sep 29	DERBY COUNTY	W 1-0	Coates	31,408
Oct 6	Ipswich Town	D 0-0		23,903
Oct 13	ARSENAL	W 2-0	Gilzean, Chivers	41,856
Oct 20	Norwich City	D 1-1	Gilzean	24,819
Oct 27	NEWCASTLE UNITED	L 0-2		31,259
Nov 3	Everton	D 1-1	Perryman	37,827
Nov 10	MANCHESTER UNITED	W 2-1	Knowles, Chivers	42,756
Nov 17	Southampton	D 1-1	Chivers	22,882
Nov 24	WOLVERHAMPTON WANDERERS	L 1-3	Chivers (pen)	22,541
Dec 1	Leicester City	L 0-3		22,088
Dec 8	STOKE CITY	W 2-1	Evans, Pratt	14,034
Dec 15	MANCHESTER CITY	L 0-2		17,066
Dec 22	Derby County	L 0-2		23,672
Dec 26	QUEENS PARK RANGERS	D 0-0		30,762
Dec 29	WEST HAM UNITED	W 2-0	Pratt, Chivers	33,176
Jan 1	Leeds United	D 1-1	McGrath	46,545
Jan 12	Sheffield United	D 2-2	McGrath, Coates	20,367
Jan 19	COVENTRY CITY	W 2-1	Peters 2	20,985
Feb 2	Manchester City	D 0-0		24,652
Feb 6	BIRMINGHAM CITY	W 4-2	Dillon, Chivers 3	14,345
Feb 16	Arsenal	W 1-0	McGrath	38,892
Feb 23	IPSWICH TOWN	D 1-1	Pratt	26,289
Mar 2	Queens Park Rangers	L 1-3	Chivers (pen)	25,775
Mar 16	NORWICH CITY	D 0-0		18,476
Mar 23	Manchester United	W 1-0	Coates	36,278
Mar 30	EVERTON	L 0-2		19,839
Apr 3	CHELSEA	L 1-2	Evans	23,646
Apr 6	Wolverhampton Wanderers	D 1-1	McGrath	24,073
Apr 13	SOUTHAMPTON	W 3-1	Pratt, Chivers 2	21,456
Apr 15	Chelsea	D 0-0		26,258
Apr 20	Stoke City	L 0-1		20,189
Apr 27	LEICESTER CITY	W 1-0	Chivers	20,110
May 8	LIVERPOOL	D 1-1	McGrath	24,618
May 11	Newcastle United	W 2-0	Chivers, Gilzean	21,601

FA Cup

Jan 5	Leicester City	(Rd3) L 0-1		28,280

League Cup

Oct 8	Queens Park Rangers	(Rd2) L 0-1		23,353

UEFA Cup

Sep 19	Grasshoppers	(Rd1/1L) W 5-1	Evans, Chivers 2, Gilzean 2	11,200
Oct 3	GRASSHOPPERS	(Rd1/2L) W 4-1	England, Peters 2, Lador o.g.	18,105
Oct 24	Aberdeen	(Rd2/1L) D 1-1	Coates	30,000
Nov 7	ABERDEEN	(Rd2/2L) W 4-1	Peters, Neighbour, McGrath 2	21,785
Nov 28	Dinamo Tbilisi	(Rd3/1L) D 1-1	Coates	45,000
Dec 12	DINAMO TBILISI	(Rd3/2L) W 5-1	McGrath, Chivers 2, Peters 2	18,602
Mar 6	1FC Cologne	(Rd4/1L) W 2-1	McGrath, Peters	28,000
Mar 20	1FC COLOGNE	(Rd4/2L) W 3-0	Chivers, Peters, Coates	40,968
Apr 10	Lokomotive Leipzig	(SF/1L) W 2-1	Peters, Coates	74,000
Apr 24	LOKOMOTIVE LEIPZIG	(SF/2L) W 2-0	McGrath, Chivers	41,280
May 21	FEYENOORD	(F/1L) D 2-2	England, Van Deele o.g.	46,281
May 29	Feyenoord	(F/2L) L 0-2		62,988

MANAGER: Bill Nicholson

CAPTAIN: Martin Peters

TOP SCORER: Martin Chivers

BIGGEST WIN: 5-1 v Grasshoppers (A), 19 September 1973, UEFA Cup 1st Round 1st leg; 5-1 v Dinamo Tbilisi (H), 12 December 1973, UEFA Cup 3rd Round 2nd leg

HIGHEST ATTENDANCE: 74,000 v Lokomotive Leipzig, 10 April 1974, UEFA Cup Semi-final 1st leg

MAJOR TRANSFERS IN: Neil McNab from Morton

League and Cup Appearances

PLAYER	LEAGUE	CUP COMPETITION			TOTAL
		FA CUP	LC	UEFA	
Beal	41	1	1	12	55
Chivers	39 (1)	1	1	11	52 (1)
Coates	36		1	10	47
Daines	5		1	2	8
Dillon	13 (3)	1		1 (1)	15 (4)
England	33	1	1	12	47
Evans	40	1	1	11	53
Gilzean	21 (4)	1	1	3 (1)	26 (5)
Holder	5 (2)			0 (4)	5 (6)
Jennings	36	1		10	47
Kinnear	3 (4)			2	5 (4)
Knowles	20		1	4	25
Lee	1				1
McGrath	22 (3)			7 (1)	29 (4)
McNab	0 (1)				0 (1)
Naylor	27 (1)		1	8 (1)	36 (2)
Neighbour	11 (3)	1		3 (1)	15 (4)
Osgood	0 (1)				0 (1)
Perryman	39	1	1	12	53
Peters	35	1	1	12	49
Pratt	35	1	0 (1)	12	48 (1)

Goalscorers

PLAYER	LEAGUE	CUP COMPETITION			TOTAL
		FA CUP	LC	UEFA	
Chivers	17			6	23
Peters	6			8	14
McGrath	5			5	10
Coates	3			4	7
Gilzean	3			2	5
Pratt	4				4
Evans	2			1	3
England				2	2
Knowles	2				2
Dillon	1				1
Holder	1				1
Neighbour				1	1
Perryman	1				1
Opp's o.gs.				2	2

Fact File

Spurs were only the second club to beat Cologne on their own pitch in European competition.

Final Division One Table

		P	W	D	L	F	A	Pts
1	LEEDS UNITED	42	24	14	4	66	31	62
2	LIVERPOOL	42	22	13	7	52	31	57
3	DERBY CO	42	17	14	11	52	42	48
4	IPSWICH T	42	18	11	13	67	58	47
5	STOKE C	42	15	16	11	54	42	46
6	BURNLEY	42	16	14	12	56	53	46
7	EVERTON	42	16	12	14	50	48	44
8	QPR	42	13	17	12	56	52	43
9	LEICESTER C	42	13	16	13	51	41	42
10	ARSENAL	42	14	14	14	49	51	42
11	TOTTENHAM HOTSPUR	42	14	14	14	45	50	42
12	WOLVERHAMPTON W	42	13	15	14	49	49	41
13	SHEFFIELD U	42	14	12	16	44	49	40
14	MANCHESTER C	42	14	12	16	39	46	40
15	NEWCASTLE U	42	13	12	17	49	48	38
16	COVENTRY C	42	14	10	18	43	54	38
17	CHELSEA	42	12	13	17	56	60	37
18	WEST HAM U	42	11	15	16	55	60	37
19	BIRMINGHAM C	42	12	13	17	52	64	37
20	SOUTHAMPTON	42	11	14	17	47	68	36
21	MANCHESTER U	42	10	12	20	38	48	32
22	NORWICH CITY	42	7	15	20	37	62	29

Season 1974-75

Football League Division One

DATE	OPPONENTS	SCORE	GOALSCORERS	ATTENDANCE
Aug 17	IPSWICH TOWN	L 0-1		26,444
Aug 21	Manchester City	L 0-1		31,549
Aug 24	Carlisle United	L 0-1		18,426
Aug 28	MANCHESTER CITY	L 1-2	Peters	20,079
Aug 31	DERBY COUNTY	W 2-0	Neighbour 2	20,670
Sep 7	Liverpool	L 2-5	Perryman, Chivers	47,538
Sep 14	WEST HAM UNITED	W 2-1	England, Chivers	27,959
Sep 21	Wolverhampton Wanderers	W 3-2	Chivers 2, Peters	20,647
Sep 28	MIDDLESBROUGH	L 1-2	Neighbour	23,282
Oct 5	BURNLEY	L 2-3	Pratt, England	18,441
Oct 12	Chelsea	L 0-1		32,660
Oct 16	CARLISLE UNITED	D 1-1	Chivers	12,813
Oct 19	ARSENAL	W 2-0	Perryman, Chivers	36,294
Oct 26	Luton Town	D 1-1	Chivers	22,420
Nov 2	Stoke City	D 2-2	Duncan 2	24,667
Nov 9	EVERTON	D 1-1	Chivers	29,052
Nov 16	Leicester City	W 2-1	Coates, Peters	23,244
Nov 23	BIRMINGHAM CITY	D 0-0		27,761
Nov 30	Sheffield United	W 1-0	Duncan	20,289
Dec 4	Leeds United	L 1-2	Duncan	25,832
Dec 7	NEWCASTLE UNITED	W 3-0	Knowles 2, Chivers	23,422
Dec 14	Ipswich Town	L 0-4		20,812
Dec 21	QUEENS PARK RANGERS	L 1-2	Duncan	21,150
Dec 26	West Ham United	D 1-1	Peters	37,682
Dec 28	COVENTRY CITY	D 1-1	Smith o.g.	20,307
Jan 11	Newcastle United	W 5-2	Conn 3, Knowles, Duncan	39,679
Jan 18	SHEFFIELD UNITED	L 1-3	Duncan	15,812
Feb 1	Everton	L 0-1		40,912
Feb 8	STOKE CITY	L 0-2		22,941
Feb 15	Coventry City	D 1-1	Duncan	15,227
Feb 18	Birmingham City	L 0-1		24,240
Feb 22	LEICESTER CITY	L 0-3		20,937
Mar 1	Derby County	L 1-3	Jones	22,995
Mar 15	Middlesbrough	L 0-3		25,637
Mar 22	LIVERPOOL	L 0-2		34,331
Mar 28	WOLVERHAMPTON WANDERERS	W 3-0	Perryman 2, Duncan	27,238
Mar 29	Queens Park Rangers	W 1-0	Duncan	25,461
Apr 5	LUTON TOWN	W 2-1	Conn, Duncan	25,796
Apr 12	Burnley	L 2-3	Perryman, Duncan	17,865
Apr 19	CHELSEA	W 2-0	Conn, Perryman	50,998
Apr 26	Arsenal	L 0-1		43,762
Apr 28	LEEDS UNITED	W 4-2	Knowles (1 pen) 2, Conn, Chivers	49,886

FA Cup

Jan 4	Nottingham Forest	(Rd3) D 1-1	Chivers		23,355
Jan 8	NOTTINGHAM FOREST	(R) L 0-1			27,996

League Cup

Sep 11	MIDDLESBROUGH	(Rd2) L 0-4		15,216

League and Cup Appearances

PLAYER	LEAGUE	CUP COMPETITION		TOTAL
		FA CUP	LC	
Beal	28		1	29
Chivers	27 (1)	1	1	29 (1)
Coates	26 (4)	2	1	29 (4)
Conn	16 (1)	1	0 (1)	17 (2)
Daines	1			1
Duncan	28	2		30
England	31	2		33
Evans	20 (1)		1	21 (1)
Jennings	41	2	1	44
Jones	16			16
Kinnear	17	2		19
Knowles	31	2		33
McAllister	7 (1)			7 (1)
McGrath	5 (4)		1	6 (4)
McNab	2			2
Naylor	37 (1)	2	1	40 (1)
Neighbour	21 (4)	0 (1)	1	22 (5)
Osgood	10		1	11
Perryman	42	2	1	45
Peters	29	2		31
Pratt	27 (2)	2	1	30 (2)

Goalscorers

PLAYER	LEAGUE	CUP COMPETITION		TOTAL
		FA CUP	LC	
Duncan	12			12
Chivers	10	1		11
Conn	6			6
Perryman	6			6
Knowles	5			5
Peters	4			4
Neighbour	3			3
England	2			2
Coates	1			1
Jones	1			1
Pratt	1			1
Opp's o.gs.	1			1

Fact File

Terry Neill called upon the service of a hypnotherapist prior to the crucial last game of the season against Leeds United.

MANAGER: Bill Nicholson until September then Terry Neill

CAPTAIN: Mmartin Peters/Steve Perryman

TOP SCORER: John Duncan

BIGGEST WIN: 5-2 v Newcastle United (A), 11 January 1975, Football League Division One

HIGHEST ATTENDANCE: 50,998 v Chelsea, 19 April 1975, Football League Division One

MAJOR TRANSFERS IN: Alfie Conn from Rangers, John Duncan from Dundee, Don McAllister from Bolton Wanderers

MAJOR TRANSFERS OUT: Ray Evans to Millwall, Alan Gilzean to Highland Park (South Africa), Martin Peters to Norwich City

Final Division One Table

		P	W	D	L	F	A	Pts
1	DERBY CO	42	21	11	10	67	49	53
2	LIVERPOOL	42	20	11	11	60	39	51
3	IPSWICH T	42	23	5	14	66	44	51
4	EVERTON	42	16	18	8	56	42	50
5	STOKE C	42	17	15	10	64	48	49
6	SHEFFIELD U	42	18	13	11	58	51	49
7	MIDDLESBROUGH	42	18	12	12	54	40	48
8	MANCHESTER C	42	18	10	14	54	54	46
9	LEEDS UNITED	42	16	13	13	57	49	45
10	BURNLEY	42	17	11	14	68	67	45
11	QPR	42	16	10	16	54	54	42
12	WOLVERHAMPTON W	42	14	11	17	57	35	39
13	WEST HAM U	42	13	13	16	58	59	39
14	COVENTRY C	42	12	15	15	51	62	39
15	NEWCASTLE U	42	15	9	18	59	72	39
16	ARSENAL	42	13	11	18	47	49	37
17	BIRMINGHAM C	42	14	9	19	53	61	37
18	LEICESTER C	42	12	12	18	46	60	36
19	TOTTENHAM HOTSPUR	42	13	8	21	52	63	34
20	LUTON TOWN	42	11	11	20	47	65	33
21	CHELSEA	42	9	15	18	42	72	33
22	CARLISLE U	42	12	5	25	43	59	29

Season 1975-76

Football League Division One

DATE	OPPONENTS	SCORE	GOALSCORERS	ATTENDANCE
Aug 16	MIDDLESBROUGH	W 1-0	Perryman	25,502
Aug 20	IPSWICH TOWN	D 1-1	Duncan	28,351
Aug 23	Liverpool	L 2-3	Jones, Duncan	42,729
Aug 25	West Ham United	L 0-1		36,567
Aug 30	NORWICH CITY	D 2-2	Pratt, Duncan	23,140
Sep 6	Manchester United	L 2-3	Chivers, Jones	51,641
Sep 13	DERBY COUNTY	L 2-3	Chivers, Duncan	28,455
Sep 20	Leeds United	D 1-1	Pratt	27,372
Sep 27	ARSENAL	D 0-0		37,064
Oct 4	Newcastle United	D 2-2	Pratt, Duncan	33,290
Oct 11	Aston Villa	D 1-1	Pratt	40,048
Oct 18	MANCHESTER CITY	D 2-2	Jones 2	30,554
Oct 25	Leicester City	W 3-2	Coates, Perryman, Chivers	22,088
Nov 1	WOLVERHAMPTON WANDERERS	W 2-1	Young, Neighbour	26,102
Nov 8	Queens Park Rangers	D 0-0		28,434
Nov 15	STOKE CITY	D 1-1	Jones	25,698
Nov 22	Manchester City	L 1-2	Osgood	31,457
Nov 29	BURNLEY	W 2-1	Duncan 2	21,222
Dec 6	Sheffield United	W 2-1	Duncan 2	22,949
Dec 10	EVERTON	D 2-2	Pratt, Duncan	18,638
Dec 13	LIVERPOOL	L 0-4		29,891
Dec 20	Middlesbrough	L 0-1		22,046
Dec 26	BIRMINGHAM CITY	L 1-3	Chivers (pen)	21,651
Dec 27	Coventry City	D 2-2	Duncan 2	21,125
Jan 10	Derby County	W 3-2	McAllister, Perryman, Neighbour	28,085
Jan 17	MANCHESTER UNITED	D 1-1	Duncan	49,189
Jan 31	Ipswich Town	W 2-1	Osgood (pen), Coates	24,049
Feb 7	WEST HAM UNITED	D 1-1	Duncan	32,832
Feb 14	QUEENS PARK RANGERS	L 0-3		28,190
Feb 21	Stoke City	W 2-1	Hoddle, Duncan	17,110
Feb 24	Everton	L 0-1		18,126
Feb 28	LEICESTER CITY	D 1-1	Chivers	21,427
Mar 6	Norwich City	L 1-3	Chivers	20,460
Mar 13	ASTON VILLA	W 5-2	McAllister, Perryman, Duncan, Robinson, Nicholl o.g.	24,169
Mar 16	Wolverhampton Wanderers	W 1-0	Pratt	21,544
Mar 20	Burnley	W 2-1	Pratt, Duncan	15,490
Mar 27	SHEFFIELD UNITED	W 5-0	Young, Perryman 2, Chivers, Duncan	21,370
Apr 3	Arsenal	W 2-0	Pratt, Duncan	42,031
Apr 10	LEEDS UNITED	D 0-0		40,365
Apr 17	Birmingham City	L 1-3	Pratt	30,616
Apr 19	COVENTRY CITY	W 4-1	Pratt, Osgood, Duncan, Neighbour	21,107
Apr 24	NEWCASTLE UNITED	L 0-3		29,649

FA Cup

Jan 3	STOKE CITY	(Rd3)	D 1-1	Duncan	26,715
Jan 24	Stoke City	(R)	L 1-2	Perryman	29,751

League Cup

Sep 9	Watford	(Rd2)	W 1-0	Jones	14,997
Oct 8	Crewe Alexandra	(Rd3)	W 2-0	Pratt, Conn	10,561
Nov 12	WEST HAM UNITED	(Rd4)	D 0-0		49,161
Nov 24	West Ham United	(R)	W 2-0*	Young, Duncan	38,443
Dec 3	DONCASTER ROVERS	(Rd5)	W 7-2	Pratt, Chivers 2, Duncan 3, Chappell o.g.	25,702
Jan 14	NEWCASTLE UNITED	(SF/1L)	W 1-0	Pratt	40,215
Jan 21	Newcastle United	(SF/2L)	L 1-3	McAllister	49,657

after extra-time

MANAGER: Terry Neill

CAPTAIN: Steve Perryman

TOP SCORER: John Duncan

BIGGEST WIN: 7-2 v Doncaster Rovers (H), 3 December 1975, Football League Cup 5th Round

HIGHEST ATTENDANCE: 51,641 v Manchester United, 6 September 1975, Football League Division One

MAJOR TRANSFERS IN: Willie Young from Aberdeen

MAJOR TRANSFERS OUT: Phil Beal to Brighton & Hove Albion

League and Cup Appearances

PLAYER	LEAGUE	CUP COMPETITION		TOTAL
		FA CUP	LC	
Brotherston	1			1
Chivers	28 (4)	1	5	34 (4)
Coates	21 (3)	2	6	29 (3)
Conn	7 (1)		1 (1)	8 (1)
Daines	2		1	3
Duncan	35 (2)	2	7	44 (2)
Hoddle	6 (1)			6 (1)
Jennings	40	2	6	48
Jones	25 (9)	1 (1)	3 (1)	29 (11)
Kinnear	1			1
Knowles	10		1 (1)	11 (1)
McAllister	35	2	6	43
McGrath	3 (1)			3 (1)
McNab	11 (4)		1 (1)	12 (5)
Naylor	36	2	7	45
Neighbour	35	2	7	44
Osgood	42	2	7	51
Perryman	40	2	6	48
Pratt	41	2	7	50
Robinson	1 (1)			1 (1)
Smith	2			2
Stead	4			4
Walford	1 (1)			1 (1)
Young	35	2	6	43

Goalscorers

PLAYER	LEAGUE	CUP COMPETITION		TOTAL
		FA CUP	LC	
Duncan	20	1	4	25
Pratt	10		3	13
Chivers	7		2	9
Jones	5		1	6
Perryman	6	1		7
McAllister	2		1	3
Neighbour	3			3
Osgood	3			3
Young	2		1	3
Coates	2			2
Conn			1	1
Hoddle	1			1
Robinson	1			1
Opp's o.gs.	1		1	2

Fact File

At the end of the season Spurs undertook the most extensive tour in their history travelling to Canada, Fiji and Australia.

Final Division One Table

		P	W	D	L	F	A	Pts
1	LIVERPOOL	42	23	14	5	66	31	60
2	QPR	42	24	11	7	67	33	59
3	MANCHESTER U	42	23	10	9	68	42	56
4	DERBY CO	42	21	11	10	75	58	53
5	LEEDS UNITED	42	21	9	12	65	46	51
6	IPSWICH T	42	16	14	12	54	48	46
7	LEICESTER C	42	13	19	10	48	51	45
8	MANCHESTER C	42	16	11	15	64	46	43
9	TOTTENHAM HOTSPUR	42	14	15	13	63	63	43
10	NORWICH CITY	42	16	10	16	58	58	42
11	EVERTON	42	15	12	15	60	66	42
12	STOKE C	42	15	11	16	48	47	41
13	MIDDLESBROUGH	42	15	10	17	46	45	40
14	COVENTRY C	42	13	14	15	47	57	40
15	NEWCASTLE U	42	15	9	18	71	62	39
16	ASTON VILLA	42	11	17	14	51	59	39
17	ARSENAL	42	13	10	19	47	53	36
18	WEST HAM U	42	13	10	19	48	71	36
19	BIRMINGHAM C	42	13	7	22	57	75	33
20	WOLVERHAMPTON W	42	10	10	22	51	68	30
21	BURNLEY	42	9	10	23	43	66	28
22	SHEFFIELD U	42	6	10	26	33	82	22

Season 1976-77

Football League Division One

DATE	OPPONENTS	SCORE	GOALSCORERS	ATTENDANCE
Aug 21	Ipswich Town	L 1-3	Jones	28,490
Aug 25	NEWCASTLE UNITED	L 0-2		24,022
Aug 28	MIDDLESBROUGH	D 0-0		21,721
Sep 4	Manchester United	W 3-2	Coates, Pratt, Moores	60,723
Sep 11	LEEDS UNITED	W 1-0	Jones	34,725
Sep 18	Liverpool	L 0-2		47,421
Sep 25	NORWICH CITY	D 1-1	Hoddle	22,440
Oct 2	West Bromwich Albion	L 2-4	Jones, Taylor	23,461
Oct 16	Derby County	L 2-8	Osgood (pen), Perryman	24,216
Oct 20	BIRMINGHAM CITY	W 1-0	Osgood (pen)	20,193
Oct 23	COVENTRY CITY	L 0-1		21,877
Oct 30	EVERTON	D 3-3	McAllister, Osgood (pen), Pratt	26,047
Nov 6	West Ham United	L 3-5	Hoddle, Osgood (pen), Duncan	28,997
Nov 13	BRISTOL CITY	L 0-1		28,795
Nov 20	Sunderland	L 1-2	Moores	30,325
Nov 27	STOKE CITY	W 2-0	Osgood (1p) 2	22,500
Dec 11	MANCHESTER CITY	D 2-2	Taylor 2	24,608
Dec 18	Leicester City	L 1-2	Coates	16,397
Dec 27	ARSENAL	D 2-2	Young, Duncan	47,751
Jan 1	WEST HAM UNITED	W 2-1	Osgood (pen), Duncan	44,972
Jan 11	Queens Park Rangers	L 1-2	Duncan	24,266
Jan 22	IPSWICH TOWN	W 1-0	Taylor	35,126
Feb 5	Middlesbrough	L 0-2		21,231
Feb 12	MANCHESTER UNITED	L 1-3	Jones	46,946
Feb 19	Leeds United	L 1-2	Armstrong	26,858
Feb 26	Newcastle United	L 0-2		30,236
Mar 5	Norwich City	W 3-1	Pratt, Armstrong, Taylor	22,949
Mar 9	LIVERPOOL	W 1-0	Coates	32,098
Mar 12	WEST BROMWICH ALBION	L 0-2		28,834
Mar 19	Birmingham City	W 2-1	Jones, Hoddle	23,398
Mar 23	DERBY COUNTY	D 0-0		27,359
Mar 26	Everton	L 0-4		32,549
Apr 2	Coventry City	D 1-1	Taylor	16,210
Apr 9	QUEENS PARK RANGERS	W 3-0	Jones 2, Taylor	32,680
Apr 11	Arsenal	L 0-1		47,432
Apr 12	Bristol City	L 0-1		27,568
Apr 16	SUNDERLAND	D 1-1	Jones	34,155
Apr 20	Aston Villa	L 1-2	Armstrong	42,047
Apr 23	Stoke City	D 0-0		15,644
Apr 30	ASTON VILLA	W 3-1	Hoddle, Jones, Taylor	30,690
May 7	Manchester City	L 0-5		37,919
May 14	LEICESTER CITY	W 2-0	Pratt, Holmes	26,094

FA Cup

Jan 8	Cardiff City	(Rd3) L 0-1		27,868

League Cup

Aug 31	Middlesbrough	(Rd2) W 2-1	Moores, Neighbour	19,042
Sep 22	WREXHAM	(Rd3) L 2-3	Hoddle, Moores	19,156

League and Cup Appearances

PLAYER	LEAGUE	CUP COMPETITION		TOTAL
		FA CUP	LC	
Armstrong	20 (1)			20 (1)
Coates	28 (3)	1	2	31 (3)
Conn	12 (1)	1		13 (1)
Daines	19		1	20
Duncan	9	1		10
Gorman	15		1	16
Hoddle	39	1	2	42
Holmes	10			10
Jennings	23	1	1	25
Jones	31		2	33
Keeley	5 (1)			5 (1)
McAllister	10 (2)	0 (1)	2	12 (3)
McNab	6 (4)			6 (4)
Moores	16 (1)		2	18 (1)
Naylor	40	1	2	43
Neighbour	7		2	9
Osgood	42	1	2	45
Perryman	42	1	2	45
Pratt	30 (4)	1	0 (2)	31 (6)
Stead	8			8
Taylor	31 (1)	1		32 (1)
Young	19		2	21

Goalscorers

PLAYER	LEAGUE	CUP COMPETITION		TOTAL
		FA CUP	LC	
Jones	9			9
Taylor	8			8
Osgood	7			7
Hoddle	4		1	5
Duncan	4			4
Moores	2		2	4
Pratt	4			4
Armstrong	3			3
Coates	3			3
Holmes	1			1
McAllister	1			1
Neighbour			1	1
Perryman	1			1
Young	1			1

Fact File

Pat Jennings left at the end of the season with a record 472 Football League appearances for Spurs to his name.

MANAGER: Keith Burkinshaw

CAPTAIN: Steve Perryman

TOP SCORER: Chris Jones

BIGGEST WIN: 3-0 v Queens Park Rangers (H), 9 April 1977, Football League Division One

HIGHEST ATTENDANCE: 60,723 v Manchester United, 4 September 1976, Football League Division One

MAJOR TRANSFERS IN: John Gorman from Carlisle United, Jimmy Holmes from Coventry City, Ian Moores from Stoke, Peter Taylor from Crystal Palace

MAJOR TRANSFERS OUT: Martin Chivers to Servette, Joe Kinnear to Brighton & Hove Albion, Willie Young to Arsenal

Final Division One Table

		P	W	D	L	F	A	Pts
1	LIVERPOOL	42	23	11	8	62	33	57
2	MANCHESTER C	42	21	14	7	60	34	56
3	IPSWICH T	42	22	8	12	66	39	52
4	ASTON VILLA	42	22	7	13	76	50	51
5	NEWCASTLE U	42	18	13	11	64	49	49
6	MANCHESTER U	42	18	11	13	71	62	47
7	WBA	42	16	13	13	62	56	45
8	ARSENAL	42	16	11	15	64	59	43
9	EVERTON	42	14	14	14	62	64	42
10	LEEDS UNITED	42	15	12	15	48	51	42
11	LEICESTER C	42	12	18	12	47	60	42
12	MIDDLESBROUGH	42	14	13	15	40	29	41
13	BIRMINGHAM C	42	13	12	17	63	61	38
14	QPR	42	13	12	17	47	52	38
15	DERBY CO	42	9	19	14	50	55	37
16	NORWICH CITY	42	14	9	19	47	64	37
17	WEST HAM U	42	11	14	17	46	65	36
18	BRISTOL C	42	11	13	18	38	48	35
19	COVENTRY C	42	10	15	17	48	59	35
20	BLACKBURN R	42	11	12	19	46	54	34
21	STOKE C	42	10	14	18	28	51	34
22	TOTTENHAM HOTSPUR	42	12	9	21	48	72	33

Season 1977-78

Football League Division Two

DATE	OPPONENTS	SCORE	GOALSCORERS	ATTENDANCE
Aug 20	SHEFFIELD UNITED	W 4-2	Osgood (2 pen) 2, Duncan, Jones	27,673
Aug 24	Blackburn Rovers	D 0-0		9,540
Aug 27	NOTTS COUNTY	W 2-1	Duncan 2	25,839
Sep 3	Cardiff City	D 0-0		8,880
Sep 10	FULHAM	W 1-0	Jones	31,939
Sep 17	Blackpool	W 2-0	Hoddle, Duncan	16,910
Sep 24	LUTON TOWN	W 2-0	Osgood (pen), Jones	32,814
Oct 1	Orient	D 1-1	Taylor	24,131
Oct 4	Hull City	L 0-2		10,966
Oct 8	OLDHAM ATHLETIC	W 5-1	Duncan 2, Robinson, Taylor 2	24,636
Oct 15	Charlton Athletic	L 1-4	Taylor	30,706
Oct 22	BRISTOL ROVERS	W 9-0	Hoddle, Moores 3, Lee 4, Taylor	26,571
Oct 29	Stoke City	W 3-1	Pratt, Armstrong 2	21,012
Nov 5	BURNLEY	W 3-0	Hoddle, McNab, Taylor	30,634
Nov 12	Crystal Palace	W 2-1	Moores, Duncan	40,522
Nov 19	BRIGHTON & HOVE ALBION	D 0-0		48,613
Nov 26	Bolton Wanderers	L 0-1		34,290
Dec 3	SOUTHAMPTON	D 0-0		37,873
Dec 10	Sunderland	W 2-1	Duncan 2	31,960
Dec 17	CRYSTAL PALACE	D 2-2	Hoddle 2	34,211
Dec 26	Millwall	W 3-1	Duncan, Lee, Taylor	14,644
Dec 27	MANSFIELD TOWN	D 1-1	Duncan	36,288
Dec 31	BLACKBURN ROVERS	W 4-0	Hoddle, Pratt, Lee 2	30,520
Jan 2	Sheffield United	D 2-2	Duncan, Taylor	31,207
Jan 14	Notts County	D 3-3	Pratt 2, Lee	15,709
Jan 21	CARDIFF CITY	W 2-1	Duncan 2	29,104
Feb 4	Fulham	D 1-1	Taylor	24,763
Feb 11	BLACKPOOL	D 2-2	McAllister, Pratt	28,707
Feb 22	Luton Town	W 4-1	Hoddle 2, McAllister, Duncan	17,024
Feb 25	ORIENT	D 1-1	Lee	32,869
Mar 4	Oldham Athletic	D 1-1	McNab	14,122
Mar 11	CHARLTON ATHLETIC	W 2-1	Hoddle (pen), Pratt	34,511
Mar 18	Bristol Rovers	W 3-2	Pratt, McNab, Jones	17,708
Mar 22	STOKE CITY	W 3-1	McAllister, Lee 2	30,646
Mar 25	Mansfield Town	D 3-3	Hoddle (1 pen) 2, Jones	12,144
Mar 27	MILLWALL	D 3-3	Hoddle, Jones 2	33,074
Apr 1	Burnley	L 1-2	Taylor	16,916
Apr 8	BOLTON WANDERERS	W 1-0	McAllister	50,097
Apr 15	Brighton & Hove Albion	L 1-3	Jones	32,647
Apr 22	SUNDERLAND	L 2-3	Duncan, Taylor	38,220
Apr 26	HULL CITY	W 1-0	Perryman	36,913
Apr 29	Southampton	D 0-0		28,846

FA Cup

Jan 7	BOLTON WANDERERS	(Rd3) D 2-2	Hoddle, Duncan	43,731
Jan 10	Bolton Wanderers	(R) L 1-2	Taylor (pen)	31,314

League Cup

Aug 31	WIMBLEDON	(Rd2) W 4-0	Osgood (pen), Duncan 3	22,807
Oct 26	COVENTRY CITY	(Rd3) L 2-3	Pratt, Armstrong	35,099

League and Cup Appearances

PLAYER	LEAGUE	CUP COMPETITION		TOTAL
		FA CUP	LC	
Armstrong	10 (9)	0 (2)	1	11 (11)
Coates	1 (2)			1 (2)
Daines	42	2	2	46
Duncan	27	2	1	30
Hoddle	41	2	2	45
Holmes	38	2		42
Jones	20		1	21
Lee	23 (2)		2	25 (2)
McAllister	25	2	1	28
McNab	42	2	2	46
Moores	7 (3)		1	8 (3)
Naylor	37	2	2	41
Osgood	18		1	19
Perryman	42	2	2	46
Pratt	42	2	2	46
Robinson	4			4
Stead	2 (1)			2 (1)
Taylor	41	2	2	45

Goalscorers

PLAYER	LEAGUE	CUP COMPETITION		TOTAL
		FA CUP	LC	
Duncan	16	1	3	20
Hoddle	12	1		13
Taylor	11	1		12
Lee	11			11
Jones	8			8
Pratt	7		1	8
McAllister	4			4
Moores	4			4
Osgood	3		1	4
Armstrong	2		1	3
McNab	3			3
Perryman	1			1
Robinson	1			1

Fact File

Spurs' average home Football League attendance of 33,417 was far and away the best in the Second Division, over 8,000 more than closest rivals, Brighton & Hove Albion, and surpassed by only six First Division clubs.

MANAGER: Keith Burkinshaw
CAPTAIN: Steve Perryman
TOP SCORER: John Duncan
BIGGEST WIN: 9-0 v Bristol Rovers (H), 22 October 1977, Football League Division Two
HIGHEST ATTENDANCE: 50,097 v Bolton Wanderers, 8 April 1978, Football League Division Two
MAJOR TRANSFERS IN: Colin Lee from Torquay United
MAJOR TRANSFERS OUT: Pat Jennings to Arsenal, Keith Osgood to Coventry City

Final Division Two Table

		P	W	D	L	F	A	Pts
1	BOLTON W	42	24	10	8	63	33	58
2	SOUTHAMPTON	42	22	13	7	70	39	57
3	TOTTENHAM HOTSPUR	42	20	16	6	83	49	56
4	BRIGHTON & HA	42	22	12	8	63	38	56
5	BLACKBURN R	42	16	13	13	56	60	45
6	BLACKBURN R	42	14	16	12	67	59	44
7	STOKE C	42	16	10	16	53	49	42
8	OLDHAM A	42	13	16	13	54	58	42
9	CRYSTAL P	42	13	15	14	50	47	41
10	FULHAM	42	14	13	15	49	49	41
11	BURNLEY	42	15	10	17	56	64	40
12	SHEFFIELD U	42	16	8	18	62	46	40
13	LUTON TOWN	42	14	10	18	54	52	38
14	ORIENT	42	10	18	14	43	49	38
15	NOTTS COUNTY	42	11	16	15	54	62	38
16	MILLWALL	42	12	14	16	49	57	38
17	CHARLTON A	42	13	12	17	55	68	38
18	BRISTOL R	42	13	12	17	61	77	38
19	CARDIFF C	42	13	12	17	51	71	38
20	BLACKPOOL	42	12	13	17	59	60	37
21	MANSFIELD T	42	10	11	21	49	69	31
22	HULL CITY	42	8	12	22	34	52	28

The Essential History of Tottenham Hotspur

Season 1978-79

Football League Division One

DATE	OPPONENTS	SCORE	GOALSCORERS	ATTENDANCE
Aug 19	Nottingham Forest	D 1-1	Villa	41,223
Aug 23	ASTON VILLA	L 1-4	Hoddle (pen)	47,892
Aug 26	CHELSEA	D 2-2	Armstrong, Duncan	40,632
Sep 2	Liverpool	L 0-7		50,705
Sep 9	BRISTOL CITY	W 1-0	Rodgers o.g.	34,035
Sep 16	Leeds United	W 2-1	Lee, Taylor	36,062
Sep 23	Manchester City	L 0-2		43,471
Sep 30	COVENTRY CITY	D 1-1	Hoddle	35,806
Oct 7	West Bromwich Albion	W 1-0	Taylor	33,068
Oct 14	BIRMINGHAM CITY	W 1-0	Ainscow o.g.	41,230
Oct 21	Derby County	D 2-2	McAllister, Taylor	26,181
Oct 28	BOLTON WANDERERS	W 2-0	Pratt, Lee	37,337
Nov 4	Norwich City	D 2-2	Lee, Taylor	27,031
Nov 11	NOTTINGHAM FOREST	L 1-3	Pratt	50,541
Nov 18	Chelsea	W 3-1	Lee 2, Hoddle	42,328
Nov 22	LIVERPOOL	D 0-0		50,393
Nov 25	WOLVERHAMPTON WANDERERS	W 1-0	Taylor	35,430
Dec 9	IPSWICH TOWN	W 1-0	Pratt	33,882
Dec 16	Manchester United	L 0-2		52,026
Dec 23	ARSENAL	L 0-5		42,273
Dec 26	Queens Park Rangers	D 2-2	Lee, Taylor (pen)	24,845
Dec 30	Everton	D 1-1	Taylor	44,572
Jan 13	Bristol City	D 0-0		29,122
Jan 20	LEEDS UNITED	L 1-2	Hoddle	36,838
Feb 3	MANCHESTER CITY	L 0-3		32,037
Feb 10	Coventry City	W 3-1	Lee, Taylor 2	25,071
Feb 24	Birmingham City	L 0-1		20,980
Mar 3	DERBY COUNTY	W 2-0	Ardiles 2	28,089
Mar 17	NORWICH CITY	D 0-0		24,982
Mar 24	Aston Villa	W 3-2	Jones, Hoddle 2	35,486
Mar 28	SOUTHAMPTON	D 0-0		23,570
Mar 31	Middlesbrough	L 0-1		19,172
Apr 3	Wolverhampton Wanderers	L 2-3	Jones 2	19,819
Apr 7	MIDDLESBROUGH	L 1-2	Taylor (pen)	21,580
Apr 10	Arsenal	L 0-1		53,896
Apr 14	QUEENS PARK RANGERS	D 1-1	Perryman	28,854
Apr 16	Southampton	D 3-3	Pratt, Jones, Taylor	22,096
Apr 21	MANCHESTER UNITED	D 1-1	Jones	36,665
Apr 28	Ipswich Town	L 1-2	Hoddle (pen)	28,179
May 5	EVERTON	L 1-1	Ardiles	26,077
May 8	Bolton Wanderers	W 3-1	Holmes, Falco, Villa	17,879
May 14	WEST BROMWICH ALBION	W 1-0	Villa	24,789

FA Cup

Jan 10	ALTRINCHAM	(Rd3)	D	1-1	Taylor (pen)	31,081
Jan 16	Altrincham *	(R)	W	3-0	Lee 3	27,878
Feb 12	WREXHAM	(Rd4)	D	3-3	Hoddle, Jones, Roberts o.g.	27,120
Feb 21	Wrexham	(R)	W	3-2	Jones 3	16,050
Feb 28	Oldham Athletic	(Rd5)	W	1-0	Perryman	16,097
Mar 10	MANCHESTER UNITED	(Rd6)	D	1-1	Ardiles	51,800
Mar 14	Manchester United	(R)	L	0-2		54,510

* played at Maine Road, Manchester

League Cup

Aug 29	Swansea City	(Rd2)	D	2-2	Hoddle (pen), Armstrong	24,335
Sep 6	SWANSEA CITY	(R)	L	1-3	Villa	33,672

Fact File

When Ossie Ardiles played for Argentina against Holland in May 1979 he became Spurs' first foreign international.

MANAGER: Keith Burkinshaw

CAPTAIN: Steve Perryman

TOP SCORER: Peter Taylor

BIGGEST WIN: 3-0 v Altrincham (A), 16 January 1979, FA Cup 3rd Round replay

HIGHEST ATTENDANCE: v Manchester United, 14 March 1979, FA Cup 6th Round replay

MAJOR TRANSFERS IN: Milija Aleksic from Luton Town, Ossie Ardiles from Huracan, John Lacy from Fulham, Ricky Villa from Racing Club

MAJOR TRANSFERS OUT: John Duncan to Derby County, Neil McNab to Bolton Wanderers, Ian Moores to Orient

League and Cup Appearances

PLAYER	LEAGUE	CUP COMPETITION		TOTAL
		FA CUP	LC	
Aleksic	5	1		6
Ardiles	38	5	2	45
Armstrong	7 (3)	1 (2)	1 (1)	9 (6)
Beavon	1			1
Daines	14		2	16
Duncan	2		2	4
Falco	1			1
Galvin	1			1
Gorman	15	1		16
Hoddle	34 (1)	5	2	41 (1)
Holmes	33	7		40
Jones	18 (1)	6 (1)		24 (2)
Kendall	23	6		29
Lacy	35	7	1	43
Lee	26 (1)	4 (1)		30 (2)
McAllister	38	5	2	45
McNab	2		2	4
Miller	7			7
Moores	2			2
Naylor	22	5 (1)	2	29 (1)
Perryman	42	7	2	51
Pratt	37 (1)	7		44 (1)
Smith	1 (1)			1 (1)
Taylor	32 (1)	5 (2)	2	39 (3)
Villa	26 (6)	5	2	33 (6)

Goalscorers

PLAYER	LEAGUE	CUP COMPETITION		TOTAL
		FA CUP	LC	
Taylor	11	1		12
Lee	7	3		10
Hoddle	7	1	1	9
Jones	5	4		9
Ardiles	3	1		4
Pratt	4			4
Villa	3		1	4
Armstrong	1		1	2
Perryman	1	1		2
Duncan	1			1
Falco	1			1
Holmes	1			1
McAllister	1			1
Opp's o.gs.	2	1		3

Final Division One Table

		P	W	D	L	F	A	Pts
1	LIVERPOOL	42	30	8	4	85	16	68
2	NOTTINGHAM F	42	21	18	3	61	26	60
3	WBA	42	24	11	7	72	35	59
4	EVERTON	42	17	17	8	52	40	51
5	LEEDS UNITED	42	18	14	10	70	52	50
6	IPSWICH T	42	20	9	13	63	49	49
7	ARSENAL	42	17	14	11	61	48	48
8	ASTON VILLA	42	15	16	11	59	49	46
9	MANCHESTER U	42	15	15	12	60	63	45
10	COVENTRY C	42	14	16	12	58	68	44
11	TOTTENHAM HOTSPUR	42	13	15	14	48	61	41
12	MIDDLESBROUGH	42	15	10	17	57	45	40
13	BRISTOL C	42	15	10	17	47	51	40
14	SOUTHAMPTON	42	12	16	14	47	53	40
15	MANCHESTER C	42	13	13	16	58	56	39
16	NORWICH CITY	42	7	23	12	51	57	37
17	BOLTON W	42	12	11	19	54	75	35
18	WOLVERHAMPTON W	42	13	8	21	44	68	34
19	DERBY CO	42	10	11	21	44	71	31
20	QPR	42	6	13	23	45	73	25
21	BIRMINGHAM C	42	6	10	26	37	64	22
22	CHELSEA	42	5	10	27	44	92	20

Season 1979-80

Football League Division One

DATE	OPPONENTS	SCORE	GOALSCORERS	ATTENDANCE
Aug 18	MIDDLESBROUGH	L 1-3	Hoddle	32,743
Aug 22	Norwich City	L 0-4		16,647
Aug 25	Stoke City	L 1-3	Perryman	22,832
Sep 1	MANCHESTER CITY	W 2-1	Jones, Hoddle	30,901
Sep 8	BRIGHTON & HOVE ALBION	W 2-1	Armstrong, Hoddle (pen)	34,107
Sep 15	Southampton	L 2-5	Jones, Hoddle	22,573
Sep 22	WEST BROMWICH ALBION	D 1-1	Hoddle (pen)	29,914
Sep 29	Coventry City	D 1-1	Jones	20,085
Oct 6	Crystal Palace	D 1-1	Villa	45,274
Oct 10	NORWICH CITY	W 3-2	Hoddle 2, Villa	26,488
Oct 13	DERBY COUNTY	W 1-0	Armstrong	33,269
Oct 20	Leeds United	W 2-1	Jones, Armstrong	25,203
Oct 27	NOTTINGHAM FOREST	W 1-0	Hoddle	49,038
Nov 3	Middlesbrough	D 0-0		19,557
Nov 10	BOLTON WANDERERS	W 2-0	Yorath, Hoddle (pen)	33,155
Nov 17	Liverpool	L 1-2	Jones	51,092
Nov 24	Everton	D 1-1	Jones	31,079
Dec 1	MANCHESTER UNITED	L 1-2	Hoddle	51,389
Dec 8	Bristol City	W 3-1	Miller, Hoddle (1 pen) 2	25,090
Dec 15	ASTON VILLA	L 1-2	Ardiles	30,555
Dec 21	Ipswich Town	L 1-3	McAllister	18,945
Dec 26	Arsenal	L 0-1		44,560
Dec 29	STOKE CITY	W 1-0	Pratt	28,810
Jan 12	Manchester City	D 1-1	Hoddle	34,837
Jan 19	Brighton & Hove Albion	W 2-0	Hughton, Villa	29,406
Feb 2	SOUTHAMPTON	D 0-0		37,155
Feb 9	West Bromwich Albion	L 1-2	Hoddle	26,319
Feb 23	Derby County	L 1-2	Galvin	21,183
Feb 27	COVENTRY CITY	W 4-3	Falco, Hoddle (2 pen) 3	22,536
Mar 1	LEEDS UNITED	W 2-1	Falco, Hoddle	35,331
Mar 11	Nottingham Forest	L 0-4		25,633
Mar 15	CRYSTAL PALACE	D 0-0		28,419
Mar 22	Bolton Wanderers	L 1-2	Jones	14,474
Mar 29	LIVERPOOL	W 2-0	Pratt, Hoddle (pen)	32,114
Apr 2	IPSWICH TOWN	L 0-2		26,423
Apr 5	Wolverhampton Wanderers	W 2-1	Jones, Galvin	30,713
Apr 7	ARSENAL	L 1-2	Jones	41,365
Apr 12	Manchester United	L 1-4	Ardiles	53,151
Apr 19	EVERTON	W 3-0	Miller, Ardiles, Galvin	25,245
Apr 23	WOLVERHAMPTON WANDERERS	D 2-2	Armstrong, Galvin	19,843
Apr 26	Aston Villa	L 0-1		29,549
May 3	BRISTOL CITY	D 0-0		23,585

FA Cup

Jan 5	MANCHESTER UNITED	(Rd3)	D 1-1	Ardiles	45,207
Jan 9	Manchester United	(R)	W 1-0*	Ardiles	53,762
Jan 26	Swindon Town	(Rd4)	D 0-0		26,000
Jan 30	SWINDON TOWN	(R)	W 2-1	Armstrong 2	46,707
Feb 16	BIRMINGHAM CITY	(Rd5)	W 3-1	Armstrong, Hoddle (1 pen) 2	49,936
Mar 8	LIVERPOOL	(Rd6)	L 0-1		48,033

* after extra time

League Cup

Aug 29	MANCHESTER UNITED	(Rd2/1L)	W 2-1	Pratt, Hoddle	29,163
Sep 5	Manchester United	(Rd2/2L)	L 1-3	Armstrong	48,292

Fact File

Glenn Hoddle scored on his full England debut in November 1979.

MANAGER: Keith Burkinshaw

CAPTAIN: Steve Perryman

TOP SCORER: Glenn Hoddle

BIGGEST WIN: 3-0 v Everton (H), 19 April 1908, Football League Division One

HIGHEST ATTENDANCE: 53,762 v Manchester United, 9 January 1980, FA Cup 3rd Round

MAJOR TRANSFERS IN: Graham Roberts from Weymouth, Terry Yorath from Coventry City

MAJOR TRANSFERS OUT: Colin Lee to Chelsea, John Pratt to Portland Timbers

League and Cup Appearances

PLAYER	LEAGUE	CUP COMPETITION		TOTAL
		FA CUP	LC	
Aleksic	8	2		10
Ardiles	40	6	1	47
Armstrong	28 (2)	5	1	34 (2)
Beavon	2 (1)		0 (1)	2 (2)
Daines	32	4	2	38
Falco	7 (2)	2 (1)		9 (3)
Galvin	7 (3)			7 (3)
Gibson	1	2		3
Hazard	3			3
Hoddle	41	6	2	49
Hughton	39	6	2	47
Jones	36 (1)	3	1	40 (1)
Kendall	2			2
Lacy	4		1	5
Lee	8 (2)	2		10 (2)
McAllister	35 (1)	5	1	41 (1)
Miller	27	6	2	35
Naylor	6 (1)	1		7 (1)
Perryman	40	6	2	48
Pratt	19 (5)	1 (5)	2	22 (10)
Smith	14	1		15
Southey	1			1
Taylor	7 (2)	0 (1)		7 (3)
Villa	22	6		28
Yorath	33	5	2	40

Goalscorers

PLAYER	LEAGUE	CUP COMPETITION		TOTAL
		FA CUP	LC	
Hoddle	19	2	1	22
Jones	9			9
Armstrong	4	3	1	8
Ardiles	3	2		5
Galvin	4			4
Pratt	2		1	3
Villa	3			3
Falco	2			2
Miller	2			2
Hughton	1			1
McAllister	1			1
Perryman	1			1
Yorath	1			1

Final Division One Table

		P	W	D	L	F	A	PTS
1	LIVERPOOL	42	25	10	7	81	30	60
2	MANCHESTER U	42	24	10	8	65	35	58
3	IPSWICH T	42	22	9	11	68	39	53
4	ARSENAL	42	18	16	8	52	36	52
5	NOTTINGHAM F	42	20	8	14	63	43	48
6	WOLVERHAMPTON W	42	19	9	14	58	47	47
7	ASTON VILLA	42	16	14	12	51	50	46
8	SOUTHAMPTON	42	18	9	15	65	53	45
9	MIDDLESBROUGH	42	16	12	14	50	44	44
10	WBA	42	11	19	12	54	50	41
11	LEEDS UNITED	42	13	14	15	46	50	40
12	NORWICH CITY	42	13	14	15	58	66	40
13	CRYSTAL P	42	12	16	14	41	50	40
14	TOTTENHAM HOTSPUR	42	15	10	17	52	62	40
15	COVENTRY C	42	16	7	19	56	66	39
16	BRIGHTON & HA	42	11	15	16	47	57	37
17	MANCHESTER C	42	12	13	17	43	66	37
18	STOKE C	42	13	10	19	44	58	36
19	EVERTON	42	9	17	16	43	51	35
20	BRISTOL C	42	9	13	20	37	66	31
21	DERBY CO	42	11	8	23	47	67	30
22	BOLTON W	42	5	15	22	38	73	25

Season 1980-81

Football League Division One

DATE	OPPONENTS	SCORE	GOALSCORERS	ATTENDANCE
Aug 16	NOTTINGHAM FOREST	W 2-0	Hoddle (pen), Crooks	43,398
Aug 19	Crystal Palace	W 4-3	Archibald, Hoddle, Crooks 2	27,841
Aug 23	BRIGHTON & HOVE ALBION	D 2-2	Hoddle, Crooks	39,763
Aug 30	Arsenal	L 0-2		54,045
Sep 6	MANCHESTER UNITED	D 0-0		40,995
Sep 13	Leeds United	D 0-0		21,947
Sep 20	SUNDERLAND	D 0-0		32,030
Sep 27	Leicester City	L 1-2	Villa	22,616
Oct 4	Stoke City	W 3-2	Hughton, Archibald, Taylor (pen)	18,614
Oct 11	MIDDLESBROUGH	W 3-2	Archibald, Villa, Crooks	27,380
Oct 18	Aston Villa	L 0-3		30,940
Oct 22	Manchester City	L 1-3	Hoddle	28,788
Oct 25	COVENTRY CITY	W 4-1	Archibald 2, Hoddle 2	25,484
Nov 1	Everton	D 2-2	Archibald 2	26,223
Nov 8	WOLVERHAMPTON WANDERERS	D 2-2	Hoddle (pen), Crooks	29,244
Nov 12	CRYSTAL PALACE	W 4-2	Archibald, Crooks 3	25,777
Nov 15	Nottingham Forest	W 3-0	Ardiles, Archibald 2	25,400
Nov 22	Birmingham City	L 1-2	Ardiles	24,817
Nov 29	WEST BROMWICH ALBION	L 2-3	Lacy, Perryman	27,372
Dec 6	Liverpool	L 1-2	Archibald	39,545
Dec 13	MANCHESTER CITY	W 2-1	Archibald, Hoddle	23,883
Dec 17	IPSWICH TOWN	W 5-3	Perryman, Ardiles, Archibald, Hoddle, Crooks	22,741
Dec 20	Middlesbrough	L 1-4	Lacy	15,990
Dec 26	SOUTHAMPTON	D 4-4	Brooke 2, Archibald, Crooks	28,792
Dec 27	Norwich City	D 2-2	Archibald, Hoddle	23,145
Jan 10	BIRMINGHAM CITY	W 1-0	Crooks	24,909
Jan 17	ARSENAL	W 2-0	Archibald 2	32,944
Jan 31	Brighton & Hove Albion	W 2-0	Ardiles, Crooks	23,610
Feb 7	LEEDS UNITED	D 1-1	Archibald	32,372
Feb 17	Manchester United	D 0-0		40,642
Feb 21	LEICESTER CITY	L 1-2	Archibald	27,326
Feb 28	Sunderland	D 1-1	Crooks	22,382
Mar 11	STOKE CITY	D 2-2	Ardiles, Brooke	28,742
Mar 14	Ipswich Town	L 0-3		32,044
Mar 21	ASTON VILLA	W 2-0	Archibald, Crooks	35,091
Mar 28	Coventry City	W 1-0	Roberts o.g.	18,654
Apr 4	EVERTON	D 2-2	Galvin, Crooks	27,208
Apr 18	NORWICH CITY	L 2-3	Miller, Hoddle (pen)	34,413
Apr 20	Southampton	D 1-1	Miller	23,735
Apr 25	LIVERPOOL	D 1-1	Hoddle	35,334
Apr 30	Wolverhampton Wanderers	L 0-1		18,350
May 2	West Bromwich Albion	L 2-4	Smith, Falco	20,549

FA Cup

Jan 3	Queens Park Rangers	(Rd3) D 0-0		28,829
Jan 7	QUEENS PARK RANGERS	(R) W 3-1	Galvin, Hoddle, Crooks	36,294
Jan 24	HULL CITY	(Rd4) W 2-0	Archibald, Brooke	37,532
Feb 14	COVENTRY CITY	(Rd5) W 3-1	Hughton, Ardiles, Archibald	36,688
Mar 7	EXETER CITY	(Rd6) W 2-0	Miller, Roberts	40,629
Apr 11	Wolverhampton Wanderers *	(SF) D 2-2†	Archibald, Hoddle	50,174
Apr 15	Wolverhampton Wanderers **	(R) W 3-0	Villa, Crooks 2	52,539
May 9	Manchester City ††	(F) D 1-1†	Hutchinson o.g.	100,000
May 14	Manchester City ††	(R) W 3-2	Villa 2, Crooks	96,000

* played at Hillsborough, Sheffield. † after extra time
** played at Highbury, London. †† played at Wembley, London

League Cup

Aug 27	Orient	(Rd2/1L) W 1-0	Lacy	20,087
Sep 3	ORIENT	(Rd2/2L) W 3-1	Archibald 2, Crooks	25,806
Sep 24	CRYSTAL PALACE	(Rd3) D 0-0		29,654
Sep 30	Crystal Palace	(R) W 3-1	Villa, Hoddle, Crooks	26,885
Nov 4	ARSENAL	(Rd4) W 1-0	Ardiles	42,511
Dec 2	West Ham United	(Rd5) L 0-1		36,003

MANAGER: Keith Burkinshaw

CAPTAIN: Steve Perryman   **TOP SCORER:** Steve Archibald

BIGGEST WIN: 4-1 v Coventry City (H), 25 October 1980, Football League Division One

HIGHEST ATTENDANCE: 100,000 v Manchester City, 9 May 1981, FA Cup Final

MAJOR TRANSFERS IN: Steve Archibald from Aberdeen, Garth Crooks from Stoke City

MAJOR TRANSFERS OUT: Gerry Armstrong to Watford, Peter Taylor to Orient, Terry Yorath to Vancouver Whitecaps

League and Cup Appearances

PLAYER	LEAGUE	CUP COMPETITION		TOTAL
		FA CUP	LC	
Aleksic	10	4		14
Archibald	40 (1)	9	6	55 (1)
Ardiles	36	7	6	49
Armstrong	0 (4)			0 (4)
Brooke	10 (8)	2 (5)		12 (13)
Crooks	40	9	6	55
Daines	28	5	5	38
Falco	3			3
Galvin	17	8 (1)		25 (1)
Hazard	2 (2)			2 (2)
Hoddle	38	9	6	53
Hughton	34	6	6	46
Kendall	4		1	5
Lacy	31	3	6	40
Mazzon	1 (1)	1		2 (1)
McAllister	18	2	1	21
Miller	24 (1)	9	1	34 (1)
O'Reilly	1 (1)			1 (1)
Perryman	42	9	6	57
Roberts	21 (3)	9	0 (1)	30 (4)
Smith	18 (2)		5	23 (2)
Taylor	5 (3)		0 (2)	5 (5)
Villa	28 (1)	5	6	39 (1)
Yorath	11 (4)	2	5	18 (4)

Goalscorers

PLAYER	LEAGUE	CUP COMPETITION		TOTAL
		FA CUP	LC	
Archibald	20	3	2	25
Crooks	16	4	2	22
Hoddle	12	2	1	15
Ardiles	5	1	1	7
Villa	2	3	1	6
Brooke	3	1		4
Lacy	2		1	3
Miller	2	1		3
Galvin	1	1		2
Hughton	1	1		2
Perryman	2			2
Falco	1			1
Roberts		1		1
Smith	1			1
Taylor	1			1
Opp's o.gs.	1	1		2

Fact File

Steve Perryman made his 473rd Football League appearance for Spurs against Wolverhampton Wanderers on 30 April, surpassing Pat Jennings' record.

Final Division One Table

		P	W	D	L	F	A	Pts
1	ASTON VILLA	42	26	8	8	72	40	60
2	IPSWICH T	42	23	10	9	77	43	56
3	ARSENAL	42	19	15	8	61	45	53
4	WBA	42	20	12	10	60	42	52
5	LIVERPOOL	42	17	17	8	62	42	51
6	SOUTHAMPTON	42	20	10	12	76	56	50
7	NOTTINGHAM F	42	19	12	11	62	44	50
8	MANCHESTER U	42	15	18	9	51	36	48
9	LEEDS UNITED	42	17	10	15	39	47	44
10	TOTTENHAM HOTSPUR	42	14	15	13	70	68	43
11	STOKE C	42	12	18	12	51	60	42
12	MANCHESTER C	42	14	11	17	56	46	39
13	BIRMINGHAM C	42	13	12	17	50	61	38
14	MIDDLESBROUGH	42	16	5	21	53	61	37
15	EVERTON	42	13	10	19	55	58	36
16	COVENTRY C	42	13	10	19	48	68	36
17	BLACKBURN R	42	14	7	21	52	53	35
18	WOLVERHAMPTON W	42	13	9	20	43	55	35
19	BRIGHTON & HA	42	14	7	21	54	67	35
20	NORWICH CITY	42	13	7	22	49	73	33
21	LEICESTER C	42	13	6	23	40	67	32
22	CRYSTAL P	42	6	7	29	47	83	19

Season 1981-82

Football League Division One

DATE	OPPONENTS	SCORE	GOALSCORERS	ATTENDANCE
Aug 29	Middlesbrough	W 3-1	Villa, Hoddle, Falco	20,490
Sep 2	WEST HAM UNITED	L 0-4		41,200
Sep 5	ASTON VILLA	L 1-3	Villa	31,265
Sep 12	Wolverhampton Wanderers	W 1-0	Galvin	18,675
Sep 19	EVERTON	W 3-0	Hughton, Roberts, Hoddle (pen)	31,219
Sep 22	Swansea City	L 1-2	Hoddle (pen)	22,352
Sep 26	Manchester City	W 1-0	Falco	39,085
Oct 3	NOTTINGHAM FOREST	W 3-0	Hazard, Falco 2	34,870
Oct 10	STOKE CITY	W 2-0	Ardiles, Crooks	30,520
Oct 17	Sunderland	W 2-0	Hazard, Archibald	25,317
Oct 24	BRIGHTON & HOVE ALBION	L 0-1		37,294
Oct 31	Southampton	W 2-1	Roberts, Corbett	24,131
Nov 7	WEST BROMWICH ALBION	L 1-2	Crooks	32,436
Nov 21	MANCHESTER UNITED	W 3-1	Roberts, Hazard, Archibald	35,534
Nov 28	Notts County	D 2-2	Crooks 2	15,550
Dec 5	COVENTRY CITY	L 1-2	Hazard	27,972
Dec 12	Leeds United	D 0-0		28,780
Jan 27	MIDDLESBROUGH	W 1-0	Crooks	22,819
Jan 30	Everton	D 1-1	Villa	30,709
Feb 6	WOLVERHAMPTON WANDERERS	W 6-1	Villa 3, Falco, Hoddle (pen), Crooks	29,960
Feb 17	Aston Villa	D 1-1	Crooks	23,877
Feb 20	MANCHESTER CITY	W 2-0	Hoddle (1 pen) 2	46,181
Feb 27	Stoke City	W 2-0	Crooks 2	20,592
Mar 9	Brighton & Hove Albion	W 3-1	Ardiles, Archibald, Crooks	27,082
Mar 20	SOUTHAMPTON	W 3-2	Roberts 3	46,827
Mar 23	Birmingham City	D 0-0		17,708
Mar 27	West Bromwich Albion	L 0-1		20,151
Mar 29	ARSENAL	D 2-2	Hughton, Archibald	40,940
Apr 10	IPSWICH TOWN	W 1-0	Hoddle	45,215
Apr 12	Arsenal	W 3-1	Hazard, Crooks 2	48,897
Apr 14	SUNDERLAND	D 2-2	Galvin, Hoddle	39,898
Apr 17	Manchester United	L 0-2		50,724
Apr 24	NOTTS COUNTY	W 3-1	Villa, Archibald, Galvin	38,017
Apr 28	BIRMINGHAM CITY	D 1-1	Villa	25,470
May 1	Coventry City	D 0-0		15,408
May 3	LIVERPOOL	D 2-2	Perryman, Archibald	38,091
May 5	SWANSEA CITY	W 2-1	Brooke (1 pen) 2	26,348
May 8	LEEDS UNITED	W 2-1	Brooke, Burns o.g.	35,020
May 10	West Ham United	D 2-2	Hoddle (pen), Brooke	27,667
May 12	Nottingham Forest	L 0-2		15,273
May 15	Liverpool	L 1-3	Hoddle	48,122
May 17	Ipswich Town	L 1-2	Crooks	21,202

FA Cup

Jan 2	ARSENAL	(Rd3) W 1-0	Crooks	38,421
Jan 23	LEEDS UNITED	(Rd4) W 1-0	Crooks	46,126
Feb 13	ASTON VILLA	(Rd5) W 1-0	Falco	43,419
Mar 6	Chelsea	(Rd6) W 3-2	Archibald, Hazard, Hoddle	42,557
Apr 3	Leicester City *	(SF) W 2-0	Crooks, Wilson o.g.	46,606
May 22	Queens Park Rangers **	(F) D 1-1†	Hoddle	100,000
May 27	Queens Park Rangers **	(F) W 1-0	Hoddle (pen)	92,000

* played at Villa Park, Birmingham. ** played at Wembley, London. † after extra time

League Cup

Oct 7	MANCHESTER UNITED	(Rd2/1L) W 1-0	Archibald	39,333
Oct 28	Manchester United	(Rd2/2L) W 1-0	Hazard	55,890
Nov 11	WREXHAM	(Rd3) W 2-0	Hughton, Hoddle	24,084
Dec 2	FULHAM	(Rd4) W 1-0	Hazard	30,214
Jan 18	NOTTINGHAM FOREST	(Rd5) W 1-0	Ardiles	31,192
Feb 3	West Brom Albion	(SF/1L) D 0-0		32,238
Feb 10	WEST BROM ALBION	(SF/2L) W 1-0	Hazard	47,241
Mar 13	Liverpool **	(F) L 1-3†	Archibald	100,000

** played at Wembley, London. † after extra time

European Cup-Winners' Cup

Sep 16	Ajax	(Rd1/1L) W 3-1	Villa, Falco 2	21,742
Sep 29	AJAX	(Rd1/2L) W 3-0	Ardiles, Galvin, Falco	34,606
Oct 21	Dundalk	(Rd2/1L) D 1-1	Crooks	17,500
Nov 4	DUNDALK	(Rd2/2L) W 1-0	Crooks	33,455
Mar 3	EINTRACHT FRANKFURT	(Rd3/1L) W 2-0	Miller, Hazard	38,172
Mar 17	Eintracht Frankfurt	(Rd3/2L) L 1-2	Hoddle	45,000
Apr 7	BARCELONA	(SF/1L) D 1-1	Roberts	41,545
Apr 21	Barcelona	(SF/2L) L 0-1		80,000

FA Charity Shield

Aug 22	Aston Villa **		D 2-2	Falco 2	92,500

** played at Wembley, London

League and Cup Appearances

PLAYER	LEAGUE	CUP COMPETITION			OTHER	TOTAL
		FA CUP	LC	ECWC		
Aleksic	2					2
Archibald	26 (1)	4 (1)	5	7	1	43 (1)
Ardiles	26	5	8	6	1	46
Brooke	12 (4)	0 (2)				12 (6)
Clemence	38	7	8	8	1	62
Corbett	0 (1)					0 (1)
Crook	3 (1)					3 (1)
Crooks	27	7	7	5		46
Dick	1					1
Falco	21	3	4	3 (2)	1	32 (2)
Galvin	32	7	8	8	1	56
Gibson	1					1
Hazard	26 (2)	4 (1)	5 (1)	6		41 (4)
Hoddle	34	7	8	8	1	58
Hughton	37	7	8	8	1	61
Jones	3 (4)			0 (1)		3 (5)
Lacy	7 (5)	0 (1)				7 (6)
Mazzon		0 (1)				0 (1)
Miller	35	6 (1)	8	7	1	57 (1)
O'Reilly	4 (1)					4 (1)
Parks	2					2
Perryman	42	7	8	8	1	66
Price	18 (3)	5	3	4		30 (3)
Roberts	35 (2)	6	5	6 (1)	1	53 (3)
Smith	1 (1)				0 (1)	1 (2)
Villa	26 (1)	2	3 (1)	4 (1)	1	36 (3)

Goalscorers

PLAYER	LEAGUE	CUP COMPETITION			OTHER	TOTAL
		FA CUP	LC	ECWC		
Crooks	13	3		2		18
Hoddle	10	3	1	1		15
Falco	5	1		3	2	11
Hazard	5	1	3	1		10
Archibald	6	1	2			9
Villa	8			1		9
Roberts	6			1		7
Ardiles	2		1	1		4
Brooke	4					4
Galvin	3			1		4
Hughton	2		1			3
Corbett	1					1
Miller				1		1
Perryman	1					1
Opp's o.gs.	1	1				2

Fact File

The new West Stand was officially opened by Sir Stanley Rous before the match against Wolverhampton Wanderers on 6 February.

Final Division One Table

		P	W	D	L	F	A	Pts
1	LIVERPOOL	42	26	9	7	80	32	87
2	IPSWICH T	42	26	5	11	75	53	83
3	MANCHESTER U	42	22	12	8	59	29	78
4	TOTTENHAM HOTSPUR	42	20	11	11	67	48	71
5	ARSENAL	42	20	11	11	48	37	71
6	SWANSEA C	42	21	6	15	58	51	69
7	SOUTHAMPTON	42	19	9	14	72	67	66
8	EVERTON	42	17	13	12	56	50	64
9	WEST HAM U	42	14	16	12	66	57	58
10	MANCHESTER C	42	15	13	14	49	50	58
11	ASTON VILLA	42	15	12	15	55	53	57
12	NOTTINGHAM F	42	15	12	15	42	48	57
13	BRIGHTON & HA	42	13	13	16	43	52	52
14	COVENTRY C	42	13	11	18	56	62	50
15	NOTTS COUNTY	42	13	8	21	61	69	47
16	BIRMINGHAM C	42	10	14	18	53	61	44
17	WBA	42	11	11	20	46	57	44
18	STOKE C	42	12	8	22	44	63	44
19	BLACKBURN R	42	11	11	20	38	58	44
20	LEEDS UNITED	42	10	12	20	39	61	42
21	WOLVERHAMPTON W	42	10	10	22	32	63	40
22	MIDDLESBROUGH	42	8	15	19	34	52	39

Season 1982-83

Football League Division One

DATE	OPPONENTS	SCORE	GOALSCORERS	ATTENDANCE
Aug 28	LUTON TOWN	D 2-2	Hazard, Mabbutt	35,195
Aug 31	Ipswich Town	W 2-1	Archibald, Crooks	23,224
Sep 4	Everton	L 1-3	Archibald	30,563
Sep 8	SOUTHAMPTON	W 6-0	Brooke (pen), Perryman, Galvin 2, Villa, Crooks	26,579
Sep 11	MANCHESTER CITY	L 1-2	Mabbutt	32,483
Sep 18	Sunderland	W 1-0	Brooke	21,137
Sep 25	NOTTINGHAM FOREST	W 4-1	Mabbutt 2, Crooks 2	30,662
Oct 2	Swansea City	L 0-2		16,381
Oct 9	COVENTRY CITY	W 4-0	Brooke (pen) 3, Crooks	25,188
Oct 16	Norwich City	D 0-0		21,668
Oct 23	NOTTS COUNTY	W 4-2	Brooke, Mabbutt, Crooks 2	26,183
Oct 30	Aston Villa	L 0-4		25,992
Nov 6	WATFORD	L 0-1		42,634
Nov 13	Manchester United	L 0-1		47,869
Nov 20	WEST HAM UNITED	W 2-1	Archibald 2	41,960
Nov 27	Liverpool	L 0-3		40,691
Dec 4	WEST BROMWICH ALBION	D 1-1	Villa o.g.	26,608
Dec 11	Stoke City	L 0-2		15,849
Dec 18	BIRMINGHAM CITY	W 2-1	Mabbutt 2	20,946
Dec 27	Arsenal	L 0-2		51,497
Dec 28	BRIGHTON & HOVE ALBION	D 2-0	Villa, Hughton	23,994
Jan 1	West Ham United	L 0-3		33,383
Jan 3	EVERTON	W 2-1	Gibson 2	28,455
Jan 15	Luton Town	D 1-1	Hoddle	21,231
Jan 22	SUNDERLAND	D 1-1	Gibson	25,250
Feb 5	Manchester City	D 2-2	Brooke (pen), Gibson	26,357
Feb 12	SWANSEA CITY	W 1-0	Crooks	24,632
Feb 26	NORWICH CITY	D 0-0		23,342
Mar 5	Notts County	L 0-3		11,841
Mar 12	Coventry City	D 1-1	Miller	11,027
Mar 19	Watford	W 1-0	Falco	27,373
Mar 23	ASTON VILLA	W 2-0	Falco 2	22,455
Apr 2	Brighton & Hove Albion	L 1-2	Roberts	20,341
Apr 4	ARSENAL	W 5-0	Hughton 2, Brazil, Falco 2	43,642
Apr 9	Nottingham Forest	D 2-2	Mabbutt, Brazil	18,265
Apr 16	IPSWICH TOWN	W 3-1	Mabbutt, Brazil 2	30,587
Apr 23	West Bromwich Albion	W 1-0	Archibald	14,879
Apr 30	LIVERPOOL	W 2-0	Archibald 2	44,907
May 3	Southampton	W 2-1	Mabbutt, Brazil	21,602
May 7	Birmingham City	L 0-2		18,947
May 11	MANCHESTER UNITED	W 2-0	Roberts, Archibald	32,803
May 14	STOKE CITY	W 4-1	Brazil, Archibald 3	33,691

FA Cup

Jan 8	SOUTHAMPTON	(Rd3) W 1-0	Hazard	38,040
Jan 29	WEST BROMWICH ALBION	(Rd4) W 2-1	Gibson, Crooks	38,208
Feb 19	Everton	(Rd5) L 0-2		42,995

League Cup

Oct 6	BRIGHTON & HOVE ALBION	(Rd2/1L) D 1-1	Brooke (pen)	20,416
Oct 26	Brighton & Hove Albion	(Rd2/2L) W 1-0	Crooks	20,755
Nov 9	Gillingham	(Rd3) W 4-2	Archibald 2, Crooks 2	14,366
Dec 1	LUTON TOWN	(Rd4) W 1-0	Villa	27,861
Jan 19	BURNLEY	(Rd5) L 1-4	Gibson	30,771

European Cup-Winners' Cup

Sep 15	Coleraine	(Rd1/1L) W 3-0	Archibald, Crooks 2	12,000
Sep 28	COLERAINE	(Rd1/2L) W 4-0	Brooke, Mabbutt, Crooks, Gibson	20,925
Oct 20	BAYERN MUNICH	(Rd2/1L) D 1-1	Archibald	36,488
Nov 3	Bayern Munich	(Rd2/2L) L 1-4	Hughton	55,000

FA Charity Shield

Aug 21	Liverpool *		L 0-1	82,500

* played at Wembley, London

MANAGER: Keith Burkinshaw   **CAPTAIN:** Steve Perryman

TOP SCORER: Steve Archibald and Garth Crooks

BIGGEST WIN: 6-0 v Southampton (H), 8 September 1982, Football League Division One

HIGHEST ATTENDANCE: 82,500 v Liverpool, 21 August 1982, FA Charity Shield

MAJOR TRANSFERS IN: Alan Brazil from Ipswich Town, Gary Mabbutt from Bristol Rovers

MAJOR TRANSFERS OUT: Chris Jones to Manchester City

League and Cup Appearances

PLAYER	LEAGUE	CUP COMPETITION			OTHER	TOTAL
		FA CUP	LC	ECWC		
Archibald	31	1	4	4	1	41
Ardiles	2	1	1			4
Brazil	12					12
Brooke	19 (4)	1 (1)	3 (1)	4		27 (6)
Clemence	41	3	5	4	1	54
Corbett	0 (1)					0 (1)
Crook	1 (3)					1 (3)
Crooks	26	2	4	4	1	37
Dick	2		2		4	
Falco	11 (5)		1 (1)	0 (1)	0 (1)	12 (8)
Galvin	26	1	1	1	1	30
Gibson	14 (2)	3	1	0 (2)		18 (4)
Hazard	15 (3)	2	3	3 (1)	1	24 (4)
Hoddle	22 (2)	0 (1)	3	0 (1)	1	26 (4)
Hughton	38	3	4	3	1	49
Lacy	22	2	3	4	1	32
Mabbutt	38	2 (1)	5	4	1	50 (1)
Mazzon	2		0 (1)			2 (1)
Miller	23		2	2	1	28
O'Reilly	25 (1)	1	4	1	1	32 (1)
Parks	1			0 (1)		1 (1)
Perryman	32 (1)	3	2	2 (1)	0 (1)	39 (3)
Price	16	1	3	4		24
Roberts	20 (4)	2	2			24 (4)
Villa	22 (1)	3	4	4		33 (1)
Webster	1 (1)					1 (1)

Goalscorers

PLAYER	LEAGUE	CUP COMPETITION			OTHER	TOTAL
		FA CUP	LC	ECWC		
Archibald	11		2	2		15
Crooks	8	1	3	3		15
Mabbutt	10			1		11
Brooke	7		1	1		9
Gibson	4	1	1	1		7
Brazil	6					6
Falco	5					5
Hughton	3			1		4
Villa	2		1			3
Galvin	2					2
Hazard	1	1				2
Roberts	2					2
Hoddle	1					1
Miller	1					1
Perryman	1					1
Opp's o.gs.	1					1

Fact File

Spurs broke new ground playing two end-of-season games against Manchester United in Swaziland.

Final Division One Table

		P	W	D	L	F	A	PTS
1	LIVERPOOL	42	24	10	8	87	37	82
2	WATFORD	42	22	5	15	74	57	71
3	MANCHESTER U	42	19	13	10	56	38	70
4	TOTTENHAM HOTSPUR	42	20	9	13	65	50	69
5	NOTTINGHAM F	42	20	9	13	62	50	69
6	ASTON VILLA	42	21	5	16	62	50	68
7	EVERTON	42	18	10	14	66	48	64
8	WEST HAM U	42	20	4	18	68	62	64
9	IPSWICH T	42	15	13	14	64	50	58
10	ARSENAL	42	16	10	16	58	56	58
11	WBA	42	15	12	15	51	49	57
12	SOUTHAMPTON	42	15	12	15	54	40	57
13	STOKE C	42	16	9	17	53	64	57
14	NORWICH CITY	42	14	12	16	52	58	54
15	NOTTS COUNTY	42	15	7	20	55	71	52
16	BLACKBURN R	42	12	14	16	48	61	50
17	BIRMINGHAM C	42	12	14	16	40	55	50
18	LUTON TOWN	42	12	13	17	65	84	49
19	COVENTRY C	42	13	9	20	48	59	48
20	MANCHESTER C	42	13	8	21	47	70	47
21	SWANSEA C	42	10	11	21	51	69	41
22	BRIGHTON & HA	42	9	13	20	38	68	40

Season 1983-1984

Football League Division One

DATE	OPPONENTS	SCORE	GOALSCORERS	ATTENDANCE
Aug 27	Ipswich Town	L 1-3	Archibald	26,562
Aug 29	COVENTRY CITY	D 1-1	Hoddle (pen)	35,454
Sep 3	WEST HAM UNITED	L 0-2		38,042
Sep 7	West Bromwich Albion	D 1-1	Roberts	14,830
Sep 10	Leicester City	W 3-0	Stevens, Mabbutt, Crooks	15,886
Sep 17	EVERTON	L 1-2	Falco	29,125
Sep 24	Watford	W 3-2	Hughton, Hoddle, Archibald	21,056
Oct 2	NOTTINGHAM FOREST	W 2-1	Stevens, Archibald	30,596
Oct 15	Wolverhampton Wanderers	W 3-2	Archibald 2, Falco	12,523
Oct 22	BIRMINGHAM CITY	W 1-0	Archibald	18,937
Oct 29	NOTTS COUNTY	W 1-0	Archibald	29,198
Nov 5	Stoke City	D 1-1	Falco	14,726
Nov 12	LIVERPOOL	D 2-2	Archibald, Hoddle (pen)	44,348
Nov 19	Luton Town	W 4-2	Dick, Archibald 2, Cooke	17,275
Nov 26	QUEENS PARK RANGERS	W 3-2	Archibald, Falco 2	38,789
Dec 3	Norwich City	L 1-2	Dick	21,987
Dec 10	SOUTHAMPTON	D 0-0		29,711
Dec 16	Manchester United	L 2-4	Brazil, Falco	33,616
Dec 26	ARSENAL	L 2-4	Roberts, Archibald	38,756
Dec 27	Aston Villa	D 0-0		30,125
Dec 31	West Ham United	L 1-4	Stevens	30,939
Jan 2	WATFORD	L 2-3	Hughton, Hoddle (pen)	32,495
Jan 14	IPSWICH TOWN	W 2-0	Roberts, Falco	25,832
Jan 21	Everton	L 1-2	Archibald	17,990
Feb 4	Nottingham Forest	D 2-2	Hughton, Falco	21,482
Feb 8	SUNDERLAND	W 3-0	Perryman, Archibald 2	19,327
Feb 11	Leicester City	W 3-2	Archibald, Falco, Galvin	28,410
Feb 21	Notts County	D 0-0		7,943
Feb 25	BIRMINGHAM CITY	L 0-1		23,564
Mar 3	STOKE CITY	W 1-0	Falco (pen)	18,271
Mar 10	Liverpool	L 1-3	Stevens	36,718
Mar 17	WEST BROMWICH ALBION	L 0-1		22,385
Mar 24	Coventry City	W 4-2	Roberts, Hazard, Brazil (1 pen) 2	12,847
Mar 31	WOLVERHAMPTON WANDERERS	W 1-0	Hazard	19,296
Apr 7	Sunderland	D 1-1	Falco	15,433
Apr 14	LUTON TOWN	W 2-1	Roberts, Falco	25,390
Apr 18	ASTON VILLA	W 2-1	Roberts (pen), Mabbutt	18,668
Apr 21	Arsenal	L 2-3	Archibald 2	48,831
Apr 28	Queens Park Rangers	L 1-2	Archibald	24,937
May 5	NORWICH CITY	W 2-0	Archibald, Falco	18,874
May 7	Southampton	L 0-5		21,141
May 12	MANCHESTER UNITED	D 1-1	Archibald	39,790

FA Cup

Jan 7	Fulham	(Rd3)	D 0-0		23,398
Jan 11	FULHAM	(R)	W 2-0	Roberts, Archibald	32,898
Jan 28	NORWICH CITY	(Rd4)	D 0-0		37,792
Feb 1	Norwich City	(R)	L 1-2	Falco	26,811

League Cup

Oct 5	LINCOLN CITY	(Rd2/1L)	W 3-1	Galvin, Archibald, Houghton o.g.	20,241
Oct 26	Lincoln City	(Rd2/2L)	L 1-2	Falco	12,239
Nov 9	ARSENAL	(Rd3)	L 1-2	Hoddle (pen)	48,200

UEFA Cup

Sep 14	Drogheda United	(Rd1/1L)	W 6-0	Mabbutt 2, Falco 2, Galvin, Crooks	7,000
Sep 28	DROGHEDA UNITED	(Rd1/2L)	W 8-0	Hughton, Roberts 2, Archibald, Falco 2, Brazil 2	19,831
Oct 19	FEYENOORD	(Rd2/1L)	W 4-2	Galvin 2, Archibald 2	35,404
Nov 2	Feyenoord	(Rd2/2L)	W 2-0	Hughton, Galvin	49,241
Nov 23	Bayern Munich	(Rd3/1L)	L 0-1		20,000
Dec 7	BAYERN MUNICH	(Rd3/2L)	W 2-0	Archibald, Falco	41,977
Mar 7	AUSTRIA VIENNA	(Rd4/1L)	W 2-0	Archibald, Brazil	34,069
Mar 21	Austria Vienna	(Rd4/2IL)	D 2-2	Ardiles, Brazil	21,000
Apr 11	Hadjuk Split	(SF/1L)	L 1-2	Falco	40,000
Apr 25	HADJUK SPLIT	(SF/2L)	W 1-0	Hazard	43,969
May 9	Anderlecht	(F/1L)	D 1-1	Miller	38,000
May 23	ANDERLECHT	(F/2L)	D 1-1*	Roberts	46,258

*after extra time – Spurs won 4-3 on penalties

Fact File

Spurs started the season with a testimonial match against West Ham United for Bill Nicholson and finished it with another against an England XI for Keith Burkinshaw.

League and Cup Appearances

PLAYER	LEAGUE	CUP COMPETITION			TOTAL
		FA CUP	LC	UEFA	
Archibald	31 (1)	3	3	11	48 (1)
Ardiles	8 (1)	1		2 (1)	11 (2)
Bowen	6 (1)	3			9 (1)
Brace	0 (1)				0 (1)
Brazil	17 (2)	1	0 (1)	3 (2)	21 (5)
Brooke	7 (5)	1	1	2 (2)	11 (7)
Clemence	26	1	3	7	37
Cockram	2				2
Rihard Cooke	9	1		1	11
Crook	3	0 (1)	1	0 (2)	4 (3)
Crooks	6 (4)	0 (1)	1		7 (5)
Culverhouse	1 (1)				1 (1)
Dick	10 (1)		3 (1)		13 (2)
Falco	32 (4)	4	3	10 (1)	49 (5)
Galvin	30	3	3	9	45
Hazard	9 (2)	1 (2)	0 (1)	6	16 (5)
Hoddle	24	3	3	5 (1)	35 (1)
Hughton	34	1	3	12	50
Mabbutt	21	2	2	7 (2)	32 (2)
Miller	20 (1)	3		6	29 (1)
O'Reilly	9 (3)	1		1 (2)	11 (1)
Parks	16	3		5	24
Perryman	41	4	3	11	59
Price	1 (1)		1	2	4 (1)
Roberts	35	4	3	12	54
Stevens	37 (3)	4	3	9	53 (3)
Thomas	26 (1)		1	7 (1)	34 (2)
Webster	1				1

Goalscorers

PLAYER	LEAGUE	CUP COMPETITION			TOTAL
		FA CUP	LC	UEFA	
Archibald	21	1	1	5	28
Falco	13	1	1	6	21
Roberts	6	1		3	10
Brazil	3			4	7
Galvin	1		1	4	6
Hoddle	4	1			5
Hughton	3		2		5
Mabbutt	2		2		4
Stevens	4				4
Hazard	2		1		3
Crooks	1		1		2
Dick	2				2
Cooke	1				1
Miller			1		1
Perryman	1				1
Opp's o.gs.			1		1

Final Division One Table

		P	W	D	L	F	A	Pts
1	LIVERPOOL	42	22	14	6	73	32	80
2	SOUTHAMPTON	42	22	11	9	66	38	77
3	NOTTINGHAM F	42	22	8	12	76	45	74
4	MANCHESTER U	42	20	14	8	71	41	74
5	QPR	42	22	7	13	67	37	73
6	ARSENAL	42	18	9	15	74	60	63
7	EVERTON	42	16	14	12	44	42	62
8	TOTTENHAM HOTSPUR	42	17	10	15	64	65	61
9	WEST HAM U	42	17	9	16	60	55	60
10	ASTON VILLA	42	17	9	16	59	61	60
11	WATFORD	42	16	9	17	68	77	57
12	IPSWICH T	42	15	8	19	55	44	53
13	BLACKBURN R	42	13	13	16	42	53	52
14	NORWICH CITY	42	12	15	15	48	49	51
15	LEICESTER C	42	13	12	17	65	68	51
16	LUTON TOWN	42	14	9	19	53	66	51
17	WBA	42	14	9	19	48	62	51
18	STOKE C	42	13	11	18	44	63	50
19	COVENTRY C	42	13	11	18	57	77	50
20	BIRMINGHAM C	42	12	12	18	39	50	48
21	NOTTS COUNTY	42	10	11	21	50	72	41
22	WOLVERHAMPTON W	42	6	11	25	27	80	29

Season 1984-85

Football League Division One

DATE	OPPONENTS	SCORE	GOALSCORERS	ATTENDANCE
Aug 25	Everton	W 4-1	Falco, Allen 2, Chiedozie	35,630
Aug 27	LEICESTER CITY	D 2-2	Roberts (1 pen) 2	30,046
Sep 1	NORWICH CITY	W 3-1	Chiedozie, Falco, Galvin	24,947
Sep 4	Sunderland	L 0-1		18,895
Sep 8	Sheffield Wednesday	L 1-2	Falco	33,421
Sep 15	QUEENS PARK RANGERS	W 5-0	Falco 2, Allen 2, Hazard	31,655
Sep 22	Aston Villa	W 1-0	Chiedozie	22,409
Sep 29	LUTON TOWN	W 4-2	Roberts (pen), Perryman, Falco, Hazard	30,204
Oct 6	Southampton	L 0-1		21,825
Oct 12	LIVERPOOL	W 1-0	Crooks	28,599
Oct 20	Manchester United	L 0-1		54,516
Oct 27	STOKE CITY	W 4-0	Roberts (pen), Chiedozie, Allen 2	23,477
Nov 3	WEST BROMWICH ALBION	L 2-3	Chiedozie, Hazard	24,494
Nov 10	Nottingham Forest	W 2-1	Hazard, Galvin	21,306
Nov 17	Ipswich Town	W 3-0	Mabbutt, Allen, Hoddle	21,894
Nov 24	CHELSEA	D 1-1	Falco	31,197
Dec 1	Coventry City	D 1-1	Falco	14,518
Dec 8	NEWCASTLE UNITED	W 3-1	Roberts (pen), Falco 2	29,695
Dec 15	Watford	W 2-1	Falco, Crooks	24,225
Dec 22	Norwich City	W 2-1	Galvin, Crooks	17,682
Dec 26	WEST HAM UNITED	D 2-2	Mabbutt, Crooks	37,186
Dec 29	SUNDERLAND	W 2-0	Hoddle, Crooks	26,930
Jan 1	Arsenal	W 2-1	Falco, Crooks	48,714
Jan 12	Queens Park Rangers	D 2-2	Falco, Crooks	27,404
Feb 2	Luton Town	D 2-2	Roberts, Falco	17,511
Feb 23	West Bromwich Albion	W 1-0	Falco	15,418
Mar 2	Stoke City	W 1-0	Crooks	12,552
Mar 12	MANCHESTER UNITED	L 1-2	Falco	42,918
Mar 16	Liverpool	W 1-0	Crooks	43,852
Mar 23	SOUTHAMPTON	W 5-1	Ardiles, Falco, Hoddle, Crooks, Brooke	33,772
Mar 30	ASTON VILLA	L 0-2		27,971
Apr 3	EVERTON	L 1-2	Roberts	48,108
Apr 6	West Ham United	D 1-1	Ardiles	24,435
Apr 13	Leicester City	W 2-1	Falco, Hoddle	15,609
Apr 17	ARSENAL	L 0-2		40,399
Apr 20	IPSWICH TOWN	L 2-3	Leworthy 2	20,348
Apr 27	Chelsea	D 1-1	Galvin	26,310
May 4	COVENTRY CITY	W 4-2	Falco 2, Hoddle, Hughton	16,711
May 6	Newcastle United	W 3-2	Leworthy, Hoddle, Crook	29,702
May 11	WATFORD	L 1-5	Hoddle (pen)	23,167
May 14	SHEFFIELD WEDNESDAY	W 2-0	Falco, Hoddle (pen)	15,669
May 17	NOTTINGHAM FOREST	W 1-0	Falco	20,075

FA Cup

Jan 5	CHARLTON ATHLETIC	(Rd3) D 1-1	Crooks	29,029
Jan 23	Charlton Athletic	(R) W 2-1	Falco, Galvin	21,409
Jan 27	Liverpool	(Rd4) L 0-1		27,905

League Cup

Sep 26	Halifax Town	(Rd2/1L) W 5-1	Falco 2, Crooks 3	7,027
Oct 9	HALIFAX TOWN	(Rd2/2L) W 4-0	Hughton, Hazard 2, Crooks	14,802
Oct 31	LIVERPOOL	(Rd3) W 1-0	Allen	38,690
Nov 21	Sunderland	(Rd4) D 0-0		27,421
Dec 5	SUNDERLAND	(R) L 1-2	Roberts (pen)	25,835

UEFA Cup

Sep 19	SC Braga	(Rd1/1L) W 3-0	Falco 2, Galvin	30,000
Oct 3	SC BRAGA	(Rd2/2L) W 6-0	Stevens, Hughton, Falco, Crooks 3	22,478
Oct 24	Club Brugge KV	(Rd2/1L) L 1-2	Allen	27,000
Nov 7	CLUB BRUGGE KV	(Rd2/2L) W 3-0	Roberts, Allen, Hazard	34,356
Nov 28	BOHEMIANS PRAG	(Rd3/1L) W 2-0	Stevens, Ondra o.g.	27,971
Dec 12	Bohemians Prague	(Rd3/2L) D 1-1	Falco	17,500
Mar 6	REAL MADRID	(Rd4/1L) L 0-1		39,914
Mar 20	Real Madrid	(Rd4/2L) D 0-0		95,000

MANAGER: Peter Shreeve

CAPTAIN: Steve Perryman   **TOP SCORER:** Mark Falco

BIGGEST WIN: 6-0 v SC Braga (H), 3 October 1984, UEFA Cup 1st Round 2nd leg

HIGHEST ATTENDANCE: 95,000 v Real Madrid, 20 March 1985, UEFA Cup 4th Round 2nd leg

MAJOR TRANSFERS IN: Clive Allen from Queens Park Rangers, John Chiedozie from Notts County

MAJOR TRANSFERS OUT: Steve Archibald to Barcelona, Alan Brazil to Manchester United, Paul Price to Minnesota Strikers

League and Cup Appearances

PLAYER	LEAGUE	CUP COMPETITION			TOTAL
		FA CUP	LC	UEFA	
Allen	12 (1)		3	3 (1)	18 (2)
Ardiles	10 (1)				10 (1)
Bowen	6				6
Brooke	1 (3)			0 (3)	1 (6)
Chiedozie	31 (3)	3	5	7	46 (3)
Clemence	42	3	5	8	58
Cooke				0 (2)	0 (2)
Crook	2 (3)				2 (3)
Crooks	22	3	2	5 (1)	32 (1)
Dick	2			0 (2)	2 (2)
Falco	42	3	5	8	58
Galvin	38	3	3	7	51
Hazard	15 (8)		3 (1)	7	25 (9)
Hoddle	26 (2)	3	3	4 (2)	36 (4)
Hughton	29 (2)	2 (1)	4	6 (1)	41 (4)
Leworthy	6				6
Mabbutt	15 (10)	1 (1)	2 (2)	3 (1)	21 (14)
Miller	39	3	5	8	55
Perryman	42	3	5	8	58
Roberts	40	3	4	7	54
Stevens	28	3	5	6	42
Thomas	14 (2)		1	1 (3)	16 (5)

Goalscorers

PLAYER	LEAGUE	CUP COMPETITION			TOTAL
		FA CUP	LC	UEFA	
Falco	22	1	2	4	29
Crooks	10	1	4	3	18
Allen	7		1	2	10
Roberts	7		1	1	9
Hoddle	8				8
Hazard	4		2	1	7
Galvin	4	1		1	6
Chiedozie	5				5
Hughton	1		1	1	3
Leworthy	3				3
Ardiles	2				2
Mabbutt	2				2
Stevens				2	2
Brooke	1				1
Crook	1				1
Perryman	1				1
Opp's o.gs.				1	1

Fact File

Real Madrid's victory made them the first club to beat Spurs at White Hart Lane in European competition. 42 previous visitors had tried and failed.

Final Division One Table

		P	W	D	L	F	A	Pts
1	EVERTON	42	28	6	8	88	43	90
2	LIVERPOOL	42	22	11	9	68	35	77
3	TOTTENHAM HOTSPUR	42	23	8	11	78	51	77
4	MANCHESTER U	42	22	10	10	77	47	76
5	SOUTHAMPTON	42	19	11	12	56	47	68
6	CHELSEA	42	18	12	12	63	48	66
7	ARSENAL	42	19	9	14	61	49	66
8	SHEFFIELD W	42	17	14	11	58	45	65
9	NOTTINGHAM F	42	19	7	16	56	48	64
10	ASTON VILLA	42	15	11	16	60	60	56
11	WATFORD	42	14	13	15	81	71	55
12	WBA	42	16	7	19	58	45	55
13	LUTON TOWN	42	15	9	18	57	61	54
14	NEWCASTLE U	42	13	13	16	55	70	52
15	LEICESTER C	42	15	6	21	65	73	51
16	WEST HAM U	42	13	12	17	51	68	51
17	IPSWICH T	42	13	11	18	46	57	50
18	COVENTRY C	42	15	5	22	47	64	50
19	QPR	42	13	11	18	53	72	50
20	NORWICH CITY	42	13	10	19	46	64	49
21	BLACKBURN R	42	10	10	22	40	62	40
22	STOKE C	42	3	8	31	24	91	17

Season 1985-86

Football League Division One

DATE	OPPONENTS	SCORE		GOALSCORERS	ATTENDANCE
Aug 17	WATFORD	W	4-0	Allen P, Waddle 2, Falco	29,884
Aug 21	Oxford United	D	1-1	Thomas	10,634
Aug 24	Ipswich Town	L	0-1		17,758
Aug 26	EVERTON	L	0-1		29,720
Aug 31	Manchester City	L	1-2	Miller	27,789
Sep 4	CHELSEA	W	4-1	Roberts, Miller, Falco, Chiedozie	23,642
Sep 7	NEWCASTLE UNITED	W	5-1	Falco, Chiedozie 2, Hoddle, Hazard	23,883
Sep 14	Nottingham Forest	W	1-0	Hughton	17,554
Sep 21	SHEFFIELD WEDNESDAY	W	5-1	Falco 2, Hoddle, Waddle 2	23,601
Sep 28	Liverpool	L	1-4	Chiedozie	41,521
Oct 5	West Bromwich Albion	D	1-1	Waddle	12,040
Oct 20	Coventry City	W	3-2	Falco, Hoddle (pen), Chiedozie	13,545
Oct 26	LEICESTER CITY	L	1-3	Falco	17,944
Nov 2	Southampton	L	0-1		17,440
Nov 9	LUTON TOWN	L	1-3	Cooke	19,163
Nov 16	Manchester United	D	0-0		54,575
Nov 23	QUEENS PARK RANGERS	D	1-1	Mabbutt	20,334
Nov 30	Aston Villa	W	2-1	Mabbutt, Falco	14,099
Dec 7	OXFORD UNITED	W	5-1	Falco, Allen C 2, Hoddle, Waddle	17,698
Dec 14	Watford	L	0-1		16,327
Dec 21	IPSWICH TOWN	W	2-0	Allen C, Hoddle	18,845
Dec 26	WEST HAM UNITED	W	1-0	Perryman	33,835
Dec 28	Chelsea	L	0-2		37,115
Jan 1	Arsenal	D	0-0		45,109
Jan 11	NOTTINGHAM FOREST	L	0-3		19,043
Jan 18	MANCHESTER CITY	L	0-2		17,009
Feb 1	Everton	L	0-1		33,178
Feb 8	COVENTRY CITY	L	0-1		13,135
Feb 22	Sheffield Wednesday	W	2-1	Chiedozie, Howells	23,232
Mar 2	LIVERPOOL	L	1-2	Waddle	16,436
Mar 8	WEST BROMWICH ALBION	W	5-0	Mabbutt, Falco 2, Galvin, Waddle	10,841
Mar 15	Birmingham City	W	2-1	Stevens, Waddle	9,394
Mar 22	Newcastle United	D	2-2	Hoddle, Waddle	30,615
Mar 29	ARSENAL	W	1-0	Stevens	33,427
Mar 31	West Ham United	L	1-2	Ardiles	27,497
Apr 5	Leicester City	W	4-1	Bowen, Falco 3	9,574
Apr 12	Luton Town	D	1-1	Allen C	13,141
Apr 16	BIRMINGHAM CITY	W	2-0	Chiedozie, Falco	9,359
Apr 19	MANCHESTER UNITED	D	0-0		32,357
Apr 26	Queens Park Rangers	W	5-2	Falco 2, Allen C 2, Hoddle	17,768
May 3	ASTON VILLA	W	4-2	Falco 2, Allen C 2	14,854
May 5	SOUTHAMPTON	W	5-3	Galvin 3, Allen C, Waddle	13,036

FA Cup

Jan 4	Oxford United	(Rd3)	D	1-1	Chiedozie	10,638
Jan 8	OXFORD UNITED	(R)	W	2-1*	Waddle, Allen C	19,136
Jan 25	Notts County	(Rd4)	D	1-1	Allen C	17,546
Jan 29	NOTTS COUNTY	(R)	W	5-0	Chiedozie, Falco, Allen C, Hoddle, Waddle	17,393
Mar 4	EVERTON	(Rd5)	L	1-2	Falco	23,338

* after extra time

League Cup

Sep 23	Orient	(Rd2/1L)	L	0-2		13,828
Oct 30	ORIENT	(Rd2/2L)	W	4-0	Roberts 2, Galvin, Waddle	21,046
Nov 6	WIMBLEDON	(Rd3)	W	2-0	Leworthy, Mabbutt	16,899
Nov 20	PORTSMOUTH	(Rd4)	D	0-0		28,619
Nov 27	Portsmouth	(R)	D	0-0*		28,100
Dec 10	Portsmouth	(2R)	L	0-1		26,306

* after extra time

Screen Sport Super Cup

Oct 2	SOUTHAMPTON	(Grp A)	W	2-1	Falco 2	11,549
Dec 3	Liverpool	(Grp A)	L	0-2		14,855
Dec 17	Southampton	(Grp A)	W	3-1	Falco, Allen C, Leworthy	4,680
Jan 14	LIVERPOOL	(Grp A)	L	0-3		10,078
Feb 5	EVERTON	(SF/1L)	D	0-0		7,54
Mar 19	Everton	(SF/2L)	L	1-3*	Falco	12,008

* after extra time

Fact File

Ray Clemence made his 1,000th senior appearance of his career against Newcastle United in September.

League and Cup Appearances

PLAYER	LEAGUE	CUP COMPETITION		OTHER	TOTAL
		FA CUP	LC		
Allen C	16 (3)	3 (1)	1	5 (1)	25 (5)
Allen P	29 (4)	4 (1)	3 (1)	5 (1)	41 (7)
Ardiles	20 (3)	2	3 (1)	2 (1)	27 (5)
Bowen	1 (1)			0 (1)	1 (2)
Chiedozie	13 (5)	2 (3)	2	3 (1)	20 (9)
Clemence	42	5	6	5	58
Cooke	(2)		1 (1)	0 (2)	1 (5)
Crook	1 (3)			1	2 (3)
Dick	1				1
Falco	40	3	6	5	54
Galvin	23		3	2	28
Hazard	3 (1)				3 (1)
Hoddle	31	5	5	2	43
Howells	1				1
Hughton	33	4	6	5 (1)	48 (1)
Jennings			1		1
Leworthy	2 (3)		0 (1)	0 (1)	2 (5)
Mabbutt	29 (3)	5	5	5 (1)	44 (4)
Miller	29	3	2	3	37
Perryman	22 (1)	5	4	5	36 (1)
Roberts	32	3	6	5	46
Stevens	28 (1)	5	5	5	43 (1)
Thomas	27	1	2 (1)	3 (1)	33 (2)
Waddle	39	5	6	4	54

Goalscorers

PLAYER	LEAGUE	CUP COMPETITION		OTHER	TOTAL
		FA CUP	LC		
Falco	19	2		4	25
Waddle	11	2	1		14
Allen C	9	3		1	13
Chiedozie	7	2			9
Hoddle	7	1			8
Galvin	4		1		5
Mabbutt	3		1		4
Roberts	1		2		3
Leworthy			1	1	2
Miller	2				2
Stevens	2				2
Allen P	1				1
Ardiles	1				1
Bowen	1				1
Cooke	1				1
Hazard	1				1
Howells	1				1
Hughton	1				1
Perryman	1				1
Thomas	1				1

Final Division One Table

		P	W	D	L	F	A	Pts
1	Liverpool	42	26	10	6	89	37	88
2	Everton	42	26	8	8	87	41	86
3	West Ham U	42	26	6	10	74	40	84
4	Manchester U	42	22	10	10	70	36	76
5	Sheffield W	42	21	10	11	63	54	73
6	Chelsea	42	20	11	11	57	56	71
7	Arsenal	42	20	9	13	49	47	69
8	Nottingham F	42	19	11	12	69	53	68
9	Luton Town	42	18	12	12	61	44	66
10	Tottenham Hotspur	42	19	8	15	74	52	65
11	Newcastle U	42	17	12	13	67	72	63
12	Watford	42	16	11	15	69	51	59
13	QPR	42	15	7	20	53	64	52
14	Southampton	42	12	10	20	51	62	46
15	Manchester C	42	11	12	19	43	57	45
16	Aston Villa	42	10	14	18	51	67	44
17	Coventry C	42	11	10	21	48	71	43
18	Oxford United	42	10	12	20	62	80	42
19	Leicester C	42	10	12	20	54	76	42
20	Ipswich T	42	11	8	23	32	55	41
21	Birmingham C	42	8	5	29	30	73	29
22	WBA	42	4	12	26	35	89	24

Season 1986-87

Football League Division One

DATE	OPPONENTS	SCORE	GOALSCORERS	ATTENDANCE
Aug 23	Aston Villa	W 3-0	Allen C 3	24,712
Aug 25	NEWCASTLE UNITED	D 1-1	Allen C	25,381
Aug 30	MANCHESTER CITY	W 1-0	Roberts	23,164
Sep 2	Southampton	L 0-2		17,911
Sep 6	Arsenal	D 0-0		44,703
Sep 13	CHELSEA	L 1-3	Allen C (pen)	28,202
Sep 20	Leicester City	W 2-1	Allen C 2	13,141
Sep 27	EVERTON	W 2-0	Allen C 2	28,007
Oct 4	LUTON TOWN	D 0-0		22,738
Oct 11	Liverpool	W 1-0	Allen C	43,139
Oct 18	SHEFFIELD WEDNESDAY	D 1-1	Allen C	26,876
Oct 25	Queens Park Rangers	L 0-2		18,579
Nov 1	WIMBLEDON	L 1-2	Thomas M	21,820
Nov 8	Norwich City	L 1-2	Claesen	22,019
Nov 15	COVENTRY CITY	W 1-0	Allen C	20,255
Nov 22	Oxford United	W 4-2	Allen C 2, Waddle 2	12,143
Nov 29	NOTTINGHAM FOREST	L 2-3	Allen C 2	30,042
Dec 7	Manchester United	D 3-3	Mabbutt, Allen C, Moran o.g.	35,267
Dec 13	WATFORD	W 2-1	Gough, Hoddle	23,137
Dec 20	Chelsea	W 2-0	Allen C 2	21,576
Dec 26	WEST HAM UNITED	W 4-0	Hodge, Allen C 2, Waddle	39,019
Dec 27	Coventry City	L 3-4	Allen C 2, Claesen	22,175
Jan 1	Charlton Athletic	W 2-0	Claesen, Galvin	19,744
Jan 4	ARSENAL	L 1-2	Thomas M	37,723
Jan 24	ASTON VILLA	W 3-0	Hodge 2, Claesen	19,121
Feb 14	SOUTHAMPTON	W 2-0	Hodge, Gough	22,066
Feb 25	LEICESTER CITY	W 5-0	Allen C 2 (1 pen), Allen P, Claesen 2	16,038
Mar 7	QUEENS PARK RANGERS	W 1-0	Allen C (pen)	21,071
Mar 22	LIVERPOOL	W 1-0	Waddle	32,763
Mar 25	Newcastle United	D 1-1	Hoddle	30,836
Mar 28	Luton Town	L 1-3	Waddle	13,447
Apr 4	NORWICH CITY	W 3-0	Allen C 3	22,400
Apr 7	Sheffield Wednesday	W 1-0	Allen C	19,488
Apr 15	Manchester City	D 1-1	Claesen	21,460
Apr 18	CHARLTON ATHLETIC	W 1-0	Allen C	26,926
Apr 20	West Ham United	L 1-2	Allen C	23,972
Apr 22	Wimbledon	D 2-2	Claesen, Bowen	7,917
Apr 25	OXFORD UNITED	W 3-1	Allen P, Waddle, Hoddle	20,064
May 2	Nottingham Forest	L 0-2		19,837
May 4	MANCHESTER UNITED	W 4-0	Thomas M 2, Allen C (pen), Allen P	36,692
May 9	Watford	L 0-1		20,024
May 11	Everton	L 0-1		28,287

FA Cup

Jan 10	SCUNTHORPE UNITED	(Rd3) W 3-2	Waddle, Mabbutt, Claesen	19,339
Jan 31	CRYSTAL PALACE	(Rd4) W 4-0	Mabbutt, Allen C (pen), Claesen, O'Reilly o.g.	29,603
Feb 21	NEWCASTLE UNITED	(Rd5) W 1-0	Allen C (pen)	38,033
Mar 15	Wimbledon	(Rd6) W 2-0	Waddle, Hoddle	15,636
Apr 11	Watford *	(SF) W 4-1	Hodge 2, Allen C, Allen P	46,151
May 16	Coventry City **	(F) L 2-3†	Allen C, Mabbutt	98,000

* played at Villa Park, Birmingham. ** played at Wembley, London. † after extra time

League Cup

Sep 23	Barnsley	(Rd2/1L) W 3-2	Roberts, Allen C, Waddle	10,079
Oct 8	BARNSLEY	(Rd2/2L) W 5-3	Close, Hoddle 2, Galvin, Allen C	12,299
Oct 29	BIRMINGHAM CITY	(Rd3) W 5-0	Roberts, Allen C 2, Hoddle, Waddle	15,542
Nov 26	Cambridge United	(Rd4) W 3-1	Allen C, Close, Waddle	10,033
Jan 27	West Ham United	(Rd5) D 1-1	Allen C	28,648
Feb 2	WEST HAM UNITED	(R) W 5-0	Allen C (1 pen) 3, Hoddle, Claesen	41,995
Feb 8	Arsenal	(SF/1L) W 1-0	Allen C	41,256
Mar 1	ARSENAL	(SF/2L) L 1-2†	Allen C	37,099
Mar 4	ARSENAL	(R) L 1-2	Allen C	41,005

† after extra time

League and Cup Appearances

PLAYER	LEAGUE	CUP COMPETITION		TOTAL
		FA CUP	LC	
Allen C	38 (1)	6	8 (1)	52 (2)
Allen P	34 (3)	6	8 (1)	48 (4)
Ardiles	16 (9)	4	7	27 (9)
Bowen	1 (1)			1 (1)
Chiedozie	1			1
Claesen	18 (8)	1 (5)	5	24 (13)
Clemence	40	6	9	55
Close	1 (1)		2	3 (1)
Falco	5 (1)		0 (1)	5 (2)
Galvin	20 (5)	1	2 (3)	23 (8)
Gough	40	6	9	55
Gray	1			1
Hoddle	34 (1)	6	8	48 (1)
Hodge	19	6		25
Howells	1			1
Hughton	9	2		11
Mabbutt	37	6	8	51
Miller	2		2 (1)	4 (1)
Moncur	1			1
Moran	1			1
O'Shea	1 (1)			1 (1)
Parks	2			2
Polston	6		0 (1)	6 (1)
Roberts	17		4	21
Ruddock	4	0 (1)		4 (1)
Samways	1 (1)			1 (1)
Stevens	20	1 (4)	2 (1)	23 (5)
Stimson	1			1
Thomas D	13 (4)	3	7 (1)	23 (5)
Thomas M	39	6	9	54
Waddle	39	6	9	54

Goalscorers

PLAYER	LEAGUE	CUP COMPETITION		TOTAL
		FA CUP	LC	
Allen C	33	4	12	49
Claesen	8	2	1	11
Waddle	6	2	3	11
Hoddle	3	1	4	8
Hodge	4	2		6
Allen P	3	1		4
Mabbutt	1	3		4
Thomas M	4			4
Roberts	1		2	3
Close			2	2
Galvin	1		1	2
Gough	2			2
Bowen	1			1
Opp's o.g.s.	1	1		2

Final Division One Table

		P	W	D	L	F	A	Pts
1	EVERTON	42	26	8	8	76	31	86
2	LIVERPOOL	42	23	8	11	72	42	77
3	TOTTENHAM HOTSPUR	42	21	8	13	68	43	71
4	ARSENAL	42	20	10	12	58	35	70
5	NORWICH CITY	42	17	17	8	53	51	68
6	WIMBLEDON	42	19	9	14	57	50	66
7	LUTON TOWN	42	18	12	12	47	45	66
8	NOTTINGHAM F	42	18	11	13	64	51	65
9	WATFORD	42	18	9	15	67	54	63
10	COVENTRY C	42	17	12	13	50	45	63
11	MANCHESTER U	42	14	14	14	52	45	56
12	SOUTHAMPTON	42	14	10	18	69	49	52
13	SHEFFIELD W	42	13	13	16	58	59	52
14	CHELSEA	42	13	13	16	53	64	52
15	WEST HAM U	42	14	10	18	52	67	52
16	QPR	42	13	11	18	48	64	50
17	NEWCASTLE U	42	12	11	19	47	65	47
18	OXFORD UNITED	42	11	13	18	44	69	46
19	CHARLTON A	42	11	11	20	45	55	44
20	LEICESTER C	42	11	9	22	54	76	42
21	MANCHESTER C	42	8	15	19	36	57	39
22	ASTON VILLA	42	8	12	22	45	79	36

Fact File

Four Spurs players made their debuts at Everton as David Pleat prepared for the FA Cup Final. Despite only losing by a solitary goal they were fined by the Football League for fielding a weakened team.

Season 1987-88

Football League Division One

DATE	OPPONENTS	SCORE	GOALSCORERS	ATTENDANCE
Aug 15	Coventry City	L 1-2	Mabbutt	23,947
Aug 19	NEWCASTLE UNITED	W 3-1	Allen C, Waddle, Hodge	26,261
Aug 22	CHELSEA	W 1-0	Claesen	37,079
Aug 29	Watford	D 1-1	Allen C	19,073
Sep 1	OXFORD UNITED	W 3-0	Allen C, Claesen 2	21,811
Sep 5	Everton	D 0-0		32,389
Sep 12	SOUTHAMPTON	W 2-1	Allen C (pen), Claesen	24,728
Sep 19	West Ham United	W 1-0	Fairclough	27,750
Sep 26	Manchester United	L 0-1		47,601
Oct 3	SHEFFIELD WEDNESDAY	W 2-0	Allen P, Claesen	24,311
Oct 10	Norwich City	L 1-2	Claesen	18,669
Oct 18	ARSENAL	L 1-2	Claesen	36,680
Oct 24	Nottingham Forest	L 0-3		23,543
Oct 31	WIMBLEDON	L 0-3		22,282
Nov 4	Portsmouth	D 0-0		15,302
Nov 14	QUEENS PARK RANGERS	D 1-1	Allen P	28,113
Nov 21	Luton Town	L 0-2		10,091
Nov 28	LIVERPOOL	L 0-2		47,362
Dec 13	CHARLTON ATHLETIC	L 0-1		20,392
Dec 20	Derby County	W 2-1	Allen C, Claesen	17,593
Dec 6	Southampton	L 1-2	Claesen	18,456
Dec 28	WEST HAM UNITED	W 2-1	Fairclough, Waddle	39,456
Jan 1	WATFORD	W 2-1	Allen C, Moran	25,235
Jan 2	Chelsea	D 0-0		29,317
Jan 16	COVENTRY CITY	D 2-2	Allen C 2	25,650
Jan 23	Newcastle United	L 0-2		24,616
Feb 13	Oxford United	D 0-0		9,906
Feb 23	MANCHESTER UNITED	D 1-1	Allen C	25,731
Feb 27	Sheffield Wednesday	W 3-0	Allen C, Allen P, Claesen	18,046
Mar 1	DERBY COUNTY	D 0-0		15,986
Mar 6	Arsenal	L 1-2	Allen C	37,143
Mar 9	EVERTON	W 2-1	Fairclough, Walsh	18,662
Mar 12	NORWICH CITY	L 1-3	Claesen	19,322
Mar 19	Wimbledon	L 0-3		8,616
Mar 26	NOTTINGHAM FOREST	D 1-1	Foster o.g.	25,306
Apr 2	PORTSMOUTH	L 0-1		18,616
Apr 4	Queens Park Rangers	L 0-2		14,738
Apr 23	Liverpool	L 0-1		44,798
May 2	Charlton Athletic	D 1-1	Hodge	13,977
May 4	LUTON TOWN	W 2-1	Mabbutt, Hodge	15,437

FA Cup

Jan 9	Oldham Athletic	(Rd3) W 4-2	Thomas, Allen C 2, Waddle	16,931
Jan 30	Port Vale	(Rd4) L 1-2	Ruddock	20,045

League Cup

Sep 23	Torquay United	(Rd2/1L) L 0-1		5,000
Oct 7	TORQUAY UNITED	(Rd2/2L) W 3-0	Claesen 2, Cole o.g.	20,970
Oct 28	Aston Villa	(Rd3) L 1-2	Ardiles	29,114

League and Cup Appearances

PLAYER	LEAGUE	CUP COMPETITION		TOTAL
		FA CUP	LC	
Allen C	31 (3)	2	1	34 (3)
Allen P	39	1	3	43
Ardiles	26 (2)	1	3	30 (2)
Claesen	19 (5)		2	21 (5)
Clemence	11		2	13
Close	2 (5)		1	3 (5)
Fairclough	40	2	3	45
Fenwick	17	2		19
Gough	9		1	10
Gray	0 (1)			0 (1)
Hodge	25 (1)	1	2	28 (1)
Howells	3 (8)	0 (2)	1	4 (10)
Hughton	12 (1)	2	0 (1)	14 (2)
Mabbutt	37	2	3	42
Metgod	5 (7)		2	7 (7)
Mimms	13			13
Moncur	3 (2)			3 (2)
Moran	9 (4)	2	0 (3)	11 (7)
O'Shea	0 (1)			0 (1)
Parks	16	2	1	19
Polston	0 (2)			0 (2)
Ruddock	3 (2)		1	4 (2)
Samways	21 (5)		2	23 (5)
Statham	14 (4)	0 (1)		14 (5)
Stevens	18		2	20
Thomas	35 (1)	2	3	40 (1)
Waddle	21 (1)	2	1	24 (1)
Walsh	11			11

Goalscorers

PLAYER	LEAGUE	CUP COMPETITION		TOTAL
		FA CUP	LC	
Allen C	11	2		13
Claesen	10		2	12
Fairclough	4			4
Allen P	3			3
Hodge	3			3
Waddle	2	1		3
Mabbutt	2			2
Ardiles			1	1
Moran	1			1
Ruddock		1		1
Thomas		1		1
Walsh	1			1
Opp's o.g.s.	1		1	2

Fact File

During the season Spurs played testimonial matches for no less than three players – Tony Galvin, Chris Hughton and Danny Thomas.

MANAGER: David Pleat until October, Terry Venables from December

CAPTAIN: Richard Gough/Gary Mabbutt

TOP SCORER: Clive Allen

BIGGEST WIN: 3-0 v Oxford United (H), 1 September 1987, Football League Division One; 3-0 v Torquay United (H), 7 October 1987, League Cup 2nd Round 2nd leg; 3-0 v Sheffield Wednesday (A), 27 February 1988, Football League Division One

HIGHEST ATTENDANCE: 47,601 v Manchester United, 26 September 1987, Football League Division One

MAJOR TRANSFERS IN: Chris Fairclough from Nottingham Forest, Terry Fenwick from Queens Park Rangers, Johnny Metgod from Nottingham Forest, Bobby Mimms from Everton, Paul Walsh from Liverpool

MAJOR TRANSFERS OUT: Tony Galvin to Sheffield Wednesday, Glenn Hoddle to Monaco

Final Division One Table

		P	W	D	L	F	A	Pts
1	LIVERPOOL	40	26	12	2	87	24	90
2	MANCHESTER U	40	23	12	5	71	38	81
3	NOTTINGHAM F	40	20	13	7	67	39	73
4	EVERTON	40	19	13	8	53	27	70
5	QPR	40	19	10	11	48	38	67
6	ARSENAL	40	18	12	10	58	39	66
7	WIMBLEDON	40	14	15	11	58	47	57
8	NEWCASTLE U	40	14	14	12	55	53	56
9	LUTON TOWN	40	14	11	15	57	58	53
10	COVENTRY C	40	13	14	13	46	53	53
11	SHEFFIELD W	40	15	8	17	52	66	53
12	SOUTHAMPTON	40	12	14	14	49	53	50
13	TOTTENHAM HOTSPUR	40	12	11	17	38	48	47
14	NORWICH CITY	40	12	9	19	40	52	45
15	DERBY CO	40	10	13	17	35	45	43
16	WEST HAM U	40	9	15	16	40	52	42
17	CHARLTON A	40	9	15	16	38	52	42
18	CHELSEA	40	9	15	16	50	68	42
19	PORTSMOUTH	40	7	14	19	36	66	35
20	WATFORD	40	7	11	22	27	51	32
21	OXFORD UNITED	40	6	13	21	44	80	31

Season 1988-89

Football League Division One

DATE	OPPONENTS	SCORE	GOALSCORERS	ATTENDANCE
Sep 3	Newcastle United	D 2-2	Fenwick, Waddle	32,977
Sep 10	ARSENAL	L 2-3	Gascoigne, Waddle	32,621
Sep 17	Liverpool	D 1-1	Fenwick	40,929
Sep 24	MIDDLESBROUGH	W 3-2	Fenwick (pen), Waddle, Howells	23,427
Oct 1	MANCHESTER UNITED	D 2-2	Walsh, Waddle	29,318
Oct 8	Charlton Athletic	D 2-2	Fenwick (pen), Allen	14,384
Oct 22	Norwich City	L 1-3	Fairclough	20,330
Oct 25	SOUTHAMPTON	L 1-2	Wallace [Ray] o.g.	19,517
Oct 29	Aston Villa	L 1-2	Fenwick (pen)	26,238
Nov 5	DERBY COUNTY	L 1-3	Stewart	22,868
Nov 12	WIMBLEDON	W 3-2	Butters, Fenwick (pen), Samways	23,589
Nov 20	Sheffield Wednesday	W 2-0	Stewart 2	15,386
Nov 23	COVENTRY CITY	D 1-1	Stewart	21,961
Nov 26	QUEENS PARK RANGERS	D 2-2	Gascoigne, Waddle	26,698
Dec 3	Everton	L 0-1		29,657
Dec 10	MILLWALL	W 2-0	Gascoigne, Waddle	27,660
Dec 17	West Ham United	W 2-0	Thomas, Mabbutt	28,365
Dec 26	LUTON TOWN	D 0-0		27,337
Dec 31	NEWCASTLE UNITED	W 2-0	Walsh, Waddle	27,739
Jan 2	Arsenal	L 0-2		45,129
Jan 15	NOTTINGHAM FOREST	L 1-2	Waddle	16,903
Jan 21	Middlesbrough	D 2-2	Stewart 2	23,692
Feb 5	Manchester United	L 0-1		41,423
Feb 11	CHARLTON ATHLETIC	D 1-1	Stewart	22,803
Feb 21	NORWICH CITY	W 2-1	Gascoigne, Waddle	19,120
Feb 25	Southampton	W 2-0	Nayim, Waddle	16,702
Mar 1	ASTON VILLA	W 2-0	Waddle 2	19,090
Mar 11	Derby County	D 1-1	Gascoigne	18,206
Mar 18	Coventry City	D 1-1	Waddle	17,156
Mar 22	Nottingham Forest	W 2-1	Howells, Samways	23,098
Mar 26	LIVERPOOL	L 1-2	Fenwick (pen)	30,012
Mar 28	Luton Town	W 3-1	Howells, Walsh, Gascoigne	11,146
Apr 1	WEST HAM UNITED	W 3-0	Fenwick (pen), Nayim, Stewart	28,375
Apr 12	SHEFFIELD WEDNESDAY	D 0-0		17,270
Apr 5	Wimbledon	W 2-1	Waddle, Stewart	12,366
Apr 22	EVERTON	W 2-1	Walsh 2	28,568
Apr 29	Millwall	W 5-0	Walsh, Stewart 3, Samways	16,551
May 13	Queens Park Rangers	L 0-1		21,873

FA Cup

Jan 7	Bradford City	(Rd3)	L 0-1		15,917

League Cup

Sep 27	Notts County	(Rd2/1L)	D 1-1	Samways	9,269
Oct 11	NOTTS COUNTY	(Rd2/2L)	W 2-1	Fenwick (pen), Gascoigne	14,953
Nov 1	BLACKBURN ROVERS	(Rd3)	D 0-0*		18,814
Nov 9	Blackburn Rovers	(R)	W 2-1	Thomas, Stewart	12,961
Nov 29	Southampton	(Rd4)	L 1-2	Osman o.g.	17,357

* after extra time

League and Cup Appearances

PLAYER	LEAGUE	CUP COMPETITION		TOTAL
		FA CUP	LC	
Allen	35 (2)	1	5	41 (2)
Bergsson	8	1		9
Butters	27 (1)	1	1 (1)	29 (2)
Fairclough	20	1	4	25
Fenwick	34	1	5	40
Gascoigne	31 (1)		5	36 (1)
Gray	0 (1)			0 (1)
Howells	12 (15)	0 (1)	0 (1)	12 (17)
Hughton	20 (1)			20 (1)
Mabbutt	38	1	5	44
Mimms	20	1	5	26
Moncur	0 (1)			0 (1)
Moran	4 (4)	0 (1)	1 (1)	5 (6)
Nayim	8 (3)			8 (3)
Polston	0 (3)			0 (3)
Robson	3 (2)			3 (2)
Samways	12 (7)		3 (2)	15 (9)
Statham	6		2	8
Stevens	5		2	7
Stewart	29 (1)	1	4	34 (1)
Stimson	0 (1)			0 (1)
Thomas	22 (3)	1	5	28 (3)
Thorstvedt	18			18
Waddle	38	1	5	44
Walsh	28 (5)	1	3	32 (5)

Goalscorers

PLAYER	LEAGUE	CUP COMPETITION		TOTAL
		FA CUP	LC	
Waddle	14			14
Stewart	12		1	13
Fenwick	8		1	9
Gascoigne	6		1	7
Walsh	6			6
Samways	3		1	4
Howells	3			3
Nayim	2			2
Thomas	1		1	2
Allen	1			1
Butters	1			1
Fairclough	1			1
Mabbutt	1			1
Opp's o.gs.	1		1	2

Fact File

The cockerel that had perched on the roof of the East Stand since 1958 was removed during refurbishment work. The myth that it contained souvenirs of Spurs' entry into the First Division in 1909 was dispelled when it was opened up to reveal nothing more than a dilapidated handbook.

MANAGER: Terry Venables

CAPTAIN: Gary Mabbutt **TOP SCORER:** Chris Waddle

BIGGEST WIN: 5-0 v Millwall (A), 29 April 1989, Football League Division One

HIGHEST ATTENDANCE: 45,129 v Arsenal, 2 January 1989, Football League Division One

MAJOR TRANSFERS IN: Paul Gascoigne from Newcastle United, Paul Stewart from Manchester City, Erik Thorstvedt from IFK Gothenburg

MAJOR TRANSFERS OUT: Clive Allen to Bordeaux, Ossie Ardiles to QPR, Nico Claesen to Antwerp, Johnny Metgod to Feyenoord

Final Division One Table

		P	W	D	L	F	A	Pts
1	ARSENAL	38	22	10	6	73	36	76
2	LIVERPOOL	38	22	10	6	65	28	76
3	NOTTINGHAM F	38	17	13	8	64	43	64
4	NORWICH CITY	38	17	11	10	48	45	62
5	DERBY CO	38	17	7	14	40	38	58
6	TOTTENHAM HOTSPUR	38	15	12	11	60	46	57
7	COVENTRY C	38	14	13	11	47	42	55
8	EVERTON	38	14	12	12	50	45	54
9	QPR	38	14	11	13	43	37	53
10	MILLWALL	38	14	11	13	47	52	53
11	MANCHESTER U	38	13	12	13	45	35	51
12	WIMBLEDON	38	14	9	15	50	39	51
13	SOUTHAMPTON	38	10	15	13	52	66	45
14	CHARLTON A	38	10	12	16	44	58	42
15	SHEFFIELD W	38	10	12	16	34	51	42
16	LUTON TOWN	38	10	11	17	42	52	41
17	ASTON VILLA	38	9	13	16	45	56	40
18	MIDDLESBROUGH	38	9	12	17	44	61	39
19	WEST HAM U	38	10	8	20	37	62	38
20	NEWCASTLE U	38	7	10	21	32	63	31

Season 1989-90

Football League Division One

DATE	OPPONENTS	SCORE	GOALSCORERS	ATTENDANCE
Aug 19	LUTON TOWN	W 2-1	Stewart, Allen	17,668
Aug 22	Everton	L 1-2	Allen	34,402
Aug 26	Manchester City	D 1-1	Gascoigne	32,004
Sep 9	Aston Villa	L 0-2		24,769
Sep 16	CHELSEA	L 1-4	Gascoigne	16,260
Sep 23	Norwich City	D 2-2	Gascoigne, Lineker	20,095
Sep 30	QUEENS PARK RANGERS	W 3-2	Lineker 3	23,781
Oct 14	Charlton Athletic	W 3-1	Gascoigne, Lineker, Thomas	17,692
Oct 18	ARSENAL	W 2-1	Walsh, Samways	33,944
Oct 21	SHEFFIELD WEDNESDAY	W 3-0	Lineker 2, Moran	26,909
Oct 29	Liverpool	L 0-1		36,550
Nov 4	Southampton	D 1-1	Gascoigne	19,601
Nov 11	WIMBLEDON	L 0-1		26,876
Nov 18	Crystal Palace	W 3-2	Howells, Samways, Lineker (pen)	26,366
Nov 25	DERBY COUNTY	L 1-2	Stewart	28,075
Dec 2	Luton Town	D 0-0		12,620
Dec 9	EVERTON	W 2-1	Stewart, Lineker	29,374
Dec 16	Manchester United	W 1-0	Lineker	36,230
Dec 26	MILLWALL	W 3-1	Samways, Lineker, McCleary o.g.	26,874
Dec 30	NOTTINGHAM FOREST	L 2-3	Lineker 2	33,401
Jan 1	Coventry City	D 0-0		19,599
Jan 13	MANCHESTER CITY	D 1-1	Howells	26,384
Jan 20	Arsenal	L 0-1		46,132
Feb 4	NORWICH CITY	W 4-0	Lineker (1 pen) 3, Howells	19,599
Feb 10	Chelsea	W 2-1	Howells, Lineker	29,130
Feb 21	ASTON VILLA	L 0-2		32,472
Feb 24	Derby County	L 1-2	Moncur	19,676
Mar 3	CRYSTAL PALACE	L 0-1		26,181
Mar 10	CHARLTON ATHLETIC	W 3-0	Polston J, Lineker, Howells	21,104
Mar 17	Queens Park Rangers	L 1-3	Walsh	16,691
Mar 21	LIVERPOOL	W 1-0	Stewart	25,656
Mar 31	Sheffield Wednesday	W 4-2	Allen, Lineker 2, Stewart	26,582
Apr 7	Nottingham Forest	W 3-1	Stewart, Allen 2	21,669
Apr 14	COVENTRY CITY	W 3-2	Lineker 2, Stewart	23,317
Apr 16	Millwall	W 1-0	Lineker	10,573
Apr 21	MANCHESTER UNITED	W 2-1	Gascoigne, Lineker	33,317
Apr 28	Wimbledon	L 0-1		12,800
May 5	SOUTHAMPTON	W 2-1	Stewart, Allen	31,038

FA Cup

Jan 6	SOUTHAMPTON	(Rd3) L 1-3	Howells	33,134

League Cup

Sep 20	SOUTHEND UNITED	(Rd2/1L) W 1-0	Fenwick	15,734
Oct 4	Southend United	(Rd2/2L) L 2-3*	Allen Nayim	10,400
Oct 25	Manchester United	(Rd3) W 3-0	Lineker, Samways, Nayim	45,759
Nov 22	Tranmere Rovers	(Rd4) D 2-2	Gascoigne, Higgins o.g.	13,789
Nov 29	TRANMERE ROVERS	(R) W 4-0	Allen, Howells, Mabbutt, Stewart	22,720
Jan 17	Nottingham Forest	(Rd5) D 2-2	Lineker, Sedgley	30,044
Jan 24	NOTTINGHAM FOREST	(R) L 2-3	Nayim, Walsh	32,357

* after extra-time

League and Cup Appearances

PLAYER	LEAGUE	CUP COMPETITION		TOTAL
		FA CUP	LC	
Allen	29 (3)	1	6	36 (3)
Bergsson	17 (1)	1	1	19 (1)
Butters	7		1	8
Fenwick	10		3	13
Gascoigne	34		4	38
Howells	33 (1)	1	5 (1)	39 (2)
Hughton	8		1 (1)	9 (1)
Lineker	38	1	6	45
Mabbutt	36	1	7	44
Mimms	4	1		5
Moncur	2 (3)			2 (3)
Moran	0 (5)		0 (1)	0 (6)
Nayim	18 (1)		3 (1)	21 (2)
Polston A	0 (1)			0 (1)
Polston J	11 (2)		3	14 (2)
Robson	0 (3)		1	1 (3)
Samways	18 (5)	1	4 (1)	23 (6)
Sedgley	31 (1)	1	6	38 (1)
Stevens	4 (3)		0 (1)	4 (4)
Stewart	24 (4)	1	6	31 (4)
Thomas	17 (9)	1	7	25 (9)
Thorstvedt	34		7	41
Van den Hauwe	31		6	37
Walsh	12 (14)	0 (1)	1 (3)	13 (18)

Goalscorers

PLAYER	LEAGUE	CUP COMPETITION		TOTAL
		FA CUP	LC	
Lineker	24		2	26
Stewart	8		1	9
Allen	6		2	8
Gascoigne	6		1	7
Howells	5	1	1	7
Samways	3		1	4
Nayim			3	3
Walsh	2		1	3
Fenwick			1	1
Mabbutt			1	1
Moncur	1			1
Moran	1			1
Polston	1			1
Sedgley			1	1
Thomas	1			1
Opp's o.g.s.	1		1	2

Fact File

In March, Andy and John Polston became the first brothers to play for Spurs in a Football League game since John and Bobby McTavish in 1912.

Final Division One Table

		P	W	D	L	F	A	PTS
1	LIVERPOOL	38	23	10	5	78	37	79
2	ASTON VILLA	38	21	7	10	57	38	70
3	TOTTENHAM HOTSPUR	38	19	6	13	59	47	63
4	ARSENAL	38	18	8	12	54	38	62
5	CHELSEA	38	16	12	10	58	50	60
6	EVERTON	38	17	8	13	57	46	59
7	SOUTHAMPTON	38	15	10	13	71	63	55
8	WIMBLEDON	38	13	16	9	47	40	55
9	NOTTINGHAM F	38	15	9	14	55	47	54
10	NORWICH CITY	38	13	14	11	44	42	53
11	QPR	38	13	11	14	45	44	50
12	COVENTRY C	38	14	7	17	39	40	49
13	MANCHESTER U	38	13	9	16	46	47	48
14	MANCHESTER C	38	12	12	14	43	52	48
15	CRYSTAL P	38	13	9	16	42	66	48
16	DERBY CO	38	13	7	18	43	40	46
17	LUTON TOWN	38	10	13	15	43	57	43
18	SHEFFIELD W	38	11	10	17	35	51	43
19	CHARLTON A	38	7	9	22	31	57	30
20	MILLWALL	38	5	11	22	39	65	26

MANAGER: Terry Venables

CAPTAIN: Gary Mabbutt

TOP SCORER: Gary Lineker

BIGGEST WIN: 4-0 v Norwich City (H), 4 February 1990, Football League Division One; 4-0 v Tranmere Rovers (H), 29 November 1989, League Cup 4th Round replay

HIGHEST ATTENDANCE: 46,132 v Arsenal, 20 January 1990, Football League Division One

MAJOR TRANSFERS IN: Gary Lineker from Barcelona, Nayim from Barcelona, Steve Sedgley from Coventry City, Pat Van den Hauwe from Everton

MAJOR TRANSFERS OUT: Chris Fairclough to Leeds United, Gary Stevens to Portsmouth, Chris Waddle to Marseille

The Essential History of Tottenham Hotspur

Season 1990-91

Football League Division One

DATE	OPPONENTS	SCORE	GOALSCORERS	ATTENDANCE
Aug 25	MANCHESTER CITY	W 3-1	Gascoigne, Lineker 2	33,501
Aug 28	Sunderland	D 0-0		30,214
Sep 1	Arsenal	D 0-0		40,009
Sep 8	DERBY COUNTY	W 3-0	Gascoigne 3	23,614
Sep 15	Leeds United	W 2-0	Howells, Lineker	31,342
Sep 22	CRYSTAL PALACE	D 1-1	Gascoigne	34,859
Sep 29	ASTON VILLA	W 2-1	Lineker, Allen	34,939
Oct 6	Queens Park Rangers	D 0-0		21,405
Oct 20	SHEFFIELD UNITED	W 4-0	Nayim, Walsh 3	34,612
Oct 27	Nottingham Forest	W 2-1	Howells 2	27,347
Nov 4	LIVERPOOL	L 1-3	Lineker	35,003
Nov 10	WIMBLEDON	W 4-2	Mabbutt, Stewart, Lineker (pen), Walsh	28,769
Nov 18	Everton	D 1-1	Howells	23,716
Nov 24	NORWICH CITY	W 2-1	Lineker 2	33,942
Dec 1	Chelsea	L 2-3	Gascoigne, Lineker	33,478
Dec 8	SUNDERLAND	D 3-3	Lineker, Walsh 2	30,431
Dec 15	Manchester City	L 1-2	Gascoigne	31,236
Dec 22	LUTON TOWN	W 2-1	Stewart 2	27,007
Dec 26	Coventry City	L 0-2		22,731
Dec 29	Southampton	L 0-3		21,405
Jan 1	MANCHESTER UNITED	L 1-2	Lineker (pen)	29,399
Jan 12	ARSENAL	D 0-0		34,753
Jan 20	Derby County	W 1-0	Lineker	17,747
Feb 2	LEEDS UNITED	D 0-0		32,253
Feb 23	Wimbledon	L 1-5	Bergsson	10,500
Mar 2	CHELSEA	D 1-1	Lineker (pen)	26,168
Mar 16	Aston Villa	L 2-3	Samways, Allen	32,638
Mar 23	QUEENS PARK RANGERS	D 0-0		30,860
Mar 30	COVENTRY CITY	D 2-2	Nayim 2	29,033
Apr 1	Luton Town	D 0-0		11,322
Apr 6	SOUTHAMPTON	W 2-0	Lineker 2	24,291
Apr 10	Norwich City	L 1-2	Hendry	19,014
Apr 17	Crystal Palace	L 0-1		26,285
Apr 20	Sheffield United	D 2-2	Edinburgh, Walsh	25,706
Apr 24	EVERTON	D 3-3	Allen, Mabbutt, Nayim	21,675
May 4	NOTTINGHAM FOREST	D 1-1	Nayim	30,891
May 11	Liverpool	L 0-2		36,192
May 20	Manchester United	D 1-1	Hendry	46,791

FA Cup

Jan 5	Blackpool	(Rd3)	W 1-0	Stewart	9,563
Jan 26	OXFORD UNITED	(Rd4)	W 4-2	Mabbutt, Gascoigne 2, Lineker	31,665
Feb 16	Portsmouth	(Rd5)	W 2-1	Gascoigne 2	26,049
Mar 10	NOTTS COUNTY	(Rd6)	W 2-1	Nayim, Gascoigne	29,686
Apr 14	Arsenal *	(SF)	W 3-1	Gascoigne, Lineker 2	77,893
May 18	Nottingham Forest *	(F)	W 2-1†	Stewart, Walker o.g.	80,000

* played at Wembley, London. † after extra time

League Cup

Sep 26	HARTLEPOOL UNITED	(Rd2/1L)	W 5-0	Gascoigne (1 pen) 4, Lineker	19,760
Oct 9	Hartlepool United	(Rd2/2L)	W 2-1	Stewart 2	9,631
Oct 30	BRADFORD CITY	(Rd3)	W 2-1	Stewart, Gascoigne	25,451
Nov 27	Sheffield United	(Rd4)	W 2-1	Gascoigne, Stewart	25,852
Jan 16	Chelsea	(Rd5)	D 0-0		34,178
Jan 23	CHELSEA	(R)	L 0-3		33,861

Fact File

Des Walker, whose own goal proved decisive in the FA Cup Final, had played for Spurs at youth level in 1981-82.

MANAGER: Terry Venables

CAPTAIN: Gary Mabbutt

TOP SCORER: Paul Gascoigne and Gary Lineker

BIGGEST WIN: 5-0 v Hartlepool United (H), 26 September 1990, League Cup 2nd Round 1st leg

HIGHEST ATTENDANCE: 80,000 v Nottingham Forest, 18 May 1991, FA Cup Final

MAJOR TRANSFERS IN: Justin Edinburgh from Southend United

MAJOR TRANSFERS OUT: Chris Hughton to West Ham United

League and Cup Appearances

PLAYER	LEAGUE	CUP COMPETITION		TOTAL
		FA CUP	LC	
Allen	34 (2)	6	6	46 (2)
Bergsson	9 (3)			9 (3)
Dearden			1	1
Edinburgh	14 (2)	5	5	24 (2)
Fenwick	4	2	2	8
Garland	0 (1)			0 (1)
Gascoigne	26	6	4 (1)	36 (1)
Gray	3 (3)	0 (1)		3 (4)
Hendon	0 (2)			0 (2)
Hendry	2 (2)			2 (2)
Howells	29	4	6	39
Lineker	32	6	5	43
Mabbutt	35	6	6	47
Moncur	4 (5)		1 (1)	5 (6)
Moran	0 (1)	1		1 (1)
Nayim	32 (1)	3 (2)	2 (3)	37 (6)
Samways	14 (9)	4 (1)	4	22 (10)
Sedgley	33 (1)	4 (1)	4 (2)	41 (4)
Stewart	35	5	6	46
Thomas	23 (8)	2	4 (1)	29 (9)
Thorstvedt	37	6	5	48
Tuttle	4 (2)		0 (1)	4 (3)
Van den Hauwe	31 (1)	5	2	38 (1)
Walker	1			1
Walsh	16 (13)	1 (3)	3 (3)	20 (19)

Goalscorers

PLAYER	LEAGUE	CUP COMPETITION		TOTAL
		FA CUP	LC	
Gascoigne	7	6	6	19
Lineker	15	3	1	19
Stewart	3	2	4	9
Walsh	7			7
Nayim	5	1		6
Howells	4			4
Allen	3			3
Mabbutt	2	1		3
Hendry	2			2
Bergsson	1			1
Edinburgh	1			1
Samways	1			1
Opp's o.gs.		1		1

Final Division One Table

		P	W	D	L	F	A	Pts
1	ARSENAL*	38	24	13	1	74	18	83
2	LIVERPOOL	38	23	7	8	77	40	76
3	CRYSTAL P	38	20	9	9	50	41	69
4	LEEDS UNITED	38	19	7	12	65	47	64
5	MANCHESTER C	38	17	11	10	64	53	62
6	MANCHESTER U†	38	16	12	10	58	45	59
7	WIMBLEDON	38	14	14	10	53	46	56
8	NOTTINGHAM F	38	14	12	12	65	50	54
9	EVERTON	38	13	12	13	50	46	51
10	TOTTENHAM HOTSPUR	38	11	16	11	51	50	49
11	CHELSEA	38	13	10	15	58	69	49
12	QPR	38	12	10	16	44	39	46
13	SHEFFIELD U	38	13	7	18	36	55	46
14	SOUTHAMPTON	38	12	9	17	58	69	45
15	NORWICH CITY	38	13	6	19	41	64	45
16	COVENTRY C	38	11	11	16	42	49	44
17	ASTON VILLA	38	9	14	15	46	58	41
18	LUTON TOWN	38	10	7	21	42	61	37
19	BLACKBURN R	38	8	10	20	38	60	34
20	DERBY CO	38	5	9	24	37	75	24

* Arsenal had 2 points deducted. † Manchester U had 1 point deducted.

Season 1991-92

Football League Division One

DATE	OPPONENTS	SCORE	GOALSCORERS	ATTENDANCE
Aug 17	Southampton	W 3-2	Durie, Lineker 2	18,581
Aug 24	CHELSEA	L 1-3	Lineker	34,645
Aug 28	Nottingham Forest	W 3-1	Durie, Lineker, Bergsson	24,018
Aug 31	Norwich City	W 1-0	Lineker	19,460
Sep 7	Aston Villa	D 0-0		33,096
Sep 14	QUEENS PARK RANGERS	W 2-0	Lineker 2	30,059
Sep 21	Wimbledon	W 5-3	Samways, Lineker (1 pen) 4	11,927
Sep 28	MANCHESTER UNITED	L 1-2	Durie	35,087
Oct 5	Everton	L 1-3	Lineker	29,505
Oct 19	MANCHESTER CITY	L 0-1		30,502
Oct 26	West Ham United	L 1-2	Lineker	23,946
Nov 2	Sheffield Wednesday	D 0-0		31,573
Nov 16	LUTON TOWN	W 4-1	Lineker 2, Houghton 2	27,543
Nov 23	SHEFFIELD UNITED	L 0-1		28,168
Dec 1	Arsenal	L 0-2		38,892
Dec 7	NOTTS COUNTY	W 2-1	Mabbutt, Walsh	23,364
Dec 14	Leeds United	D 1-1	Howells	31,404
Dec 18	LIVERPOOL	L 1-2	Walsh	27,434
Dec 22	Crystal Palace	W 2-1	Walsh, Lineker	22,491
Dec 26	NOTTINGHAM FOREST	L 1-2	Stewart	31,079
Dec 28	NORWICH CITY	W 3-0	Nayim, Lineker, Allen	27,969
Jan 1	Coventry City	W 2-1	Stewart, Lineker	19,639
Jan 11	Chelsea	L 0-2		28,628
Jan 18	SOUTHAMPTON	L 1-2	Mabbutt	23,191
Jan 25	OLDHAM ATHLETIC	D 0-0		20,843
Feb 1	Manchester City	L 0-1		30,123
Feb 16	CRYSTAL PALACE	L 0-1		19,834
Feb 22	ARSENAL	D 1-1	Stewart	33,124
Mar 7	LEEDS UNITED	L 1-3	Allen	27,622
Mar 11	Luton Town	D 0-0		11,494
Mar 14	SHEFFIELD WEDNESDAY	L 0-2		23,027
Mar 21	Liverpool	L 1-2	Stewart	39,968
Mar 28	COVENTRY CITY	W 4-3	Durie 3, Lineker	22,744
Apr 1	WEST HAM UNITED	W 3-0	Lineker 3	31,809
Apr 4	ASTON VILLA	L 2-5	Lineker, Teale o.g.	26,370
Apr 7	Notts County	W 2-0	Lineker 2	9,205
Apr 11	Queens Park Rangers	W 2-1	Gray A, Durie	20,678
Apr 14	Sheffield United	L 0-2		21,526
Apr 18	WIMBLEDON	W 3-2	Lineker 2, Hendry	23,934
Apr 20	Oldham Athletic	L 0-1		15,443
Apr 25	EVERTON	D 3-3	Stewart, Minton, Allen	36,340
May 2	Manchester United	L 1-3	Lineker	44,595

FA Cup

Jan 5	Aston Villa	(Rd3) D 0-0		29,316
Jan 14	ASTON VILLA	(R) L 0-1		25,462

League Cup

Sep 25	Swansea City	(Rd2/1L) L 0-1		11,416
Oct 9	SWANSEA CITY	(Rd2/2L) W 5-1	Stewart, Samways, Lineker, Allen, Brazil o.g.	20,198
Oct 29	Grimsby Town	(Rd3) W 3-0	Howells, Durie, Lineker	17,017
Dec 4	Coventry City	(Rd4) W 2-1	Durie, Allen	20,095
Jan 8	NORWICH CITY	(Rd5) W 2-1	Walsh, Lineker	29,471
Feb 9	Nottingham Forest	(SF/1L) D 1-1	Lineker (pen)	21,402
Mar 1	NOTTINGHAM FOREST	(SF/2L) L 1-2	Lineker	28,216

European Cup-Winners' Cup

Aug 21	Stockerau *	(PRd/1L) W 1-0	Durie	17,700
Sep 4	STOCKERAU	(PRd/2L) W 1-0	Mabbutt	28,072
Sep 17	Hadjuk Split **	(Rd1/1L) L 0-1		7,000
Oct 2	HADJUK SPLIT	(Rd1/2L) W 2-0	Tuttle, Durie	24,297
Oct 23	PORTO	(Rd2/1L) W 3-1	Durie, Lineker 2	23,621
Nov 7	Porto	(Rd2/2L) D 0-0		55,000
Mar 4	Feyenoord	(Rd3/1L) L 0-1		38,385
Mar 18	FEYENOORD	(Rd3/2L) D 0-0		29,834

*played at Prater Stadium, Vienna. ** played at Linz, Austria.

FA Charity Shield

Aug 10	Arsenal †		D 0-0	65,483

† played at Wembley, London

MANAGER: Peter Shreeve

CAPTAIN: Gary Mabbutt

TOP SCORER: Gary Lineker

BIGGEST WIN: 5-1 v Swansea City (H), 9 October 1991, League Cup 2nd Round 2nd leg

HIGHEST ATTENDANCE:65,483 v Arsenal, 10 August 1991, FA Charity Shield

League and Cup Appearances

PLAYER	LEAGUE	CUP COMPETITION			OTHER	TOTAL
		FA CUP	LC	ECWC		
Allen	38 (1)	2	7	6 (1)	1	54 (2)
Bergsson	17 (11)	0 (1)	3 (2)	5 (1)		25 (15)
Cundy	10					10
Durie	31	1	6	8		46
Edinburgh	22 (1)		1 (2)	3		26 (3)
Fenwick	22 (1)	2	4	4	1	33 (1)
Gray	14					14
Hendon	0 (2)		1	0 (2)		1 (4)
Hendry	1 (4)			0 (1)		1 (5)
Houghton	0 (10)		0 (2)	0 (2)		0 (14)
Howells	27 (4)	1	5	6	1	40 (4)
Lineker	35	2	5	8	1	51
Mabbutt	40	2	6	8	1	57
Minton	2					2
Moncur			0 (1)			0 (1)
Moran			0 (1)			0 (1)
Nayim	22 (9)	0 (1)	4 (2)	6	1	33 (12)
Samways	26 (1)	2	6 (1)	6 (1)	1	41 (3)
Sedgley	21 (13)	2	6 (1)	4 (3)	1	34 (17)
Stewart	38	2	7	8	1	56
Thorstvedt	24	2	6	6	1	39
Tuttle	2		1	1		4
Van den Hauwe	35	2	6	6	1	50
Walker	18		1	2		21
Walsh	17 (12)	2	2 (1)	1 (3)		22 (16)

Goalscorers

PLAYER	LEAGUE	CUP COMPETITION			OTHER	TOTAL
		FA CUP	LC	ECWC		
Lineker	28		5	2		35
Durie	7		2			9
Allen	3		2	3		8
Stewart	5		1			6
Walsh	3		1			4
Mabbutt	2			1		3
Houghton	2					2
Howells	1		1			2
Samways	1		1			2
Bergsson	1					1
Gray	1					1
Hendry	1					1
Minton	1					1
Nayim	1					1
Tuttle	1					1
Opp's o.gs.	1		1			2

Fact File

Liverpool's December visit was Spurs 3,000th Football League game.

Final Division One Table

		P	W	D	L	F	A	Pts
1	LEEDS U	42	22	16	4	74	37	82
2	MANCHESTER U	42	21	15	6	63	33	78
3	SHEFFIELD W	42	21	12	9	62	49	75
4	ARSENAL	42	19	15	8	81	47	72
5	MANCHESTER C	42	20	10	12	61	48	70
6	LIVERPOOL	42	16	16	10	47	40	64
7	ASTON VILLA	42	17	9	16	48	44	60
8	NOTTINGHAM F	42	16	11	15	60	58	59
9	SHEFFIELD U	42	16	9	17	65	63	57
10	CRYSTAL P	42	14	15	13	53	61	57
11	QPR	42	12	18	12	48	47	54
12	EVERTON	42	13	14	15	52	43	53
13	WIMBLEDON	42	13	14	15	53	53	53
14	CHELSEA	42	13	14	15	50	60	53
15	TOTTENHAM HOTSPUR	42	15	7	20	58	63	52
16	SOUTHAMPTON	42	14	10	18	39	55	52
17	OLDHAM A	42	14	9	19	63	67	51
18	NORWICH C	42	11	12	19	47	63	45
19	COVENTRY C	42	11	11	20	35	44	44
20	LUTON T	42	10	12	20	39	71	42
21	NOTTS CO	42	10	10	22	40	62	40
22	WEST HAM U	42	9	11	22	37	59	38

Season 1992-93

FA Premier League

DATE	OPPONENTS	SCORE	GOALSCORERS	ATTENDANCE
Aug 15	Southampton	D 0-0		19,654
Aug 19	COVENTRY CITY	L 0-2		24,388
Aug 22	CRYSTAL PALACE	D 2-2	Durie, Sedgley	25,237
Aug 25	Leeds United	L 0-5		28,218
Aug 30	Ipswich Town	D 1-1	Cundy	20,100
Sep 2	SHEFFIELD UNITED	W 2-0	Sheringham, Durie	21,322
Sep 5	EVERTON	W 2-1	Allen, Turner	26,503
Sep 14	Coventry City	L 0-1		15,348
Sep 19	MANCHESTER UNITED	D 1-1	Durie	33,296
Sep 27	Sheffield Wednesday	L 0-2		24,895
Oct 3	Queens Park Rangers	L 1-4	Sheringham	19,845
Oct 11	MIDDLESBROUGH	D 2-2	Sheringham (pen), Barmby	24,735
Oct 25	Wimbledon	D 1-1	Barmby	8,628
Oct 31	LIVERPOOL	W 2-0	Nayim, Ruddock	32,917
Nov 7	Blackburn Rovers	W 2-0	Sheringham (pen), Howells	17,305
Nov 21	ASTON VILLA	D 0-0		32,852
Nov 28	Manchester City	W 1-0	Phelan o.g.	25,496
Dec 5	CHELSEA	L 1-2	Campbell	31,540
Dec 12	ARSENAL	W 1-0	Allen	33,707
Dec 19	Oldham Athletic	L 1-2	Sheringham	11,735
Dec 26	Norwich City	D 0-0		19,413
Dec 28	NOTTINGHAM FOREST	W 2-1	Barmby, Mabbutt	32,118
Jan 9	Manchester United	L 1-4	Barmby	35,648
Jan 16	SHEFFIELD WEDNESDAY	L 0-2		25,702
Jan 27	IPSWICH TOWN	L 0-2		23,738
Jan 30	Crystal Palace	W 3-1	Sheringham 2, Gray	20,937
Feb 7	SOUTHAMPTON	W 4-2	Sheringham 2, Anderton, Barmby	20,098
Feb 10	Everton	W 2-1	Mabbutt, Allen	16,164
Feb 20	LEEDS UNITED	W 4-0	Sheringham (1 pen) 3, Ruddock	32,040
Feb 27	QUEENS PARK RANGERS	W 3-2	Sheringham 2, Anderton	32,341
Mar 2	Sheffield United	L 0-6		16,654
Mar 10	Aston Villa	D 0-0		37,727
Mar 20	Chelsea	D 1-1	Sheringham (pen)	25,157
Mar 24	MANCHESTER CITY	W 3-1	Nayim, Anderton, Turner	27,247
Apr 9	NORWICH CITY	W 5-1	Sheringham 2, Barmby, Nayim, Ruddock	31,425
Apr 12	Nottingham Forest	L 1-2	Sedgley	25,682
Apr 17	OLDHAM ATHLETIC	W 4-1	Sheringham (2 pen) 2, Turner, Anderton	26,663
Apr 20	Middlesbrough	L 0-3		13,472
May 1	WIMBLEDON	D 1-1	Anderton	24,473
May 5	BLACKBURN ROVERS	L 1-2	Anderton	23,097
May 8	Liverpool	L 2-6	Sedgley, Sheringham	43,385
May 11	Arsenal	W 3-1	Sheringham, Hendry 2	26,393

FA Cup

Jan 2	Marlow *	(Rd3) W 5-1	Barmby 2, Samways 2, Sheringham	19,365
Jan 24	Norwich City	(Rd4) W 2-0	Sheringham 2	15,005
Feb 14	WIMBLEDON	(Rd5) W 3-2	Anderton, Sheringham, Barmby	26,529
Mar 7	Manchester City	(Rd6) W 4-2	Nayim 3, Sedgley	34,050
Apr 4	Arsenal †	(SF) L 0-1		76,263

* played at White Hart Lane, London. † played at Wembley, London

League Cup

Sep 21	BRENTFORD	(Rd2/1L) W 3-1	Sheringham, Watson, Durie	19,365
Oct 7	Brentford	(Rd2/2L) W 4-2	Sheringham (1 pen) 2, Turner, Anderton	11,445
Oct 28	Manchester City	(Rd3) W 1-0	Samways	18,399
Dec 2	Nottingham Forest	(Rd4) L 0-2		22,812

FIRST TEAM COACHES: Doug Livermore and Ray Clemence

CAPTAIN: Gary Mabbutt

TOP SCORER: Teddy Sheringham

BIGGEST WIN: 5-1 v Marlow (A), 2 January 1993, FA Cup 3rd Round; 5-1 v Norwich City (H), 9 April 1993, FA Premier League

HIGHEST ATTENDANCE: 76,263 v Arsenal, 4 April 1993, FA Cup Semi-final

MAJOR TRANSFERS IN: Darren Anderton from Portsmouth, Dean Austin from Southend United, Neil Ruddock from Southampton, Teddy Sheringham from Nottingham Forest

MAJOR TRANSFERS OUT: Paul Gascoigne to Lazio, Gary Lineker to Grampus Eight, Paul Stewart to Liverpool, Paul Walsh to Portsmouth

League and Cup Appearances

PLAYER	LEAGUE	CUP COMPETITION		TOTAL
		FA CUP	LC	
Allen	38	5	4	47
Anderton	32 (2)	4 (1)	2	38 (3)
Austin	33 (1)	5	2 (1)	40 (2)
Barmby	17 (5)	3 (1)	2 (1)	22 (7)
Bergsson	0 (5)	0 (1)		0 (6)
Campbell	0 (1)			0 (1)
Cundy	13 (2)		2	15 (2)
Dearden	0 (1)			0 (1)
Durie	17	1	2	20
Edinburgh	31 (1)	5	3 (1)	39 (2)
Fenwick	3 (2)			3 (2)
Gray	9 (8)			9 (8)
Hendry	2 (3)			2 (3)
Hill	2 (2)			2 (2)
Hodges	0 (4)			0 (4)
Howells	16 (2)	2 (1)	0 (1)	18 (4)
Mabbutt	29	5	2	36
McDonald	2			2
Minton			0 (1)	0 (1)
Moran	0 (3)			0 (3)
Nayim	15 (3)	3	2	20 (3)
Nethercott	3 (2)			3 (2)
Ruddock	38	5	4	47
Samways	34	5	3	42
Sedgley	20 (2)	2	3	25 (2)
Sheringham	38	5	4	47
Thorstvedt	25 (2)	5	2	32 (2)
Turner	7 (11)	0 (1)	0 (2)	7 (14)
Tuttle	4 (1)		2	6 (1)
Van den Hauwe	13 (5)		2	15 (5)
Walker	17		2	19
Watson	4 (1)	0 (1)	1 (1)	5 (3)

Goalscorers

PLAYER	LEAGUE	CUP COMPETITION		TOTAL
		FA CUP	LC	
Sheringham	21	4	3	28
Barmby	6	3		9
Anderton	6	1	1	8
Nayim	3	3		6
Durie	3		1	4
Sedgley	3	1		4
Turner	3		1	4
Allen	3			3
Ruddock	3			3
Samways		2	1	3
Hendry	2			2
Mabbutt	2			2
Campbell	1			1
Cundy	1			1
Gray	1			1
Howells	1			1
Watson			1	1
Opp's o.gs.	1			1

Final Premier League Table

		P	W	D	L	F	A	Pts
1	MANCHESTER U	42	24	12	6	67	31	84
2	ASTON VILLA	42	21	11	10	57	40	74
3	NORWICH CITY	42	21	9	12	61	65	72
4	BLACKBURN R	42	20	11	11	68	46	71
5	QPR	42	17	12	13	63	55	63
6	LIVERPOOL	42	16	11	15	62	55	59
7	SHEFFIELD W	42	15	14	13	55	51	59
8	TOTTENHAM HOTSPUR	42	16	11	15	60	66	59
9	MANCHESTER C	42	15	12	15	56	51	57
10	ARSENAL	42	15	11	16	40	38	56
11	CHELSEA	42	14	14	14	51	54	56
12	WIMBLEDON	42	14	12	16	57	47	54
13	EVERTON	42	15	8	19	53	55	53
14	SHEFFIELD U	42	14	10	18	54	53	52
15	COVENTRY C	42	13	13	16	52	57	52
16	IPSWICH T	42	12	16	14	50	55	52
17	LEEDS UNITED	42	12	15	15	57	62	51
18	SOUTHAMPTON	42	13	11	18	54	61	50
19	OLDHAM A	42	13	10	19	63	74	49
20	CRYSTAL P	42	11	16	15	48	61	49
21	MIDDLESBROUGH	42	11	11	20	54	75	44
22	NOTTINGHAM F	42	10	10	22	41	62	40

Season 1993-94

FA Premier League

DATE	OPPONENTS	SCORE	GOALSCORERS	ATTENDANCE
Aug 14	Newcastle United	W 1-0	Sheringham	35,216
Aug 16	ARSENAL	L 0-1		28,355
Aug 21	MANCHESTER CITY	W 1-0	Sedgley	24,535
Aug 25	Liverpool	W 2-1	Sheringham (1 pen) 2	42,456
Aug 28	Aston Villa	L 0-1		32,498
Sep 1	CHELSEA	D 1-1	Sheringham (1 pen)	27,567
Sep 11	Sheffield United	D 2-2	Sheringham 2	21,325
Sep 18	OLDHAM ATHLETIC	W 5-0	Sedgley 2, Durie, Dozzell, Sheringham	24,614
Sep 26	Ipswich Town	D 2-2	Dozzell, Sheringham	19,411
Oct 3	EVERTON	W 3-2	Caskey, Sheringham, Anderton	27,487
Oct 16	Manchester United	L 1-2	Caskey	44,655
Oct 23	SWINDON TOWN	D 1-1	Dozzell	31,394
Oct 30	Blackburn Rovers	L 0-1		16,849
Nov 6	Southampton	L 0-1		16,017
Nov 20	LEEDS UNITED	D 1-1	Anderton	31,275
Nov 24	WIMBLEDON	D 1-1	Barmby	17,744
Nov 27	Queens Park Rangers	D 1-1	Anderton	17,694
Dec 4	NEWCASTLE UNITED	L 1-2	Barmby (pen)	30,780
Dec 6	Arsenal	D 1-1	Anderton	35,669
Dec 11	Manchester City	W 2-0	Dozzell 2	21,566
Dec 18	LIVERPOOL	D 3-3	Samways, Hazard (pen), Caskey	31,394
Dec 27	NORWICH CITY	L 1-3	Barmby	31,130
Dec 28	West Ham United	W 3-1	Dozzell, Hazard, Anderton	20,787
Jan 1	COVENTRY CITY	L 1-2	Caskey	26,015
Jan 3	Sheffield Wednesday	L 0-1		32,514
Jan 15	MANCHESTER UNITED	L 0-1		31,343
Jan 22	Swindon Town	L 1-2	Barmby	16,563
Feb 5	SHEFFIELD WEDNESDAY	L 1-3	Rosenthal	23,078
Feb 12	BLACKBURN ROVERS	L 0-2		30,236
Feb 27	Chelsea	L 3-4	Sedgley, Dozzell, Gray (pen)	16,807
Mar 2	ASTON VILLA	D 1-1	Rosenthal	17,452
Mar 5	SHEFFIELD UNITED	D 2-2	Scott, Dozzell	25,741
Mar 19	IPSWICH TOWN	D 1-1	Barmby	26,653
Mar 26	Everton	W 1-0	Sedgley	23,580
Apr 2	Norwich City	W 2-1	Sheringham, Woodthorpe o.g.	21,181
Apr 4	WEST HAM UNITED	L 1-4	Sheringham (pen)	31,502
Apr 9	Coventry City	L 0-1		14,491
Apr 17	Leeds United	L 0-2		33,658
Apr 23	SOUTHAMPTON	W 3-0	Anderton, Samways, Sedgley	25,959
Apr 30	Wimbledon	L 1-2	Sheringham (pen)	20,875
May 5	Oldham Athletic	W 2-0	Samways, Howells	14,283
May 7	QUEENS PARK RANGERS	L 1-2	Sheringham (pen)	26,105

FA Cup

Jan 08	Peterborough United	(Rd3) D 1-1	Dozzell	19,169
Jan 19	PETERBOROUGH UNITED	(R) D 1-1*	Barmby	24,893
Jan 29	Ipswich Town	(Rd4) L 0-3		22,539

*after extra time – Spurs won 5-4 on penalties

League Cup

Sep 22	Burnley	(Rd2/1L) D 0-0		16,844
Oct 6	BURNLEY	(Rd2/2L) W 3-1	Sheringham 2, Howells	20,614
Oct 27	Derby County	(Rd3) W 1-0	Barmby	19,885
Dec 1	BLACKBURN ROVERS	(Rd4) W 1-0	Campbell	22,295
Jan 12	ASTON VILLA	(Rd5) L 1-2	Caskey	31,408

MANAGER: Ossie Ardiles

CAPTAIN: Gary Mabbutt

TOP SCORER: Teddy Sheringham

BIGGEST WIN: 5-0 v Oldham Athletic (H), 18 September 1993, FA Premier League

HIGHEST ATTENDANCE: 44,655 v Manchester United, 16 October 1993, FA Premier League

MAJOR TRANSFERS IN: Colin Calderwood from Swindon Town, Jason Dozzell from Ipswich Town, Mike Hazard from Swindon Town, David Kerslake from Leeds United, Ronnie Rosenthal from Liverpool, Kevin Scott from Newcastle United

MAJOR TRANSFERS OUT: Paul Allen to Southampton, Gordon Durie to Rangers, Nayim to Real Zaragoza, Neil Ruddock to Liverpool

League and Cup Appearances

PLAYER	LEAGUE	CUP COMPETITION		TOTAL
		FA CUP	LC	
Allen	0 (1)			0 (1)
Anderton	35 (2)	3	5	43 (2)
Austin	20 (3)	2	0 (1)	22 (4)
Barmby	27	3	3	33
Calderwood	26	3	5	34
Campbell	27 (7)	1 (2)	5	33 (9)
Carr	1		1	2
Caskey	16 (9)	3	3 (1)	22 (10)
Dozzell	28 (4)	2	4	34 (4)
Durie	10		2	12
Edinburgh	24 (1)	3	3	30 (1)
Gray	0 (2)			0 (2)
Hazard	13 (4)	2		15 (4)
Hendry	0 (3)	0 (1)	0 (1)	0 (5)
Hill	1 (2)			1 (2)
Howells	15 (3)		1 (1)	16 (4)
Kerslake	16 (1)	1 (1)	3	20 (2)
Mabbutt	29		3	32
Mahorn	1			1
Moran	0 (5)		0 (1)	0 (6)
Nethercott	9 (1)		1	10 (1)
Robinson	1 (1)			1 (1)
Rosenthal	11 (4)			11 (4)
Samways	39	3	5	47
Scott	12			12
Sedgley	42	3	5	50
Sheringham	17 (2)		2	19 (2)
Thorstvedt	32	1	4	37
Turner	0 (1)			0 (1)
Walker	10 (1)	2	1	13 (1)

Goalscorers

PLAYER	LEAGUE	CUP COMPETITION		TOTAL
		FA CUP	LC	
Sheringham	13		2	15
Dozzell	8	1		9
Barmby	5	1	1	7
Anderton	6			6
Sedgley	6			6
Caskey	4		1	5
Samways	3			3
Hazard	2			2
Howells	1		1	2
Rosenthal	2			2
Campbell			1	1
Durie	1			1
Gray	1			1
Scott	1			1
Opp's o.gs.	1			1

Final Premier League Table

		P	W	D	L	F	A	Pts
1	MANCHESTER U	42	27	11	4	80	38	92
2	BLACKBURN R	42	25	9	8	63	36	84
3	NEWCASTLE U	42	23	8	11	82	41	77
4	ARSENAL	42	18	17	7	53	28	71
5	LEEDS UNITED	42	18	16	8	65	39	70
6	WIMBLEDON	42	18	11	13	56	53	65
7	SHEFFIELD W	42	16	16	10	76	54	64
8	LIVERPOOL	42	17	9	16	59	55	60
9	QPR	42	16	12	14	62	61	60
10	ASTON VILLA	42	15	12	15	46	50	57
11	COVENTRY C	42	14	14	14	43	45	56
12	NORWICH CITY	42	12	17	13	65	68	53
13	WEST HAM U	42	13	13	16	47	58	52
14	CHELSEA	42	13	12	17	49	53	51
15	TOTTENHAM HOTSPUR	42	11	12	19	54	59	45
16	MANCHESTER C	42	9	18	15	38	49	45
17	EVERTON	42	12	8	22	42	63	44
18	SOUTHAMPTON	42	12	7	23	49	66	43
19	IPSWICH T	42	9	16	17	35	58	43
20	SHEFFIELD U	42	8	18	16	42	60	42
21	OLDHAM A	42	9	13	20	42	68	40
22	SWINDON T	42	5	15	22	47	100	30

Season 1994-95

FA Premier League

DATE	OPPONENTS	SCORE	GOALSCORERS	ATTENDANCE
Aug 20	Sheffield Wednesday	W 4-3	Sheringham, Anderton, Barmby, Klinsmann	34,051
Aug 24	EVERTON	W 2-1	Klinsmann 2	24,553
Aug 27	MANCHESTER UNITED	L 0-1		24,502
Aug 30	Ipswich Town	W 3-1	Dumitrescu, Klinsmann 2	22,559
Sep 12	SOUTHAMPTON	L 1-2	Klinsmann	22,387
Sep 19	Leicester City	L 1-3	Klinsmann	21,300
Sep 24	NOTTINGHAM FOREST	L 1-4	Dumitrescu	24,558
Oct 1	Wimbledon	W 2-1	Sheringham, Popescu	16,802
Oct 8	QUEENS PARK RANGERS	D 1-1	Barmby	25,799
Oct 15	Leeds United	D 1-1	Sheringham	39,224
Oct 24	Manchester City	L 2-5	Dumitrescu (1 pen)	25,473
Oct 29	WEST HAM UNITED	W 3-1	Klinsmann, Sheringham, Barmby	26,271
Nov 5	Blackburn Rovers	L 0-2		26,933
Nov 19	ASTON VILLA	L 3-4	Sheringham, Bosnich o.g. Klinsmann (pen),	26,899
Nov 23	CHELSEA	D 0-0		27,037
Nov 26	Liverpool	D 1-1	Ruddock o.g.	35,007
Dec 3	NEWCASTLE UNITED	W 4-2	Sheringham 3, Popescu	28,002
Dec 10	SHEFFIELD WEDNESDAY	W 3-1	Barmby, Klinsmann, Calderwood	25,912
Dec 17	Everton	D 0-0		32,809
Dec 26	Norwich City	W 2-0	Barmby, Sheringham	21,814
Dec 27	CRYSTAL PALACE	D 0-0		27,730
Dec 31	Coventry City	W 4-0	Darby o.g., Barmby, Anderton, Sheringham	19,951
Jan 2	ARSENAL	W 1-0	Popescu	28,747
Jan 14	West Ham United	W 2-1	Sheringham, Klinsmann	24,573
Jan 25	Aston Villa	L 0-1		40,017
Feb 5	BLACKBURN ROVERS	W 3-1	Barmby, Anderton, Klinsmann	28,124
Feb 11	Chelsea	D 1-1	Sheringham	30,812
Feb 25	WIMBLEDON	L 1-2	Klinsmann	27,258
Mar 4	Nottingham Forest	D 2-2	Sheringham, Calderwood	28,711
Mar 8	IPSWICH TOWN	W 3-0	Barmby, Klinsmann, Youds o.g.	24,930
Mar 15	Manchester United	D 0-0		43,802
Mar 18	LEICESTER CITY	W 1-0	Klinsmann	30,851
Mar 22	LIVERPOOL	D 0-0		31,988
Apr 2	Southampton	L 3-4	Sheringham 2, Klinsmann	15,105
Apr 11	MANCHESTER CITY	W 2-1	Howells, Klinsmann	27,410
Apr 14	Crystal Palace	D 1-1	Klinsmann	18,149
Apr 17	NORWICH CITY	W 1-0	Sheringham	32,304
Apr 29	Arsenal	D 1-1	Klinsmann	38,377
May 3	Newcastle United	D 3-3	Klinsmann, Barmby, Anderton	35,603
May 6	Queens Park Rangers	L 1-2	Sheringham	18,637
May 9	COVENTRY CITY	L 1-3	Anderton	24,134
May 14	LEEDS UNITED	D 1-1	Sheringham	33,040

FA Cup

Jan 7	ALTRINCHAM	(Rd3) W 3-0	Sheringham, Rosenthal, Nethercott	25,057
Jan 29	Sunderland	(Rd4) W 4-1	Mabbutt, Sheringham, Klinsmann (1 pen) 2	21,135
Feb 18	SOUTHAMPTON	(Rd5) D 1-1	Klinsmann	28,091
Mar 1	Southampton	(R) W 6-2*	Rosenthal 3, Sheringham, Barmby, Anderton	15,172
Mar 11	Liverpool	(Rd6) W 2-1	Sheringham, Klinsmann	39,592
Apr 9	Everton †	(SF) L 1-4	Klinsmann (pen)	38,226

* after extra time. † played at Elland Road, Leeds

League Cup

Sep 21	Watford	(Rd2/1L) W 6-3	Klinsmann 3, Anderton, Sheringham, Dumitrescu	13,659
Oct 4	WATFORD	(Rd2/2L) L 2-3	Barmby, Klinsmann	17,798
Oct 26	Notts County	(Rd3) L 0-3		16,952

MANAGER: Ossie Ardiles until October then Gerry Francis

CAPTAIN: Gary Mabbutt   **TOP SCORER:** Jurgen Klinsmann

BIGGEST WIN: 6-2 v Southampton (A), 1 March 1995, FA Cup 5th Round replay

HIGHEST ATTENDANCE: 43,802 v Manchester United, 15 March 1995, FA Premier League

MAJOR TRANSFERS IN: Ilie Dumitrescu from Steaua Bucharest, Jurgen Klinsmann from Monaco, Gica Popescu from PSV Eindhoven

MAJOR TRANSFERS OUT: Vinny Samways to Everton, Steve Sedgley to Ipswich Town

League and Cup Appearances

PLAYER	LEAGUE	CUP COMPETITION		TOTAL
		FA CUP	LC	
Anderton	37	6	2	45
Austin	23 (1)	4 (1)	2	29 (2)
Barmby	37 (1)	6	2	45 (1)
Calderwood	35 (1)	6		42 (1)
Campbell	29 (1)	3	3	35 (1)
Caskey	1 (3)	0 (1)		1 (4)
Dozzell	6 (1)	2		8 (1)
Dumitrescu	11 (2)			13 (2)
Edinburgh	29 (2)	4	2	35 (2)
Hazard	2 (9)		1 (1)	3 (10)
Hill	1 (2)		0 (2)	1 (4)
Howells	26	6	1 (1)	33 (1)
Kerslake	16 (2)		2	18 (2)
Klinsmann	41	6	3	50
Mabbutt	33 (3)	6	2	41 (3)
McMahon	2			2
Nethercott	8 (9)	2	0 (2)	10 (11)
Popescu	23	3	2	28
Rosenthal	14 (6)	2 (2)	1	17 (8)
Scott	4			4
Sheringham	41 (1)	6	2	49 (1)
Thorstvedt	1		1	2
Turner	1			1
Walker	41	6	2	49

Goalscorers

PLAYER	LEAGUE	CUP COMPETITION		TOTAL
		FA CUP	LC	
Klinsmann	20	5	4	29
Sheringham	18	4	1	23
Barmby	9	1	1	11
Anderton	5	1	1	7
Dumitrescu	4		1	5
Rosenthal		4		4
Popescu	3			3
Calderwood	2			2
Howells	1			1
Mabbutt		1		1
Nethercott		1		1
Opp's o.gs.	4			4

Fact File

Both Jurgen Klinsmann (Germany) and Erik Thorstvedt (Norway) captained their countries.

Final Premier League Table

		P	W	D	L	F	A	Pts
1	BLACKBURN R	42	27	8	7	80	39	89
2	MANCHESTER U	42	26	10	6	77	28	88
3	NOTTINGHAM F	42	22	11	9	72	43	77
4	LIVERPOOL	42	21	11	10	65	37	74
5	LEEDS UNITED	42	20	13	9	59	38	73
6	NEWCASTLE U	42	20	12	10	67	47	72
7	TOTTENHAM HOTSPUR	42	16	14	12	66	58	62
8	QPR	42	17	9	16	61	59	60
9	WIMBLEDON	42	15	11	16	48	65	56
10	SOUTHAMPTON	42	12	18	12	61	63	54
11	CHELSEA	42	13	15	14	50	55	54
12	ARSENAL	42	13	12	17	52	46	51
13	SHEFFIELD W	42	13	12	17	49	57	51
14	WEST HAM U	42	13	11	18	44	48	50
15	EVERTON	42	11	17	14	44	51	50
16	COVENTRY C	42	12	14	16	44	62	50
17	MANCHESTER C	42	12	13	17	53	64	49
18	ASTON VILLA	42	11	15	16	51	56	48
19	CRYSTAL P	42	11	12	19	34	49	45
20	NORWICH CITY	42	10	13	19	37	54	43
21	LEICESTER C	42	6	11	25	45	80	29
22	IPSWICH T	42	7	6	29	36	93	27

Season 1995-96

FA Premier League

DATE	OPPONENTS	SCORE	GOALSCORERS	ATTENDANCE
Aug 19	Manchester City	D 1-1	Sheringham	30,827
Aug 23	ASTON VILLA	L 0-1		26,726
Aug 26	LIVERPOOL	L 1-3	Barnes o.g.	31,254
Aug 30	West Ham United	D 1-1	Rosenthal	23,516
Sep 9	LEEDS UNITED	W 2-1	Howells, Sheringham	30,034
Sep 16	Sheffield Wednesday	W 3-1	Sheringham (1 pen) 2, Walker o.g.	26,565
Sep 25	Queens Park Rangers	W 3-2	Sheringham (1 pen) 2, Dozzell	15,659
Sep 30	WIMBLEDON	W 3-1	Sheringham 2, Elkins o.g.	25,321
Oct 14	NOTTINGHAM FOREST	L 0-1		32,876
Oct 22	Everton	D 1-1	Armstrong	33,629
Oct 29	NEWCASTLE UNITED	D 1-1	Armstrong	32,279
Nov 4	Coventry City	W 3-2	Fox, Sheringham, Howells	17,545
Nov 18	ARSENAL	W 2-1	Sheringham, Armstrong	32,894
Nov 21	Middlesbrough	W 1-0	Armstrong	29,487
Nov 25	Chelsea	D 0-0		31,059
Dec 2	EVERTON	D 0-0		32,894
Dec 9	QUEENS PARK RANGERS	W 1-0	Sheringham	28,851
Dec 16	Wimbledon	W 1-0	Fox	16,193
Dec 23	BOLTON WANDERERS	D 2-2	Sheringham, Armstrong	30,702
Dec 26	Southampton	D 0-0		15,238
Dec 30	Blackburn Rovers	L 1-2	Sheringham	30,004
Jan 1	MANCHESTER UNITED	W 4-1	Sheringham, Armstrong 2, Campbell	32,852
Jan 13	MANCHESTER CITY	W 1-0	Armstrong	31,438
Jan 21	Aston Villa	L 1-2	Fox	35,666
Feb 3	Liverpool	D 0-0		40,826
Feb 12	WEST HAM UNITED	L 0-1		29,781
Feb 24	SHEFFIELD WEDNESDAY	W 1-0	Armstrong	32,047
Mar 2	SOUTHAMPTON	W 1-0	Dozzell	26,320
Mar 16	BLACKBURN ROVERS	L 2-3	Sheringham, Armstrong	32,387
Mar 20	Bolton Wanderers	W 3-2	Howells, Fox, Armstrong	17,829
Mar 24	Manchester United	L 0-1		50,157
Mar 30	COVENTRY CITY	W 3-1	Sheringham, Fox 2	26,808
Apr 6	Nottingham Forest	L 1-2	Armstrong	27,053
Apr 8	MIDDLESBROUGH	D 1-1	Armstrong	32,036
Apr 15	Arsenal	D 0-0		38,273
Apr 27	CHELSEA	D 1-1	Armstrong	32,918
May 2	Leeds United	W 3-1	Armstrong, Anderton 2	30,061
May 5	Newcastle United	D 1-1	Dozzell	36,589

FA Cup

Jan 6	Hereford United	(Rd3) D 1-1	Rosenthal	8,806
Jan 17	HEREFORD UNITED	(R) W 5-1	Sheringham 3, Armstrong 2	31,534
Jan 27	WOLVERHAMPTON W	(Rd4) D 1-1	Wilson	32,816
Feb 7	Wolverhampton Wanderers	(R) W 2-0	Sheringham, Rosenthal	27,846
Feb 28	Nottingham Forest	(Rd5) D 2-2	Armstrong 2	18,600
Mar 9	NOTTINGHAM FOREST	(R) D 1-1	Sheringham	31,055

League Cup

Sep 20	Chester City	(Rd2/1L) W 4-0	Sheringham, Armstrong 2, Rosenthal	17,645
Oct 4	Chester City	(Rd2/2L) W 3-1	Sheringham 2, Howells	5,372
Oct 25	Coventry City	(Rd3) L 2-3	Armstrong, Busst o.g.	18,227

League and Cup Appearances

PLAYER	LEAGUE	CUP COMPETITION		TOTAL
		FA CUP	LC	
Anderton	6 (2)		1	7 (2)
Armstrong	36	6	3	45
Austin	28	4	3	35
Calderwood	26 (3)	4	3	33 (3)
Campbell	31	6	2	39
Caskey	3	3		6
Cundy	0 (1)			0 (1)
Dozzell	24 (4)	2 (1)	1 (2)	27 (7)
Dumitrescu	5			5
Edinburgh	15 (7)	4	1 (1)	20 (8)
Fox	26	6		32
Howells	29	2	2	33
Kerslake	2			2
Mabbutt	32	6	3	41
McMahon	7 (7)	0 (1)	3	10 (8)
Nethercott	9 (4)	2 (1)		11 (5)
Rosenthal	26 (7)	5	2	33 (7)
Scott	3		0 (1)	0 (3)
Sheringham	38	6	3	47
Sinton	8 (1)			8 (1)
Slade	1 (4)	0 (2)	0 (1)	1 (7)
Walker	38	6	3	47
Wilson	28	4 (1)	3	35 (1)

Goalscorers

PLAYER	LEAGUE	CUP COMPETITION		TOTAL
		FA CUP	LC	
Sheringham	16	5	3	24
Armstrong	15	4	3	22
Fox	6			6
Howells	3		1	4
Rosenthal	1	2	1	4
Dozzell	3			3
Anderton	2			2
Campbell	1			1
Wilson		1		1
Opp's o.gs.	3		1	4

Fact File

A record of 602 minutes without conceding a League goal was set between 18 November and 23 December.

MANAGER: Gerry Francis

CAPTAIN: Gary Mabbutt

TOP SCORER: Teddy Sheringham

BIGGEST WIN: 5-1 v Hereford United (H), 17 January 1996, FA Cup 3rd Round replay

HIGHEST ATTENDANCE:, 50,157 v Manchester United, 24 March 1996 FA Premier League

MAJOR TRANSFERS IN: Chris Armstrong from Crystal Palace, Ruel Fox from Newcastle United, Andy Sinton from Sheffield Wednesday, Clive Wilson from Queens Park Rangers

MAJOR TRANSFERS OUT: Nick Barmby to Middlesbrough, Jurgen Klinsmann to Bayern Munich, Gica Popescu to Barcelona

Final Premier League Table

		P	W	D	L	F	A	Pts
1	MANCHESTER U	38	25	7	6	73	35	82
2	NEWCASTLE U	38	24	6	8	66	37	78
3	LIVERPOOL	38	20	11	7	70	34	71
4	ASTON VILLA	38	18	9	11	52	35	63
5	ARSENAL	38	17	12	9	49	32	63
6	EVERTON	38	17	10	11	64	44	61
7	BLACKBURN R	38	18	7	13	61	47	61
8	TOTTENHAM HOTSPUR	38	16	13	9	50	38	61
9	NOTTINGHAM F	38	15	13	10	50	54	58
10	WEST HAM U	38	14	9	15	43	52	51
11	CHELSEA	38	12	14	12	46	44	50
12	MIDDLESBROUGH	38	11	10	17	35	50	43
13	LEEDS UNITED	38	12	7	19	40	57	43
14	WIMBLEDON	38	10	11	17	55	70	41
15	SHEFFIELD W	38	10	10	18	48	61	40
16	COVENTRY C	38	8	14	16	42	60	38
17	SOUTHAMPTON	38	9	11	18	34	52	38
18	MANCHESTER C	38	9	11	18	33	58	38
19	QPR	38	9	6	23	38	57	33
20	BOLTON W	38	8	5	25	39	71	29

Season 1996-97

FA Premier League

DATE	OPPONENTS	SCORE	GOALSCORERS	ATTENDANCE
Aug 17	Blackburn Rovers	W 2-0	Armstrong 2	26,960
Aug 21	DERBY COUNTY	D 1-1	Sheringham	28,219
Aug 24	EVERTON	D 0-0		29,696
Sep 4	Wimbledon	L 0-1		17,506
Sep 7	NEWCASTLE UNITED	L 1-2	Allen	32,535
Sep 14	Southampton	W 1-0	Armstrong (pen)	15,251
Sep 22	LEICESTER CITY	L 1-2	Wilson (pen)	24,159
Sep 29	Manchester United	L 0-2		54,943
Oct 12	ASTON VILLA	W 1-0	Nielsen	32,847
Oct 19	Middlesbrough	W 3-0	Fox, Sheringham 2	30,215
Oct 26	Chelsea	L 1-3	Armstrong	28,373
Nov 2	WEST HAM UNITED	W 1-0	Armstrong	32,999
Nov 16	SUNDERLAND	W 2-0	Sinton, Sheringham	31,867
Nov 24	Arsenal	L 1-3	Sinton	38,264
Dec 2	LIVERPOOL	L 0-2		32,899
Dec 7	Coventry City	W 2-1	Sheringham, Sinton	19,675
Dec 14	Leeds United	D 0-0		33,783
Dec 21	SHEFFIELD WEDNESDAY	D 1-1	Nielsen	30,996
Dec 26	SOUTHAMPTON	W 3-1	Nielsen, Iversen 2	30,549
Dec 28	Newcastle United	L 1-7	Nielsen	36,308
Jan 12	MANCHESTER UNITED	L 1-2	Allen	33,026
Jan 19	Nottingham Forest	L 1-2	Sinton	27,303
Jan 29	BLACKBURN ROVERS	W 2-1	Iversen, Sinton	22,943
Feb 1	CHELSEA	L 1-2	Howells	33,027
Feb 15	ARSENAL	D 0-0		33,039
Feb 24	West Ham United	L 3-4	Sheringham, Anderton, Howells	23,998
Mar 1	NOTTINGHAM FOREST	L 0-1		32,805
Mar 4	Sunderland	W 4-0	Nielsen, Iversen 3	20,785
Mar 15	LEEDS UNITED	W 1-0	Anderton	33,040
Mar 19	Leicester City	D 1-1	Sheringham	20,593
Mar 22	Derby County	L 2-4	Rosenthal, Dozzell	18,083
Apr 5	WIMBLEDON	W 1-0	Dozzell	32,654
Apr 9	Sheffield Wednesday	L 1-2	Nielsen	22,667
Apr 12	Everton	L 0-1		36,380
Apr 19	Aston Villa	D 1-1	Vega	39,339
Apr 24	MIDDLESBROUGH	W 1-0	Sinton	29,947
May 3	Liverpool	L 1-2	Anderton	40,003
May 11	COVENTRY CITY	L 1-2	McVeigh	33,029

FA Cup

Jan 5	Manchester United	(Rd3) L 0-2		52,495

League Cup

Sep 17	Preston North End	(Rd2/1L) D 1-1	Anderton	16,258
Sep 25	PRESTON NORTH END	(Rd2/2L) W 3-0	Anderton, Allen 2	20,080
Oct 23	SUNDERLAND	(Rd3) W 2-1	Campbell, Armstrong	24,867
Nov 27	Bolton Wanderers	(Rd4) L 1-6	Sheringham	18,621

League and Cup Appearances

PLAYER	LEAGUE	CUP COMPETITION		TOTAL
		FA CUP	LC	
Allen	9 (3)	1	2 (1)	12 (4)
Anderton	14 (2)		3	17 (2)
Armstrong	12		3	15
Austin	13 (2)	1		14 (2)
Baardsen	1 (1)			1 (1)
Calderwood	33 (1)	1	4	38 (1)
Campbell	38	1	4	43
Carr	24 (2)	1	3	28 (2)
Clapham	0 (1)			0 (1)
Dozzell	10 (7)		1	11 (7)
Edinburgh	21 (3)	1	2	24 (3)
Fenn	0 (4)	1		1 (4)
Fox	19 (6)		3 (1)	22 (7)
Howells	32	1	4	37
Iversen	16			16
Mabbutt	1			1
McVeigh	2 (1)			2 (1)
Nethercott	2 (7)			2 (7)
Nielsen	28 (1)	1	2 (1)	31 (2)
Rosenthal	4 (16)			4 (16)
Scales	10 (2)			10 (2)
Sheringham	29		3	32
Sinton	32 (1)	1	2	35 (1)
Vega	8			8
Walker	37	1	4	42
Wilson	23 (3)		4	27 (3)

Goalscorers

PLAYER	LEAGUE	CUP COMPETITION		TOTAL
		FA CUP	LC	
Sheringham	7		1	8
Armstrong	5		1	6
Iversen	6			6
Nielson	6			6
Sinton	6			6
Anderton	3		2	5
Allen	2		2	4
Dozzell	2			2
Howells	2			2
Campbell			1	1
Fox	1			1
McVeigh	1			1
Rosenthal	1			1
Vega	1			1
Wilson	1			1

Fact File

Alan Nielsen was voted Player of the Year by his fellow Danish professionals.

MANAGER: Gerry Francis

CAPTAIN: Gary Mabbutt/Teddy Sheringham

TOP SCORER: Teddy Sheringham

BIGGEST WIN: 4-0 v Sunderland (A), 4 March 1997, FA Premier League

HIGHEST ATTENDANCE: 54,943 v Manchester United, 29 September 1996, FA Premier League

MAJOR TRANSFERS IN: Steffen Iversen from Rosenborg, Allan Nielsen from Brondby, John Scales from Liverpool, Ramon Vega from Cagliari

MAJOR TRANSFERS OUT: Darren Caskey to Reading, Ilie Dumitrescu to West Ham United

Final Premier League Table

		P	W	D	L	F	A	Pts
1	MANCHESTER U	38	21	12	5	76	44	75
2	NEWCASTLE U	38	19	11	8	73	40	68
3	ARSENAL	38	19	11	8	62	32	68
4	LIVERPOOL	38	19	11	8	62	37	68
5	ASTON VILLA	38	17	10	11	47	34	61
6	CHELSEA	38	16	11	11	58	55	59
7	SHEFFIELD W	38	14	15	9	50	51	57
8	WIMBLEDON	38	15	11	12	49	46	56
9	LEICESTER C	38	12	11	15	46	54	47
10	TOTTENHAM HOTSPUR	38	13	7	18	44	51	46
11	LEEDS U	38	11	13	14	28	38	46
12	DERBY CO	38	11	13	14	45	42	46
13	BLACKBURN R	38	9	15	14	42	43	42
14	WEST HAM U	38	10	12	16	39	48	42
15	EVERTON	38	10	12	16	44	57	42
16	SOUTHAMPTON	38	10	11	17	50	56	41
17	COVENTRY C	38	9	14	15	38	54	41
18	SUNDERLAND	38	10	10	18	35	53	40
19	MIDDLESBROUGH*	38	10	12	16	51	60	39
20	NOTTINGHAM F	38	6	16	16	31	59	34

* Middlesbrough had three points deducted

Season 1997-98

FA Premier League

DATE	OPPONENTS	SCORE	GOALSCORERS	ATTENDANCE
Aug 10	MANCHESTER UNITED	L 0-2		26,359
Aug 13	West Ham United	L 1-2	Ferdinand	25,354
Aug 23	DERBY COUNTY	W 1-0	Calderwood	25,886
Aug 27	ASTON VILLA	W 3-2	Ferdinand 2, Fox	26,317
Aug 30	Arsenal	D 0-0		38,102
Sep 13	Leicester City	L 0-3		20,683
Sep 20	BLACKBURN ROVERS	D 0-0		26,573
Sep 23	Bolton Wanderers	D 1-1	Armstrong	23,433
Sep 27	WIMBLEDON	D 0-0		26,261
Oct 4	Newcastle United	L 0-1		36,709
Oct 19	SHEFFIELD WEDNESDAY	W 3-2	Ginola, Armstrong, Dominguez	25,097
Oct 25	Southampton	L 2-3	Ginola, Dominguez	15,255
Nov 1	LEEDS UNITED	L 0-1		26,441
Nov 8	Liverpool	L 0-4		38,006
Nov 24	CRYSTAL PALACE	L 0-1		25,634
Nov 29	EVERTON	W 2-0	Vega, Ginola	36,670
Dec 6	Chelsea	L 1-6	Vega	28,476
Dec 13	Coventry City	L 1-4		19,499
Dec 20	BARNSLEY	W 3-0	Nielsen, Ginola 2	28,232
Dec 26	Aston Villa	L 0-4	Calderwood	38,644
Dec 28	ARSENAL	D 1-1	Nielsen	29,610
Jan 10	Manchester United	L 0-2		55,281
Jan 17	WEST HAM UNITED	W 1-0	Klinsmann	27,909
Jan 31	Derby County	L 1-2	Fox	30,187
Feb 7	Blackburn Rovers	W 3-0	Fox, Armstrong, Berti	30,388
Feb 14	LEICESTER CITY	D 1-1	Calderwood	28,355
Feb 21	Sheffield Wednesday	L 0-1		29,871
Mar 1	BOLTON WANDERERS	W 1-0	Nielsen	29,032
Mar 4	Leeds United	L 0-1		31,394
Mar 14	LIVERPOOL	D 3-3	Vega, Klinsmann, Ginola	30,245
Mar 28	Crystal Palace	W 3-1	Berti, Klinsmann, Armstrong	26,116
Apr 4	EVERTON	D 1-1	Armstrong	35,646
Apr 11	Chelsea	L 0-2		34,149
Apr 13	COVENTRY CITY	D 1-1	Berti	35,646
Apr 18	Barnsley	D 1-1	Calderwood	18,692
Apr 25	NEWCASTLE UNITED	W 2-0	Klinsmann, Ferdinand	35,847
May 2	Wimbledon	W 6-2	Ferdinand, Klinsmann 4, Saib	25,820
May 10	SOUTHAMPTON	D 1-1	Klinsmann	35,995

FA Cup

Jan 5	FULHAM	(Rd3) W 3-1	Calderwood, Clemence, Taylor o.g.	27,909
Jan 24	BARNSLEY	(Rd4) D 1-1	Campbell	28,722
Feb 4	Barnsley	(R) L 1-3	Ginola	18,220

League Cup

Sep 17	CARLISLE UNITED	(Rd2/1L) W 3-2	Fox, Fenn, Mahorn	19,255
Sep 30	Carlisle United	(Rd2/2L) W 2-0	Ginola (pen), Armstrong	13,571
Oct 15	Derby County	(Rd3) L 1-2	Ginola	20,390

League and Cup Appearances

PLAYER	LEAGUE	CUP COMPETITION		TOTAL
		FA CUP	LC	
Rory Allen	1 (3)			1 (3)
Anderton	7 (8)			7 (8)
Armstrong	13 (6)	0 (1)	2	15 (7)
Baardsen	9	2 (1)		11 (1)
Berti	17	2		19
Brady	0 (9)	1 (1)		1 (10)
Calderwood	21 (5)	1 (1)	1 (1)	23 (7)
Campbell	34	3	3	40
Carr	37 (1)	3		42 (1)
Clemence	12 (5)	2	2	16 (5)
Dominguez	8 (10)	1	2 (1)	11 (11)
Edinburgh	13 (3)		2	15 (3)
Fenn	0 (4)		1	1 (4)
Ferdinand	19 (2)	2	1	22 (2)
Fox	32	2	3	37
Ginola	34	3	3	40
Howells	14 (6)	0 (1)	1	15 (7)
Iversen	8 (5)			8 (5)
Klinsmann	15	3		18
Mabbutt	8 (3)		1	9 (3)
Mahorn	2	0 (1)	0 (1)	2 (2)
Nielsen	21 (4)		1	22 (4)
Saib	3 (6)			3 (6)
Scales	9 (1)		2	11 (1)
Sinton	14 (5)	1	1	16 (5)
Vega	22 (3)	3	2	27 (3)
Walker	29	1	3	33
Wilson	16	3		19

Goalscorers

PLAYER	LEAGUE	CUP COMPETITION		TOTAL
		FA CUP	LC	
Ginola	6	1	2	9
Klinsmann	9			9
Armstrong	5		1	6
Calderwood	4	1		5
Ferdinand	5			5
Fox	3		1	4
Berti	3			3
Nielsen	3			3
Vega	3			3
Dominguez	2			2
Campbell		1		1
Clemence		1		1
Fenn			1	1
Mahorn			1	1
Saib	1			1
Opp's o.gs.		1		1

Fact File

Sol Campbell captained England against Belgium on 29 May, the fifth post-war Spurs player to do so following Alf Ramsey, Alan Mullery, Martin Peters and Gary Lineker.

MANAGER: Gerry Francis until November then Christian Gross

CAPTAIN: Gary Mabbutt/David Howells/Sol Campbell

TOP SCORER: David Ginola and Jurgen Klinsmann

BIGGEST WIN: 6-2 v Wimbledon (A), 2 May 1998, FA Premier League

HIGHEST ATTENDANCE: 55,281 v Manchester United, 10 January 1998, FA Premier League

MAJOR TRANSFERS IN: Nicola Berti from Internazionale, Jose Dominguez from Sporting Club de Portugal, Les Ferdinand from Newcastle United, David Ginola from Newcastle United, Jurgen Klinsmann from Sampdoria, Moussa Saib from Valencia

MAJOR TRANSFERS OUT: Jason Cundy to Ipswich Town, Kevin Scott to Norwich City, Teddy Sheringham to Manchester United

Final Premier League Table

		P	W	D	L	F	A	Pts
1	ARSENAL	38	23	9	6	68	33	78
2	MANCHESTER U	38	23	8	7	73	26	77
3	LIVERPOOL	38	18	11	9	68	42	65
4	CHELSEA	38	20	3	15	71	43	63
5	LEEDS U	38	17	8	13	57	46	59
6	BLACKBURN R	38	16	10	12	57	52	58
7	ASTON VILLA	38	17	6	15	49	48	57
8	WEST HAM U	38	16	8	14	56	57	56
9	DERBY CO	38	16	7	15	52	49	55
10	LEICESTER C	38	13	14	11	51	41	53
11	COVENTRY C	38	12	16	10	46	44	52
12	SOUTHAMPTON	38	14	6	18	50	45	48
13	NEWCASTLE U	38	11	11	16	35	44	44
14	TOTTENHAM HOTSPUR	38	11	11	16	44	56	44
15	WIMBLEDON	38	10	14	14	34	46	44
16	SHEFFIELD W	38	12	8	18	52	67	44
17	EVERTON	38	9	13	16	41	56	40
18	BOLTON W	38	9	13	16	41	61	40
19	BARNSLEY	38	10	5	23	37	82	35
20	CRYSTAL P	38	8	9	21	37	71	33

Season 1998-99

FA Premier League

DATE	OPPONENTS	SCORE	GOALSCORERS	ATTENDANCE
Aug 15	Wimbledon	L 1-3	Fox	23,031
Aug 22	SHEFFIELD WEDNESDAY	L 0-3		32,129
Aug 29	Everton	W 1-0	Ferdinand	39,378
Sep 9	BLACKBURN ROVERS	W 2-1	Ferdinand, Nielsen	28,338
Sep 13	MIDDLESBROUGH	L 0-3		30,437
Sep 19	Southampton	D 1-1	Fox	15,204
Sep 26	LEEDS UNITED	D 3-3	Vega, Iversen, Campbell	35,535
Oct 3	Derby County	W 1-0	Campbell	30,083
Oct 19	Leicester City	L 1-2	Ferdinand	20,787
Oct 24	NEWCASTLE UNITED	W 2-0	Iversen 2	36,047
Nov 2	CHARLTON ATHLETIC	D 2-2	Nielsen, Armstrong	32,202
Nov 7	Aston Villa	L 2-3	Anderton (pen), Vega	39,241
Nov 14	Arsenal	D 0-0		38,278
Nov 21	NOTTINGHAM FOREST	W 2-0	Armstrong, Nielsen	35,832
Nov 28	West Ham United	L 1-2	Armstrong	26,044
Dec 5	LIVERPOOL	W 2-1	Fox, Carragher o.g.	36,521
Dec 12	MANCHESTER UNITED	D 2-2	Campbell 2	36,079
Dec 19	Chelsea	L 0-2		34,881
Dec 26	Coventry City	D 1-1	Campbell	23,098
Dec 28	EVERTON	W 4-1	Armstrong 3, Ferdinand	36,053
Jan 9	Sheffield Wednesday	D 0-0		28,204
Jan 16	WIMBLEDON	D 0-0		32,422
Jan 30	Blackburn Rovers	W 1-1	Iversen	29,643
Feb 6	COVENTRY CITY	D 0-0		34,376
Feb 20	Middlesbrough	D 0-0		34,687
Feb 27	DERBY COUNTY	D 1-1	Sherwood	35,392
Mar 2	SOUTHAMPTON	W 3-0	Armstrong, Iversen, Dominguez	28,580
Mar 10	Leeds United	L 0-2		34,521
Mar 13	ASTON VILLA	W 1-0	Sherwood	35,963
Apr 3	LEICESTER CITY	L 0-2		35,415
Apr 5	Newcastle United	D 1-1	Anderton (pen)	36,655
Apr 17	Nottingham Forest	W 1-0	Iversen	25,181
Apr 20	Charlton Athletic	W 4-1	Iversen, Campbell, Dominguez, Ginola	20,034
Apr 24	WEST HAM UNITED	L 1-2	Ginola	36,089
May 1	Liverpool	L 2-3	Carragher o.g., Iversen	44,007
May 5	ARSENAL	L 1-3	Anderton	36,019
May 10	CHELSEA	D 2-2	Iversen, Ginola	35,878
May 16	Manchester United	L 1-2	Ferdinand	55,189

FA Cup

Jan 2	WATFORD	(Rd4)	W 5-2	Iversen 2, Anderton (pen), Nielsen, Fox	36,022
Jan 23	Wimbledon	(R)	D 1-1	Ginola	22,229
Feb 2	WIMBLEDON	(Rd4)	W 3-0	Sinton, Nielsen 2	24,049
Feb 13	Leeds United	(Rd5)	D 1-1	Sherwood	39,696
Feb 24	LEEDS UNITED	(R)	W 2-0	Anderton, Ginola	32,307
Mar 16	Barnsley	(Rd6)	W 1-0	Ginola	18,793
Apr 11	Newcastle United *	(SF)	L 0-2†		53,609

* played at Old Trafford, Manchester. † after extra time

League Cup

Sep 15	Brentford	(Rd2/1L)	W 3-2	Carr, Dominguez, Vega	11,831
Sep 23	BRENTFORD	(Rd2/2L)	W 3-2	Nielsen, Campbell, Armstrong	22,980
Oct 27	Northampton Town	(Rd3)	W 3-1	Armstrong 2, Campbell	7,422
Nov 10	Liverpool	(Rd4)	W 3-1	Iversen, Scales, Nielsen	20,772
Dec 2	MANCHESTER UNITED	(Rd5)	W 3-1	Armstrong 2, Ginola	35,702
Jan 27	WIMBLEDON	(SF/1L)	D 0-0		35,997
Feb 16	Wimbledon	(SF/2L)	W 1-0	Iversen	25,204
Mar 21	Leicester City **	(F)	W 1-0	Nielsen	77,892

** played at Wembley, London

League and Cup Appearances

PLAYER	LEAGUE	CUP COMPETITION		TOTAL
		FA CUP	LC	
Allen	0 (5)		1 (2)	1 (7)
Anderton	31 (1)	7	7	45 (1)
Armstrong	24 (10)	3 (2)	5	32 (12)
Baardsen	12			15
Berti	4			4
Calderwood	11 (1)		5	16 (1)
Campbell	37	7	8	52
Carr	37	7	8	52
Clemence	9 (9)	0 (1)	2 (1)	11 (11)
Dominguez	2 (11)		0 (2)	2 (13)
Edinburgh	14 (2)	4 (1)	5	23 (3)
Ferdinand	22 (2)	6 (1)	2 (2)	30 (5)
Fox	17 (3)	2	1 (2)	20 (5)
Freund	17	6	3	26
Ginola	30	6	8	44
Gower			0 (2)	0 (2)
Iversen	22 (5)	5 (2)	6	33 (7)
King	0 (1)			0 (1)
Nielsen	24 (4)	2 (2)	7	33 (6)
Nilsen	3			3
Saib	0 (4)			0 (4)
Scales	7		2	9
Segers	1		1	2
Sherwood	12 (2)	4		16 (2)
Sinton	12 (10)	2 (4)	3 (3)	17 (17)
Taricco	12 (1)	2 (1)		14 (2)
Tramezzani	6		1	7
Vega	13 (3)	4	5	22 (3)
Walker	25	7	4	36
Wilson		0 (1)		0 (1)
Young	14 (1)	3 (2)	1 (1)	18 (4)

Goalscorers

PLAYER	LEAGUE	CUP COMPETITION		TOTAL
		FA CUP	LC	
Iversen	9	2	2	13
Armstrong	7		5	12
Nielsen	3	3	3	9
Campbell	6		2	8
Ginola	3	3	1	7
Anderton	3	2		5
Ferdinand	5			5
Fox	3	1		4
Dominguez	2		1	3
Sherwood	2	1		3
Vega	2		1	3
Carr			1	1
Scales			1	1
Sinton		1		1
Opp's o.gs.	2			2

MANAGER: Christian Gross until October then George Graham

CAPTAIN: Sol Campbell

TOP SCORER: Steffen Iversen

BIGGEST WIN: 5-2 v Watford (H), 2 January 1999, FA Cup 3rd Round

HIGHEST ATTENDANCE: 77,892 v Leicester City, 21 March 1999, League Cup Final

MAJOR TRANSFERS IN: Steffen Freund from Borussia Dortmund, Tim Sherwood from Blackburn Rovers, Mauricio Taricco from Ipswich Town, Paolo Tramezzani from Piacenza

MAJOR TRANSFERS OUT: Nicola Berti to Alaves, Colin Calderwood to Aston Villa

Final Premier League Table

		P	W	D	L	F	A	Pts
1	MANCHESTER U	38	22	13	3	80	37	79
2	ARSENAL	38	22	12	4	59	17	78
3	CHELSEA	38	20	15	3	57	30	75
4	LEEDS U	38	18	13	7	62	34	67
5	WEST HAM U	38	16	9	13	46	53	57
6	ASTON VILLA	38	15	10	13	51	46	55
7	LIVERPOOL	38	15	9	14	68	49	54
8	DERBY CO	38	13	13	12	40	45	52
9	MIDDLESBROUGH	38	12	15	11	48	54	51
10	LEICESTER C	38	12	13	13	40	46	49
11	TOTTENHAM HOTSPUR	38	11	14	13	47	50	47
12	SHEFFIELD W	38	13	7	18	41	36	46
13	NEWCASTLE U	38	11	13	14	48	54	46
14	EVERTON	38	11	10	17	42	47	43
15	COVENTRY C	38	11	9	18	39	51	42
16	WIMBLEDON	38	10	12	16	40	63	42
17	SOUTHAMPTON	38	11	8	19	37	64	41
18	CHARLTON A	38	8	12	18	41	56	36
19	BLACKBURN R	38	7	14	17	38	52	35
20	NOTTINGHAM F	38	7	9	22	35	69	30

Season 1999-2000

FA Premier League

DATE	OPPONENTS	SCORE	GOALSCORERS	ATTENDANCE
Aug 7	West Ham United	L 0-1		26,010
Aug 9	NEWCASTLE UNITED	W 3-1	Iversen, Ferdinand, Sherwood	28,701
Aug 14	EVERTON	W 3-2	Sherwood, Leonhardsen, Iversen	34,539
Aug 21	Sheffield Wednesday	W 2-1	Ferdinand, Leonhardsen	24,027
Aug 28	LEEDS UNITED	L 1-2	Sherwood	36,012
Sep 12	Bradford City	D 1-1	Perry	18,143
Sep 19	COVENTRY CITY	W 3-2	Iversen, Armstrong, Leonhardsen	35,224
Sep 26	Wimbledon	D 1-1	Carr	17,368
Oct 3	LEICESTER CITY	L 2-3	Iversen 2	35,591
Oct 16	Derby County	W 1-0	Armstrong	29,815
Oct 23	MANCHESTER UNITED	W 3-1	Iversen, Scholes o.g., Carr	36,072
Oct 31	Sunderland	L 1-2	Iversen	41,904
Nov 7	ARSENAL	W 2-1	Iversen, Sherwood	36,085
Nov 20	Southampton	W 1-0	Leonhardsen	15,248
Nov 28	Newcastle United	L 1-2	Armstrong	36,460
Dec 6	WEST HAM UNITED	D 0-0		36,233
Dec 18	Middlesbrough	L 1-2	Vega	33,129
Dec 26	WATFORD	W 4-0	Ginola, Iversen, Sherwood 2	36,089
Dec 29	Aston Villa	D 1-1	Sherwood	39,217
Jan 3	LIVERPOOL	W 1-0	Armstrong	36,044
Jan 12	Chelsea	L 0-1		34,969
Jan 15	Everton	D 2-2	Armstrong, Ginola	36,144
Jan 22	SHEFFIELD WEDNESDAY	L 0-1		35,897
Feb 5	CHELSEA	L 0-1		36,041
Feb 12	Leeds United	L 0-1		40,127
Feb 26	Coventry City	W 1-0	Armstrong	23,077
Mar 4	BRADFORD CITY	D 1-1	Iversen	35,472
Mar 11	SOUTHAMPTON	W 7-2	Richards o.g., Anderton, Armstrong 2, Iversen 3	36,024
Mar 19	Arsenal	L 1-2	Armstrong	38,131
Mar 25	Watford	D 1-1	Armstrong	20,050
Apr 3	MIDDLESBROUGH	L 2-3	Armstrong, Ginola	31,796
Apr 9	Liverpool	L 0-2		44,536
Apr 15	ASTON VILLA	L 2-4	Iversen, Armstrong	35,304
Apr 19	Leicester City	W 1-0	Ginola	19,764
Apr 22	WIMBLEDON	W 2-0	Armstrong, Anderton	33,086
Apr 29	DERBY COUNTY	D 1-1	Clemence	33,044
May 6	Manchester United	L 1-3	Armstrong	61,629
May 14	SUNDERLAND	W 3-1	Anderton (pen), Sherwood, Carr	36,070

FA Cup

Dec 12	NEWCASTLE UNITED	(Rd3) D 1-1	Iversen	33,116
Dec 23	Newcastle United	(R) L 1-6	Ginola	35,415

League Cup

Oct 13	CREWE ALEXANDRA	(Rd3) W 3-1	Leonhardsen, Ginola, Sherwood	25,486
Dec 1	Fulham	(Rd4) L 1-3	Iversen	18,134

UEFA Cup

Sep 16	ZIMBRU CHISINAU	(Rd1/1L) W 3-0	Leonhardsen, Perry, Sherwood	32,660
Sep 30	Zimbru Chisinau	(Rd1/2L) D 0-0		6,000
Oct 28	KAISERSLAUTERN	(Rd2/1L) W 1-0	Iversen (pen)	35,177
Nov 4	1FC Kaiserslautern	(Rd 2/2L) L 0-2		29,044

MANAGER: George Graham

CAPTAIN: Sol Campbell

TOP SCORER: Steffen Iversen

BIGGEST WIN: 7-2 v Southampton (H), 11 March 2000, FA Premier League

HIGHEST ATTENDANCE: 61,629 v Manchester United, 6 May 2000, FA Premier League

MAJOR TRANSFERS IN: Oyvind Leonhardsen from Liverpool, Chris Perry from Wimbledon

MAJOR TRANSFERS OUT: Justin Edinburgh to Portsmouth, Moussa Saib to El Nasr, Andy Sinton to Wolverhampton Wanderers

League and Cup Appearances

PLAYER	LEAGUE	CUP COMPETITION			TOTAL
		FA CUP	LC	UEFA	
Anderton	22				22
Armstrong	29 (2)	0 (2)	2	3	34 (4)
Campbell	29	2	2	2	35
Carr	34		1	4	39
Clemence	16 (4)	1		2 (1)	19 (5)
Davies	1 (2)				1 (2)
Doherty	0 (2)				0 (2)
Dominguez	2 (10)	1 (1)	0 (1)	0 (2)	3 (14)
Edinburgh	7 (1)	1	1	1 (2)	10 (3)
Etherington	1 (4)				1 (4)
Ferdinand	5 (4)				5 (4)
Fox	1 (2)	1 (1)		1	3 (3)
Freund	24 (3)	1	2	4	31 (3)
Ginola	36	2	2	2 (1)	42 (1)
Iversen	36	2	1 (1)	4	43 (1)
King	2 (1)				2 (1)
Korsten	4 (5)				4 (5)
Leonhardsen	21 (1)		2	4	27 (1)
McEwen	0 (1)				0 (1)
Nielsen	5 (9)	2		1	8 (9)
Perry	36 (1)	2	2	4	44 (1)
Piercy	1 (2)		1		2 (2)
Scales	3 (1)				3 (1)
Sherwood	23 (4)	1	2	3	29 (4)
Taricco	29	1	2	3	35
Vega	2 (3)	1 (1)	0 (1)		3 (5)
Walker	38	2	2	4	46
Young	11 (9)	2 (1)	2 (1)		15 (11)

Goalscorers

PLAYER	LEAGUE	CUP COMPETITION			TOTAL
		FA CUP	LC	UEFA	
Iversen	14	1	1	1	17
Armstrong	14				14
Sherwood	8		1	1	10
Ginola	4	1	1		6
Leonhardsen	4		1	1	6
Anderton	3				3
Carr	3				3
Ferdinand	2				2
Perry	1			1	2
Clemence	1				1
Vega	1				1
Opp's o.gs.	2				2

Fact File

John Piercy became the 500th player to appear for Spurs in Football/Premier League matches when he went on as a substitute against Derby County on 16 October.

Final Premier League Table

		P	W	D	L	F	A	PTS
1	MANCHESTER U	38	28	7	3	97	45	91
2	ARSENAL	38	22	7	9	73	43	73
3	LEEDS U	38	21	6	11	58	43	69
4	LIVERPOOL	38	19	10	9	51	30	67
5	CHELSEA	38	18	11	9	53	34	65
6	ASTON VILLA	38	15	13	10	46	35	58
7	SUNDERLAND	38	16	10	12	57	56	58
8	LEICESTER CITY	38	16	7	15	55	55	55
9	WEST HAM U	38	15	10	13	52	53	55
10	TOTTENHAM HOTSPUR	38	15	8	15	57	49	53
11	NEWCASTLE U	38	14	10	14	63	54	52
12	MIDDLESBROUGH	38	14	10	14	46	49	52
13	EVERTON	38	12	14	12	59	49	50
14	COVENTRY C	38	12	8	18	47	54	44
15	SOUTHAMPTON	38	12	8	18	45	62	44
16	DERBY CO	38	9	11	18	44	57	38
17	BRADFORD C	38	9	9	20	38	68	36
18	WIMBLEDON	38	7	12	19	46	74	33
19	SHEFFIELD W	38	8	7	23	38	70	31
20	WATFORD	38	6	6	26	35	77	24

Season 2000-01

FA Premier League

DATE	OPPONENTS	SCORE	GOALSCORERS	ATTENDANCE
Aug 19	IPSWICH TOWN	W 3-1	Anderton (pen), Carr, Ferdinand	36,550
Aug 22	Middlesbrough	D 1-1	Leonhardsen	31,254
Aug 26	Newcastle United	L 0-2		51,573
Sep 5	EVERTON	W 3-2	Rebrov (1 pen) 2, Ferdinand	35,316
Sep 11	WEST HAM UNITED	W 1-0	Campbell	32,282
Sep 16	Charlton Athletic	L 0-1		20,043
Sep 23	MANCHESTER CITY	D 0-0		36,069
Sep 30	Leeds United	L 3-4	Rebrov 2, Perry	37,562
Oct 14	Coventry City	L 1-2	Rebrov	21,435
Oct 21	DERBY COUNTY	W 3-1	Carr, Leonhardsen 2	34,483
Oct 28	Chelsea	L 0-3		34,966
Nov 4	SUNDERLAND	W 2-1	Sherwood, Armstrong	36,016
Nov 11	Aston Villa	L 0-2		33,608
Nov 19	LIVERPOOL	W 2-1	Ferdinand, Sherwood	36,036
Nov 25	LEICESTER CITY	W 3-0	Ferdinand 3	35,636
Dec 2	Manchester United	L 0-2		67,583
Dec 9	Bradford City	D 3-3	King, Campbell, Armstrong	17,225
Dec 18	ARSENAL	D 1-1	Rebrov	36,062
Dec 23	MIDDLESBROUGH	D 0-0		35,638
Dec 27	Southampton	L 0-2		15,237
Dec 30	Ipswich Town	L 0-3		22,234
Jan 2	NEWCASTLE UNITED	W 4-2	Anderton (pen), Doherty, Rebrov, Ferdinand	34,324
Jan 13	Everton	D 0-0		32,290
Jan 20	SOUTHAMPTON	D 0-0		36,095
Jan 31	West Ham United	D 0-0		26,048
Feb 3	CHARLTON ATHLETIC	D 0-0		35,368
Feb 10	Manchester City	W 1-0	Rebrov	34,399
Feb 24	LEEDS UNITED	L 1-2	Ferdinand	36,070
Mar 3	Derby County	L 1-2	West o.g.	29,410
Mar 17	COVENTRY CITY	W 3-0	Ferdinand, Iversen, Rebrov	35,606
Mar 31	Arsenal	L 0-2		38,121
Apr 10	BRADFORD CITY	W 2-1	Iversen, Davies	28,306
Apr 14	Sunderland	W 3-2	Doherty 2, Clemence	48,029
Apr 17	CHELSEA	L 0-3		36,074
Apr 22	Liverpool	L 1-3	Korsten	43,547
Apr 28	ASTON VILLA	D 0-0		36,096
May 5	Leicester City	L 2-3	Davies, Carr	21,056
May 19	MANCHESTER UNITED	W 3-1	Korsten 2, Ferdinand	36,072

FA Cup

Jan 6	Leyton Orient	(Rd3) W 1-0	Doherty	12,336
Feb 7	Charlton Athletic	(Rd4) W 4-2	Rufus o.g., Anderton, Leonhardesn, Rebrov	18,101
Feb 17	STOCKPORT COUNTY	(Rd5) W 4-0	King, Flynn o.g., Davies 2	36,040
Mar 11	West Ham United	(Rd6) W 3-2	Rebrov 2, Doherty	26,048
Apr 8	Arsenal *	(SF) L 1-2	Doherty	63,541
			* played at Old Trafford, Manchester	

League Cup

Sep 19	Brentford	(Rd2/1L) D 0-0		8,580
Sep 26	BRENTFORD	(Rd2/2L) W 2-0	Leonhardsen, Iversen	26,909
Oct 31	BIRMINGHAM CITY	(Rd3) L 1-3	Anderton (pen)	27,096

Fact File

Ledley King's 10 second strike at Bradford on 9 December is the fastest goal scored in the Premiership.

MANAGER: George Graham until March then Glenn Hoddle

CAPTAIN: Sol Campbell

TOP SCORER: Sergei Rebrov

BIGGEST WIN: 4-0 v Stockport County (H), 17 February 2001, FA Cup 5th Round

HIGHEST ATTENDANCE: 67,583 v Manchester United, 2 December 2000, FA Premier League

MAJOR TRANSFERS IN: Sergei Rebrov from Dynamo Kiev, Neil Sullivan from Wimbledon, Ben Thatcher from Wimbledon

MAJOR TRANSFERS OUT: Jose Dominguez to Kaiserslautern, Ruel Fox to West Bromwich Albion, David Ginola to Aston Villa, Allan Nielsen to Watford, John Scales to Ipswich Town

League and Cup Appearances

PLAYER	LEAGUE	CUP COMPETITION		TOTAL
		FA CUP	LC	
Anderton	22 (1)	2	1	25 (1)
Armstrong	3 (6)			3 (6)
Booth	3 (1)			3 (1)
Campbell	21	5	1	27
Carr	27 (1)	1 (1)	3	31 (2)
Clemence	27 (2)	4	2	33 (2)
Davies	9 (4)	0 (1)	0 (1)	9 (6)
Doherty	18 (4)	5		23 (4)
Dominguez	0 (2)		0 (2)	0 (4)
Etherington	1 (5)		1	2 (5)
Ferdinand	25 (3)	4	2 (1)	31 (4)
Freund	19 (2)	3	3	25 (2)
Gardner	5 (3)			5 (3)
Iversen	10 (4)	2	2	14 (4)
King	18	4 (1)		22 (1)
Korsten	8 (6)	0 (3)	1	9 (9)
Leonhardsen	23 (2)	3 (1)	2	28 (3)
McEwen	0 (3)			0 (3)
Perry	30 (2)	4	3	37 (2)
Piercy	0 (5)			0 (5)
Rebrov	28 (1)	5	2	35 (1)
Sherwood	31 (2)	4	2	37 (2)
Sullivan	35	5	3	43
Taricco	2 (3)			2 (3)
Thatcher	10 (2)	3		13 (2)
Thelwell	13 (3)	0 (2)		13 (5)
Vega	8 (2)		2 (1)	10 (3)
Walker	3 (1)		0 (1)	3 (2)
Young	19 (4)	4	0 (1)	23 (5)

Goalscorers

PLAYER	LEAGUE	CUP COMPETITION		TOTAL
		FA CUP	LC	
Rebrov	9	3		12
Ferdinand	10			10
Doherty	3	3		6
Leonhardsen	3	1	1	5
Anderton	2	1	1	4
Davies	2	2		4
Carr	3			3
Iversen	2		1	3
Korsten	3			3
Armstrong	2			2
Campbell	2			2
King	1	1		2
Sherwood	2			2
Clemence	1			1
Perry	1			1
Opp's o.gs.	1	2		3

Final Premier League Table

		P	W	D	L	F	A	Pts
1	MANCHESTER U	38	24	8	6	79	31	80
2	ARSENAL	38	20	10	8	63	38	70
3	LIVERPOOL	38	20	9	9	71	39	69
4	LEEDS U	38	20	8	10	64	43	68
5	IPSWICH T	38	20	6	12	57	42	66
6	CHELSEA	38	17	10	11	68	45	61
7	SUNDERLAND	38	15	12	11	46	41	57
8	ASTON VILLA	38	13	15	10	46	43	54
9	CHARLTON A	38	14	10	14	50	57	52
10	SOUTHAMPTON	38	14	10	14	40	48	52
11	NEWCASTLE U	38	14	9	15	44	50	51
12	TOTTENHAM HOTSPUR	38	13	10	15	47	53	49
13	LEICESTER C	38	14	6	18	39	51	48
14	MIDDLESBROUGH	38	9	15	14	44	44	42
15	WEST HAM U	38	10	12	16	45	50	42
16	EVERTON	38	11	9	18	45	59	42
17	DERBY CO	38	10	12	16	37	59	42
18	MANCHESTER C	38	8	10	20	41	65	34
19	COVENTRY C	38	8	10	20	36	63	34
20	BRADFORD C	38	5	11	22	30	70	26

Tottenham in celebration. Top: FA Cup 1991; FA Cup 1981. Middle: League Cup 1973. Bottom: Dave Mackay with the FA Cup, 1967;Ralph Coates with the League Cup 1973.

Complete Players' Career Records

These records cover all players who have played a senior competitive match for Spurs since they first entered the FA Cup in 1894-95 until summer 2001. 'Period' covers the seasons in which a competitive appearance was made, thus 1922-29 covers seasons 1922-23 to 1928-29 inclusive. 'League' covers all major League competitions – the Southern League, Football League and FA Premier League. 'League Cup' includes all names by which the competition has been known,

Player		Birthplace	From	Year Joined	Year Left	To	League Apps	Sub	G
Adams	Chris	Hornchurch	Romford	1951	1953	Norwich City	6		
Adams	William	Arlecdon	Northfleet	1945	1946	Carlisle United	1		
Aleksic	Milija	Newcastle-Under-Lyme	Luton Town	1978	1982	Released	25		
Alexander	Stan	Percy Main	Millwall	1936	1937	Accrington Stanley	9		1
Allen	Clive	Stepney, London	Queens Park Rangers	1984	1988	Bordeaux	97	8	
Allen	Jimmy		Clapton	1896	1997	Mansfield	4		
Allen	Joe	Bilsthorpe	Mansfield Town	1932	1933	Queens Park Rangers	1	1	
Allen	Les	Dagenham	Chelsea	1959	1965	Queens Park Rangers	119		4
Allen	Paul	Aveley	West Ham United	1985	1994	Southampton	276	0	
Allen	Rory	Beckenham	School	1996	1999	Portsmouth	10	11	2
Almond	Bill	Blackburn	Millwall Athletic	1895	1897	Millwall Athletic	16	2	7
Alsford	Wally	Edmonton, London	Northfleet	1930	1937	Nottingham forest	81		
Ambler	Charlie	Alverstone	Luton Town	1894	1899	Gravesend	22		
Anderton	Darren	Southampton	Portsmouth	1992		Still at club	206	18	3
Anson	William	Islington, London		1900	1901	Released	4		
Archibald	Jimmy	Falkirk	Motherwell	1919	1922	Aberdare Athletic	24	1	1
Archibald	Steve	Glasgow	Aberdeen	1980	1984	Barcelona	128	3	5
Ardiles	Ossie	Cordoba, Argentina	Huracan	1978	1988	Queens Park Rangers	222	16	1
Armstrong	Chris	Newcastle	Crystal Palace	1995		Still at club	117	24	4
Armstrong	Gerry	Belfast	Bangor	1975	1981	Watford	65	19	1
Armstrong	Jimmy	Swalwell-on-Tyne	Chelsea	1927	1930	Luton Town	28		5
Atherton	Tom	West Derby	Hibernian	1898	1899	Partick Thistle	2		
Austin	Dean	Hemel Hempstead	Southend United	1992	1997	Crystal Palace	117	7	0
Austin	Percy	Watford	Farnham United Breweries	1927	1928	Released	1		0
Baardsen	Espen	San Rafael, USA	San Francisco All Blacks	1996	1999	Watford	22	1	0
Badenoch	George	Castlehouse	Glossop	1906	1907	Watford	1		0
Baily	Eddie	Clapton, London	Juniors	1946	1956	Port Vale	296		6
Baker	Peter	Hampstead, London	Enfield	1952	1965	Durban United	299		3
Banks	Jimmy	Ashington	Willington Athletic	1913	1923	Norwich City	69		6
Bann	Bill	Broxburn	Broxburn United	1923	1929	Brentford	12		0
Barlow	John	Prescot	Reading	1901	1903	Reading	6		0
Barmby	Nicky	Hull	School	1992	1995	Middlesbrough	81	6	2
Barnett	Fred	Dartford	Northfleet	1922	1929	Southend United	16		1
Barton	Ken	Caernarvon	School	1955	1964	Millwall	4		0
Bauchop	Jimmy	Sauchie	Derby County	1913	1914	Bradford Park Avenue	10		6
Beal	Phil	Godstone	School	1963	1975	Brighton & Hove Albion	330	3	1
Beavon	Stuart	Wolverhampton	School	1978	1980	Reading	3	1	0
Bell	Sammy	Burnhope	Luton Town	1934	1937	Southend United	15		6
Bellamy	Walter	Tottenham, London	Dulwich Hamlet	1926	1935	Brighton & Hove Albion	70		9
Bennett	Les	Wood Green, London	Wood Green Town	1946	1955	West Ham United	272		1
Bentley	Frank	Butt Lane	Stoke	1909	1912	Brentford	36		0
Bergsson	Gudni	Reykjavik, Iceland	Valur	1988	1993	Valur	51	20	2
Berry	Frank		Edmonton White Star	1900	1901	Released	1		0
Berry	William	Sunderland	Sunderland	1903	1907	Manchester United	19		1
Berti	Nicola	Salsomaggiore, Italy	Internazionale	1997	1999	Deportivo Alaves	21		3
Bing	Tommy	Broadstairs	Margate	1957	1958	Margate	1		0
Birnie	Ted	Sunderland	Chelsea	1910	1911	Mulheim	4		1
Black	David	Irvine	Burnley	1897	1998	Woolwich Arsenal	20		8
Blair	John	Neilston	Third Lanark	1926	1928	Sheffield United	29		1
Blake	Bert	Bristol	Mid-Rhondda	1921	1924	Kettering Town	51		0
Blanchflower	Danny	Belfast	Aston Villa	1954	1964	Retired	337		1
Bliss	Bert	Willenhall	Willenhall Swifts	1911	1923	Clapton Orient	194		9
Blyth	Jim	Stobhill	Arniston Rovers	1936	1937	Hull City	11		0
Bolan	Len	Lowestoft	Lowestoft Town	1933	1935	Southend United	10		3
Bond	Dennis	Walthamstow, London	Watford	1966	1971	Charlton Athletic	20	3	1
Booth	Andy	Huddersfield	Sheffield Wednesday	2000	1901	Sheffield Wednesday	3	1	0
Boreham	Fred	Rye	Leyton	1908	1910	Leyton	20		
Bowen	Mark	Neath	School	1983	1987	Norwich City	14	3	2
Bowering	Ernest	Wandsworth, London	Tottenham Thursday	1911	1912	Fulham	7		0

eg Coca-Cola Cup, Rumbelows Cup etc. 'Europe' covers the three major European competitions – the European Champions Cup, European Cup-Winners' Cup and UEFA Cup. The category 'Others' includes the Charity Shield, Texaco Cup, Anglo-Italian League Cup Winners' Cup and Screen Sport Super Cup.

| FAC | | | FLC | | | European | | | Others | | | Totals | | |
Apps	Sub	Goals	Apps	Sub	Goals	Apps	Sub	Goals	Apps	Sub	Goals	Apps	Sub	Goals
0		0	0		0	0		0	0		0	6		1
0		0										1		0
7		0	0		0	0		0	0		0	32		0
0		0										9		1
11	1	9	13	1	13	3	1	2	5	1	1	129	12	85
0		0										4		0
0	0	0	0	0	0	0	0	0	0	0	0	1	0	1
15		13	0		0	3		1	1		2	138		63
23	26	1	1	42	2	4	6	1	6	1	0	356	21	28
1	0	0	3	3	2	0	0	0	0	0	0	14	14	4
1	0	0	0	0	0	0	0	0	0	0	0	17	2	7
9		0										90		0
12		0										34		0
22	1	5	21	0	5	0			0			249	19	40
0		0										4		0
0	0	0	0	0	0	0	0	0	1	0	0	26	0	1
17	1	5	18		7	22	0	7	2	0	0	187	4	77
32	0	4	31	1	3	8	1	2	3	1	0	296	19	25
9	5	4	15		10	3	0	0	0	0	0	144	29	62
6	4	3	3	1	3	0	0	0	0	0	0	74	24	16
5		0	0		0	0			0		0	33		5
0		0										2		0
16	1	0	7	2	0	0			0			140	10	0
0		0										1		0
2	1	0	3	0	0	0			0			27	2	0
0		0										1		0
29		5										325		69
27		0	0		0	16	0	2	0			344		3
9		4	0		0	0		0	2		0	80		10
0		0										12		0
0		0										6		0
12	1	5	7	1	2	0	0	0	0	0	0	100	8	27
0		0										16		1
0		0										4		0
0		0										10		6
30	0	0	27	0	0	30	0	0	5	0	0	422	3	1
0	0	0	0	1	0	0	0	0	0	0	0	3	2	0
1		0										16		6
3		0										73		9
22	14	0	0		0	0		0	0		1	294		118
5		0										41		0
2	2	0	4	2	0	5	1	0	0	0	0	62	24	2
0									1		0	2		1
1		0	0		0	0			0		0	20		1
2		0										23		3
0		0										1		0
0		0										4		1
2	2	0	0		0	0		0	0			22		10
1		0										30		15
5		0										56		0
33	4	0	0			12	2	2	0			384		21
21	13	0	0			0			2		1	217		106
0		0										11		0
0		0										10		3
0	0	0	2	1	0	1		0	0	0	0	23	4	1
0	0	0	0	0	0	0			0	0	0	3	1	0
0		0										20		0
3	0	0	0	0	0	0		0	1		0	16	4	2
0		0										7		0

The Essential History of Tottenham Hotspur

Player		Birthplace	From	Year Joined	Year Left	To	League Apps	Sub	Go
Bowler	George	Newhall	Derby County	1913	1914	Luton Town	3		0
Brace	Robert	Waltham Abbey	School	1983	1984	Waterschei	0	1	0
Bradshaw	Tom	Liverpool	Liverpool	1898	1899	Thames Ironworks	24		5
Brady	Gary	Glasgow	School	1997	1998	Newcastle United	0	9	0
Brain	Jimmy	Bristol	Arsenal	1931	1935	Kings Lynn	45		10
Brazil	Alan	Simshill	Ipswich Town	1982	1984	Manchester United	29	2	9
Brearley	John	Liverpool	Everton	1903	1907	Crystal Palace	70		7
Brewster				1907	1908	Released	1		0
Briggs	Stanley	Stamford Hill, London	Tottenham FC	1891	1898	Clapton	101		8
Brittan	Charlie	Isle of Wight	Northampton Town	1911	1913	Cardiff City	40		0
Brittan	Colin	Bristol	Bristol North Old Boys	1950	1958	Bedford Town	41		1
Britton	Jock	Lennoxtown	Dundee	1925	1928	Released	40		0
Brooke	Garry	Bethnal Green, London	School	1980	1985	Norwich City	49	24	15
Brooks	Johnny	Reading	Reading	1952	1960	Chelsea	166		46
Brooks	Sammy	Brierley Hill	Wolverhampton W	1922	1924	Kidderminster Harriers	10		1
Brotherston	Noel	Dundonald	School	1975	1976	Blackburn Rovers	1		0
Brough	Joe	Burslem	Stoke	1908	1909	Burslem Port Vale	1		0
Brown	Charles	Greenock	Everton	1902	1904	Released	16		0
Brown	David	Broughty Ferry	Forthill Athletic	1909	1910	Morton	1		0
Brown	Ivor	Shardlow	Ripley Town	1909	1911	Coventry City	12		0
Brown	Jimmy	Troon	Brentford	1936	1937	Guildford City	4		0
Brown	Laurie	Shildon	Arsenal	1963	1966	Norwich City	62		3
Brown	Roy	Hove	School	1966	1967	Reading	1		0
Brown	Sandy	Glenbuck	Portsmouth	1900	1902	Portsmouth	46		30
Brown	Robert	Southampton	Thorneycrofts	1919	1924	Retired	37		0
Brown	William	Arbroath	Dundee	1959	1966	Northampton Town	222		0
Buckingham	Vic	Greenwich	Northfleet	1935	1949	Bradford Park Avenue	204		1
Buckingham	W		Novocastrians	1900	1901	Coventry City	6		0
Bull	Walter	Nottingham	Notts County	1904	1909	Heanor United	117		8
Bulling	Ed	East Retford	Nottingham Olympic	1910	1911	Released	2		0
Burgess	Ron	Cwm	Northfleet	1938	1954	Swansea Town	297		15
Burgon	Archie	Nottingham	Grantham Town	1934	1935	Wrexham	4		0
Burne	R			1895	1896		0		0
Burrows	Ly	Ashton-Under-Lyme	Woolwich Arsenal	1894	1898	Sheffield United	27		1
Burton	John	Derby	Chatham	1900	1905	Preston North End	32		3
Burton	Ollie	Derby		1903	1910	Released	95		0
Butters	Guy	Hillingdon	School	1988	1990	Portsmouth	34	1	1
Cable	Tommy	Barking, London	Leyton	1928	1932	Southampton	42		0
Cain	Bob	Slamannan	Sheffield United	1898	1999	Albion Rovers	24		0
Calderwood	Colin	Stranraer	Swindon Town	1993	1999	Aston Villa	152	11	6
Cameron	John	Ayr	Everton	1898	1804	Resigned	117		43
Campbell	Sol	Newham, London	School	1992	2001	Arsenal	246	9	10
Cantrell	Jimmy	Sheepbridge	Notts County	1912	1923	Sutton Town	159		74
Carr	Steve	Dublin	School	1993		Still at club	160	4	6
Carrick	Chris	Stockton	West Ham United	1905	1906	Reading	15		4
Cartwright	Bill	Burton-on-Trent	Chelsea	1913	1914	Swansea Town	13		0
Caskey	Darren	Basildon	School	1993	1996	Reading	20	12	4
Castle	Sid	Basingstoke	Guildford City	1919	1921	Charlton Athletic	5		0
Cattell	C		Old St Marks	1895	1996	Old St Marks	0	1	0
Chalmers	Jimmy	Old Luce	Watford	1902	1904	Swindon Town	10		1
Channell	Fred	Edmonton, London	Northfleet	1933	1936	Retired	95		1
Chaplin	John	Dundee	Dundee	1906	1908	Dundee	66		0
Chapman	Herbert	Kiveton Park	Northampton Town	1904	1907	Northampton Town	43		16
Chiedozie	John	Owerri, Nigeria	Notts County	1984	1987	Derby County	45	8	12
Chipperfield	Jimmy	Bethnal Green, London	Luton Town	1919	1920	Notts County	15		6
Chisholm	Jack	Enfield	Juniors	1947	1948	Brentford	2		0
Chivers	Martin	Southampton	Southampton	1967	1976	Servette	268	10	118
Claesen	Nico	Leut, Belgium	Standard Liege	1986	1988	Antwerp	37	13	18
Clapham	Jamie	Lincoln	School	1996	1997	Ipswich	0	1	0
Clarke	Harry	Woodford	Lovells Athletic	1948	1957	Llanelli	295		4
Clarke	Ray	Hackney, London	School	1972	1973	Swindon Town	0	1	0
Clawley	George	Scholar Green	Stoke City	1899	1803	Southampton	82		0
Clay	Tommy	Leicester	Leicester Fosse	1913	1929	Northfleet	318		23
Clayton	Eddie	Bethnal Green	Eton Manor	1957	1968	Southend United	88	4	20
Clemence	Ray	Skegness	Liverpool	1981	1988	Retired	240	0	0
Clemence	Stephen	Liverpool	School	1997		Still at club	64	20	2
Clements	Bob	Greenwich		1895	1897	Chatham	21		14
Close	Shaun	Islington, London	School	1986	1988	AFC Bournemouth	3	6	0

Complete Players' Career Records: Bowler – Close

FAC			FLC			European			Others			Totals		
Apps	Sub	Goals	Apps	Sub	Goals	Apps	Sub	Goals	Apps	Sub	Goals	Apps	Sub	Goals
0		0										3		0
0	0	0	0	0	0	0	0	0	0	0	0	0	1	0
9		5	0		0	0		0	0		0	33		10
1	1	0	0	0	0	0	0	0	0	0	0	1	10	0
2		0										47		10
1	0	0	1	0	0	3	2	4	0	0	0	33	5	13
8		0										78		7
0		0										1		0
10		0										111		8
2		0	0		0	0		0	0		0	42		0
4		0	0		0	0		0	0		0	45		1
0		0										40		0
4	8	1	4	1	1	6	5	1	0	0	0	63	38	18
13		5										179		51
0		0										10		1
0		0	0		0	0		0	0		0	1		0
1		0	0		0	0		0	0		0	2		0
0		0										16		0
0		0										1		0
0		0										12		0
0		0										4		0
3		0	0		0	0		0	0		0	65		3
0		0										1		0
11		15										57		45
8		0	0		0	0		0	0	1	0	46		0
23		0	0		0	17		0	2		0	264		0
26		0										230		1
0		0										6		0
15	1	1	0		0	0		0	0		0	132		9
0		0										2		0
27		1	0		0	0		0	0	1	0	321		16
0		0										4		0
1		0	0		0	0		0	0		0	1		0
12		0	0		0	0		0	0		0	39		1
0		0										32		3
5		0										100		0
1	0	0	2	1	0	0		0	0		0	37	2	1
2		0										44		0
10		0										34		0
15	1	1	19	1	0	0						186	13	6
25		7										142		50
28	2	1	28	0	4	2	0	0	0	0	0	304	11	15
15		10							2		1	176		85
12	1	0	18	0	1	4	0	0	0	0	0	190	5	7
4		4										19		8
2		0										15		0
6	1	0	3	1	1	0	0	0	0	0	0	29	14	6
0		0										5		0
0		0										1		0
0		0										10		1
14		0	0		0	0		0	0		0	109		1
1		0	0		0	0		0	0		0	67		0
7		1	0		0	0		0	0		0	50		17
5	3	2	7	0	0	7	0	0	3	1	0	67	12	14
0		0										15		6
0		0										2		0
22	2	11	33	0	23	32	0	22	6	0	7	361	12	181
1	5	2	7	0	3	0	0	0	0	0	0	45	18	23
0	0	0	0	0	0	0	0	0	0	0	0	0	1	0
27		0	0		0	0		0	1		0	323		4
0		0										1		0
12		0	0		0	0		0	0		0	94		0
33		1									2	353		24
9	0	0	1	0	0	1	0	0	0	0	0	99	4	20
25	0	0	38	0	0	27	0	0	7	0	0	337		0
7	1	1	6	1	0	2	1	0	0	0	0	79	23	3
9		4	0		0	0		0	0		0	30		18
0	0	0	0	0	0	3	0	2	0	0	0	6	6	2

Player		Birthplace	From	Year Joined	Year Left	To	League Apps	Sub	Go
Coates	Ralph	Hetton-Le-Hole	Burnley	1971	1978	Orient	173	15	14
Cockram	Alan	Kensington, London	School	1983	1984	Bristol Rovers	2	0	0
Coleman	Alf			1894	1895	Novocastrians	0		0
Collins	James	Woolwich, London		1895	1897	Sheppey United	2		0
Collins	Jimmy	Lorn	Lugar Boswell Thistle	1961	1962	Brighton & Hove Albion	2		0
Collins	John	Rhymney	School	1965	1966	Portsmouth	2		0
Collins	Peter	Chelmsford	Chelmsford City	1968	1973	Retired	77	6	4
Collins	Tom	Leven	Heart of Midlothian	1910	1915	Retired	113		1
Colquhoun	David	Motherwell	St Mirren	1931	1935	Luton Town	81		2
Conn	Alfie	Kirkcaldy	Rangers	1974	1977	Celtic	35	3	6
Cook	Billy	Evenwood	Aston Villa	1929	1931	Brentford	63		22
Cook	Bobby	Letchworth	Reading	1949	1950	Watford	3		0
Cooke	Richard	Islington, London	School	1983	1986	AFC Bournemouth	9	2	2
Copeland	David	Ayr	Bedminster	1899	1905	Chelsea	144		51
Coquet	Ernie	Durston-on-Tyne	Reading	1907	1911	Burslem Port Vale	82		0
Corbett	Pat	Hackney, London	School	1980	1983	Orient	3	2	1
Cousins	Albert	Pancras		1907	1908	St Leonards & Hastings Utd	2		0
Cox	Freddie	Reading	Northfleet	1938	1949	Arsenal	99		15
Crompton	Arthur	Birmingham	Army football	1928	1930	Southend United	15		2
Crompton	Ellis	Ramsbottom	Blackburn Rovers	1910	1912	Exeter City	8		0
Crook	Ian	Romford	School	1981	1986	Norwich City	10	10	1
Crooks	Garth	Stoke-on-Trent	Stoke City	1980	1985	West Bromwich Albion	121	4	48
Crowl	Sid	Enfield	Enfield	1913	1914	Enfield	1		0
Crump	Harry		Hereford Thistle	1896	1898	Luton Town	} 31		2
			Luton Town	1899	1900	Doncaster Rovers			
Cubberley	Archie	Bermondsey, London	Asplin Rovers	1894	1895	Asplin Rovers	0		0
Cullen	Joe	Glasgow	Celtic	1897	1899	Lincoln	43		0
Culverhouse	Ian	Bishops Stortford	Hoddesdon United	1983	1984	Norwich City	1	1	0
Cundy	Jason	Wimbledon, London	Chelsea	1991	1996	Ipswich Town	23	3	1
Curtis	John	Southbank	Gainsborough Trinity	1908	1913	Fulham	82		5
Daines	Barry	Witham	School	1971	1981	Bulova	146		0
Darnell	Jabez	Potton	Northampton Town	1905	1915	Trainer	184		4
Davidson	Jimmy	Edinburgh	Burnley	1897	1898	Brighton United	17		5
Davies	Simon	Haverfordwest	Peterborough United	1999		Still at club	10	6	2
Davies	Willie	Troedrhiwfuwch	Notts County	1929	1933	Swansea Town	109		19
Day	Alf	Ebbw Vale	Northfleet	1933	1936	Millwall	13		0
Dearden	Kevin	Luton	School	1990	1993	Brentford	0	1	0
Devlin	James		Airdrie	1896	1897	Millwall Athletic	21		1
Dick	Ally	Stirling	School	1981	1986	Ajax	16	1	2
Dicker	Les	Lambeth, London	Chelmsford City	1952	1953	Southend United	10		2
Dillon	Matt	Highgate, London	School	1972	1974	New York Cosmos	21	3	1
Dimmock	Jimmy	Edmonton, London	Edmonton Ramblers	1919	1931	Thames	400		10
Ditchburn	Ted	Gillingham	Northfleet	1946	1959	Romford	418		0
Dix	Ronnie	Bristol	Derby County	1945	1948	Reading	36		5
Dixon	Arthur	Barrowford	Burnley	1907	1908	Bradford Park Avenue	5		0
Dodge	Bill	Hackney, London	Eton Manor	1958	1960	Crystal Palace	6		0
Doherty	Gary	Carndonagh	Luton Town	1999		Still at club	18	6	3
Dominguez	Jose	Lisbon, Portugal	Sporting Club de Portugal	1997	2001	1FC Kaiserslautern	12	33	4
Dow	Willie	Edinburgh	Bury	1906	1907	Released	9		3
Downie	Ed		Heart of Midlothian	1897	1999	Chesterfield	11		0
Dowsett	Dickie	Wickford	Sudbury Town	1954	1955	Southend United	1		1
Dozzell	Jason	Ipswich	Ipswich Town	1993	1997	Ipswich Town	68	16	13
Drabble	Fred	Southport	Southport YMCA	1909	1910	Nottingham Forest	1		0
Dryburgh	William		Cowdenbeath	1902	1903	Released	16		2
Dulin	Micky	Stepney, London	Welwyn Garden City	1955	1958	Retired	10		2
Dumitrescu	Ilie	Bucharest	Steaua Bucharest	1994	1996	West Ham United	16	0	2
Duncan	Andy	Renton	Hull City	1934	1939	Chelmsford City	93		22
Duncan	John	Dundee	Dundee	1974	1979	Derby County	101	2	53
Dunmore	Dave	Whitehaven	York City	1953	1960	West Ham United	75		23
Duquemin	Len	Cobo, Guernsey	Vauxbelet	1947	1958	Bedford Town	274		11
Durie	Gordon	Paisley	Chelsea	1991	1994	Rangers	58	0	11
Dyson	Terry	Malton	Scarborough	1954	1965	Fulham	184		41
Eadon	John	Glasgow	Maryhill	1914	1915	Albion Rovers	5		0
Eames	Wally	Watford	Watford	1906	1907	Watford	7		2
Eccles	J		Queens Park	1894	1896	London Caledonians	0		0
Edinburgh	Justin	Brentwood	Southend United	1990	2000	Portsmouth	190	23	1
Edrich	Bill	Lingwood	Northfleet	1935	1937	Chelmsford City	20		4
Eggett	John	Wisbech	West Ham United	1904	1907	Croydon Common	66		0

FAC			FLC			European			Others			Totals		
Apps	Sub	Goals	Apps	Sub	Goals	Apps	Sub	Goals	Apps	Sub	Goals	Apps	Sub	Goals
11	1	0	19	3	1	26	0	9	2	0	0	231	19	24
0	0	0	0	0	0	0	0	0	0	0	0	2	0	0
1		0	0		0	0		0	0		0	1		0
6		0	0		0	0		0	0		0	8		0
0		0										2		0
0		0										2		0
8	1	0	5	2	1	1	1	0	0	0	0	91	10	5
9		0										122		1
6		0										87		2
2	0	0	1	2	1	0	0	0	0	0	0	38	5	7
4		2										67		24
0		0										3		0
1	0	0	1	1	0	1	2	0	0	2	0	12	7	2
20		3										164		54
8		1										90		1
0	0	0	0	0	0	0	0	0	0	0	0	3	2	1
												2		0
6		2										105		17
0		0										15		2
2		0										10		0
0	1	0	0	1	0	0	2	0	1	0	0	12	13	1
21	0	9	19	1	9	15	1	9	1	0	0	176	1	75
0	0	0	0		0	0			0		0	1		0
4		3										35		5
5		1										5		1
12		0										55		0
0	0	0	0	0	0	0	0	0	0	0	0	1	1	0
0	0	0	2	0	0	0	0	0	0	0	0	25	3	1
7		0										89		5
11		0	14		0	2			0			172		0
11		0										195		4
0		0										17		5
0	1	2	0	1	0	0	0	0	0	0	0	10	8	4
6		0										115		19
1		0										14		0
0	0	0	1	0	0	0	0	0	0	0	0	1	1	0
3		0										24		1
2	0	0				3	3		0			21	4	2
												10		2
1	0	0	1	0	0	2	1	0	0	0	0	25	4	1
38		12							2		0	440		112
34		0							1		0	453		0
4		0										40		5
0		0										5		0
4		0										10		0
5	0	3	0	0	0	0	0	0	0	0	0	23	6	6
2	1	0	2	6	1	0	2	0	0	0	0	16	42	5
0		0										9		3
0		0										11		0
0		0										1		1
4	1	1	8	2	0	0	0	0	0	0	0	80	19	14
0		0										1		0
4		1										20		3
1		0										11		3
4	0	0	2	0	1	0	0	0	0	0	0	18	2	5
10		4										103		26
7	0	2	10	0	7	0	0	0	0	0	0	118	2	62
6		3										81		26
33		17							1		0	308		131
2	0	0	10	3	0	8	0	3	0	0	0	78		17
16	6		0		0	9	8		1		0	210		55
0		0										5		0
0		0										7		2
6		3										6		3
27	1	0	25	4	0	4	2	0	0	0	0	246	30	1
0		0										20		4
8		0										74		0

Player		Birthplace	From	Year Joined	Year Left	To	League Apps	Sub	Goa
Elkes	Jack	Snedshill	Southampton	1923	1929	Middlesbrough	191		50
Elkin	Bert	Neasden, London	Stockport County	1909	1911	Released	26		0
Elliott	Jimmy	Peterborough	Peterborough	1911	1920	Brentford	13		4
England	Mike	Greenfield	Blackburn Rovers	1966	1975	Retired	300	0	14
Etherington	Matt	Truro	Peterborough United	1999		Still at club	2	9	0
Erentz	Harry	Dundee	Newton Heath	1898	1904	Swindon Town	132		0
Evans	Albert	Camberwell, London	Woking	1927	1929	Grantham	5		0
Evans	Ray	Edmonton, London	School	1968	1975	Millwall	132	4	2
Evans	Tom	Ton Pentre	Northfleet	1929	1937	West Bromwich Albion	94		4
Evans	Willie	Wannllwyd	Hayward Sports	1931	1937	Fulham	178		78
Fairclough	Chris	Nottingham	Nottingham Forest	1987	1989	Leeds United	60		5
Falco	Mark	Hackney, London	School	1978	1987	Watford	162	12	68
Farley	Brian	Ross-on-Wye	Chelmsford City	1951	1952	Sittingbourne	1		0
Felton	Bill	Heworth	Manchester City	1931	1934	Altrincham	73		1
Fenn	Neale	Edmonton, London	School	1996	1998	Peterborough United	0	8	0
Fenwick	Terry	Camden, County Durham	Queens Park Rangers	1987	1993	Swindon Town	90	3	8
Ferdinand	Les	Ladbroke Grove, London	Newcastle United	1997		Still at club	71	11	22
Fitchie	Tom	Edinburgh	West Norwood	1901	1902	West Norwood	1		0
Fleming	Jim	Musselburgh	Newcastle United	1913	1915	Armadale Thistle	19		3
Fleming	Willie		Bury	1896	1897	Released	2		1
Flint	Ken	Selston	Bedford Town	1947	1948	Aldershot	5		1
Foreman	George	Walthamstow, London	West Ham United	1946	1947	Released	36		14
Forman	Tom	Basford	Barnsley	1910	1912	Sutton Junction	8		1
Forster	Matt	Newburn-on-Tyne	Newburn	1920	1930	Reading	236		0
Fortnum	W		Novocastrians	1900	1901	Novocastrians	2		1
Fox	Ruel	Ipswich	Newcastle United	1995	2000	West Bromwich Albion	95	11	13
Freund	Steffen	Brandenburg, Germany	Borussia Dortmund	1998		Still at club	60	5	0
Fredericks	George		Chelmsford	1902	1903	Released	1		0
Freeborough	James	Stockport	Stockport County	1904	1906	Leeds City	2		0
Fullwood	James	Ilkeston	Thorne Colliery	1934	1938	Reading	34		1
Galloway	Randolph	Sunderland	Coventry City	1928	1929	Grantham Town	3		2
Galvin	Tony	Huddersfield	Goole Town	1978	1987	Sheffield Wednesday	194	7	20
Gardner	Anthony	Stafford	Port Vale	2000		Still at club	5	3	0
Garland	Peter	Croydon	School	1990	1991	Newcastle United	0	1	0
Garwood	Len	Ranikwet, India	Eton Bray	1948	1949	Bedford Town	2		0
Gascoigne	Paul	Gateshead	Newcastle United	1988	1992	Lazio	91	1	19
Gavin	Johnny	Limerick	Norwich City	1954	1956	Norwich City	32		15
Gemmill	George	Kings Lynn	Ilford	1913	1914	Ilford	0		0
George	John	Irchester	Kettering	1904	1906	Leeds City	5		1
Gibbins	Eddie	Shoreditch, London	Tottenham Juniors	1952	1953	Coaching staff	1		0
Gibbons	Jack	Fulham, London	Kingstonians	1937	1938	Brentford	27		13
Gibson	Terry	Walthamstow, London	School	1979	1983	Coventry City	16	2	4
Gilberg	Harry	Tottenham, London	Northfleet	1946	1949	Queens Park Rangers	2		0
Gilhooley	Patrick	Draffan	Sheffield United	1901	1904	Brighton & Hove Albion	18		2
Gilmore	J			1895	1896		0		0
Gilzean	Alan	Coupar, Angus	Dundee	1964	1974	Highland Park	335	8	93
Ginola	David	Gassin, France	Newcastle United	1997	2000	Aston Villa	100	0	13
Glen	Alexander	Kilsyth	Notts County	1904	1906	Southampton	32		12
Goldsmith	George	Loftus	Hull City	1934	1935	Bolton Wanderers	1		0
Goodall	Donald		Old St Stephens	1894	1895	Clapton			
Goodman	Bert	Dalston, London	Maidstone United	1919	1920	Margate	16		1
Gorman	John	Winchburgh	Carlisle United	1976	1979	Tampa Bay Rowdies	30		0
Gosnell	Albert	Colchester	Newcastle United	1910	1911	Darlington	5		0
Gough	Richard	Stockholm, Sweden	Dundee United	1986	1988	Rangers	49	0	2
Gower	Mark	Edmonton, London	School	1998	1999	Barnet	0	0	0
Gray	Andy	Lambeth, London	Crystal Palace	1992	1994	Released	23	10	3
Gray	James	Bristol	Rangers	1907	1908	Leyton	15		0
Gray	Phil	Belfast	School	1986	1991	Luton Town	4	5	0
Greaves	Jimmy	East Ham, London	AC Milan	1961	1970	West Ham United	321		220
Greenfield	George	Hackney, London	Lea Bridge GasWorks	1931	1935	Retired	31		11
Grice	Frank	Derby	Notts County	1935	1939	Released	47		1
Griffiths	Fred	Presteigne	Millwall	1901	1902	Preston North End	9		0
Grimsdell	Arthur	Watford	Watford	1912	1929	Clapton Orient	324		26
Groves	Vic	Stepney, London	Leytonstone	1952	1954	Leytonstone	4		3
Grubb	Alan	Leven	Gloucester City	1952	1953	Walsall	2		0
Haddow	David	Dalserf	New Brighton Tower	1899	1901	Albion Rovers	26		0
Haig-Brown	Alan	Charterhouse	Corinthians	1901	1903	Corinthians	4		0
Hall	Alan	Deepcar	Lincoln City	1933	1934	Blackpool	2		0

FAC			FLC			European			Others			Totals		
Apps	Sub	Goals	Apps	Sub	Goals	Apps	Sub	Goals	Apps	Sub	Goals	Apps	Sub	Goals
10		1										201		51
2	0											28		0
0	0											13		4
32	0	2	30	0	0	35	0	3	8	0	1	405	0	20
0	0	0	1	0	0	0	0	0	0	0	0	2	9	0
21	0											153		0
0	0											5		0
7	0	0	13	0	0	22	3	2	0	0	0	174	7	4
7	0											101		4
17		8										195		86
3	0		7									70		5
15	0	5	19	3	3	21	4	13	6	1	6	223	20	95
0	0											1		0
2	0											75		1
1	0	0	1	1	0	0	0	0	0	0	0	2	8	1
7	0	0	14	0	2	4	0	0	1	0	0	116	3	10
12	1	0	5	3	0	0	0	0	0	0	0	88	15	22
0	0											1		0
0	0											19		3
0	0											2		1
0	0											5		1
2	0											38		14
0	0											8		1
8	0											244		0
0	0											2		1
11	1	1	7	3	1	1	0	0	0	0	0	114	15	15
10	0	0	8	0	0	4	0	0	0	0	0	82	5	0
0	0											1		0
0	0											2		0
1	0											35		1
0	0											3		2
23	1	2	20	3	3	25	0	6	4	0	0	256	11	31
0	0	0	0	0	0	0	0	0	0	0	0	5	3	0
0	0	0											1	0
0	0											2		0
6		6	13	1	8	0	0	0	0	0	0	110	2	33
2	1											34		16
1	0											1		0
0	0											5		1
3	0											4		0
6		5										33		18
5	0	1	1	0	1	0	2	1	0	0	0	22	4	7
1	0											3		0
3	0											21		2
2	0											2		0
40	0	21	27	1	6	27	1	13	7	0	1	436	10	134
11	0	5	13	0	4	2	1	0	0	0	0	126	1	22
8	1											40		13
0	0											1		0
4		4										4		4
1	0											17		1
2	0											32		0
2	0											7		0
6	0	0	10	0	0	0	0	0	0	0	0	65	0	2
0	0	0	0	2	0	0	0	0	0	0	0	0	2	0
0	0	0	0	0	0	0	0	0	0	0	0	23	10	3
1	0											15		0
0	1	0	0	0	0	0	0	0	0			4	6	0
36		32	8		5	14		9	2		2	381		268
0	0											31		11
8	0											55		1
3	0											12		0
36		1							2		0	362		27
0	0											4		3
0	0											2		0
1	0											27		0
0	0											4		0
0	0											2		0

Player		Birthplace	From	Year Joined	Year Left	To	League Apps	Sub
Hall	Albert	Barry	Tottenham Juniors	1935	1947	Plymouth Argyle	41	
Hall	Alex		Dundee	1897	1899	Retired	24	
Hall	Almer	Hove	Brighton & Hove Albion	1934	1936	Southend United	16	
Hall	Jack	Prestwich	Manchester United	1936	1939	Stalybridge	53	
Hall	Willie	Newark	Notts County	1932	1944	Retired	201	
Hancock	Ken	Stoke-on-Trent	Ipswich Town	1969	1971	Bury	3	0
Handley	Charlie	Edmonton, London	Edmonton Juniors	1921	1929	Swansea Town	120	
Hargreaves	Harry	Higham	Pontypridd	1923	1926	Burnley	34	
Harmer	Tommy	Hackney, London	Tottenham Juniors	1948	1960	Watford	205	
Harper	Ted	Sheerness	Sheffield Wednesday	1928	1932	Preston North End	63	
Harris	William	Glasgow	Rutherglen	1909	1910	Released	7	
Hartley	Frank	Shipton-Under-Wychwood	Oxford City	1922	1930	Released	7	
Hartley	Jimmy	Dumbarton	Burnley	1897	1899	Lincoln City	18	
Hatfield	Tom	Woolwich, London	Woolwich Arsenal	1896	1897	Released	1	
Hawley	Alf			1900	1901	Southampton	3	
Hay	William	Maryhill	London Caledonians	1895	1896	London Caledonians	0	
Hazard	Micky	Sunderland	School	1979	1985	Chelsea	} 88	31
			Swindon Town	1993	1995	Hitchin Town		
Hedley	Foster	Monkseaton	Chester	1933	1935	Millwall	4	
Helliwell	Sid	Sheffield	Reading	1927	1929	Walsall	8	
Hendon	Ian	Hornchurch	School	1990	1992	Leyton Orient	0	4
Hendry	John	Glasgow	Dundee	1990	1994	Motherwell	5	12
Henry	Ron	Shoreditch, London	Redbourne	1954	1966	Retired	247	
Herod	Edwin	Ilford	Brentford	1928	1931	Chester City	57	
Hewitson	Bob	Blyth	Oldham Athletic	1908	1909	Croydon Common	30	
Hewitt	Charlie	Greatham	Middlesbrough	1906	1907	Liverpool	30	
Hill	Danny	Enfield	School	1992	1995	Oxford United	4	6
Hills	John	Gravesend	Gravesend & Northfleet	1957	1960	Bristol Rovers	29	
Hinton	Bill	Swindon	Bolton Wanderers	1924	1926	Swindon Town	57	
Hitchins	Arthur	Devonport	Northfleet	1937	1939	Retired	35	
Hoddle	Glenn	Hayes	School	1975	1987	Monaco	370	7
Hodge	Steve	Nottingham	Aston Villa	1986	1988	Nottingham Forest	44	1
Hodges	Lee	Epping	School	1992	1993	Barnet	0	4
Hodgkinson	Bert	Peniston	Barnsley	1930	1932	Colwyn Bay United	56	
Holder	Phil	Kilburn, London	School	1971	1974	Crystal Palace	9	4
Hollis	Roy	Great Yarmouth	Norwich City	1952	1953	Southend United	3	
Hollowbread	John	Enfield	Enfield	1958	1964	Southampton	67	
Holmes	Jimmy	Dublin	Coventry City	1976	1979	Vancouver Whitecaps	81	0
Hooper	Percy	Westminster, London	Northfleet	1934	1939	Swansea Town	97	
Hopkins	Mel	Ystrad Rhondda	Ystrad Boys Club	1952	1964	Brighton & Hove Albion	219	
Houghton	Scott	Hitchin	School	1991	1992	Luton Town	0	10
Houston	Bob	Leven	Heart of Midlothian	1902	1903	Released	9	
Howe	Les	Bengeo	Northfleet	1930	1938	Retired	165	
Howells	David	Guildford	School	1985	1998	Southampton	238	39
Hoy	Roger	Poplar, London	School	1965	1968	Crystal Palace	10	
Hudson	E		Novocastrians	1900	1901	Novocastrians	1	
Hughes	Archie	Colwyn Bay	Huddersfield Town	1945	1948	Blackburn Rovers	2	
Hughes	Ted	Ruabon	Everton	1899	1908	Clyde	152	
Hughton	Chris	Forest Gate, London	School	1979	1990	West Ham United	293	4
Humphreys	Percy	Cambridge	Chelsea	1909	1912	Leicester Fosse	45	
Hunt	Doug	Shipton Bellinger	Northfleet	1934	1937	Barnsley	17	
Hunt	George	Barnsley	Chesterfield	1930	1937	Arsenal	185	
Hunter	Alex	Renfrew	Queens Park	1920	1922	Wigan Borough	23	
Hunter	Peter		London Caledonians	1894	1896	London Caledonians		
Hutchinson	George	Allerton Bywater	Sheffield United	1953	1954	Guildford	5	
Hyde	Leon	Birmingham	Wellingborough	1899	1802	Wellingborough	18	
Iley	Jim	Kirkby	Sheffield United	1957	1959	Nottingham Forest	53	
Illingworth	John	Castleford	Northfleet	1929	1935	Swansea Town	10	
Ireland	Jeff	Paddington, London	Finchley	1957	1959	Shrewsbury Town	3	
Iversen	Steffen	Oslo	Rosenborg	1996		Still at club	92	14
Jacques	Bill	Erith	Coventry City	1914	1923	Retired	123	
Jeffrey	George	Motherwell	Wishaw Juniors	1937	1938	Motherwell	1	
Jenkins	David	Bristol	Arsenal	1968	1970	Brentford	11	3
Jennings	Pat	Newry	Watford	1964	1977	Arsenal	} 472	0
			Arsenal	1985	1986	Retired		
Johnson	Neil	Grimsby	School	1965	1971	Torquay United	27	7
Jones	Arthur	St Pancras, London	Market Drayton	1900	1901	Doncaster Rovers	8	
Jones	Charlie	Penmaer	Northfleet	1934	1936	Southend United	18	

FAC Apps	Sub	Goals	FLC Apps	Sub	Goals	European Apps	Sub	Goals	Others Apps	Sub	Goals	Totals Apps	Sub	Goals
4		1										45		11
2		1										26		1
5		0										21		3
5		0										58		0
20		2										221		29
0	0	0	1	0	0	0	0	0	2	0	0	6	0	0
11		9										131		35
0		0										34		7
17		4										222		51
4		1										67		63
0		0										7		0
0		0										7		1
3		1										21		10
0		0										1		0
0		0										3		2
1		0										1		0
9	3	2	12	4	5	22	1	3	1	0	0	132	39	25
1		0										5		1
1		0										9		0
0	0	0	1	0	0	0	2	0	0	0	0	1	6	0
0	1	0	0	2	0	0	0					5	15	5
23		0	0		0	17		0	2		0	289		1
2		0										59		0
4		0										34		0
5		0										35		11
0	0	0	0	2	0	0	0	0	0	0	0	4	8	0
3		0										32		0
7		0										64		0
7		0										42		1
47	1	11	44	0	10	17	4	1	4	0	0	482	12	110
7	0	2	2	0	0	0	0	0	0	0	0	53	1	9
0	0	0	0	0	0	0	0	0	0	0	0		4	0
2												58		0
0	0	0	0	0	0	0	6	1	0	0	0	9	10	2
1		2										4		3
6												73		0
9	0	0	2	0	0	0	0	0	0	0	0	92	0	2
11												108		0
20		0										239		0
0	0	0	0	2	0	0	2	0	0	0	0	0	14	2
0		0										9		2
17		2										182		28
17	4	1	26	5	4	6	0	0	1	0	0	288	48	27
0		0				2						12		0
0		0										1		0
2												4		0
31		2										183		11
34	2	1	33	2	2	29	1	4	7	1	0	396	10	19
5		5										50		29
2		0										19		6
13		13										198		138
3		0							1		0	27		0
11		6										11		6
0		0										5		1
0		0										18		5
4		0										57		1
2		0										12		0
0		0										3		0
9	2	3	9	1	4	4	0	1	0	0	0	114	17	39
15		0							1		0	139		0
0		0										1		1
2	1	0										13	4	2
43	0	0	39		0	36		0	6		1	596		1
4		1										31	7	6
0		0										8		1
0		0										18		0

Player		Birthplace	From	Year Joined	Year Left	To	League Apps	Sub	G
Jones	Chris	Jersey	School	1974	1982	Manchester City	149	15	3
Jones	Cliff	Swansea	Swansea Town	1958	1968	Fulham	314	4	1
Jones	Gordon	Birkenhead	Bolton Wanderers	1912	1913	Released	7		0
Jones	John	West Bromwich	Bristol Rovers	1902	1904	Died	32		1
Jones	John L.	Rhuddlan	Sheffield United	1897	1904	Watford	131		7
Jones	Billy	Brighton	Bristol City	1906	1907	Swindon Town	8		5
Jones	Ernie	Cwmbwrla	Swansea Town	1946	1949	Southampton	55		1
Jordon	Johnny	Romford	Grays Athletic	1947	1948	Juventus	24		1
Joseph	Leon	Stepney, London	Leytonstone	1946	1947	Leytonstone	1		0
Joyce	John	Burton-on-Trent	Millwall	1909	1915	Millwall	73		1
Joyce	Bill		Bolton Wanderers	1897	1899	Thames Ironworks	40		3
Julian	Bill	Boston	Luton Town	1894	1895	Dartford	0		0
Jull	Jack	Edmonton, London	Founder	1882	1896	Retired	142		2
Kaine	Bill	East Ham, London	West Ham United	1925	1926	Luton Town	11		0
Keeley	Andy	Basildon	School	1975	1977	Sheffield United	5	1	0
Kendall	Mark	Tredegar	School	1978	1981	Newport County	29	0	0
Kennedy	Jimmy	Dundee	Stockport County	1909	1912	Swindon Town	13		1
Kerry	Arthur	Headington	Oxford City	1909	1910	Oxford City	1		0
Kerslake	David	Stepney, London	Leeds United	1993	1996	Charlton Athletic	34	3	0
King	Arthur	Kentore	Aberdeen	1913	1914	Belfast Celtic	19		0
King	Derek	Hackney, London	Juniors	1951	1955	Swansea Town	19		0
King	Eddie	Hackney, London	Northfleet	1934	1935	Retired	1		0
King	Ledley	Bow, London	School	1998		Still at club	20	2	1
Kinnear	Joe	Dublin	St Albans City	1965	1976	Brighton & Hove Albion	189	7	2
Kirwan	Jack	Wicklow	Everton	1899	1805	Chelsea	155		4
Klinsmann	Jurgen	Goppingen, Germany	Monaco	1994	1995	Bayern Munich }			
			Sampdoria	1997	1998	Retired }	56	0	2
Knight	John	Edmonton, London	Corinthians	1928	1929	Released	1		0
Knowles	Cyril	Fitzwilliam	Middlesbrough	1964	1976	Retired	400	1	1
Knowles	Joe	Monkwearmouth	Sunderland	1897	1898	South Shields	19		0
Korsten	Willem	Boxtel, Holland	Vitesse Arnhem	1999		Still at club	12	11	3
Kyle	Peter	Rutherglen	Larkhall Thistle	1905	1906	Woolwich Arsenal	25		8
Lacy	John	Liverpool	Fulham	1978	1983	Crystal Palace	99	5	2
Lane	Bill	Tottenham, London	Northfleet	1924	1927	Leicester City	25		7
Lanham	Charlie	Stanley		1895	1897	Millwall Athletic	2		0
Leach	George	Malta	Brighton & Hove Albion	1905	1906	Released	2		2
Leach-Lewis	Allan	Margate	Cambridge University	1903	1904	Casuals	2		0
Lee	Colin	Torquay	Torquay United	1977	1980	Chelsea	57	5	1
Lee	Terry	Stepney, London	School	1973	1974	Torquay United	1		0
Leech	Billy	Newcastle-under-Lyme	Newcastle Swifts	1898	1899	Burslem Port Vale	4		2
Leonhardsen	Oyvind	Kristiansund, Norway	Liverpool	1999		Still at club	44	3	7
Leslie	Tom	Tollcross	Vale of Clyde	1908	1911	Leyton	10		0
Levene	David	Bethnal Green, London	Northfleet	1932	1935	Crystal Palace	8		0
Leworthy	David	Portsmouth	Fareham Town	1984	1986	Oxford United	8	3	3
Lightfoot	Ed	Liverpool	Southport Central	1911	1915	Killed in action	61		2
Lindsay	Alex	Dundee	Raith Rovers	1919	1930	Thames	211		4
Lineker	Gary	Leicester	Barcelona	1989	1992	Grampus Eight	105	0	6
Lorimer	Hugh	Paisley	St Mirren Juniors	1919	1922	Dundee	5		0
Low	Roy	Watford	School	1964	1967	Watford	6	2	1
Lowdell	Arthur	Edmonton, London	Sheffield Wednesday	1927	1930	Released	86		0
Lowe	Harry	Northwich	Brighton & Hove Albion	1914	1927	Fulham	65		0
Ludford	George	Barnet	Northfleet	1936	1950	Coaching staff	75		8
Lunn	Tommy	Bishop Auckland	Wolverhampton W	1909	1913	Stockport	86		0
Lyle	Archie	Maryhill		1909	1910	Released	1		0
Lyman	Colin	Northampton	Northampton Town	1937	1946	Port Vale	46		1
Lyons	Bert	Hednesford	Clapton Orient	1930	1932	Colwyn Bay	54		3
Mabbutt	Gary	Bristol	Bristol Rovers	1982	1998	Retired	458	19	2
MacFarlane	Doug	Barrow	Burnley	1908	1910	Barrow	21		0
Mackay	Dave	Musselburgh	Heart of Midlothian	1959	1968	Derby County	268		4
Madden	John	Dumbarton	Dundee	1897	1898	Slavia Prague	2		0
Maddison	Geordie	Birtley	Birtley Colliery	1922	1924	Hull City	40		0
Mahorn	Paul	Whipps Cross	School	1993	1998	Port Vale	3	0	0
Mair	Jimmy	Glenboig		1896	1897	Released	2		0
Manning	Gordon	Prescot	Preston North End	1907	1908	Released	33		0
Mapley	Percy	Poplar, London	West Ham United	1903	1904	Released	5		0
Marchi	Tony	Edmonton, London	School	1949	1957	Juventus }			
			Torino	1959	1965	Cambridge City }	232		7
Markham	Ernie	Edmonton, London	Gravesend United	1896	1897	Ilford	3		0
Marshall	Harry	Hucknall	Port Vale	1931	1932	Kidderminster Harriers	1		0

FAC			FLC			European			Others			Totals		
Apps	Sub	Goals	Apps	Sub	Goals	Apps	Sub	Goals	Apps	Sub	Goals	Apps	Sub	Goals
10	2	4	7	1	1	0	1	0	0	0	0	166	19	42
35	4	16	2	0	1	19	0	7	2	0	0	372	8	159
0		0										7		0
5		2										37		21
31		1										162		8
0		0										8		0
2		0										57		14
3		3										27		13
0		0										1		0
8		0										81		1
12		7										52		41
5		0										5		0
8		0										150		24
1		0										12		0
0	0	0	0	0	0	0	0	0	0	0	0	5	1	0
6	0	0	1	0	0	0	0	0	0			36		0
0		0										13		1
0		0										1		0
1	1	0	5	0	0	0	0	0	0	0	0	40	4	0
1		0										20		0
0		0										19		0
0		0										1		0
4	1	1	0	0	0	0	0	0	0	0	0	24	3	2
24	0	0	20	0	0	18	0	0	7	0	0	258	7	2
24		2										179		42
9	0	5	3	0	4	0	0	0	0	0	0	68	0	38
0		0										1		0
42	0	1	32	1	0	30	0	1	5	0	0	509	2	17
1		0										19		1
0	3	0	1	0	0	0	0	0	0	0	0	13	14	1
4		3										29		11
12	0	0	11	0	1	4	1	0	1	0	0	127	6	3
4		2										29		9
1		0										3		0
0		0										2		2
0		0										2		0
6	1	3	2	0	0	0	0	0	0	0	0	65	6	21
0		0										1		0
0		0										4		2
3	1	1	4	0	2	4	0	1	0	0	0	55	4	11
2		0										12		0
2		0										10		0
0	0	0	0	1	1	0	0	0	0	1	1	8	5	5
5												66		2
15		8										226		50
9	0	3	16	0	8	8	0	2	1	0	0	139	0	80
0		0										5		0
0	0	0	0	0	0	0	0	0	0	0	0	6	2	1
4		0										90		0
7		0										72		0
6		1										81		9
5		0										91		0
0		0										1		0
8		1										54		11
3		0										57		3
45	2	5	60	2	2	22	3	4	7	1	0	592	27	38
0		0										21		2
33		4	0		0	17		5	3		0	321		51
0		0										2		0
1		0										41		0
0	1	0	0	1	1	0	0	0	0	0	0	3	2	1
0		0										2		0
1		0										34		0
0		0										5		0
16	0	0	0		0	12		0	0	0	0	260		7
0		0										3		0
0		0										1		0

Player		Birthplace	From	Year Joined	Year Left	To	League Apps	Sub	Goal
Mason	Tom	Portsmouth		1911	1912	Southend United	7		1
Massey	Fred	East Ham, London	Leyton	1908	1909	West Ham United	1		0
Mazzon	Georgio	Waltham Cross	Waltham New Town	1980	1983	Aldershot	3	1	0
McAllister	Don	Radcliffe	Bolton Wanderers	1974	1981	Charlton Athletic	168	4	9
McClellan	Sid	Dagenham	Chelmsford City	1950	1956	Portsmouth	68		29
McConnachie	John	Alexandria	Rangers	1903	1904	Southampton	}		
			Southampton	1905	1906	Leyton	6		0
McCormick	Jimmy	Rotherham	Chesterfield	1903	1904	Fulham	137		26
McCurdy	Bill	Bridgton	New Brompton	1904	1905	New Brompton	12		0
McDiarmid	Frank	Dundee	Dundee	1906	1907	Northampton Town	7		0
McDonald	David	Dublin	Home Farm	1992	1993	Peterborough United	2	0	0
McDonald	Bob	Inverness	Inverness Caledonians	1919	1925	Clapton Orient	109		0
McElhaney	Richard		Partick Thistle	1896	1897	Swindon Town	19		6
McEwen	Dave	Westminster, London	Dulwich Hamlet	1999	2001	Queens Park Rangers	0	4	0
McGrath	Chris	Belfast	School	1973	1976	Manchester United	30	8	5
McKay	Kenny	Larkhall	Sheffield United	1898	1899	Thames Ironworks	18		5
McKenzie	L		London Caledonians	1895	1896	Released	0		0
McMahon	Gerry	Belfast	Glenavon	1994	1996	Stoke City	9	7	0
McNab	Neil	Greenock	Morton	1973	1979	Bolton Wanderers	63	9	3
McNair	Willie	Caldarwan	Falkirk	1907	1908	Aberdeen	15		5
McNaught	Jimmy	Dumbarton	Newton Heath	1898	1805	Maidstone	104		0
McTavish	John	Govan	Oldham Athletic	1910	1912	Newcastle United	38		3
McTavish	Bob		Falkirk	1910	1911	Brentford	10		3
McVeigh	Paul	Belfast	School	1996	1997	Norwich City	2	1	1
Meade	Tom	Plumstead	Woolwich Arsenal	1897	1899	Released	15		5
Meads	Tommy	Grassmoor	Reading	1929	1935	Notts County	184		6
Mearns	Fred	Sunderland	Kettering	1903	1904	Bradford City	5		0
Medley	Les	Edmonton, London	Juniors	1939	1947	Toronto Greenbacks	}		
			Ulster United	1948	1953	Retired	150		45
Medwin	Terry	Swansea	Swansea Town	1956	1963	Retired	197		65
Meek	Joe	Hazelrigg	Bradford Park Avenue	1935	1939	Swansea Town	45		15
Melia	Jimmy	Darlington	Sheffield Wednesday	1898	1901	Preston North End	37		1
Messer	Alf	Deptford, London	Reading	1930	1932	Bournemouth & B A	50		2
Metgod	Johnny	Amsterdam, Holland	Nottingham Forest	1987	1988	Feyenoord	5	7	0
Middlemiss	Bert	New Benwell	Stockport County	1907	1920	Queens Park Rangers	270		58
Miller	Les	Barking	Sochaux	1936	1939	Chesterfield	56		22
Miller	Paul	Stepney, London	School	1978	1987	Charlton Athletic	206	2	7
Milliken	Jimmy		St Mirren	1896	1897	Clyde	19		6
Milton	Harold	Hackney, London	New Crusaders	1903	1904	Clapton	1		0
Mimms	Bobby	York	Everton	1987	1990	Blackburn Rovers	37	0	0
Minter	Billy	Woolwich, London	Reading	1907	1921	Trainer	253		99
Minton	Jeff	Hackney, London	School	1991	1993	Brighton & Hove Albion	2	0	1
Moffatt	Joe	Paisley	Walsall	1900	1901	St Mirren	6		3
Moles	Walter	Tottenham, London	Waverley	1900	1902	Bristol City	}		
			Bristol City	1901	1902	Released	3		0
Moncur	John	Mile End, London	School	1986	1992	Swindon Town	10	11	1
Monk	Cuthbert	Hackney, London	Tottenham College	1894	1896	Old Tottonians	0		0
Montgomery	Jock	Chryston		1895	1898	Notts County	36		0
Moores	Ian	Newcastle-Under-Lyme	Stoke City	1976	1979	Orient	25	4	6
Moran	Jack	Wigan	Wigan Borough	1931	1932	Watford	12		0
Moran	Paul	Enfield	School	1986	1994	Peterborough United	14	22	2
Morgan	Roger	Walthamstow, London	Queens Park Rangers	1968	1972	Retired	66	2	8
Morris	Tom	Grantham	Gainsborough Trinity	1899	1912	Retired	301		24
Morrison	Johnny	Belvedere	Northfleet	1932	1939	Retired	133		87
Morton	James	Leith	Stoke	1908	1909	Released	2		0
Mullery	Alan	Notting Hill, London	Fulham	1964	1972	Fulham	312		25
Murphy	Peter	Hartlepool	Coventry City	1950	1952	Birmingham City	38		14
Murray	Willie	Forres	Northampton Town	1904	1906	Leeds City	21		0
Nayim		Ceuta, Morocco	Barcelona	1988	1993	Real Zaragoza	95	17	11
Naylor	Terry	Islington, London	School	1968	1980	Charlton Athletic	237	6	0
Neighbour	Jimmy	Chingford	School	1970	1977	Norwich City	104	15	8
Nethercott	Stuart	Chadwell Heath	School	1992	1997	Millwall	31	23	0
Newbigging	Willie	Larkhall	Lanark County	1896	1897	Folkestone	10		2
Newman	Ernie	Birmingham	Stockport County	1909	1914	Released	30		6
Nicholls	Joe	Carlton	Grenadier Guards	1926	1936	Bristol Rovers	124		0
Nicholson	Bill	Scarborough	Northfleet	1938	1955	Coaching staff	314		6
Nielsen	Allan	Esbjerg, Denmark	Brondby	1996	2000	Watford	78	18	12
Nilsen	Roger	Tromso, Norway	Sheffield United	1998	1999	Released	3		0
Norman	Maurice	Mulbarton	Norwich City	1955	1966	Retired	357		16

Complete Players' Career Records: Mason – Norman

FAC Apps	Sub	Goals	FLC Apps	Sub	Goals	European Apps	Sub	Goals	Others Apps	Sub	Goals	Totals Apps	Sub	Goals
0		0										7		1
0		0										1		0
1	0	0	0	2	0	0	0	0	0	0	0	4	3	0
16	1	0	13	0	1	0	0	0	0	0	0	197	5	10
2		3										70		32
0		0										6		0
13		2										150		28
0		0										12		0
0		0										7		0
0	0	0	0	0	0	0	0	0	0	0	0	2	0	0
16		0							1		0	126		0
3		1										22		7
0	0	0	0	0	0	0	0	0	0	0	0	0	4	0
0	0	1	0	0	0	7	1	5	0	0	0	38	9	10
9		1										27		6
1		0										1		0
0	1	0	3	0	0	0	0	0	0	0	0	12	8	1
2	0	0	5	1	0	0	0	0	0	0	0	70	10	3
1		0										16		5
13		1										117		1
2		0										40		3
1		0										11		3
0	0	0	0	0	0	0	0	0	0	0	0	2	1	1
2		3										17		8
5		0										189		6
												5		0
14		1							1		0	165		46
13		7	0		0	5		0	1		1	216		73
6		1										51		16
3		0										40		1
2		0										52		2
0	0	0	2		0	0	0	0	0	0	0	7	7	0
17		3										287		61
9		4										65		26
30	1	1	22	1	0	23	2	0	5	0	0	286	4	10
3		0										22		6
0		0										1		0
2	0	0	5	0	0	0	0	0	0	0	0	44	0	0
19		6										272		105
0	0	0	0	1	0	0	0	0	0	0	0	2	1	1
												6		3
0		0										3		0
0	0	0	1	2	0	0	0	0	0	0	0	12	13	1
2		0										2		0
5		0										41		0
0	0	0	3	0	2	0	0	0	0	0	0	28	4	8
0		0										12		0
3	1	0	1	6	0	0	1	0	0	0	0	18	30	2
6	0	2	3	0	1	2	1	1	2	0	0	79	3	12
38		1										339		25
21		14										154		101
0		0										2		0
33		1	18		0	10		4	7		0	380		30
0		0							1		1	39		15
1		0										22		0
6	3	4	11	6	3	6	0	0	1	0	0	119	26	18
17	1	0	23	1	1	13	6	0	2	0	0	292	14	1
10	1	1	14	3	1	6	3	1	0	1	0	134	23	11
5	3	1	0	0	0	0	0	0	0	0	0	36	26	1
3		3										13		5
2		0										32		6
5		0										129		0
27		0							1		0	342		6
5	2	3	10	1	3	1	0	0	0	0	0	94	21	18
0		0										3		0
37		2	0		0	17		0	2		1	413		18

The Essential History of Tottenham Hotspur

Player		Birthplace	From	Year Joined	Year Left	To	League Apps	Sub	Goals
O'Callaghan	Taffy	Ebbw Vale	Ebbw Vale	1926	1935	Leicester City	252		92
O'Hagan	Charlie	Buncara	Everton	1904	1906	Middlesborough	19		5
Oliver	William	Walthamstow, London	Walthamstow Grange	1913	1914	Released	2		0
O'Reilly	Gary	Isleworth	School	1980	1984	Brighton & Hove Albion	39	6	0
Osborne	Frank	Wynberg, South Africa	Fulham	1923	1931	Southampton	210		78
Osgood	Keith	Isleworth	School	1973	1978	Coventry City	112	1	13
O'Shea	Tim	Westminster, London	School	1986	1988	Leyton Orient	1	2	0
Owen	Aled	Brynteg	Bangor City	1953	1954	Ipswich Town	1		0
Owen	M		London Welsh	1895	1896	London Welsh	0		0
Page	Albert	Walthamstow, London	Leyton	1936	1939	Colchester United	55		0
Page	George	London	Cheshunt	1905	1906	Leeds City	1		0
Pangbourne	Tom	Birmingham	New Brompton	1900	1901	Reading	2		0
Parks	Tony	Hackney, London	School	1981	1988	Brentford	37	0	0
Pass	Jimmy	Juffulpore, India	Stockport County	1907	1908	New Brompton	18		5
Payne	Ernie	Fulham, London	Fulham	1894	1899	Retired	20		6
Payne	George	Hitchin	Barnet Alston	1907	1908	Crystal Palace	7		3
Pearce	Jimmy	Tottenham, London	School	1968	1973	Retired	108	33	21
Pearson	John	Arbroath	Arbroath	1914	1923	Luton Town	47		0
Perry	Chris	Carshalton	Wimbledon	1999		Still at club	66	3	2
Perryman	Steve	Ealing, London	School	1969	1986	Oxford United	653	2	31
Peters	Martin	Plaistow, London	West Ham United	1970	1975	Norwich City	189	0	46
Phypers	Ernie	Walthamstow, London	Northfleet	1934	1937	Doncaster Rovers	30		0
Piercy	John	Forest Gate, London	School	1999		Still at club	1	7	0
Pickett	Arthur	Bristol	Workington	1906	1908	New Brompton	28		6
Piper	Ron	Lowestoft	Arsenal	1962	1963	Released	1		0
Pitt	Steve	Willesden, London	Corinthian Casuals	1965	1966	Colchester United	1		0
Polston	Andy	Bethnal Green, London	School	1989	1990	Brighton & Hove Albion	0	1	0
Polston	John	Walthamstow, London	School	1986	1990	Norwich City	17	7	1
Popescu	Gica	Romania	PSV Eindhoven	1994	1995	Barcelona	23	0	3
Possee	Derek	Southwark, London	School	1963	1966	Millwall	19		4
Poynton	Cecil	Brownhills	Ton Pentre	1923	1933	Coaching staff	152		3
Pratt	John	Hackney, London	School	1969	1980	Portland Timbers	307	24	39
Pratt	Tom	Fleetwood	Preston North End	1899	1900	Preston North End	29		23
Price	Paul	St Albans	Luton Town	1981	1984	Minnesota Strikers	35	4	0
Pryor	Harry		Old Castle Swifts	1895	1896	Dartford	0		0
Quinn	David	Tyrone	Darwen	1903	1904	Released	1		0
Raby	Joe	Heighington	Gainsborough Trinity	1899	1900	Wellingborough	2		0
Ramsey	Alf	Dagenham	Southampton	1949	1955	Ipswich Town	226		24
Rance	Charlie	Bow, London	Clapton	1910	1921	Derby County	103		0
Rebrov	Sergei	Gorlovka, Ukraine	Dynamo Kiev	2000		Still at club	28	1	9
Reddish	Jack	Nottingham	Boots Athletic	1929	1932	Lincoln City	6		0
Rees	Billy	Blaengarw	Cardiff City	1949	1950	Leyton Orient	11		3
Reid	Jimmy	Bells Hill	Watford	1906	1908	Reading	36		20
Reilly	Matt	Donnybrook	Notts County	1906	1907	Shelbourne	19		0
Reynolds	Ron	Haslemere	Aldershot	1953	1958	Southampton	86		0
Richardson	Jock	Motherwell	Northfleet	1926	1929	Reading	38		0
Ringrose	Bert	Tottenham, London	Northfleet	1936	1937	Notts County	10		0
Robb	George	Finsbury Park, London	Finchley	1951	1959	Retired	182		53
Roberts	Graham	Southampton	Weymouth	1980	1987	Rangers	200	9	23
Roberts	Tom	Handsworth	Preston North End	1928	1929	Dick Kerr's FC	4		2
Robertson	Jimmie		Dundee	1896	1897	Released	1		1
Robertson	Jimmy	Cardonald	St Mirren	1963	1969	Arsenal	153	4	25
Robinson	Martin	Chadwell St Marys	School	1975	1978	Charlton Athletic	5	1	2
Robinson	Steve	Lisburn	School	1993	1994	Bournemouth	1	1	0
Robshaw	Harry	Edmonton, London	Golders Green	1951	1952	Reading	1		
Robson	Mark	Stratford, London	Exeter City	1988	1990	West Ham United	3	5	0
Roe	Tommy	Evenwood	Northfleet	1925	1927	Nottingham Forest	6		4
Rosenthal	Ronny	Haifa	Liverpool	1993	1997	Watford	55	33	4
Ross	Jimmy	Bonnyrigg	Raith Rovers	1922	1924	Released	7		0
Rowe	Arthur	Tottenham, London	Northfleet	1931	1938	Retired	182		0
Rowley	Dick	Enniskillen	Southampton	1929	1932	Preston North End	24		10
Ruddock	Neil	Battersea, London	Millwall	1986	1988	Millwall			
			Southampton	1992	1993	Liverpool	45	2	3
Rule	Art		Sheppey United	1898	1900	Portsmouth	7		1
Rundle	Charlie	Par	St Blazey	1946	1949	Crystal Palace	28		12
Ryden	John	Alexandria	Accrington Stanley	1955	1959	Watford	63		2
Sage	Willie	Edmonton, London	Corinthians	1919	1926	Clapton Orient	13		0
Saib	Moussa	Theniet-el-Had, Algeria	Auxerre	1997	1999	El Nasr	3	10	1
Samways	Vinny	Bethnal Green, London	School	1986	1994	Everton	165	28	11

Complete Players' Career Records: O'Callaghan – Samways

FAC			FLC			European			Others			Totals		
Apps	Sub	Goals	Apps	Sub	Goals	Apps	Sub	Goals	Apps	Sub	Goals	Apps	Sub	Goals
11		6										263		98
3		1										22		6
0		0										2		0
2	0	0	4	0	0	2	2	0	1	0	0	48	8	0
9		4										219		82
3	0	0	11	0	1	0	0	0	0	0	0	126	1	14
0	0	0	0	0	0	0	0	0	0	0	0	1	2	0
0		0										1		0
1		1										1		1
1												56		0
0		0										1		0
0												2		0
5	0	0	1	0	0	5	1	0	0	0	0	48	1	0
1												19		5
14		6										34		12
0												7		3
4	6	3	21	6	7	8	7	4	2	2	1	143	54	36
3												50		0
6	0	0	5	0	0	4	0	1	0	0	0	81	3	3
69	0	2	66		3	63	1	3	11	1	0	862	4	39
16	0	5	23	0	12	32	0	13	6	0	4	266	0	80
3		0										33		0
0	0	0	1	0	0	0	0	0	0	0	0	2	7	0
0		0										28		6
0		0										1		0
0		0										1		0
0	0	0	0	0	0	0	0	0	0	0	0		1	0
0	0	0	3	1	0	0	0	0	0	0	0	20	8	1
3	0	0	2	0	0	0	0	0	0	0	0	28	0	3
0		0										19		4
6		0										158		3
23	5	2	27	4	7	24	1	1	0	0	0	381	34	49
1												30		23
6	0	0	7	0	0	10	0	0	0	0	0	58	4	0
6		4										6		4
0		0										1		0
0		0										2		0
24		0										250		24
7		1										110		1
5	0	3	2	0	0	0	0	0	0	0	0	35	1	12
1		0										7		0
2		0										13		3
7		2										43		22
7												26		0
9												95		0
3												41		0
												10		0
18		5										200		58
27	0	2	24	1	5	25	1	5	6	0	0	282	11	35
0		0										4		2
0		0										1		1
18	0	3	2	0	0	4	0	3	1	0	1	178	4	32
0	0	0	0	0	0	0	0	0	0	0	0	5	1	2
0	0	0	0	0	0	0	0	0	0	0	0	1	1	0
												1		0
0	0	0	1	0	0	0	0	0	0	0	0	4	5	0
												6		4
7	2	6	3	0	1	0	0	0	0	0	0	65	35	11
0		0										7		0
19		0										201		0
0		0										24		10
6	1	1	4	0	0	0	0	0	0	0	0	55	3	4
7												7		1
1		0										29		12
5		0										68		2
0		0										13		0
0		0										3	10	1
15	1	2	27	4	4	6	1	0	1	0	0	214	34	17

Player		Birthplace	From	Year Joined	Year Left	To	League Apps	Sub	Goal
Sanders	Arthur	Edmonton, London	Northfleet	1926	1928	Northfleet	13		7
Sargent	Fred	Islington, London	Northfleet	1934	1939	Chelmsford City	93		24
Saul	Frank	Canvey Island	School	1960	1968	Southampton	112	4	37
Scales	John	Harrogate	Liverpool	1996	2000	Ipswich Town	29	4	0
Scarth	Jimmy	North Shields	Percy Main	1949	1952	Gillingham	7		3
Scott	Joe	Lye	Barnsley	1928	1931	Cradley Heath	18		4
Scott	Kevin	Easington	Newcastle United	1993	1996	Norwich City	16	2	1
Sedgley	Steve	Enfield	Coventry City	1989	1994	Ipswich Town	147	17	9
Seeburg	Max	Leipzig, Germany	Chelsea	1907	1909	Leyton	16		5
Seed	Jimmy	Blackhill	Mid-Rhondda	1920	1927	Sheffield Wednesday	229		65
Segers	Hans	Eindhoven, Holland	Wolverhampton W	1998	1999	Coaching Staff	1	0	0
Shackleton	John	Keighley	Darlington	1905	1906	Bury	3		1
Sharp	Buchanan	Alexandria	Chelsea	1922	1925	Leicester City	3		0
Sharpe	Fred	Greenwich, London	School	1958	1959	Norwich City	2		1
Shepherd	Jack		Shaftesbury Rovers	1894	1896	Millwall Athletic	0		0
Sheringham	Teddy	Highams Park	Nottingham Forest	1992	1997	Manchester United			
			Manchester United	2001		Still at club	163	3	75
Sherwood	Tim	St Albans	Blackburn Rovers	1998		Still at club	66	8	12
Sinton	Andy	Newcastle	Sheffield Wednesday	1995	1999	Wolverhampton W	66	17	6
Skinner	George	Belvedere	Northfleet	1946	1947	Gillingham	1		0
Skinner	Jimmy	Beckenham	Beckenham	1919	1926	Released	87		3
Skitt	Harry	Portobello	Northfleet	1924	1931	Chester	213		0
Slade	Steve	Hackney, London	School	1995	1996	Queens Park Rangers	1	4	0
Smailes	Jimmy	South Moor	Huddersfield Town	1930	1932	Blackpool	16		3
Smith	Bert	Higham	Huddersfield Town	1919	1929	Northfleet	291		9
Smith	Bobby	Lingdale	Chelsea	1955	1964	Brighton & Hove Albion	271		176
Smith	Gordon	Partick	Aston Villa	1978	1982	Wolverhampton W	34	4	1
Smith	Ian	Rotherham	School	1975	1976	Rotherham United	2	0	0
Smith	Jimmy	Leith	Rosyth Recreation	1925	1927	St Johnstone	30		0
Smith	John	Shoreditch, London	West Ham United	1959	1964	Coventry City	21		1
Smith	Tom	Maryport	Preston North End	1898	1902	Retired	93		25
Smy	Jimmy	Edmonton, London	Hampstead Town	1928	1931	Released	17		6
Souness	Graeme	Edinburgh	School	1971	1972	Middlesborough	0	0	0
Southey	Peter	Parsons Green, London	School	1979	1980	Deceased	1		0
Sparrow	Harry	Faversham	Leicester Fosse	1913	1915	Released	18		7
Spelman	Isaac	Newcastle-Upon-Tyne	Southend United	1937	1939	Hartlepool United	28		2
Spiers	Cyril	Whitton	Aston Villa	1927	1932	Wolverhampton W	158		0
Sproston	Bert	Ebworth	Leeds United	1938	1939	Manchester City	9		0
Stansfield	Harry	Manchester	Stockport County	1904	1908	Luton Town	48		9
Statham	Brian	Zimbabwe	School	1987	1989	Brentford	20	4	0
Stead	Micky	West Ham, London	School	1975	1978	Southend United	14	1	0
Steel	Alex	Newmilns	Manchester City	1909	1910	Kilmarnock	1		0
Steel	Danny	Newmilns	Rangers	1906	1912	Third Lanark	160		4
Steel	Robert	Newmilns	Port Glasgow	1908	1919	Released	227		41
Stephenson	John	Leigh	Swindon Town	1901	1902	Retired	1		0
Stevens	Bob	Cheshunt		1900	1901	Fulham	3		0
Stevens	Gary	Hillingdon	Brighton & Hove Albion	1983	1990	Portsmouth	140	7	6
Stevens	Les	Croydon	Northfleet	1946	1949	Bradford Park Avenue	54		5
Stewart	Paul	Manchester	Manchester City	1988	1992	Liverpool	126	5	28
Stimson	Mark	Plaistow, London	School	1986	1989	Newcastle United	1	1	0
Stokes	Alfie	Hackney, London	Clapton	1952	1959	Fulham	65		40
Stormont	Bob	Dundee		1897	1901	Brentford	92		8
Sullivan	Neil	Sutton	Wimbledon	2000		Still at club	35	0	0
Swan	Andrew	Dalbeattie	Mexborough United	1904	1905	Released	2		0
Tait	Sandy	Glenbuck	Preston North End	1899	1908	Leyton	206		3
Tannahill	Bob	Kilmarnock	Bolton Wanderers	1897	1898	Millwall Athletic	11		3
Taricco	Mauricio	Buenos Aires, Argentina	Ipswich Town	1998		Still at club	43	4	0
Tate	John	Chester-Le-Street	West Stanley	1913	1915	West Stanley	4		0
Tattersall	Walter	Warsop	Watford	1911	1915	Released	44		3
Taylor	Alan	North Shields	South Shields	1931	1936	Hartlepool United	60		0
Taylor	Peter	Rochford	Crystal Palace	1976	1981	Orient	116	7	31
Thatcher	Ben	Swindon	Wimbledon	2000		Still at club	10	2	0
Thelwell	Alton	Holloway, London	School	2000		Still at club	13	3	0
Thomas	Danny	Worksop	Coventry City	1983	1987	Retired	80	7	1
Thomas	Mitchell	Luton	Luton Town	1986	1991	West Ham United	136	21	6
Thompson	Andy	Newcastle-Upon-Tyne	Wickham Park Villa	1920	1930	Norwich City	153		19
Thorstvedt	Erik	Stavanger, Norway	IFK Gothenburg	1988	1995	Retired	171	2	0
Tickridge	Sid	Stepney, London	Northfleet	1946	1951	Chelsea	95		0
Tomkin	Albert	Barrow-in-Furness	Northfleet	1938	1939	Released	2		0

FAC Apps	Sub	Goals	FLC Apps	Sub	Goals	European Apps	Sub	Goals	Others Apps	Sub	Goals	Totals Apps	Sub	Goals
0		0										13		7
16		8										109		32
7	0	6	1	0	0	5	0	2	1	0	1	126	4	46
0	0	0	4	0	1	0	0	0	0	0	0	33	4	1
0												7		3
0												18		4
0	0	0	0	1	0	0	0	0	0	0	0	16	3	1
12	1	1	24	3	1	4	3	0	1	0	0	188	24	11
0		0										16		5
25		12							2		0	256		77
0	0	0	1	0	0	0	0	0	0	0	0	2	0	0
0												3		1
0												3		0
0												2		1
8												8		0
17	0	13	14	0	10	0	0	0	0	0	0	194	3	98
9	0	1	4	0	1	3	0	1	0	0	0	82	8	15
4	4	1	6	3	0	0	0	0	0	0	0	76	24	7
0												1		0
6												93		3
17												230		0
0	2	0	0	1	0	0	0	0	0	0	0	1	7	0
0												16		3
28		1							2		0	321		10
32		22	0		0	14		10	2		2	319		210
0	0	0	6	0	0	0	1	0	0	0	0	40	5	1
0	0	0	0	0	0	0	0	0	0	0	0	2	0	0
1												31		0
2	0	0	0	0	0	1	0	0	0	0	0	24	0	1
20		2										113		27
0		0										17		6
0	0	0	0	0	0	0	1	0	0	0	0	1	1	0
0		0										1		0
1		0										19		7
4		0										32		2
11		0										169		0
0		0										9		0
6		0										54		9
0	1	0	2	0	0	0	0	0	0	0	0	22	5	0
0	0	0	0	0	0	0	0	0	0	0	0	14	1	0
0		0										1		0
13		0										173		4
19		5										246		46
0		0										1		0
0		0										3		0
13	4	0	19	2	0	15	0	2	5	0	0	192	13	8
5		0										59		5
9	0	2	23	0	7	8	0	0	1	0	0	167	5	37
0	0	0	0	0	0	0	0	0	0	0	0	1	1	0
4		2										69		42
14		1										106		9
5	0	0	3	0	0	0	0	0	0	0	0	43		0
0		0										2		0
36		0										242		3
2		0										13		3
3	1	0	0	2	0	0	3	0	0	0	0	51	4	0
0		0										4		0
3		2										47		5
10		0										70		0
8	3	2	4	2	0	0	0	0	0	0	0	128	12	33
0	0	0	3	0	0	0	0	0	0	0	0	13	2	0
0	2	0	0	0	0	0	0	0	0	0	0	13	5	0
4	0	0	11	2	0	8	4	0	3	1	0	106	14	1
12	0	1	28	1	1	0	0	0	0	0	0	176	22	8
13		2										166		21
14	0	25	0	6	0	0	0	0	1	0	0	217	2	0
6		0										101		0
0		0										2		0

Player		Birthplace	From	Year Joined	Year Left	To	League Apps	Sub	Goals
Toulouse	Cyril	Acton, London	Brentford	1948	1949	Guildford City	2		0
Townley	Jimmy	Blackburn	St Gallen	1927	1928	Brighton & Hove Albion	3		2
Trailor	Cyril	Merthyr Tydfil	Northfleet	1946	1948	Clapton Orient	11		0
Tramezzani	Paolo	Reggio-Elilia, Italy	Piacenza	1998	1999	Pistoiese	6	0	0
Tull	Walter	Folkestone	Clapton	1909	1911	Northampton Town	10		2
Turner	Andy	Woolwich, London	School	1992	1995	Portsmouth	8	12	3
Turner	Archie	Farnborough	Newcastle United	1903	1904	Southampton	6		5
Tuttle	David	Reading	School	1989	1993	Sheffield United	10	3	0
Uphill	Dennis	Bath	Peasedown Colliery	1950	1953	Reading	6		2
Upton	Solomon	Higham Ferrers	Kettering	1912	1913	Portsmouth	2		0
Van den Hauwe	Pat	Dendermode, Belgium	Everton	1989	1993	Millwall	110	6	0
Vega	Ramon	Olten, Switzerland	Cagliari	1996	2001	Celtic	53	11	7
Venables	Terry	Dagenham	Chelsea	1965	1969	Queens Park Rangers	114	1	5
Villa	Ricky	Buenos Aires, Argentina	Racing Club	1978	1983	Fort Lauderdale Strikers	124	9	18
Waddle	Chris	Gateshead	Newcastle United	1985	1989	Olympique de Marseille	137	1	33
Walden	Fanny	Wellingborough	Northampton Town	1912	1926	Northampton Town	214		21
Walford	Steve	Islington, London	School	1975	1976	Arsenal	1	1	0
Walker	Ian	Watford	School	1990	1901	Leicester City	257	2	0
Walker	Bob	Northallerton	Middlesbrough	1906	1908	New Brompton	24		3
Waller	Wilfred	South Africa	Richmond Association	1898	1900	Richmond Association	4		0
Walley	Ernie	Caernarvon	School	1955	1958	Middlesbrough	5		0
Walsh	Paul	Plumstead, London	Liverpool	1987	1992	Portsmouth	84	44	19
Walters	Charlie	Sandford-on-Thames	Oxford City	1919	1926	Fulham	106		0
Walters	Sonny	Edmonton, London	Finchley	1946	1956	Aldershot	210		66
Walton	Joe	Lunes	Preston North End	1903	1909	Sheffield United	126		25
Want	Tony	Hackney, London	School	1967	1972	Birmingham City	46	4	0
Ward	Ralph	Oadby	Bradford Park Avenue	1935	1946	Crewe Alexandra	115		10
Warner	Alf	Hyson Green	Notts County	1902	1905	Luton Town	47		13
Watson	John	Dundee	Everton	1902	1908	Released	104		0
Watson	Kevin	Hackney, London	School	1992	1993	Swindon Town	4	1	0
Webster	Fred	Sheffield	Gainsborough Trinity	1911	1915	Brentford	82		0
Webster	Simon	Earl Shildon	School	1983	1985	Huddersfield Town	2	1	0
Weir	Finlay	Glasgow	Sheffield Wednesday	1912	1915	Killed in action	96		2
Welham	Jack		Bedminster	1894	1895	Bristol South End	0		0
Weller	Keith	Islington, London	School	1964	1967	Millwall	19	2	1
Wetton	Ralph	Rowland Gill	Cheshunt	1951	1955	Plymouth Argyle	45		0
Whatley	Bill	Ebbw Vale	Northfleet	1932	1939	Retired	226		2
Whitbourne	Jack	Middlesbrough	Sunderland	1906	1908	Leyton	19		0
Whitchurch	Charlie	Grays	West Ham United	1946	1947	Southend United	8		2
White	John	Musselburgh	Falkirk	1959	1964	Deceased	183		40
White	Roy	Bootle	Army	1945	1946	Bradford Park Avenue	0		0
White	Sid	Tottenham, London	Edmonton Ramblers	1923	1926	Retired	20		0
Whyman	Alf	Edmonton, London	Edmonton Rovers	1905	1908	New Brompton	18		1
Wilding	Harry	Wolverhampton	Chelsea	1928	1929	Bristol Rovers	12		1
Wilkes	Fred	Bedford-On-Avon	Reading	1908	1912	Reading	57		0
Wilkie	Bob	Dundee	Lochee Harps	1956	1957	Romford	1		0
Wilkinson	John	Hucknall	Notts County	1906	1907	Released	2		0
William	Charlie	Welling	Manchester City	1902	1905	Norwich City	37		0
Williams	T		Trialist	1895	1896		0		0
Willis	Arthur	Denaby Main	Northfleet	1945	1954	Swansea	144		1
Wilson	Charlie	Atherstone	Coventry City	1919	1923	Huddersfield Town	55		27
Wilson	Clive	Rusholme	Queens Park Rangers	1995	1999	Cambridge United	67	3	1
Wilson	Frank		Aston Villa	1896	1897	Released	5		3
Withers	Charlie	Edmonton, London	Tottenham Juniors	1947	1956	Boston United	153		0
Woodruff	Charlie	Grantham	Grantham Avenue	1907	1909	Doncaster Rovers	15		4
Woods	Alan	Dinnington	School	1954	1955	Swansea Town	6		0
Woodward	Horace	Islington, London	Tottenham Juniors	1946	1949	Queens Park Rangers	63		1
Woodward	Vivian	Kennington, London	Chelmsford City	1901	1909	Chelmsford City	132		63
Wooloctt	Roy	Leyton, London	Eton Manor	1969	1970	Chelmsford City	1		0
Worley	Len	Amersham	Wycombe Wanderers	1959	1960	Wycombe Wanderers	1		0
Wright	Alex	Kirkcaldy	Barnsley	1950	1951	Bradford Park Avenue	2		1
Yorath	Terry	Cardiff	Coventry City	1979	1981	Vancouver Whitecaps	44	4	1
Young	Alex	Slamannan	Everton	1911	1912	Manchester City	5		3
Young	Chris	Cleethorpes	Gainsborough Trinity	1912	1913	Burslem Port Vale	4		0
Young	Luke	Harlow	School	1998	1901		44	14	0
Young	Willie	Heriot	Aberdeen	1975	1977	Arsenal	54		3
Own	Goals								88

| FAC | | | FLC | | | European | | | Others | | | Totals | | |
Apps	Sub	Goals	Apps	Sub	Goals	Apps	Sub	Goals	Apps	Sub	Goals	Apps	Sub	Goals
0		0										2		0
0		0										3		2
1		0										12		0
0	0	0	1	0	0	0	0	0	0	0	0	7		0
0		0										10		2
0	1	0	0	2	1	0	0	0	0	0	0	8	15	4
0		0										6		5
0	0	0	0	3	1	0	1	0	1	0	0	14	4	1
0		0										6		2
0		0										2		0
7	0	0	16	0	0	6	0	0	1	0	0	140	6	0
8	1	0	9	2	1	0	0	0	0	0	0	70	13	8
15	1	2	6	0	1	4	0	1	1	0	0	140	2	9
21	0	3	15	1	3	8	1	1	2	0	0	170	11	25
14	0	5	21	0	4	0	0	0	4	0	0	176	1	42
22		4										236		25
0	0	0	0	0	0	0	0	0	0	0	0	1	1	0
25	0	0	22	1	0	6	0	0	0	0	0	310	3	0
1		0										25		3
0		0										4		0
0		0										5		0
4	4	0	9	7	2	1	3	0	0	0	0	98	49	21
11		0							1		0	118		0
23		5							1		0	234		71
18		4										144		29
3	0	0	3	0	0	0	0	0	2	0	0	54	4	0
17		1										132		11
5		0										52		13
23		0										127		0
0	1	0	1	1	1	0	0	0	0	0	0	5	3	1
4		0										86		0
0	0	0	0	0	0	0	0	0	0	0	0	2	1	0
5		0										101		2
3		0										3		0
0	0	0	0	0	0	0	0	0	0	0	0	19	2	1
1		0										46		0
28		0										254		2
0		0										19		0
0		0										8		2
19		1	0		0	17		6	2		1	222	0	48
2		0										2		0
2		0										22		0
0		0										18		1
0		0										12		1
3		0										60		0
0		0										1		0
0		0										2		0
5		0										42		0
1		0										1		0
16		0							1		0	161		0
7		6										62		33
7	1	1	7	1	0	0	0	0	0	0	0	81	5	2
0		0										5		3
11		2							1		0	165		2
0		0										15		4
0		0										6		0
4		0										67		1
24		5										156		68
0		0										1		0
0		0										1		0
0		0										2		1
7	0	0	7	0	0	0	0	0	0	0	0	58	4	1
0		0										5		3
0		0										4		0
9	2	0	1	3	0	2	1	0	0	0	0	56	20	0
2			8	1								64		4
		13			7			4						112

Representative Honours (to June 2001)

FULL INTERNATIONALS

ALGERIA
Moussa Saib: (8 apps) 28.2.1999 Liberia, 9.4.1999 Liberia, 6.6.1999 Tunisia, 20.6.1999 Uganda, 24.1.2000 Congo, 29.1.2000 Gabon, 2.2.2000 South Africa, 6.2.2000 Cameroon

ARGENTINA
Ossie Ardiles: (12 apps, 1 goal) 22.5.1979 Holland, 25.6.1979 Rest of the World, 1.1.1981 West Germany, 4.1.1981 Brazil, 14.1.1982 USSR, 5.5.1982 Bulgaria, 12.5.1982 Romania, 13.6.1982 Belgium, 18.6.1982 Hungary (1), 23.6.1982 El Salvador, 29.6.1982 Italy, 2.7.1982 Brazil

BELGIUM
Nico Claesen: (9 apps, 6 goals) 14.10.1986 Luxembourg (3), 19.11.1986 Bulgaria, 4.2.1987 Portugal, 1.4.1987 Scotland (3), 29.4.1987 Republic of Ireland, 9.9.1987 Holland, 23.9.1987 Bulgaria, 14.10.1987 Scotland, 11.11.1987 Luxembourg

DENMARK
Allan Nielsen: (30 apps, 5 goals) 1.9.1996 Slovenia (1), 9.10.1996 Greece, 9.11.1996 France, 29.3.1997 Croatia, 30.4.1997 Slovenia (2), 8.6.1997 Bosnia-Herzegovina, 20.8.1997 Bosnia-Herzegovina, 10.9.1997 Croatia, 11.10.1997 Greece, 25.3.1998 Scotland, 22.4.1998 Norway, 28.5.1998 Sweden, 5.6.1998 Cameroon (sub), 12.6.1998 Saudi Arabia (sub), 18.6.1998 South Africa (1), 24.6.1998 France, 28.6.1998 Nigeria, 3.7.1998 Brazil,

19.8.1998 Czech Republic, 5.9.1998 Belarus, 10.2.1999 Croatia, 27.3.1999 Italy, 6.6.1999 Belarus, 9.6.1999 Wales, 4.9.1999 Switzerland (1), 8.9.1999 Italy, 10.10.1999 Iran, 3.6.2000 Belgium, 11.6.2000 France, 16.6.00 Holland

ENGLAND
Clive Allen: (2 apps) 29.4.1987 Turkey, 11.2.19 Israel
Wally Alsford: (1 app) 6.4.1935 Scotland
Darren Anderton: (29 apps, 7 goals) 9.3.1994 Denmark, 17.5.1994 Greece (1), 22.5.1994 Norway, 7.9.1994 USA, 15.2.1995 Republic of Ireland (aban), 29.3.1995 Uruguay, 3.6.1995 Japan (1), 8.6.1995 Sweden (1), 11.6.1995 Brazil, 17.5.1996 Hungary (2), 23.5.1996 China, 8.6.1996 Switzerland, 15.6.1996 Scotland, 18.6.1996 Holland, 22.6.1996 Spain, 26.6.1996 Germany, 23.5.1998 Saudi Arabia, 27.5.1998 Morocco, 15.6.1998 Tunisia, 22.6.1998 Romania, 26.6.1998 Colombia (1), 30.6.1998 Argentina, 5.9.1998 Sweden, 10.10.1998 Bulgaria, 14.10.1998 Luxembourg, 18.11.1998 Czech Republic (1), 10.2.1999 France, 2.9.2000 France, 15.11.2000 Italy (sub)
Eddie Baily: (9 apps, 5 goals) 2.7.1950 Spain, 7.10.1950 Northern Ireland (2), 15.11.1950 Wales (2), 22.11.1950 Yugoslavia, 20.10.1951 Wales (1), 28.11.1951 Austria, 25.5.1952 Austria, 28.5.1952 Switzerland, 4.10.1952 Northern Ireland
Nicky Barmby: (2 apps) 29.3.1995 Uruguay (sub), 8.6.1995 Sweden (sub)
Bert Bliss: (1 app) 9.4.1921 Scotland
Johnny Brooks: (3 apps, 2 goals) 14.11.Wales (1), 28.11.1956 Yugoslavia (1), 5.12.1956 Denmark
Sol Campbell: (40 apps, 1 goal) 17.5.1996 Hungary (sub),

World Cup winner Ossie Ardiles won 12 caps for Argentina as a Spurs player.

15.6.1996 Scotland (sub), 9.11.1996 Georgia, 12.2.1997 Italy, 30.4.1997 Georgia, 24.5.1997 South Africa (sub), 31.5.1997 Poland, 7.6.1997 France, 10.6.1997 Brazil, 10.9.1997 Moldova, 11.10.1997 Italy, 15.11.1997 Cameroon, 11.2.1998 Chile, 22.4.1998 Portugal, 27.5.1998 Morocco, 29.5.1998 Belgium, 15.6.1998 Tunisia, 19.6.1998 Romania, 26.6.1998 Colombia, 30.6.1998 Argentina, 5.9.1998 Sweden, 10.10.1998 Bulgaria, 14.10.1998 Luxembourg, 18.11.1998 Czech Republic (1), 27.3.1999 Poland, 5.6.1999 Sweden, 9.6.1999 Bulgaria, 13.11.1999 Scotland, 17.11.1999 Scotland, 23.2.2000 Argentina, 27.5.2000 Brazil, 31.5.2000 Ukraine, 3.6.2000 Malta, 12.6.2000 Portugal, 17.6.2000 Germany, 20.6.2000 Romania, 2.9.2000 France, 28.2.2001 Spain, 24.3.2001 Finland, 28.3.2001 Albania
Martin Chivers: (24 apps, 13 goals) 3.2.1971 Malta, 21.4.1971 Greece (1), 12.5.1971 Malta (2), 15.5.1971 Northern Ireland, 22.5.1971 Scotland (2), 13.10.1971 Switzerland (1), 10.11.1971 Switzerland (sub), 1.12.1971 Greece (1), 29.4.1972 West Germany, 13.5.1972 West Germany, 23.5.1972 Northern Ireland (sub), 27.5.1972 Scotland, 15.11.1972 Wales, 24.1.1973 Wales, 14.2.1973 Scotland (1), 12.5.1973 Northern Ireland (2), 15.5.1973 Wales (1), 19.5.1973 Scotland, 27.5.1973 Czechoslovakia, 6.6.1973 Poland, 10.6.1973 USSR (1), 14.6.1973 Italy, 26.9.1973 Austria (1), 17.10.1973 Poland
Harry Clarke: (1 app) 3.4.1954 Scotland
Tommy Clay: (4 apps) 15.3.1920 Wales, 22.10.1921 Northern Ireland, 13.3.1922 Wales, 8.4.1922 Scotland
Ray Clemence: (5 apps) 9.9.1981 Norway, 23.2.1982 Northern Ireland, 3.6.1982 Finland, 15.12.1982 Luxembourg, 16.11.1983 Luxembourg
Ralph Coates: (2 apps) 12.5.1971 Malta, 19.5.1971 Wales
Jimmy Dimmock: (3 apps) 9.4.1921 Scotland, 1.3.1926 Wales, 24.5.1926 Belgium
Ted Ditchburn: (6 apps) 1.12.1948 Switzerland, 13.5.1949 Sweden, 8.6.1953 USA, 14.11.1956 Wales, 28.11.1956 Yugoslavia, 5.12.1956 Denmark
Terry Fenwick: (1 app) 11.2.1988 Israel (sub)
Les Ferdinand: (4 apps) 10.9.1997 Moldova, 23.5.1998 Saudi Arabia (sub), 27.5.1998 Morocco (sub), 29.5.1998 Belgium
Paul Gascoigne: (20 apps, 2 goals) 14.9.1988 Denmark (sub), 16.11.1988 Saudi Arabia (sub), 26.4.1989 Albania (sub) (1), 23.5.1989 Chile, 27.5.1989 Scotland (sub), 6.9.1989 Sweden (sub), 28.3.1990 Brazil (sub), 25.4.1990 Czechoslovakia (1), 15.5.1990 Denmark, 22.5.1990 Uruguay, 2.6.1990 Tunisia, 11.6.1990 Republic of Ireland, 16.6.1990 Holland, 21.6.1990 Egypt, 26.6.1990 Belgium, 1.7.1990 Cameroon, 4.7.1990 West Germany, 12.9.1990 Hungary, 17.10.1990 Poland, 6.2.1991 Cameroon
Jimmy Greaves: (42 apps, 28 goals) 14.4.1962 Scotland, 9.5.1962 Switzerland, 20.5.1962 Peru (3), 31.5.1962 Hungary, 2.6.1962 Argentina (1), 7.6.1962 Bulgaria, 10.6.1962 Brazil, 3.10.1962 France, 20.10.1962 Northern Ireland (1), 22.11.1962 Wales (1), 27.2.1963 France, 6.4.1963 Scotland, 8.5.1963 Brazil, 20.5.1963 Czechoslovakia (2), 5.6.1963 Switzerland, 17.10.1963 Wales (1), 23.10.1963 Rest of the World (1), 20.11.1963 Northern Ireland (4), 6.5.1964 Uruguay, 17.5.1964 Portugal, 24.5.1964 Republic of Ireland (1), 30.5.1964 Brazil (1), 4.6.1964 Portugal, 6.6.1964 Argentina, 3.10.1964 Northern Ireland (3), 21.10.1964 Belgium, 9.12.1964 Holland (1), 10.4.1965 Scotland (1), 5.5.1965 Hungary (1), 9.5.1965 Yugoslavia, 2.10.1965 Wales, 20.10.1965 Austria, 4.5.1966 Yugoslavia (1), 29.6.1966 Norway (4), 3.7.1966 Denmark, 5.7.1966 Poland, 11.7.1966 Uruguay, 16.7.1966 Mexico, 20.7.1966 France, 15.4.1967 Scotland, 24.5.1967 Spain (1), 27.5.1967 Austria
Arthur Grimsdell: (6 apps) 15.3.1920 Wales, 10.4.1920 Scotland, 23.10.1920 Northern Ireland, 9.4.1921

With 48 goals Gary Lineker is England's second highest ever goalscorer. Bobby Charlton leads the way with 49.

Scotland, 21.10.1922 Northern Ireland, 5.3.1923 Wales
Willie Hall: (10 apps, 9 goals) 6.12.1933 France, 23.10.1937 Northern Ireland (1), 17.11.1937 Wales (1), 1.12.1937 Czechoslovakia, 9.4.1938 Scotland, 26.10.1938 Rest of Europe (1), 10.11.1938 Northern Ireland (5), 15.4.1939 Scotland, 13.5.1939 Italy (1), 18.5.1939 Yugoslavia
Ron Henry: (1 app) 27.2.1963 France
Glenn Hoddle: (44 apps, 8 goals) 22.11.1979 Bulgaria (1), 17.5.1980 Wales, 31.5.1980 Australia (1), 18.6.1980 Spain, 25.3.1981 Spain (1), 20.5.1981 Wales, 23.5.1981 Scotland, 9.9.1981 Norway, 23.2.1982 Northern Ireland (1), 27.4.1982 Wales, 2.6.1982 Iceland, 20.6.1982 Czechoslovakia (sub), 25.6.1982 Kuwait, 15.12.1982 Luxembourg (sub) (1), 28.5.1983 Northern Ireland, 1.6.1983 Scotland, 12.10.1983 Hungary (1), 16.11.1983 Luxembourg, 29.2.1984 France, 26.3.1985 Republic of Ireland (sub), 25.5.1985 Scotland, 6.6.1985 Italy (sub), 9.6.1985 Mexico, 12.6.1985 West Germany, 16.6.1985 USA, 11.9.1985 Romania (1), 16.10.1985 Turkey, 13.11.1985 Northern Ireland, 26.2.1986 Israel, 26.3.1986 USSR, 23.4.1986 Scotland (1), 17.5.1986 Mexico, 24.5.1986 Canada, 3.6.1986 Portugal, 6.6.1986 Morocco, 11.6.1986 Poland, 18.6.1986 Paraguay, 22.6.1986 Argentina, 10.9.1986 Sweden, 15.10.1986 Northern Ireland, 12.11.1986 Yugoslavia, 10.2.1987 Spain, 29.4.1987 Turkey, 23.5.1987 Scotland
Steve Hodge: (4 apps) 10.2.1987 Spain, 1.4.1987 Northern Ireland, 29.4.1987 Turkey, 23.5.1987 Scotland
George Hunt: (3 apps, 1 goal) 13.3.1933 Italy, 1.4.1933 Scotland (1), 20.5.1933 Switzerland
Cyril Knowles: (4 apps) 6.12.1967 USSR, 3.4.1968 Spain, 22.5.1968 Sweden, 1.6.1968 West Germany

Gary Lineker: (38 apps, 19 goals) 6.9.1989 Sweden, 11.10.1989 Poland, 15.11.1989 Italy, 13.12.1989 Yugoslavia, 28.3.1990 Brazil (1), 25.4.1990 Czechoslovakia, 15.5.1990 Denmark (1), 22.5.1990 Uruguay, 2.6.1990 Tunisia, 11.6.1990 Republic of Ireland (1), 16.6.1990 Holland, 21.6.1990 Egypt, 26.6.1990 Belgium, 1.7.1990 Cameroon (2), 4.7.1990 West Germany (1), 7.7.1990 Italy, 12.9.1990 Hungary (1), 17.10.1990 Poland (1), 13.11.1990 Republic of Ireland, 6.2.1991 Cameroon (2), 27.3.1991 Republic of Ireland, 1.5.1991 Turkey, 25.5.1991 Argentina (1), 1.6.1991 Australia, 3.6.1991 New Zealand (1), 12.6.1991 Malaysia (4), 11.9.1991 Germany, 16.10.1991 Turkey, 13.11.1991 Poland (1), 19.2.1992 France (sub) (1), 25.3.1992 Czechoslovakia (sub), 29.4.1992 CIS (1), 12.5.1992 Hungary, 17.5.1992 Brazil, 3.6.1992 Finland, 11.6.1992 Denmark, 14.6.1992 France, 17.6.1992 Sweden

Gary Mabbutt: (16 apps, 1 goal) 13.10.1982 West Germany, 17.11.1982 Greece, 15.12.1982 Luxembourg, 23.2.1983 Wales, 30.3.1983 Greece, 27.4.1983 Hungary, 28.5.1983 Northern Ireland, 1.6.1983 Scotland (sub), 12.10.1983 Hungary, 12.11.1986 Yugoslavia (1), 1.4.1987 Northern Ireland, 29.4.1987 Turkey, 9.9.1987 West Germany, 16.10.1991 Turkey, 13.11.1991 Poland, 25.3.1992 Czechoslovakia

Les Medley: (6 apps, 1 goal) 15.11.1950 Wales, 22.11.1950 Yugoslavia, 3.10.1951 France (1), 20.10.1951 Wales, 14.11.1951 Northern Ireland, 28.11.1951 Austria

Alan Mullery: (35 apps, 1 goal) 9.12.1964 Holland, 24.5.1967 Spain, 27.5.1967 Austria, 21.10.1967 Wales, 22.11.1967 Northern Ireland, 6.12.1967 USSR, 24.2.1968 Scotland, 3.4.1968 Spain, 8.5.1968 Spain, 22.5.1968 Sweden, 5.6.1968 Yugoslavia, 1.6.1968 Romania, 11.12.1968 Bulgaria, 12.3.1969 France, 3.5.1969 Northern Ireland, 10.5.1969 Scotland, 1.6.1969 Mexico, 8.6.1969 Uruguay, 12.6.1969 Brazil, 5.11.1969 Holland, 10.12.1969 Portugal, 14.1.1970 Holland (sub), 18.4.1970 Wales, 21.4.1970 Northern Ireland, 25.4.1970 Scotland (sub), 20.5.1970 Colombia, 24.5.1970 Ecuador, 2.6.1970 Romania, 7.6.1970 Brazil, 11.6.1970 Czechoslovakia, 14.6.1970 West Germany (1), 25.11.1970 East Germany, 3.2.1971 Malta, 21.4.1971 Greece, 13.10.1971 Switzerland

Bill Nicholson: (1 app, 1 goal) 19.5.1951 Portugal (1)

Maurice Norman: (23 apps) 20.5.1962 Peru, 31.5.1962 Hungary, 2.6.1962 Argentina, 7.6.1962 Bulgaria, 10.6.1962 Brazil, 3.10.1962 France, 6.4.1963 Scotland, 8.5.1963 Brazil, 20.5.1963 Czechoslovakia, 2.6.1963 East Germany, 12.10.1963 Wales, 23.10.1963 Rest of World, 20.11.1963 Northern Ireland, 11.4.1964 Scotland, 6.5.1964 Uruguay, 17.5.1964 Portugal, 27.5.1964 USA, 30.5.1964 Brazil, 4.6.1964 Portugal, 6.6.1964 Argentina, 3.10.1964 Northern Ireland, 21.10.1964 Belgium, 9.12.1964 Holland

Frank Osbourne: (2 apps, 3 goals) 8.12.1924 Belgium, 24.5.1926 Belgium (3)

Steve Perryman: (1 app) 2.6.1982 Iceland (sub)

Martin Peters: (34 apps, 9 goals) 18.4.1970 Wales, 21.4.1970 Northern Ireland (1), 25.4.1970 Scotland, 20.5.1970 Colombia (2), 24.5.1970 Ecuador, 2.6.1970 Romania, 7.6.1970 Brazil, 11.6.1970 Czechoslovakia, 14.6.1970 West Germany (1), 25.11.1970 East Germany (1), 3.2.1971 Malta (1), 21.4.1971 Greece, 12.5.1971 Malta, 15.5.1971 Northern Ireland, 19.5.1971 Wales, 22.5.1971 Scotland (1), 13.10.1971 Switzerland, 1.12.1971 Greece, 29.4.1972 West Germany, 13.5.1972 West Germany (sub), 23.5.1972 Northern Ireland (sub), 14.2.1973 Scotland, 12.5.1973 Northern Ireland, 15.5.1973 Wales (1), 19.5.1973 Scotland (1), 27.5.1973 Czechoslovakia, 6.6.1973 Poland, 10.6.1973 USSR, 14.6.1973 Italy, 26.9.1973 Austria, 17.10.1973 Poland, 14.11.1973 Italy, 3.4.1974 Portugal, 18.5.1974 Scotland

Alf Ramsey: (31 apps, 3 goals) 30.11.1949 Italy, 15.4.1950 Scotland, 14.5.1950 Portugal, 18.5.1950 Belgium, 15.6.1950 Chile, 29.6.1950 United States, 2.7.1950 Spain, 7.10.1950 Northern Ireland, 15.11.1950 Wales, 22.11.1950 Yugoslavia, 14.4.1951 Scotland, 9.5.1951 Argentina, 19.5.1951 Portugal, 3.10.1951 France, 20.10.1951 Wales, 14.11.1951 Northern Ireland, 28.11.1951 Austria (1), 5.4.1952 Scotland, 18.5.1952 Italy, 25.5.1952 Austria, 28.5.1952 Switzerland, 4.10.1952 Northern Ireland, 12.11.1952 Wales, 26.11.1952 Belgium, 18.4.1953 Scotland, 17.5.1953 Argentina, 24.5.1953 Chile, 31.5.1953 Uruguay, 8.6.1953 United States, 21.10.1953 Rest of Europe (1), 25.11.1953 Hungary (1)

George Robb: (1 app) 25.11.1953 Hungary

Graham Roberts: (6 apps) 29.5.1983 Northern Ireland, 1.6.1983 Scotland, 29.2.1984 France, 4.4.1984 Northern Ireland, 26.5.1984 Scotland, 2.6.1984 USSR

Arthur Rowe: (1 app) 6.12.1933 France

Jimmy Seed: (5 apps, 1 goal) 21.5.1921 Belgium, 21.10.1922 Northern Ireland, 5.3.1923 Wales, 19.3.1923 Belgium (1), 4.4.1925 Scotland

Teddy Sheringham: (28 apps, 8 goals) 29.5.1993 Poland, 2.6.1993 Norway, 7.9.1994 USA, 12.10.1994 Romania (sub), 16.11.1994 Nigeria (sub), 29.3.1995 Uruguay, 3.6.1995 Japan (sub), 8.6.1995 Sweden (1), 11.6.1995 Brazil, 6.9.1995 Colombia (sub), 11.10.1995 Norway (sub), 15.11.1995 Switzerland (1), 27.3.1996 Bulgaria, 24.4.1996 Croatia, 18.5.1996 Hungary, 8.6.1996 Switzerland, 15.6.1996 Scotland, 18.6.1996 Holland (2), 22.6.1996 Spain, 26.6.1996 Germany, 9.11.1996 Georgia (1), 29.3.1997 Mexico (1), 30.4.1997 Georgia (1), 24.5.1997 South Africa, 31.5.1997 Poland (1), 4.6.1997 Italy, 7.6.1997 France (sub), 10.6.1997 Brazil

Tim Sherwood: (3 apps) 27.3.1999 Poland, 27.4.1999 Hungary, 5.6.1999 Sweden

Bert Smith: (2 apps) 9.4.1921 Scotland, 13.3.1922 Wales

Bobby Smith: (15 apps, 13 goals) 8.10.1960 Northern Ireland (1), 19.10.1960 Luxembourg (2), 26.10.1960 Spain (2), 23.11.1960 Wales (1), 15.4.1961 Scotland (2), 21.5.1961 Portugal, 14.4.1962 Scotland, 27.2.1963 France (1), 6.4.1963 Scotland, 8.5.1963 Brazil, 20.5.1963 Czechoslovakia (1), 2.6.1963 East Germany, 12.10.1963 Wales (2), 23.10.1963 Rest of the World, 20.11.1963 Northern Ireland (1)

Bert Sproston: (2 apps) 22.10.1938 Wales, 26.10.1938 Rest of Europe

Gary Stevens: (7 apps) 17.10.1984 Finland (sub), 14.11.1984 Turkey (sub), 27.2.1985 Northern Ireland, 23.4.1986 Scotland (sub), 17.5.1986 Mexico (sub), 3.6.1986 Morocco (sub), 18.6.1986 Paraguay (sub)

Paul Stewart: (3 apps) 11.9.1991 Germany (sub), 25.3.1992 Czechoslovakia (sub), 29.4.1992 CIS (sub)

Chris Waddle: (36 apps, 6 goals) 11.9.1985 Romania, 16.10.1985 Turkey (1), 13.11.1985 Northern Ireland, 26.2.1986 Israel, 26.3.1986 USSR (1), 23.4.1986 Scotland, 17.5.1986 Mexico, 24.5.1986 Canada, 3.6.1986 Portugal, 6.6.1986 Morocco, 11.6.1986 Poland (sub), 22.6.1986 Argentina (sub), 10.9.1986 Sweden (sub), 15.10.1986 Northern Ireland (1), 12.11.1986 Yugoslavia, 10.2.1987 Spain, 1.4.1987 Northern Ireland (1), 29.4.1987 Turkey, 19.5.1987 Brazil, 23.5.1987 Scotland, 9.9.1987 West Germany, 11.2.1988 Israel, 27.4.1988 Hungary, 21.5.1988 Scotland (sub), 24.5.1988 Colombia, 28.5.1988 Switzerland (sub), 12.6.1988 Republic of Ireland, 15.6.1988 Holland, 19.10.1988 Sweden, 16.11.1988 Saudi Arabia, 8.3.1989 Albania, 26.4.1989 Albania (1), 23.5.1989 Chile, 27.5.1989 Scotland (1), 3.6.1989 Poland, 7.6.1989 Denmark

Fanny Walden: (2 apps) 4.4.1914 Scotland, 13.3.1922 Wales

Ian Walker: (3 apps) 18.5.1996 Hungary (sub), 23.5.1996 China (sub), 12.2.1997 Italy

Arthur Willis: (1 app) 3.10.1951 France

Vivian Woodward: (21 apps, 27 goals) 14.2.1903 Ireland (2), 2.3.1903 Wales (1), 4.4.1903 Scotland (1), 12.3.1904 Ireland, 9.4.1904 Scotland, 25.2.1905 Ireland, 27.3.1905 Wales (2), 1.4.1905 Scotland, 6.4.1907 Scotland, 15.2.1908 Ireland (1), 16.3.1908 Wales (3), 4.4.1908 Scotland, 6.6.1908 Austria (1), 8.6.1908 Austria (4), 10.6.1908 Hungary (1), 12.6.1908 Bohemia, 13.2.1909 Ireland (2), 15.3.1909 Wales, 29.5.1909 Hungary (2), 31.5.1909 Hungary (4), 1.6.1909 Austria (3)

GERMANY
Jurgen Klinsmann: (17 apps, 8 goals) 7.9.1994 Russia, 12.10.1994 Hungary, 16.11.1994 Albania (1), 14.12.1994 Moldova (1), 18.12.1994 Albania (1), 22.2.1995 Spain, 29.3.1995 Georgia (2), 26.4.1995 Wales, 7.6.1995 Bulgaria (1), 25.3.1998 Brazil, 30.5.1998 Colombia (sub), 5.6.1998 Luxembourg (1), 15.6.1998 USA (1), 21.6.1998 Yugoslavia, 25.6.1998 Iran (1), 29.6.1998 Mexico (1), 4.7.1998 Croatia

ICELAND
Gudni Bergsson: (30 apps) 19.5.1989 England 'B', 31.5.1989 USSR, 14.6.1989 Austria, 23.8.1989 Austria, 6.9.1989 East Germany, 20.9.1989 Turkey, 28.3.1990 Luxembourg, 30.5.1990 Albania, 5.9.1990 France, 26.9.1990 Czechoslovakia, 10.10.1990 Spain, 27.4.1991 England 'B', 1.5.1991 Wales, 26.5.1991 Albania, 5.6.1991 Czechoslovakia, 17.7.1991 Turkey, 25.9.1991 Spain, 20.11.1991 France, 8.4.1992 Israel, 13.5.1992 Greece, 3.6.1992 Hungary, 8.8.1992 Israel, 7.10.1992 Greece, 14.10.1992 Russia, 17.4.1993 USA, 20.5.1993 Luxembourg, 2.6.1993 Russia, 16.6.1993 Hungary, 8.9.1993 Luxembourg, 17.10.1993 Tunisia

IRELAND
John Kirwan: (12 apps, 2 goals) 24.2.1900 Wales, 22.2.1902 Wales, 22.3.1902 England, 14.2.1903 England, 21.3.1903 Scotland (1), 28.3.1903 Wales, 12.3.1904 England (1), 21.3.1904 Wales, 26.3.1904 Scotland, 25.2.1905 England, 18.3.1905 Scotland, 8.4.1905 Wales
Charlie O'Hagan: (5 apps, 1 goal) 18.3.1905 Scotland, 8.4.1905 Wales (1), 17.2.1906 England, 17.3.1906 Scotland, 2.4.1906 Wales

ISRAEL
Ronny Rosenthal: (19 apps, 4 goals) 31.5.1994 Argentina, 17.8.1994 Croatia, 4.9.1994 Poland, 12.10.1994 Slovakia, 16.11.1994 Azerbaijan (1), 29.11.1994 Cyprus (1), 14.12.1994 Romania (1), 29.3.1995 France, 25.4.1995 Poland (1), 6.9.1995 Slovakia (sub), 11.10.1995 Azerbaijan, 15.11.1995 France, 1.9.1996 Bulgaria. 9.10.1996 Russia (sub), 10.11.1996 Cyprus, 26.2.1997 Germany, 12.3.1997 Sweden, 31.3.1997 Luxembourg, 8.6.1997 Russia

NIGERIA
John Chiedozie: (3 apps) 20.10.1984 Liberia, 6.7.1985 Tunisia, 20.7.1985 Tunisia

NORTHERN IRELAND
Gerry Armstrong: (28 apps, 6 goals) 27.4.1977 West Germany, 28.5.1977 England, 3.6.1977 Wales (sub), 11.6.1977 Iceland (sub), 16.11.1977 Belgium (2), 13.5.1978 Scotland, 16.5.1978 England, 19.5.1978 Wales, 20.9.1978 Republic of Ireland, 25.10.1978 Denmark, 29.11.1978 Bulgaria (1), 7.2.1979 England, 2.5.1979 Bulgaria (1), 19.5.1979 England, 22.5.1979 Scotland. 25.5.1979 Wales, 6.6.1979 Denmark, 17.10.1979 England, 21.11.1979 Republic of Ireland (1), 26.3.1980 Israel, 16.5.1980 Scotland, 20.5.1980 England,

23.5.1980 Wales, 11.6.1980 Australia, 15.6.1980 Australia, 18.6.1980 Australia, 22.6.1980 Western Australia (1), 15.10.1980 Sweden
Danny Blanchflower: (43 apps) 2.10.1954 England, 3.11.1954 Scotland, 20.4.1955 Wales, 8.10.1955 Scotland, 2.11.1955 England, 11.4.1956 Wales, 6.10.1956 England, 7.11.1956 Scotland, 16.1.1957 Portugal, 10.4.1957 Wales, 25.4.1957 Italy, 1.5.1957 Portugal, 5.10.1957 Scotland, 6.11.1957 England, 4.12.1957 Italy, 15.1.1958 Italy, 16.4.1958 Wales, 8.6.1958 Czechoslovakia, 11.6.1958 Argentina, 15.6.1958 West Germany, 17.6.1958 Czechoslovakia, 19.6.1958 France, 4.10.1958 England, 15.10.1958 Spain, 5.11.1958 Scotland, 22.4.1959 Wales, 3.10.1959 Scotland, 18.11.1959 England, 6.4.1960 Wales, 8.10.1960 England, 26.10.1960 West Germany. 9.11.1960 Scotland, 12.4.1961 Wales, 10.5.1961 West Germany, 7.10.1961 Scotland, 17.10.1961 Greece, 22.11.1961 England, 11.4.1962 Wales, 9.5.1962 Holland, 10.10.1962 Poland, 20.10.1962 England, 7.11.1962 Scotland, 28.11.1962 Poland
Pat Jennings: (75 apps) 3.10.1964 England, 14 .10.1964 Switzerland, 14.11.1964 Switzerland, 25.11.1964 Scotland, 7.4.1965 Holland, 7.5.1965 Albania, 2.10.1965 Scotland, 10.11.1965 England, 24.11.1965 Albania, 30.3.1966 Wales, 7.5.1966 West Germany, 22.10.1966 England, 16.11.1966 Scotland, 21.10.1967 Scotland, 22.11.1967 England, 2.2.1968 Wales, 10.9.1968 Israel, 23.10.1968 Turkey, 11.12.1968 Turkey, 3.5.1969 England, 6.5.1969 Scotland, 10.5.1969 Wales, 10.9.1969 USSR, 22.10.1969 USSR, 18.4.1970 Scotland, 21.4.1970 England, 3.2.1971 Cyprus, 21.4.1971 Cyprus, 15.5.1971 England, 18.5.1971 Scotland, 22.5.1971 Wales, 13.10.1971 USSR, 16.2.1972 Spain, 20.5.1972 Scotland, 23.5.1972 England, 27.5.1972 Wales, 18.10.1972 Bulgaria, 14.2.1973 Cyprus, 28.3.1973 Portugal, 12.5.1973 England, 16.5.1973 Scotland, 19.5.1973 Wales, 14.11.1973 Portugal, 11.5.1974 Scotland, 15.5.1974 England, 18.5.1974 Wales, 4.9.1974 Norway, 30.10.1974 Sweden, 16.3.1975 Yugoslavia, 17.5.1975 England, 20.5.1975 Scotland, 23.5.1975 Wales, 3.9.1975 Sweden, 23.10.1975 Norway, 19.11.1975 Yugoslavia, 24.3.1976 Israel, 8.5.1976 Scotland, 11.5.1976 England, 14.5.1976 Wales, 13.10.1976 Holland, 10.11.1976 Belgium, 27.4.1977 West Germany, 28.5.1977 England, 1.6.1977 Scotland, 3.6.1977 Wales, 11.6.1977 Iceland, 11.9.1985 Turkey, 16.10.1985 Romania, 13.11.1985 England, 26.2.1986 France, 26.3.1986 Denmark, 23.4.1986 Morocco, 3.6.1986 Algeria, 7.6.1986 Spain, 12.6.1986 Brazil
Chris McGrath: (6 apps, 1 goal) 1.5.1974 Scotland, 15.5.1974 England, 18.5.1974 Wales, 4.9.1974 Norway, 24.3.1976 Israel (sub), 13.10.1976 Holland (1)
Gerard McMahon: (7 apps, 1 goal) 22.5.1995 Canada (sub), 26.5.1995 Chile, 7.6.1995 Latvia, 10.10.1995 Leichenstein (1), 27.3.1996 Norway (sub), 24.4.1996 Sweden, 29.5.1996 Germany
Paul McVeigh: (1 app, 1 goal) 27.4.1999 Canada (sub) (1)
Dick Rowley: (2 apps, 1 goal) 22.4.1931 Wales (1), 19.9.1931 Scotland

NORWAY
Espen Baardsen: (4 apps) 6.9.1998 Latvia, 20.2.1999 Israel (sub), 18.8.99 Lithuania (sub), 31.1.2000 Iceland
Frode Grodas: (8 apps) 25.2.1998 France, 22.4.1998 Denmark, 20.5.1998 Mexico, 27.5.1998 Saudi Arabia, 10.6.1998 Morocco, 16.6.1998 Scotland, 23.6.1998 Brazil, 27.6.1998 Italy
Steffen Iversen: (24 apps, 7 goals) 14.10.1998 Albania (sub), 18.11.1998 Egypt, 27.3.1999 Greece, 28.4.1999 Georgia (1), 20.5.1999 Jamaica (1), 30.5.1999 Georgia (1), 5.6.1999 Albania (1), 18.8.1999 Lithuania, 4.9.1999

Gica Popescu earned 6 caps for Romania while at Tottenham.

Greece, 8.9.99 Slovenia (1), 9.10.1999 Latvia, 14.11.1999 Germany, 29.3.2000 Switzerland, 26.4.2000 Belgium, 27.5.2000 Slovakia (sub) (1), 13.6.2000 Spain (1), 18.6.2000 Yugoslavia, 21.6.2000 Slovenia, 16.8.2000 Finland, 2.9.2000 Armenia, 7.10.2000 Wales, 11.10.2000 Ukraine, 24.3.2001 Poland (sub), 28.3.2001 Belarus
Oyvind Leonhardsen: (11 apps, 4 goals) 18.8.1999 Lithuania, 4.9.1999 Greece (1), 8.9.1999 Slovenia (1), 9.10.1999 Latvia, 14.11.1999 Germany, 2.9.2000 Armenia, 7.10.2000 Wales, 11.10.2000 Ukraine, 25.4.2001 Bulgaria, 2.6.2001 Ukraine (2), 6.6.2001 Belarus
Erik Thorstvedt: (46 apps) 2.5.1989 Poland, 21.5.1989 Cyprus, 23.8.1989 Greece, 5.9.1989 France, 11.10.1989 Yugoslavia, 15.11.1989 Scotland, 7.2.1990 Malta, 27.3.1990 Northern Ireland, 22.8.1990 Sweden, 12.9.1990 USSR, 10.10.1990 Hungary, 31.10.1990 Cameroons, 14.11.1990 Cyprus, 1.5.1991 Cyprus, 22.5.1991 Romania, 5.6.1991 Italy, 28.8.1991 USSR, 25.9.1991 Czechoslovakia, 13.11.1991 Italy, 9.9.1992 San Marino, 23.9.1992 Holland, 7.10.1992 San Marino, 14.10.1992 England, 30.3.1993 Qatar, 2.6.1993 England, 9.6.1993 Holland, 8.9.1993 USA, 22.9.1993 Poland, 10.11.1993 Turkey, 19.1.1994 Costa Rica, 22.5.1994 England, 1.6.1994 Denmark, 5.6.1994 Sweden, 19.6.1994 Mexico, 23.6.1994 Italy, 28.6.1994 Republic of Ireland, 12.10.1994 Holland, 6.2.1995 Estonia, 29.3.1995 Luxembourg, 25.5.1995 Ghana, 7.6.1995 Malta, 22.7.1995 France, 16.8.1995 Czech Republic, 6.9.1995 Czech Republic, 10.10.1995 England, 27.3.1996 Northern Ireland (sub)

REPUBLIC OF IRELAND
Steve Carr: (18 apps) 28.4.1999 Sweden, 29.5.1999 Northern Ireland, 9.6.1999 Macedonia, 1.9.1999 Yugoslavia (sub), 4.9.1999 Croatia, 8.9.1999 Malta, 13.11.1999 Turkey, 17.11.1999 Turkey, 30.5.2000 Scotland, 4.6.2000 Mexico, 6.6.2000 USA, 11.6.2000 South Africa, 2.9.2000 Holland, 7.10.2000 Portugal, 11.10.2000 Estonia, 25.4.2001 Andorra (sub), 2.6.2001 Portugal, 6.6.2001 Estonia
Gary Doherty: (7 apps) 6.6.2000 USA, 11.6.2000 South Africa (sub), 24.3.2001 Cyprus (sub), 28.3.2001 Andorra (sub), 25.4.2001 Andorra, 2.6.2001 Portugal (sub), 6.6.2001 Estonia (sub)
Tony Galvin: (19 apps, 1 goal) 22.9.1982 Holland, 30.3.1983 Malta, 12.10.1983 Holland (sub), 4.4.1984 Israel (sub), 8.8.1984 Mexico, 12.9.1984 USSR, 17.10.1984 Norway, 14.11.1984 Denmark, 5.2.1985 Italy, 1.5.1985 Norway, 26.5.1985 Spain, 23.4.1986 Uruguay, 25.5.1986 Iceland, 27.5.1986 Czechoslovakia, 10.9.1986 Belgium, 18.2.1987 Scotland, 1.4.1987 Bulgaria, 29.4.1987 Belgium, 28.5.1987 Luxembourg (1)
Johnny Gavin: (2 apps) 1.5.1955 Holland, 28.5.1955 West Germany
Jimmy Holmes: (12 apps) 30.3.1977 France, 24.4.1977 Poland, 1.6.1977 Bulgaria, 12.10.1977 Bulgaria, 5.4.1978 Turkey, 12.4.1978 Poland, 21.5.1978 Norway, 24.5.1978 Denmark, 20.9.1978 Northern Ireland, 25.10.1978 England, 2.5.1979 Denmark, 19.5.1979 Bulgaria
Chris Hughton: (51 apps, 1 goal) 29.10.1979 USA, 6.2.1980 England, 30.4.1980 Switzerland, 16.5.1980 Argentina, 10.9.1980 Holland, 15.10.1980 Belgium, 28.10.1980 France, 19.11.1980 Cyprus (1), 24.2.1981 Wales, 25.3.1981 Belgium, 23.5.1981 Poland, 14.10.1981 France, 22.9.1982 Holland, 17.11.1982 Spain, 30.3.1983 Malta, 27.4.1983 Spain, 21.9.1983 Iceland, 12.10.1983 Holland, 16.11.1983 Malta, 8.8.1984 Mexico (sub), 12.9.1984 USSR, 17.10.1984 Norway, 5.2.1985 Italy, 27.2.1985 Israel, 26.3.1985 England, 26.5.1985 Spain, 11.9.1985 Switzerland, 16.10.1985 USSR, 23.4.1986 Uruguay, 25.5.1986 Iceland, 10.9.1986 Belgium, 1.4.1987 Bulgaria, 10.11.1987 Israel, 27.4.1988 Yugoslavia, 27.5.1988 Poland, 1.6.1988 Norway, 12.6.1988 England, 15.6.1988 USSR, 18.6.1988 Holland, 14.9.1988 Northern Ireland, 7.2.1989 France, 8.3.1989 Hungary, 26.4.1989 Spain, 28.5.1989 Malta, 4.6.1989 Hungary, 28.3.1990 Wales (sub), 25.4.1990 USSR (sub), 16.5.1990 Finland, 27.5.1990 Turkey (sub), 2.6.1990 Malta, 17.10.1990 Turkey

ROMANIA
Ilie Dumitrescu: (10 apps, 2 goals) 7.9.1994 Azerbaijan, 8.10.1994 France, 12.10.1994 England (1), 12.11.1994 Slovakia, 14.12.1994 Israel, 29.3.1995 Poland, 26.4.1995 Azerbaijan (1), 7.6.1995 Israel, 10.10.1995 France, 15.11.1995 Slovakia (sub)
Gica Popescu: (6 apps, 1 goal) 8.10.1994 France, 12.10.1994 England, 12.11.1994 Slovakia (1), 14.12.1994 Israel, 29.3.1995 Poland, 26.4.1995 Azerbaijan

SCOTLAND
Steve Archibald: (22 caps, 3 goals) 16.5.1980 Northern Ireland, 28.5.1980 Poland, 31.5.1980 Hungary (1), 10.9.1980 Sweden (sub), 25.2.1981 Israel, 25.3.1981 Northern Ireland, 28.4.1981 Israel, 19.5.1981 Northern Ireland (1), 23.5.1981 England, 14.10.1981 Northern Ireland, 18.11.1981 Portugal, 24.2.1982 Spain (sub), 23.3.1982 Holland, 15.6.1982 New Zealand (sub) (1), 18.6.1982 Brazil, 23.6.1982 Russia, 13.10.1982 East Germany, 17.11.1982 Switzerland (sub), 15.12.1982

Belgium, 16.11.1983 East Germany, 26.5.1984 England, 1.6.1984 France
Alan Brazil: (2 apps, 1 goal) 28.5.1983 Wales (1), 1.6.1983 England (sub)
Sandy Brown: (1 app) 5.4.1902 England (later declared unofficial due to Ibrox disaster)
Bill Brown: (24 apps) 3.10.1959 Wales, 14.11.1959 Northern Ireland, 4.5.1960 Poland, 29.5.1960 Austria, 5.6.1960 Hungary, 8.6.1960 Turkey, 26.9.1961 Czechoslovakia, 7.10.1961 Northern Ireland, 8.11.1961 Wales, 14.4.1962 England, 20.10.1962 Wales, 7.11.1962 Northern Ireland, 6.4.1963 England, 8.5.1963 Austria, 12.10.1963 Northern Ireland, 7.11.1963 Wales, 20.11.1963 Norway, 10.4.1965 England, 8.5.1965 Spain, 23.5.1965 Poland, 27.5.1965 Finland, 2.10.1965 Northern Ireland, 13.10.1965 Poland, 9.11.1965 Italy
Colin Calderwood: (33 apps, 1 goal) 29.3.1995 Russia, 26.4.1995 San Marino (1), 21.5.1995 Ecuador, 7.6.1995 Faroe Islands, 16.8.1995 Greece, 6.9.1995 Finland, 10.10.1995 Sweden, 15.11.1995 San Marino, 26.5.1996 USA, 30.5.1996 Colombia, 10.6.1996 Holland, 15.6.1996 England, 18.6.1996 Switzerland, 31.8.1996 Austria, 5.10.1996 Latvia, 9.10.1996 Estonia (aban), 10.11.1996 Sweden, 11.2.1997 Estonia, 29.3.1997 Estonia, 2.4.1997 Austria, 30.4.1997 Sweden, 7.9.1997 Belarus, 11.10.1997 Latvia, 12.11.1997 France, 25.3.1998 Denmark, 22.4.1998 Finland, 23.5.1998 Colombia, 30.5.1998 USA, 10.6.1998 Brazil, 16.6.1998 Norway, 5.9.1998 Lithuania, 10.10.1998 Estonia
Alfie Conn: (2 apps) 20.5.1975 Northern Ireland (sub), 24.5.1975 England
Gordon Durie: (13 apps, 2 goals) 11.9.1991 Switzerland (1), 16.10.1991 Romania, 13.11.1991 San Marino (1), 19.2.1992 Northern Ireland (sub), 25.3.1992 Finland, 21.5.1992 Canada, 3.6.1992 Norway (sub), 12.6.1992 Holland, 15.6.1992 Germany, 9.9.1992 Switzerland, 18.11.1992 Italy, 8.9.1993 Switzerland, 13.10.1993 Italy
Alan Gilzean: (17 apps, 8 goals) 8.5.1965 Spain, 2.10.1965 Northern Ireland (2), 13.10.1965 Poland, 9.11.1965 Italy, 24.11.1965 Wales, 22.11.1967 Wales (2), 6.11.1968 Austria (sub), 11.12.1968 Cyprus (2), 16.4.1969 West Germany, 3.5.1969 Wales (1), 10.5.1969 England, 12.5.1969 Cyprus, 22.10.1969 West Germany (1), 5.11.1969 Austria, 18.4.1970 Northern Ireland, 25.4.1970 England (sub), 21.4.1971 Portugal
Richard Gough: (8 apps) 10.9.1986 Bulgaria, 15.10.1986 Republic of Ireland, 12.11.1986 Luxembourg, 18.2.1987 Republic of Ireland, 1.4.1987 Belgium, 23.5.1987 England, 26.5.1987 Brazil, 9.9.1987 Hungary
Dave Mackay: (18 apps, 4 goals) 11.4.1959 England, 6.5.1959 West Germany, 3.10.1959 Northern Ireland, 14.11.1959 Wales, 4.5.1960 Poland, 29.5.1960 Austria (1), 5.6.1960 Hungary, 8.6.1960 Turkey, 22.10.1960 Wales, 9.11.1960 Northern Ireland, 15.4.1961 England (1), 6.4.1963 England, 8.5.1963 Austria, 4.6.1963 Norway, 12.10.1963 Northern Ireland, 7.11.1963 Norway (2), 20.11.1963 Wales, 2.10.1965 Northern Ireland
Jimmy Robertson: (1 app) 3.10.1964 Wales
Neil Sullivan: (6 apps) 2.9.2000 Latvia, 7.10.2000 San Marino, 11.10.2000 Croatia, 24.3.2001 Belgium, 28.3.2001 San Marino, 25.4.2001 Poland
John White: (18 apps, 1 goal) 14.11.1959 Wales, 4.5.1960 Poland, 29.5.1960 Austria, 8.6.1960 Turkey, 22.10.1960 Wales, 26.9.1961 Czechoslovakia, 7.10.1961 Northern Ireland, 8.11.1961 Wales, 29.11.1961 Czechoslovakia, 14.4.1962 England, 20.10.1962 Wales, 7.11.1962 Northern Ireland, 6.4.1963 England, 12.10.1963 Northern Ireland, 7.11.1963 Norway, 20.11.1963 Wales (1), 11.4.1964 England, 12.5.1964 West Germany

John White earned 18 Scotland caps with Spurs before his tragic death in 1964.

SWITZERLAND
Ramon Vega: (6 apps, 1 goal) 30.4.1997 Hungary, 11.10.1997 Azerbaijan, 25.3.1998 England (1), 22.4.1998 Northern Ireland, 2.9.1998 Yugoslavia (sub), 10.10.1998 Italy

UKRAINE
Sergei Rebrov: (7 apps) 2.9.2000 Poland, 7.10.2000 Armenia, 11.10.2000 Norway, 24.3.2001 Belarus, 28.3.2001 Wales, 2.6.2001 Norway, 6.6.2001 Wales

WALES
Mark Bowen: (2 apps) 10.5.1986 Canada (sub), 20.5.1986 Canada (sub)
Ron Burgess: (32 apps, 1 goal) 19.10.1946 Scotland, 13.11.1946 England, 16.4.1947 Northern Ireland, 18.10.1947 England, 12.11.1947 Scotland, 23.101948 Scotland, 10.11.1948 England, 9.3.1949 Northern Ireland, 15.5.1949 Portugal, 23.5.1949 Belgium, 26.5.1949 Switzerland, 15.10.1949 England, 9.11.1949 Scotland, 23.11.1949 Belgium, 8.3.1950 Northern Ireland, 21.10.1950 Scotland, 7.3.1951 Northern Ireland, 12.5.1951 Portugal, 16.5.1951 Switzerland (1), 20.10.1951 England, 20.11.1951 Scotland, 5.12.1951 Rest of the UK, 19.3.1952 Northern Ireland, 18.10.1952 Scotland, 12.11.1952 England, 15.4.1953 Northern Ireland, 14.5.1953 France, 21.5.1953 Yugoslavia, 10.10.1953 England, 4.11.1953 Scotland, 31.3.1954 Northern Ireland, 9.5.1954 Austria
Simon Davies: (2 apps) 28.3.2001 Ukraine (sub), 6.6.2001 Ukraine
Alf Day: (1 app) 4.11.1933 Northern Ireland
Mike England: (24 apps, 2 goals) 22.10.1966 Scotland, 16.11.1966 England, 21.10.1967 England, 28.2.1968 Northern Ireland, 8.5.1968 West Germany, 16.4.1969 East Germany, 28.6.1969 Rest of U.K., 22.10.1969 East Germany, 4.11.1969 Italy (1), 18.4.1970 England, 22.4.1970

Scotland, 25.4.1970 Northern Ireland, 11.11.1970 Romania, 13.10.1971 Finland, 20.5.1972 England, 24.5.1972 Scotland, 27.5.1972 Northern Ireland, 15.11.1972 England, 24.1.1973 England, 12.5.1973 Scotland, 15.5.1973 England, 26.9.1973 Poland, 30.10.1974 Hungary, 20.11.1974 Luxembourg (1)
Willie Evans: (6 apps, 1 goal) 7.12.1932 Northern Ireland, 4.10.1933 Scotland (1), 15.11.1933 England, 29.9.1934 England, 5.2.1936 England, 11.3.1936 Northern Ireland
Mel Hopkins: (34 apps) 11.4.1956 Northern Ireland, 20.10.1956 Scotland, 14.11.1956 England, 10.4.1957 Northern Ireland, 1.5.1957 Czechoslovakia, 19.5.1957 East Germany, 26.5.1957 Czechoslovakia, 25.9.1957 East Germany, 19.10.1957 England, 13.11.1957 Scotland, 15.1.1958 Israel, 5.2.1958 Israel, 10.4.1958 Northern Ireland, 8.6.1958 Hungary, 11.6.1958 Mexico, 15.6.1958 Sweden, 17.6.1958 Hungary, 19.6.1958 Brazil, 18.10.1958 Scotland, 26.11.1958 England, 22.4.1959 Northern Ireland, 17.10.1959 England, 4.11.1959 Scotland, 12.4.1961 Northern Ireland, 19.4.1961 Spain, 18.5.1961 Spain, 26.5.1961 Hungary, 11.4.1962 Northern Ireland, 12.5.1962 Brazil, 16.5.1962 Brazil, 22.5.1962 Mexico, 20.10.1962 Scotland, 7.11.1962 Hungary, 3.4.1963 Northern Ireland
Ted Hughes: (12 apps) 2.3.1901 Scotland, 18.3.1901 England, 22.2.1902 Ireland, 29.2.1904 England, 12.3.1904 Scotland, 21.3.1904 Ireland, 6.3.1905 Scotland, 27.3.1905 England, 8.4.1905 Ireland, 3.3.1906 Scotland, 2.4.1906 Ireland, 18.3.1907 England
Cliff Jones: (41 apps, 12 goals) 16.4.1958 Northern Ireland, 8.6.1958 Hungary, 11.6.1958 Mexico, 15.6.1958 Sweden, 17.6.1958 Hungary, 19.6.1958 Brazil, 22.4.1959 Northern Ireland, 17.10.1959 England, 4.11.1959 Scotland, 6.4.1960 Northern Ireland, 28.9.60 Republic of Ireland (2), 22.10.1960 Scotland (1), 23.11.1960 England, 12.4.1961 Northern Ireland (2), 18.5.1961 Spain, 28.5.1961 Hungary (1), 14.10.1961 England, 8.11.1961 Scotland, 11.4.1962 Northern Ireland, 12.5.1962 Brazil, 16.5.1962 Brazil, 22.5.1962 Mexico, 20.10.1962 Scotland, 20.3.1963 Hungary (1), 3.4.1963 Northern Ireland (3), 12.10.1963 England, 20.11.1963 Scotland, 15.4.1964 Northern Ireland, 3.10.1964 Scotland, 21.10.1964 Denmark, 18.11.1964 England (1), 9.12.1964 Greece, 17.3.1965 Greece, 31.3.1965 Northern Ireland (1), 1.5.1965 Italy, 30.5.1965 USSR, 22.10.1966 Scotland, 16.11.1966 England, 21.10.1967 England, 22.11.1967 Scotland, 8.5.1968 West Germany
John L. Jones: (12 apps) 19.2.1898 Ireland, 19.3.1898 Scotland, 28.3.1898 England, 4.3.1899 Ireland, 18.3.1899 Scotland, 3.2.1900 Scotland, 22.2.1902 Ireland, 3.3.1902 England, 15.3.1902 Scotland, 29.2.1904 England, 12.3.1904 Scotland, 21.3.1904 Ireland
Ernie Jones: (2 apps) 23.10.1948 Scotland, 10.11.1948 England
Terry Medwin: (27 apps, 6 goals) 28.10.1956 Scotland (1), 14.11.1956 England, 10.4.1957 Northern Ireland, 1.5.1957 Czechoslovakia, 19.5.1957 East Germany, 26.5.1957 Czechoslovakia, 19.10.1957 England, 13.11.1957 Scotland (1), 15.1.1958 Israel, 5.2.1958 Israel, 16.4.1958 Northern Ireland, 8.6.1958 Hungary, 11.6.1958 Mexico, 17.6.1958 Hungary (1), 19.6.1958 Brazil, 18.10.1958 Scotland, 26.11.1958 England, 22.4.1959 Northern Ireland, 17.10.1959 England, 4.11.1959 Scotland, 6.4.1960 Northern Ireland (2), 28.9.1960 Republic of Ireland, 22.10.1960 Scotland, 23.11.1960 England, 19.4.1961 Spain, 7.11.1962 Hungary (1), 21.11.1962 England
Taffy O'Callaghan: (11 apps, 3 goals) 2.2.1929 Northern Ireland, 26.10.1929 Scotland (1), 31.10.1931 Scotland, 18.11.1931 England, 26.10.1932 Scotland (2),

16.11.1932 England, 7.12.1932 Northern Ireland, 4.10.1933 Scotland, 4.11.1933 Northern Ireland, 15.11.1933 England, 29.9.1934 England
Paul Price: (14 apps) 18.11.1981 USSR, 24.3.1982 Spain, 2.6.1982 France, 22.9.1982 Norway, 15.12.1982 Yugoslavia, 23.2.1983 England, 27.4.1983 Bulgaria, 28.5.1983 Scotland, 31.5.1983 Northern Ireland, 21.9.1983 Norway, 12.10.1983 Romania, 16.11.1983 Bulgaria, 14.12.1983 Yugoslavia, 28.2.1984 Scotland (sub)
Billy Rees: (1 app) 8.3.1950 Northern Ireland
Bill Whatley: (2 apps) 22.10.1938 England, 9.11.1938 Scotland
Terry Yorath: 8 (apps) 11.9.1979 Republic of Ireland, 21.11.1979 Turkey, 17.5.1980 England, 21.5.1980 Scotland, 23.5.1980 Northern Ireland, 2.6.1980 Iceland, 15.10.1980 Turkey, 19.11.1980 Czechoslovakia

INTERNATIONAL TRIALS

ENGLAND
Wally Alsford: 27.3.1935 Rest v England
Bert Bliss: 9.2.1920 South v England, 7.2.1921 South v England
Tom Bradshaw: 1.2.1899 South v North
John Brearley: 16.1.1905 Professionals of the South v Amateurs of the South
Walter Bull: 13.2.1905 South v North, 8.1.1906 Professionals of South v. Amateurs of South, 22.1.1906 South v North
Fred Channell: 27.3.1935 Rest v England
George Clawley: 21.1.1903 South v North
Tommy Clay: 14.4.1919 South v North, 22.2.1922 England v South, 12.2.1923 South v England
John Curtis: 31.1.1910 Whites v Stripes
Jimmy Dimmock: 7.2.1921 South v England, 28.2.1921 England v North (1), 10.2.1926 Rest v England
Jack Elkes: 21.1.1924 South v North, 11.2.1924 Rest v England, 19.1.1925 South v North, 18.1.1926 Rest v England
Matt Forster: 7.2.1927 Rest v England
Arthur Grimsdell: 24.11.1913 South v England, 14.4.1919 South v North, 9.2.1920 England v South, 25.2.1920 England v North (1), 7.2.1921 England v South, 28.2.1921 England v North, 6.1.1922 England v North, 22.2.1922 England v South, 12.2.1923 South v England
Willie Hall: 13.10.1937 Probables v Possibles
George Hunt: 22.3.1933 Rest v England (2)
Bert Middlemiss: 25.1.1909 South v North, 22.1.1912 Stripes v Whites, 25.11.1912 South v England, 24.11.1913 South v North
Tom Morris: 7.3.1900 South v North, 26.1.1903 South v North
Joe Nicholls: 21.3.1934 Rest v England
Frank Osbourne: 19.1.1925 South v North (2), 18.1.1926 England v Rest
Jimmy Seed: 22.2.1922 South v England, 12.2.1923 South v England, 19.1.1925 South v North (1), 9.2.1925 England v Rest
Bert Smith: 9.2.1920 South v England, 7.2.1921 England v South, 22.2.1922 South v England, 21.1.1924 South v North
Cyril Spiers: 4.3.1931 Rest v England
Fanny Walden: 21.1.1914 England v North, 22.2.1922 South v England, 12.2.1923 South v England
Joe Walton: 16.1.1905 Southern Professionals v Southern Amateurs, 13.2.1905 South v North (1), 8.1.1906 Southern Professionals v Southern Amateurs
Vivian Woodward: 26.1.1903 South v North (1), 25.1.1904

South v North, 13.2.1905 South v North, 3.1.1906
Amateurs v Professionals, 8.1.1906 Southern Amateurs v
Southern Professionals, 22.1.1906 South v North (1),
27.1.1908 South v North, 25.1.1909 South v North

SCOTLAND
Sandy Brown: 24.3.1902 Anglo-Scots v Home Scots
Tom Collins: 20.3.1911 Anglo-Scots v Home Scots, 11.3.1912
Anglo-Scots v Home Scots
David Copeland: 23.3.1903 Anglo-Scots v Home Scots
Alex Lindsay: 20.3.1923 Anglo-Scots v Home Scots
James McNaught: 28.3.1899 Anglo-Scots v Home Scots
Danny Steel: 22.3.1908 Anglo-Scots v Home Scots,
21.3.1910 Anglo-Scots v Home Scots, 11.3.1912 Anglo-Scots
v Home Scots
Bobby Steel: 22.3.1909 Anglo-Scots v Home Scots
Sandy Tait: 23.3.1903 Anglo-Scots v Home Scots

'B' INTERNATIONALS

ENGLAND
Darren Anderton: 21.4.1998 Russia
Nicky Barmby: 13.12.1994 Republic of Ireland
Sol Campbell: 13.12.1994 Republic of Ireland
Eddie Baily: 18.1.1950 Switzerland, 11.5.1950 Italy,
17.5.1950 Holland
Harry Clarke: 24.3.1954 West Germany
Ted Ditchburn: 18.5.1949 Holland, 18.1.1950 Switzerland
Chris Fairclough: 14.10.1987 Malta
Les Ferdinand: 21.4.1998 Russia (1)
Paul Gascoigne: 16.5.1989 Switzerland (1), 19.5.1989
Iceland, 14.11.1989 Italy, 12.12.1989 Yugoslavia
Tommy Harmer: 26.3.1952 Holland
Glenn Hoddle: 12.6.1979 Austria (abandoned), 15.10.1979
New Zealand (1)
Gary Mabbutt: 16.5.1989 Switzerland, 19.5.1989 Iceland,
22.5.1989 Norway, 11.12.1990 Algeria, 5.2.1991 Wales,
27.4.1991 Iceland, 18.2.1992 France, 28.4.1992 CIS
Tony Marchi: 6.2.1957 Scotland
Bill Nicholson: 18.1.1950 Switzerland, 11.5.1950 Italy,
17.5.1950 Holland
George Robb: 24.3.1954 West Germany, 16.5.1954
Yugoslavia, 22.5.1954 Switzerland
Graham Roberts: 13.11.1984 New Zealand
Paul Stewart: 16.5.1989 Switzerland (sub), 19.5.1989
Iceland, 22.5.1989 Norway, 27.4.1991 Iceland,
18.2.1992 France (1)
Alfie Stokes: 6.2.1957 Scotland
Mitchell Thomas: 14.10.1987 Malta
Ian Walker: 21.4.1998 Russia
Sonny Walters: 22.2.1950 Holland
Charlie Withers: 26.3.1952 Holland

NORTHERN IRELAND
Gerard McMahon: 10.5.1994 England (sub), 21.2.1995
Scotland (sub)
Steve Robinson: 10.5.1994 England

REPUBLIC OF IRELAND
Ross Darcy: 17.3.1997 FAI National League
Neale Fenn: 9.2.1999 FAI National League (2)
Peter Gain: 17.3.1997 FAI National League
David McDonald: 12.2.1992 Denmark
Kevin Maher: 17.3.1997 FAI National League (sub)

*Martin Chivers represented England at both
Under-23 and full international level during his
career at Spurs.*

UNDER-23 INTERNATIONALS

ENGLAND
Les Allen: 8.2.1961 Wales
Martin Chivers: 7.2.1968 Scotland (1), 1.5.1968 Hungary
(1), 26.5.1968 Italy, 30.5.1968 Hungary, 2.6.1968
West Germany
Jimmy Greaves: 28.2.1962 Scotland (2)
Jim Iley: 23.4.1958 Wales
Cyril Knowles: 4.11.1964 Wales, 12.10.1966 Wales (1),
1.3.1967 Scotland, 31.5.1967 Greece, 4.6.1967 Bulgaria,
7.6.1967 Turkey
Roger Morgan: 8.4.1970 Bulgaria (2)
Maurice Norman: 8.2.1956 Scotland, 24.5.1957 Romania,
31.5.1957 Czechoslovakia
Steve Perryman: 1.6.1972 East Germany, 4.6.1972 Poland,
7.6.1972 USSR, 13.2.1973 Scotland, 24.5.1973
Denmark, 29.5.1973 Holland, 1.6.1973 Czechoslovakia,
16.10.1973 Poland, 13.11.1973 Denmark, 16.1.1974
Wales, 13.3.1974 Scotland, 11.5.1974 Turkey, 15.5.1974
Yugoslavia, 28.10.1974 Czechoslovakia, 19.11.1974
Portugal, 18.12.1974 Scotland, 21.1.1975 Wales
Alfie Stokes: 28.9.1955 Denmark (2)

NORTHERN IRELAND
Phil Gray: 15.5.1990 Republic of Ireland
Richard Johnston: 11.4.1989 Republic of Ireland (sub)

NORWAY
Espen Baardsen: 11.3.1998 Greece, 24.3.1998 Belgium 'B',
21.4.1998 Scotland B, 24.5.1998 Sweden, 27.5.1998
Spain, 31.5.1998 Holland
Steffen Iversen: 21.4.1998 Scotland 'B', 24.5.1998 Sweden
(1), 27.5.1998 Spain, 31.5.98 Holland (2)

SCOTLAND
Alfie Conn: 31.5.1975 Romania, 28.10.1975 Denmark, 16.12.1975 Romania
Jimmy Robertson: 17.5.1964 France (2), 2.12.1964 Wales, 7.2.1968 England
John White: 25.11.1959 Wales

WALES
John Collins: 12.10.1966 England, 22.2.1967 Northern Ireland (aban), 1.11.1967 England, 20.3.1968 Northern Ireland, 2.10.1968 England
Mel Hopkins: 23.4.1958 England
Cliff Jones: 23.4.1958 England

UNDER-21 INTERNATIONALS

ENGLAND
Paul Allen: 10.9.1985 Romania
Rory Allen: 14.5.1998 France (sub), 16.5.98 South Africa, 18.5.98 Argentina (sub).
Darren Anderton: 8.9.1992 Spain (1), 16.2.1993 San Marino (1), 27.4.1993 Holland (1), 28.5.1993 Poland (1), 1.6.1993 Norway, 7.6.1993 Portugal, 9.6.1993 Czechoslovakia, 11.6.1993 Brazil, 14.6.1993 Scotland, 15.6.1993 France, 7.9.1993 Poland, 17.11.1993 San Marino (1)
Nicky Barmby: 8.3.1994 Denmark, 6.9.1994 Portugal, 11.10.1994 Austria (sub)
Guy Butters: 5.6.1989 Bulgaria, 7.6.1989 Senegal, 9.6.1989 Republic of Ireland (sub)
Sol Campbell: 8.3.1994 Denmark, 29.5.1994 Russia, 31.5.1994 France, 2.6.1994 USA, 5.6.1994 Belgium (1), 7.6.1994 Portugal, 6.9.1994 France, 11.10.1994 Austria, 15.11.1994 Republic of Ireland, 9.10.1995 Norway (1), 14.11.1995 Austria
Stephen Clemence: 4.9.1998 Sweden (sub)
Richard Cooke: 12.3.1986 Denmark (sub)
Chris Day: 23.4.1996 Croatia, 24.5.1996 Belgium, 1.6.1996 Brazil
Chris Fairclough: 10.11.1987 Yugoslavia, 27.4.1988 France
Ian Hendon: 12.5.1992 Hungary, 24.5.1992 Mexico, 26.5.1992 Czechoslovakia, 28.5.1992 France, 8.9.1992 Spain, 13.10.1992 Norway, 17.11.1992 Turkey
Danny Hill: 6.6.1995 Brazil, 8.6.1995 Malaysia, 10.6.1995 Angola, 12.6.95 France
Glenn Hoddle: 15.12.1976 Wales (sub), 12.10.1977 Finland (sub), 8.3.1978 Italy, 5.4.1978 Italy, 19.4.1978 Yugoslavia, 19.9.1978 Denmark (1), 6.2.1979 Wales (1), 5.6.1979 Bulgaria, 12.2.1980 Scotland, 4.3.1980 Scotland, 16.4.1980 East Germany, 23.4.1980 East Germany
Chris Jones: 1.5.1978 Yugoslavia (sub)
Ledley King: 3.9.1999 Luxembourg (sub), 7.9.1999 Poland, 27.5.200 Italy, 29.5.2000 Turkey (1), 1.6.2000 Slovakia, 14.11.2000 Italy (abandoned), 27.2.2001 Spain (sub), 23.3.2001 Finland
Gary Mabbutt: 21.9.1982 Denmark (2), 28.3.1984 France, 12.3.1986 Denmark, 9.4.1986 Italy
Stuart Nethercott: 8.3.1994 Denmark, 29.5.1994 Russia, 31.5.1994 France, 2.6.1994 USA, 5.6.1994 Belgium, 7.6.1994 Portugal, 25.4.1995 Latvia, 7.6.1995 Latvia
Vinny Samways: 28.5.1988 Switzerland (sub), 7.6.1988 USSR (1), 12.6.1988 France, 13.9.1988 Denmark, 18.10.1988 Sweden
Steve Sedgley: 5.9.1989 Sweden
Steve Slade: 24.5.1996 Belgium (1), 28.5.1996 Angola, 30.5.1996 Portugal (1), 1.6.1996 Brazil
Brian Statham: 28.5.1988 Switzerland, 13.9.1988 Denmark (sub), 18.11.1988 Sweden

Gary Stevens: 11.10.1983 Hungary, 28.2.1984 France, 28.3.1984 France (sub), 2.5.1984 Italy (sub), 17.5.1984 Spain, 24.5.1984 Spain (sub), 9.4.1986 Italy
Alton Thelwell: 27.2.2001 Spain (sub)
Danny Thomas: 2.5.1984 Italy, 17.5.1984 Spain
Ian Walker: 5.12.1990 Wales, 12.5.1992 Hungary, 26.5.1992 Czechoslovakia, 28.5.1992 France, 8.9.1992 Spain, 13.10.1992 Norway, 17.11.1992 Turkey, 16.2.19San Marino, 7.9.1993 Poland
Luke Young: 27.4.1999 Hungary, 7.9.1999 Poland, 22.2.2000 Argentina (sub), 29.5.2000 Turkey, 1.6.2000 Slovakia, 31.8.2000 Georgia, 23.3.2001 Finland, 27.3.2001 Albania, 24.5.2001 Mexico, 5.6.2001 Greece

NORTHERN IRELAND
Phil Gray: 3.4.1990 Israel (1)
Gerard McMahon: 22.3.1994 Romania (sub)
Paul McVeigh: 21.4.1998 Switzerland, 20.5.1998 Scotland (sub), 22.5.1998 Republic of Ireland, 4.9.1998 Turkey, 17.11.1998 Moldova, 26.3.1999 Germany, 31.3.1999 Moldova, 2.6.1999 Republic of Ireland, 8.6.1999 Republic of Ireland, 17.8.1999 France, 3.9.1999 Turkey (sub), 7.9.1999 Germany (sub), 8.10.1999 Finland,
Steve Robinson: 22.3.1994 Romania
Ciaran Toner: 28.3.2000 Malta (sub), 29.5.2000 Scotland (sub), 2.6.2000 Wales, 6.10.2000 Denmark, 10.10.2000 Iceland, 23.3.2001 Czech Republic, 27.3.2001 Bulgaria, 1.6.2001 Bulgaria, 5.6.2001 Czech Republic

NORWAY
Espen Baardsen: 31.7 1996 Poland, 31.8.1996 France, 8.10.1996 Hungary, 31.10.1996 Sweden, 9.11.1996 Switzerland, 13.2.1997 South Korea, 3.4.1997 Lebanon, 29.4.1997 Finland, 20.7.1997 Iceland, 19.8.1997 Finland, 9.9.1997 Switzerland, 8.10.1997 South Africa, 29.10.1997 France, 9.10.1998 Slovenia, 13.10.98 Albania, 3.9.1999 Greece, 7.9.99 Slovenia
Steffen Iversen: 19.8.1997 Finland, 9.9.1997 Switzerland (1)

REPUBLIC OF IRELAND
Steve Carr: 9.3.1993 Germany, 15.11.1994 England, 27.3.1995 England, 25.4.1995 Portugal, 10.6.1995 Austria, 5.9.1995 Austria, 10.10.1995 Latvia, 26.3.1996 Russia, 30.5.1996 Norway, 8.10.1996 Macedonia (1), 9.11.1996 Iceland, 1.4.1997 Macedonia, 5.9.1997 Iceland
Owen Coll: 14.11.1995 Portugal, 26.3.1996 Russia (sub), 30.5.1996 Norway, 8.10.1996 Macedonia, 29.4.1997 Romania
Ross Darcy: 8.10.1996 Macedonia, 9.11.1996 Iceland, 9.9.1997 Lithuania, 24.3.1998 Czech Republic, 4.9.98 Croatia (sub), 18.11.1998 Yugoslavia 18.11.98
Gary Doherty: 1.9.2000 Netherlands, 6.10.2000 Portugal, 10.10.2000 Estonia
Neale Fenn: 29.4.97 Romania, 19.8.1997 Lithuania (2), 5.9.1997 Iceland, 22.5.1998 Northern Ireland, 22.5.1998 Northern Ireland, 27.4.1999 Sweden, 31.5.1999 Scotland, 8.6.1999 Macedonia 8.6.99, 3.9.1999 Croatia, 7.9.99 Malta
Peter Gain: 9.9.1997 Lithuania (1)
Eddie Gormley: 5.6.1989 Senegal (sub), 7.6.1989 Bulgaria, 10.6.1989 France (sub)
David McDonald: 30.4.1991 Poland, 15.10.1991 Poland, 12.11.1991 Turkey
Kevin Maher: 26.3.1996 Russia, 1.4.1997 Macedonia, 29.4.1997 Romania, 19.8.1997 Lithuania, 9.9.98 Lithuania
Andy Turner: 27.4.1993 Denmark, 12.10.1993 Spain, 15.11.1994 England, 27.3.1995 England, 5.9.1995 Austria, 14.11.1995 Portugal (sub), 26.3.1996 Russia

SCOTLAND
Steve Archibald: 18.11.1980 Denmark
Neil McNab: 8.2.1978 Wales

WALES
Mark Bowen: 22.9.1982 Norway, 15.11.1984 Bulgaria, 13.12.1984 Yugoslavia
Simon Davies: 31.5.2000 Scotland, 1.9.2000 Belarus, 6.10.2000 Norway, 10.10 2000 Poland, 23.3.2001 Armenia
Ian Hillier: 27.3.2001 Ukraine (sub), 1.6.2001 Poland (sub), 5.6.2001 Ukraine
Mark Kendall: 8.2.1978 Scotland
Gareth Knott: 1.6.1996 San Marino

WARTIME INTERNATIONALS

ENGLAND
Vic Buckingham: 26.4.1941 Wales, 7.6.1941 Wales
Ted Ditchburn: 19.2.1944 Scotland, 6.5.1944 Wales
Jack Gibbons: 24.10.1942 Wales
Willie Hall: 11.11.1939 Wales, 13.4.1940 Wales, 9.5.1942

WALES
Ron Burgess: 11.11.1939 England, 18.11.1939 England, 26.4.1941 England, 25.9.1943 England, 6.5.1944 England, 16.9.1944 England, 5.5.1945 England, 20.10.1945 England, 10.11.1945 Scotland, 4.5.1946 Northern Ireland
Bill Whatley: 11.11.1939 England

VICTORY INTERNATIONALS

ENGLAND
Arthur Grimsdell: 26.4.1919 Scotland, 3.5.1919 Scotland (2)

FOOTBALL LEAGUE

Clive Allen: 8.8.1987 Rest of the World
Les Allen: 29.11.1962 Italian League (1)
Ossie Ardiles: 8.8.1987 Rest of the World (sub), 8.9.1987 Irish League
Eddie Baily: 15.2.1950 League of Ireland (1), 22.3.1950 Scottish League, 18.10.1950 Irish League, 4.4.1951 League of Ireland, 24.9.1952 Irish League, 20.10.1954 Irish League
Danny Blanchflower: 12.10.1960 Irish League (1)
Ron Burgess: 12.3.1947 Scottish League
Tommy Clay: 4.10.1922 Irish League
Ted Ditchburn: 12.3.1947 Scottish League, 30.4.1947 League of Ireland, 17.3.1948 Scottish League, 14.4.1948 League of Ireland, 20.9.1948 Irish League, 29.11.1950 Scottish League
Jack Elkes: 11.10.1924 Irish League, 14.3.1925 Scottish League, 19.3.1927 Scottish League (1)
Richard Gough: 8.8.1987 Rest of World
Jimmy Greaves: 29.11.1962 Italian League (1), 18.3.1964 Scottish League (1), 17.3.1965 Scottish League, 16.3.1966 Scottish League (1), 15.3.1967 Scottish League, 8.11.1967 League of Ireland (1)
Arthur Grimsdell: 20.3.1920 Scottish League
Willie Hall: 31.10.1934 Scottish League, 6.10.1937 Irish League (1), 2.11.1938 Scottish League
David Howells: 13.11.1990 Irish League

Jim Iley: 8.10.1958 Scottish League
Cliff Jones: 23.3.1960 Scottish League, 12.10.1960 Irish League, 1.11.1960 Italian League
Cyril Knowles: 20.3.1968 Scottish League
Tommy Lunn: 14.11.1910 Southern League
Gary Mabbutt: 13.11.1990 Irish League
Dave Mackay: 23.3.1960 Scottish League, 12.10.1960 Irish League
Les Medley: 31.10.1951 Scottish League
Johnny Metgod: 8.9.1987 Irish League
Bert Middlemiss: 11.4.1910 Southern League
Alan Mullery: 9.5.1964 Italian League, 28.10.1964 Irish League
Bill Nicholson: 15.2.1950 League of Ireland
Maurice Norman: 9.5.1964 Italian League
Martin Peters: 18.3.1970 Scottish League (sub), 23.9.1970 Irish League (1)
Alf Ramsey: 22.3.1950 Scottish League, 4.4.1951 League of Ireland, 31.10.1951 Scottish League, 24.9.1952 Irish League (1), 5.5.1953 Danish Combination
George Robb: 23.9.1953 Irish League
Bert Smith: 18.2.1922 Scottish League
Cyril Spiers: 5.11.1930 Scottish League
Bert Sproston: 21.9.1938 Irish League, 2.11.1938 Scottish League
Alfie Stokes: 13.3.1957 Scottish League
Chris Waddle: 8.8.1987 Rest of World
Fanny Walden: 26.10.1914 Southern League
John White: 12.10.1960 Irish League
Vivian Woodward: 10.10.1908 Irish League (2)

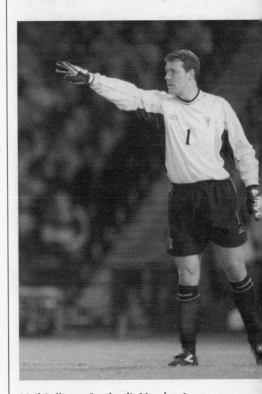

Neil Sullivan, Scotland's Number 1.

Record Appearances

Southern League

1.	Tom Morris	238
2.	Sandy Tait	206
3.	John Kirwan	155
4.	Edward Hughes	152
5.	David Copeland	144
6.	Harry Erentz	132
7.	John L. Jones	131
8.	John Cameron	117
9. =	Walter Bull	105
	Vivian Woodward	105
11. =	James McNaught	104
	John Watson	104
13.	Joseph Walton	102
14.	Tom Smith	93
15.	Bob Stormont	92
16.	George Clawley	82
17.	John Brearley	70
18. =	John Chaplin	66
	John Eggett	66
20.	Ollie Burton	58

Football League

1.	Steve Perryman	655
2.	Gary Mabbutt	477
3.	Pat Jennings	472
4.	Ted Ditchburn	418
5.	Cyril Knowles	404
6.	Jimmy Dimmock	400
7.	Glenn Hoddle	377
8.	Maurice Norman	357
9.	Alan Gilzean	343
10.	Danny Blanchflower	337
11.	Phil Beal	333
12.	John Pratt	331
13.	Arthur Grimsdell	324
14.	Jimmy Greaves	321
15. =	Tommy Clay	318
	Cliff Jones	318
17.	Bill Nicholson	314
18.	Alan Mullery	312
19.	Mike England	300
20.	Peter Baker	299

FA Cup

1.	Steve Perryman	69
2.	Glenn Hoddle	48
3.	Gary Mabbutt	47
4.	Pat Jennings	43
5.	Cyril Knowles	42

Steve Perryman, Spurs leading appearance-maker, played 655 league games for the club.

6.	Alan Gilzean	40
7.	Cliff Jones	39
8. =	Tom Morris	38
	Jimmy Dimmock	38
10.	Maurice Norman	37
11. =	Jimmy Greaves	36
	Arthur Grimsdell	36
	Sandy Tait	36
	Chris Hughton	36
15.	Ted Ditchburn	34
16. =	Danny Blanchflower	33
	Tommy Clay	33
	Len Duquemin	33
	Dave Mackay	33
	Alan Mullery	33

League Cup

1.	Steve Perryman	66
2.	Gary Mabbutt	62
3. =	Glenn Hoddle	44
	Paul Allen	44
5.	Pat Jennings	39
6.	Ray Clemence	38
7.	Chris Hughton	35
8. =	Martin Chivers	33
	Cyril Knowles	33
10.	Osvaldo Ardiles	32
11. =	David Howells	31
	John Pratt	31
	Vinny Samways	31
14.	Mike England	30
15. =	Justin Edinburgh	29
	Mitchell Thomas	29
17. =	Alan Gilzean	28
	Sol Campbell	28
19. =	Phil Beal	27
	Steve Sedgley	27
	Jimmy Pearce	27

Europe (all competitions)

1.	Steve Perryman	64
2.	Pat Jennings	36
3.	Mike England	35
4. =	Martin Chivers	32
	Martin Peters	32
6. =	Phil Beal	30
	Chris Hughton	30
	Cyril Knowles	30
9.	Alan Gilzean	28
10.	Ray Clemence	27
11. =	Ralph Coates	26
	Graham Roberts	26
13. =	Ray Evans	25
	Mark Falco	25
	Tony Galvin	25
	Gary Mabbutt	25
	John Pratt	25
18. =	Mike Hazard	23
	Paul Miller	23
20.	Steve Archibald	22

All Matches (includes 'Others' and Anglo-Italian Cup-Winners' Cup)

1.	Steve Perryman	866
2.	Gary Mabbutt	619
3.	Pat Jennings	596
4.	Cyril Knowles	511

5.	Glenn Hoddle	494
6.	Ted Ditchburn	453
7.	Alan Gilzean	446
8.	Jimmy Dimmock	440
9.	Phil Beal	425
10.	John Pratt	415
11.	Maurice Norman	413
12.	Chris Hughton	406
13.	Mike England	405
14.	Danny Blanchflower	384
15.	Jimmy Greaves	381
16. =	Alan Mullery	380
	Cliff Jones	380
18.	Paul Allen	377
19.	Arthur Grimsdell	362
20.	Tommy Clay	353

Alan Gilzean clocked up 446 appearances for Tottenham Hotspur.

Top Goalscorers

Jimmy Greaves, Spurs' supreme goalscorer, registered 220 league goals during his career.

Southern League		
1.	David Copeland	51
2.	Vivian Woodward	45
3.	John Cameron	43
4.	John Kirwan	40
5.	William Joyce	34
6.	Sandy Brown	30
7. =	Tom Smith	25
8. =	Tom Pratt	23
	John Walton	23
10.	Tom Morris	22
11.	James Reid	20
12.	John Jones	19
13.	Herbert Chapman	16
14.	Robert Clements	14
15.	Alfred Warner	13
16.	Alex Glen	12
17.	Charles Hewitt	11
18. =	James Hartley	9
	Edward Hughes	9
	Harold Stansfield	9

Football League		
1.	Jimmy Greaves	220
2.	Bobby Smith	176
3.	Cliff Jones	135
4.	George Hunt	125
5.	Martin Chivers	118
6.	Len Duquemin	114
7.	Les Bennett	103
8.	Jimmy Dimmock	100
9.	Billy Minter	99
10.	Alan Gilzean	93
11. =	Bert Bliss	92
	Taffy O'Callaghan	92
12.	Glenn Hoddle	88
13.	John Morrison	87
14. =	Willie Evans	78
	Frank Osborne	78
16.	Jimmy Cantrell	74
17.	Mark Falco	68
18.	Sonny Walters	66
19. =	Terry Medwin	65
	Jimmy Seed	65

FA Cup

1.	Jimmy Greaves	32
2.	Bobby Smith	22
3.	Alan Gilzean	21
4.	Len Duquemin	17
5.	Cliff Jones	16
6.	Sandy Brown	15
7. =	Les Bennett	14
	John Morrison	14
9. =	Les Allen	13
	Bert Bliss	13
	George Hunt	13
	Teddy Sheringham	13
13. =	Jimmy Dimmock	12
	Jimmy Seed	12
15. =	Martin Chivers	11
	Glenn Hoddle	11
17.	Jimmy Cantrell	10
18.	Clive Allen	9
	Garth Crooks	9
	Charlie Handley	9

League Cup

1.	Martin Chivers	23
2.	Clive Allen	13
3.	Martin Peters	12
4. =	Chris Armstrong	10
	Glenn Hoddle	10
	Teddy Sheringham	10
7.	Garth Crooks	9
8. =	Paul Gascoigne	8
	Gary Linker	8
10. =	Steve Archibald	7
	John Duncan	7
	Jimmy Pearce	7
	John Pratt	7
	Paul Stewart	7
15.	Alan Gilzean	6
16. =	Darren Anderton	5
	Jimmy Greaves	5
	Mike Hazard	5
	Graham Roberts	5
20. =	Paul Allen	4
	David Ginola	4
	David Howells	4
	Steffan Iversen	4
	Jurgen Klinsmann	4
	Vinny Samways	4
	Chris Waddle	4

Europe

1.	Martin Chivers	22
2. =	Mark Falco	13
	Alan Gilzean	13
	Martin Peters	13
5.	Bobby Smith	10
6. =	Ralph Coates	9
	Garth Crooks	9
	Jimmy Greaves	9
9.	Terry Dyson	8
10. =	Steve Archibald	7
	Cliff Jones	7
12. =	Tony Galvin	6
	John White	6

14. =	Graham Roberts	5
	Dave Mackay	5
	Chris McGrath	5
17. =	Alan Brazil	4
	Chris Hughton	4
	Gary Mabbutt	4
	Alan Mullery	4
	Jimmy Pearce	4

All Matches

1.	Jimmy Greaves	268
2.	Bobby Smith	210
3.	Martin Chivers	181
4.	Cliff Jones	159
5.	George Hunt	138
6.	Alan Gilzean	134
7.	Len Duquemin	131
8.	Les Bennett	118
9.	Jimmy Dimmock	112
10.	Glenn Hoddle	110
11.	Bert Bliss	106
12.	Billy Minter	105
13.	John Morrison	101
14. =	Taffy O'Callaghan	98
	Teddy Sheringham	98
16.	Mark Falco	95
17.	Willie Evans	86
18.	Clive Allen	85
19.	Frank Osborne	82
20. =	Gary Lineker	80
	Martin Peters	80

Martin Chivers, scorer of 23 League Cup goals leads the attack in the 1973 final against Norwich.

Record Transfer Fees

Joining Tottenham Hotspur

Date	Name	From	Fee
1913	Fanny Walden	Northampton Town	£1,700
1949	Alf Ramsey	Southampton	£21,000
1954	Danny Blanchflower	Aston Villa	£30,000
1961	Jimmy Greaves	AC Milan	£96,000
1968	Martin Chivers	Southampton	£125,000
1970	Martin Peters	West Ham	£200,000
1976	Peter Taylor	Crystal Palace	£400,000
1980	Steve Archibald	Aberdeen	£800,000
1988	Paul Stewart	Manchester City	£1,700,000
1988	Paul Gascoigne	Newcastle United	£2,000,000
1991	Gordon Durie	Chelsea	£2,000,000
1992	Darren Anderton	Portsmouth	£2,000,000
1992	Teddy Sheringham	Nottingham Forest	£2,100,000
1994	Ilie Dumitrescu	Steaua Bucharest	£2,600,000
1994	Gheorge Popescu	PSV Eindhoven	£2,900,000
1995	Chris Armstrong	Crystal Palace	£4,500,00
1997	Les Ferdinand	Newcastle United	£6,000,000
2000	Sergie Rebrov	Dynamo Kiev	£11,000,000

The fee received for Paul Gascoigne is still a record even though it was reduced after his injury in the 1991 FA Cup final.

Leaving Tottenham Hotspur

Date	Name	To	Fee
1956	Eddie Bailey	Port Vale	£6,000
1960	Tommy Harmer	Watford	£16,000
1965	Tony Marchi	Lanerossi	£42,000
1969	Terry Venables	QPR	£70,000
1976	Martin Chivers	Servette	£80,000
1977	Keith Osgood	Coventry City	£130,000
1978	Neil McNab	Bolton	£250,000
1984	Steve Archibald	Barcelona	£1,500,000
1989	Chris Waddle	Marseilles	£4,250,000
1992	Paul Gascoigne	Lazio	£5,500,000

Many of Spurs' early transfer dealings involved undisclosed sums. Those listed include only publicly revealed transfer fees.

Sergei Rebrov, Spurs record signing – £11 million brought him to White Hart Lane from Dynamo Kiev in 2000.